Violence and Maltreatment in Intimate Relationships

Second Edition

Cindy and Robin dedicate this book to their fathers, Emerson Miller and Kenneth Perrin, and to their mothers, Helen Miller and Libby Perrin, who cared for Emy and Ken in times of need. Our parents have taught us about self-sacrifice, the vulnerability of seniors, and the importance of tender loving care.
Claire dedicates this book to her parents, the late Joseph and Clara Renzetti, for modeling a loving and supportive relationship and for their never-ending support.

Sara Miller McCune founded SAGE Publishing in 1965 to support the dissemination of usable knowledge and educate a global community. SAGE publishes more than 1000 journals and over 800 new books each year, spanning a wide range of subject areas. Our growing selection of library products includes archives, data, case studies and video. SAGE remains majority owned by our founder and after her lifetime will become owned by a charitable trust that secures the company's continued independence.

Los Angeles | London | New Delhi | Singapore | Washington DC | Melbourne

Violence and Maltreatment in Intimate Relationships

Second Edition

Cindy L. Miller-Perrin
Pepperdine University

Robin D. Perrin
Pepperdine University

Claire M. Renzetti
University of Kentucky

Los Angeles | London | New Delhi
Singapore | Washington DC | Melbourne

FOR INFORMATION:

SAGE Publications, Inc.
2455 Teller Road
Thousand Oaks, California 91320
E-mail: order@sagepub.com

SAGE Publications Ltd.
1 Oliver's Yard
55 City Road
London, EC1Y 1SP
United Kingdom

SAGE Publications India Pvt. Ltd.
B 1/I 1 Mohan Cooperative Industrial Area
Mathura Road, New Delhi 110 044
India

SAGE Publications Asia-Pacific Pte. Ltd.
18 Cross Street #10-10/11/12
China Square Central
Singapore 048423

Acquisitions Editor: Josh Perigo
Content Development Editor:
  Megan O'Heffernan
Editorial Assistant: Tiara Beatty
Production Editor: Bennie Clark Allen
Copy Editor: Melinda Masson
Typesetter: Hurix Digital
Proofreader: Scott Oney
Indexer: Integra
Cover Designer: Scott Van Atta
Marketing Manager: Jill Ragusa

Printed in Canada

Library of Congress Cataloging-in-Publication Data

Names: Miller-Perrin, Cindy L. (Cindy Lou), 1962- author. | Perrin, Robin D., author. | Renzetti, Claire M., author.
Title: Violence and Maltreatment in Intimate Relationships / Cindy L. Miller-Perrin, Pepperdine University, Robin D. Perrin, Pepperdine University, Claire M. Renzetti, University of Kentucky.

Description: Second edition. | Los Angeles : SAGE, [2021] | Includes bibliographical references.

Identifiers: LCCN 2020021893 | ISBN 9781544371085 (paperback) | ISBN 9781544371092 (epub) | ISBN 9781544371108 (epub) | ISBN 9781544371115 (ebook)

Subjects: LCSH: Intimate partner violence. | Child abuse.

Classification: LCC HV6626 .M542 2021 | DDC 362.82/92–dc23 LC record available at https://lccn.loc.gov/2020021893

This book is printed on acid-free paper.

20 21 22 23 24 10 9 8 7 6 5 4 3 2 1

BRIEF CONTENTS

DETAILED CONTENTS

LIST OF ABBREVIATIONS

A Safety Awareness Program (ASAP)

Abusive head trauma (AHT)

Activity of daily living (ADL)

Adoption and Foster Care Analysis and Reporting System (AFCARS)

Adoption and Safe Families Act (ASFA)

Adult Protective Services (APS)

Adults and Children Together (ACT)

Adverse childhood experiences (ACEs)

Aid to Families With Dependent Children (AFDC)

Alcohol myopia theory (AMT)

Alternatives for Families: A Cognitive Behavioral Therapy (AF-CBT)

American Association of University Women (AAUW)

American Civil Liberties Union (ACLU)

American Indian Institute (AII)

American Professional Society on the Abuse of Children (APSAC)

American Psychological Association (APA)

Americans With Disabilities Act (ADA)

Attention-deficit/hyperactivity disorder (ADHD)

Bachelor of arts (BA)

Batterer intervention program (BIP)

California Social Work Education Center (CalSWEC)

Centers for Disease Control and Prevention (CDC)

Centers for independent living (CILs)

Child Abuse Prevention and Treatment Act (CAPTA)

Child physical abuse (CPA)

Child Protective Services (CPS)

Child psychological maltreatment (CPM)

Child sexual abuse (CSA)

Child Welfare League of America (CWLA)

Cognitive behavioral therapy (CBT)

Commercial sexual exploitation of children (CSEC)

Commission to Eliminate Child Abuse and Neglect Fatalities (CECANF)

Community-Based Child Abuse Prevention (CBCAP)

Conflict Tactics Scales (CTS)

Corporal punishment (CP)

Court-Appointed Special Advocates (CASA)

Danger Assessment Scale (DAS)

Developmental Victimization Survey (DVS)

Diagnostic and Statistical Manual of Mental Disorders (DSM)

Elder Justice Act (EJA)

Failure to thrive (FTT)

Federal Bureau of Investigation (FBI)

Healthy Families America (HFA)

Home Visiting Evidence of Effectiveness (HomVEE)

Hypothalamic-pituitary-adrenal (HPA)

Incredible Years (IY)

Institute on Violence, Abuse and Trauma (IVAT)

Integrated theory of sexual offending (ITSO)

International Labour Organization (ILO)

International Organization for Migration (IOM)

International Society for the Prevention of Child Abuse and Neglect (ISPCAN)

International Society for Traumatic Stress Studies (ISTSS)

Intimate partner violence (IPV)

Juvenile Victimization Questionnaire (JVQ)

Lesbian, gay, bisexual, transgender, and queer (LGBTQ)

Longitudinal Studies of Child Abuse and Neglect (LONGSCAN)

Major League Baseball (MLB)

Master of arts (MA)

Maternal, Infant, and Early Childhood Home Visiting (MIECHV)

Metropolitan Action Committee on Violence Against Women and Children (METRAC)

Minnesota Center Against Violence and Abuse (MINCAVA)

Modified Maltreatment Classification Scheme (MMCS)

National Association of Counsel for Children (NACC)

National Basketball Association (NBA)

National Center for Missing and Exploited Children (NCMEC)

National Center on Child Abuse and Neglect (NCCAN)

National Center on Elder Abuse (NCEA)

National Child Abuse and Neglect Data System (NCANDS)

National Clearinghouse on Families and Youth (NCFY)

National College Women Sexual Victimization (NCWSV)

National Crime Survey (NCS)

National Crime Victimization Survey (NCVS)

National Epidemiologic Survey on Alcohol and Related Conditions (NESARC)

National Football League (NFL)

National Hockey League (NHL)

National Incidence Study (NIS)

National Institute of Child Health and Human Development (NICHD)

National Intimate Partner and Sexual Violence Survey (NISVS)

National Organization for Women (NOW)

National Partnership to End Interpersonal Violence Across the Lifespan (NPEIV)

National Survey of Children's Exposure to Violence (NatSCEV)

National Survey on Drug Use and Health (NSDUH)

National Violence Against College Women (NVACW)

National Violence Against Women Survey (NVAWS)

National Women's Study (NWS)

Neonatal abstinence syndrome (NAS)

Nongovernmental organizations (NGOs)

North American Man/Boy Love Association (NAMBLA)

Nurse–Family Partnership (NFP)

Office of Juvenile Justice and Delinquency Prevention (OJJDP)

Parent–Child Conflict Tactics Scales (CTSPC)

Parent–Child Interaction Therapy (PCIT)

Personal assistance services (PAS)

Postpartum depression (PPD)

Post-traumatic stress disorder (PTSD)

Prevent Child Abuse America (PCAA)

Public Law (PL)

Randomized controlled trial (RCT)

Rape, Abuse & Incest National Network (RAINN)

Safe Environment for Every Kid (SEEK)

Sex Offender Treatment and Evaluation Project (SOTEP)

Sexual Assault Nurse Examiners (SANEs)

Sexual Experiences Survey (SES)

Shaken baby syndrome (SBS)

Socioeconomic status (SES)

Spousal Assault Risk Assessment (SARA)

Spouse Assault Replication Program (SARP)

Substance Abuse and Mental Health Services Administration (SAMHSA)

Sudden infant death syndrome (SIDS)

Temporary Assistance for Needy Families (TANF)

Trafficking Victims Protection Act (TVPA)

Trauma-focused cognitive behavioral therapy (TF-CBT)

Uniform Crime Report (UCR)

United Nations (UN)

United Nations Children's Fund (UNICEF)

United Nations Convention on the Rights of the Child (UNCRC)

United States Department of Health and Human Services (U.S. DHHS)

University of Southern California (USC)

U.S. Trans Survey (USTS)

Violence Against Women Act (VAWA)

Violence and maltreatment in intimate relationships (VMIR)

World Health Organization (WHO)

Youth Internet Safety Survey (YISS)

Youth Relationships Project (YRP)

Youth Risk Behavior Surveillance System (YRBSS)

PREFACE

There is but one coward on Earth, and that is the
coward that dares not know.

W. E. B. Du Bois

We know that violence and maltreatment in intimate relationships (VMIR) is a pervasive and often devastating problem that impacts people of all ages, from newborn infants to the elderly. We also know that it remains largely hidden from public view—hidden behind the closed doors of homes in every neighborhood in the United States and around the world. It is our intent, through this volume, to shed light on what is known about this serious social problem in order to lift the veil of secrecy that often surrounds it so that efforts are mobilized to stop it.

There is something especially tragic about violence and maltreatment between intimates. Intimates are supposed to love each other. Intimates are supposed to protect each other. Is there anything more tragic than a child who is physically abused by a parent, an elderly parent who is physically abused by an adult child, or a wife who is physically abused by her husband? A few years back, while researching a paper on corporal punishment, we encountered the story of Hana Williams (see K. Joyce, 2013). Hana was adopted from Ethiopia. Her parents, who felt she was openly defiant, regularly spanked her, locked her in a closet, and denied her food. Hana died when she was 13 years old from hypothermia after spending the night outside. Her mother had sent Hana outside as punishment, telling her to do jumping jacks to stay warm. She weighed only 78 pounds, and her malnourished body simply couldn't retain enough heat. Her story has stuck with us because it reflects the opposite of love and protection.

The farther back in history we go, the more gruesome the story of intimate violence becomes. At its core, violence and maltreatment in intimate relationships is about power, and power differentials describe the history of women and children throughout the world. Child abuse was not "discovered" until the rights of children were "discovered." Spousal abuse and rape were not "discovered" until women's rights were "discovered." The mistreatment of children did not receive serious attention as a social problem until the child-saving movement of the mid- to late 1800s, and the research community essentially ignored the problem until the 1960s, when medical doctors began to raise awareness. The victimization of women was similarly ignored until the late 1800s, and the social problem of woman battering was not fully identified until feminists successfully raised awareness in the early 1970s. Other forms of intimate violence—dating violence, marital rape, acquaintance rape, and elder abuse—were discovered even more recently. Indeed, our understanding and awareness of VMIR continues even into the present day as we consider how our understanding of sexual assault was radically transformed with the fall of Harvey Weinstein and the birth of the #MeToo movement.

Since the exposure of these various forms of intimate violence, progress in the field has been rapid; grassroots organizations, mental health professionals, university researchers, lawmakers, medical personnel, social service professionals, criminal justice workers, and the media have mobilized their efforts to understand the problem. The combined efforts of these groups have led to a growing national concern about VMIR. Today, with news coverage of highly publicized cases, cover stories in magazines, television programs, and movies, our society is now very familiar with VMIR.

Despite increasing awareness, however, much is still unknown about this complex and multifaceted problem. It is our hope that *Violence and Maltreatment in Intimate Relationships* will serve us all in our ongoing attempt to discover and understand this significant social problem. We, as authors, want to continue to bring the topic into the mainstream of public knowledge. To achieve these goals, we have drawn together a voluminous research literature that describes the magnitude, risk factors, and consequences of intimate violence. We also discuss the professional and social response to VMIR in hopes of furthering our understanding of how to treat victims and how to prevent future intimate violence. Throughout the book, we have attempted to keep our commitment to responsible scholarship and have made every attempt to control our own biases when presenting research. At the same time, however, it is only fair to acknowledge that we do indeed bring our passions to the discussion. These passions contribute to a lofty goal: We hope that we have presented the content in such a way that readers can find their own personal roles in the struggle to end violence and maltreatment in intimate relationships. Intimate violence is a pervasive problem that affects families and communities throughout the world. An effective response to the problem will require the commitment of many individuals from a variety of segments within society. We hope this text will increase your understanding of VMIR and motivate you to join the effort to combat this problem.

Cindy L. Miller-Perrin
Robin D. Perrin
Pepperdine University

Claire M. Renzetti
University of Kentucky

Teaching Resources

This text includes an array of instructor teaching materials designed to save you time and to help you keep students engaged. To learn more, visit sagepub.com or contact your SAGE representative at sagepub.com/findmyrep.

ACKNOWLEDGMENTS

We have many people to thank for their contributions to the second edition of *Violence and Maltreatment in Intimate Relationships*. First, we wish to acknowledge Josh Perigo for his editorial guidance. We also wish to thank Tiara Beatty, Bennie Clark Allen, and Melinda Masson for their support and involvement with this volume. We have worked with SAGE Publishing on a number of different projects, and through both the expected and the unexpected, our colleagues at SAGE have always been encouraging and helpful, especially Kassie Graves, Jerry Westby, and Terry Hendrix. The reviewers deserve everlasting praise for their careful reading of the text, in the previous edition as well as the current edition. Thanks to Amanda Admire of University of California, Riverside; Laurel Anderson of Palomar College; Alan Bittel of Corban University; Stephanie Bonnes of University of New Haven; Christina Byrne of Western Washington University; Patrick Cheek of University of Maine; Candan Duran-Aydintug of University of Colorado, Denver; Danielle Leihua Edstrom of Northwest University; Danielle M. Ficco of Washington & Jefferson College; Brenda Gill of Alabama State University; Patricia M. Henry of California State University, Bakersfield; Mary Ellen Keith of New Mexico State University, Alamogordo; Maissa Khatib, University of Texas at El Paso; Alexandrea Park of California State University, Los Angeles; Janet Reynolds of Northern Illinois University; Jay Slosar of Chapman University; Karen Slovak of Malone University; Justin Smith of Phoenix Seminary; Sherria Taylor of San Francisco State University; Lynn A. Tovar of Lewis University; Stephen Wofsey of Northern Virginia Community College; Gerrian Wuts of California State University, Los Angeles; and Theresa Wyatt of University of Detroit Mercy McAuley School of Nursing. We learned much from their insights. We also want to thank our colleagues at Pepperdine University and the University of Kentucky, where our work is supported by a number of individuals ranging from our provost and deans to our numerous faculty colleagues and students.

Cindy and Robin: We wish to thank our parents, Helen and Emerson Miller and Libby and Ken Perrin, who have always unwaveringly provided us with love and support. Among their many gifts to us is their 117 combined years of marriage—a legacy of love, marriage, and family. We are blessed to have two marvelous children, Madison and Jacob, and an equally marvelous daughter-in-law, Rachael. All three have hearts of gold and daily teach us about ourselves and how to love our neighbors as ourselves. Finally, we are thankful for one another. Not a day goes by when we do not thank God that he led us to each other—to be husband and wife, colleagues, and best friends for life.

Claire: I wish to thank my parents, the late Joseph and Clara Renzetti, for modeling a loving and supportive relationship and for their never-ending support of all my endeavors. I miss them both every single day. And to my sons, Sean and Aidan, my daughter-in-law, Pammi, and my granddaughter, Ide, thank you for the daily smiles and the reminders that love and kindness are truly the sustenance of life.

SAGE also wishes to thank the following reviewers:

Britni Adams of University of Florida

Rufaro Chitiyo of Tennessee Tech University

JulieAnn Jones of College of the Sequoias

Kirsten Kemmerer of SUNY College at Oneonta

Maissa Khatib of University of Texas at El Paso

Sandra Morgan of Vanguard University of Southern California

Susan Reid of St. Thomas University

ABOUT THE AUTHORS

Cindy L. Miller-Perrin is Distinguished Professor of Psychology at Pepperdine University. She enjoys teaching undergraduates and is the recipient of the 2008 Howard A. White Award for Teaching Excellence at Pepperdine. She is a licensed clinical psychologist who has worked with maltreated and developmentally delayed children and their families. Dr. Miller-Perrin has authored numerous journal articles and book chapters covering a range of topics, including child maltreatment, family violence, interventions to reduce physical punishment of children, vocation and life purpose, and faith development in college students. She has coauthored five books, including *Violence and Maltreatment in Intimate Relationships* (with R. Perrin and C. Renzetti, 2017), *Why Faith Matters: A Positive Psychology Perspective* (with E. Krumrei, 2014), *Family Violence Across the Lifespan* (with O. Barnett & R. Perrin, SAGE, 1997, 2005, 2011), *Child Maltreatment: An Introduction* (with R. Perrin, SAGE, 1999, 2007, 2013), and *Preventing Child Sexual Abuse: Sharing the Responsibility* (with S. Wurtele, University of Nebraska Press, 1992). She serves on the editorial boards of *Journal of Aggression, Maltreatment, and Trauma*; *Journal of Child Sexual Abuse*; *Journal of Child and Adolescent Trauma*; and *Advances in Child and Family Policy and Practice*. She is a fellow in the American Psychological Association (APA) and has served as the president of the Section on Child Maltreatment and president as well as member-at-large for the Society for Child and Family Policy and Practice (APA Division 37). She also served on the board of the Committee on Division/APA Relations (CODAPAR) and currently serves on the board of the APA Fellows Committee. She received her doctorate in clinical psychology from Washington State University.

Robin D. Perrin is Professor of Sociology at Pepperdine University. His research interests and publications are in the areas of interpersonal violence, deviance theory, the social construction of social problems, and the sociology of religion. He is the coauthor of four books: *Violence and Maltreatment in Intimate Relationships* (with C. Miller-Perrin and C. Renzetti, 2017), *Social Deviance: Being, Behaving, and Branding* (with D. Ward & T. Carter, 1991), *Child Maltreatment: An Introduction* (with C. Miller-Perrin, SAGE, 1999, 2007), and *Family Violence Across the Lifespan* (with O. Barnett & C. Miller-Perrin, SAGE, 1997, 2005, 2011). He is the author or coauthor of numerous articles on a variety of topics related to religion, deviance, and interpersonal violence. He is the recipient of the 2004 Howard A. White Award for Teaching Excellence. He received his doctorate in sociology from Washington State University in 1989. Following his doctoral studies, he was assistant professor of sociology at Seattle Pacific University.

Claire M. Renzetti is the Judi Conway Patton Endowed Chair in the Center for Research on Violence Against Women, and Professor and Chair of the Sociology Department at the University of Kentucky. She is founding editor of the international, interdisciplinary journal, *Violence Against Women*, published by SAGE. She is also coeditor with Jeffrey Edleson of the Interpersonal Violence book series for Oxford University Press, editor of the Gender and Justice book series for the University of California Press, and editor of the Family and Gender-Based Violence book series for Cognella. She has authored or edited 26 books as well as numerous book chapters and articles in professional journals. Much of her research has focused on the violent victimization experiences of socially and economically marginalized women. Her current research includes a federally funded evaluation of a therapeutic horticulture program at a shelter for battered women, studies examining the relationship between religiosity and intimate partner violence perpetration and victimization, an analysis of how college students perceive "justice" in the adjudication of campus sexual misconduct cases, and an evaluation of a human trafficking training program for first responders and emergency room staff. Dr. Renzetti has held elected and appointed positions on the governing bodies of several national professional organizations. She is the recipient of several awards and honors, most recently the Doris Wilkinson Faculty Leadership Award from the Society for the Study of Social Problems; the Peterson-Krivo Mentoring Award from the Section on Crime, Law, and Deviance and the Section on the Sociology of Law of the American Sociological Association; and the Lifetime Achievement Award from the Division on Crime and Juvenile Delinquency of the Society for the Study of Social Problems. She is also an inductee on the Alumni Wall of Fame at the University of Delaware.

1

HISTORY AND DEFINITIONS OF INTIMATE VIOLENCE AND MALTREATMENT

LEARNING OBJECTIVES

1. Describe the key issues that are present in determining the scope of violence and maltreatment in intimate relationships (VMIR).
2. Demonstrate the ways in which VMIR can be viewed as a social construction.
3. Summarize the historical events that have led to the discovery of VMIR.
4. Identify and discuss the VMIR forms of abuse and victim groups that are less well recognized in today's society, including elder abuse, LGBTQ violence, and male victims of intimate partner violence and sexual assault.
5. Describe the various definitional components of VMIR including intimate relationships, violence, and maltreatment.
6. Discuss the various intervention and prevention efforts that have been developed to address VMIR.

INTRODUCTION

Women, children, and the elderly are more likely to be victimized *in their own home* than they are on the streets of America's most dangerous cities. Admittedly, this is a dramatic claim. Yet, we would argue this claim is supported by research. We know that violence and maltreatment in intimate relationships (VMIR) is a pervasive and often devastating problem that impacts people of all ages, from newborn infants to the elderly. We also know that it remains largely hidden from public view—hidden behind the closed doors of homes in every neighborhood in America.

We begin with a story from, of all places, Major League Baseball (MLB). October 19, 2019, was a memorable day for the Houston Astros. Leading the American League Championship Series against the New York Yankees 3 games to 2, and hoping to close out the Yankees in game 6, Houston star José Altuve came to bat in the ninth with the score tied and a runner on first base. Altuve's towering, two-run, walk-off homer ended the series, and sent the Houston crowd into a frenzy.

The locker room celebration was predictable—excitement, laughter, hugs, tears, and a room wet with champagne. Four days later, however, the Astros were in trouble. Not only had they lost the first two games of the World Series against the Washington Nationals, but Assistant General Manager Brandon Taubman was attracting unwanted national attention. His job was in jeopardy. And it had nothing to do with baseball.

During the celebration, Taubman had "turned to a group of three female reporters, including one wearing a purple domestic-violence awareness bracelet, and yelled, half a dozen times, 'Thank God we got Osuna! I'm so f----- glad we got Osuna!'" (Apstein, 2019). Why was Taubman yelling "Thank God we got Osuna" to female reporters? Why was one of the reporters wearing a purple domestic-violence awareness bracelet? And who is Osuna?

Before addressing these questions it is important to look back to 2014, when Baltimore Ravens running back Ray Rice and Minnesota Vikings running back Adrian Peterson were both arrested in unrelated cases involving charges of intimate violence. Rice was arrested in February for felony assault after a physical altercation with his fiancée, Janay Palmer, at an Atlantic City hotel. Peterson was arrested in September for felony child abuse.

Both cases attracted considerable attention and contributed to a fascinating national discussion about intimate violence. In the Ray Rice case, the celebrity news website TMZ released a video the day after the arrest. In the video, which was taken outside a hotel elevator, Rice is seen dragging Palmer from the elevator. He leaves her lying facedown with her feet still inside the elevator door as he is approached by a hotel security official. As Palmer begins to stir, Rice walks away, shaking his head.

Initial reactions of National Football League (NFL) officials were cautious and muted. Ravens coach John Harbaugh, while acknowledging that all the facts were yet to be established, defended Rice's character: "You guys know his character. So you start with that" (CNN Staff, 2014). In July, five months after the altercation, NFL commissioner Roger Goodell announced the penalty: a two-game suspension for the 2014 season.

One can only assume that NFL executives anticipated that the announced decision would settle the issue. They were wrong. Experts on intimate violence, women's rights advocates, and many journalists openly criticized the decision. *New York Times* columnist Michael Powell (2014), for example, wondered why Rice, in the aftermath of the decision, "got to hear his putative bosses talk about what a fine, good, upstanding man he is." Powell also wondered why the NFL was seemingly more troubled by the use of steroids, a banned performance-enhancing substance (warranting a four-game suspension for first-time users), than intimate partner violence (warranting only a two-game suspension). Powell concluded his critique with this astute observation: "What's fascinating about domestic abuse is the delicacy with which men treat any mention of it. The original Atlantic City police report is a triumph of the passive voice. It notes that Janay Palmer stepped onto the elevator with Rice and was 'rendered unconscious.' One minute she's in the elevator, the next—shazam!—she's out."

In September 2014, seven months after the original video surfaced, TMZ released a second video that clarified exactly how Palmer had been "rendered unconscious." The video begins in the hotel lobby with Palmer and Rice noticeably agitated. Palmer takes a backhanded swipe at Rice as they approach the elevator. Inside, she pushes him, he punches her, and she collapses. This time the NFL acted swiftly and decisively, suspending him indefinitely. The Baltimore Ravens released him from the team.

NFL commissioner Goodell had defended the original two-game suspension because, in his words, it was "ambiguous what actually happened" (Dowd, 2014). But the second video removed all ambiguity. Had Commissioner Goodell seen the video before TMZ released it? Was there indeed "ambiguity" in his mind about what had happened?

In response to the criticism, the NFL appointed a former Federal Bureau of Investigation (FBI) director to review the league's handling of the case. The report, released in January 2015, affirmed that Commissioner Goodell had not seen the in-elevator video prior to the TMZ release. However, Goodell had seen the report written by police officers who had viewed the in-elevator video. He had also seen the grand jury indictment that claimed Rice "did recklessly cause significant bodily injury" to Palmer. There were also numerous reports suggesting that Rice had admitted to Goodell that he had hit Palmer and knocked her out (Dowd, 2014). By the time the report was released, however, media interest in the case had run its course, and the fact that Goodell was likely well aware when he imposed the two-game suspension that Rice had assaulted Palmer inside the elevator went largely unnoticed.

In another case occurring in the fall of 2014, Minnesota Vikings player Adrian Peterson was arrested after doctors discovered bruises and cuts on the ankles, legs, and back of his 4-year-old son. Media reports suggested that Peterson was angry that the young boy had pushed one of his brothers while playing video games. According to *New York Times* columnist Charles M. Blow (2014), Peterson had "retrieved a tree branch—called a 'switch'—stripped off its leaves, shoved leaves into the boy's mouth and beat him with his pants down until he bled."

Peterson released a statement in which he apologized for causing an injury he "never intended or thought would happen" and that he had merely "disciplined my son the way I was disciplined as a child" (Blow, 2014). Peterson went on to acknowledge that, after having met with a psychologist, he had learned that "there are alternative ways of disciplining a child that may be more appropriate. But deep in my heart, I have always believed I could have been one of those kids that was lost in the streets without the discipline instilled in me by my parents and other relatives. I have always believed that the way my parents disciplined me has a great deal to do with the success I have enjoyed as a man. I love my son and I will continue to become a better parent and learn from any mistakes I ever make" (Blow, 2014).

In a compromise with prosecutors, the felony charges were dropped, and Peterson pled no contest to a misdemeanor charge, was fined $4,000, and was ordered to perform community service. The NFL suspended him without pay for the remainder of the 2014 season (Belson, 2014). Commissioner Goodell, in a scathing letter addressed to Peterson, admonished the Minnesota star for the use of a switch, "the functional equivalent of a weapon," in causing physical and emotional injury of the boy. In addition, he scolded

Peterson for defending his actions and showing no "meaningful remorse for your conduct" (*Boston Globe*, 2014).

What have these two cases taught us about intimate violence? What questions do they raise? What lessons did we learn? What impact, if any, have these cases had on policy? And, finally, how are these cases relevant to the Houston Astros, Assistant General Manager Brandon Taubman, and the female reporter with a purple bracelet?

First, both cases illustrate the evolving recognition of intimate violence as a social problem, and the role societal reactions play in this evolution. Sociologists maintain that social problems are a **social construction** (Best, 1989; Spector & Kitsuse, 1977). This means that the social conditions only become recognized as social problems as a result of successful advocacy by those concerned about the issue. Social problems are essentially negotiated, with a variety of **claims makers** weighing in on the nature and seriousness of the problem. In the Ray Rice case, for example, the initial two-game suspension imposed by NFL commissioner Roger Goodell communicated *his* perception of the seriousness of Rice's actions. Subsequent criticisms from the media and a variety of advocates likewise communicated *their* perception of the nature and seriousness of Rice's actions. It is indeed telling that Goodell only imposed severe sanctions (a one-year suspension) *after* the world had seen, and reacted to, the video. By the time the Adrian Peterson case reached Goodell's desk, he had endured months of criticism for his perceived indifference to intimate violence, and he imposed a swift and serious sanction. We discuss the social construction of VMIR in more detail in a subsequent section of this chapter.

A second observation focuses on Peterson's attempts to defend his behavior. He acknowledged that he had crossed a line and would learn from his mistakes, but he wanted to emphasize that he still believed that physical discipline was part of being a good parent, as he believed he would have become a "street kid" were it not for his own parents' use of violent discipline. In his statements, Peterson defended not only his own personal actions but also the use of **corporal punishment** more generally. According to the General Social Survey, three-quarters of Americans agree or strongly agree that it is "sometimes necessary to discipline a child with a good, hard spanking" (T. Smith, Davern, Freese, & Morgan, 2019). But is it? Children most certainly need discipline, but does a child need to be hit? And does the fact that a discipline strategy is normative legitimize its use?

As for Peterson's attitude toward child discipline a mere four years removed from his misdemeanor plea, he has admitted that he still sometimes disciplines his child with a belt (Keim, 2018).

Third, should there have been greater legal consequences for Ray Rice and Adrian Peterson? Charges were eventually dropped against Rice (Palmer chose not to press charges), and Peterson pled no contest to a misdemeanor charge. Without speculating about the particulars of these two specific cases, we can say this: Too often, especially historically, society, through its legal responses to VMIR, has not recognized its significance. As we will see in subsequent sections of this chapter that describe the history and discovery of VMIR, social and legal policies addressing this social problem have been relatively recent.

Our fourth observation relates to the Rice case and illustrates the ongoing relevance of gender in discussions of adult intimate violence. During the Rice incident, we read, or heard, many variations of this: *A gentleman* never hits *a woman*. Needless to say, we agree. But in passively hearing and repeating this seemingly benign phrase, do we miss an important point? Hitting between intimate partners—whoever is doing the hitting—is never an acceptable option. In the in-elevator video that TMZ released in September 2014, we see the couple arguing, and we see Palmer slap Rice as they approach the elevator. Inside the elevator the argument continues, and Palmer pushes Rice before he punches her in the face. The reciprocal nature of intimate partner violence has always been a sensitive topic to discuss, as women suffer far greater consequences of intimate violence than do men. And we must always be careful not to blame the victim. Palmer did nothing to "deserve" being punched. She did not "ask for it." She is the victim. But her actions are relevant to the discussion. Can we discuss the consequences of all violence within intimate relationships while at the same time acknowledging the greater consequences for women? We think this is both possible and necessary in order to fully understand VMIR.

Finally, these two cases are important because they immediately impacted the response to intimate violence within professional sports. Each of the major professional male leagues in the United States (MLB, NBA, NFL, and NHL) give their commissioners broad authority to discipline players who engage in behavior that is deemed "detrimental" to the league. This could include criminal behavior as well as noncriminal behavior like use of performance-enhancing supplements. Prior to the Rice and Peterson cases, however, intimate violence had very rarely been deemed "detrimental" by pro sports organizations. Commissioners either minimized it or ignored it. Bud Selig, who was the MLB commissioner from 1992 to 2014, never suspended a player for intimate violence. David Stern, who was commissioner of the National Basketball Association (NBA) from 1984 to 2004, never suspended a player for more than five games for intimate violence (M. Brown & Essay, 2016). In the NFL, Commissioner Goodell had seen over 50 cases, most of which he had treated with leniency (M. Brown & Essay, 2016).

The angry reactions to the initial two-game suspension imposed on Rice were a reminder that the era of indifference was changing. Society, it seemed, was suddenly appalled by such behavior.

All of this brings us back to the controversial Houston Astros locker room celebration in October 2019. Recall from the earlier discussion that in his 22 years as MLB commissioner Bud Selig *never* suspended a player for intimate violence. By the time Robert Manfred succeeded Selig as commissioner in 2014, however, the climate had changed. Manfred has already suspended 14 MLB players for intimate violence, with penalties ranging from 20 games to 100 games. One of those players was Roberto Osuna, the relief pitcher at the center of the Astros controversy. Osuna was suspended for 85 games in 2018 (Hoffman, 2019).

So why was Assistant General Manager Brandon Taubman yelling "Thank God we got Osuna! I'm so f------ glad we got Osuna!" to female reporters? As Stephanie Apstein (2019) writes in her *Sports Illustrated* description of the interaction, Taubman's timing was, to say the least, odd. Closer Roberto Osuna had surrendered a two-run home run in the top of the ninth that had tied the game. He was hardly the hero. He had *blown* the save. Taubman's taunts, it turns out, were directed at a female reporter who is known to tweet out the National Domestic Violence Hotline number when Osuna pitches. Her purple bracelet was a sign of her solidarity with victims of domestic violence.

The Houston Astros initially disputed the Apstein report, arguing that it was "misleading," "irresponsible," and a "fabrication" (Hoffman, 2019). Three days later, however, they released the following statement:

During the past two days, the Astros proactively assisted Major League Baseball in interviewing Astros employees as part of MLB's investigation of the events published in the recent Sports Illustrated article. Major League Baseball also separately interviewed members of the media over the past 24 hours.

Our initial investigation led us to believe that Brandon Taubman's inappropriate comments were not directed toward any reporter. We were wrong. We sincerely apologize to Stephanie Apstein, Sports Illustrated and to all individuals who witnessed this incident or were offended by the inappropriate conduct. The Astros in no way intended to minimize the issues related to domestic violence.

Our initial belief was based on witness statements about the incident. Subsequent interviews have revealed that Taubman's inappropriate comments were, in fact, directed toward one or more reporters. Accordingly we have terminated Brandon Taubman's employment with the Houston Astros. His conduct does not reflect the values of our organization and we believe this is the most appropriate course of action.

We are thankful to Major League Baseball and to everyone that cooperated in the investigation. As previously stated, the Astros are very committed to using our voice to create awareness and support on the issue of domestic violence. We fully support MLB and baseball's stance and values regarding domestic violence. We will continue to make this cause a priority for our organization.

Source: Astros release updated statement following investigation. (2014, October 24). *MLB News.* Retrieved from https://www.mlb.com/press-release/press-release-astros-statement-following-investigation

ESTIMATING THE SCOPE OF THE PROBLEM

Books of this nature often begin with a series of statistics, presumably because the writer wants to impress upon the reader the seriousness of the issue at hand. The problem with this approach, especially with topics like VMIR, is that statistics cannot be summarized in simple, bullet-point form. A seemingly simple question like "How common is child sexual abuse?" is far from simple to answer.

Why is this question so difficult to answer? If we google "U.S. homicide rate," we can quickly find our way to the Uniform Crime Report, where we discover that the 2018 rate was 5.0 homicides per 100,000 people. To be sure, this statistic is not perfect. Some homicides go unreported, and others are misclassified as accidents or suicides. Yet in general we know that homicide statistics are reasonably reliable, requiring little explanation or elaboration.

Googling "prevalence rate of child sexual abuse," on the other hand, will likely be frustrating and confusing. Yes, the United States collects data on **child sexual abuse (CSA)**. In 2017, **Child Protective Services (CPS)** agencies in the United States investigated approximately 3.5 million reports of neglect, physical abuse, or sexual abuse. About 700,000 of these reports were substantiated (i.e., CPS authorities concluded that abuse did in fact occur). Of these substantiated cases, the overwhelming majority were for neglect (75%) and physical abuse (18%). The remaining 9 percent (about 60,000) were for sexual abuse (U.S. Department of Health and Human Services [U.S. DHHS], 2019b). Needless to say, this number, while important, simply does not answer the question we asked to begin this section. It tells us little to nothing about how common child sexual abuse is.

The problem, of course, is that most sexual abuse, unlike most homicides, goes unreported. To borrow from the title of an early and influential book on the topic, VMIR occurs *Behind Closed Doors* (Straus, Gelles, & Steinmetz, 1980). The most vulnerable victims cannot always speak for themselves, or may not even understand that they have been abused. As a result, their abuse goes unnoticed and unreported. Social scientists and criminologists often use the term **dark figure** to refer to the gap between the number of crimes that are committed and the number of crimes that are reported and recorded in official statistics collected by government agencies. Homicide has a small dark figure. VMIR has a huge dark figure.

Can we estimate the dark figure? With surveys we can indeed, but it is an ominous task. Think about the various problems we would inevitably face. First of all, we would have to define an inevitably ambiguous term like *sexual abuse.* Even if we could agree on a definition, we would face the very difficult issue of actually measuring this concept in a real-world population. Second, we would have to operationalize the variable. That is, we would have to create specific questions about sexual acts and sexual circumstances that constitute "child sexual abuse" as we have defined it. We would also face unavoidable problems when we actually collect the data. We can't reasonably ask children, especially young children. We can't get the information from abusive parents. And adults asked about their own childhood victimization history may not recall childhood abuse. All of this means that if we do look to self-reports to find the prevalence rate of child sexual abuse, we will find wildly varying estimates, depending on how child sexual abuse has been defined and measured.

In the chapters that follow, we will, of course, revisit the prevalence issue in more detail. For now, we are content to remind the reader that we simply do not know how "big" the problem is. We do, however, know it is big. We know that women, children, and the elderly are especially vulnerable in intimate relationships. We know that they are often victimized in many different ways (see Box 1.1 on **polyvictimization**).

BOX 1.1
POLYVICTIMIZATION

Most books on the topic of intimate violence are organized similarly. After an introductory chapter and a theory/methods chapter, subsequent chapters are arranged by topic; child physical abuse, child sexual abuse, sexual assault, intimate partner violence, and so on. It is hard to imagine another organizational strategy, and we have ourselves organized this book in a similar way. The problem with compartmentalizing the various forms of intimate violence in this way, however, is that it masks a very important empirical reality: The various forms of violence and maltreatment that comprise these chapters do not typically occur independent of one another. That is, many victims, arguably most victims, are victimized in more than one way.

Polyvictimization is the term we use to describe the empirical reality that victims are often exposed to multiple forms of violence and maltreatment. One child, for example, might be physically abused, sexually abused, psychologically abused, neglected, and exposed to other violence as well (Finkelhor, Ormrod, & Turner, 2007). He might witness his parents fighting. He might live in a violent neighborhood. He might be bullied at school. Senior citizens might be at the same time physically abused and neglected, financially exploited, and abandoned. Intimate partners, as well, may be abused psychologically, physically, and sexually (Sabina & Straus, 2008).

Yale psychologist Alan Kazdin (2011) maintains that *all* forms of intimate violence—child, intimate partner, and elder—are interconnected. Because their causes and effects intersect, studying them together has the potential to produce interventions that could potentially impact multiple forms of intimate violence. The Centers for Disease Control and Prevention (CDC), acknowledging the interconnectedness of all forms of intimate violence, has introduced a five-year vision plan to prevent violence, summarized in the document *Preventing Multiple Forms of Violence: A Strategic Vision for Connecting the Dots* (CDC, 2016b). This vision is based on the mounting empirical evidence that (1) victims of one form of violence are likely to experience other forms, (2) those who are violent in one context are likely to be violent in another context, (3) different forms of violence share similar consequences, and (4) different forms of violence share common risk and protective factors (CDC, 2016b).

And we would argue, as we did in the opening sentence of this chapter, that women, children, and the elderly are more likely to be victimized *in their own home* than they are on the streets of America's most dangerous cities.

INTIMATE VIOLENCE AND MALTREATMENT AS A SOCIAL CONSTRUCTION

Presumably, few would question our assertion that VMIR is a serious social problem. Stories of VMIR commonly appear in the U.S. news media. College courses are taught on the topic. Several academic journals are specifically devoted to publishing research on the topic.

Concern about VMIR has also increased around the world, and some international treaties explicitly acknowledge protection from intimate violence as a human right. The 1989 **United Nations Convention on the Rights of the Child (UNCRC)** declares that all children should be protected from "physical or mental violence, injury or abuse, neglect or negligent treatment, maltreatment or exploitation including sexual abuse, while in the care of parent(s), legal guardian(s) or any other person who has the care of the child" (quoted in Levesque, 2001, p. 7). The **United Nations Declaration on the Elimination of Violence Against Women**, adopted in 1994, condemns any "act of gender-based violence that results in, or is likely to result in, physical, sexual, or psychological harm or suffering to women, including threats of such acts, coercion or arbitrary deprivation of liberty, whether occurring in public or private life" (quoted in Levesque, 2001, p. 7). In these documents, the United Nations rejects **cultural relativism**, declaring that all UN member countries must eliminate any cultural practices or customs that contribute to the abuse of women or children.

This attention from the United Nations sends a clear message: VMIR is a universal concern, occupying a very high position on the social agendas of the United States and many other nations. Even a cursory look at human history, however, reminds us that intimate maltreatment was a social *condition* long before it was recognized as a social *problem*. When and how did VMIR come to be recognized as a social problem?

Social conditions become social problems through a process of social constructionism. From this perspective, *societal reactions* are central to the process through which a social condition is redefined as a social problem, as we noted earlier in our discussion of the Rice and Peterson cases. Societal reactions can come from many sources: individual citizens, religious groups, social movement organizations, political interest groups, and the media, to name a few. Through their reactions to particular social conditions, individuals and institutions play a crucial role in transforming public perceptions.

The term *claims making* has been applied to the activities of such groups; it refers to advocacy and grievances of those concerned about an unrecognized condition.

Generally speaking, the process begins when the members of an interest group, or *claims makers*, express concern about a particular condition that they see as unacceptable. Claims makers may have vested interests in the outcomes of their protests, or they may be **moral entrepreneurs** engaged in what they see as purely moral crusades (Becker, 1963). As the cause of a particular claims making group comes to be recognized by society more generally, the social condition comes to be defined as a social problem. Social problems, then, are essentially discovered through this process of societal reactions and social definition. From this perspective, social problems come and go as societal reactions to given conditions and responsive behaviors change.

The social constructionist perspective on social problems is important because it gives us a theoretical framework within which to understand the discovery, definition, and extent of VMIR in the United States and around the world. The social constructionist perspective not only helps explain the history of VMIR as a social problem, but also explains cross-cultural variations in recognizing certain practices as VMIR. Sexual abuse serves as a fascinating example. As historian Philip Jenkins (1998) reminds us, "Sexually appropriate behavior is a socially constructed phenomenon, the definition and limits of which vary greatly among different societies, and this is especially true where children and young people are concerned" (p. 14). One widely cited example of this comes from anthropologist Gilbert Herdt (1987), who describes the Sambia, a tribe in Papua New Guinea, who believe that the only way a boy can grow into manhood is by orally ingesting the semen of older boys and men. In other words, a boy becomes masculine, strong, and sexually attractive to women only after performing fellatio. In the United States, such behavior is illegal. We can imagine a situation where the Sambia might redefine this behavior as deviant, and we can envision *how* that redefinition could occur. For this social change to occur, claims makers would have to successfully challenge the cultural practice. This practice could only come to be perceived as a problem if claims makers were successful in redefining it as such.

We need not look to primitive cultures, however, to illustrate a constructionist perspective. There is an even more obvious illustration that is a common practice in contemporary cultures. As many as a billion people around the world are subjected to a form of genital "manipulation" that is most typically performed on a subset of the population that has no say in the matter. This practice is "demanded or approved by religious consensus, is virtually never regulated by secular law, and is never mentioned in literatures on sex crimes or ritual abuse" (Jenkins, 1998, p. 14). Sounds pretty heinous, right? But in countries like the United States, circumcision (yes, you guessed it) is not a heinous act of "genital mutilation" or "foreskin amputation" or "child sexual abuse." The point, at least for our purposes at the moment, is not whether circumcision should or should not be considered abusive. The point is that it is *not* considered abusive, at least not in the United States.

In Europe, however, the "genital autonomy" movement has gained considerable traction. Circumcision is seen by many as a violation of children's rights (Svoboda, Adler, & Van Howe, 2019). For example, the advocacy organization Genital Autonomy, in its "Helsinki Declaration 2012," declared that children have a fundamental right to "personal control of their own genital and reproductive organs" (genitalautonomy.org). A German court essentially agreed in 2012, ruling that circumcision violates a child's "fundamental right to physical integrity," essentially making circumcision illegal in Germany (Kulish, 2012).

There are most certainly U.S. claims makers who make similar arguments (e.g., see Denniston & Milos, 2013). It is not unreasonable to assume that their arguments will gain broader support over time. Circumcision rates in the United States are declining, and anti-circumcision voices are getting louder. In San Francisco, for example, opponents of circumcision, citing international human rights and "genital autonomy," gathered enough signatures to put a referendum on the November 2011 ballot that would have made it illegal to circumcise a child in the city. The referendum did not pass, but the fact that it was on the ballot reminds us that attitudes toward circumcision are changing.

The social constructionist perspective also helps illustrate how research is used in ongoing debates about VMIR. Intimate violence research is one of the most contentious areas of social science, and disagreements among scholars are often intense. Although one might hope that research findings could settle these debates, the reality is that the data that researchers collect are often interpreted differently by competing claims makers. Those on both sides in any given debate typically arm themselves with their own sets of empirical findings, which they espouse as the truth. From a social constructionist perspective, the nature of social problems and the facts about those problems are defined for the general public by the winners of such debates (Best, 2001).

The social constructionist perspective helps us understand what is recognized as a problem and how it came to be recognized as such. It is important to consider, however, what the perspective *does not* tell us. To conclude that a particular social problem is a social construction is merely to acknowledge that social problems, like all human knowledge, are "created through people's actions; everything we know is shaped by our language, culture, and society" (Best, 2001, p. 30). When we say, for example, that child sexual abuse is a social construction, therefore, we are merely saying that the actions of people produce and define concepts like "child," "sexual," and "abuse." In a similar way, if we argue that sexual assault on college campuses is a social construction, we are merely arguing people produce and define concepts like "sexual" and "assault" and "consent." Unfortunately, some people may misunderstand, believing that to call child sexual abuse or sexual assault on college campuses "social constructions" is to suggest that they are false, fanciful, or arbitrary. No doubt there have been some fascinating examples of nonexistent (or nearly so) phenomena that have come to be seen as social problems.

But to assume that socially constructed problems are not *really* problems or that people are not *really* harmed is to misunderstand the concept. "Constructionism means more than simply debunking," writes Jenkins (1998, p. 5). "Although a constructionist might challenge the factual claims used to support a particular cause, he or she does not argue that the problem itself has no basis in reality. Child molestation does occur and can cause severe physical and psychic damage; there are in fact human predators who rape, mutilate, and kill children." A researcher who takes a social constructionist perspective merely acknowledges and examines the contributions of social processes to the creation of all knowledge. One area where this perspective and these processes are evident is in examining historical developments as they relate to VMIR, which is our topic in the following sections.

THE DISCOVERY OF CHILDHOOD AND THE RECOGNITION OF CHILD ABUSE

The history of childhood is a nightmare from which we have only recently begun to awaken. The further back in history one goes, the lower the level of child care, and the more likely children are to be killed, abandoned, beaten, terrorized, and sexually abused. (deMause, 1974, p. 1)

The contemporary conception of children and childhood—that children should be loved, nurtured, and protected from the cruel world—is a relatively modern notion. In earlier times, the harshness of life, high rates of disease, and the visibility of death all contributed to a general devaluation of life and of children's lives in particular. Most societies regarded children as the property of their parents, who were allowed to treat their property as they saw fit. In some cases, parents probably viewed their children as economic liabilities—as little more than extra mouths to feed (Wolfe, 1991).

One illustration of the previous indifference to children is found in the historical practice of **infanticide.** Prior to the fourth century, in Rome and Greece, infanticide was a legal and culturally approved solution to unwanted births. Children who were too big or too small, cried too much, had physical defects, were born to unwed mothers, or were simply unwanted were sometimes killed or abandoned (see Box 1.2).

Through the centuries the concept of childhood evolved. The end result, we would argue, is that today children are more valued, more nurtured, and perceived to be more fragile than at any other time in history. These evolving conceptions have produced a variety of social policy changes, such as child labor laws, the creation of a juvenile court system, mandatory education requirements, and, of course, the recognition of child abuse as a social problem.

BOX 1.2
HIGH-TECH FETICIDE: SEX-SELECTIVE ABORTIONS

Historians report that most human societies have practiced and condoned infanticide (the killing of one's infant, up to age 1), in one form or another. Some scholars maintain infanticide was the most frequent crime in all of Europe before modern times and remained a relatively common practice until about 1800 (Piers, 1978). In a world generally ruled by patriarchy, most commonly it is young girls who have been killed.

Although infanticide is no longer condoned internationally, this does not mean it does not occur. In fact, researchers estimate that 45 million girls were identified as missing from 1970 to 2017 (Chao, Gerland, Cook, & Alkema, 2019). These estimates are derived from country-by-country analyses of sex ratios. The historical norm for male-to-female births is approximately 105 for every 100 (Chao et al., 2019). Certain human practices, however, can alter the ratios. Wars, for example, tend to produce low male-to-female ratios because men are more likely to be killed in battle, whereas infanticide tends to produce high male-to-female ratios because females are more likely to be victims of infanticide.

During the Middle Ages, the practice of infanticide was not openly condoned, but with sex ratios of approximately 170 males for every 100 females in Europe in 1400 CE, it seems clear that infanticide was common. The practice continued there through the 19th century. In London, for example, dead babies lying in the streets were not uncommon as late as 1890 (deMause, 1974). In 19th-century China, male-to-female ratios were nearly 400 to 100 in some rural areas primarily dependent on farming (Ho, 1959).

Infanticide is no longer practiced openly around the world. However, in the last few decades, several Asian and Eastern European countries, including Albania, Armenia, Azerbaijan, China, Georgia, Hong Kong (a special administrative region of China), India, Montenegro, the Republic of Korea, Taiwan (a province of China), Tunisia, and Vietnam, have produced troubling ratios (Chao et al., 2019). Several factors have contributed to

the rising ratios. First, there is a strong cultural preference for boys in each of the countries listed. Second, as medical technology has advanced and identification of the sex of an unborn child has become more reliable, female **feticide**—killing a fetus—has become increasingly common. Third, with fertility rates declining around the world, families have more actively tried to produce the "perfect" family, in terms of both size and sex composition (Chao et al., 2019).

In China, which has the most imbalanced ratios in the world, the cultural devaluation of females, a family planning policy that for many years limited family size (commonly referred to as the **one-child policy**), and rural farmers' economic preference for male labor resulted in widespread sex-selective abortions (Almond, Li, & Zhang, 2019). The demographic data are impossible to deny. Because the one-child policy has typically allowed for a second child if the first child is a female, most of these selective abortions have occurred in second births. In a massive study of almost 5 million Chinese, Zhu, Lu, and Hesketh (2009) reported male-to-female ratios that were slightly unbalanced for first births (108 to 100). For second births, however, the imbalance increased to 143 males for every 100 females. In rural areas, the imbalance was especially dramatic and alarming, often more than 160 to 100.

Whether the unbalanced ratios can be blamed primarily on culture or on government policies was a matter of some debate through the early 2000s. Regardless, it is a problem the Chinese government has openly acknowledged (J. Yardley, 2005). In 2013, China eased some of the restrictions of the one-child policy, allowing a second child for families where one of the spouses was a single child. In 2015, the policy was further modified, when the government announced that all married couples would be allowed to have two children. China remains a patriarchal society, so it is doubtful that this policy shift will fully balance the ratios. The Chinese government hopes, however, that the ratio gaps shrink in the coming years (Buckley, 2015).

Recognizing Child Physical Abuse

In the 17th century, Protestant reformers in the New World had mixed perceptions of children, suggesting that they were valued gifts of God but that they also possessed wrongdoing hearts inclined toward evil. There were laws that prohibited parents from inflicting severe punishment, but because children were seen as innately inclined toward evil, the laws were enforced only in those cases where the child was considered completely blameless. According to Pleck (1987), some Puritan laws actually stated that any child over the age of 16 who had cursed at or struck a parent could be put to death. Although there is no evidence that a child was ever executed for such insubordination, the fact that these laws existed illustrates the Puritans' intolerance of stubbornness and disobedience in children.

Many scholars trace the actual discovery of child abuse in the United States to the **House of Refuge movement** of the early 1800s. This movement was guided by the principle of *parens patriae*, a Latin term that essentially means that the state has a right and responsibility to protect those who cannot protect themselves (Levesque, 2001). As a result of reforms brought about by the movement, children in the early to mid-1800s who were neglected, abused, or otherwise "on the road to ruin" were housed in one of the many state-supported institutions. It is important to note that many of these institutions were no better, and sometimes worse, than the homes from which the children were removed. Regardless, however, the House of Refuge movement is historically important because it represents the government's first attempt to intervene in neglect and abuse cases (Empey, Stafford, & Hay, 1999).

In a widely cited child abuse case in 1874, church social worker Etta Wheeler discovered that 8-year-old Mary Ellen Wilson was being beaten and starved by her stepmother. After unsuccessfully seeking help to remedy the situation from several sources, Wheeler took the case to Henry Bergh, founder of the American Society for the Prevention of Cruelty to Animals. Mary Ellen was, after all, a member of the animal kingdom. According to Pleck (1987), a courtroom full of concerned New Yorkers, many of them upper-class women, heard the shocking details of Mary Ellen's life. She had been beaten almost daily and not been allowed to play with friends or to leave the house. She had an unhealed gash on the left side of her face, where her stepmother had struck her with a pair of scissors. The jury took only 20 minutes to find the stepmother guilty of assault and battery.

The case of Mary Ellen attracted considerable attention, and the resulting public outcry eventually led to the founding of the New York Society for the Prevention of Cruelty to Children in 1874 (Pagelow, 1984). This organization, and the larger child-saving movement of which it was a part, advocated for dramatic changes in society's treatment of children. Increasingly, child protection advocates argued that children need to be loved and nurtured and that they need to be protected by the state when their parents fail to do so. They argued, in effect, that parents should not have complete authority over their children (Finkelhor, 1996).

Throughout the 1900s concern for child protection grew, but public outcry and legal reactions to the problem of child abuse remained somewhat sporadic and muted. Yes, child abuse was perceived as a social problem, but a relatively rare and insignificant one. This changed in 1962, when Dr. C. Henry Kempe and his colleagues described the **battered child syndrome** and suggested that physicians should report any observed cases of abuse (Kempe, Silverman, Steele, Droegemueller, & Silver, 1962). They defined **child physical abuse (CPA)** as a clinical condition with diagnosable medical and physical symptoms resulting from deliberate physical assault. This work was important in large part because it marked the addition of the medical community to claims making about the child abuse problem. When medical doctors combined forces with other professionals and advocacy groups already fighting for child protection, the movement rapidly gained momentum. By the end of the 1960s, child abuse was widely recognized as a pervasive problem, and every U.S. state had created laws mandating that professionals report suspected cases of abuse (Levesque, 2001).

In 1974, Congress passed the Child Abuse Prevention and Treatment Act (CAPTA). CAPTA, which has been reauthorized and amended several times, mandates state-level CPS agencies to investigate suspected incidents of child maltreatment and also provides federal funding and guidance for research and services related to child protection (Child Welfare Information Gateway, 2019a).

Recognizing Child Sexual Abuse

Throughout history, and particularly in certain cultures, sexual interactions involving children have been commonplace. These interactions have often been seen as appropriate and, in some cases, have been believed to be healthy for children. In his disturbing review of the history of abuse of children, deMause (1974) notes that the children of ancient Greece, especially the boys, were often sexually exploited. Aristotle, for example, believed that masturbation of boys by adult males hastened their manhood. Greek authors made reference to "adults feeling the 'immature little tool' of boys" (p. 44). Although it is not clear how common these practices were, their matter-of-fact depiction in the literature and art of the time suggests that they were not widely condemned. Jenkins (1998), likewise, acknowledges the "huge disparities" in sexual norms between adults and children over time. Parents in 16th- and 17th-century Europe, he argues, "treated infants and toddlers with a playful sexual frankness that today would not just be wildly inappropriate but criminal" (p. 14).

The recognition of sexual maltreatment and abuse can be traced, to some degree, to Sigmund Freud (1856–1939) and his contemporaries. At the turn of the century, there was considerable disagreement among European physicians concerning the prevalence of sexual abuse. In one camp were physicians who argued that the overwhelming majority of sex abuse allegations were fabrications concocted by attention-seeking and highly suggestible children. Any father from a "respectable" background would be incapable of abusing his daughter, so women who accused "honorable" fathers of childhood abuse were clearly "hysterical" and belonged in mental institutions (Olafson, Corwin, & Summit, 1993).

Freud, however, challenged this view. In a series of three articles written in 1896, Freud articulated a view that was a radical departure from the common understandings of the time. He argued that incest (sexual abuse within families) was not uncommon, even among the respectable classes, and that it was the cause of many of the neuroses he observed in his female patients. Incest was especially heinous and damaging, he argued, because children were helpless and powerless (Olafson et al., 1993).

Interestingly, Freud famously changed his mind late in his career, concluding that the vast majority of stories of sexual abuse revealed by his patients over the years were fictitious and imagined childhood fantasies (Olafson et al., 1993). Reflecting on earlier writings some 30 years later, he wrote: "I believed these stories, and consequently supposed that I had discovered the roots of the subsequent neurosis in these experiences of sexual seduction in childhood. . . . If the reader feels inclined to shake his head at my credulity, I cannot altogether blame him" (as cited in Olafson et al., 1993, p. 11).

Recognizing Other Forms of Child Maltreatment

Child neglect and **child psychological maltreatment (CPM)** were the last forms of child maltreatment to attract attention. The limited interest in neglect is surprising, given that it is far more common than physical or sexual child abuse. Child psychological maltreatment is also pervasive; indeed, it is a central component of all child maltreatment. Although physical wounds may heal, psychological wounds often run deep.

Why do child neglect and child psychological maltreatment receive less attention than other forms of abuse? The most obvious reason is that physical and sexual abuse are far more likely to result in observable harm. Child physical abuse tends to be defined only by the physical harm the child experiences. Sometimes neglect results in signs of physical harm (e.g., malnutrition), but often the negative effects of neglect and psychological maltreatment are insidious and never become fully apparent to observers outside the family.

THE WOMEN'S RIGHTS MOVEMENT, THE RISE OF FEMINISM, AND THE RECOGNITION OF INTIMATE PARTNER VIOLENCE

WOMEN'S RIGHTS CONVENTION. A Convention to discuss the social, civil, and religious condition and rights of women, will be held in the Wesleyan Chapel, at Seneca Falls, N.Y., on Wednesday and Thursday, the 19th and 20th of July, current; commencing at 10 o'clock am. (Seneca Falls Convention, 1848)

The seed for the women's rights movement was planted in 1848 in a Wesleyan Methodist church in Seneca Falls, New York. The Seneca Falls Convention was organized by Lucretia Mott, the wife of an antislavery reformer and Quaker preacher, and women's rights advocate Elizabeth Stanton. In the days prior to the convention, Stanton wrote the convention's **"Declaration of Sentiments,"** a document modeled after the Declaration of Independence. The declaration begins with the following pronouncement:

> We hold these truths to be self-evident; that all men and women are created equal; that they are endowed by their Creator with certain inalienable rights; that among these are life, liberty, and the pursuit of happiness; that to secure these rights governments are instituted, deriving their just powers from the consent of the governed. (Seneca Falls Convention, 1848)

In surprisingly strong language, the document asserts that throughout history men have injured and controlled women in hopes of establishing "absolute tyranny" over them. It concludes: "In view of this entire disenfranchisement of one-half the people of this country . . . we insist that they have immediate admission to all the rights and privileges which belong to them as citizens of the U.S." (Seneca Falls Convention, 1848).

Stanton fully recognized the vulnerability of women within marital relationships. In the Declaration of Sentiments, she argued that the rights of women should be acknowledged in all spheres of life. In doing so, she listed a number of "facts submitted to a candid world," several of which related specifically to the family:

> He has made her, if married, in the eye of the law, civilly dead. He has taken from her all right in property, even to the wages she earns.

> In the covenant of marriage, she is compelled to promise obedience to her husband, he becoming, to all intents and purposes, her master—the law giving him power to deprive her of her liberty and to administer chastisement.

> He has so framed the laws of divorce, as to what shall be the proper causes, and in case of separation, to whom the guardianship of the children shall be given, as to be wholly regardless of the happiness of women—the law, in all cases, going upon a false supposition of the supremacy of man, and giving all power into his hands. (Seneca Falls Convention, 1848)

Recognizing Women as Victims of IPV

Despite the efforts of Stanton and other influential reformers, the problem of the physical abuse of women attracted little attention in the first half of the 20th century.

The campaign was, "compared to the child abuse movement of roughly the same time period, an abysmal failure" (Pleck, 1987, p. 109). Ake and Arnold (2018) argue that during this era the problem of wife beating was essentially handed over to social scientists who, in using language like "marital discord" and "domestic difficulties," implied that husbands and wives were equally to blame. Feminist challenges to these views were often dismissed by a public suspicious of a movement it perceived to be radical and antifamily. By the mid-1970s, however, feminists had regained control of the issue, ushering in the "beginnings of an analysis of oppression and male dominance that located the problem of domestic violence in the inequality inherent in patriarchy itself" (Ake & Arnold, 2018, p. 5).

Chiswick Women's Aid, the first shelter for battered women to gain widespread public attention, opened in England in 1971. Chiswick's founder, Erin Pizzey, published the influential book *Scream Quietly or the Neighbours Will Hear* in 1974. The publicity that surrounded the book, and the subsequent radio and television exposure it generated, helped to spread the battered women's movement in Europe. American activists, some of whom visited Chiswick in the early 1970s, were eager to open similar shelters in the United States. A flood of media attention in the mid-1970s further increased public awareness of the domestic violence problem (Dobash & Dobash, 1979; Pleck, 1987). The first shelters in the United States were Rainbow Retreat in Phoenix (opened in 1973) and Haven House in Pasadena (opened in 1974). These shelters, and others that opened soon thereafter, became the "iconic symbols" of the movement and the physical base from which the social movement was organized (Ake & Arnold, 2018).

In 1976, the **National Organization for Women (NOW)** decided to make wife battering a priority issue. The organization announced the formation of a task force to examine the problem and demanded government support for research and shelter funding. As battered women moved higher up the list of feminist concerns, women's organizations more effectively exerted pressure on police and government officials to protect abused women. Advocacy organizations such as the **National Coalition Against Domestic Violence**, founded in 1978, effectively voiced the concerns of battered women on a national level, and this led to improvements in social services for battered wives and changes in legal statutes to protect women (Studer, 1984). Arguably, the culmination of the movement was the **Violence Against Women Act (VAWA)**, which passed through Congress with bipartisan support and was signed by Bill Clinton into law in 1994. The passage of the VAWA, along with its three subsequent renewals, "unmistakably signaled that domestic violence was finally being taken seriously on a national scale" (Ake & Arnold, 2018, pp. 3–4). Today, domestic violence is commonly referred to as intimate partner violence (discussed in greater detail in Chapter 8).

Recognizing the Sexual Assault of Women

Rape laws in the United States can be traced to the 17th century. These early laws, like rape laws historically around the world, primarily protected the property interests of men.

Sir Matthew Hale, chief justice of the Court of Kings Bench in England, summed up the thinking of the times, writing in 1680: "Rape is an accusation easily to be made, hard to be proved, and harder to be defended by the party accused" (quoted in Ake & Arnold, 2018, p. 4). Furthermore, to the degree that rape laws existed, they pertained only to sexual assault *outside* of marriage. These attitudes influenced statutes and courtroom proceedings until the 1900s. Sir Hale originated the **marital exemption law**, which held that by mutual matrimonial consent and contract, a wife had given her consent to sexual intercourse with her husband. These issues are further discussed in Chapter 8.

Hasday (2000) maintains that many historians have incorrectly characterized the women's rights movement of the late 1800s as focusing exclusively on access to the public sphere, with suffrage being the movement's overriding goal. Instead, she argues, prominent feminists held that "economic and political equality, including even the vote, would prove hollow, if women did not win the right to set the terms of marital intercourse. Indeed, feminists explained a woman's lack of control over her person as the key foundation of her subordination" (p. 1379). These same advocates waged "a vigorous, public, and extraordinarily frank campaign against a man's right to forced sex in marriage" (p. 1380). In addition to feminist advocacy of the late 19th century, instructional literature at the time maintained that a wife's right to say no to sex is essential to a happy marriage and urged men to acknowledge women's sexual rights. Early attempts to change marital exemption laws, however, were unsuccessful, and there were no attempts made in the 19th century to charge a husband criminally for raping his wife (Hasday, 2000; Pleck, 1987).

The modern feminist movement of the 1960s and 1970s worked diligently to draw attention to rape, framing it as yet another illustration of **patriarchal** privilege and control. Activists focused their attention on male-dominated institutions, most specifically law enforcement, the courts, and hospitals, that they argued revictimized women and contributed to a cultural misunderstanding of rape (Ake & Arnold, 2018). Beginning in the early 1970s, rape crisis centers opened, and rape hotlines were established. These activists challenged the prevailing perceptions of rape victims as ultimately asking for it, and of rapists as a few sick men jumping out of bushes. Rape, they countered, was an expression of male dominance, and they openly challenged the "rape myth" that a woman's no might mean yes. No, 1970s feminists maintained, means *no!*

Marital exemption laws also became a significant topic of debate during this time. Defenders of marital exemption made the argument that it was in the best interests of the man and the woman to protect the privacy of the marital union and keep the judicial system out of the bedroom. Defenders raised concerns that once the state intervenes, "the delicate shoots of love, trust, and closeness in a marriage will be trampled in a way unlikely ever to be undone" (Hasday, 2000, p. 1381). Despite feminist objections, this line of reasoning proved reasonably successful, and it was well into the 1970s before the first marital rape laws were passed. It was not until the early 1990s that all 50 states had criminalized marital rape. It is important to note, however, that many states continue to have exemptions. For example, in some states the couple must be separated (Ake & Arnold, 2018).

According to some observers, rape was not fully recognized as a social problem until the late 1980s, when the results of a study called the *Ms. Magazine Campus Project on Sexual Assault* were published in a series of articles by University of Arizona psychologist Mary Koss (e.g., 1992, 1993). The study, which was funded by the National Institute of Mental Health, found that 27 percent of the college women surveyed (a sample of 6,159 women on 32 college campuses) had been victims of rape (15%) or attempted rape (12%). Although critics questioned the study as "**advocacy statistics**" (N. Gilbert, 1998), the research undoubtedly put sexual assault on the map. The findings were widely cited in the popular press and were the subject of a 1991 U.S. Senate hearing on sexual assault and date rape. The Koss findings were also the primary source of data for the "one in four" statistic (percentage of college women who are victims of rape or attempted rape), which on many college campuses became the mantra of rape awareness programs. Young women were warned to be careful about who they dated, to stay sober, and to be assertive in informing their dates of their physical boundaries.

With evolving perceptions of rape, state laws began to change. At the federal level, however, change was much more glacial. In fact, until fairly recently, the FBI relied on a definition of rape that was written in 1927. In 2012, Attorney General Eric Holder announced that the old definition of rape, "the carnal knowledge of a female, forcibly and against her will," would be replaced by a new definition, "the penetration, no matter how slight, of the vagina or anus with any body part or object, or oral penetration by a sex organ of another person, without the consent of the victim" (U.S. Department of Justice, 2012). In the old definition rape was "carnal knowledge" (i.e., typically understood as vaginal penetration), and in the new definition it is any penetration (oral, vaginal, anal, or with an object) of another person. Additionally, the phrase "forcibly and against her will" was replaced with the phrase "without the consent of the victim," emphasizing that a key element of the crime is lack of consent and that rape can occur if the victim is intimidated (e.g., verbally coerced or threatened) or is unable to consent (e.g., passed out, or too intoxicated or under the influence of drugs to consent).

Finally, it is important to recognize the #MeToo movement that has attracted so much attention in recent years. On October 5, 2017, *New York Times* journalists Jodi Kantor and Megan Twohey reported allegations that Hollywood producer Harvey Weinstein had, for three decades, sexually harassed or assaulted multiple women. Many of the women had, according to the journalists, been paid off to remain silent. Five days later, the *New Yorker* published the first of several articles by Ronan Farrow, in which even more women went on record accusing Weinstein of assault.

Ten days after the *New York Times* article, actor Alyssa Milano posted to Twitter: "If you've been sexually harassed or assaulted write 'me too' as a reply to this tweet." Women began to respond with their own stories. The hashtag #MeToo was used more than 500,000 times in its first 24 hours, and a social movement was born (Rutenberg, Adams, & Ryzik, 2017).

In May 2019, *Glamour* magazine published a list of 100 powerful men who faced allegations of sexual misconduct during the #MeToo era (*Glamour*, 2019). Listed as follows are some of the more prominent names from the *Glamour* article:

- U.S. Supreme Court justice Brett Kavanaugh was accused of sexually harassing Christine Blasey Ford when he was in high school.

- CBS executive Les Moonves was terminated by CBS after acknowledging that he engaged in sexual acts with women hoping to be cast in CBS shows.

- Actor Morgan Freeman was accused by eight women of making sexual comments, trying to lift up their skirts, and asking if they were wearing underwear. He has lost advertising contracts as a result of the allegations.

- Musician R. Kelly has been accused of having sex with minors. In February 2019, Kelly was charged with 10 counts of criminal assault.

- News anchor Charlie Rose was fired by CBS after several women accused him of making obscene phone calls, groping them, and exposing himself.

- *Today Show* host Matt Lauer was terminated by NBC after several women complained of sexual misconduct.

- Minnesota senator Al Franken resigned after a photo emerged of him pretending to grope a sleeping colleague.

- Actor Kevin Spacey was accused by Anthony Rapp of making sexual advances on him when he was 14. Several other men came forward with similar accusations. Spacey was dropped from the very popular Netflix show *House of Cards*, as well as several other projects on which he was scheduled to work.

OTHER SOMETIMES FORGOTTEN VICTIMS

We can imagine that the reader might be somewhat confused about the limited scope of our discussion to this point, perhaps wondering if women and children are the only victims of VMIR. Most of the empirical literature does indeed focus on women and children. As we have mentioned, there are historical reasons for this. But, of course, there are other victim groups that are worthy of attention.

Elder Abuse

The earliest federal government involvement in attempts to address elder abuse in the United States came in 1962, when Congress authorized payments to states to provide protective services for "persons with physical and/or mental limitations, who are unable to manage their own affairs . . . or who are neglected or exploited" (U.S. DHHS, as quoted in Wolf, 2000, p. 6). In 1974, Congress mandated **Adult Protective Services (APS)** for all states. Public concern escalated even more in 1978, when a congressional subcommittee heard testimony on "parent battering." The image of the stressed and burdened adult daughter abusing an elderly parent linked elder abuse to child abuse and resulted in considerable media attention. Following the child abuse model, claims makers successfully advocated for laws that made the reporting of suspected elder abuse mandatory for certain professionals (Wilber & McNeilly, 2001).

In 2010, Congress passed the **Elder Justice Act (EJA)** as part of the Patient Protection and Affordable Care Act ("Obamacare"). The EJA seeks to promote "elder justice," defined as efforts to "prevent, detect, treat, intervene in, and prosecute elder abuse, neglect and exploitation and protect elders with diminished capacity while maximizing their autonomy" (Elder Justice Act, 2009).

The EJA has, to date, received very little federal funding. Congress did not provide its first direct appropriations until 2015, when it allocated $4 million for the EJA (the Obama administration had requested $25 million). Interestingly, this $4 million was seen as a victory for advocacy organizations like the National Council on Aging, which had aggressively, but to that point unsuccessfully, lobbied for EJA funding (Colello, 2014). In two subsequent federal budgets (fiscal years 2016 and 2017), funding has remained well below what the Obama administration requested.

LGBTQ Violence

Another sometimes neglected group is lesbian, gay, bisexual, transgender, and queer (LGBTQ) couples. This neglect is not surprising, given the ambivalence and uneasiness with which society has historically responded to LGBTQ couples. As acceptance has grown, however, so too has interest in violence within these relationships (Renzetti & Miley, 2014). Research suggests that LGBTQ couples likely experience as much violence as heterosexual couples, or perhaps even more (Ard & Makadon, 2011; Dank, Lachman, Zweig, & Yahner, 2014).

Male Victims of IPV and Sexual Assault

Intimate partner violence most typically focuses on heterosexual female victims. Given the place of patriarchy in the world's history, such a focus seems warranted. Research suggests, however, that violence among intimates is often reciprocal. Murray Straus and his colleagues (Straus & Gelles, 1986; Straus et al., 1980), who conducted the earliest national surveys on marital violence, found that wives pushed and hit husbands as frequently as husbands pushed and hit wives. Demi Kurz (1991) was openly critical of the Straus findings, arguing that his conclusions "vastly underestimated the harm done to women and greatly exaggerated their responsibility for that violence" (p. 158). Indeed, research that focuses specifically on criminal victimization suggests that approximately four in five victims of IPV are women (Catalano, 2012). Taken as a whole, the research would seem to suggest that women are in fact much more likely to be victims, but many men are also victimized and deserving of attention (Kimberg, 2008).

The sexual assault literature is even more heavily focused on women as victims. In our earlier discussion about the FBI definition of sexual assault, we purposely chose not to highlight what is, arguably, the most significant change from 1927 to 2012. Perhaps the reader noticed it? In 1927, rape was defined as "carnal knowledge of a *female*" (emphasis added). In other words, at least according to the FBI, prior to 2012 a male could not be a victim of rape. In the academic literature the sexual assault of males has been a subject of discussion since at least 1980 (Groth & Burgess, 1980). Yet it remains fascinating that the FBI did not formally acknowledge male victimization until very recently. Not surprisingly, this broadened understanding has led to a growing literature on sexual assault within the LGBTQ community as well (e.g., M. Davies, 2002; Pérez & Hussey, 2014).

DEFINING "VIOLENCE" AND "MALTREATMENT" AND "INTIMATE RELATIONSHIPS"

Just as the claims making process is an important part of the history and discovery of intimate violence and maltreatment, as noted earlier, it plays an important role in how these concepts are defined as well. When, for example, is a child or an elder or an intimate partner a victim of "violence" or "maltreatment"? The answer to this question is not self-evident; it is negotiated, debated, and argued. Of course, to argue that subject matter is socially constructed does not solve the immediate problem. *We need to define the subject matter of this volume.* In the following subsections, we briefly examine some of the conceptual definitional assumptions that direct our investigation.

What Is an Intimate Relationship?

Deciding on a title for this book, and defining the scope of this book, has not been an easy task. Historically, books on this topic have used the word *family* in the title: husbands hitting wives, wives hitting husbands, parents hitting children, children hitting each other. Yet consideration of the topic of family violence invariably led to discussion of intimate violence outside the bounds of the *traditional* family. And, of course, cultural and legal definitions of what constitutes a family are changing. The question "What is a family?" is more frequently asked today than it has been in the past. In 2010, for example, the Pew Research Center published results from a national survey that asked Americans when a household meets the requirement of being a family. The results are interesting. Essentially everyone agreed that a married couple with children is a family. The percentages drop from there, however, with respondents identifying the following circumstances as a family: 88 percent, a married couple without children; 86 percent, single parents with children; 80 percent, unmarried heterosexual parents with children; and 63 percent, unmarried same-sex couples with children. Perhaps most telling of all, almost 50 percent of Americans indicate that a childless unmarried couple (either homosexual or heterosexual) makes a family.

Given these trends, terms like *family violence* or *marital violence* seem to raise more questions than answers. Certainly, violence that occurs between unmarried adult cohabiters, dating partners, and same-sex intimates clearly fits within the scope of this book. Given these various trends, the term **intimate** seems appropriately inclusive. This is not to say that we will abandon the use of the word *family* altogether. Many times in our writing, the term *family* seems most appropriate. When we use the term *family*, however, keep in mind that we are thinking broadly and inclusively.

What Is Violence?

Violence can be defined as "an act carried out with the intention of, or an act perceived as having the intention of, physically hurting another person" (Steinmetz, 1987, p. 729). Some might complain that this definition is too broad and inclusive. According to this definition, for example, spanking is a violent act. Many parents who physically punish their children may choose not to see it this way, preferring minimizing language like "swat," "paddle," or "smack." But a spanking *is* a violent act. It *is* intended to hurt the child. That is why parents do it. The pain caused by the spanking is supposed to produce compliance. In the same way, intimate partners who hit are also engaged in violent acts. From our perspective, however, this seems to be the only consistent place to start. We will reserve terms like *assault* and *abuse*, however, for the most extreme forms of VMIR.

What Is Maltreatment?

Our interests extend far beyond violence to other acts of **maltreatment**. Sexual abuse, for example, may only occasionally involve physical violence but can have damaging effects that last a lifetime. Child neglect and emotional abuse are forms of maltreatment that can be even more devastating than physical violence. A woman can be psychologically tormented and controlled by a man who never touches her. Elders can be harmed through neglect rather than physical assault. Our intent is to discuss all forms of intimate maltreatment, whether it is violent or not.

SOCIAL POLICY: PREVENTION AND INTERVENTION

Two pervasive tensions dominate social policy discussions. The first concerns the relative importance of **prevention** versus **intervention strategies**. *Prevention* refers to social support and education programs designed to prevent intimate violence from occurring in the first place. *Intervention* refers to societal responses to intimate violence after it occurs. The second tension focuses on competing perspectives on how society should approach prevention and intervention. Is the problem most effectively addressed with support and treatment models, or punishment and protection models?

History helps put the current social policy debates in context. Once VMIR became fully recognized in the 1960s and 1970s, the most immediate and urgent concerns were identification and protection of abuse victims and the punishment of offenders. Given the history of indifference, this policy emphasis seems reasonable. However, this response has sometimes come at the expense of a societal commitment to supporting, mentoring, and protecting families. Yes, sometimes offenders need to be in prison. But there are other times when support and services for vulnerable families are needed. Balancing the two is no easy task. In the sections that follow we briefly introduce several prevention and intervention programs and policies, many of which will be discussed in more detail in subsequent chapters.

Child and Adult Welfare Policy

There is no single entity called the child welfare system or the adult welfare system. Nor is there a single entity called Child Protective Services or Adult Protective Services. Instead, these are general terms used to describe various efforts at the state level to protect children, elders, and, in many states, younger adults with significant disabilities. State CPS and APS agencies engage in both prevention and intervention efforts. They promote child and adult support and protection policies; they receive and investigate reports of maltreatment; they assess needs and arrange and/or mandate services; and they monitor service delivery. These entities are discussed further in Chapters 3, 5, and 10.

Of critical importance to the work of these agencies are **mandatory reporting laws**, which apply to individuals who have regular contact with vulnerable populations including children, adults who are dependent due to a disability, and elderly adults. Such individuals are **mandated reporters**, because they are legally required to report observed or suspected cases of abuse, which are often received and processed by CPS and APS.

Most state statutes include some type of penalty for failure to report, depending on the particular circumstances of a case. Sanctions range from fines to felony criminal charges (Child Welfare Information Gateway, 2019c; N. Dube, 2012; Jirik & Sanders, 2014).

Within five years following the publication of Kempe's influential article on child abuse (Kempe et al., 1962), every U.S. state had enacted mandatory child abuse reporting laws. Protections for adult victims have been slower to develop, but today mandatory reporting laws for elders are the norm (Jirik & Sanders, 2014). Only a few states, however, specifically mandate the reporting of suspicions of IPV (Durborow, Lizdas, Flaherty, & Marjavi, 2010; Futures Without Violence, n.d.).

Initially, the laws for children focused primarily on the need for doctors to report injurious physical abuse. But the list of reportable behaviors has grown to include all forms of child maltreatment that might *potentially* harm a child (National Center for Prosecution of Child Abuse, 2014). The list of professionals required to report has also grown, and now includes social workers, mental health professionals, teachers, and other school staff (Child Welfare Information Gateway, 2019c).

Those identified as mandated reporters for elder abuse include doctors, nurses, nursing home administrators and staff, and social workers, among others. All laws require the reporting of observed or suspected physical abuse, neglect, and financial or material exploitation, and the large majority also include emotional or psychological abuse, sexual abuse, and self-neglect (Jirik & Sanders, 2014).

While mandatory reporting laws have generally been heralded as a triumph of intimate violence advocacy, there are a number of unintended problems associated with mandatory reporting. Some advocates for women, for example, have expressed concern that mandatory reporting laws might inhibit women from seeking care or make them vulnerable to retaliation (Hyman, Schillinger, & Lo, 1995). These laws also often put people in the helping professions in a difficult position, essentially forcing them to violate the confidences of their clients. Many professionals who are required to report suspected abuse see themselves as better equipped to help needy families than the overburdened CPS and APS systems, so they choose to ignore the reporting laws (Melton, 2002; Rodríguez, Wallace, Woolf, & Mangione, 2006; Zellman & Fair, 2002). Research evidence suggests, for example, that the more professionals know about the protection system (i.e., the more formal training they have), the less likely they are to report suspected cases of abuse (Melton, 2002). Others have found that while mandatory reporting laws are associated with an increased number of investigations, they have not been associated with an increased number of substantiated cases (Ainsworth, 2002; Jogerst et al., 2003). In addition, there is considerable variability in how reporting laws are interpreted by professionals, and the specific wording used in mandatory reporting laws can influence those interpretations (Levi & Portwood, 2011). Although all U.S. states and many international societies have enacted mandatory reporting laws, to date, their impact has rarely been empirically examined; more research is needed on the benefits and drawbacks to mandatory reporting laws (Jirik & Sanders, 2014; Mathews, Lee, & Norman, 2016).

Family Preservation, Foster Care, and Adoption

One of the most controversial issues within child protection circles is the question of when children should be temporarily or permanently removed from their homes. (See Chapter 5 for further discussion of this issue.) CPS agencies are mandated to make child protection their top priority, and no one questions this mandate. But when a child is being abused, what course of action will serve the best interests of the child? Should CPS attempt to maintain the family unit, offering support and training in hopes that abuse will not occur again in the future? Should CPS remove the child from the home and place the child in a temporary setting with the hope of eventually returning the child to the home? Or should the state seek a more permanent solution for the child, such as adoption or placement in an orphanage?

Proponents of the family preservation model maintain that the best place to raise a child is in a nuclear family, and that children can be safely left in their homes *if* their communities offer vulnerable families the social services and training they need. These advocates point out that the foster care system is not a panacea, noting the relatively high rates of abuse in foster families (U.S. DHHS, 2019a). The commitment to family reunification is not without its critics, of course, who point to some troubling child fatality data to illustrate their point. In 2017, for example, 1,720 children died as a result of abuse and neglect; 10.7 percent of these victims were in families who had received family preservation services in the previous five years, and 1.7 percent (20 children) of child fatalities involved children who had been in foster care and were reunited with their families in the previous five years (U.S. DHHS, 2019a).

Criminal Justice Issues

Because most of the behaviors discussed in this book are against the law, the actions of the criminal justice system are important in policy discussions. For example, despite the fact that IPV has long been recognized as a crime, police discretion in making arrests, combined with family privacy norms, cultural tolerance, and the reluctance of women to press charges, has meant that historically arrest has been the exception rather than the rule. In the 1980s, only about 1 in 10 police interventions in IPV resulted in arrest (Gelles & Straus, 1988). A related problem was that many victims of IPV do not press charges, and criminal prosecutions were therefore often abandoned.

Many researchers and women's advocates saw these data as a sign of societal indifference to, and continuing tolerance of, the abuse of women. Citing the **deterrence doctrine** (see Chapter 2), they argued that a society that punishes violent family members should have less family violence. A husband who hits his wife is guilty of criminal assault, and he should be punished as a criminal. Punishing family offenders would begin, these advocates argued, with the limiting of discretion in the criminal justice system. Mandatory arrest policies and preferred arrest policies soon became the most widely implemented and highly publicized way of placing limits on justice system discretion in cases of domestic violence (Barner & Carney, 2011). Many jurisdictions also initiated "no-drop" prosecution policies, which require prosecutors to move forward with criminal proceedings even if the victim has recanted or asked that the prosecution cease (Barner & Carney, 2011). These policies are discussed further in Chapter 8.

Community Awareness Campaigns

One of the easiest and most cost-efficient prevention techniques is public education through advertisements and public service announcements. Many of the social movement organizations and federal agencies devoted to the family violence problem see themselves, at least in part, as public educators.

Community awareness campaigns are too numerous and varied to discuss at length here and are discussed further in subsequent chapters. One particular campaign worth highlighting is "No Hit Zones" in hospitals and other settings frequented by parents and small children. This campaign focuses specifically on corporal punishment, politely asking visitors to refrain from hitting of any kind. Given that corporal punishment remains the norm in the United States and has been associated with child physical abuse, "No Hit Zone" campaigns have attracted some attention in the press, as well as in the academic literature (Frazier, Liu, & Dauk, 2014).

Shelters and Hotlines

Perhaps the most visible form of intervention in IPV is the battered women's shelter. Since the first such shelter opened in England in the early 1970s, battered women's shelters have become commonplace. Today, most large metropolitan areas have shelters that provide numerous services, including counseling, social support groups, child care, economic support, and job training. The U.S. government took an active role in promoting the shelter movement in 1994 when it passed the first Violence Against Women Act. The VAWA, which was reauthorized in 2000, has provided funding for shelters and established the National Domestic Violence Hotline (1-800-799-SAFE). Some observers have argued that although implementing VAWA provisions has been expensive, the law meets the needs of battered women so effectively that it may have saved U.S. taxpayers billions of dollars in medical costs and social services (Clark, Biddle, & Martin, 2002). This topic is discussed further in Chapter 8.

CHAPTER SUMMARY

Our intent in this chapter, in part, is to impress upon the reader the significance and prevalence of VMIR. Compared to other wealthy democracies, the United States is, arguably, the most violent country in the world. An unacceptably high proportion of this violence occurs within intimate relationships.

We take a social constructionist perspective in our description of how VMIR came to be recognized as a social problem. The social constructionist perspective focuses on the role claims makers have played in this history. Each of the forms of VMIR discussed in this book has, at various times in history, been treated with indifference. The mistreatment of children began to receive serious attention during the child-saving movement of the mid- to late 1800s, and the research community essentially ignored child abuse until the 1960s, when medical doctors began to raise awareness. The victimization of women was similarly ignored until the late 1800s, and the social problem of woman battering was not fully discovered until feminists successfully raised awareness in the early 1970s. Other forms of family violence—sibling violence, dating violence, marital rape, acquaintance rape, and elder abuse—were only discovered after claims makers successfully raised awareness.

Specific definitions of VMIR are also shaped by the claims making process. Words such as *abuse, battering, assault, maltreatment,* and *violence* are commonly used in discussions of VMIR, but there is little agreement, or even discussion, on exactly what these words mean. Their meanings are negotiated by claims makers, and the winners in these negotiations earn the right to define particular behaviors and estimate their prevalence.

Social scientific progress in the field of VMIR depends, to some extent, on a shared understanding of what constitutes VMIR, so we have offered our own conceptualizations. *Violence* is a physical act meant to hurt another person. *Maltreatment* is a more inclusive term meant to encompass various forms of nonviolent acts such as psychological mistreatment, neglect, or inappropriate sexual contact. And finally, the term *intimate* has historically referred to family members, but as conceptualizations of family have broadened, so too have our understandings of intimates.

Any history of the recognition of VMIR as a social problem is incomplete without a consideration of the prevention and intervention strategies that have been introduced to address this problem. Prevention efforts are attempts to keep VMIR from occurring in the first place, whereas intervention strategies are responses to VMIR after it occurs. U.S. social policies have tended to emphasize intervention rather than prevention, and these intervention strategies have most typically focused on protecting victims and deterring perpetrators from committing further violence.

Recommended Resources

Best, J. (2001). *Damned lies and statistics: Untangling numbers from the media, politicians, and activists.* Berkeley: University of California Press.

Centers for Disease Control and Prevention (CDC). (2016). *Preventing multiple forms of violence: A strategic vision for connecting the dots.* Atlanta, GA: Division of Violence Prevention, National Center for Injury Prevention and Control, Centers for Disease Control and Prevention.

deMause, L. (1974). *The history of childhood.* New York, NY: Psychotherapy Press.

Dobash, R. F., & Dobash, R. P. (1979). *Violence against wives: A case against patriarchy.* New York, NY: Free Press.

Gelles, R. J., & Straus, M. A. (1988). *Intimate violence.* New York, NY: Simon & Schuster.

Levesque, R. J. R. (2001). *Culture and family violence.* Washington, DC: American Psychological Association.

Pleck, E. (1987). *Domestic tyranny: The making of American social policy against family violence from colonial times to present.* New York, NY: Oxford University Press.

Renzetti, C. M., Edleson, J. L., & Kennedy Bergen, R. (Eds.). (2018). *Sourcebook on violence against women* (3rd ed.). Thousand Oaks, CA: Sage.

2

METHODS AND PERSPECTIVES IN VIOLENCE AND MALTREATMENT IN INTIMATE RELATIONSHIPS

LEARNING OBJECTIVES

1. Describe the various explanations for violence and maltreatment in intimate relationships (VMIR) that have been proposed, including structural characteristics of intimate relationships, cultural acceptance of violence, the low costs of VMIR, and the intergenerational transmission of VMIR.

2. Interpret the funnel metaphor as it is used in measuring VMIR.

3. Compare and contrast the important data sets and self-report survey instruments used in VMIR research.

4. Identify the various methodological issues relevant in conducting research on VMIR, including those related to defining VMIR, establishing cause-and-effect relationships, and research designs.

The invisibility and secrecy of violence and maltreatment in intimate relationships (VMIR), as well as the ongoing debates about definitions and measurement of VMIR, create empirical and methodological hurdles that are difficult to overcome. Our task in this chapter is to try to simplify these complicated issues. We begin with a discussion of several broad explanatory perspectives that provide a context for our understanding. We then turn to measurement issues, and the important data sets and self-report instruments that are used to study VMIR. We conclude with a discussion of several important methodological issues relevant to the study of VMIR.

AN EXPLANATORY CONTEXT

We begin with a discussion of several factors that help explain why VMIR is so common. Our intent in this section is *not* to introduce specific theories. Instead, we hope to provide a contextual beginning point for understanding why VMIR occurs. Although we often discuss this topic under the stated assumption that VMIR is "inexplicable," the reality is that it is in many ways quite understandable and predictable. Why is this so? Why might we reasonably *expect* VMIR to be a common occurrence under specific conditions?

Structural Characteristics of Intimate Relationships

All families and intimate relationships have tensions, and it is reasonable to expect that these tensions will not always be resolved in the most appropriate ways. Even the best parents and the most loving couples sometimes lose their temper, say intentionally hurtful things to one another, or raise their voices when arguing. Sometimes, they even lash out physically.

Part of the reason why these behaviors occur is structural. Intimates spend a lot of time together, which increases the opportunity for VMIR. Intimate interactions are often emotional, and therefore potentially volatile. Power differentials often exist among intimates: Children are subordinate to parents, elderly parents may be subordinate to adult children, and wives may be subordinate to husbands. No doubt patriarchy and the historical devaluation of children, as discussed in Chapter 1, also contribute to dynamics within intimate relationships. Further complicating matters is the fact that victims are often physically weaker and thus more vulnerable. Intimates also cannot always choose with whom they will or will not interact. Whereas many interpersonal conflicts can be resolved simply through the dissolution of relationships, family relationships are protected by law and are not so easily severed. Spouses can easily feel trapped by the cultural, legal, and economic constraints of marriage. Children are dependent both financially and emotionally on their parents. The elderly may be similarly dependent on their adult children or other caregivers. Finally, the privacy and autonomy traditionally granted to families in our society make violence relatively easy to hide (Brinkerhoff & Lupri, 1988).

Levesque (2001) asserts that the problem begins with an idealized notion of the family, and intimate relationships more broadly, that offers rights and protections that are sometimes undeserved. The apparent reasonableness of this notion serves to "justify what otherwise could be construed as violent, abusive, and worthy of intervention" (p. 5). According to Levesque, this idealized image of "the family" includes several beliefs: (a) that parental rights supersede children's rights and that parents can and should have control over the development of their children; (b) that family members will act in the best interests of children and elderly parents who are not capable of caring for themselves; (c) that families rooted in traditional cultures are "strong families," even though some of their cultural customs justify intimate maltreatment; and (d) that families have the right to privacy and autonomy, even though this right often results in harm to vulnerable members (this assumed right may also indirectly result in society's reluctance to provide social services or criminal justice assistance).

A Culture of Acceptance

Too often, we would argue, interactions that would not be tolerated outside intimate relationships are seen as inevitable and unavoidable within intimate relationships. Intimate partners sometimes hit and push. Siblings fight. Parents sometimes get frustrated and spank harder than they should. Men push sexual boundaries beyond agreed-upon limits. "It just happens," observers might respond.

The "it just happens" argument is troubling, in large part because we generally do not accept this argument outside of intimate relationships. We might see hitting a child, for example, as an "inevitable part of childhood or family life" that is "educational" and "builds character" (Finkelhor, 2008, p. 9). Even intimate partner hitting is, to a limited degree, tolerated (Simon et al., 2001).

This issue will be discussed in more detail in Chapter 11. For now, our point is simply to provide a cultural context for this implied acceptance. The more we as a society accept physical, emotional, and sexual aggression as "appropriate" or "inevitable," the more likely it is that abuses will occur. Physical, emotional, and sexual aggressions generally deemed "legitimate" in American society (e.g., a slap on the hand of a misbehaving child) and aggression deemed "illegitimate" (e.g., a fist to the face of a misbehaving child) exist on a hitting continuum. It stands to reason that the more society accepts minor forms of VMIR as legitimate and inevitable, the more abusive VMIR will occur.

Low Costs of VMIR

Sociologists define **social control** as the collective efforts of a society to ensure conformity and prevent deviance. Theories of social control begin with the assumption that humans are rational beings who maximize benefits and minimize costs. We would argue that part of the reason why VMIR exists is because social costs for these behaviors are often low.

Famed sociologist Peter Berger envisions social control as a series of concentric circles, with the individual sitting at the center. The outer rings represent the political and legal system that coerces conformity: what we will call *formal* mechanisms of social control. This is the system that, in the words of Berger (1963, pp. 73–74), "will tax one, draft one into the military, and make one obey its innumerable rules and regulations, if need be put one in prison, and in the last resort will kill one." The formal mechanisms of control relevant to topics in this book include the criminal justice system, Child Protective Services, and Adult Protective Services, each of which has the power to impose costs on intimate offenders. The outer circles describe what criminologists refer to as **deterrence theory**. For deterrence theorists, *costs* are defined as the perceived probability of getting caught by formal agents of social control (*certainty* of punishment) and the perceived seriousness of the punishment these agents will impose (*severity* of punishment).

The inner circles represent *informal* mechanisms, where we imagine the approval (rewards) or disapproval (costs) of others (e.g., frowns, judgments, ridicule, gossip). Where these social bonds are weak, and where the inner circle does not condemn the behavior, deviance is more common.

This system of formal and informal social control ensures that most of us, most of the time, play by the rules. But when we perceive the potential costs to be low, as they often are with VMIR, we are more likely to deviate. Gelles and Straus (1988) provide an interesting illustration of the relatively low costs of VMIR, arguing that one of the reasons why family members hit other family members is "because they can." That is, there are insufficient controls, or "costs," to keep them from hitting one another when they are inclined to do so. To illustrate, they tell the story of David, who is at the hospital with his son Peter. Peter had been playing with the family's new television set and had knocked it over. In anger, David "lost it" and hit Peter, who fell onto the coffee table and was injured.

If we apply what we know about social control, we might reasonably conclude that people are far less likely to "lose control" when the costs are high—when they cannot afford to "lose control." What would happen, for example, if Peter was not David's son? What if Peter is a neighborhood boy who is visiting David's son when he knocks over the TV? How is David likely to respond? "Does David slap, spank, or even beat the wayward 3-year-old? Absurd" (Gelles & Straus, 1988, p. 21).

Family members hit one another "because they can" (Gelles & Straus, 1988). In many ways it is that simple. There are insufficient costs—both formal (outer circle) and informal (inner circle)—to keep them from hitting one another.

Note that the Gelles and Straus book cited earlier was written in 1988, long before VMIR was fully discovered. As societal concern about VMIR has risen, so too have the costs. And as costs have risen, rates of VMIR have declined. Researchers have been tracking victimization rates since the early 1990s, and these data suggest that, almost without exception, rates of intimate partner violence, adult sexual assault, child sexual abuse, and child physical abuse are all down (Finkelhor, Saito, & Jones, 2016; Finkelhor, Shattuck, Turner, & Hamby, 2014a; Langton, Krebs, Berzofsky, & Smiley-McDonald, 2013; Truman & Morgan, 2014). There is every reason to believe, furthermore, that as costs continue to rise, VMIR will continue to decline. (Declining rates of VMIR are discussed in more detail in Chapter 11.)

Intergenerational Transmission: VMIR as Learned Behavior

How are parents *supposed to* discipline children? How are married couples *supposed to* interact? How are men and women *supposed to* navigate sexual interactions? Each of us is likely to answer these questions very differently, in part because we are each socialized to answer these questions differently. Human behavior is not instinctual; human behavior is learned.

Most social science students will remember the research of psychologist Albert Bandura (1978), who placed an adult in a room with a "bobo" doll (a large clown blow-up doll) while a child watched the interaction from another room. Some of the adults acted both verbally and physically aggressively (i.e., yelling, hitting, and punching the doll), while others acted nonaggressively. When the children were placed in the room with the doll, the reaction was predictable; those who observed the adults acting aggressively acted aggressively themselves, and those who observed nonaggression acted nonaggressively. The implications for VMIR are obvious. Some children grow up in families where violence is common: Parents hit children, children hit each other, and parents hit each other. Other children grow up in families where nobody hits. There is an inherent logic in the observation that children who experience or observe VMIR are more likely to act aggressively as adults (Widom & Wilson, 2015).

While learning theory is logical, and is generally supported empirically, it is important to note that the research on **intergenerational transmission** is not as strong as many imagine (see Widom & Wilson, 2015, for a review). For example, in an important article published in the prestigious journal *Science*, Widom, Czaja, and DuMont (2015) found support for the intergenerational transmission of sexual abuse and neglect but not physical abuse—a finding that is difficult to explain theoretically.

Scholars remind us that there are many factors that complicate what would seem to be a "common sense" association. For example, if the individual who is observed reaps rewards from the violence, or if the aggressive model is someone the observer greatly admires, the observer is more likely to model the behavior (see Leve, Khurana, & Reich, 2015; Thornberry & Henry, 2013; Widom & Wilson, 2015).

Evidence for intergenerational transmission is described in more detail in subsequent chapters that address the different forms of VMIR.

MEASUREMENT ISSUES: THE FUNNEL METAPHOR

Social phenomena are inherently difficult to study. We don't know the percentage of high school students who have tried alcohol, for example. We only know how many *tell us* they have done so. However, because alcohol use is relatively easy to operationalize, and it is not an overly sensitive topic (since most teens do it), if we read that a national survey has found that 80 percent of 12th graders have consumed alcohol at some point in their lives we can trust that the estimate is reasonably accurate.

With VMIR, however, the issues are much more complex. To demonstrate the problems associated with measuring crimes and other deviant behaviors, criminologists sometimes use the metaphor of a funnel. Figure 2.1 illustrates what this funnel might look like with respect to VMIR. Keep in mind that while the funnel metaphor applies to all forms of VMIR, the specifics encountered along the way vary with each specific type of VMIR. The discussion that follows, therefore, details the general issues that apply to all forms of VMIR.

At the top of the funnel sits the actual amount of VMIR present within society (Level I). This is an unknowable number and can only be estimated with surveys. Level II represents the cases that are actually reported to official agents of social control. This would include reports made to Child Protective Services (CPS), Adult Protective Services (APS), and/or law enforcement. Level III represents cases that, upon investigation, are determined to have occurred. For example, if a concerned neighbor calls CPS to report a case of child neglect, authorities must investigate. If CPS determines that a preponderance

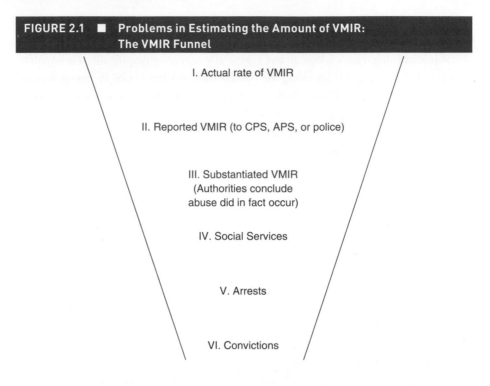

FIGURE 2.1 ■ Problems in Estimating the Amount of VMIR: The VMIR Funnel

I. Actual rate of VMIR

II. Reported VMIR (to CPS, APS, or police)

III. Substantiated VMIR
(Authorities conclude
abuse did in fact occur)

IV. Social Services

V. Arrests

VI. Convictions

of evidence suggests that the abuse did in fact occur, the case is said to be **substantiated**. Typically, approximately one-fifth of the children investigated are found to be victims of abuse or neglect (U.S. Department of Health and Human Services [U.S. DHHS], 2019b). In cases reported as a crime, law enforcement authorities must essentially do the same thing. If a wife reports to law enforcement that she has been raped by her husband, police must decide whether there is sufficient evidence to conclude that the rape did in fact occur. At Level IV the funnel narrows even further as authorities must decide how to proceed. In the case of child maltreatment, the assumption is that the state will mandate services (e.g., counseling for the parents, foster care for the child, permanent removal of the child). In reality, however, CPS intervenes in only approximately two-thirds of substantiated cases (U.S. DHHS, 2019b). At Levels V and VI the funnel narrows even more, as a small number of cases move through the criminal justice system.

The funneling metaphor is helpful as we turn our attention to specific data sources and survey instruments that are commonly used to study VMIR. Each source examines a different level in the funnel. **Self-report surveys** (Level I) are mail, phone, or face-to-face surveys of the general public concerning VMIR. Self-report surveys can question people about their own history of VMIR toward intimates (**perpetration surveys**) or question people about their experiences with VMIR as victims (**victimization surveys**). There are many unavoidable methodological problems associated with perpetration and victimization surveys. The most obvious problem with perpetration surveys is that people may well minimize, or lie about, their behavior. Or perpetrators may perceive their own violence as justified and therefore not reportable. Victims, on the other hand, may not feel free to share their story in an interview or on a survey, especially if they are still living with the abuser. And adults who are asked to recall childhood victimization may have memory lapses and distortions. One of the most contentious debates about child sexual abuse, for example, is the question of whether adults can recover previously **repressed memories** of childhood victimization. Some question the accuracy of these **recovered memories**, suggesting that false memories are easily constructed (Loftus & Davis, 2006).

Level II and Level III are two different levels of **official statistics** compiled by formal agents of social control. This would include, for example, the Uniform Crime Report and the National Child Abuse and Neglect Data System, both of which are discussed in the next section of this chapter. Recall from Chapter 1 that the gap between the *actual* rate and the officially recorded rate is termed the *dark figure*. In our funnel, this represents the difference between Level I (actual rate of VMIR) and Level II (reported VMIR) or the difference between Level I and Level III (substantiated VMIR). Since VMIR has a very large dark figure, official statistics must be interpreted with a degree of caution. An increase or decrease in a particular form of VMIR could reflect a change in the actual behavior, a change in the reporting of that behavior, or both.

Imagine, for example, that we have reliable official statistics from the Federal Bureau of Investigation (FBI) on marital rape from 100 years ago. How would we expect these data to compare to present-day rates? Since marital rape was not a crime 100 years ago, the official rate would have been *zero*. Today, marital rape *is* a crime (by the mid-1990s, all states had criminalized marital rape). As a result of these legal changes, official statistics obviously indicate that there has been a dramatic *increase* in marital rape. Logic, however, suggests otherwise. With criminalization, increased awareness, the empowerment of women, and cultural challenges to a patriarchal model of marriage, we would fully expect that the *actual* rates would have declined dramatically over the past 100 years. And if we had reliable self-report data from 100 years ago to compare to current patterns, we can imagine what they might reveal: a dramatic decline. In this case we would simply conclude the obvious: Increased awareness and criminalization have driven up official rates and driven down self-report rates. The point is that self-report statistics and official statistics provide very different information, reminding us that questions of prevalence will always be difficult to answer.

IMPORTANT DATA SETS AND SELF-REPORT SURVEY INSTRUMENTS

There are several data sources and survey instruments that attempt to track and estimate the occurrence of VMIR in society. These sources are described in this section as they relate to the measurement funnel described earlier, as well as in terms of the advantages and disadvantages of each.

Uniform Crime Report

The Uniform Crime Reporting Program is a nationwide effort by the FBI to collect and report crimes, number of arrests, and persons arrested. These official statistics (Levels II, III, V, and VI from Figure 2.1) are published annually in the **Uniform Crime Report (UCR)**, the most important and commonly cited crime data in the United States.

Because most of the cases of VMIR discussed in this book are *not* typically reported as crimes, the UCR is of limited value in the study of VMIR. However, for the most serious forms of violence the UCR is an invaluable resource. Consider, for example, what the UCR can tell us about intimate homicide. Overall, women are, when compared to men, unlikely to be victims of homicide. Only about 25 percent of homicide victims are female. However, when women are killed, they are especially likely to have been killed by a male intimate (which the UCR defines as husbands, ex-husbands, boyfriends, or ex-boyfriends). According to the UCR, each year approximately 40 percent of female homicide victims are killed by an intimate (U.S. Department of Justice, Federal Bureau of Investigation, 2019). Less than 5 percent of male homicide victims are killed by an intimate. However, these data do not, and cannot, tell the entire story. Think about it. Not every homicide is reported. Most are, of course, but not all. Additionally, not all homicide cases are solved. In fact, in approximately 40 percent of homicides each year, the victim–offender relationship is unknown when the UCR is published for that year. Since no doubt *some* of these unknowns are intimates, we can reasonably assume that the actual percentage of female homicide victims killed by intimates is well above 40 percent. Perhaps it is closer to 50 percent? The UCR, therefore, tells us a great deal about intimate homicide. Male homicide victims are rarely killed by an intimate, but we can reasonably conclude that approximately one-half of female homicide victims are killed by intimates.

National Child Abuse and Neglect Data System

The **National Child Abuse and Neglect Data System (NCANDS)** is a federally sponsored data collection system on reported child abuse and neglect. Every year NCANDS compiles CPS data from all 50 states on a variety of important issues relevant to child maltreatment such as source of child abuse reports, investigation outcomes, types of maltreatment reported, description of the victims of maltreatment, the relationship of perpetrators to victims, CPS caseloads and response time, and services provided. These official statistics (Levels II, III, and IV from Figure 2.1) are disseminated annually in the publication *Child Maltreatment*. This publication is now in its 26th edition, *Child Maltreatment 2017* (U.S. DHHS, 2019b).

National Incidence Studies

The **National Incidence Studies (NIS)** are unique in that they actually sit between Level I and Level II on our funnel (Figure 2.1). These are surveys of professionals who are mandated to report cases of child maltreatment to CPS. The logic behind the NIS is that mandated professionals do not always report suspected cases of child maltreatment, and this fact must be taken into consideration in determining the extent of child maltreatment. Professionals may fail to report, for example, because they have conflicting responsibilities (e.g., they may be in a counseling relationship with a victim or perpetrator), because they may not want to get involved with CPS, or because they may not trust CPS or the reporting system.

The NIS uses sampling procedures to select community professionals who work in agencies where it is common to come into contact with abused and neglected children (e.g., police departments, school and day care centers, hospitals, social service agencies, shelters). In the NIS-4, nearly 11,000 professionals were selected. These mandated reporters essentially served as lookouts for child abuse and neglect. Researchers then extrapolated from the reports filed by these professionals to create national estimates of child maltreatment (Sedlak et al., 2010). There have been four NIS studies published—in 1981, 1988, 1996, and 2010.

National Crime Victimization Survey

The **National Crime Victimization Survey (NCVS)** is a semiannual victim survey (Level I from Figure 2.1) conducted by the U.S. Census Bureau on behalf of the U.S. Department of Justice. The NCVS has been conducted since 1973 and is the primary source of information in the United States on the characteristics of criminal victimization.

Approximately 45,000 households and 100,000 individuals are interviewed every six months for three consecutive years. Respondents are asked about a variety of victimizations during the previous six months, including sexual and physical assaults. Children under the age of 12 are not interviewed, so the NCVS is not especially useful in the study of child maltreatment. However, because respondents are asked if and how they are connected to the offender, the NCVS is a valuable source of information on adult intimate partner violence, or IPV (Bureau of Justice Statistics, 2019).

There are two significant limitations with the NCVS as a measure of IPV. First, because the respondent is typically home for the interview (interviews are over the phone or face-to-face in the home), they may not always feel free to openly discuss VMIR. How many women, for example, are going to openly discuss their husband's abuse if he is in the next room watching television? Second, the NCVS is introduced to respondents as a *crime* survey. The survey actually begins, "I am going to read some examples that will give you an idea of the kinds of crimes the study covers" (Bachman, 2015, p. 24).

The concern is that a respondent who is primed in this way will likely think of acts he or she perceives to be a crime. A woman who has a very narrow understanding of sexual assault, or who may not realize that a husband can sexually assault his wife, may not respond affirmatively to questions on sexual assault, even if she has had experiences that would satisfy legal definitions of rape (Bachman, 2015). Despite the limitation, since the NCVS provides biannual data on crime victimization, it is a very important source of data on IPV.

National Intimate Partner and Sexual Violence Survey

The **National Intimate Partner and Sexual Violence Survey (NISVS)** is a victimization survey (Level I from Figure 2.1) that measures adult respondents' recollections about physical violence and sexual assault experienced by the respondent. It is an ongoing, nationally representative victimization phone survey of approximately 18,000 adult men and women that assesses the past 12 months as well as lifetime rates for VMIR (S. Smith et al., 2018).

In the NISVS, unlike the NCVS, researchers make a more conscious effort to avoid preconceptions of what terms like *crime*, or *violence*, or *rape* might mean to a respondent. The NISVS introduces the topics of violence and sexual assault as a "health concern," which is a much less imposing and threatening approach to measuring sensitive and misunderstood topics like rape. In addition, unlike earlier measures of sexual assault, the NISVS includes measures of sexual contact where consent was compromised by drugs or alcohol. The preamble reads (National Center for Injury Prevention and Control, 2014, p. 3):

> Sometimes sex happens when a person is unable to consent to it or stop it from happening because they were drunk, high, drugged, or passed out from alcohol, drugs, or medications. This can include times when they voluntarily consumed alcohol or drugs or they were given drugs or alcohol without their knowledge or consent. . . .

> When you were drunk, high, drugged, or passed out and unable to consent, how many people have ever . . .

The survey then goes on to ask the respondent about several sex acts. For example, how many people have ever "had vaginal sex with you?" or "made you perform anal sex?"

Another strength of the NISVS is that it measures maltreatment that has not typically been studied in national surveys, including sexual violence other than rape, psychological coercion, control of reproductive/sexual health, and stalking (S. Smith et al., 2018).

Conflict Tactics Scales

The **Conflict Tactics Scales (CTS)**, originally created by Murray Straus (1979), are the most historically significant and widely used scales in self-reported VMIR (Level I from Figure 2.1). The CTS are based on the assumption that conflict is an inevitable part of intimate interactions. Introducing the questionnaire in this way "normalizes" conflict in hopes that respondents will speak more freely and honestly about the "tactics" they use to resolve intimate conflict. The CTS use several questions to measure three categories of conflict resolution: reasoning/negotiation (e.g., "suggested a compromise to a disagreement"), verbal/psychological aggression (e.g., "shouted or yelled at my partner"), and physical aggression (e.g., "kicked my partner"). In 1996, Straus and his colleagues introduced the CTS2, a revised version that includes additional items and new scales for physical injury (e.g., "had a sprain, bruise, or small cut because of a fight with my partner") and sexual coercion (e.g., "used force to make my partner have sex") (Straus, Hamby, Boney-McCoy, & Sugarman, 1996).

The original CTS was designed to measure marital or dating violence, but it could be altered to measure child maltreatment by changing the reference from "your partner" to a specific child. Eventually Straus, Hamby, Finkelhor, Moore, and Runyan (1998) created a modified version of the CTS specifically to measure child maltreatment: the **Parent–Child Conflict Tactics Scale (CTSPC)**. Like the CTS, the CTSPC normalizes conflict in a preamble that acknowledges that children often engage in wrongful or disobedient behavior that might make parents angry. Respondents are asked several questions about a variety of conflict tactics their mother or father might have used when they misbehaved. Three conflict tactics are measured in the CTSPC: nonviolent responses (e.g., "explained why something was wrong"), psychological aggression responses (e.g., "cursed or swore at me"), and physical aggression responses that measure everything from various forms of corporal punishment (e.g., "spanked me on the bottom with her hand") to extreme forms of child maltreatment (e.g., "grabbed me around the neck and choked me"). The CTSPC also includes a series of optional supplemental questions designed to measure weekly discipline (including more measures of corporal punishment), neglect, and sexual abuse.

It is worth noting that the Conflict Tactics Scales, especially the two versions that measure IPV (CTS and CTS2), have been somewhat controversial. Critics maintain that because the CTS merely counts violent acts, it ignores the context and consequences of those acts. In doing so, it underestimates the consequences of IPV for women (DeKeseredy & Schwartz, 1998).

National Survey of Children's Exposure to Violence and Juvenile Victimization Questionnaire

The **National Survey of Children's Exposure to Violence (NatSCEV)** uses the **Juvenile Victimization Questionnaire (JVQ)** to measure exposure to a wide variety of childhood victimization, including conventional crime, child maltreatment, peer and sibling victimization, sexual assault, and witnessing an indirect victimization. It was defined specifically to measure the *polyvictimization* of children (Finkelhor, Turner, Shattuck,

Hamby, & Kracke, 2015). As discussed in Chapter 1, child maltreatment research is often fragmented, with studies focusing on the measurement of one specific form of child maltreatment. In reality, of course, there is considerable overlap between the various forms of child maltreatment. If we read, for example, that 10 percent of children are physically abused and 10 percent are neglected, we cannot conclude that 20 percent of children are victims of physical abuse or neglect, because it is likely that a high percentage experienced both abuse and neglect.

The JVQ measures not only the most serious forms of direct childhood victimization but also a wide variety of indirect forms of exposure (e.g., witnessing fights in and outside the home, hearing gunfire) as well as relatively common forms of victimization, including bullying and teasing. The NatSCEV has been conducted three times, in 2008 (NatSCEV I), 2011 (NatSCEV II), and 2014 (NatSCEV III; Finkelhor, Turner, Shattuck, & Hamby, 2015).

METHODOLOGICAL ISSUES: CONDUCTING BETTER RESEARCH

During the 1980s, editors of major social science journals were asked why they seemed unwilling to publish research on VMIR. They responded that they would like to publish more but that the research they had seen generally did not meet minimal standards of scientific rigor (Rosenbaum, 1988). Researchers interested in VMIR, therefore, were faced with two alternatives: either improve the quality of their research or find alternative outlets. In many respects, the past years have seen both alternatives occur.

Today, numerous journals are devoted specifically to VMIR (e.g., *Child Abuse and Neglect: The International Journal, Child Maltreatment, Journal of Child Sexual Abuse, Journal of Family Violence, Sexual Abuse: A Journal of Research and Treatment, Violence Against Women*).

Methodological rigor has also increased, and dramatically so. The federal government, for one, has become active in collecting, funding, and disseminating important data. And increasingly the top social science and medical journals are publishing VMIR research. For example, the Widom et al. (2015) research on intergenerational transmission, as discussed previously in this chapter, was published in *Science*, one of the most prestigious journals in the world.

Despite improvements, however, research on VMIR can never be perfect. There will always be tensions associated with the study of a topic so emotional and personal (see Box 2.1). Additionally, there are many methodological hurdles that sometimes stand in the way of full understanding. In the following sections, we consider several of these problems.

BOX 2.1

IS IMPARTIAL EMPIRICISM IN THE STUDY OF VMIR POSSIBLE?

The scientific method, we are told, is "value-free." Empiricists report what they see, not what they hope to see. Given the passions that many bring to the study of VMIR, however, a truly value-free approach is extremely challenging. Most professionals who study VMIR want to make the world a safer place for victims and do not want their research and writing to be completely void of that passion. At the same time, however, one must be careful not to discard the scientific method in favor of an advocacy-driven approach to knowledge. How do we, and how should we, balance advocacy and research? (See Perrin & Miller-Perrin, 2011, for a more detailed discussion of the ideas presented in this section.)

We would argue that advocacy, absent scientific objectivity, is inherently problematic and may do more harm than good. To consider why, we must briefly revisit the social constructionist perspective on social problems, as discussed in Chapter 1. Social conditions become social problems when claims makers successfully define them as such. Claims makers may employ many strategies for raising awareness, including the use—and sometimes misuse—of statistical facts and dramatic rhetoric. Because social conditions essentially compete for attention, claims makers will inevitably be drawn to larger numbers and dramatic rhetoric (Best, 2001).

Why is this a potential problem? Consider the debate between Dianna Russell and Neil Gilbert. Gilbert (1997) is critical of Russell's (1984) claim that 54 percent of children are victims of sexual abuse. This estimate from Russell, Gilbert argues, is an exaggerated "advocacy statistic." In fairness, Russell is clear that the 54 percent figure is based on a very broad definition of sexual abuse that includes unwanted kisses and nongenital sexual touching as well as exposure to exhibitionism (D. Russell & Bolen, 2000). However, it is also fair to remind the reader that Russell, like advocates more generally, likely assumes that broad definitions and large numbers will further her cause. The potential problem, Perrin and Miller-Perrin argue (2011), is that if the public *perceives* that advocacy is driving social science, that social scientists manipulate or misuse data to support certain causes, or that social scientists make claims beyond what the data can justify, public confidence in social scientific findings are undermined. It is easy for the public to dismiss social scientific claims about particular issues if they perceive that the claims are ideologically motivated. And having dismissed the claims, it is easy for the public to dismiss the issues themselves.

Furthermore, if almost everyone is a victim of abuse, do the terms *victim* and *abuse* not lose their meaning? If marital pushing and shoving is abuse, then many marital couples have engaged in "abusive" behavior. If spanking is child abuse, then almost all children are "victims of abuse." If sibling pushing or hitting is abusive, then almost all siblings are victims or perpetrators or both. In each of these scenarios, the meaning of the terms *victim* and *abuse* have been diluted. However inappropriate and indefensible these relatively minor forms of VMIR are, they should be clearly distinguished from more serious and damaging forms of VMIR. Giving a child an occasional swat on the bottom may not be good or effective, and we might want to advocate that society not accept these behaviors, but do they constitute *abuse*? Certainly, we must acknowledge that the effects of spanking are minor compared with severe assault. If our advocacy leads us to claim otherwise and our attention is diverted from more serious forms of abuse, then we may do more harm than good.

The notion of *value-free inquiry* can be traced to the very beginnings of the social sciences. Sociologist Max Weber (1949) reasoned that if values influence research, the findings will be rejected and the discipline discredited. But Weber also reminds us that the topics we choose, and the ways we approach these topics, are always "value relevant."

We cannot be, nor should we be, completely value-free. It simply is not possible. Yet we must be careful. If our advocacy commitments lead to poor scholarship and shoddy research, then we may win a battle here and there, but we may be less likely to win the war.

Negotiated Definitions

It is very important to remember that the behaviors we categorize as abuse will always be debated and negotiated. They will never be, and can never be, "objectively defined." The definitional criteria deemed important vary from one audience to the next and from one generation to the next.

The problem, at least in part, is that we want our facts delivered neatly and succinctly (see Best, 2001). Yet there are very few neat and succinct facts in the study of VMIR. Consider as an example these two empirical statements (Leve et al., 2015, p. 1429): "Official statistics from the National Center for Injury Prevention and Control [2014] indicate that the rate of victimization in the United States is as high as 9.2 children per 1,000 children. Self-report studies reveal that as many as one-in-four U.S. children will experience some form of maltreatment in their lifetime." We would argue that these two statements essentially tell us nothing. In no way do we intend to criticize Dr. Leve and her colleagues with this critique. They have appropriately cited statistics, and readers who want to know more can go to the source of those statistics. And, quite frankly, we are all, including the authors of this book, often guilty of oversimplifying statistics in this way. It is likely not feasible to *always* provide the definitional details of the statistics we cite. But the fact of the matter is that without the definitional details of the terms *victimization* (first sentence) and *maltreatment* (second sentence), these statistics tell us very little. In subsequent chapters addressing the various forms of VMIR, we attempt to clarify the definitions used as much as possible.

Correlation Isn't Causation: Problems Establishing Cause-and-Effect Relationships

Most of the research on VMIR is **retrospective**, **cross-sectional**, and **correlational**, making causal connections difficult to identify. If a researcher wanted to study the effects of IPV on women, for example, he or she might examine a sample of IPV victims for emotional, behavioral, or cognitive problems and compare them to a sample of individuals who were not abused. In general, this is how research on the effects of abuse is conducted (Dillon, Hussain, Loxton, & Rahman, 2013). Predictably, most of this research reveals that IPV is associated with a range of behavioral and emotional problems (e.g., depression, post-traumatic stress disorder, anxiety, self-harm, and sleep disorders). Does the violence cause these emotional and behavioral problems? This is a much more difficult question to answer. Two variables can be associated without necessarily being causally related.

A causal link between correlated variables can only be established if two criteria are met: **time order** and **nonspuriousness**. Time order refers to the obvious fact that a cause must occur before an effect. For example, the correlation between spanking and behavioral problems in children is well established in the literature (see Gershoff & Grogan-Kaylor, 2016). If one hopes to argue that spanking causally contributes to behavioral problems in children, however, it must be established that the spanking occurred before the behavior problems. Obviously, parents who spank are likely to make the opposite argument, since it is misbehaving children who must be spanked. Nonspuriousness refers to the requirement that the relationship be nonaccidental. A spurious relationship is one in which a third unknown and uncontrolled variable accounts for the correlation between the two variables in question. The number of fire trucks is indeed correlated with the amount of financial damage caused by a fire, but not because fire trucks cause fire damage. Perhaps spanking and behavioral problems are correlated because emotionally detached parents (or poor parents, or physically aggressive parents) are more likely to hit and have poorly behaved children. Or perhaps child maltreatment victims are more likely than nonvictims to suffer from adult depression because of other factors that are also correlated with abuse and depression (e.g., living in a chaotic family environment, living in poverty, and having few social supports).

Randomized Controlled Trials (Experimental Design)

Researchers, of course, are keenly aware of the issues discussed in the previous section, and make every effort to control for as many potential intervening variables as possible. But the only way to establish clear cause-and-effect relationships is to devise an **experimental design** using a **randomized controlled trial** (**RCT**). The experimental design is considered the "gold standard" in research design. In this methodological design, the researcher randomly assigns participants to two or more groups and then introduces an independent variable into one or more of the groups. Because subjects are randomly assigned, one can reasonably assume that the groups are alike on any trait that might be causally relevant, essentially controlling for all extraneous effects. Any observed differences between the groups can then be attributed to the independent variables.

Of course, RCTs are rarely feasible in the study of VMIR. It is hardly ethical, for example, to take a sample of 200 infants who are up for adoption and randomly assign 100 to abusive families and 100 to nonabusive families and observe the outcome. Interestingly, one area where RCTs are feasible is evaluation research of prevention and intervention programs. Even here, however, ethical dilemmas present themselves. For example, researchers who randomly assign at-risk families to prevention and intervention programs must consider the potential consequences of excluding at-risk families that are in the control group and therefore miss out on the potential benefit of such programs.

Longitudinal Studies and Matched Comparison Groups

With **longitudinal designs** and **matched control groups** we can approximate the methodological power of RCTs. Longitudinal studies allow us to track effects over time, thus controlling for the time order problem inherent in many correlation studies. And with a matched comparison group we have a reference point with which we can compare our research participants. Unfortunately, these studies are expensive, participants are difficult to obtain, and attrition rates for participants are high. In addition, sometimes researchers are under pressure to produce immediate results. A researcher who needs tenure today may not be able to wait for results tomorrow (i.e., over several years). Consequently, most research designs are cross-sectional, using retrospective self-report survey data.

With increased funding and interest in VMIR research, longitudinal studies are becoming more common. For example, Widom has been following a **prospective cohort** of child abuse victims since the late 1960s. The original sample included almost 1,000 children, ages 11 years and under, all of whom were court-substantiated victims of abuse and neglect. Widom also selected a comparison group, matched for known correlates of abuse and criminality (e.g., age, sex, race, class). Making the two groups as similar as possible is important, of course, because causal assertions are dependent on the assumption that the primary difference between the two groups is the abuse they endured as children. A prospective design like this is powerful because both cohorts, the abused children and the matched comparison group, were free of the "outcome" (intergenerational transmission, the effects of abuse, etc.) when the study began. Widom has been following these two cohorts for 50 years now, and she and various colleagues have evaluated the effects of abuse as well as the intergenerational transmission of abuse in the original cohort (generation 1), their children (generation 2), and their children's children (generation 3). It is a fascinating and impressive endeavor, and effectively demonstrates not only the power of the longitudinal research, but also how sophisticated some VMIR research has become (see, for example, Widom et al., 2015).

CHAPTER SUMMARY

We have approached this chapter with three goals in mind. First, we try to explain VMIR. This section is not intended to be a detailed discussion of theory. Rather, it is an attempt to provide a context for understanding why VMIR is so common. Second, we introduce the various measurement issues that all researchers must navigate. This includes a discussion of important data sources and measurement instruments. Finally, we discuss the many methodological issues that make VMIR, and frankly all social science, so complicated.

Many cultural and social-structural antecedents contribute to physically violent and verbally aggressive intimate interactions. The structural characteristics of intimate relationships partly explain why VMIR is so common. Intimates spend a great deal of time together, and interactions tend to be intense. The subordination and in some cases dependency of intimates also make them vulnerable to abuse, and privacy norms make VMIR relatively easy to conceal. The culture sometimes encourages, condones, and accepts verbal and physical aggression between parents that, arguably, could indirectly contribute to VMIR. VMIR is also a relatively low-cost form of deviant behavior, which partially explains why it is so common. Finally, we introduce the concept of intergenerational transmission: the idea that VMIR is learned behavior and is passed on across generations. We conclude that learning factors are relevant, but that intergenerational transmission theory is not as powerfully predictive as many suspect.

The many difficulties associated with determining the extent of VMIR are illustrated in Figure 2.1. The top of the funnel (Level I) is the actual amount of VMIR that exists in society. Although this figure is obviously unknown and unknowable, it can be estimated with self-report perpetration or victim surveys, such as the National Crime Victimization Survey (NCVS), the National Intimate Partner and Sexual Violence Survey (NISVS), the Conflict Tactics Scales (CTS and CTS2), and the Juvenile Victimization Questionnaire (JVQ). Self-report and victim surveys are the only way we can estimate the *dark figure*, which is the gap between the actual rate of VMIR (Level I) and the officially reported and recorded rate (Level II). Level II data sets include the Uniform Crime Report (UCR) and the National Child Abuse and Neglect Data System (NCANDS). Our funnel narrows even more at this point, through various stages of substantiation (determining whether or not the alleged abuse did in fact occur), social services, or criminal proceedings.

Many methodological problems continue to plague the field. The most glaring of these may be definitional ambiguity. For example, terms like *sexual assault* or *child neglect* or *intimate partner violence* are commonly used in popular and professional circles, but there is not always agreement on exactly what these terms mean, and how they should be operationalized. This ambiguity makes findings difficult to compare across studies. Another problem is that most VMIR research is retrospective and correlational. This makes it very difficult to establish cause-and-effect relationships. Randomized controlled trials (RCTs), also called experimental designs, are rarely feasible. Longitudinal research is expensive and difficult to conduct.

Despite these many difficulties, research on VMIR has become increasingly sophisticated in recent years, and we fully expect this trend to continue.

Recommended Resources

Finkelhor, D., Turner, H. A., Shattuck, A., & Hamby, S. L. (2015). Prevalence of childhood exposure to violence, crime, and abuse: Results from the National Survey of Children's Exposure to Violence. *JAMA Pediatrics, 169*(8), 746–754.

Perrin, R. D., & Miller-Perrin, C. (2011). Interpersonal violence as social construction: The potentially undermining role of claims-making and advocacy statistics. *Journal of Interpersonal Violence, 26*, 3033–3049.

U.S. Department of Health and Human Services, Administration on Children, Youth and Families. (2019). *Child Maltreatment 2017*. Washington, DC: Government Printing Office.

Widom, C. S., Czaja, S. J., & DuMont, K. A. (2015). Intergenerational transmission of child abuse and neglect: Real or detection bias? *Science, 347*(6229), 1480–1485.

3

CHILD PHYSICAL ABUSE

LEARNING OBJECTIVES

1. Describe the definition and scope of child physical abuse, including problems inherent in measuring this form of abuse.

2. Identify the various risk factors associated with child physical abuse.

3. Summarize the consequences of child physical abuse, including both short- and long-term outcomes.

4. Discuss the various intervention and prevention efforts that have been developed to address child physical abuse, including evidence of their effectiveness.

CASE HISTORY

KEVIN FELL OFF HIS RAZOR

Kevin was placed in foster care because his community's Child Protective Services (CPS) department determined that his family was in conflict. The placement was made after 10-year-old Kevin was seen at the local hospital's emergency room for bruises, welts, and cuts on his back. According to his mother's report to emergency room personnel, the boy fell off of his Razor (scooter) while riding down a hill near the family home. Kevin was very quiet during the visit, never speaking but occasionally nodding his head in affirmation of his mother's report. The attending physician, however, believed that Kevin's injuries were unlikely to have occurred as the result of such a fall. Rather, they appeared consistent with the kinds of injuries a child might have from being slapped repeatedly or possibly whipped with a belt or another object.

Initially, Kevin's mother persisted in her story that Kevin had fallen from his Razor, but after the doctor told her that the injuries could not have resulted from such an accident, she confessed that her boyfriend, Sam, had some strong opinions about how children should behave and how

they should be disciplined. She reported that Sam had a short temper when it came to difficult behavior in children and that he sometimes "lost his cool" in disciplining Kevin. She also mentioned that Sam had been depressed for the past several months because of their difficult financial circumstances. She wondered if these circumstances might have contributed to Sam's violence but also suggested that Kevin's behavior could often be very difficult to control. She said that Kevin had numerous problems, including difficulties in school (e.g., trouble with reading) and with peers (e.g., physically fighting with other children); she described both acting-out behaviors (e.g., setting fire to objects, torturing and killing small animals, stealing) and oppositional behaviors (e.g., skipping school, refusing to do homework, breaking curfew, being noncompliant with requests).

In interviews with a CPS worker, Kevin revealed that he was, in fact, experiencing physical abuse inflicted by his mother's boyfriend. Kevin reluctantly acknowledged that Sam frequently disciplined him by repeatedly slapping

(Continued)

(Continued)

a belt across his back. Kevin reported that on these occasions he tried hard not to cry but often the whippings hurt so much that he couldn't help himself. He also talked about an incident that had taken place when he was several years younger. He had been playing with some baby ducks that lived in the pond in his backyard, trying to teach the ducks to swim underwater. When Sam saw Kevin submerging the ducklings' heads under the water, he became very angry and "taught Kevin a lesson" by holding Kevin's head underwater repeatedly. Kevin was tearful as he told this story and stated that, at the time, he thought he was going to drown. Kevin also mentioned that he was worried about Sam's violence toward his mother,

reporting that Sam would angrily slap and kick his mother after having been out drinking with his buddies.

After Kevin had been in foster care for several weeks, his foster mother indicated that he was doing very well and described him as a remarkably adaptive child. She said she found him to be a "warm, loving kid," and he had not exhibited "any behavior problems other than what you might expect from a 10-year-old boy." She reported also that Kevin "hoped to go home soon" because he missed his mother and Sam. He believed that he was placed in foster care because he was disobedient toward his mother and her boyfriend and because he hadn't been doing well in school.

This case history describes the violence characteristic of the life of a child who is being abused. Until the 1960s, however, and as discussed in Chapter 1, U.S. society was relatively indifferent to the violent world of such children. Child maltreatment was considered a mythical or rare phenomenon that occurred only in some people's imaginations or in "sick" lower-class families. As is now more widely known, however, child maltreatment is an ugly reality for many children in the United States and worldwide (World Health Organization, 2014).

In this chapter, we focus on one form of child maltreatment—child physical abuse (CPA). We first examine issues related to the definition of the physical abuse of children and the use of official statistics and self-report surveys for determining the magnitude of the problem. We then shift our attention to some of the characteristics that research has found to be typical of children who are physically abused and the adults who abuse them in an attempt to understand factors that might explain why physical abuse occurs. We also present evidence of the short- and long-term consequences associated with CPA. We conclude the chapter with a discussion of recommendations for addressing the problem.

SCOPE OF THE PROBLEM

What Is Child Physical Abuse?

Defining CPA is no easy task. Consider, for example, the following situations. Which of these would you consider CPA?

- Jimmy, a 3-year-old, was playing with his puppy in his backyard when he tried to make the puppy stay near him by pulling roughly on the dog's ear. Jimmy's father saw the child vigorously pulling on the puppy's ear and yelled at him to stop. When Jimmy did not respond quickly, his father grabbed Jimmy's arm and pulled him away from the dog. The father then began pulling on Jimmy's ear—actually tearing the skin a bit—to teach him a lesson about the appropriate way to treat a dog.

- Angela's baby, Maria, had colic from the day she was born. This meant that from 4:00 in the afternoon until 8:00 in the evening every day, Maria cried inconsolably. No matter what Angela did, she could not get Maria to stop crying. One evening, after 5-month-old Maria had been crying for three hours straight, Angela became so frustrated that she began shaking Maria. The shaking caused Maria to cry more loudly, which in turn caused Angela to shake the infant more vigorously. Angela shook Maria until the baby lost consciousness.

- Ryan and his brother, Matthew, were playing Super Smash Brothers in Ryan's bedroom when they got into a disagreement and began hitting and arguing. Their mother heard the commotion and came running into the room and separated the two boys. She then took each boy, pulled down his trousers, put him over her knee, and spanked him several times.

One way to define CPA is to focus on observable harm. A child who is injured is abused. However, is this definition too restrictive? Is a father who shoots a gun at his child and misses not also guilty of CPA (Gelles & Cornell, 1990)? Beginning in 1988, the National Center on Child Abuse and Neglect (NCCAN) began to include an **endangerment standard** in addition to a **harm standard** (U.S. Department of Health and Human Services [U.S. DHHS], 1988, 1996). While the harm standard recognizes children as CPA victims if they have observable injuries that last at least 48 hours, children without observable injuries may also be recognized as abuse victims if they are deemed substantially at risk for injury or endangerment.

This broadened understanding leads us to the following definition: CPA is *the intentional use of physical force against a child that results in or has the potential to result in physical injury*. Behaviors that could be defined as abusive include hitting a child with one's fist or an object such as a belt; kicking, biting, choking, shaking, or burning a child; throwing or knocking down a child; or threatening a child with a weapon. Armed with this definition, we can more effectively evaluate the earlier vignettes. The behaviors of Jimmy's father as described in the first vignette qualify as abuse, since pulling on Jimmy's ear results in physical harm.

The second vignette describes a mother whose behavior is clearly abusive. Vigorously shaking a child can result in a particularly dangerous type of head injury known as **shaken baby syndrome (SBS)** or **abusive head trauma (AHT)**, which can result in serious injury or even death (see Box 3.1).

The third vignette illustrates the complicated issue of spanking and corporal punishment. The two boys were spanked, but since there is no indication that they were injured, this is not *defined* as CPA. Of course, there is considerable debate about whether it *should* be defined as abusive, or at least unacceptable. Consider, for example, the recent case of California assemblyman Joaquin Arambula, who was found not guilty of misdemeanor child abuse (Appleton, 2019). Arambula was arrested and charged with misdemeanor child abuse after school officials called police to report a one-inch bruise on the temple of Arambula's 7-year-old daughter. The daughter testified that the bruise was the result of her father's actions; her initial statements claimed that her father "hit her." Arambula claimed that his actions only went as far as spanking his daughter as a form of discipline, and his defense focused on his character as someone who would never be violent toward his family (Amaro, 2018; Appleton, 2019). Despite the fact that the 7-year-old sustained a physical injury, CPS concluded there was insufficient evidence to confirm child abuse, which contributed to Arambula's not guilty verdict (Appleton, 2019).

Determining the boundaries of abuse and discipline is also complicated by the social context of a family's culture and beliefs with regard to child-rearing. We know, for example, that certain cultural values and beliefs are associated with greater endorsement and/or use of harsh physical punishment, which in turn is associated with CPA. Several studies indicate that endorsement and use of corporal punishment among U.S. parents is more common among southerners, African Americans, and

BOX 3.1
SHAKEN BABY SYNDROME

The leading cause of death among children who are physically abused is death associated with some type of injury to the head, referred to in the medical community as abusive head trauma, or AHT (R. Berger & Bell, 2014; Choudhary et al., 2018; Lind et al., 2016). The large majority of these children are under the age of 5, with children under the age of 1 at greatest risk (Joyce & Huecker, 2019). Although the precise mechanisms leading to AHT in cases of child physical abuse have been hotly debated, one common cause of head injury to children is referred to as shaken baby syndrome, or SBS. The National Center on Shaken Baby Syndrome estimates that 1,300 children are injured or killed by abusive head injuries each year in the United States (dontshake.org/learn-more).

SBS results when a caregiver violently shakes a child, causing the child's brain to move within the skull. Such shaking can result in severe brain injury, coma, or even death. Indeed, of children diagnosed with SBS, approximately 20–25 percent die as a result of their injuries, and only 8–36 percent achieve a "good" recovery (K. Barlow, Thomson, Johnson, & Minns, 2005; Chevignard & Lind, 2014; Lind et al., 2016). The damage can result from any number of causes, such as stretching and tearing of blood vessels and brain tissue, retinal bleeding, and oxygen deprivation (Joyce & Huecker, 2019; Strouse, 2018). The children who do survive frequently have lifelong problems such as intellectual disability, cerebral palsy, impaired vision or blindness, seizure disorders, learning disabilities, behavioral difficulties, or delays in physical and emotional growth (Lind et al., 2016; Ornstein & Ward, 2012). In addition to permanent neurologic and associated damage, SBS carries tremendous familial and societal consequences. SBS can result in children being removed from their homes, parents losing their parental rights, and adults being convicted and imprisoned for their actions (Antonietti et al., 2019; Joyce & Huecker, 2019).

Individuals who confess to shaking a child most commonly report difficulty trying to console a crying baby as the antecedent to the behavior. They often report that they felt frustrated, lost control, or "snapped" at the time the shaking occurred (E. Bell, Shouldice, & Levin, 2011; Feld, Banaschak, Remschmidt, & Rothschild, 2018). In one case, a man was accused of assaulting his girlfriend's 3-year-old child (E. Bell et al., 2011). At the time of the abuse, the man was the only adult in the home and was feeling frustrated because one child under his care was screaming in one room while he was bathing the 3-year-old child (who was also upset) in another room. The man began shaking the 3-year-old over and over again for approximately 10–30 seconds. Within that short amount of time, the 3-year-old suffered permanent serious injury including severe mental and physical disabilities.

Innumerable programs have been launched throughout the country via both public and private organizations to inform and educate the public on the hazards of shaking babies. These programs have been successful, with surveys conducted over the last 20 years showing that over 80 percent of adults report some familiarity with SBS (Dias et al., 2005). Although public awareness is an important first step, it is equally important to equip caregivers with appropriate methods to deal with their frustration and respond to inconsolable infants. Intervention studies designed to educate about appropriate response methods have been created, such as the Period of PURPLE Crying program, which helps parents understand and cope with the stress of normal infant crying. The program has a parent education component that includes a 10-minute DVD and 11-page booklet that addresses the risks of shaking a baby and the reasons for early infant crying (Barr et al., 2009). In one evaluation study, 4,200 parents participated in a randomized controlled trial of the program, and results indicated that the program not only enhanced mothers' knowledge about infant crying, but mothers who participated in the program were more likely to leave a situation where an infant was crying inconsolably compared to a control group of mothers (Barr et al., 2009). In another study, pediatric providers gave an educational baby book, *Calm Baby Gently*, to caregivers at the 1-month well-child visit and then assessed knowledge and responses to infant crying at the 2-month well-child visit (Eismann et al., 2019). Parents who had read the book, which describes safe parenting and health practices related to infant crying through gentle rhymes, simple language, and culturally sensitive illustrations, were more confident and had more knowledge on how to respond appropriately to infant crying compared to parents who had not read the book. Findings from several studies following implementation of such programs have also indicated an actual reduction in abusive head injuries (Altman et al., 2011; Barr et al., 2018; Dias et al., 2005).

conservative Protestants (Ellison, Musick, & Holden, 2011; Gershoff, Lansford, Sexton, Davis-Kean, & Sameroff, 2012), and that corporal punishment often escalates into CPA (Gershoff & Grogan-Kaylor, 2016). The controversy surrounding spanking and corporal punishment is fueled by disagreement about the sanctity of cultural norms, the impact of harsh physical punishment on children, and the importance of children's rights, all issues we discuss further in Chapter 11.

Legal Perspectives

Federal law defines physical abuse as actions that result in "serious physical or emotional harm" (Child Abuse Prevention and Treatment Reauthorization Act, 2010; 42 U.S.C.A. § 5106g). Individual states, however, are left to define the specifics of what constitutes "serious physical or emotional harm" (Child Welfare Information Gateway, 2015). In general, all U.S. entities acknowledge the harm and endangerment standards discussed earlier. However, key features of U.S. definitions vary according to the specificity of the acts included as physically abusive. Most emphasize the overt consequences of abuse, such as bruises or broken bones. Parents in all states are permitted to use corporal punishment as long as it is not "injurious," "excessive," or "cruel" (Child Welfare Information Gateway, 2015). In California, for example, physical abuse does not include "reasonable and age-appropriate spanking to the buttocks where there is no evidence of serious physical injury" (California Welfare and Institutions Code §§ 300; 300.5).

How Common Is Child Physical Abuse?

Looking at the various data sources discussed in Chapter 2 provides a sense of just how prevalent CPA is within the United States. According to the most recent figures available from the National Child Abuse and Neglect Data System (NCANDS), approximately 3.5 million children were reported for abuse to CPS in 2017 (U.S. DHHS, 2019b). This number has remained remarkably stable for the last several years. Twenty years ago, for example, 3.14 million suspected cases of abuse were reported to CPS (U.S. DHHS, 2016). Keep in mind that this figure also includes reports of *suspected* cases and includes all forms of child maltreatment (including physical and sexual abuse, neglect, and psychological maltreatment). If we consider only substantiated cases (i.e., those in which upon investigation CPS concluded the children were indeed physically abused), approximately 18 percent of maltreatment reports were instances of CPA in 2017. Furthermore, if we standardize by population size, we find a physical abuse rate of approximately 3 per 1,000 children. Importantly, this is a significant *decrease* from 20 years ago, when the rate was over 7 per 1,000 children (Finkelhor, Saito, & Jones, 2016; U.S. DHHS, 2016).

A second source of data, the National Incidence Study (NIS), conducted by the NCCAN, is a much broader measure of child abuse and neglect because it is designed to measure not only reports to CPS agencies, but also the number of cases of CPA reported to police and sheriff's departments, schools and day care centers, hospitals, and other mental health and social service agencies. Between the first NIS, known as NIS-1 (published in 1981), and NIS-3 (published in 1996), the reporting of CPA steadily increased, from 3.1 to 9.1 per 1,000 children. The most recent National Incidence Study (NIS-4), published in 2010, however, shows an overall decrease in the general incidence of CPA for a rate of 6.5 per 1,000 children (Sedlak et al., 2010). These trends are discussed further in Chapter 11.

A third important data source, the National Family Violence Survey, is a telephone survey that used the Conflict Tactics Scales, or CTS (Gelles & Straus, 1987, 1988). The CTS asks parents about the conflict techniques they used with their children in the past year, selecting their responses from a scale that ranges from mild forms of violence (e.g., slapped or spanked child) to severe forms of violence (e.g., beat up child, burned or scalded child, used a knife or gun). Some 75 percent of parents admitted to having used at least one violent act while rearing their children. Approximately 2 percent of the parents had engaged in at least one act of abusive violence (i.e., an act with a high probability of injuring the child) during the year prior to the survey. The most frequent type of violence in either case was slapping or spanking the child; 39 percent of respondents reported slapping or spanking their children more than 2 times in the previous year.

Recall from Chapter 2 that the original CTS was designed to measure violence between adult intimates. Straus and colleagues (Straus, Hamby, Finkelhor, Moore, & Runyan, 1998) used a redesigned CTS, the Parent–Child Conflict Tactics Scales (CTSPC), to estimate child abuse in a nationally representative sample of 1,000 parents. Two-thirds of the parents surveyed reported using at least one physically violent tactic during the previous year, and three-fourths reported using some method of physical violence during the rearing of their children. Most of the reporting of physical violence by parents involved acts considered minor assaults, such as spanking, slapping, and pinching. As Straus and his colleagues (1998) point out, however, although the majority of physical assaults were in the minor assault category and included corporal punishment tactics, *nearly half* of all the parents surveyed said that they had engaged in behaviors from the severe physical assault subscale at some point during their parenting. These behaviors included hitting the child with an object such as a stick or belt, slapping the child on the face, hitting the child with a fist, kicking the child, and throwing or knocking down the child. Each of the very severe physical assault tactics (e.g., beating up or burning the child or threatening the child with a knife or gun) was used by less than 1 percent of the sample.

Finally, the third National Survey of Children's Exposure to Violence (NatSCEV III), which was conducted in 2014 and used the Juvenile Victimization Questionnaire (see Chapter 2), measured victimization in a nationally representative sample of 4,000 American children from ages 1 month to 17 years (parents or caregivers responded to questions for children under the age of 10) (Finkelhor, Turner, Shattuck, & Hamby, 2015). Findings indicated that approximately 15 percent of the youth and parents surveyed reported some experience of child maltreatment (i.e., physical abuse, psychological/emotional abuse, neglect, or sexual abuse) in the previous year and nearly 25 percent reported experiencing child maltreatment at some point during their lifetime. For the oldest children, those 14–17 years old, the lifetime prevalence rates jump to 38 percent. In terms of CPA specifically (defined as being hit, beaten, or kicked), 5 percent of the sample reported such experiences in the past year, and about 10 percent reported experiencing physical abuse over their lifetime. The rates of physical abuse across NatSCEV I to NatSCEV II and NatSCEV II to NatSCEV III, though slightly higher, were not statistically significant (Finkelhor, Turner, Shattuck, & Hamby, 2015; Finkelhor, Turner, Shattuck, Hamby, & Kracke, 2015).

RISK FACTORS ASSOCIATED WITH CHILD PHYSICAL ABUSE

What specific characteristics and traits are common among children who are physically abused and the adults who perpetrate violent acts against them? In the sections that follow, we hope to shed some light on the most common characteristics of child victims and adult perpetrators of CPA to help inform our understanding of **risk factors** associated with both physical violence perpetration and victimization. These risk factors are discussed as follows and summarized in Table 3.1. Research examining these characteristics has demonstrated the heterogeneity of both victim and offender populations, suggesting that, although CPA occurs in all types of families, several factors are predictors of higher risk of abuse. Research also indicates that the risk for CPA increases as the risk factors accumulate and interact with one another (Lamela & Figueiredo, 2018).

Characteristics of Children Who Are Physically Abused

Age of the Child

Data from official reports (U.S. DHHS, 2016), the NIS-4 (Sedlak et al., 2010), and self-report surveys such as the NatSCEV III (e.g., Finkelhor, Turner, Shattuck, & Hamby, 2015) indicate that the risk of CPA *increases* with age. It is hard to know how to interpret these data, however, because we would fully expect significant *underreporting* for very young children. The NIS data, for example, come from mandated reporters. As children grow, they become more visible, and their abuse presumably becomes more visible to mandated reporters. For self-report surveys, like the NatSCEV, it is actually

TABLE 3.1 ■ Characteristics of Children Who Are Physically Abused and the Adults Who Abuse Them	
Child Characteristics	**Examples**
Demographic factors	Young age
	Male gender
Special characteristics	Birth complications
	Physical, cognitive, and developmental disabilities
Adult Characteristics	**Examples**
Mental health and behavioral difficulties	Self-expressed anger and anger control problems
	Depression
	Low frustration tolerance
	Low self-esteem
	Rigidity
	Deficits in empathy
	Anxiety
	Perceived life stress and personal distress
	Substance abuse/dependence
	Reports of physical health problems and disabilities
Biological factors	Physiological overreactivity/heightened arousal
	Neuropsychological deficits and intellectual impairment (e.g., problem-solving, conceptual ability)
Parenting deficits	Disregard for children's needs/abilities
	Unrealistic expectations of children
	Deficits in child management skills
	View of parenting role as stressful
	Negative bias/perceptions regarding children
	Poor problem-solving ability with regard to child-rearing
	Intrusive/inconsistent parenting
	High rates of verbal and physical aggression toward children
	Living with a single parent, unmarried parents, in a large family

(Continued)

TABLE 3.1 ■ (Continued)	
Adult Characteristics	**Examples**
Economic and family contextual factors	Poverty, low socioeconomic status
	Spousal disagreement, tension, abuse
	Parental history of abuse in childhood
	Deficits in positive parental interactions with children and other family members
	Verbal and physical conflict among family members; sibling violence
	Deficits in family cohesion and expressiveness
	Isolation from friends and the community

Sources: A representative but not exhaustive list of sources for the information displayed in this table includes the following: Berkout & Kolko, 2016; Crouch et al., 2018; Éthier, Couture, & Lacharite, 2004; Hartley, 2012b; H. Kim & Drake, 2018; Scott & Pinderhughes, 2019; Sedlak et al., 2010; Shimada, Kasaba, Yao, & Tomoda, 2019; Smokowski & Evans, 2019; U.S. DHHS, 2016.

the parents who provide the information on abuse for children under the age of 10, and they might obviously be reluctant to do so. We become especially suspicious of the data suggesting older children are more at risk when we examine child fatalities. Recall from earlier discussions that the dark figure for fatalities is small. Most homicides are recorded. When we look at fatalities data, we find that it is *young children* who are, by far, most at risk. Almost three-fourths of child fatality victims are under the age of 3 (U.S. DHHS, 2019b). This leads us to speculate that, despite what we generally see in the official reports of CPA, it is actually young children who are most at risk and most often forgotten.

Gender of the Child

In terms of gender, self-report surveys indicate that males are at slightly greater risk for CPA than females. The NatSCEV III, for example, found that boys experienced significantly higher rates of CPA compared to girls both in the past year (6.4% vs. 3.7%) and during their lifetime (11.1% vs. 8.4%) (Finkelhor, Turner, Shattuck, & Hamby, 2015).

Race and Ethnicity of the Child

Official reports suggest that CPA varies slightly across racial and ethnic groups with Hispanic children victimized most commonly (19%), followed by Asian children (16.6%), black children (14%), Pacific Islanders (11.5%), white children (10.3%), and American Indians or Alaska Natives (7.3%) (U.S. DHHS, 2005). The NIS-4, which is collected from mandated reporters, likewise found that the incidence of CPA was higher for blacks and Hispanics compared to white children (Sedlak et al., 2010). Furthermore, both black and Hispanic children were at greater risk of suffering serious harm and injury relative to whites.

It is difficult to interpret findings related to race and ethnicity because such differences may be related to socioeconomic status (SES), with a disproportionate likelihood of nonwhite children living in poverty. Indeed, Hyunil Kim and Brett Drake (2019) found that racial disproportionality of official maltreatment reports is largely driven by poverty.

Physical, Cognitive, and Developmental Disabilities of the Child

Many researchers in the field of CPA have argued that special characteristics may put some children at increased risk for abuse and neglect. Several studies, for example, have found an association between CPA and birth complications such as low birth weight and premature birth (J. Brown, Cohen, Johnson, & Salzinger, 1998; DiScala, Sege, Li, & Reece, 2000). Research findings have also implicated physical, cognitive, and developmental disabilities as risk factors for CPA (e.g., Duan et al., 2015; L. Jones et al., 2012; A. Roberts, Koenen, Lyall, Robinson, & Weisskopf, 2015) (see Chapter 10 for a discussion of abuse in adults with disabilities). In one study, for example, children with autism spectrum disorder and intellectual disability were 2–3 times more likely to experience child maltreatment compared to a control group, and were especially likely to experience physical abuse (McDonnell et al., 2019). Parents of these children with special needs may become frustrated by the challenges such children present and therefore become more punitive in their parenting. Such children may be more hyperactive, oppositional, noncompliant, and socially impaired, and parents may not feel that they can either successfully reason with or be understood by such children (Helton & Cross, 2011; A. Roberts et al., 2015). Although some research has failed to find any evidence that either prematurity or disability is a risk factor for abuse, or increases a child's risk above and beyond parental characteristics (e.g., parental employment, SES) (see Sedlak et al., 2010), this lack of findings could be due, in part, to the failure of CPS workers to recognize and document disabilities in child abuse cases (Algood, Hong, Gourdine, & Williams, 2011) or to variations in the way states define and collect data on child maltreatment (Child Welfare Information Gateway, 2012).

Characteristics of Adults Who Physically Abuse Children

Parents and Siblings as Perpetrators

Who are the adults who physically abuse children? Official statistics indicate that the parents of the maltreated child are the perpetrators of the abuse in the majority (91.6%) of reported cases (U.S. DHHS, 2019b). Official statistics are difficult to interpret, however, because many states, by definition, report only those child abuse cases in which perpetrators are in primary caretaking roles. In the NIS-4, a **primary caregiver** was defined as "an adult in charge of the child's care (such as a parent, adult baby-sitter, etc.) or, if the abuser did not meet this requirement, then a parent or caregiver had to permit the abuse of the child" (Sedlak et al., 2010, pp. 6–11). Using this broader NIS-4 definition, 72 percent of perpetrators of CPA were biological parents, 19 percent were nonbiological parents, and 9 percent were other individuals (e.g., babysitters, nonparent family members). The severity of injury or harm resulting from the abuse differed significantly depending on the perpetrator of the abuse. Children who were physically abused were more likely to sustain severe harm when someone other than a parent or parent figure perpetrated the abuse, while they were more likely to sustain moderate harm when either their biological or nonbiological parent physically abused them.

It is important to note that in some cases, siblings have been identified as perpetrators of CPA (L. Jones et al., 2012). Research demonstrates, in fact, that violence between siblings is one of the most common forms of interpersonal violence. Some surveys suggest that over 80 percent of children have experienced violence perpetrated by a sibling (e.g., Straus, Gelles, & Steinmetz, 1980). Because sibling violence is so common, it is sometimes rationalized as harmless "sibling rivalry." A number of family violence experts, however, strongly disagree, and argue that sibling violence should be recognized as one of the most serious forms of family violence *because* it is so common (Finkelhor, 2008). Violence between siblings as a potential form of abuse is discussed in Box 3.2.

Gender of the Perpetrator

In terms of perpetrator gender, CPS receives slightly more reports of child maltreatment perpetrated by females (53.1%) compared to males (45%) (U.S. DHHS, 2019b). One likely explanation for this is that mothers spend more time with their children than do fathers. The gender distribution of CPA perpetrators in particular may depend, however, on the specific relationship between perpetrator and child. The NIS-4, for example, found that children who had been physically abused by biological parents were more likely to be abused by mothers (56%) than by fathers (48%), but the reverse was true (74% by fathers and 29% by mothers) when the perpetrators were nonbiological parents or parent substitutes (Sedlak et al., 2010).

Mental Health and Behavioral Difficulties of the Perpetrator

In the case example that opened the chapter, we saw that part of the mother's explanation for her boyfriend's abusive behavior toward Kevin was attributed to his "short temper," or anger control problems. Studies comparing nonabusive parents with physically abusive parents have identified several mental health and behavioral problems typical of abusive parents, including not only anger control problems but hostility, low frustration tolerance, depression, low self-esteem, substance abuse or dependence, deficits in empathy,

BOX 3.2
SIBLING VIOLENCE AND ABUSE

I can't remember a time when my brother didn't taunt me, usually trying to get me to respond so he would be justified in hitting me. Usually he would be saying I was a crybaby or a sissy or stupid or ugly and that no one would like me, want to be around me, or whatever. Sometimes he would accuse me of doing something, and if I denied it, he would call me a liar. I usually felt overwhelmingly helpless because nothing I said or did would stop him. If no one else was around, he would start beating on me, after which he would stop and go away. (quoted in Wiehe, 1997, p. 34)

Most individuals who have brothers or sisters can undoubtedly remember a time when they engaged in some altercation with their siblings: pulling hair, name-calling, pinching, pushing, and so on. Rivalry, jealousy, and anger commonly exist between siblings as they compete for the attention of their parents. Many of the behaviors that siblings exhibit toward each other are described as the products of "normal" sibling rivalry. Because such behaviors are very common, they are rarely defined as family violence (Gelles & Cornell, 1990; Wiehe, 1990). At what point should such interactions be labeled as *violent* or *abusive*? The answer to this question is a matter of some debate. Emery and Laumann-Billings (1998) have argued that, although many sibling interactions may be inappropriate, most should not be considered a form of family violence because they are very common and largely involve relatively minor physical acts that result in little or no measurable harm. Others argue that negative interactions between siblings, which are often rationalized as sibling rivalry and considered a normal part of development, should be recognized as one of the most serious forms of family violence *because* they are so common (Finkelhor, 2008; Finkelhor, Turner, & Ormrod, 2006; Wiehe, 1997).

Using data from the first National Family Violence Survey, Straus et al. (1980) found that 82 percent of American children with siblings between the ages of 3 and 17 engaged in at least one violent act toward a sibling during the 1-year period preceding the survey. Straus et al. measured violence using the Conflict Tactics Scales and included minor acts as well as severe forms of violence. These findings suggest that the majority of violence between siblings is minor and does not meet the criteria for abuse outlined previously. Several studies, however, suggest that more severe violence between siblings is not uncommon. In a nationally representative sample of 2,030 children and youth, Finkelhor and colleagues (2006) interviewed the parents of children aged 2–9 years and directly interviewed youth aged 10–17 years. The interviews focused on experiences of physical violence perpetrated by siblings including being hit or attacked with an object (e.g., sticks, rocks, guns, knives), being hit or attacked without an object, experiencing an attempted attack, or being hit or kicked in the genitals. Results indicated that 35 percent of children experienced some form of sibling violence with 6 percent being hit or attacked with a weapon or some other object. For 40 percent of the children who experienced some form of sibling violence, the violence was reoccurring (more than 4 repeat occurrences in the same year). Similar rates have been found in more recent studies using similar methodologies (Tucker, Finkelhor, Turner, & Shattuck, 2013).

One starting point in defining sibling violence and abuse is to define what should be considered *normal* sibling interaction. Normal behavior of any kind is often defined by a statistical standard that relies on a bell curve; in such a definition, approximately 68 percent of individual behavior falls within the "normal" range, within one standard deviation of the mean. In this case, abusive behavior may be defined as those behaviors falling at the outer extreme of such a distribution—that is, behaviors that are exceedingly severe

(Continued)

(Continued)

or occur excessively frequently. Abusive sibling interaction defined in this way stands in stark contrast to definitional conceptualizations of sibling abuse that are so inclusive that 80 percent of the U.S. child population could be considered victims (e.g., Straus et al., 1980).

Many claims makers prefer to define sibling violence and abuse broadly, arguing that the time has come to redefine what society views as normal sibling behavior. From this perspective, even such common behaviors as siblings hitting or pushing one another might be considered wrong and, as a result, recognized as problematic. It is true that, in times past, many behaviors now generally considered to be wrong, such as adult–child sexual relations, were not disapproved by society (as noted in Chapter 1). Adult–child sexual interactions came to be labeled as *abusive* only in relatively recent times. Similarly, much of what we label *child physical abuse* today was viewed as merely stern discipline or punishment 30 years ago. How many of the interactions between siblings that we are aware of today does society rationalize as legitimate simply because they occur frequently?

Other scholars have argued that overly inclusive definitions of sibling violence and abuse may make it difficult for professionals to discern appropriate interventions and, ultimately, understand this form of violence (Emery & Laumann-Billings, 1998). Consider, for example, an 8-year-old boy who frequently pushes his 4-year-old sister. His behavior is inappropriate and should be addressed, but it may not be helpful to label it *abusive*, as that may diminish the significance of the term. In response to these concerns, one approach is to delineate specific criteria against which professionals can judge sibling interactions to determine whether they rise to the level of violence or abuse. Several scholars have proposed specific factors that might distinguish between sibling abuse and normal sibling rivalry (e.g., Smokowski & Evans, 2019; Wiehe, 1997). Table 3.2 lists some criteria that professionals might find helpful in identifying sibling violence and abuse. In some cases, it may be necessary for

sibling interactions to meet only one of these criteria to be established as abusive. In other cases, professionals will need to evaluate whether sibling interactions meet a number of these criteria.

The first criterion of interest is *power disparity* between the siblings. That is, is one sibling older or physically more powerful than the other, or both? In one family we know, for example, the 4-year-old sister actually displays more violent behavior (e.g., kicking and hitting) than the 8-year-old brother. Because she is both younger and physically weaker than her brother, however, by definition her violent behaviors directed toward her brother are not considered abusive. Her behavior is inappropriate, and her parents try to respond to her aggression, but it is unreasonable to label it as abuse. Some scholars have argued that the power differential criterion should additionally include power differences based on societal stereotypes involving gender, whereby males dominate females regardless of age differences (Smokowski & Evans, 2019).

The second criterion to consider is the *frequency and duration of the interaction*. Most cases of severely negative sibling interactions involve multiple incidents occurring over several months or years (Adler & Schutz, 1995; Finkelhor et al., 2006; Wiehe, 1997).

The *outcome of the interaction* is another factor that professionals should consider. In most abusive sibling interactions, there is an aspect of victimization whereby the recipient of the behavior is "hurt or injured by the action or actions of another" (Wiehe, 1997, p. 167). Hurt or injury might take a physical form, such as bruises or cuts, or it might be more psychological in nature, including feelings of anger, fear, or sadness. In a study using data from the Developmental Victimization Survey, Finkelhor and colleagues (2006) found that 13 percent of 2- to 17-year-old children who reported being treated violently by a sibling experienced some form of physical injury such as bruising, pain the next day, a cut that bled, or a broken bone. They assessed the effects of being physically hit or attacked (or threatened by such) on various trauma symptoms including

TABLE 3.2 ■ Potential Criteria for Sibling Abuse	
Criterion	**Description**
Power disparity between siblings	Negative sibling interactions that involve significant differences in the distribution of power in age, physical size or strength, or social status
Frequency and duration of the interactions	Negative sibling interactions that occur over many months or years and that include multiple incidents
Outcomes of the interactions	Negative sibling interactions that result in some type of harm to the child who is the recipient of the behavior; includes physical and psychological injury
Lack of appropriate parental intervention	Negative sibling interactions that occur without appropriate intervention from parents or guardians; inappropriate parental reactions/interventions that include no response, indifference to the victim's suffering, and blame directed at the victim

anger, depression, and anxiety. After controlling for family factors, other adversities, and demographic factors (e.g., SES, ethnicity, city size, age, and gender), as well as other forms of victimization (e.g., child maltreatment, bullying, sexual assaults, and witnessing family and community violence), sibling violence continued to predict trauma symptoms. Other studies conducted have demonstrated some consistency in the types of difficulties that sibling abuse victims experience, finding that these problems are similar to those reported by victims of other forms of child maltreatment such as substance abuse, delinquency, aggression, depression, anxiety, and self-harm (Bowes, Wolke, Joinson, Lereya, & Lewis, 2014;

Button & Gealt, 2010; Tucker et al., 2013; Van Berkel, Tucker, & Finkelhor, 2018).

A final key criterion that distinguishes sibling abuse from nonabusive sibling interactions appears to be *lack of appropriate parental intervention*. Adler and Schutz (1995) examined sibling abuse cases and found that 58 percent of siblings exposed to abuse experienced continued abuse because of ineffective parental intervention. Other scholars have found that parents who discover inappropriate interactions between siblings often fail to protect the victims, deny any suffering on the part of the victims, or respond negatively toward the victims with blame or disbelief (Laviola, 1992; Wiehe, 1997).

and rigidity (e.g., Berkout & Kolko, 2016; Mammen, Kolko, & Pilkonis, 2003). Many studies have also found that physically abusive adults report more anxiety, life stress, and personal distress than do nonabusive adults (e.g., Scott & Pinderhughes, 2019). Such negative emotional and behavioral states may increase the risk of CPA by interfering with the ways these parents perceive events, by decreasing their parenting abilities, or by lowering their tolerance for specific child behaviors (Hillson & Kupier, 1994; Lahey, Conger, Atkeson, & Treiber, 1984; Milner, 2003). In some cases, the CPA perpetrated by adults with mental health issues is unintentional, as is the case when mothers are suffering from **postpartum depression (PPD)**. In one case, a woman with PPD tried to drown her 4-month-old twin babies in a bathtub; she received probation and was required to obtain psychiatric care because the judge recognized that her PPD led to her behavior (Carter, 2016).

Biological and Physical Risk Factors of the Perpetrator

Research suggests that some physically abusive parents possess a physiological trait that predisposes them to hyperreactive responses (or heightened physiological reactions) to stressful stimuli such as a crying child. Frodi and Lamb (1980), for example, conducted one of the seminal studies in this area by measuring the physical responses of physically abusive mothers and a control group of nonabusive mothers. The two groups of mothers were presented with three videotapes: one showing a crying infant, one showing a quiet but alert infant, and one showing a smiling infant. Comparisons revealed that although both the abusive and the nonabusive mothers responded to the crying infant with increased heart rate, blood pressure, and skin conductance, the abusive mothers displayed greater increases in heart rate. In addition, only the abusive mothers showed increased physiological reactivity in response to the smiling infant, suggesting that abusive parents may view their children as aversive regardless of how the children behave.

These findings have been replicated in studies comparing nonabusive but high-risk participants with low-risk participants and in studies using stressful non-child-related stimuli (e.g., Crouch et al., 2018; Crowe & Zeskind, 1992; McCanne & Hagstrom, 1996). Although it appears that abusive parents exhibit a general physiological overreactivity, it is unclear exactly how this pattern contributes to parents' physical maltreatment of their children. It may be that heightened physiological reactivity influences the way a parent cognitively processes or perceives a child's behavior or the way a parent subsequently reacts to a child (Milner, 2003). It is also difficult to determine whether this physiological pattern is the result of a genetic trait or environmental event that predisposes parents toward abusive behavior or whether the physiological pattern develops as a *result* of continuing negative parent–child interactions.

Several studies that have evaluated additional physical risk factors have demonstrated that adults who abuse children report more health problems and physical disabilities than do nonabusing adults (e.g., Lahey et al., 1984). Other research has found evidence that particular neuropsychological factors are characteristic of physically abusive parents. Physically abusive adults demonstrate intellectual impairment and deficits in problem-solving skills (Cantos, Neale, O'Leary, & Gaines, 1997; Éthier, Couture, & Lacharite, 2004). Nayak and Milner (1998) found that mothers at high risk for CPA performed worse than mothers at low risk for CPA on measures of problem-solving ability and conceptual ability as well as on measures of cognitive flexibility. Researchers need to evaluate the variables of physical health and neurological functioning further before they can determine the precise nature of the link between biological risk factors and CPA.

Parenting Deficits of the Perpetrator

Compared with nonabusive adults, abusive individuals have been found to have unrealistic expectations and negative perceptions regarding their children (Azar, 1997; Young et al., 2018). Such parents often regard their children as bad, slow, or difficult to discipline and view their children's behavior as if it were intended to annoy them. Abusive parents may expect their children to be toilet trained at an unreasonably early age, for instance, and so interpret the children's soiling of their diapers as deliberate misbehavior. In one prospective study, parents who described their infants 12 months of age or younger with negative or developmentally unrealistic words (e.g., *fussy, spoiled, stubborn*) were more likely to physically abuse their children than parents who described their children with positive or neutral words (e.g., *happy, hungry*) (Young et al., 2018). Similarly, research examining parents at high risk for engaging in CPA (those who use physical methods of discipline) finds that they are more likely to process negative stimuli, such as anger or hostility, and less likely to process positive stimuli, such as happiness, suggesting that their distorted social cognitive schemas may increase the risk of maladaptive parenting behaviors (Shimada, Kasaba, Yao, & Tomoda, 2019).

Several studies have found that abusive parents tend to view the parenting role as stressful and dissatisfying and that such parents exhibit numerous deficits in child management skills (Berkout & Kolko, 2016; McPherson, Lewis, Lynn, Haskett, & Behrend, 2009). Compared with nonabusive parents, physically abusive parents interact with their children less; when they do interact with their children, they display higher rates of directive, critical, and controlling behavior and a higher frequency of verbal and physical aggression (Chaffin et al., 2004). Tuteur, Ewigman, Peterson, and Hosokawa (1995) observed mother–child dyads at a public health clinic, with each dyad spending 10 minutes in a private room equipped with toys, a table, and paper and crayons. The researchers asked each mother to sit at the table with her child, who was allowed to use the paper and crayons but was not permitted to play with the toys. They found that abusive mothers, compared with nonabusive mothers, used more negative and rigid control (e.g., chased child under the table) rather than positive control (e.g., comfortably directed child) and made requests of their children that were either neutral (e.g., "Keep going") or negative (e.g., "Draw a circle right now") rather than positive (e.g., "Can you please draw a circle for Mommy?").

Economic and Family Contextual Risk Factors

In addition to psychological, biological, and health risk factors, broader contextual conditions serve as risk factors for CPA. According to the NIS-4, children living with two biological parents are significantly less likely to be victims of CPA (2 per 1,000 children) than are children living with a single parent (6 per 1,000 children), with unmarried parents (8 per 1,000), with other married parents such as a biological parent and stepparent or adoptive parent (10 per 1,000), and with single parents with an unmarried, live-in partner (20 per 1,000). There is also some evidence that children from larger families are at greater risk (Sedlak et al., 2010). It is difficult to know the causal significance of these various family structures because other relevant factors, such as rates of poverty and stress, are also common in such families.

CPA occurs more often, for example, among economically and socially disadvantaged families (H. Kim & Drake, 2019; McLeigh, McDonell, & Lavenda, 2018; Sedlak et al., 2010; U.S. DHHS, 2019b). The NIS-4 found that children living in poverty, defined as those living in households with an income below $15,000 a year, parents' highest education level less than high school, or any member of the household being a participant in a poverty program (e.g., food stamps, public housing, energy assistance, or subsidized school meals), were 3 times more likely to be at risk for CPA by the harm standard as well as the endangerment standard (Sedlak et al., 2010). A clear association between income inequality and substantiated child maltreatment has also been found, suggesting an impact of low income that extends beyond child poverty (Eckenrode, Smith, McCarthy, & Dineen, 2014). Low income also appears to be related to the severity of abuse, with serious or fatal injuries being more likely among families with annual incomes below the poverty level (e.g., Pelton, 1994; Sedlak et al., 2010).

Lack of financial resources, in turn, likely contributes to a number of parental stressors including an inability to provide adequate food, shelter, health care, child care, and education for their children. The mechanisms through which low income and its related stressors increase risk of child maltreatment are not well understood. It may be that these stressors impact the way parents relate to their children, increasing negative forms of parenting (Duva & Metzger, 2010). Another possibility is that low income is associated with other conditions that are associated with increased risk of child maltreatment such as single parenthood, high-crime neighborhoods, poor physical health, and increased risk for substance-use problems and mental health problems (Cancian, Clack, & Yang, 2010; Prinz, 2016; Torquati, 2002). The stress of single parenting, for example, in combination with low income, may lead to child maltreatment.

CPA is also associated with a variety of family struggles and dysfunctions. Risk factors include social isolation from other family members and friends, family conflict and lack of positive interactions, and intimate partner violence. Perpetrators of CPA, for example, report more social isolation, limited support from friends and family members, and loneliness than do nonperpetrators (e.g., Chan, 1994; Coohey, 2000; Kelleher, Chaffin, Hollenberg, & Fischer, 1994). Abusive and high-risk individuals also report more verbal and physical conflict among family members, higher levels of spousal disagreement and tension, and greater deficits in family cohesion and expressiveness (e.g., Justice & Calvert, 1990; L. Merrill, Hervig, & Milner, 1996; Mollerstrom, Patchner, & Milner, 1992). In addition, abusive parents engage in fewer positive interactions with their children, such as playing together, providing positive responses to their children, and demonstrating affection (e.g., Alessandri, 1991; Bousha & Twentyman, 1984; Lahey et al., 1984). Indeed, there is evidence of disruption in the parent–child bond, reflecting **insecure attachment style** (e.g., increased avoidance of and resistance to the parent) in infants exposed to CPA (Cicchetti & Toth, 1995) as well as **disorganized attachment style** (e.g., having no organized strategy to secure safety when frightened), sometimes referred to as Type D attachment (Barnett, Ganiban, & Cicchetti, 1999). For these children, the parent–child relationship presents an irresolvable paradox, because the caregiver is at once the child's source of safety and protection and the source of danger or harm (Hesse & Main, 2000).

Studies have also demonstrated a significant relationship between the occurrence of CPA and more extreme forms of family conflict such as intimate partner violence between parents (Hartley, 2012b). Research also suggests the frequent presence of violence between siblings (Button & Gealt, 2010), as noted in Box 3.2. Some studies also suggest that abusive parents are more likely to report their own childhood abuse compared to nonabusive parents, suggesting that intergenerational transmission of abuse may occur in some of these families. Jinseok Kim (2009), for example, analyzed data from the original National Longitudinal Study of Adolescent Health (now referred to as the National Longitudinal Study of Adolescent to Adult Health) and found that parents who reported having been slapped, hit, or kicked by parental figures during childhood were 5 times as likely to report engaging in similar parenting behaviors with their own children than were parents who did not report having been physically abused as children. Other studies have failed to find evidence for intergenerational transmission or have found evidence for transmission of neglect and sexual abuse but not CPA (Renner & Slack, 2006; Widom, Czaja, & DuMont, 2015). Findings appear to vary depending on the source of information used to determine maltreatment, such as parents versus their children and CPS records versus self-report (Widom et al., 2015).

CONSEQUENCES ASSOCIATED WITH CHILD PHYSICAL ABUSE

Isolating the effects of CPA, displayed in Table 3.3, is a very complicated task. As we have discussed, CPA typically accompanies other problems within the family or environment, such as marital violence, alcohol or drug use by family members, parental depression, psychological maltreatment, and low SES. It is therefore difficult to conclude with any certainty that the psychological problems associated with CPA result solely—or even primarily—from violent interactions between parent and child. For example, imagine that you are working with Kevin from the opening case example. In assessing the family, you would find that he is having trouble in school (a possible negative effect of CPA).

TABLE 3.3 ■ Possible Effects Associated With Physical Child Abuse for Children and Adolescents and Adults		
Age Group	**Effects**	**Examples**
Children	Medical and neurobiological complications	Bruises; traumatic brain injury and neurological impairment; chest, throat, and abdominal injuries; bites and burns; fractures; compromised brain development; visual deficits; sleep disorders; alteration of biological stress system; emotional, behavioral, and cognitive dysregulation
	Cognitive deficits	Decreased intellectual and cognitive functioning; deficits in verbal abilities, memory, problem solving, and perceptual-motor skills; decreased reading and math skills; poor school achievement; increase in need for special education services
	Behavioral problems	Aggression; fighting; noncompliance; defiance; property offenses; arrests; delinquency
	Socioemotional deficits	Delayed play skills; infant attachment problems; poor social interaction skills; peer rejection; deficits in social competence with peers; avoidance of adults; difficulty making friends; deficits in positive social behaviors; hopelessness; anxiety; depressive symptoms; suicidal ideation and behavior; low self-esteem; post-traumatic stress symptoms
	Psychiatric disorders	Major depressive disorder; oppositional defiant disorder; conduct disorder; ADHD; borderline personality disorder; PTSD
Adolescents and adults	Criminal/antisocial/violent behavior	Arrests for delinquency; violent and/or criminal behavior; marital violence (for adult males); received and inflicted dating violence; physical abuse of own children; aggression; prostitution
	Substance abuse	Abuse of alcohol; illicit drug use and addiction; polydrug use
	Emotional, cognitive, and interpersonal problems	Self-destructive behavior; suicidal ideation and behavior; anxiety; anger and hostility; dissociation; depression and mania; unusual thoughts; narcissistic vulnerability; shame-proneness; interpersonal difficulties; poor self-concept; low academic competence
	Psychiatric disorders	Antisocial and other personality disorders; ADHD; major depressive disorder; bipolar disorder; PTSD
	Physical health problems/risk	Obesity; chronic pain; risk of diabetes vision problems, malnutrition, and lung disease

Sources: A representative but not exhaustive list of sources for information displayed in this table includes the following: Alvarez-Alonso et al., 2016; R. Berger & Bell, 2014; Chaney et al., 2014]; Cheung et al., 2018; DeBellis & Zisk, 2014; Fuller-Thomson & Lewis, 2015; Gardner, Thomas, & Erskine, 2019; Grady, Yoder, & Brown, 2018; Gorka, Hanson, Radtke, & Hairi, 2014; Greger, Myhre, Lydersen, & Jozefiak, 2015; Halpern et al., 2018; Hanson et al., 2015; Hughes et al., 2019; Jardim et al., 2018; Keene & Epps, 2016; Kleinman, 2015; Lee, Herrenkohl, Jung, Skinner, & Klika, 2015; Lueger-Schuster et al., 2014; P. Mitchell et al., 2019; Raby et al., 2019; Runyon, Deblinger, & Steer, 2014; Simon et al., 2018; Sousa et al., 2018.

But Kevin is also from a very poor family and regularly witnesses violence between his mother and her boyfriend when Sam has been drinking heavily. Determining which factors (or combination of factors) are responsible for the school problems is a difficult task. Fortunately, research has become increasingly sophisticated, and as a result we know more than we ever have about the negative effects of CPA (e.g., Font & Maguire-Jack, 2016; Klika, Herrenkohl, & Lee, 2012).

Medical and Neurological Problems

Some of the most frequent outcomes associated with CPA in children are *medical and neurobiological problems*. The medical consequences of CPA are numerous and range from minor physical injuries (e.g., bruising) to death (see Box 3.3 on child maltreatment fatalities). The NatSCEV studies indicate that among physically abused children, nearly 43 percent are injured during the abuse including bruises, cuts, and broken bones (Simon et al., 2018).

BOX 3.3
WHAT CAN BE DONE TO PREVENT CHILD FATALITIES?

NCANDS data indicate that an estimated 1,720 children died in 2017 as a result of child abuse. The two most common causes of death were neglect (75%) and physical abuse (42%). Most of these children were very young (72% under the age of 3 and about 50% younger than age 1), and most were killed by their parents (80%). The most common perpetrators (31%) were mothers (U.S. DHHS, 2019). According to the U.S. Commission to Eliminate Child Abuse and Neglect Fatalities (CECANF, 2016), established by the **Protect Our Kids Act** in 2013, although the overall safety of children has increased in the United States, child fatalities are *not* declining, and somewhere between 1,500 and 3,000 U.S. children will die each year from maltreatment. In the report, the chairperson of the commission ironically notes that "child protection is perhaps the only field where some child deaths are assumed to be inevitable, no matter how hard we work to stop them. This is certainly not true in the airline industry, where safety is paramount

and commercial airline crashes are never seen as inevitable" (p. 11).

There are few things more tragic than a child being killed by a parent or caregiver. Inevitably, we must come to grips with the fact that we—society—failed that child. But where and when did we fail the child? At the very least we must acknowledge that we failed to notice what, presumably, would have been warning signs. Children with prior allegations of child maltreatment died from intentional injuries at a rate 5.9 times greater than children not reported for child maltreatment, and the risk was greater for victims of CPA compared to neglect (Putnam-Horenstein, 2011; Putnam-Horenstein, Cleves, Licht, & Needell, 2013). According to 2017 NCANDS data (U.S. DHHS, 2019), approximately 27 percent of child fatality victims had prior CPS contact in the three years prior to the date of death (U.S. DHHS, 2019). Approximately 11 percent of the child fatalities in 2017 involved families who received family preservation services in the past

(Continued)

(Continued)

five years. Most troubling of all, 20 children died in 2017 after spending time in foster care and being reunited with their abusive families (U.S. DHHS, 2019). Not every child death, of course, is evidence of a faulty child protection system. But 1,720 child abuse deaths are too many, and must be addressed.

According to the CECANF (2016), the answer to preventing child fatalities lies not in simply improving the current system of child protection, but in requiring fundamental reform such as a national strategy to create a reinvigorated child welfare system. Such reform would include CPS agencies as leaders in the effort to respond quickly but would also include expanding responsibility for child safety to additional community partners who come into contact with families (e.g., health care and public health agencies and professionals). In addition, the commission recommended greater sharing of CPS data on families, both electronically and in real time, to enhance CPS response, as well as increased identification of children and families at greatest risk for child maltreatment fatality by retrospectively reviewing child fatality cases over the past five years.

What else can be done to help prevent fatalities? One response that has been helpful is the establishment of **child fatality review teams** (Krugman & Lane, 2014; Palusci & Covington,

2014). Such teams are typically composed of community professionals representing multiple agencies who retrospectively review the circumstances under which a child died, including interviewing family members, teachers, neighbors, and others, in order to reconstruct the circumstances and events that may have contributed to the death. Although the functions of these teams vary, typically they identify the prevalence of deaths from abuse and neglect, improve the policies and procedures of CPS to prevent future child deaths and serious injuries, protect siblings of children whose causes of death are unexplained, and increase professional and public awareness of child death due to maltreatment (Block, 2002; Durfee, Durfee, & West, 2002). One study found a 9 percent decrease in the number of child deaths associated with child fatality review team activities (Palusci, Yager, & Covington, 2010). Other suggestions for preventing child fatalities include parent education during the newborn period (see Box 3.1); support for new, especially high-risk, parents through home visitation programs (see Chapter 5); community involvement in promoting healthy families (CECANF, 2016; Krugman & Lane, 2014); and the application of sophisticated predictive analytic systems to more accurately identify child fatality risk (Camasso & Jagannathan, 2019; CECANF, 2016).

Several neurobiological consequences are also associated with CPA, including structural and functional brain changes and alterations of systems within the body involved in emotion, memory, executive control, and the stress response (e.g., Gonzalez & Oshri, 2019; Hanson et al., 2015; Hart & Rubia, 2012). Hanson and colleagues (2015), for example, found smaller amygdala and hippocampal volumes in the brains of children exposed to various forms of early life stress, such as physical abuse, compared to those who had not experienced such events. These brain areas are responsible for storing and processing memories and emotional responses (e.g., fear). In one seminal study of brain systems, researchers found that a sample of physically and sexually abused children exhibited greater concentrations of urinary dopamine, norepinephrine, and free cortisol than did children in a control group (De Bellis et al., 1999). They also found that a number of specific brain regions were smaller in the children who were abused. Several other studies are consistent with these results in finding compromised brain development and impairment in the **hypothalamic-pituitary-adrenal (HPA) axis** (a neurobiological system involved in the stress response system of the body) associated with various forms of abuse and neglect (Edmiston et al., 2011; Hart & Rubia, 2012).

Changes in neurobiological systems are not just an outcome of CPA in and of themselves, but these changes can then ultimately influence other areas of functioning to impact the developmental trajectories of the health, behavior, and cognitive functioning of children who are maltreated and adults with a history of child maltreatment (Gonzalez & Oshri, 2019). This idea—that early childhood experiences such as child maltreatment can alter underlying biological systems to produce stable and long-lasting impacts—has been referred to as **biological embedding** (Gonzalez & Oshri, 2019). A significant body of empirical evidence is mounting that identifies a number of biological mechanisms as the link between child maltreatment and various negative developmental outcomes. A number of biological systems have demonstrated a link between child maltreatment experiences and various outcomes including decreased brain structure volume in the hippocampus and amygdala with alcohol use (De Bellis et al., 2019) and internalizing behavior problems (Oshri et al., 2019), respectively; dysregulated autonomic nervous system (i.e., resting heart period) and shyness (Poole, MacMillan, & Schmidt, 2019); and reduced neural activity in various brain regions (i.e., the parietal lobe) and impulsivity (Hallowell et al., 2019). Research findings also suggest that child maltreatment might influence the way our genes function, turning on or off the action of some genes, and influencing how susceptible a child is to negative behavioral, psychological, and health outcomes associated with abuse (McCrory, De Brito, & Viding, 2012; Yang et al., 2013).

Cognitive Problems

Studies have shown that children who are physically abused exhibit *cognitive problems* such as lower intellectual and cognitive functioning relative to comparison groups of children on general intellectual measures as well as on specific measures of verbal facility, memory, **dissociation** (separation of normally related mental processes), verbal language, communication ability, problem-solving skills, and perceptual-motor skills (e.g., Hart & Rubia, 2012). Children who are physically abused also perform relatively poorly in school, receive more special education services, score lower on standardized tests, have more learning disabilities, and are more likely to repeat a grade (e.g., Rouse & Fantuzzo, 2009; Stone, 2007). These effects persist even after controlling for potential extraneous variables like socioeconomic disadvantage (Kurtz, Gaudin, Wodarski, & Howing, 1993). The cognitive deficits that are observed in children who have been physically abused may be the result of direct physical injury (e.g., head injury), environmental factors (e.g., low levels of stimulation and communication), or both.

Behavioral and Socioemotional Problems

Children who are physically abused also suffer from a variety of *behavioral and socioemotional problems*. Youth who are abused have been found to show more **externalizing behavior problems** such as aggression and antisocial behavior than nonabused children, even after the researchers have statistically controlled for the poverty, family instability, and spousal abuse that often accompany CPA (e.g., Fantuzzo, 1990). As illustrated in the case example that opened the chapter, Kevin exhibited many externalizing problems including physically fighting with other children and other acting-out behaviors (setting fire to objects, skipping school, refusing to do homework, etc.). Youth who are physically abused also exhibit higher levels of **internalizing behavior problems**, such as anxiety and depression (Dube et al., 2001; Fantuzzo, delGaudio, Atkins, Meyers, & Noone, 1998; Runyon, Deblinger, & Steer, 2014). Finally, social interaction deficits are common, including difficulty in making friends, deficits in positive social behavior (e.g., smiling), peer rejection, and delays in interactive play skills (e.g., Prino & Peyrot, 1994; Rogosch, Cicchetti, & Abre, 1995).

These various cognitive, behavioral, and socioemotional difficulties may sometimes form a constellation of symptoms characteristic of specific *psychiatric disorders*. Kaplan, Pelcovitz, and Labruna (1999) estimated that approximately 40 percent of CPA victims will meet criteria for major depressive disorders during their lifetimes, and at least 30 percent will meet criteria for disruptive behavior disorders, as Kevin in our case example may, such as **oppositional defiant disorder** or **conduct disorder**. **Post-traumatic stress disorder (PTSD)** is also a common outcome for children who have been physically abused; in one study, 36 percent of CPA victims met criteria for PTSD (Famularo, Fenton, Kinscherff, Ayoub, & Barnum, 1994). In a meta-analysis of 604 studies, Gardner, Thomas, and Erskine (2019) found that CPA was associated with both depressive disorders and anxiety disorders. A history of CPA has also been associated with **attention-deficit/hyperactivity disorder (ADHD)** and **borderline personality disorder** (Famularo, Kinscherff, & Fenton, 1991; Ouyang, Fang, Mercy, Perou, & Grosse, 2008).

Studies have also empirically examined the *long-term sequelae* associated with CPA, and the evidence suggests that many of the difficulties that emerge in childhood are also evident in adulthood. Various emotional, cognitive, and behavioral symptoms, such as higher incidence of self-destructive behavior, suicidal thoughts and behavior, poor academic competence, interpersonal problems, anxiety, anger and hostility, aggression, depression, and mania, have been observed in adults with CPA histories (e.g., Font & Maguire-Jack, 2016; Jardim et al., 2018; Keene & Epps, 2016; Raby et al., 2019). Psychiatric disorders are also common and include ADHD, personality disorders, major depressive disorder, bipolar disorder, PTSD, and substance abuse (P. Cohen, Brown, & Smailes, 2001; Font & Maguire-Jack, 2016; Fuller-Thomson & Lewis, 2015; Fuller-Thomson, Mehta, & Valeo, 2014; Lueger-Schuster et al., 2014; Sugaya et al., 2012). Many of these impairments that began in childhood and persisted into adulthood were discussed previously as adult risk factors for CPA and therefore may contribute to the intergenerational transmission of violence (Currie & Tekin, 2012).

One of the most widely studied long-term outcomes of child maltreatment is *criminal behavior* (see Allwood & Widom, 2013; Currie & Tekin, 2012; Jung, Herrenkohl, Klika, Lee, & Brown, 2015; Klika et al., 2012; Lee, Herrenkohl, Jung, Skinner, & Klika, 2015). Many of these studies utilize longitudinal designs, in which validated cases of child maltreatment are followed over time and compared to individuals matched on key characteristics. Currie and Tekin (2012) argue that there is a unique relationship, in particular, between CPA and criminal activity. These researchers examined 13,509 adolescents who were assessed 3 times over a seven-year period, and their findings indicated that having a parent who ever struck, hit, or kicked them increased the probability of criminal activity, and the effect tended to be greater if the parent struck them frequently. In a longitudinal study that compared adults who had been physically abused as children to a control group matched on age, sex, race, and SES, Widom and Maxfield (2001) reached a similar conclusion: Adults who were physically abused as children were much more likely to be arrested for a violent crime. Other cross-sectional studies have focused uniquely on CPA and identified specific interpersonally violent behaviors in adults who were victims of CPA, including being more likely to receive and inflict dating violence (L. Marshall & Rose, 1990; D. Riggs, O'Leary, & Breslin, 1990), becoming perpetrators of CPA as adults (J. Kim, 2009), and inflicting physical abuse on intimate partners (Gil-González, Vives-Cases, Ruiz, Carrasco Portiño, & Álvarez-Dardet, 2008).

One topic that has increasingly become the focus of research attention is the adult *health risks* associated with child maltreatment. The **Adverse Childhood Experiences (ACE) Study**, supported by the Centers for Disease Control and Prevention (CDC) and Kaiser Permanente, is a population-based effort to assess associations between adverse childhood experiences (e.g., child maltreatment, parental divorce, parental drug and alcohol abuse) and health and well-being in later life (CDC, n.d.). Results from the ACE Study, which frequently focuses on child maltreatment generally as opposed to CPA specifically, suggest that child maltreatment is indeed associated with poor health behaviors and outcomes such as self-rated health and number of health problems, depression, tobacco and alcohol use, and obesity (e.g., Anda et al., 2001; Dube et al., 2001; Felitti et al., 2019). Results from research studies on adverse childhood experiences (ACEs) that specifically focus on CPA have also identified negative health effects, as has non-ACEs research (Chartier, Walker, & Naimark, 2010; Font and Maguire-Jack, 2016; Schneiderman, Negriff, & Trickett, 2016). ACEs research is further highlighted in Chapter 5 (see Box 5.2 on page 154).

Risk and Protective Factors Associated With Abuse Effects

CPA victims do not respond to being abused in consistent or predictable ways. For some, the effects of their victimization may be pervasive and long-standing, but for many others the effects may be minimally negative or disruptive. What factors might contribute to the variability researchers have found in the effects associated with CPA? To date, we know very little about potential factors that might mediate or moderate the pathway from CPA to abuse effects. Exceptions are beginning to appear that examine such factors (e.g., Keene & Epps, 2016; Klika et al., 2012; Lee et al., 2015; Raby et al., 2019).

Not surprisingly, the more severe the abuse, the longer it continues, the more frequent it is, and the greater the number of subtypes of maltreatment experienced (e.g., physical abuse, sexual abuse, neglect), the more negative the outcome for the child (e.g., Currie & Tekin, 2012; Rehan, Antfolk, Johansson, & Santtila, 2019; Simon et al., 2018; Sugaya et al., 2012). Research from the ACE Study also confirms the cumulative effects of adverse childhood experience on health problems (e.g., Chartier, Walker, & Naimark, 2010).

The child's *perceptions* of the abuse may also serve an important mediating role. Elissa Brown and David Kolko (1999), for example, found that children who tended to blame themselves for the abuse exhibited greater internalizing symptoms such as anxiety and depression. Other studies have suggested that various emotional processes, such as poor emotion regulation, narcissistic vulnerability, and shame-proneness, underlie angry and aggressive behavior in victims of CPA (Gratz, Paulson, Jakupcak, & Tull, 2009; Keene & Epps, 2016; Stevens et al., 2013; Teisl & Cicchetti, 2008).

The earlier children experience abuse, the greater the negative effects. Keiley, Howe, Dodge, Bates, and Pettit (2001) evaluated internalizing behavior and externalizing behavior problems in three physical maltreatment groups: children maltreated prior to age 5, children maltreated at age 5 or older, and a nonmaltreated control group. Results indicated that the earlier children experienced harsh physical maltreatment by caregivers, the more likely they were to experience adjustment problems in early adolescence. In addition, the children maltreated prior to age 5 demonstrated higher levels of both internalizing and externalizing behavior problems, while the children maltreated at age 5 or older experienced higher levels of externalizing problems.

Reports are also beginning to appear that demonstrate the influence of family and sociocultural variables. Some studies find, for example, that the negative effects of abuse are greatest for children in families in which there are high levels of stress, parent–child conflict, and parental mental health problems such as schizophrenia or depression (E. Herrenkohl, Herrenkohl, Rupert, Egolf, & Lutz, 1995; Kurtz, Gaudin, Howing, & Wodarski, 1993; Walker, Downey, & Bergman, 1989). Lee and colleagues (2015) examined peer and partner influences on the pathway between CPA and adult crime as part of the Lehigh Longitudinal Study, which analyzed data from adult participants who were followed from early childhood. These researchers found that although CPA predicted adult crime, it did so indirectly through child and adolescent antisocial behavior, as well as adult partner and antisocial peer influences. The researchers concluded that CPA leads to adult criminal behavior because such experiences trigger persistent involvement in anti-social behavior throughout one's lifetime, which includes compromised social networks.

Researchers have also begun to examine the role of various protective factors that affect the resilience of individuals who have experienced CPA. Studies have suggested that certain factors, such as high intellectual functioning in the victim of CPA (Klika et al., 2012) and the presence of a supportive parent figure (E. Herrenkohl et al., 1995), may have a protective influence. In one study, Sachs-Ericsson and colleagues (2010) conducted an analysis of a population sample of more than 1,000 participants aged 50 years or older, who were assessed at two time points, three years apart. The researchers examined the role of self-esteem in explaining the relationship between anxiety and depression and childhood abuse. Findings indicated that abuse had a more negative impact on those with lower self-esteem than on those with higher self-esteem, suggesting that self-esteem may serve as a buffer against the negative impact of abuse. Other studies have also documented the protective effects of positive self-esteem, as well as positive coping strategies and an internal locus of control (Cheung et al., 2018).

INTERVENTION AND PREVENTION OF CHILD PHYSICAL ABUSE

Proposed solutions to the CPA problem include both intervention and prevention strategies. Recall from Chapter 1 that *intervention* refers to strategies designed to treat the problems of abused children or to modify the behaviors of abusive parents. *Prevention* refers to strategies designed to prevent abuse from occurring in the first place. Although the conceptual distinction between intervention and prevention is clear, in practice, intervention and prevention are overlapping goals in many approaches that attempt to address CPA. Indeed, the CDC, in its recommendations for the prevention of child abuse and neglect, identified several strategies (see Table 3.4) based on the best available evidence to guide communities in their efforts to both *prevent* and *reduce* child abuse and neglect in general (Fortson, Klevens, Merrick, Gilbert, & Alexander, 2016). The CDC website provides a number of web-based resources for the prevention of child abuse and neglect (see cdc.gov/violenceprevention/childabuseandneglect/prevention.html). Many of these strategies will be discussed in the current chapter while others will be discussed in subsequent chapters focusing on other forms of child maltreatment.

In the following paragraphs, we briefly contemplate how we, as a society, should respond to CPA, in particular, although many of these strategies apply to other forms of child maltreatment as well. How do we address the needs of children who have been abused and the parents who have abused them? How do we attempt to alleviate the occurrence of CPA altogether in our society? Most experts in the field of child maltreatment

TABLE 3.4 ■ CDC Guidelines for Preventing Child Abuse and Neglect	
Strategy	**Approach**
Strengthen economic supports to families	• Strengthening household financial security • Family-friendly work policies
Change social norms to support parents and positive parenting	• Public engagement and education campaigns • Legislative approaches to reduce corporal punishment
Provide quality care and education early in life	• Preschool enrichment with family engagement • Improved quality of child care through licensing and accreditation
Enhance parenting skills to promote healthy child development	• Early childhood home visitation • Parenting skill and family relationship approaches
Intervene to lessen harms and prevent future risk	• Enhanced primary care • Behavioral parent training programs • Treatment to lessen harms of abuse and neglect exposure • Treatment to prevent problem behavior and later involvement in violence

Source: US Centers for Disease Control and Prevention.

agree that in order to be successful, strategies for addressing CPA must be broad, aimed at all levels of society (Child Welfare Information Gateway, 2013b; K. Oates, 2015). Many strategies have been developed, and we describe these efforts by focusing on children who are physically abused, their parents, and the communities in which they live. The discussion here focuses on formal programs and strategies; personal responses to address the problem are included in Chapter 11.

Focusing on Physically Abused Children

First and foremost, children who have been identified as physically abused need child protection services. CPS agencies provide a number of different services to children who have been maltreated as well as to those at risk for abuse. Approximately 1.3 million children reported for child maltreatment (whether or not maltreatment was substantiated) received services in 2017, including foster care, family support, and family preservation services, representing approximately 60 percent of substantiated victims and 30 percent of nonvictims (U.S. DHHS, 2019). The role of CPS in providing services to child maltreatment victims will be discussed further in Chapter 5.

One needed intervention for many children who are physically abused is treatment to address the many consequences associated with abuse that we discussed earlier, including developmental, psychological, and behavioral problems. In the past, children who were physically abused were not typically referred for treatment because CPA was viewed as a family problem and the individual impact on children was not recognized (Fitzgerald & Berliner, 2012). Today, however, several interventions have been developed and proven effective in treating this group of children including therapeutic day-treatment programs, individual therapy, and group therapy (R. Culp, Little, Letts, & Lawrence, 1991; Runyon, Deblinger, & Steer, 2010; Swenson & Kolko, 2000). Some newer approaches focus on cognitive skills development such as language stimulation (Manso, Garcia-Baamonde, & Alonso, 2011). There is some evidence that these treatment approaches can be successful in decreasing aggressive and coercive behaviors in victims of CPA and in improving social behavior, cognitive development, and self-esteem (Fantuzzo et al., 1996; R. Oates & Bross, 1995; Wolfe & Wekerle, 1993).

The treatment of choice for children who have experienced traumatic events, including physical abuse, however, is some type of trauma-focused therapy that includes cognitive behavioral components that focus specifically on the abuse experience. As summarized by Fitzgerald and Berliner (2012), **cognitive behavioral therapy (CBT)** for abused children includes five components: (1) providing corrective information about abuse, (2) building coping skills to manage stress and regulate emotional distress, (3) achieving mastery over trauma-related memories through gradual exposure, (4) contextualizing and reframing the abuse experience through cognitive restructuring, and (5) enhancing future safety. **Trauma-focused cognitive behavioral therapy (TF-CBT)** is a specific form of trauma-focused therapy and has the greatest evidence of effectiveness to date for children of all ages and across multiple types of child maltreatment (Silverman et al., 2008); this specific form of treatment is discussed in detail in Chapter 4. Another trauma-focused approach that has demonstrated some effectiveness is **Integrative Treatment of Complex Trauma for Children (ITCT-C)** (Lanktree & Briere, 2016). ITCT-C includes multiple targets and is responsive to a number of contextual issues such as family dynamics, caretaker support, cultural factors, and institutional demands (e.g., school, CPS). The main components of ITCT-C are described in Table 3.5. Similarly effective approaches have been developed specifically for adolescents (Briere & Lanktree, 2012; Briere, Lanktree, & Semple, 2019).

Focusing on Physically Abusive Adults

In previous sections, we described what we know about who is most likely to be abusive and who is most likely to be abused. When we speak of "correlates," or "risk factors," we often find ourselves imagining the "typical" abusive family. It makes sense that we would engage in this typification process, but we must continually remind ourselves that this process is inherently flawed. Abuse can, and often does, occur in unexpected households.

TABLE 3.5 ■ Components of Integrative Treatment of Complex Trauma for Children (ITCT-C)	
Component	**Description**
Assessment-Driven Treatment	Ongoing review of symptoms/problems based on interviews and trauma-specific tests.
Attention to Complex Trauma Issues	Targets common trauma-related outcomes (e.g., PTSD, depression, interpersonal difficulties, affect dysregulation) using affect regulation training, cognitive therapy, therapeutic exposure, trigger management, and relational/attachment-oriented approaches through individual, group, caretaker, and family therapy.
Early Focus on Immediate Issues	Prioritizes trauma-related symptoms and problematic environments (i.e., dangerous or nonprotective aspects of physical environment).
Focus on Positive Working Relationship With the Therapist	Includes a nonjudgmental and caring client–therapist relationship.
Customization	Adapts treatment approaches and components to individual child's specific demographics, history, family constellation, and needs.
Attention to Attachment Difficulties	Devotes attention to processing attachment-related issues in individual and caretaker therapy sessions.
Skills Development	Includes skills training and development of coping skills (e.g., affect regulation, identifying triggers, mindfulness strategies).
Titrated Therapeutic Exposure and Exploration of Trauma Memories	Exposes child to traumatic memories through therapeutic play, art, writing exercises, or discussion that is titrated within a developmentally appropriate and safe context so that affect regulation capacities are not unduly challenged.
A Flexible Time Frame	Adapts to flexible time frame rather than manualized or standardized time frame.
Advocacy and Interventions at the System Level	Focuses on child's and family's interface with various social systems such as school, foster care, CPS, medical services, and juvenile justice system.
Positive Professional Collaborations and Therapist Self-Care	Emphasizes support for clinician including collaborations with colleagues and healthy self-care strategies.

Source: Lanktree, C. B., & Briere, J. N. (2016). *Treating complex trauma in children and their families: An integrative approach.* Thousand Oaks, CA: SAGE Publications.

And it is important to remember that most high-risk households are not abusive. Yet, as we begin to think about prevention and intervention, it seems reasonable to begin with these risk factors. We know, for example, that abusive parents are more likely to be poor and socially isolated, and experience more life stress than other families. Parents have likely experienced or witnessed violence in their own childhoods and demonstrate significant deficits in their own parenting. We also know that the parents in these families often experience multiple problems including substance abuse, mental health disorders, and domestic violence, like the family in our opening case study, which make them unable or unwilling to take care of their children. Several intervention and prevention approaches have been developed to target specific populations (e.g., abusive parents, young parents, disadvantaged families) and specific risk factors, and we describe these approaches in the following paragraphs.

Parent Training and Support Efforts

When and how do parents learn how to parent? Perhaps some have taken a class, or read a parenting book. Hospitals send parents home with a list of dos and don'ts, and many offer parents training and support. Most parents, however, were never taught *how to parent*. Most of what parents know they have learned by observation, with the most salient observations likely stemming from how they themselves were parented. Since the 1970s, both intervention and prevention efforts have attempted to provide parents with education and skills training through parent education and support programs. Programs of this kind focus on educating parents about child development, improving parenting skills, modifying attitudes associated with harsh parenting, reducing negative emotions such as anger and stress, and providing settings where parents can share their concerns and work on problem solving with one another (Daro, 2012; Lundahl, Nimer, & Parsons, 2006). Strategies employed include providing parents with written information, video or live demonstrations, training with child discipline experts on increasing child compliance, and role playing and other techniques designed to teach parenting skills (e.g., Daro, 2012). Although most of these programs are intended for high-risk populations, some experts argue that all parents or prospective parents might benefit from this type of education and training (Krug, Dahlberg, Mercy, Zwi, & Lozno, 2002).

One such program is **Incredible Years (IY)**, which targets children with behavior problems and aims to reduce coercive parent–child interactions by providing parents with information about child development along with strategies to enhance parent–child interactions, such as the use of positive discipline, the reduction of negative affect during parenting interactions, and the reinterpretation of negative cognitive attributions about the parent–child relationship (Webster-Stratton, Reid, & Beauchaine, 2011, 2013). Several randomized controlled trials of IY have found that it is effective at reducing physical punishment and at enhancing parent–child interactions, which in turn leads to improvements in the behavior of young children with oppositional defiant or conduct disorders (Webster-Stratton & Reid, 2010) and ADHD (Webster-Stratton et al., 2011). Several components of these programs have been identified as particularly effective in enhancing parenting skills, reducing risk of abuse, changing attitudes and emotions, and reducing children's problematic behaviors. In a meta-analysis conducted by the CDC (2009), for example, particularly effective components included teaching parents various skills in emotional communication and positive parent–child interactions, as well as providing parents with the opportunity to demonstrate and practice these skills.

Other empirically evaluated parent education and support approaches target the family as a unit, such as integrated parent–child approaches. These interventions focus on both the child and the parent, along with their interaction, and constitute a family-oriented approach that has been used extensively with physically abusive families. Runyon and Urquiza (2011) argue that a coercive parent–child relationship leads to CPA and, as a result, effective treatment needs to address the following four elements: "(1) parenting skills, (2) distorted cognitions/attributions, (3) development of adaptive and nonviolent coping strategies, and (4) development of greater affective regulation" (p. 197).

Several interventions exist that incorporate all four of these elements and are based on the principles of CBT. **Alternatives for Families: A Cognitive Behavioral Therapy (AF-CBT)** is one approach that has been empirically evaluated that targets both parents who are physically abusive and their children. Kolko (1996b), for example, randomly assigned children who were physically abused and their parents to either family therapy or separate individual cognitive behavioral treatments, and then compared these two groups with families who received routine community services. Both family therapy and cognitive behavioral treatment were found to be superior to routine community services in reducing child-to-parent violence, child behavior problems, and parental distress. AF-CBT has also been shown to be effective in reducing levels of parental anger, abuse risk, and re-abuse (e.g., Kolko, 1996a).

In other studies, the effectiveness of **Parent–Child Interaction Therapy (PCIT)** has been examined (Chaffin, Funderbunk, Bard, Valle, & Gurwitch, 2011; Chaffin et al., 2004). This form of therapy involves behavioral parent training whereby the parent is coached in parenting skills during live parent–child interactions. Chaffin and colleagues (2004) assigned parent–child dyads to one of three conditions: PCIT only, PCIT with enhanced services (services targeting additional family problems such as parental depression, substance abuse, and marital or domestic violence), or a community parenting group. Families assigned to the PCIT condition had fewer reports of CPA and greater improvement in parent–child interactions compared to the community parenting condition. Results of several other studies examining the effectiveness of PCIT have indicated it is effective in decreasing child behavior problems, child post–traumatic stress, parental stress, and risk for future abuse (e.g., Borrego, Timmer, Urquiza, & Follette, 2004; Chaffin et al., 2011; Runyon et al., 2010; Timmer, Urquiza, & Zebell, 2006).

In a recent systematic review of parenting intervention programs, Melendez-Torres, Leijten, and Gardner (2019) identified several potentially important components in reducing CPA. These components included psychoeducation (e.g., explanation of child development stages), positive reinforcement techniques (e.g., praise and rewards), discipline techniques (e.g., time out), proactive parenting techniques (e.g., rule setting), attachment enhancement techniques (e.g., parent–child play), and parent self-management skills (e.g., problem solving, emotion regulation, relaxation). Results of the review indicated that the most effective interventions included teaching specific strategies such as parental self-management strategies, alternative nonviolent punishment strategies, and proactive parenting strategies.

Focusing on Communities

As noted in Chapter 1, primary prevention efforts are designed to prevent child maltreatment from occurring in the first place and are often offered at the community level. These prevention strategies are typically designed to improve the larger community environment of children through either wide-scale training, information dissemination and changing community norms, or changes in public policy. Such approaches address the complex and interactive nature of CPA by targeting multiple systems and integrating complementary services. Both theory and research evidence suggest that prevention programs that focus on multiple levels or systems of the ecological model tend to be more effective than programs that focus on a single ecological level (Child Welfare Information Gateway, 2013b; Daro, 2012).

Improving Community Environments

Although enhancing parenting skills, reducing negative parent–child interactions, and decreasing child behavior problems are important intervention and prevention goals, experts also recognize the value in shifting attention from individual- and family-focused strategies to efforts that additionally focus on creating supportive community environments (Daro, 2012; Daro & Dodge, 2009; Gomez & Fliss, 2019). The intention of such efforts is to create supportive communities where citizens and professionals alike share the belief that keeping children safe from abuse is a collective responsibility and one that requires expanding and coordinating services and support for parents. According to Daro and Dodge (2009), "It is increasingly recognized that environmental forces can overwhelm even well-intended parents, that communities can support parents in their role, and that public expenditures might be most cost-beneficial if directed toward community strategies" (p. 68). Indeed, specific federal funding is available to each U.S. state through the Community-Based Child Abuse Prevention (CBCAP) program to support community-based programs and activities designed to prevent child maltreatment (Gomez & Fliss, 2019).

These prevention strategies are typically designed to improve the larger community environment of children through wide-scale dissemination of information, expansion of service and support for parents, and provision of efficient delivery of services. Daro and Dodge (2009) identified four intervention strategies often used by community prevention initiatives: (1) expanding service capacity and access either by offering a new service or by improving families' ability to access services; (2) improving intervention practices either by training providers to deliver services in a unique way or by improving the relationship between provider and participant; (3) improving agency functionality by altering either institutional culture or interinstitutional communication to foster partnerships; and (4) altering community standards to increase mutual reciprocity among neighbors, collective responsibility for child protection and safety, healthy parent–child interaction, and acceptability of seeking services to resolve personal and parenting difficulties.

One such initiative is the American Psychological Association's ACT Raising Safe Kids Program (ACT-RSK). The program is a universal violence prevention program—community-based and cost-effective—based on theories of behaviorism and social learning that is available to all parents of young children, regardless of risk (J. Silva, 2009). The program trains caregivers on a variety of topics based on empirical evidence suggesting a role in CPA including nonviolent discipline, child development, anger management and social problem-solving skills, effects of media on children, and methods to protect children from exposure to violence (Knox, Burkhart, & Hunter, 2011). One of the strengths of the program is that it is low-cost based on a dissemination model whereby those trained in the program train other professionals who then train parents using existing facilities and staff. The program has been implemented in more than 80 communities in 12 different countries (Howe et al., 2017). A recent systematic literature of ACT-RSK evaluating 10 caregiver training programs indicated that all studies reported positive effects of the program such as a decrease in harsh discipline and an increase in positive parenting (Pontes, Siqueira, & de Albuquerque Williams, 2019). ACT-RSK was recently identified by the World Health Organization (WHO, 2018) as one of the most promising evidence-based strategies for reducing violence against children.

One of the most widely researched community prevention strategies is the **Triple P—Positive Parenting Program**. Triple P is a multilevel parenting and family support program that was originally developed by a group of researchers at the University of Queensland in Australia. The primary aim of Triple P is to "promote family harmony and reduce parent–child conflict by helping parents develop a safe, nurturing environment and promote positive, caring relationships with their children and to develop effective, non-violent management strategies for dealing with a variety of childhood behavioral problems and common developmental issues" (Turner & Sanders, 2006, p. 184). The program includes a series of five integrated intervention levels of increasing intensity to meet the varying levels of need among families. The interventions focus on positive parenting principles and practices, ranging from broad public or universal forms of dissemination of parenting information (e.g., newspaper articles, radio spots, websites), to brief parenting sessions offered in various primary care facilities for parents needing parenting advice, to more intensive behavioral family interventions for multiple-risk families (Prinz, Sanders, Shapiro, Whitaker, & Lutzker, 2009; Sanders & Prinz, 2012).

A series of controlled outcome studies has demonstrated the effectiveness of the various levels of intervention among a variety of populations and problem areas in improving the quality of parenting (Prinz et al., 2009; Sanders & Prinz, 2012). Triple P has proven effective on community-wide outcomes as well. In one study, Prinz and colleagues (2009) randomly assigned 18 counties in South Carolina to either the Triple P program or a control group who received services as usual. Findings suggested a lack of growth in child maltreatment rates in the counties receiving the Triple P program compared to the control counties, which showed considerable growth in substantiated child maltreatment. Other child maltreatment–related indicators (such as out-of-home placements and hospital admissions for child injuries) showed significant decreases in the intervention counties compared to the control counties.

Other community prevention programs take advantage of school-based interventions for preschoolers and school-age children. One promising school-based program is the **Chicago Child–Parent Centers program**, which provides preschool education and a variety of family support services for low-income children aged 3 to 9 years (Reynolds & Robertson, 2003). The preschool education component focuses on basic skills in language arts and math, while the family support component includes home visitation, parenting skills, vocational skills, and social supports but primarily focuses on enhancing parents' involvement in their children's education. Research evaluating the effectiveness of the Chicago program indicated a 52 percent reduction in court petitions of child maltreatment for children who participated in the Child–Parent Centers program compared with children who participated in alternative kindergarten interventions. Among children who attended a Child–Parent Centers program, those enrolled for longer periods (e.g., more than four years) experienced lower rates of child maltreatment than those enrolled for a shorter time. In addition, unlike previous studies, the research of Reynolds and Robertson (2003) found that these benefits were maintained. The greatest difference in child maltreatment rates between children who attended a Child–Parent Centers program and those who did not, for example, occurred at least six years after the children attended the Chicago program. Components of the program that appear to be particularly salient include family support processes such as increased parent involvement in school and maternal educational attainment as well as decreased family problems (Mersky, Topitzes, & Reynolds, 2011).

Other community prevention programs, such as the **Durham Family Initiative (DFI)**, attempt to expand universal assessments designed to identify families at risk for child maltreatment and then connect them to appropriate community-based services (Dodge et al., 2004). The aim of the initiative is to enhance community social and professional coordination and cooperation to improve a community's ability to not only provide, but also access, evidence-based resources. The effectiveness of this initiative was supported by findings indicating that the rate of substantiated child maltreatment in Durham County decreased by 49 percent between the year prior to the implementation of the DFI program and five years later, compared to 21 percent in five demographically matched comparison counties (Daro & Dodge, 2009).

In their review of community child abuse prevention strategies, Daro and Dodge (2009) concluded that these approaches offer reasons for both encouragement and caution. On the one hand, these efforts appear to be promising on both theoretical and empirical grounds. According to their review, these approaches have been associated with a reduction in reported rates of child maltreatment, injuries to children, and parental stress as well as improvements in parental efficacy and parent–child interactions. On the other hand, this approach requires significant financial resources, and it is not yet clear, empirically, that these programs are meeting their goals.

Public Awareness Campaigns

Another approach to the prevention of CPA, and child maltreatment more generally, is that of educating the public about the problem through mass media campaigns. Indeed, changing social norms though public engagement and education campaigns is one of the four pillars of the CDC's child maltreatment prevention strategy (Fortson et al., 2016) described earlier. Such campaigns employ public service announcements on radio and television; in newspapers, magazines, and brochures; and on posters and billboards. The rationale behind this approach is that changing societal beliefs and expectations (e.g., social norms about CPA), increasing knowledge, and enhancing awareness about the problem of CPA will result in lower levels of abuse. The reduction of CPA occurs directly, when abusive parents learn that their behavior is inappropriate and take action to change their behavior. Community awareness campaigns may also indirectly reduce rates of abuse by changing prevailing social norms and as professionals and laypeople begin to recognize the signs and symptoms of CPA and begin reporting suspected abuse to authorities.

The **ACT (Adults and Children Together) Media Campaign** is an example of a violence prevention media campaign. The goal of the campaign is to raise awareness about adult behaviors that can impact young children for better or worse (see APA website: apa .org/act/resources/psa). The media campaign includes public service announcements (see Figure 3.1) that are disseminated via television, radio, and print sources. The message of the campaign is to "teach carefully" because the things that adults say and do in front of children, especially verbally and physically expressing anger and aggression, can affect children's future behavior (American Psychological Association, 2020).

Another example of a media campaign is that created by a Spanish organization headquartered in Madrid called Fundación ANAR, or Aid to Children and Adolescents at Risk (see anar.org). This organization created an ingenious ad campaign using what is known as lenticular photography to create bus stop advertisements about physical abuse with much of the content of the ad only visible to children of a certain height (Isaacson, 2013). This type of photography allows companies to create images in such a way that viewers see different images depending on their height. Those taller than 4 feet, 5 inches (presumably the average height of a 10-year-old), would see a photo of a boy with the following message—"Sometimes, child abuse is only visible to the child suffering it"—while children under that would see the same image of the boy with a bruised face with the message: "If somebody hurts you, phone us and we'll help you" along with the organization's hotline number (Isaacson, 2013, p. 2). Those interested in viewing the ad can watch a YouTube video at www.youtube.com/watch?v=N0h1mgpn95s. Adolescents and children at risk in the United States can call the National Domestic Violence Hotline at 1-800-799-SAFE.

Some research evidence indicates that public education campaigns are effective in potentially reducing CPA. Some studies demonstrate evidence, for example, of a link between public education and increased reporting associated with a multimedia campaign conducted in the Netherlands from 1991 to 1992 (Hoefnagels & Baartman, 1997; Hoefnagels & Mudde, 2000). The campaign employed a variety of media and educational efforts, including a televised documentary, televised public service announcements, a radio program, teacher training, and various printed materials (e.g., posters, newspaper articles). In an evaluation of the campaign, Hoefnagels and Baartman (1997) found that it was effective in increasing awareness of abuse, as shown by the dramatic increase in the number of calls received by a national child abuse hotline in the period after the campaign. Further evidence of the potentially powerful impact of media campaigns comes from universal education programs to prevent shaken baby syndrome, as noted previously (Barr et al., 2009; Dias et al., 2005; see Box 3.1). In the United States today, 87 percent of adults view child abuse as a serious problem, believe that it is preventable, and report that they would (97%) and should (98%) take action if confronted with an abusive situation (Klika, Haboush-Deloye, & Linkenbach, 2019).

FIGURE 3.1 ■ Example of ACT Media Campaign

Source: Courtesy of the American Psychological Association and the Advertising Council.

Law and Policy

Another important way to address the problem of child maltreatment in general, and CPA in particular, is through the adoption of various laws and policies that attempt to protect children and prevent child maltreatment. Over the years, a variety of legislation has been introduced with this purpose in mind. The first comprehensive child maltreatment law in the United States, the **Child Abuse Prevention and Treatment Act (CAPTA)**, was originally passed in 1974 and has been regularly reauthorized and amended since. CAPTA provides federal funding and guidance to U.S. states to support prevention, assessment, investigation, prosecution, and treatment initiatives and to also provide grants (such as the CBCAP grants described earlier) to agencies and organizations for the same purpose (Child Welfare Information Gateway, 2019a).

In 2019, CAPTA was updated as the Stronger Child Abuse Prevention and Treatment Act (Stronger CAPTA, H.R. 2480). As of this writing, the bill has passed both the House of Representatives and the Senate, and is awaiting President Trump's signature. The bill proposed modest but important changes including increased funding for communities and states to implement strategies and programs to prevent child maltreatment, enhance coordination between agencies, and improve reporting requirements on child fatalities (Whitney, 2019).

Another strategy to reduce or eliminate CPA involves criminal justice system responses that target CPA offenders. As noted, all U.S. states and territories have child abuse statutes that define serious physical abuse as punishable by law (Myers, 2011). Although prosecution of CPA is most often considered to be a tertiary prevention strategy (e.g., it applies after abuse has already occurred), it also has a potential deterrent effect on future acts of abuse and therefore should also be considered a primary prevention strategy. Prosecutors process far more cases of child sexual abuse than cases of CPA (B. Smith, 1995). This is true due to the significant challenges associated with prosecuting CPA relative to other forms of child maltreatment. Such challenges include the hidden nature of abuse, which makes it difficult to establish proof of what occurred (i.e., who, what, and when), the lack of a clear distinction between punishment and criminal intent to harm a child, difficulties in interpreting medical evidence by both jurors and prosecutors, and lack of experience by prosecutors in handling such cases (Parrish, 2012; Smith, 1995). Since the late 1980s, significant improvements have been made in the processes of criminal investigation of CPA as well as its prosecution due to increased interdisciplinary training, networking, and professional cross-training among lawyers, social workers, and medical professionals (Parrish, 2012).

In addition to broad child maltreatment policies and criminal laws that attempt to deter CPA, other policy initiatives have the potential to impact the occurrence of CPA. According to a recent study, for example, paid family leave was associated with reduced risk of abuse-related head injuries in young children (Klevens, Luo, Xu, Peterson, & Latzman, 2016). This study compared data from 1995 through 2011 among California families, where paid family leave was introduced in 2004, with data from seven states without a paid family leave policy. Not only was there a decline in rates of hospital admission in California for abuse-related head injuries after 2004, but there was an increase in hospital admission rates for states without paid family leave. In another study, researchers examined the impact of policy associated with child support on likelihood of low-income families being reported for child maltreatment (Slack, Holl, McDaniel, Yoo, & Bolger, 2004). In the experimental group, families were able to receive child support payments with no change in benefits while families in the control group received reduced benefits because of the child support that was required by state policy; thus, the families in the control group experienced modest increases in income. Results indicated that families with modest increases in income were approximately 10 percent less likely to be reported for child maltreatment. The adoption of various policies such as these that enhance income and/or bonding time for parents and infants have the potential to reduce the occurrence of CPA. Additional policy and practice initiatives targeting child maltreatment will be discussed in subsequent chapters on other forms of child maltreatment.

CHAPTER SUMMARY

The physical abuse of children is a complex problem that is not well understood, despite nearly six decades of research. The complexity of CPA is evident in attempts to define what specific circumstances constitute abuse. Although most experts agree that CPA includes a range of behaviors that cause observable harm to children, there is less agreement about the boundary between CPA and normal parenting practices that do not result in observable harm. Despite definitional ambiguities, it is clear that thousands of children are subjected to the harm associated with CPA each year.

Research examining the characteristics of adults who are physically abusive and children who are physically abused has demonstrated the heterogeneity of both victim and offender populations, which encompass all ages, genders, races, and socioeconomic groups. A number of risk factors, however, have been consistently associated with CPA. Children who are physically abused are often quite young (i.e., 5 years old or younger); children with special needs (e.g., those with physical or mental disabilities) also appear to be at high risk for abuse. Adults who are physically abusive are found disproportionately among economically disadvantaged groups, and their environments include additional stressors such as having children at a young age and single parenthood. Many adults who inflict violence on children also display other common characteristics, including depression, anger control problems, parenting difficulties, substance abuse problems, family difficulties, and physiological overreactivity.

CPA is associated with a number of negative physical and psychological effects for child victims as well as for adults with childhood histories of CPA. These consequences affect a variety of areas of functioning, including physical, emotional, cognitive, behavioral, and social domains. The experience of CPA, however, does not affect all victims in the same way. Specific factors can mediate the effects of CPA; for example, factors associated with increased negative impact of CPA include the severity of abuse, the duration of the abuse, and the number of forms of abuse experienced.

Proposed solutions to the CPA problem include both intervention and prevention efforts. Because of the complexity of CPA, any single intervention or treatment is unlikely to be successful, particularly with high-risk families. Psychological approaches for children and their families target parenting skills, anger control and stress management, social and developmental skills, and parent–child interactions. Although enhancing parenting skills, reducing negative parent–child interactions, and decreasing child behavior problems are important intervention and prevention goals, experts also recognize the value in shifting attention from individual- and family-focused strategies to efforts that impact society more broadly (through laws and policy initiatives) as well as efforts that additionally focus on creating supportive community environments. The intention of such efforts is to create communities where citizens and professionals alike share the belief that keeping children safe from abuse is a collective responsibility. Public education campaigns have also used the mass media effectively to increase awareness, recognition, and understanding of the CPA problem. The adoption of various child maltreatment laws and policies has also contributed to prevention and intervention efforts. Although evaluation studies suggest that many intervention and prevention strategies are promising, additional research is needed to enhance the current state of knowledge about solutions to the CPA problem.

Recommended Resources

Bentovim, A. (2018). *Trauma-organized systems: Physical and sexual abuse in families.* Abingdon, Oxon, UK: Routledge.

Briere, J., Lanktree, C. B., & Semple, R. J. (2019). *Using ITCT-A to treat self-injury in traumatized youth.* Los Angeles, CA: University of Southern California.

Finkelhor, D., Turner, H. A., Shattuck, A., & Hamby, S. L. (2015). Prevalence of childhood exposure to violence, crime, and abuse. *JAMA Pediatrics, 169*(8), 746–754.

Fortson, B. L., Klevens, J., Merrick, M. T., Gilbert, L. K., & Alexander, S. P. (2016). *Preventing child abuse and neglect: A technical package for policy, norm, and programmatic activities*. Atlanta, GA: National Center for Injury Prevention and Control, Centers for Disease Control and Prevention.

Gomez, R., & Fliss, J. (2019). A community-based prevention approach: Examples from the field. *Child and Adolescent Social Work Journal*, *36*(1), 65–74.

Greeley, C. S. (2019). Prevention of child physical abuse. In A. P. Giardino, M. A. Lyn, & E. R. Giardino (Eds.), *A practical guide to the evaluation of child physical abuse and neglect* (pp. 375–404). New York, NY: Springer.

Hoehn, E. F., Wilson, P. M., Riney, L. C., Ngo, V., Bennett, B., & Duma, E. (2018). Identification and evaluation of physical abuse in children. *Pediatric Annals*, *47*(3), e97–e101.

Lanktree, C. B., & Briere, J. N. (2016). *Treating complex trauma in children and their families: An integrative approach*. Thousand Oaks, CA: SAGE.

Lieberman, A. F., Ippen, C. G., & Dimmler, M. H. (2018). Child-parent psychotherapy. *Assessing and Treating Youth Exposed to Traumatic Stress*, 223.

CHILD SEXUAL ABUSE

LEARNING OBJECTIVES

1. Describe the definition and scope of child sexual abuse including problems inherent in measuring this form of abuse.

2. Identify the various risk factors associated with child sexual abuse.

3. Summarize the consequences of child sexual abuse including both short- and long-term outcomes.

4. Discuss the various intervention and prevention efforts that have been developed to address child sexual abuse including evidence of their effectiveness.

CASE HISTORY
SASHIM'S SECRET

Sashim, an only child, was 9 years old when her parents divorced. Her father had been physically violent toward both Sashim and her mother, and they broke off all ties with him after the divorce. The next three years were difficult for Sashim, and she was frequently lonely because she rarely saw her mother, who had to work two jobs to make ends meet. When Sashim was 12 years old, her mother became romantically involved with Bhagwan, a 39-year-old construction foreman. Shortly after Sashim's mother met Bhagwan, he moved in with the family and took a serious interest in Sashim. He showered her with attention by taking her to movies, buying her new clothes, and listening to her when she complained about difficulties at school. He seemed to provide her with the parental attention and affection that she had missed for so many years.

During the course of several months, Bhagwan's behavior toward Sashim gradually changed. He became much more physical with her, putting his arm around her when they were at the movies, stroking her hair, and kissing her on the lips when he said good night. He began to go into her bedroom and the bathroom without knocking when she was changing her clothes or bathing. He also began checking on her in the middle of the night. During these visits, he would stroke and caress her body. In the beginning, he touched only her non-private areas (e.g., shoulders, arms, and legs), but after several visits, he began to touch her breasts and genitals. Eventually, he began to kiss her sexually during his touching, all the while telling her how much he loved her and enjoyed being her father. He warned her that she should not tell anyone about their time together because others would not understand their special relationship.

One night, Bhagwan forced Sashim to have sexual intercourse with him. A few days later, one of Sashim's favorite teachers noticed that Sashim seemed very quiet and asked if something was bothering her. Sashim began crying and told her teacher everything that had happened. Sashim's teacher reassured her that she believed her

(Continued)

(Continued)

and would help her. The teacher called Child Protective Services (CPS), and Bhagwan was arrested. Sashim's mother could not believe that Bhagwan could do such things or that the things Sashim described could occur without her knowledge. She refused to believe Sashim, calling her a liar and a home-wrecker.

As a result, Sashim was placed in a foster home. Shortly thereafter, she was diagnosed with leukemia; the doctors estimated that she had only six months to live. Her only request was that she

be able to die at home with her foster parents, to whom she had become quite attached. The hospital, however, was unable to grant Sashim's request without the consent of her biological mother, who still had legal custody of Sashim. Her mother refused to consent unless Sashim agreed to recant her story about Bhagwan. After much discussion and deliberation, Sashim recanted her story and was able to return to her foster parents' home where she died several months later.

As this case history demonstrates, child sexual abuse (CSA) is a multifaceted problem, extraordinarily complex in its characteristics, dynamics, causes, and consequences. This chapter examines the major issues that contribute to this complexity. We begin by addressing issues related to defining the scope of CSA, including definitions and estimates of the rates of CSA in the United States. We then focus on risk factors associated with this form of abuse including characteristics of victims and perpetrators as well as family and cultural factors that help us to understand why it occurs. We also address the myriad consequences of this form of maltreatment for victims. We conclude the chapter with a description of various responses to the problem including both intervention and prevention approaches.

SCOPE OF THE PROBLEM

What Is Child Sexual Abuse?

What sexual interactions should be defined as *abusive*? To illustrate the complexities inherent in answering this question, consider the following scenarios:

- Jamie, a 15-year-old, frequently served as babysitter for his neighbor, 4-year-old Naomi. Each time Jamie was left alone with Naomi, he had her stroke his exposed penis while they watched her favorite video.

- Manuel and Maria frequently walked around nude at home in front of their 5-year-old son, Ernesto.

- Richard, an adult, repeatedly forced his nephew Matt to have anal intercourse with him when Matt was between the ages of 5 and 9 years. After the abuse stopped when he was 10, Matt frequently sneaked into his 6-year-old sister's room and had anal intercourse with her.

- Sally, at 16 years old, was a self-proclaimed nymphomaniac. She had physical relationships (e.g., kissing, fondling, and sexual intercourse) with numerous boyfriends from school. One evening when Sally was home alone with her 45-year-old stepfather, he asked her if she wanted to "mess around." Sally willingly agreed to have sexual intercourse with him.

- Dexter, a 30-year-old man, invited 7-year-old Jimmy to his house frequently for after-school snacks. After their snacks, Dexter asked Jimmy to undress and instructed him to assume various sexual poses while Dexter videotaped him. Dexter sold the videos for profit.

These vignettes illustrate a number of important issues to consider when defining CSA. In the following sections, we discuss the importance of conceptual issues, culture and development, and legal perspectives in determining what constitutes CSA before providing an operational definition of CSA.

Conceptual Issues in Defining CSA

A number of key components are generally regarded as essential in defining CSA, and these are illustrated in the vignettes included at the beginning of this section of the chapter. First, definitions of CSA should include sexual experiences with children that involve both physical contact and noncontact activities. For example, CSA may include physical contact such as fondling or intercourse as described in the vignettes about Jamie, Matt, and Sally, but it can also include noncontact forms, such as taking photographs, as in the scenario involving Dexter and Jimmy. Furthermore, sexual activities include sexual contact performed by the perpetrator on the child but also by the child on the perpetrator, as in the vignette involving Jamie and Naomi. Controversy continues to exist, however, regarding what specific behaviors should be deemed abusive, regardless of whether those behaviors are classified as contact or noncontact experiences. The range of sexual activities we might call CSA extends from exhibitionism to intercourse. Although certain sexual acts are generally universally recognized as abusive (e.g., vaginal and anal penetration), other activities are less obviously abusive such as the vignette depicting the parental nudity (a noncontact behavior) of Manuel or Maria or when an adult kisses a child on the mouth (a contact behavior).

One way to distinguish between abusive and nonabusive behaviors is to evaluate the intent of the perpetrator. Many definitions of CSA, for example, include the requirement that the activities are intended for the sexual stimulation or gratification of the perpetrator or another person (such as in the case of child pornography as discussed in Box 4.1), thus excluding normal family and caregiving interactions such as nudity, bathing, and displays of affection (Mathews & Collin-Vézina, 2019). In practice, of course, determining whether a behavioral intention is sexual or nonsexual can be difficult. How can one determine whether a grandfather kisses his granddaughter out of innocent affection or for his sexual gratification?

A second important component of CSA definitions emphasizes adults' exploitation of their authority, knowledge, and power to achieve sexual ends. Implicit in this component is the assumption that children are incapable of providing informed consent to sexual interactions with adults for two reasons: (a) Because of their developmental status, children are not capable of fully understanding what they are consenting to and what the consequences of their consent might be, and (b) children might not be in a position to decline involvement because of their vulnerability and/or the adult's authority status. The vignette about Sally and her stepfather illustrates a case of abuse because, despite Sally's sexual experience and consent in this situation, she is not mature enough to understand the ramifications of having sexual intercourse with her stepfather. As Haugaard and Reppucci (1988) point out, "The total legal and moral responsibility for any sexual behavior between an adult and a child is the adult's; it is the responsibility of the adult not to respond to the child" (p. 193).

The third and final component of CSA definitions addresses the age or maturational advantage of the perpetrator over the victim. This component focuses on the age of the victim as well as the perpetrator. CSA, by definition, specifies that the abuse victim is a child, as defined through the victim's cognitive or psychosocial developmental status (Mathews & Collin-Vézina, 2019) or as defined through the victim's legal status (see page 96 for a discussion of legal perspectives on defining CSA). In terms of the perpetrator's age, many definitions limit abuse to situations involving an age discrepancy wherein the perpetrator is at least 2 to 5 years older than the victim. Others include children and adolescents as potential perpetrators if a situation involves the exploitation of a child by virtue of the perpetrator's size, age, sex, or status. Broader definitions of CSA include circumstances such as those described in the second scenario of anal intercourse between 10-year-old Matt and his 6-year-old sister. An increasing number of reports involving both adolescent offenders and children victimizing children younger than themselves are beginning to appear (e.g., Gewirtz-Meydan & Finkelhor, 2019; Grossi, Lee, Schuler, Ryan, & Prentky, 2016).

Culturally and Developmentally Normative Sexual Behavior

As noted in Chapter 1, sexual interactions between children and adults have occurred throughout history and only relatively recently have come to be recognized as a social problem. Recall from the discussion in Chapter 1 that the appropriateness or inappropriateness of various sexual behaviors has varied not only across time but also across societies and cultures. In some cultures, for example, young boys performing fellatio on older boys is a developmental rite of passage (Herdt, 1987). In the United States, circumcision is commonly defined and practiced as a voluntary and harmless medical procedure, whereas in Europe it is more likely to be recognized as a violation of children's rights (Kulish, 2012). There is also variability *within* cultures and societies with regard to the acceptability of adult–child sexual behaviors. In North America, for example, the North American Man/Boy Love Association (NAMBLA) supports adult–child sexual interactions advocating against "the extreme oppression of men and boys in mutually consensual relationships" as well as age-of-consent laws (see nambla.org).

We find another example of these ongoing cultural tensions in the case of Jeffrey Epstein, the American financier and convicted sexual offender who died in what was ruled a suicide in his prison cell in the fall of 2019. According to the *New York Times*, Epstein believed that "criminalizing sex with teenage girls was a cultural aberration" (Stewart, 2019). One has to wonder if many of his friends and acquaintances thought likewise. After all, many of them knew of his sexual inclination toward underage girls. Why, one wonders, were so many unwilling to step forward to report his behavior?

It is important to remind ourselves, once again, that intimate violence, including sexual abuse, is a social construction. Societal reactions produce definitions of what is considered "sexual." Societal reactions define "child." And societal reactions drive the process that deems sexual contact with children as immoral or illegal. It thus becomes apparent that any definition of CSA depends on the historical period in question, the cultural context of the behavior, and the values and orientations of specific social groups.

To define CSA today in the United States, it is also essential to know something about what types of behaviors are generally regarded as developmentally appropriate as well as acceptable within American families. Would most people consider Manuel and Maria abusive for walking around nude in front of their 5-year-old son? What if their son were 13 years old? How much variation in nudity, touching various body parts, and kissing on the lips is socially acceptable between adults and children?

One way to approach the question of acceptability is to examine what kinds of sexual behaviors are common and developmentally appropriate for children. Debra A. Poole and Michele A. Wolfe (2009), in a review of the research on normative sexual behaviors in early, middle, and late childhood, conclude that children are curious about sex and engage in sexual behaviors throughout childhood. Some of the most common behaviors in children aged 2–6 years include kissing nonfamily members, trying to look at others undressing, undressing in front of others, showing sex parts to others, touching women's breasts, and touching sex parts or masturbating. The most common sexual behaviors during middle and late childhood (for children aged 7–10 years and 11–12 years, respectively) are similar to those described for early childhood, but by middle school, sex play with friends is not uncommon, and this play sometimes involves some form of manipulation or persuasion. Several unique behaviors also increase from middle to late childhood including talking about sex, kissing and hugging, looking at pornographic pictures, sexual teasing, and interest in the opposite sex (Friedrich, Fisher, Broughton, Houston, & Shafran, 1998; Larsson & Svedin, 2002). An estimated 15 percent of middle schoolers and 50 percent of high school seniors have had sexual intercourse (Martinez & Abma, 2015).

Of course, there will be disagreement as to whether these activities are "good" or "bad," but that is not our point. Societal reactions create these boundaries. We merely want to emphasize that sexualized behavior in children is not uncommon. It is, in fact, a developmentally normal curiosity of childhood. Although a comprehensive review of cultural and developmental factors impacting CSA is beyond the scope of this chapter, we recommend Lisa Aronson Fontes's (2008) *Child Abuse and Culture: Working With Diverse Families* and John Bancroft's (2003) *Sexual Development in Childhood* for those interested in further reading.

Legal Perspectives in Defining CSA

All U.S. states have laws prohibiting the sexual abuse of children, but the specifics of criminal statutes vary from state to state. CSA laws typically identify an age of consent—that is, the age at which an individual is considered to be capable of consenting to sexual contact. In most states, the age of consent falls somewhere in the range of 16 to 18 years. Sexual contact between an adult and a minor who has not reached the age of consent is illegal. As discussed earlier, however, most states make an exception if the sexual partners are close to the same age (for example, a 19-year-old male and a 17-year-old female), and punishments tend to be much more severe if the age gap is larger. Incest is illegal regardless of the victim's age or consent (Berliner & Elliott, 2002).

Criminal statutes also vary in how they define sexual contact between an adult and a minor. Some states define CSA in relatively broad terms. In the state of Maryland, for example, *sexual abuse* is defined as "any act that involves sexual molestation or exploitation of a child" including "incest, rape, sexual offense in any degree, sodomy, and unnatural or perverted sexual practices" (Maryland Family Law § 5-701). In contrast, California law defines CSA very specifically: *Sexual abuse* includes **child sexual assault** and **child sexual exploitation**, and both of these terms are explicitly defined. In the California statute, *sexual assault* includes anal or vaginal penetration by the penis or another object, oral-genital and oral-anal contact, touching of the genitals or other intimate body parts whether clothed or unclothed, and genital masturbation of the perpetrator in the presence of a child (California Penal Code § 11165.1). California law also defines *sexual exploitation*, which primarily refers to noncontact activities involving pornography (preparing, accessing, or distributing obscene matter depicting a child) and activities that include the sexual exploitation of children for financial gain such as selling child pornography or encouraging and/or coercing child prostitution. The California Penal Code also defines *commercial* sexual exploitation of children and includes child sex trafficking as a form of CSA. Although outside the scope of the current chapter, which focuses primarily on noncommercial forms of CSA, sexual exploitation for commercial gain is an important topic that has recently gained considerable research and legislative attention (see Box 4.1).

BOX 4.1
COMMERCIAL SEXUAL EXPLOITATION OF CHILDREN

The First World Congress Against the Commercial Sexual Exploitation of Children, held in 1996, provided the first working definition of **commercial sexual exploitation of children (CSEC)** as comprising "sexual abuse by the adult and remuneration in cash or kind to the child or a third person or persons. The child is treated as a sexual and commercial object. The commercial sexual exploitation of children constitutes a form of coercion and violence against children, and amounts to forced labor and a contemporary form of slavery." Of all the major forms of child maltreatment discussed in this book, CSA is the one that is most likely to occur between a child and an adult who is not a family member. CSEC is one form of CSA that is typically extrafamilial, although reports also suggest that some elements of CSEC may also occur within the family (e.g., Miller-Perrin & Wurtele, 2017a). CSEC includes what is referred to by most laypersons as pornography, prostitution of children, and child sex trafficking activities. These forms of child sexual exploitation are often interrelated and are important to study not only because they are a violation of children's human rights but because of their negative impact on children's development (Gewirtz-Meydan, Lahav, Walsh, & Finkelhor, 2019; Miller-Perrin & Wurtele, 2017a; Oram, Khondoker, Abas, Broadbent, & Howard, 2015).

Child pornography is defined by federal law under 18 U.S.C. § 2256(8) as any "visual depiction" of an actual minor (under age 18) or a computer-generated image that "is indistinguishable from that of a minor" who is "engaging in sexually explicit conduct," "including any photograph, film, video, picture, or computer-generated image or picture, whether made or produced by electronic, mechanical, or other means" (U.S. Sentencing Commission, 2012). In 1978, the U.S. Congress passed the Protection of Children Against Sexual Exploitation Act in an attempt to halt the production and dissemination of pornographic materials involving children. In addition, the **Child Sexual Abuse and Pornography Act** of 1986 provides for federal prosecution of individuals engaged in child pornography, including parents who permit their children to engage in such activities (Otto & Melton, 1990).

Of course, as access to the internet has spread around the world, access to child pornography has spread exponentially. According to a 2012 U.S. Congress report, there are at least 5 million child pornographic images available on the internet at any given time (U.S. Sentencing Commission, 2012). Larry Nassar, the osteopathic physician who is in prison for molesting multiple American gymnasts, had over 37,000 images and videos of child pornography on his computer (Connor,

(Continued)

(Continued)

2016). According to the Internet Watch Foundation (IWF), "78,589 URLs contained child sexual abuse imagery and 3,791 domain names worldwide were used to create links to this content" (see www.iwf.org.uk). In 2018, technology companies reported over 45 million online photos and videos of children being sexually abused (Keller & Dance, 2019; see www.missingkids.org/theissues/csam#bythenumbers).

Some have objected to the use of the term *child pornography*, arguing that the term trivializes its inherently abusive content, implies consensual activity, and fails to recognize that such materials are not the same as adult pornography or erotica (Holmes & Holmes, 2009). Indeed, the IWF argues that this term acts to legitimize images by failing to acknowledge that such images are not pornography but, rather, a permanent record of a child being sexually exploited and should therefore be referred to as **child sexual abuse images** (www.iwf.org.uk). These images, then, are clearly abusive in and of themselves, and also likely contribute to the problem of CSA by stimulating adult sexual interest in children (Merdian, Curtis, Thakker, Wilson, & Boer, 2013). In addition, these images likely contribute to the exploitation of children by creating a market for the victimization of children and by serving as a tool that perpetrators use to groom victims for contact abuse or to blackmail victims into maintaining secrecy about abusive activities (A. Burgess & Hartman, 1987; P. Hunt & Baird, 1990; Seto, Hanson, & Babchishin, 2011; R. Tyler & Stone, 1985; Wolak, Finkelhor, & Mitchell, 2011).

Prostitution of children is another form of CSEC and is defined by the United Nations Optional Protocol to the Convention on the Rights of the Child (2000, article 2[b]) as "the use of a child in sexual activities for remuneration or any other form of consideration." The commercial element in prostitution of children can include any form of compensation, financial or otherwise, where the child or youth is treated as a commodity. Closely related to prostitution of children is **child sex trafficking**, defined by the U.S. Trafficking Victims Protection Act of 2000 (P.L. 106-386) and its reauthorizations in 2003,

2005, 2008, 2013, and 2018 as "the recruitment, harboring, transportation, provision, or obtaining of a person for the purpose of a commercial sex act." The use of the term *trafficking* is somewhat misleading because it implies physical movement of the child, which is not a requirement of most definitions (Miller-Perrin & Wurtele, 2017a). That transportation is not a requirement reflects the current recognition that child sex trafficking is defined by exploitation, rather than by movement (Rafferty, 2013). Thus, prostitution of children is essentially equivalent to child sex trafficking (see Reid & Jones, 2011).

Although child victims of prostitution and sex trafficking have historically been characterized as "child prostitutes" or "juvenile delinquents," most experts now argue that these minors should be viewed as victims of CSEC, rather than criminals, regardless of whether or not they seem to be engaging in sexual acts willingly (Institute of Medicine & National Research Council, 2013; Stop Exploitation Through Trafficking Act, 2013). Traditional views of children who are prostituted as voluntarily engaging in sex acts in exchange for something of value, for example, imply that children possess the maturity and cognitive ability to fully understand and consent to such acts (American Professional Society on the Abuse of Children, 2013). In addition, with victims of sex trafficking, there is often an element of force or coercion when they are recruited through kidnapping/physical coercion, false promises such as a paying job, sham marriages, or the guise of legitimate organizations such as modeling or tourist agencies (e.g., Hodge & Lietz, 2007; L. Jones, Engstrom, Hilliard, & Diaz, 2007; U.S. Department of State, 2019).

"Guesstimates" of the problem of sex trafficking and prostitution of children, such as "millions of victims of trafficking," are commonly referenced in international publications (Goodey, 2008). One must always be cautious with estimates of passionate topics like sex trafficking since advocates will tend to favor larger numbers over small ones (Best, 2012). However, even the highly respected International Labour Organization (2017) estimated that over 1 million minors are victims of forced sexual exploitation. Within the United States, estimates of prostitution of children have ranged from 1,400 to 326,000 children (Sedlak, Finkelhor, Hammer, & Schultz, 2002; Shared Hope International, 2009). The covert nature of sex trafficking and prostitution of children, as well as the lack of a uniform reporting system, contributes to the difficulty in determining the extent of the problem. In the United States, new legislation is attempting to improve documentation of CSEC. The Justice for Victims of Trafficking Act of 2015, for example, requires each state to report child victims of CSEC and will be added to the National Child Abuse and Neglect Data System over the next several years (U.S. Department of Health and Human Services [U.S. DHHS], 2016).

Miller-Perrin and Wurtele (2017a) describe a number of characteristics of victims of CSEC that have been documented repeatedly in the literature. This literature suggests that children who are vulnerable in some way are the ones typically targeted and recruited. Children who have drug and alcohol problems, physical and/or intellectual difficulties, and troubled family lives (e.g., parental substance abuse) or who are homeless are much more likely to become involved in CSEC (Clawson, Dutch, Solomon, & Grace, 2009; Cobbina & Oselin, 2011; Institute of Medicine & National Research Council, 2013; Swartz, 2014). Being female and pubescent (ages 15–19 years) is also a risk factor (Clawson et al., 2009; UNICEF, 2014). Another common vulnerability is the presence of violence in the home, including child physical and sexual abuse and neglect, which often results in youth running away to escape the abusive home (Greeson, Treglia, Wolfe, Wasch, & Gelles, 2019; Havlicek, Huston, Boughton, & Zhang, 2016; Wilson & Widom, 2010). Social and economic factors also likely contribute to sex

trafficking, such as poverty and few employment or educational opportunities (United Nations Office on Drugs and Crime, 2009; U.S. Department of State, 2005).

In response to the problem of CSEC, guidelines and standards have been set in various U.S. and international laws, treaties, and protocols to protect victims, prosecute offenders, provide services to victims, and prevent future CSEC (e.g., Justice for Victims of Trafficking Act, 2015; Preventing Sex Trafficking and Strengthening Families Act, 2013; United Nations, 2000). For example, in an effort to both protect victims and prosecute offenders, 168 countries have enacted legislation prohibiting all forms of human trafficking (U.S. Department of State, 2019). With regard to providing services for victims, the **Administration for Children and Families** has a website with resources to rescue and restore victims of human trafficking (www .acf.hhs.gov/otip/partnerships/look-beneath-the-surface). Ideally, victim services should include temporary and safe shelter, physical and mental health services, public benefits, legal and immigration assistance, substance abuse treatment, support groups, employment and training services, language education, and long-term housing or relocation assistance (Miller-Perrin & Wurtele, 2017a). The National Human Trafficking Resource Center, funded by the U.S. Department of Health and Human Services, operates a hotline where one can report CSEC and also obtain services (humantraffickinghotline .org). A number of efforts to prevent CSEC, including dissemination of resource guides, public awareness campaigns, and interventions for at-risk youth, are currently underway and hold promise (U.S. DHHS, 2019d; Wurtele & Miller-Perrin, 2012).

An Operational Definition of CSA

At this point, we have considered the complicating factors, but have not yet offered a workable definition of CSA. This oft-cited definition from the Centers for Disease Control and Prevention (CDC) will serve as our definition: "any completed or attempted (non-completed) sexual act, sexual contact with, or exploitation of (i.e., noncontact sexual interaction) a child" (Leeb, Paulozzi, Melanson, Simon, & Arias, 2008, p. 11). According to this definition, *sexual acts* include contact that involves some form of penetration "between the mouth, penis, vulva, or anus of the child and another individual" (p. 14). *Sexual contact* refers to intentional touching, by the individual on the child or by the child on the individual, of the genitalia, anus, groin, breast, inner thigh, or buttocks. *Exploitation*, or noncontact sexual abuse, includes exposing a child to activities such as pornography, voyeurism, or exhibitionism; depicting a child in a sexual act through either photographs or film; sexual harassment (see Chapter 7) of a child; and prostitution of a child.

Readers who are familiar with the CDC definition of CSA may well notice that we have deleted the final three words: "by a caregiver." Although in this chapter we will focus our attention on maltreatment in intimate relationships, it is important to recognize at the outset that CSA is frequently *not* committed by parents or caregivers (Finkelhor, Ormrod, & Turner, 2009). CSA can be committed by family members other than parents and caregivers, acquaintances, strangers, older children and adolescents, and other individuals in positions of authority over children. Indeed, news media and research publications are replete with stories of nonfamilial CSA occurring in religious organizations, day care settings and preschools, schools, and other youth-serving organizations such as organized clubs and sports (e.g., Henschel & Grant, 2019; Miller-Perrin & Wurtele, 2017b; Robert & Thompson, 2019; Speckhardt, 2011; Sturtz, 2014; W. Yardley, 2010).

Consider, for example, the case of Larry Nassar, former physician of the U.S. women's Olympic gymnastics team and osteopathic physician at Michigan State University (briefly mentioned earlier). For more than two decades, Nassar sexually abused hundreds of female athletes under the guise of providing legitimate medical treatment (Hauser, 2018). The Federal Bureau of Investigation found over 37,000 images and videos of child abuse on Nassar's computer, including a video of Nassar molesting girls in a swimming pool (Connor, 2016). He was convicted on child pornography charges and sentenced to 60 years in prison, plus an additional 40 to 175 years for criminal sexual conduct (Hauser, 2018). Additionally, Michigan State University was fined $4.5 million for Title IX violations, including not acting promptly on sexual assault reports and inadequate sexual assault policies and procedures (Jesse, 2019). As a result of these charges, as well as other charges of sexual misconduct by medical professionals, the Federation of State Medical Boards has released new guidelines in an effort to prevent future sexual misconduct (Haelle, 2019).

How Common Is Child Sexual Abuse?

According to the National Child Abuse and Neglect Data System (NCANDS), of the approximately 3.5 million children reported to CPS during 2017, 8.6 percent were victims of CSA (U.S. DHHS, 2019b). Approximately 58,000 total cases of CSA were substantiated, a number that is less than one-half what it was in the early 1990s (U.S. DHHS, 2016, 2019b). The most up-to-date examination of NCANDS data suggests a 64 percent decline in CSA between 1990 and 2014 (Finkelhor, Saito, & Jones, 2016). The four National Incidence Studies (NIS-1, NIS-2, NIS-3, NIS-4), which survey mandated professionals, similarly suggest that CSA has declined since the early 1990s. For example, NIS-3 estimated a 1993 rate of 4.5 cases of CSA per 1,000 children. NIS-4, which is the most recent study, estimated a rate of 2.4 cases of CSA per 1,000 children (Sedlak et al., 2010). These trends are discussed further in Chapter 11.

As noted previously, official statistics, such as those published by NCANDS, are difficult to interpret because most child maltreatment never comes to the attention of CPS. Underreporting of CSA, in particular, is problematic given that many incidents are not disclosed to professionals, friends, or family members. Indeed, approximately 66 percent of 10- to 17-year-olds in a community sample of youth did not disclose their CSA to a parent or other adult (Gewirtz-Meydan & Finkelhor, 2019). Surveys asking adults about childhood histories of CSA also reveal that a large percentage of adults report never having disclosed their abuse or disclosing it only after decades of living with their secret (Alaggia, Collin-Vézina, & Lateef, 2017; Romano, Moorman, Ressel, & Lyons, 2019; Tener & Murphy, 2015). In one study, less than one-third of adults disclosed their abuse during childhood, and most survivors waited to disclose their abuse, on average, 21 years (Jonzon & Lindblad, 2004). It seems clear that whatever estimates are used, they are likely underestimates of the true incidence and prevalence of CSA.

As discussed in Chapter 2, self-report surveys, compared to official statistics, often provide a clearer picture of the true rate of victimization. However, such surveys are not without their problems. Some men and women victimized as children may be reluctant to report their childhood experiences as adults. Retrospective recall might also bias reports by adults because they are recalling events that occurred many years earlier. Retrospective studies of adults are also limited because they provide rates of CSA that apply to the past and do not reflect current trends (Jud, Fegert, & Finkelhor, 2016). Even more importantly, measurement requires definition and operationalization of the ambiguous term *sexual abuse*, and definitions of this term vary widely across studies.

Despite these difficult hurdles, after nearly three decades of research examining the occurrence of CSA in the general population, consistent prevalence estimates have emerged in studies examining populations both in the United States and worldwide. In a national random sample of 1,000 U.S. adults who participated in a telephone survey sponsored by Gallup, Finkelhor, Moore, Hamby, and Straus (1997) asked respondents two questions about their own childhood experiences of sexual abuse. Overall, 23 percent of the respondents reported having been touched in a sexual way or forced to have sex before the age of 18 by a family member or by someone outside the family. The women in this survey sample were nearly 3 times as likely as the men to self-report CSA. These results are similar to those found in the most representative and methodologically sound self-report surveys in the literature, which indicate that at least 20 percent of women and between 5 percent and 10 percent of men in North America experienced some form of sexual abuse as children (Finkelhor, 1994). Studies examining the impact of CSA abuse in countries outside the United States have corroborated these findings by finding similar rates (e.g., Barth, Bermetz, Heim, Trelle, & Tonia, 2013; R. Gilbert, Widom, et al., 2009). In a meta-analysis of the prevalence of child sexual abuse in 22 countries, approximately 8 percent of men and 20 percent of women suffered some form of sexual abuse prior to the age of 18 (Pereda, Guilera, Forns, & Gómez-Benito, 2009).

When using more narrow definitions of CSA, rates are somewhat lower. Barth and colleagues (2013) conducted a meta-analysis of 55 studies from 24 countries examining children and adolescents and found that about 9 percent of girls and 3 percent of boys were victims of forced intercourse. Similarly lower rates were found by Finkelhor and colleagues (Finkelhor, Shattuck, Turner, & Hamby, 2014b), who argued that population surveys and meta-analyses generally define "sexual abuse" to include offenses perpetrated by same-age peers as well as adult perpetrators. In their study, which drew on three national U.S. telephone surveys and distinguished between juvenile and adult perpetrators, they found that lifetime experiences with sexual abuse perpetrated by adults was approximately 11 percent for females and 2 percent for males.

RISK FACTORS ASSOCIATED WITH CHILD SEXUAL ABUSE

In attempting to understand why CSA occurs, many experts in the field adhere to an ecological perspective that attempts to explain CSA using a framework that considers individuals and their environment and focuses on multiple levels of the ecology including the individual, family, community, and society (Assink et al., 2019; Lanier, Maguire-Jack, Mienko, & Panlilio, 2015; Miller-Perrin & Wurtele, 2017b). Using this approach, various risk factors associated with CSA can be identified including those that are characteristic of victims and perpetrators and the social environments, including families and society, in which they reside. Table 4.1 displays the risk factors associated with each of these systems, and this section of the chapter concludes by describing contemporary theories that attempt to integrate these various risk factors to help explain why CSA occurs. Keep in mind, however, that victims and perpetrators of CSA are not a homogeneous group and therefore no one risk factor, or group of risk factors, applies to all.

Characteristics of Children Who Are Sexually Abused

Accurately identifying risk factors for CSA victimization is difficult because, as noted earlier, much of the victim population is unidentified due to nondisclosure of abuse.

TABLE 4.1 ■ Risk Factors Associated With Child Sexual Abuse	
System Level	**Risk Factor**
Child	Demographic characteristics such as female sex, early adolescent age, and sexual minority status
	Disability status including intellectual, communication, physical, and mental health
	Psychological characteristics such as low self-esteem, susceptibility to persuasion/easily manipulated, emotional immaturity, behavioral difficulties, loneliness, having few close friends, passivity, quietness, trustingness, and emotional neediness
Perpetrator	Demographic characteristics such as male sex, adolescent or early adulthood age, and being someone with a relationship with the child
	Childhood history variables such as a history of child maltreatment (sexual, physical, psychological, or neglect), witnessing violence, poor parent–child attachment, and early sexual experience including viewing pornography
	Sexual deviances including sexual attraction to children and/or adolescents, fantasies about sexual activity with children, and high sex drive
	Presence of disinhibitors such as alcohol and drug use/abuse and cognitive distortions
	Social deficits including low social skills/competence, empathy deficiencies, loneliness, difficulties with intimate relationships, and emotional congruence with children
	Behavioral problems/disorders including externalizing (aggression/ violence, criminal behavioral, anger/hostility, paranoia/mistrust, and antisocial personality) and internalizing (anxiety, depression, and low self-esteem)
	Neurobiological/psychological markers such as deficits in IQ, increased frequency of childhood head injury, and abnormalities in brain anatomy
Socioeconomic	Low socioeconomic status, living in poverty, overcrowded living conditions, and parental unemployment
Family	Family structural characteristics such as a female child living with a nonbiological father or single parent, or absence of both parents
	Conflicted family relationships such as marital discord, divorce, intimate partner violence, absent and emotionally detached parenting, poor parent–child relationships, and absence of family cohesion, warm parenting, and family support

(Continued)

TABLE 4.1 ■ (Continued)	
System Level	**Risk Factor**
	Parent characteristics such as parental lack of education, young maternal age at first birth, nonoptimal parental monitoring, substance abuse, parental history of CSA, and mental health problems
Community and Society	Social attitudes that fail to recognize or understand CSA, sanctioning male/female power and status differentials
	Sexualization of children
	Sanctioning sexual relations between adults and children through media portrayals of children

Sources: References are representative rather than exhaustive: Assink et al., 2019; Brownlie, Graham, Bao, Koyama, & Beitchman, 2017; Butler, 2013; Cant, O'Donnell, Sims, & Harries, 2019; E. Davies & Jones, 2013; Doidge, Higgins, Delfabbro, & Segal, 2017; Euser et al., 2016; Finkelhor et al., 2013; Friedenberg et al., 2013; Gewirtz-Meydan & Finkelhor, 2019; Houtepen, Sijtsema, & Bogaerts, 2016; Lund & Vaughn-Jensen, 2012; MacMillan, Tanaka, Duku, Vaillancourt, & Boyle, 2013; Pérez-Fuentes et al., 2013; Sedlak et al., 2010; N. Smith & Harrell, 2013; Whittle et al., 2013; Widom & Massey, 2015.

One consistent risk factor, noted in both official sources and self-report surveys, is being biologically female. Girls are nearly 4 times more likely than boys to be sexually abused, according to NIS-4 findings (Sedlak et al., 2010). Data from national community surveys show that sexual victimization is more common for girls, although the gender differences are less pronounced (Gewirtz-Meydan & Finkelhor, 2019). Research also suggests that sexual orientation is a risk factor for CSA. A meta-analysis conducted on 26 school-based studies in North America indicated that sexual minority adolescents were 3.8 times more likely to experience CSA than heterosexual youth, especially male sexual minority youth (Friedman et al., 2011).

Children of all ages, from infants to adolescents, are at risk of being sexually exploited. Like Sashim in the case history that opened this chapter, older children and adolescents tend to be at greater risk (Gewirtz-Meydan & Finkelhor, 2019). The second National Survey of Children's Exposure to Violence (NatSCEV II), for example, found that rates of contact sexual abuse were highest for girls aged 14–17 years, 23 percent of whom experienced a sexual victimization in their lifetime (Finkelhor, Turner, Shattuck, & Hamby, 2013). Many have argued that risk for sexual abuse peaks in early adolescence (Bebbington et al., 2011; E. Davies & Jones, 2013; Finkelhor et al., 2013).

No clear differences in rates of sexual abuse between race and ethnic groups have been identified through official sources, although Asian American children tend to have the lowest CSA rates (Sedlak et al., 2010). A recent report based on an aggregate community sample from the NatSCEV, however, found that CSA was more likely among black youth (Gewirtz-Meydan & Finkelhor, 2019). There is also some evidence that children with intellectual, communication, or physical vulnerabilities are at increased risk for CSA. Children with disabilities are 2 to 3 times more likely to be sexually abused as children without disabilities (Reiter, Bryen, & Shachar, 2007; N. Smith & Harrell, 2013). In addition, the risk is higher for children in certain settings such as out-of-home care (Euser, Alink, Tharner, van IJzendoorn, & Bakermans-Kranenburg, 2016) and for children with certain types of disabilities such as cognitive and mental health disabilities rather than physical disabilities (Lund & Vaughn-Jensen, 2012) (see Chapter 10 for a discussion of abuse in adults with disabilities).

Some researchers have also examined various socioemotional characteristics of victims that increase their vulnerability to CSA. Low self-esteem, susceptibility to persuasion, behavior difficulties, and emotional immaturity are all victim characteristics associated with CSA (Dombrowski, LeMasney, Ahia, & Dickson, 2004; Olson, Daggs, Ellevold, & Rogers, 2007; Whittle, Hamilton-Giachritsis, Beech, & Collings, 2013). Studies of CSA offenders reveal other characteristics of victims for which offenders report a preference such as quiet, withdrawn, lonely, passive, and easily manipulated children, as well as those with low self-esteem, who have few close friends, and who are emotionally needy (Budin & Johnson, 1989; Conte, Wolf, & Smith, 1989; M. Elliott, Browne, & Kilcoyne, 1995; C. Johnson, 2004).

Characteristics of Individuals Who Sexually Abuse Children

Many people have the impression that perpetrators of CSA are frightening strangers or "dirty old men." Research findings concerning the demographic and psychological characteristics of perpetrators of CSA, however, suggest that these stereotypes are rarely accurate.

Demographic Characteristics

Data from the NIS-4 suggest a relatively equal distribution of offenders across age groups for offenders 26 years old or older (Sedlak et al., 2010). Although official statistics show that CSA offenders vary widely in age, clinical and community studies suggest that there seem to be two distinct age periods for the onset of CSA offending: one during adolescence and one during early adulthood. Studies show, for example, that most male offenders come to the attention of authorities when they are in their mid-thirties (Smallbone, Marshall, & Wortley, 2008) and the average age of female sex offenders is between 26 and 36 years (Strickland, 2008; Wijkman, Bijleveld, & Hendriks, 2010). In McLeod's (2015) large sample of sexual offenders reported to CPS, the mean ages of both male and female perpetrators were quite similar (33 years of age), although male offenders began at earlier ages and continued for a longer duration. Indeed, many sex offenders report that their sexual offending actually began while they were teenagers (Seto, 2008). Consistent estimates suggest that adolescents are responsible for approximately 40 percent of all sex offenses against children, with most of those adolescents being boys around 14 years of age (Saunders, Kilpatrick, Hanson, Resnick, & Walker, 1999; Veneziano & Veneziano, 2002). A recent report suggested even higher rates of adolescent offenders; the majority of offenses (approximately 77% for male and 70% for female victims) in an aggregate NatSCEV community sample were juvenile offenders (Gewirtz-Meydan & Finkelhor, 2019). Children are also sometimes sexually abusive toward younger children, as is sometimes the case in sibling abuse (L. Jones, Bellis, et al., 2012).

The overwhelming majority of CSA perpetrators are male. This sex discrepancy has been noted across multiple studies using a variety of samples and methodologies. Data from the 2000 National Incident-Based Reporting System indicate that of those sex offenses reported, approximately 96 percent included male offenders and 4 percent female offenders (McCloskey & Raphael, 2005). Perpetrator–victim sex differences varied depending on whether the offense was **pedophilia** (adult-to-child) or **hebephilia** (adult-to-adolescent). Male perpetrators offended against child victims nearly one-fourth of the time and chose female victims in approximately 90 percent of cases. Male perpetrators offended against adolescent victims in approximately 40 percent of cases and likewise chose female victims. In contrast, females offended against child victims in about 40 percent of cases and adolescent victims in 45 percent of cases, choosing male victims as often as female victims.

It may be that sexual abuse committed by females is more common than once believed. Kestin and Williams (2010), for example, reported that 20 percent of the student–teacher sexual misconduct cases in south Florida were women. In juvenile correctional facilities, approximately 95 percent of youth who reported being sexually abused by staff identified female correctional staff as the perpetrators, despite the fact that females made up only 42 percent of facility staff (Beck, Harrison, & Guerino, 2010). Indeed, a recent study conducted by McLeod (2015) reported that 21 percent of all substantiated CSA cases reported to U.S. CPS agencies in 2010 were perpetrated by females, particularly parents and adoptive parents. Research also suggests that boys are more likely to be abused by female offenders, with female offenders comprising 54.4 percent of perpetrators of CSA (Gewirtz-Meydan & Finkelhor, 2019). These findings suggest that perpetrator gender may vary depending on the relationship the perpetrator has to the victim as well as the gender of the child, and also support the assertion that women in caregiving roles do commit sexual offenses against children.

There are a variety of reasons to explain why female perpetration of CSA may be underreported. Because of culturally prescribed definitions of CSA, many Americans may fail to recognize women as potential offenders. As Boroughs (2004) aptly puts it, "it is difficult to understand how a woman is physically capable of sexually abusing a child in the traditional concept of rape without a genital organ for penetration" (p. 484). Abuse by females may also go unnoticed because inappropriate sexual contact may occur in the context of culturally approved routine child care (e.g., bathing, dressing, sleeping with children). In addition, some have suggested that there may be more shame associated with disclosing CSA by a female, especially a mother figure (Tsopelas, Spyridoula, & Athanasios, 2011). Even when such contact comes to light, there may be a tendency to minimize the behavior and label it as *inappropriate affection* (Turton, 2010). This minimization is illustrated in one of the most well-publicized cases of female-perpetrated sexual abuse in which Mary Kay Letourneau began having sex with one of her sixth-grade male students. The relationship was discovered when Letourneau discovered she was pregnant with the boy's child. Letourneau pled guilty to second-degree child rape, but the judge suspended all but 6 months of her 7.5-year sentence, and not even the boy's mother was pushing for prison time. Indeed, the general public views sexual abuse by women as both less harmful and less serious (Tsopelas, Tsetsou, Ntounas, & Douzenis, 2012).

Relationship to the Abused Child

There is some debate in the literature as to whether CSA is more common within or outside the family. Approximately 60 percent of sexual abuse reported to authorities is committed by either a biological or nonbiological parent/partner (Sedlak et al., 2010). However, self-report victimization surveys generally find that sexual victimization is more likely to occur outside the family (Finkelhor, Ormrod, & Turner, 2009). Sexual misconduct between school employees and their students, as illustrated in the Letourneau case discussed earlier, for example, has been reported frequently in recent years. In one study examining sexual abuse by school employees in Texas, 1,415 educators were sanctioned for sexual misconduct between 2008 and 2016 (Robert & Thompson, 2019).

Although growing evidence suggests that extrafamilial CSA may be more common than intrafamilial abuse, whether abuse occurs inside or outside the family, it is important to remember that the perpetrator of either form of abuse is a person familiar to the child in the majority of cases, with some estimates suggesting that only about 10 percent of CSA victims do not know their offender (Finkelhor & Ormrod, 2001; Richards, 2011). As we noted earlier, extrafamilial abuse often occurs in various youth-serving organizations such as those previously discussed (e.g., schools and youth sports). One of the most publicized examples of extrafamilial CSA involving the betrayal of persons familiar to children is illustrated in the CSA scandals that have plagued some faith-based organizations in recent years such as the Catholic Church (see Box 4.2).

Mental Health and Psychological Deficits

Researchers have identified various mental health problems and psychological deficits that characterize some CSA offenders and increase risk of offending.

BOX 4.2

CSA IN FAITH-BASED ORGANIZATIONS: THE CATHOLIC CHURCH

In recent years, CSA within faith-based organizations has received a great deal of attention. The sexual abuse scandal within the Catholic Church is the most often widely discussed example of CSA occurring extrafamilially in faith-based settings. In the early 2000s, with media attention escalating, the U.S. Conference of Catholic Bishops commissioned researchers from the John Jay College of Criminal Justice to assess the scope of the problem. The report, known as the John Jay Report (John Jay College of Criminal Justice, 2004), concluded that between 1950 and 2002, approximately 11,000 individuals had made allegations of sexual abuse involving more than 4,000 Catholic clergy. More than 95 percent of U.S. dioceses were impacted. Today, Americans remain concerned about the problem. A Pew Research Center survey recently examined Americans' views on sexual abuse scandals in religious organizations, including CSA in the Catholic Church, and found that 79 percent of Americans believed that reports of sexual abuse and misconduct by Catholic priests and bishops reflect ongoing problems (Gecewicz, 2019).

Children who experience CSA by personnel in religious institutions suffer some of the same negative outcomes as children who experience abuse outside of such institutions, in both the short and long term. In one study, for example, the prevalence of post-traumatic stress disorder (PTSD) in an adult sample was nearly 50 percent, with 85 percent showing clinically significant symptoms in at least one of ten psychiatric dimensions (Lueger-Schuster et al., 2014).

How could Christians, whose doctrine supports loving one's neighbor as oneself, be responsible for such horrific exploitation? Victor Vieth (2018), a noted expert on child maltreatment and religion, believes that several Bible verses inadvertently either harm sexually abused children or contribute to their victimization. For example, Vieth suggests that Matthew 18:15–18 encourages readers to first speak privately with someone who is identified as "sinning" and that this passage has been used by pastors and laypersons either to avoid reporting CSA to authorities or to urge victims to first confront their abuser. He argues that this interpretation essentially shifts the burden of protection to the child victim (Vieth, 2018). Vieth suggests that what is needed is more quality training for religious leaders as well as greater policy changes to protect children and prevent abuse. In addition, religious leaders need to speak out about the problem. In the same Pew Research Center survey described earlier, 68 percent of respondents indicated that they had never heard their clergy or other religious leader speak out about sexual abuse, assault, or harassment (Gecewicz, 2019).

Several suggestions for improving policies to protect children in the Catholic Church, as well as other youth-serving organizations, have been proposed. Risk management strategies include the adoption of employment screening, codes of conduct, general protection policies for youth stating the agency's commitment to youth safety, monitoring and supervision protocols, electronic communication and social media policies, and education and training (including a focus on boundary violation training) initiatives for staff, parents, and youth (Wurtele, 2012). Given the pervasive nature of sexual exploitation of minors in the Catholic Church, as well as other youth-serving organizations, the adoption of policies to protect children is a necessary step in protecting children from extrafamilial CSA.

Some evidence suggests that CSA perpetrators seek out sexual encounters with children primarily because they are sexually attracted to children (Houtepen, Sijtsema, & Bogaerts, 2016; Ward & Beech, 2006). Psychologists define such sexual attraction as a mental disorder called pedophilia where the individual has "recurrent, intense sexually arousing fantasies, sexual urges, or behaviors involving sexual activity with a prepubescent child or children" (American Psychiatric Association, 2013, p. 697). Some evidence suggests that CSA offenders not only are sexually attracted to children but also have an emotional attachment to children, sometimes called emotional congruence, who meet their needs for intimacy (Houtepen et al., 2016). The origins of such deviant sexual arousal or emotional congruence with children, however, are undetermined. Some researchers have suggested that biological factors may be a cause of deviant sexual arousal, such as abnormally high levels of male hormones such as testosterone (Ward & Beech, 2006). We know, for example, that measures of sex drive and hypersexuality predict deviant sexual interests in general (Dawson, Bannerman, & Lalumière, 2016) and that many CSA offenders in particular have higher sex drives, which might lead to their acting on their sexual attraction toward children (D. Whitaker et al., 2008). Others suggest that deviant sexual arousal is learned, when offenders have early sexual experiences (e.g., masturbation, playing "doctor" with other children, viewing pornography) that later become sexual fantasies, and therefore deviant sexual arousal becomes conditioned through the pairing of deviant sexual fantasies with masturbation and orgasm (e.g., Houtepen et al., 2016). Indeed, sexual fantasizing about both children and child pornography consumption was associated with contact sexual offending among a large population-based sample of German men (Klein, Schmidt, Turner, & Briken, 2015).

Because not all individuals who are sexually aroused by children act on their feelings, researchers have hypothesized that other factors, usually referred to as **disinhibitors**, must be operating. Alcohol, for example, is a disinhibitor. **Cognitive distortions** may also be disinhibitors. For example, perpetrators may rationalize and defend their behavior through distorted ideas or thoughts, such as "Having sex with children is a good way to teach them about sex" or "Children need to be liberated from the sexually repressive bonds of society." Indeed, the infamous Penn State football coach convicted of sexually abusing dozens of children, Jerry Sandusky, described his behavior as "horsing around" with the boys in the shower (Hopper, 2011). Research evidence indicates the presence of both substance abuse and cognitive distortions in CSA perpetrators (L. Cohen & Galynker, 2009; D. Whitaker et al., 2008).

CSA offenders also exhibit other psychological characteristics such as externalizing (e.g., aggression and violence, criminal behavior, anger/hostility, substance abuse, paranoia/mistrust, and antisocial personality disorder) as well as internalizing behaviors (e.g., anxiety, depression, low self-esteem, and external locus of control) (D. Whitaker et al., 2008). They are also more likely to exhibit various social deficits such as low social skills/competence, empathy deficits, loneliness, and difficulties in intimate relationships (D. Whitaker et al., 2008). Other research has identified various neuropsychological and neurobiological deficits associated with CSA perpetration such as lower mean IQ, increased frequency of childhood head injury, and abnormalities in brain anatomy (Blanchard et al., 2003; Cantor, Blanchard, Robichaud, & Christensen, 2005; Schiffer et al., 2007).

Modus Operandi of Offenders

There have been several studies, predominantly with CSA perpetrators, that attempt to understand the **modus operandi**, or method of operation, of offenders (for a review, see Clemente, 2013). We know that CSA offenders use specific tactics to recruit victims as well as to maintain their compliance. Although only a handful of studies have been undertaken in this area, their credibility is increased by the fact that some child victims' accounts closely resemble those provided by perpetrators (see Berliner & Conte, 1990).

As noted earlier, perpetrators typically select children who are vulnerable or needy in some way. Once a perpetrator has identified a target child, he or she typically engages in a process referred to as **grooming**, whereby the offender employs a series of strategies aimed at gaining the child's trust and compliance, developing a "special" relationship with the child, and gradually crossing sexual boundaries by progressing from nonsexual to sexual touch (Lanning, 2010; Leclerc, Proulx, & McKibben, 2005). As noted in the opening case study, Bhagwan showered Sashim with the attention she had been longing for by taking her to movies, buying her new clothes, and listening to her when she complained about difficulties at school. Their interactions then moved to increasingly more physical contact.

In order to build trust and establish a relationship with their victims, perpetrators attempt to provide both emotional and tangible things to their victims in an attempt to fulfill their unmet needs. They do this by providing attention, recognition, affection, kindness, romance, gifts, money, trips, jewelry, clothing, drugs, alcohol, tobacco, or special privileges (e.g., getting to drive a vehicle without a license). A consistent tactic is to make the victim feel exceptionally special. Victims comply with the demands of the offender because "they have finally found someone . . . who treats them well or tells them they are special" (Clemente, 2013, p. 7). Offenders also break down sexual boundaries that usually exist between adults and children by lowering inhibitions, being overly physical and playful, talking about or encouraging masturbation and/or sex, giving sexual instructions, or supplying pornography.

The grooming process involves not only victims but also their parents or other adults in the community. According to McAlinden (2006), grooming of the parents or organization has a dual purpose—first, to secure the trust and thus cooperation of adults in gaining access to the child; and second, to reduce the likelihood of discovery by appearing to be "above reproach." Jerry Sandusky, the perpetrator identified in the Penn State scandal, successfully groomed "child care experts, psychologists, professionals, celebrities, athletes, coaches, friends and family," all of whom believed him to be "a pillar of the community" (Clemente, 2013, pp. 3–4).

Youth may also be vulnerable to **online grooming** when children are sexually exploited over the internet (see Box 4.3), where the presumed anonymity of the perpetrator and victim contributes to abuse. Online grooming is similar to offline strategies in that the goal is to establish a relationship by making the youth feel "special." Offenders are often successful at this by promising love or romance, or by offering a sympathetic "ear" to the child or adolescent's concerns (e.g., sexual orientation) or frustrations (e.g., school problems, parent conflict) (Katz, 2013). Once rapport is established, the offender might escalate the sexualization process just as he or she would in face-to-face situations. Another potential way to form a relationship with a child or adolescent is through **sexting**, discussed further in Chapter 7, which involves sending sexually explicit messages and/or photographs electronically either via text messaging or by posting photographs on the internet (Hasinoff, 2016). Anthony Weiner, a former U.S. congressman, resigned from his position in 2011 amid allegations of sending explicit photos of himself through his Twitter account to young women ("New York Congressman," 2011). Despite his publicly humiliating resignation, he continued to send photos of himself, including to a minor, and was later sentenced to serve 21 months in prison for knowingly sending sexually explicit text messages to a 15-year-old girl (Reilly, 2017).

BOX 4.3
EXPLOITATION OVER THE INTERNET

Sexual exploitation of children can also occur as a result of internet interactions, a form of exploitation described in the research literature in recent years as **cyberexploitation** or online crimes against children. Researchers examining this issue have described the variety of ways in which children who use the internet may be at risk (Kreston, 2002; Malesky, 2005; K. J. Mitchell, Finkelhor, & Wolak, 2003; Wurtele & Miller-Perrin, 2014). First, children and adolescents may be propositioned online for sexual activity. Such propositions may be explicit proposals, or perpetrators may take a more indirect approach, using an online version of the grooming process just described to establish and maintain contact with children. Some children may provide their names, addresses, and telephone numbers to individuals they correspond with online and may even agree to meet with them. Second, children may be exposed to various forms of sexually explicit material on the internet via links that come up when they use search engines, through their own misspelling of web addresses, or through unsolicited emails and pop-up ads. Third, children may experience online sexual harassment. This can include a variety of behaviors, such as

(Continued)

(Continued)

"threatening or offensive behavior targeting the child or sharing information or pictures online about the targeted child" (Kreston, 2002, p. 13). The risks of these activities are promulgated by a number of different internet facets including newsgroups, email, websites, and chat rooms.

Researchers at the Crimes Against Children Research Center conducted three administrations of the **Youth Internet Safety Survey (YISS)** in an attempt to determine the magnitude of online exploitation of children (Finkelhor, Mitchell, & Wolak, 2000, 2005; Priebe, Mitchell, & Finkelhor, 2013). The YISS-1 was administered to a national U.S. sample of 1,501 children and adolescents aged 10–17 years in the year 2000 (Finkelhor et al., 2000). The respondents were asked about their experiences online with unwanted sexual solicitation, exposure to pornography, and harassment within the past year. Of the children in this sample, 1 in 5 reported having experienced an unwanted sexual solicitation (e.g., received an online request to engage in sexual activities or sexual talk or to give personal sexual information to an adult), 1 in 4 had experienced unwanted exposure to sexual material, and 1 in 17 had been threatened or harassed. Adolescents in the sample (aged 14–17 years) were more likely than younger children to have had these experiences online. Subsequent administrations of the survey in 2005 and 2010 showed decreases in both online sexual solicitation and pornography viewing, but slight increases in harassment (Priebe et al., 2013; Wolak, Mitchell, & Finkelhor, 2006).

Even fewer youth have face-to-face meetings with unknown online "friends." According to a survey of adolescents conducted by the Adolescent Risk Communication Institute of the Annenberg Public Policy Center, few social network users (3%) reported actually meeting strangers offline. Only 2 percent of teens in YISS-1 reported online "romances" (defined as someone met online who the youth believed to be a boyfriend or girlfriend (Wolak, Mitchell, & Finkelhor, 2003). Although the findings from these surveys suggest that children are at risk for this form of exploitation, such victimization constitutes a small proportion of the sexual abuse, exploitation, and other crimes to which children are vulnerable. In addition, the results of these surveys suggest that most of the solicitations made online by potential CSA perpetrators fail; they do not result in offline sexual assault or illegal sexual contact.

Scholars have proposed several approaches to combating the problem of internet exploitation of youth. A first step is to educate youth, parents, and professionals who work with youth and families about the potential dangers of the internet and how they can protect against this form of exploitation. Parents need to be educated, for example, about ways in which they can limit their child's internet access (e.g., browser access controls, software filters). An additional approach is for families to place any computers with internet access in family living areas rather than in private rooms and for parents to instruct their children not to enter internet chat rooms without parental permission (Kreston, 2002; Wurtele & Miller-Perrin, 2014). Others have suggested the implementation of various educational efforts to help prevent cyberexploitation such as cybersafety websites (Wurtele & Kenny, 2016). For example, there are several recommended cybersafety websites for individual youth (e.g., Getnetwise.org, Safeteens.org), parent–child communication strategies about internet safety (e.g., Mediasmarts.ca/parents, Cybertip.ca), and internet safety curricula for schools (e.g., Missingkids.org/NetSmartz). Legislation has also been enacted to address this form of exploitation. The United States has established an $11 million federal program that includes Internet Crimes Against Children Task Forces, which were developed to assist state and local law enforcement agencies in conducting undercover investigations, providing technical assistance and training, and developing prevention and education materials (Wortley & Smallbone, 2012). Additional efforts are necessary to ensure that federal and state child abuse statutes, most of which were written prior to the development of the internet, apply to illegal behaviors carried out online.

Studies also shed light on the strategies that perpetrators use to keep children engaged in sexual activities for prolonged periods. Central to a perpetrator's ability to continue sexual activities with a child is the perpetrator's ability to convince the child that the activities should be kept secret so that other adults cannot intervene to terminate the abuse. The victim might be just as motivated to keep the relationship a secret as the perpetrator, if the victim perceives that he or she has done something "wrong." As noted previously, the majority of CSA victims do not disclose their abuse immediately, and a significant number of victims do not disclose their abuse for years (Goodyear-Brown, Fath, & Myers, 2012; London, Bruck, Wright, & Ceci, 2008).

Family and Cultural Risk Factors

It is not only important to examine individual victim and perpetrator characteristics in identifying CSA risk factors but also important to examine other systems and contexts in which the individuals reside. Some of this research has focused on family characteristics while other research has focused on the broad context of societal and community forces, such as societal attitudes, that may play roles in the etiology of CSA.

Socioeconomic Characteristics

Official reporting sources have consistently suggested that low socioeconomic status (SES) is not an important risk factor for CSA (Sedlak et al., 2010). Community surveys, however, that are not subject to the same reporting biases show otherwise. A recent report based on an aggregate community sample from the NatSCEV, for example, found that CSA was more likely among low-SES youth (Gewirtz-Meydan & Finkelhor, 2019). Studies have also indicated that CSA is associated with other adverse socioeconomic factors such as living in poverty, overcrowded living conditions, and parental unemployment (Cant, O'Donnell, Sims, & Harries, 2019; Doidge, Higgins, Delfabbro, & Segal, 2017; MacMillan, Tanaka, Duku, Vaillancourt, & Boyle, 2013).

Family Characteristics

Family life that is characterized by violence, dysfunction, and instability serves as a risk factor for CSA, and this is true for the families of both victims and perpetrators. The families of CSA victims, for example, are often characterized by marital discord and divorce, intimate partner violence, and absence of family cohesion and support, as we saw in the case study of Sashim's family (e.g., Butler, 2013; Laaksonen et al., 2011; Pérez-Fuentes et al., 2013; Stith et al., 2009). Parental substance abuse, educational deficits, parental history of sexual abuse, and parental mental health problems are also risk factors (e.g., L. Berger, Slack, Waldfogel, & Bruch, 2010; Butler, 2013; Doidge et al., 2017; Pérez-Fuentes et al., 2013). Finally, the fact that CSA victims are more likely to live with a stepfather, foster father, adoptive father, or single parent is also a risk factor (e.g., Butler, 2013; Gewirtz-Meydan & Finkelhor, 2019; Olafson, 2011). The exact mechanisms through which these risk factors operate are unknown but appear to contribute to a chaotic, violent, unsupportive environment that might make it difficult to protect a child from CSA.

There is considerable research on the specific role of parenting in predicting CSA. Parent–child bonds that are strong and secure are more likely to produce healthy relationships in adult life. When the bond is insecure, on the other hand, children expect to be ignored or rejected in their relationships, and this expectation extends into adulthood (Sawle & Kear-Colwell, 2001; Waters, Hamilton, & Weinfield, 2000). As discussed in Chapter 2, we also know that a weak bond with family reduces the potential cost of deviant behavior. Anything that weakens the bond between parent and child, therefore, is a risk factor. Parenting in the families of child victims, for example, is characterized by absent and emotionally detached parenting, poor parent–child relationships, and the absence of warm parenting (Averdijk, Mueller-Johnson, & Eisner, 2011; Butler, 2013; Jack, Munn, Cheng, & MacMillan, 2006).

Parenting within the families of individuals who become perpetrators of CSA has also been examined as a risk factor. Several studies have reported a greater likelihood of insecure childhood and adult attachment styles in CSA perpetrators (e.g., W. Marshall & Marshall, 2010). Theories about why disrupted parent–child attachments might lead to CSA perpetration focus on the deficits in empathy and difficulties with intimacy that we noted earlier. These theories suggest that insecurely attached individuals have deficits in empathy that limit their ability to see the negative consequences of their actions for others and are also more likely to fulfill their intimacy needs through inappropriate relationships (Seto & Lalumière, 2010; Simons, Wurtele, & Durham, 2008).

Perhaps the most widely researched family risk factor for perpetration of CSA is a childhood history of abuse. As discussed in Chapter 2, the research on intergenerational transmission is not always definitive. Certainly, there is research that suggests that sexual offenders are indeed more likely to have been sexually victimized as children when compared either to the general population (Babchishin, Hanson, & Hermann, 2011) or to other types of offenders (Jesperson, Lalumière, & Seto, 2009; Nunes, Hermann, Malcolm, & Lavoie, 2013). In addition, the other forms of child maltreatment discussed in this book are also risk factors (e.g., Laaksonen et al., 2011). One problem with this research, especially the research on sexual victimization as a child, is that most of these studies have been conducted with special populations of male offenders who are either incarcerated or in treatment and may be motivated to exaggerate claims of childhood victimization (Richards, 2011). Indeed, data from the ongoing prospective longitudinal study conducted by Widom and Massey (2015) suggest that a history of childhood physical abuse and neglect increases the risk for being arrested for a sex crime but, interestingly, a history of CSA does not predict arrest for sex crimes.

Societal Attitudes

Societal attitudes, such as a lack of understanding and acknowledgment of CSA, represent another risk factor. In an empirical study of over 5,000 U.S. adults conducted by the advocacy organization Stop It Now! (2010), fewer than half of adults (44%) reported that CSA was a major problem in their community, leading the authors to conclude: "We either do not recognize behaviors that should raise concerns about abuse or choose not to see them" (p. 8).

The sexual abuse allegations levied against superstar Michael Jackson over the past quarter-century serve as an appropriate illustration of just how social attitudes toward CSA can influence one's inability to recognize and acknowledge abuse. Jackson was originally accused in 1993 of sexually abusing a 13-year-old boy. He was accused again in 2003 and indicted on 10 criminal counts (Tsioulcas, 2019). Jackson settled the 1993 lawsuit for $25 million and was eventually acquitted on the 10 criminal counts in 2005 (Orth, 2019). In a two-part documentary titled *Leaving Neverland*, aired by HBO in March 2019, two men tell their stories of how Jackson sexually abused them for years, beginning when one was age 7 and the other age 10. One element common to these cases of alleged abuse is the fact that the parents knew, and *permitted*, their sons to share the same bed with Jackson. In one case, parents permitted Jackson to sleep with their son for more than 30 nights in a row in the same bed (Orth, 2019). In another case, one of the boys' mothers described her son's encounters with Jackson as "slumber parties" in which "they play so hard, they fall asleep, they're exhausted. There's nothing more to it than that" (Tsioulcas, 2019). Clearly, these parents, no doubt enamored with Jackson's fame, and probably also unaware of the risk of sexual abuse, failed to identify Jackson's behavior as concerning or as a glaring red flag that abuse was occurring. A juror in the 2005 trial asked the pertinent question in relation to a parent allowing a child to sleep in the same bed with an adult nonfamily member, "What mother in her right mind would allow that to happen?" (Tsioulcas, 2019). During his lifetime, however, Jackson was never convicted of the crime of CSA.

Attitudes toward sexuality and the appropriateness of sexual behaviors between adults and children have also been implicated as potential risk factors for CSA (Swenson & Chaffin, 2006). Some would argue that too often children are sexualized. According to the American Psychological Association (APA, 2007), sexualization occurs when a person is sexually objectified or made into a thing for others' sexual use, people's value comes only from their sexual appeal or behavior, and a standard is applied that equates physical attractiveness with being sexy. According to its 2007 report, the APA found a growing trend of sexualizing young children through video games, television shows, movies, music videos, song lyrics, magazines, clothing styles, and toys. A 2011 study, for example, analyzed the presence of sexualizing characteristics in girls' clothing (sizes 6–14) on the websites of 15 popular stores in the United States

(Goodin, Van Denburg, Murnen, & Smolak, 2011). Findings indicated that approximately 30 percent of clothing items, such as those sold by Abercrombie Kids, had sexualizing characteristics (e.g., revealing or emphasizing a sexualized body part). By the time a child reaches puberty, she or he has likely been exposed to thousands if not tens of thousands of sexualized messages, leading to the creation of what Kaeser (2011) refers to as a generation of super-sexualized children. Sexualized images are sending clear messages to people who have sexual interests in children "that contrary to laws and ethical norms, children are sexually available" (Egan & Hawkes, 2008, p. 295). To sexualize children also implicitly suggests to adults that children are interested in and ready for sex, and may lead children and adults to believe that sexual activity with children is acceptable.

Integrative Theories Explaining CSA

Until relatively recently, most models and theories attempting to explain the behavior of CSA perpetrators have focused on a narrow list of individual characteristics (e.g., deviant sexual arousal or a childhood history of abuse). Contemporary theories, however, attempt to explain sexually abusive behavior by focusing on the integration of multiple contributing factors. Covell and Scalora (2002), for example, have developed a model of socio-cognitive deficiencies in sexual offenders that contribute to sexually assaultive behavior. According to this model, deficits in a variety of abilities—including social skills, interpersonal intimacy, and cognitive processes—may have an impact on the development and expression of appropriate empathy and may lead to sexually assaultive behavior. W. Marshall and Marshall (2000) have proposed a comprehensive etiological model of sexual offending that incorporates multiple components including biological, social, and attachment processes. According to their theory, the early developmental environment of a sexual offender includes several stressful events such as poor attachment between parent and child, low self-esteem, limited coping abilities, low-quality relationships with others, and a history of sexual abuse. The presence of such stressors leads the child to rely on sexualized coping methods, including masturbation and sexual acts with others, as a way to avoid current stressors. Eventually, the individual is conditioned to rely on sexualized coping mechanisms and, when other factors are present (e.g., access to a victim, disinhibition owing to alcohol use), is predisposed to engage in sexually abusive behavior.

Perhaps the most comprehensive integrative theory to date is the Integrated Theory of Sexual Offending (ITSO) proposed by Ward and Beech (2006). ITSO incorporates several single-factor theories including biological factors (e.g., brain development, genetics), neuropsychological factors (e.g., motivations, perceptions, and memory), and ecological factors (e.g., social, cultural, and personal circumstances) that continuously interact in a dynamic way. These multiple factors interact to produce both sexual offending behavior and the clinical problems observed in offenders (e.g., deviant sexual arousal, distorted cognitions, and social difficulties). According to ITSO, an individual's level of psychological functioning is determined by the confluence of biological and neuropsychological factors as well as ecological experiences. When early brain development and/or social, cultural, and personal circumstances are compromised in some way (such as through poor genetic inheritance or developmental adversity), psychological dysfunction results and leads to both clinical problems and sexually abusive behavior. The sexual offending behavior results in consequences that then affect the offender's ecological system as well as psychological functioning, which leads to maintaining and/or escalating further abusive behavior.

CONSEQUENCES ASSOCIATED WITH CHILD SEXUAL ABUSE

Investigators have identified a wide range of outcomes associated with CSA ranging from its detrimental impact on families to its serious repercussions for the child welfare system. Some researchers have also recently examined the economic burden associated with CSA and estimated that the annual financial burden of CSA for society is over $9 billion (Letourneau, Brown, Fang, Hassan, & Mercy, 2019). Of tantamount concern, of course, is the harm to those individuals exploited by CSA, which includes physical, emotional, behavioral, cognitive, and interpersonal problems. Table 4.2 displays the most common outcomes observed in child and adult victims of CSA. We discuss some of the more severe and pervasive of these outcomes, as well as protective factors, in the next section.

The Negative Effects of CSA

One of the most common symptoms identified in sexually abused children is sexualized behavior (Kendall-Tackett, Williams, & Finkelhor, 1993). **Sexualized behavior** refers to overt sexual acting out toward adults or other children, compulsive masturbation, excessive sexual curiosity, sexual promiscuity, and precocious sexual play and knowledge. Children who are sexually abused demonstrate significantly more of such symptoms compared with children who are either physically abused or neglected as well as children who are psychiatrically disturbed (Friedrich, Jaworski, Huxsahl, & Bengtson, 1997; Kendall-Tackett et al., 1993). The sexual behaviors of children who are sexually abused are often associated with intercourse, such as mimicking intercourse and inserting objects into the vagina or anus (Chaffin, 2008; Friedrich, 2007). Among children who exhibit sexualized behavior problems, 62 percent to 95 percent have a history of sexual abuse (Gray, Busconi, Houchens, & Pithers, 1997; Pithers, Gray, Busconi, & Houchens, 1998; Silovsky & Niec, 2002). Sexualized behavior is therefore the behavioral symptom that is most predictive of the occurrence of sexual abuse, although only 10 percent to 30 percent of victims exhibit this symptom (Wamser-Nanney & Campbell, 2019).

TABLE 4.2 ■ Common Effects Associated With Child Sexual Abuse in Children, Youth, and Adults

	Physical	Emotional	Behavioral	Cognitive	Interpersonal	Psychiatric Disorders
Children and Youth	Adolescent pregnancy Somatization	Anger Depression Anxiety Low self-esteem	Sexual behavior problems Aggression Self-harm Running away Substance abuse Rule-breaking	Negative self-attributions Dissociation Suicidal thoughts Academic problems Cognitive distortions	Relationship problems	PTSD Attention-deficit/hyperactivity disorder Eating disorders Borderline personality disorder Major depressive disorder Substance use disorders
Adults	Chronic pain Gastrointestinal disorders Obesity Sleep disturbance Seizures Gynecologic disorders Somatization	Anxiety Depression Anger/irritability Poor self-esteem	Substance abuse Suicidal behavior Self-harm Sexual dysfunction Sexual aggression Risky sexual behavior	Cognitive distortions Suicidal ideation Negative self-attributions Dissociation	Relationship distress Sexual revictimization Partner violence	PTSD Borderline and other personality disorders Mood disorders Substance use disorders Anxiety disorders

Sources: References are representative rather than exhaustive: Amado, Arce, & Herraiz, 2015; DeCou & Lynch, 2019; Fergusson, McLeod, & Horwood, 2013; Gardner, Thomas, & Erskine, 2019; Gewirtz-Meydan, Lahav, Walsh, & Finkelhor, 2019; Goodyear-Brown et al., 2012; Heneghan et al., 2013; King et al., 2019; Lewis, McElroy, Harlaar, & Runyan, 2016; Noll, Shenk, & Putnam, 2013; Olafson, 2011; Papalia, Luebbers, Ogloff, Cutajar, & Mullen, 2017; Runyon, Deblinger, & Steer, 2014; Steine et al., 2019; Turner, Taillieu, Cheung, & Afifi, 2017; Turniansky, Ben-Dor, Krivoy, Weizman, & Shoval, 2019; Vachon, Krueger, Rogosch, & Cicchetti, 2015; Vaillancourt-Morel et al., 2016; Wamser-Nanney & Campbell, 2019.

Another frequently observed outcome in children and youth is post-traumatic stress disorder and PTSD-related symptoms. PTSD symptoms include nightmares, fears, feelings of isolation, inability to enjoy usual activities, somatic complaints, autonomic arousal (e.g., heightened startle response), and guilt feelings. Children who are sexually abused consistently report higher levels of PTSD symptoms relative to comparison children and are more likely to receive a diagnosis of PTSD than are other children who have been maltreated (e.g., Finkelhor, 2008; Kearney, Wechsler, Kaur, & Lemos-Miller, 2010). Some children who are sexually abused also receive multiple diagnoses that include depression (including suicidal ideation) and other anxiety disorders (Deblinger, Mannarino, Cohen, & Steer, 2006; DeCou & Lynch, 2019).

The most common problems observed in adult victims of CSA are depression, anxiety, and PTSD (Goodyear-Brown et al., 2012; Sachs-Ericsson et al., 2010; Spataro, Mullen, Burgess, Wells, & Moss, 2004). Additional effects include problems with interpersonal relationships (e.g., Trickett, Negriff, Ji, & Peckins, 2011); difficulties with sexual adjustment, including sexual aggression (Bensley, Eenwyk, & Simmons, 2000; King, Khun, Strege, Russell, & Kolander, 2019; Vaillancort-Morel et al., 2016); impaired social and occupational functioning (Zielinski, 2009); physical or health problems (e.g., chronic pain and obesity; see Chartier, Walker, & Naimark, 2007; Kendall-Tackett, 2003; Meagher, 2004); and behavioral dysfunction such as substance abuse, eating disorders, and self-mutilation (e.g., Klonsky & Moyer, 2008; Smolak & Murnen, 2002; Yates, Carlson, & Egeland, 2008).

Risk and Protective Factors Associated With CSA Effects

No single symptom or pattern of symptoms is present in all victims of CSA. Many CSA victims exhibit no symptoms at all, at least in the short term (McClure, Chavez, Agars, Peacock, & Matosian, 2008; Yancey, Hansen, & Naufel, 2011). One systematic literature of CSA victims examining outcomes of both children and adolescents as well as adults found normal levels of functioning ranged from 10 percent to 53 percent of individuals studied (Domhardt, Münzer, Fegert, & Goldbeck, 2015). Why is it that some victims are severely affected, others are moderately affected, and still others are relatively unscathed by their experience of CSA?

This is a very difficult question to answer empirically. Definitions vary dramatically across studies, nonrepresentative clinical samples are common, and often the studies have failed to include comparison groups. Many CSA victims have experienced other childhood traumas or adverse life events (Finkelhor, Ormrod, & Turner, 2009), which could explain negative outcomes equally well. Or perhaps the outcomes vary depending on the relationship between the victim and the perpetrator (e.g., a father vs. a stranger) or the type of reaction the child receives following disclosure (e.g., disbelief vs. support).

Studies conducted within the past 15 years using larger numbers of participants, multiple measures, comparison groups, and longitudinal designs have contributed greatly to what we do know. Researchers attempting to understand the effects associated with CSA have explored associations between preabuse, abuse, and postabuse characteristics and differential psychological effects. Table 4.3 lists the most influential variables that impact CSA outcomes and the direction of their impact on those outcomes.

The most important *preabuse characteristics* include a history of prior traumatic experiences and a history of prior psychological problems (Berliner, 2011). Dysfunctional family environments, such as those that include parental psychopathology, illness, and domestic violence, also contribute to greater negative outcomes (Fitzgerald et al., 2008; K. Putnam, Harris, & Putnam, 2013). There is also some evidence that older age of abuse (e.g., 12–16 years) is associated with more adverse outcomes, perhaps because the teenage years are such a significant transitional developmental period (Papalia, Luebbers, Ogloff, Cutajar, & Mullen, 2017).

CSA *situations* are also associated with severity of symptoms. Perhaps the most consistent finding is that threats, force, and violence by the perpetrator are linked with increased negative outcome (Ruggiero, McLeer, & Dixon, 2000; Steine et al., 2019). Studies have also demonstrated, not surprisingly, that the least serious forms of sexual contact (e.g., unwanted kissing or touching of clothed body parts) are associated with less trauma than are more serious forms of genital contact (Amado, Arce, & Herraiz, 2015; Fergusson, McLeod, & Horwood, 2013; Gewirtz-Meydan & Finkelhor, 2019). Most studies indicate that when abuse is perpetrated by a father, father figure, or other individual who has an intense emotional relationship with the victim, the consequences are particularly severe (Trickett, Noll, & Putnam, 2011). In addition, when victims are exposed to multiple episodes of abuse or traumatic events (e.g., polyvictimization), they exhibit increased symptoms (J. Ford, Elhai, Connor, & Frueh, 2010; Ippen, Harris, Van Horn, & Lieberman, 2011).

Research has also found that specific *postabuse events* (e.g., the ways in which family members and institutions respond to disclosure) are related to the effects of CSA. In the opening case study, for example, we saw that Sashim's mother was not supportive upon hearing her daughter's disclosure; she disbelieved Sashim and actually pressured her to recant her story. Recantations are more likely when children are abused by a member of their household and when the nonperpetrating parent expresses disbelief of the allegation (Malloy, Lyon, & Quas, 2007). Studies have consistently found that negative responses tend to aggravate victims' experience of trauma (e.g., Bernard-Bonnin, Herbert, Daignault, & Allard-Dansereau, 2008; Easton, 2013). In contrast, strong social supports, such as maternal support or a supportive relationship with another adult, appear to mitigate negative effects and play a protective role (e.g., Bolen & Gergely, 2015; Domhardt et al., 2015; Godbout, Briere, Sabourin, & Lussier, 2014; Steine et al., 2019).

TABLE 4.3 ■ Mediators of the Effects of Child Sexual Abuse	
Potential Mediators	**Influence on Child Sexual Abuse Outcomes**
Preabuse Risk Factors	
Prior traumatic experiences	A history of experiencing prior traumatic events is associated with greater negative outcomes.
History of psychological problems	A prior history of psychological problems, such as anxiety, is associated with greater negative outcomes.
Dysfunctional family environment	The presence of certain family characteristics, such as parental psychopathology, illness, and domestic violence, is associated with a greater negative effect.
Abuse Characteristics	
Type of sexual activity	More severe forms of sexual activity (e.g., penetration) are associated with a greater negative effect.
Child–perpetrator relationship	A greater negative effect is associated with fathers, father figures, and intense emotional relationships.
Force or physical injury	Presence of force or physical injury is associated with a greater negative effect.
Multiple traumatic events	Different combinations of child maltreatment are associated with a greater negative effect as are multiple episodes of abuse.
Postabuse Characteristics	
Response toward the victim	Negative responses toward victims' disclosures of abuse are associated with a greater negative effect.
Available social support	Increased social support is associated with a less severe effect.

Sources: References are representative rather than exhaustive: Amado et al., 2015; Berliner, 2011; Bolen & Gergely, 2015; Fergusson et al., 2013; J. Ford et al., 2010; Gilbert, Widom, et al., 2009; Ippen et al., 2011; Macdonald, Danielson, Resnick, Saunders, & Kilpatrick, 2010; K. Putnam et al., 2013; Romano et al., 2019; Steine et al., 2019; Trickett et al., 2011; Vaillancort-Morel et al., 2016.

Additionally, some evidence suggests that a greater delay in disclosure is associated with greater negative outcomes (Romano et al., 2019).

A growing body of research has examined various protective factors, or resilience, in survivors of CSA. As indicated earlier, some individuals who are sexually abused somehow maintain normal levels of functioning. In a systematic review of literature on short-term (e.g., during childhood and adolescence) and long-term (e.g., during adulthood) resilience, Domhardt and colleagues (2015) identified several resilience factors that seemed to serve a protective function. These included higher levels of education, interpersonal and emotional competence, control beliefs (e.g., sense of empowerment and internal locus of control), active coping, optimism, social attachment, external attribution of blame, and support (as noted earlier) from the family and wider community. Enhancing such protective factors should be a focus of both intervention and prevention efforts.

INTERVENTION AND PREVENTION OF CHILD SEXUAL ABUSE

Throughout this chapter, we have described what is known about CSA in an attempt to explore the relevant issues thoroughly. Improved understanding about CSA has contributed to the establishment of a number of treatment and prevention efforts aimed at addressing the sexual abuse of children. The discussion here focuses on formal programs and strategies; personal responses to address the problem are included in Chapter 11.

Treatment for Children and Adults

Treatment programs must take into account that victims of CSA are diverse in their preabuse histories, the nature of their abuse experiences, and the social supports and coping resources available to them. CSA perpetrators are equally heterogeneous. As a result, treatment programs need to be able to tailor the services they offer to meet the particular needs of each individual client. No single treatment plan will be effective for all victims or all families, or all perpetrators. A comprehensive review of CSA treatment interventions is beyond the scope of this chapter, and we therefore focus on just a few significant interventions in the sections that follow.

Interventions for Children and Nonoffending Parents

Many treatment approaches have been developed specifically for child and adolescent victims of CSA including individual, family, and group therapies. Unfortunately, a recent review of therapeutic interventions for children and adolescent survivors of CSA revealed "an absence of culturally-specific, clear guides to therapy" and an "inconclusive, conflicting and contradictory evidence-base of therapeutic approaches, with limited scope and methodological flaws" (Narang, Schwannauer, Quayle, & Chouliara, 2019, p. 1). Despite challenges to developing effective interventions, the most well-supported treatment approach for the problems experienced by victims of CSA, to date, is trauma-focused cognitive behavioral therapy (TF-CBT, introduced in Chapter 3; see also Pollio, Deblinger, & Runyon, 2011; Saunders, 2012). This form of individual therapy targets a variety of the symptoms associated with sexual abuse victimization, including negative attributions, cognitive distortions, fear, anxiety, and other post-traumatic stress reactions.

The treatment includes a number of components that can be remembered using the acronym PRACTICE (J. Cohen, Mannarino, & Murray, 2011; Pollio et al., 2011):

- Psychoeducation: Providing accurate information about the problem of sexual abuse and common reactions to this abuse.

- Parenting skills: Training parents in various management techniques to help them become more effective parents.

- Relaxation skills: Training and practice for children in various relaxation skills to reduce fear and anxiety and physical reactions to stress.

- Affective expression: Building various skills to help children express and manage their feelings effectively.

- Cognitive coping skills: Helping children to understand and identify the connections between thoughts, feelings, and behaviors.

- Trauma narrative and processing: Recounting the narrative about the trauma and correcting cognitive distortions.

- In vivo mastery: Gradually exposing the child to elements of the abuse experience in order to decondition negative emotional responses to memories of the abuse.

- Conjoint therapy: Sessions involving both parent and child.

- Enhancing safety: Teaching safety skills to help children feel empowered and to help them protect themselves from future victimization.

Researchers who have evaluated the effectiveness of TF-CBT have found that this form of treatment is effective, particularly for reducing post-traumatic stress symptoms in children (e.g., Morina, Koerssen, & Pollet, 2016; Saunders, 2012). However, the variability of responses that children have to CSA dictates the need to additionally develop specialized treatments that complement TF-CBT. A child victim who presents problematic sexual behavior, for example, might have different treatment needs than a child with troubled social functioning (Allen, Timmer, & Urquiza, 2016; Benuto & O'Donohue, 2015). In addition, children and their families might present other problems (e.g., learning problems, marital discord, or attention-deficit/hyperactivity disorder) in addition to a history of CSA, which will need to be addressed as part of the treatment strategy. Research confirms that the best, most successful therapies are those that treat the specific needs of each individual child (Taylor & Harvey, 2010).

Nonoffending parents also have their own traumatic reactions to the abuse and need support to cope with their anger, guilt, depression, and feelings of powerlessness (Wickham & West, 2002). Providing interventions that reduce parental stress and empower parents to help their child is a critical component in the treatment of CSA

(Coohey & O'Leary, 2008). One such approach is Child–Parent Relationship Therapy (CPRT), which is a play-therapy-based intervention that combines parental support and education with the aim of fostering a healthy parent–child relationship (Bratton, Ceballos, Landreth, & Costas, 2012; Bratton, Landreth, Kellam, & Blackard, 2006). Treatment outcome studies of CPRT suggest that it is a promising intervention that is beneficial in relieving parental stress and enhancing parental empathy in nonoffending parents (Baggerly & Bratton, 2010; Bratton, Landreth, & Lin, 2010). For further reading, we recommend *Child Sexual Abuse: A Primer for Treating Children, Adolescents, and Their Nonoffending Parents* (Deblinger, Mannarino, Cohen, Runyon, & Heflin, 2015).

Interventions for Adults Sexually Abused as Children

Treatment of adult survivors likewise requires a variety of approaches, depending on the specific therapeutic needs of the victim. Some clients, for example, might need to learn effective ways to modulate emotions such as anger, anxiety, and fear (Briere, 2002). Others might be suffering from negative attributions and cognitive distortions such as guilt, shame, and stigmatization (Cahill, Llewelyn, & Pearson, 1991; Jehu, Klassen, & Gazan, 1986). Research on the effectiveness of therapy has been promising (see McDonagh et al., 2005; Taylor & Harvey, 2010). For further reading, we recommend *Healing the Incest Wound: Adult Survivors in Therapy* (Courtois, 2010) and *Working With Adult Survivors of Child Sexual Abuse* (E. Jones, 2018).

Interventions for Offenders

The most common form of treatment for adult sex offenders is multicomponent CBT (Kirsch, Fanniff, & Becker, 2011). The behavioral component focuses on altering the deviant sexual arousal patterns of CSA perpetrators. Most behavioral approaches use some form of aversive therapy that pairs an aversive outcome with sexually deviant fantasies. For example, in a technique called **masturbatory satiation**, the perpetrator is instructed to reach orgasm through masturbation as quickly as possible using *appropriate* sexual fantasies (e.g., sexual encounters between two mutually consenting adults). Once he has ejaculated, he is told to switch his fantasies to images involving children and continue to masturbate until the total masturbation time is one hour. The reasoning behind this technique is that it reinforces the appropriate fantasies through the pleasurable feelings of orgasm and diminishes the offender's inappropriate fantasies by associating them with nonpleasurable masturbation that occurs after ejaculation. Sometimes these techniques are supplemented with medical treatments such as **chemical castration**, or the administration of various drugs to reduce sex drive (L. Cohen & Galynker, 2009).

CBT can also target distorted beliefs, levels of empathy, and low self-esteem, all of which are associated with CSA perpetration (W. Marshall & Laws, 2003). Offenders can be taught, for example, how to recognize and change inaccurate beliefs that justify and maintain their deviant sexual behavior (e.g., that the perpetrator is simply teaching the victim about sex). Other therapies focus on nonsexual factors relevant to perpetration, including social and life skills, in hopes of helping perpetrators reintegrate into the community (e.g., Kirsch et al., 2011; W. Marshall & Laws, 2003).

CBT programs also often include a relapse prevention component designed to assist perpetrators in maintaining the gains they achieved in therapy. Perpetrators are taught how to (a) identify their typical offense pattern, (b) recognize factors (e.g., intoxication) and situations (e.g., being alone with a child) associated with risk, (c) identify coping skills that reduce risk, and (d) create plans to avoid risk (W. Marshall, 1999). Many of these programs also provide long-term, community-based supervision (Miner, Marques, Day, & Nelson, 1990; Pithers & Kafka, 1990).

Whether any of these treatments is successful is hotly debated. The primary goal in working with CSA offenders and in determining treatment effectiveness has been the evaluation of **recidivism rates**. Recidivism rates (the likelihood that offenders will commit repeat offenses) are all but impossible to accurately calculate. Indeed, unless the offender is arrested, it is impossible to determine if or when he or she reoffended. Despite these difficulties, there is preliminary evidence that men who freely choose medical therapy to reduce their sex drive (e.g., chemical castration) demonstrate decreased sexual behavior and offense-supportive cognitions, and increased perceptions of control over their sexual urges (Amelung, Kuhle, Konrad, Pauls, & Beier, 2012). But, of course, the body of knowledge on treatment for sex offenders is far from conclusive. Even if a particular treatment alters a perpetrator's arousal patterns to pictures and/or stories of children, we cannot know for sure whether such changes necessarily apply to arousal patterns toward actual children. For further reading, we recommend *Adult Sex Offender Management* (Lobanov-Rostovsky, 2015).

Prevention of CSA

Efforts aimed at eliminating CSA through prevention have focused primarily on equipping children with the skills they need to respond to or protect themselves from sexual abuse. Other CSA prevention programs are geared toward parents, who are often in a position to empower children to protect themselves. Other programs focus on preventing the perpetration of sexual abuse by focusing on actual or potential sexual abusers. Yet other programs focus on educating professionals who are often in positions to identify and help victims as well as influence social policy on CSA.

Education Programs for Children

During the 1980s, school-based empowerment programs to help children avoid and report victimization became popular across the United States. Such programs generally teach children knowledge and skills that experts believe will help them to protect themselves from a variety of dangers. Most focus on sexual abuse and emphasize two goals: *primary prevention* (keeping the abuse from occurring) by recognizing potentially abusive situations/abusers and by teaching children to resist advances and *detection* (encouraging children to report past and current abuse) (Miller-Perrin & Wurtele, 2017b).

Evaluations of school-based victimization prevention programs suggest that, in general, exposure to such programs increases children's knowledge and protection skills (Miller-Perrin & Wurtele, 2017b; Rudolph & Zimmer-Gembeck, 2018; Walsh, Zwi, Woolfenden, & Shlonsky, 2018). Whether these programs are effective in actually helping children to avoid abuse is a much more complicated question. There is some evidence to suggest that they are effective in this regard. Zwi and colleagues (2007), for example, found that children who had participated in an education program were 6 to 7 times more likely to demonstrate protective behavior in simulated situations than those who had not participated in such programs. Finkelhor, Asdigian, and Dziuba-Leatherman (1995b) found that among their 2,000 survey respondents aged 10–16 years, 40 percent reported specific instances in which they used information or self-protection skills taught to them in an education program. These researchers, however, found no differences in actual victimization rates for those who had and had not participated in school-based prevention programs. In contrast, a survey of 825 college women found that women who had participated in "good-touch, bad-touch" prevention programs as children were significantly less likely to report, as adults, any sexual victimization experienced in childhood compared to women who reported having no personal safety training as children (Gibson & Leitenberg, 2000). School-based prevention education has also been shown to be effective in encouraging children to disclose past or ongoing abuse (Blakey, Glaude, & Jennings, 2019; Walsh et al., 2018). These various findings offer some hope that school-based programs might help prevent CSA.

School-based CSA prevention programs are not without their critics. Reppucci, Land, and Haugaard (1998), among other researchers, have questioned whether the "relatively exclusive focus on children as their own protectors is appropriate" (p. 332). Many children, they argue, may not be developmentally ready to protect themselves. Critics have argued that the skills and concepts taught in child-focused education programs may be too complex for children to understand and that the skills required to overcome the perpetrator's authority status and manipulations may be too difficult (Finkelhor, 2009; Rudolph & Zimmer-Gembeck, 2018). In addition, there is some danger that an overreliance on these types of programs may give parents and society a false sense of security about a child's safety following participation in such programs. At the same time, it seems reasonable to conclude that children and adolescents have a right to be enlightened about sexuality and sexual abuse and to know about their right to live free from such abuse. Indeed, it might be morally reprehensible to *not* equip children with knowledge and skills to potentially help them to prevent sexual abuse (Finkelhor, 2009).

The Parental Role in Child Empowerment

Because parents potentially play an important role in empowering their own children to protect themselves, and because opponents to child-focused programs believe attention should shift from children to protectors in the child's environment, some have argued that prevention efforts should focus on parent education (Mendelson & Letourneau, 2015; Miller-Perrin & Wurtele, 2017b; Rudolph & Zimmer-Gembeck, 2018). Studies indicate that CSA prevention programs for parents not only increase knowledge about CSA, but also are effective in increasing parent–child communication about the topic, improving parents' ability to teach their children about sexual abuse and appropriate protective skills (e.g., Wurtele, Kast, & Melzer, 1992; Wurtele, Moreno, & Kenny, 2008). Parents are particularly effective if they are given specific instruction in how to talk to their children about sexual abuse (E. Burgess & Wurtele, 1998).

Perpetration Prevention

Public Education. Some education programs target actual or potential offenders. The **Stop It Now!** program was developed by a national nonprofit organization in Vermont and is one of the best-known examples of this type of program. This program encourages offenders and those at risk for offending to self-identify, report themselves to authorities, and enter treatment (Stop It Now!, 2010; Tabachnick, 2003). The program operates through public education and media campaigns targeting adult offenders, those at risk to offend, parents of youth with sexual behavior problems, and families and close friends of these individuals. Prevention messages are delivered through newspaper advertisements, television and radio ads, talk shows, articles, billboards, posters, and news features (Stop It Now!, 2010). Through these media, individuals are encouraged to contact the organization's helpline for information and referrals. The helpline provides support, information, and guidance to individuals in need, including helping them to identify and respond to warning signs of sexually abusive behaviors in adults and youth. A recent analysis of helpline data indicated that the majority of users were bystanders, family members, or friends/acquaintances of individuals at risk for CSA and 12 percent had questions or concerns about their own feelings and/or behaviors potentially at risk to a child (Grant, Shields, Tabachnick, & Coleman, 2019). Individuals can contact the helpline via phone (1-888-PREVENT), email (stopitnow.org/webform/help-inquiry), chat (stopitnow.org/get-immediate-help), or social media (facebook.com/stopitnow). According to the 2019 Stop It Now! Helpline Report (available at www.stopitnow.org/about-us/helpline-report), the helpline responded to over 1,500 requests for personal help in 2018, which comprised more inquiries than in the organization's first five years combined. Other similar approaches that specifically target juveniles with a sexual preference for children, such as the Berlin Project for Primary Prevention of Child Sexual Abuse by

Juveniles, are appearing in other countries (Beier et al., 2016). Unfortunately, program evaluation studies documenting the effectiveness of these programs in preventing future CSA are not yet available.

In Massachusetts, the **Enough Abuse Campaign** is a statewide education and community mobilization effort whose mission is "to prevent people from sexually abusing children now and to prevent children from developing sexually abusive behaviors in the future" (Massachusetts Citizens for Children, 2010). The Enough Abuse Campaign provides information about conditions and social norms associated with the occurrence of CSA and offers training for parents and child care professionals to identify and respond to sexual behaviors of children. Along with media coverage and community presentations and workshops, the campaign also provides a variety of CSA prevention materials and resources on its website (www.enoughabuse.org). The campaign also supports efforts to affect public policies related to CSA (e.g., reforming states' statutes of limitations) (Schober, Fawcett, & Bernier, 2012).

Evaluation of the Enough Abuse Campaign supports this approach as a promising avenue for CSA prevention. Following the campaign, it was demonstrated that more Massachusetts residents were likely to endorse the belief that adults, rather than children, should take responsibility for preventing CSA (an increase from 69% in 2003 to 93% in 2007; Schober, Fawcett, & Bernier, 2012). As another potential indicator of program impact, substantiated reports of CSA in Massachusetts declined by 69 percent from 1990 to 2007. Similar effects were observed in Georgia, as substantiated reports of CSA decreased over four of the five years of the implementation period (Schober, Fawcett, Thigpen, Curtis, & Wright, 2012).

Public Policy. Public policy and law are also viewed as potential perpetrator prevention strategies. As noted previously, all U.S. states have laws criminalizing CSA. There is considerable debate, however, about how severe the criminal sanctions should be. Unlike the perpetrators of other forms of violence and maltreatment discussed in this book, CSA offenders are more likely to be seen as "sick perverts." Because they are sick, their abuse is less likely to be seen as volitional. Can a "sick pervert" be deterred? Can a "sick pervert" be cured?

Those who answer "no" to both questions argue that communities must be protected from potential perpetrators with community protection policies such as lifetime offender registries, lifetime online community notification, indefinite postincarceration civil commitment, and expansive sex offender residency restrictions (Letourneau & Levenson, 2011; Lobanov-Rostovsky, 2015). Unfortunately, most legislative initiatives have not been adequately evaluated, and what research is available suggests that sex offender policies, including notification, registration, and residency restrictions, do not prevent sex offenders from repeating their crimes (e.g., Letourneau & Levenson, 2011). Thus, the impact of these legislative initiatives on primary prevention of CSA perpetration is unknown. Letourneau, Eaton, Bass, Berlin, and Moore (2014) argue that strong emotional reactions engendered by CSA often lead to reactionary legislation that may actually be counter-productive to CSA prevention efforts because such legislation leaves the impression that "legislators are doing everything that can be done," which results in complacency (p. 225). Such reactive legislation is often quickly implemented in response to a dramatic case of CSA (e.g., legislation that includes the name of the child victim in its title) in order to protect children. There are recent signs, however, that the tide of reactive legislation may be subsiding (Letourneau et al., 2014).

Training Professionals

Another key strategy to preventing CSA is educating professionals who have contact with children and families and/or serve in influential leadership roles within communities. Training for mental health professionals, for example, is important because such individuals—including counselors, psychologists, and social workers—have direct contact with children and can help identify and treat those who are victims of CSA (Kenny & Abreu, 2015; Kenny, Helpingstine, Abreu, & Duberli, 2019). Other professionals who come into contact with children and families, such as physicians, lawyers, religious leaders, teachers, and child care professionals, would also benefit from training in CSA to help them identify victims and guide them to appropriate resources. Training of professionals might also be impactful because such professionals are often in a position to influence and educate others, conduct research to improve understanding of the field, and contribute to primary prevention, as well as influence public policy (Yamaoka, Wilsie, Bard, & Bonner, 2019). Finally, training professionals in CSA and its prevention might not only increase their knowledge and awareness of CSA but also translate into an actual decrease in their own risk of engaging in abusive behavior (e.g., decreased boundary crossing by school personnel; see Grant, Shakeshaft, & Mueller, 2019).

What type of training is available to professionals, and is there evidence that such training is effective? One approach to training professionals would be to include providing information on child abuse and neglect in graduate coursework. One example of such training is the Interdisciplinary Training Program in Child Abuse and Neglect, a national training program initiated by the National Center on Child Abuse and Neglect in an effort to institutionalize interdisciplinary graduate training in child maltreatment (Gallmeier & Bonner, 1992). Although funding for the program ended in the early 1990s, the University of Oklahoma Health Sciences Center continues to operate the program and recently found that the program demonstrated effectiveness in training early professionals to contribute to advocacy, clinical treatment, primary prevention, and research related to child abuse and neglect (Yamaoka et al., 2019). Unfortunately, relatively little is known about the inclusion of specific information on CSA provided in graduate programs for early professionals (Kenny & Abreu, 2015). Another approach to training professionals includes special training workshops targeting various professional groups. One example of such training is the Stewards of Children prevention program, which includes a two-and-a-half-hour workshop designed to shift knowledge, attitudes, and behaviors related to CSA (Letourneau, Nietert, & Rheingold, 2016; Rheingold et al., 2015). One randomized controlled trial of the program with child care professionals indicated that the program was successful in impacting knowledge, attitudes, and preventive behaviors of these professionals (Rheingold et al., 2015). Other training programs have shown similar success with a more diverse group of child-serving professionals, improving knowledge and awareness of CSA (Gushwa, Bernier, & Robinson, 2019; Kenny, Helpingstine, Long, Peerez, & Harrington, 2019; Lipson, Grant, Mueller, & Sonnich, 2019). Additional program implementation and evaluation targeting various professional groups is needed.

CHAPTER SUMMARY

No one knows exactly how many children experience sexual abuse each year. The difficulty in determining accurate rates of CSA stems from the problems inherent in defining and studying any complex social problem. Although no precise figures are available, it is clear that adults sexually exploit large numbers of children. Conservative estimates derived from the most methodologically sound studies suggest that in the United States, 20 percent of women and between 5 percent and 10 percent of men have experienced some form of CSA.

Research has demonstrated the heterogeneity of CSA victim and offender populations. Victims and perpetrators represent all possible demographic and psychological profiles. A number of risk factors, however, have been consistently associated with CSA. Victims often are female, have few close friends, and live in families characterized by poor family relations and the absence or unavailability of natural parents. Perpetrators of CSA are most often male, and they are often relatives or acquaintances of their victims. The heterogeneity of victim and perpetrator populations has contributed to scholars' difficulty in establishing a single explanation for the occurrence of CSA. One perpetrator may abuse a certain type of child for one reason, and another may abuse a different type of child for a different reason. Risk factors for CSA span various individuals and systems involved in CSA, including individuals as well as the context in which they reside. Several theories have been developed in an attempt to integrate individual risk factors across multiple ecological levels.

The psychological sequelae associated with CSA are variable and consist of short-term as well as long-term effects. Difficulties associated with CSA include a variety of symptoms that affect emotional well-being, interpersonal functioning, behavior, sexual functioning, physical health, and cognitive functioning. The variability of outcomes for victims is associated with a number of factors including the severity of the sexual behavior, the degree of physical force used by the perpetrator, the response the victim received following disclosure, and the relationship of the perpetrator to the victim.

In recognition of the significance of the CSA problem, many professionals are involved in responding to the needs of victims and the treatment of perpetrators. Researchers and mental health practitioners have developed an array of treatment interventions in an effort to address the multiple causes and far-reaching consequences of CSA. Regardless of the type of approach, the therapeutic goals for child victims and adult survivors of CSA generally include addressing significant symptoms as well as common emotions associated with abuse, such as guilt, shame, anger, depression, and anxiety. Treatment programs for offenders include a variety of approaches, but most typically incorporate cognitive and behavioral components to reduce deviant sexual arousal and cognitive distortions associated with abuse. These approaches demonstrate some promise, but further studies are needed to address the limitations of extant research methodologies and to examine potential alternative treatments.

The prevention of CSA begins with social awareness and the recognition that expertise, energy, and money are needed to alleviate the conditions that produce CSA. Many experts maintain, however, that society has not yet sufficiently demonstrated a commitment to prevention. In most communities, monetary resources are tied up in responding to, rather than preventing, CSA. Increasing commitment to the prevention of CSA, however, is evidenced in the many prevention programs appearing across the United States. Several of the strategies employed in these programs seem especially promising. Although additional evaluations are needed, available research indicates that these programs have tremendous positive potential.

Recommended Resources

Assink, M., van der Put, C. E., Meeuwsen, M. W., de Jong, N. M., Oort, F. J., Stams, G. J. J., & Hoeve, M. (2019). Risk factors for child sexual abuse victimization: A meta-analytic review. *Psychological Bulletin, 145*(5), 459–489.

Deblinger, E., Mannarino, A. P., Cohen, J. A., Runyon, M. K., & Heflin, A. H. (2015). *Child sexual abuse: A primer for treating children, adolescents, and their nonoffending parents* (2nd ed.). New York, NY: Oxford University Press.

Jones, E. (2018). *Working with adult survivors of child sexual abuse.* New York, NY: Routledge.

Lobanov-Rostovsky, C. (2015). *Adult sex offender management.* Sex Offender Management Assessment and Planning Initiative. Retrieved from http://www.smart.gov/pdfs/AdultSexOffenderManagement.pdf

Walsh, K., Zwi, K., Woolfenden, S., & Shlonsky, A. (2018). School-based education programs for the prevention of child sexual abuse: A Cochrane systematic review and meta-analysis. *Research on Social Work Practice, 28*(1), 33–55.

CHILD NEGLECT

LEARNING OBJECTIVES

1. Describe the definition and scope of child neglect, including problems inherent in measuring this form of abuse.

2. Identify the various risk factors associated with child neglect.

3. Summarize the consequences of child neglect, including both short- and long-term outcomes.

4. Discuss the various intervention and prevention efforts that have been developed to address child neglect, including evidence of their effectiveness.

CASE HISTORY

WILL AND MARK: "WHERE ARE THE PARENTS?"

Will and Mark arrived at the psychiatric unit of the county hospital after being apprehended by the police the night before. Their clothes were covered with dirt, and the odor emanating from their bodies indicated that they had not bathed in quite some time. Both were thin and immediately asked the nursing staff for some food. An interview revealed that they were brothers and part of a family of seven, although many other "friends of the family" often stayed in their house. Neither of their parents worked, and Will and Mark stated that they often had the responsibility of bringing home money for their parents. Their father had taught them

how to beg for money on various street corners around the city.

After the interview, the events of the previous evening were clear. Mark and Will had been out "killing time" by wandering around the neighborhood. After roaming the city for hours, they spotted a pickup truck and took it for a ride. After a short drive, they stopped at a local furniture store, broke in, and began to vandalize the merchandise, using Will's knife. A woman from the community spotted the intruders and called the police. She told the police that two young boys, probably somewhere between 7 and 9 years of age, had broken into a local business.

The events of this case history clearly reflect parenting practices that are less than ideal. Such behaviors, however, would not be characterized as physical or sexual abuse as previously defined in this book. Rather, this vignette illustrates another form of child maltreatment: child neglect. In contrast to physical and sexual abuse, child neglect is typically viewed as an act of *omission* rather than an act of *commission*. Child neglect may sometimes be unintentional, but that does not make it any less detrimental to a child's development than intentional abuse or neglect.

Like all forms of child maltreatment, child neglect is not new. However, widespread recognition of this form of child maltreatment has often taken a backseat to concerns about child physical and sexual abuse. In recent years, however, attention has grown, and today child neglect is the most frequently reported form of child maltreatment (U.S. Department of Health and Human Services [U.S. DHHS], 2020). In this chapter, we address what is currently known about child neglect by examining issues related to defining child neglect and determining the magnitude of the problem. We then shift our attention to the characteristics researchers have found to be associated with neglectful parents and their children before focusing on an evaluation of the short- and long-term consequences associated with child neglect. The chapter concludes with a discussion of potential intervention and prevention strategies for addressing the problem.

SCOPE OF THE PROBLEM

All forms of violence and maltreatment in intimate relationships (VMIR) are difficult to conceptualize and measure. At least with physical violence and sexual maltreatment, however, we can base our definitions and criminal codes on specific outcomes (e.g., an injury) or specific actions (e.g., sexual penetration). With child neglect and child psychological maltreatment (see Chapter 6), however, the definitional task becomes much more difficult. Reaching consensus regarding conceptual and operational definitions and determining the rates of the problem are two of the greatest challenges to the field.

What Is Child Neglect?

The following scenarios illustrate a range of behaviors that may fall under the label of child neglect:

- Mark, who is 8 years old, is left to care for his 3-year-old sister, Maria, while their parents go out.

- Margaret fails to provide medication for her 10-year-old daughter, who has a seizure disorder.

- Jonathan refuses to allow his 16-year-old son into the family's home and tells him not to return.

- Tyrone and Rachel live with their three children in a home that is thick with dirt and dust, smells of urine, and has nothing but rotting food in the refrigerator.

- Alicia leaves her 10-month-old infant unattended in a bathtub full of water.

Experts generally agree that deficits in meeting a child's basic needs, including basic needs in the broad categories of physical, emotional, medical, and educational needs, constitute **child neglect** (e.g., Dubowitz, Pitts, & Black, 2012; A. M. Jackson, Kissoon, & Greene, 2015), although definitions vary significantly by state (Rebbe, 2018). There is less agreement, however, about various aspects of the scope and specificity of children's needs and parental behaviors. Determining what specific basic needs are included in each of these broad categories, and at what point a parent has failed to provide for those needs, is no easy matter.

The complicated question of what constitutes a "basic need" and what constitutes "parental failure to provide" is illustrated in the story of Mark and Maria, as described in the first scenario. Is it negligent to leave an 8-year-old boy to care for his 3-year-old sister? Obviously, the answer depends on the specific circumstances. What if Mark were responsible for Maria's care for five minutes while she played on the floor? For five minutes while she played in the bathtub? For one evening between 9 p.m. and 1 a.m.?

For every evening between 9 p.m. and 1 a.m.? What if Mark were responsible for Maria's care while their parents took a two-week vacation?

A given scenario might be interpreted as neglectful or not depending on several factors, including the *duration and frequency* of parental behavior. A single incident of neglectful behavior or an occasional lapse in adequate care, for example, is usually considered a normal characteristic of parenting or parental error rather than an indication of serious child neglect. Few would allege child neglect if a child occasionally misses a bath or a meal. In contrast, a pattern of frequent and repeated deficits in child care (e.g., few baths and numerous missed meals) is likely to be considered neglectful. Some definitions of neglect therefore focus on the *persistent* failure of parents to meet a child's basic needs. However, sometimes isolated incidents or brief omissions in care cannot be dismissed as merely caretaker error. If a caretaker leaves a young child or infant alone just once near a swimming pool, or unbuckled in a car, for example, the child could die. Perhaps there are some caretaker behaviors that are so irresponsible and dangerous for the child that, even in isolation, they should be considered negligent.

Consider, for example, a fascinating case from 2016 in which a 4-year-old boy managed to navigate a barrier and fall into a gorilla exhibit at the Cincinnati Zoo. The gorilla took a significant interest in the boy, aggressively dragging him through the water and around the gorilla habitat for approximately 10 minutes, inadvertently banging the boy's head on the concrete structures within the exhibit. The zoo staff shot and killed the gorilla, and the boy was not seriously injured. (Readers may view a video of the incident here: www.youtube.com/watch?v=BUCfY270l7k).

Who is to blame for this incident? Nobody blamed the gorilla. He was simply doing what gorillas do. But should the zoo exhibit be so accessible that a child can find his way in? And where were the adults—in this case, the mother—who presumably should have been watching the child? Many animal rights supporters, who were angered by the death of the gorilla, argued that the mother should be charged with child neglect. They collected 350,000 signatures in a petition calling for an investigation of the mother for child neglect (Dell'Antonia, 2016; McPhate, 2016). The questions that emerged from this incident are fascinating. Does this incident suggest negligence on the part of the zoo, negligence on the part of the mother in charge of supervising the boy, or simply an unfortunate accident?

The *severity of the consequences*, or demonstrable harm, of neglect is therefore another important variable (Dubowitz et al., 2012). A case in which a child dies from bleach poisoning, for example, should be considered more severe than a case in which a child receives a minor burn from an iron, even though the same parental behavior (i.e., lack of supervision) contributed to both injuries. Of course, harm is not always easy to measure and is not always immediate. The three children of Tyrone and Rachel, described in the fourth scenario, may suffer no demonstrable immediate harm as a result of living in unsanitary conditions for a month, but the parents' behavior could still be considered neglect. It may be that the effects of child neglect do not appear in childhood, but rather become evident during adolescence or adulthood (Perez & Widom, 1994).

In recognition of this dilemma, the U.S. DHHS (1988) broadened its definition of child neglect in the second National Incidence Study (NIS-2) to include an endangerment standard. This new category allowed for the reporting of cases in which children demonstrated no actual harm (i.e., present evidence of injury) but in which it was reasonable to suspect potential harm (i.e., future risk of injury). In the end, of course, determining endangerment is no easy matter, so professionals who investigate cases of alleged child neglect will inevitably be faced with some difficult choices. Definitions of child neglect should take into consideration potential harm that is both probable and severe in its consequences. Leaving a 10-month-old unattended in a bathtub full of water, as Alicia did in the last scenario, for example, is potentially likely to result in severe injury or even death.

Two decidedly more controversial issues also hover over the definitional debate. The first is the issue of poverty and parental intent. Definitions of child neglect that emphasize parental blame, parental responsibility, or both may focus narrowly on the role of the caretaker in child neglect, limiting understanding of the problem. What if parents fail to provide, for example, simply because they are poor? In the second scenario, for example, Margaret's failure to provide medication for her 10-year-old might be because she cannot afford the medication. Is her child a victim of neglect? Presumably most of us would agree that the answer is yes. The issue of whether or not Margaret should be held accountable for the neglect is less clear.

How we choose to handle the question of poverty and parental intent will obviously have a huge impact on both our estimates of the scope of the problem and how we choose to address the problem. In terms of scope, if we exclude children who are poor from our definitions of neglect, our estimates will obviously be dramatically lower. There is significant empirical evidence that child neglect rates are directly tied to environmental poverty (H. Kim & Drake, 2018). In terms of addressing the problem, if professionals designing child neglect interventions focus exclusively on the negative intent or failures of neglectful parents, they might confine their strategies to improving parental behaviors and thereby fail to address other important contributors to neglect, such as poverty. Dubowitz and colleagues have argued for a definition of neglect that focuses on the unmet needs of the child, regardless of parental intentions (Dubowitz, Pitts, & Black, 2004, 2012). The definition of child neglect used in the fourth National Incidence Study (NIS-4) took into account parental intention by distinguishing between two different kinds of neglect: parental failure to provide when options are available and parental failure to provide when options are not available (Sedlak et al., 2010).

Another controversial issue is the *cultural context* in which the child neglect occurs. Here it is important to remind the reader of the social constructionist perspective introduced in Chapter 1. Societal reactions ultimately determine what is and is not appropriate parental behavior and what is developmentally appropriate and safe for children. We are reminded of the documentary film *Babies*, released in 2006, which follows four babies and their families through their first years of life. The babies and their families are from various parts of the world—Namibia, Mongolia, Japan, and the United States. What parents consider appropriate and safe varies dramatically from one culture to the next—one of the babies takes a bath while a goat comes to drink from the same water, while another baby sits alone and unsupervised surrounded by a group of large cows. However, none of the parents profiled in the documentary is considered "neglectful."

Thus, the social context of a family's culture and beliefs is an important factor to consider in both defining and intervening in child neglect. Research examining variation in community standards of care, however, suggests general consensus on this issue. Studies examining North American parents, for example, indicate that cultural views about household cleanliness, appropriate medical and dental care, and adequate supervision vary little across demographic categories (Polansky, Ammons, & Weathersby, 1983; Polansky, Chalmers, & Williams, 1987; Polansky & Williams, 1978). Studies investigating community standards in other countries have found similar results (Shor, 2000). However, social context continues to be relevant because knowledge of culturally driven reasons for neglectful behavior might inform treatment and prevention approaches (see M. Smith & Fong, 2004, for a discussion of this issue).

Proposed Subtypes of Child Neglect

As previously noted, child neglect exists in many forms, such as physical, educational, medical, and emotional neglect. Many consider the distinction between different subtypes important because they may each have different underlying causes and can lead to differential outcomes for children (Dubowitz et al., 2012). It is important to note, however, that different subtypes of neglect can overlap conceptually and can also co-occur (Dubowitz et al., 2012; Mennen, Kim, Sang, & Trickett, 2010). Consider Will and Mark from the opening case history, for example. These boys clearly were exposed to a number of forms of neglect in terms of personal hygiene, nutrition, and supervision, among others. The various subtypes of neglect that are consistently reported in the literature are described in Table 5.1.

Physical neglect is typically defined as failure to provide a child with basic necessities of life, such as food, clothing, and shelter (Sedlak et al., 2010). An example of physical neglect could be a 2-year-old who is found naked and alone, wandering on the street late at night. **Medical neglect** is the failure or delay in seeking needed health care, refusal to allow or provide needed care for diagnosed conditions, and noncompliance with medical recommendations (A. M. Jackson et al., 2015; Sedlak et al., 2010). For example, one case of medical neglect involved a 12-year-old boy whose parents refused chemotherapy for

TABLE 5.1   ■   Subtypes of Child Neglect

Subtype	Description	Examples
Health care or medical neglect	Refusal to provide (or delay in providing) physical or mental health care	Failing to obtain child's immunizations Failing to fill prescriptions for child's needed medications or to follow health care provider's instructions Failing to attend to child's dental needs Failing to obtain prescribed psychological help for child
Personal hygiene neglect	Failure to meet basic standards of personal care and cleanliness	Infrequent bathing of child Neglecting child's dental hygiene Not providing child with clothing adequate for weather conditions or of the correct size Not providing sleeping arrangements that allow child to obtain adequate sleep
Nutritional neglect	Failure to provide a sufficient and nutritionally balanced diet	Providing insufficient calories to support child's growth Providing meals for child that do not include all the basic food groups Providing child with food that is stale or spoiled
Neglect of household safety	Failure to eliminate safety hazards in and around the child's living area	Allowing structural hazards to exist in and around the home, such as broken stairs or railings, broken windows, or holes in floors or ceilings Allowing fire hazards and burn threats to exist in and around the home, such as combustible materials close to heat sources or frayed wiring Leaving chemicals or drugs where they are accessible to child
Neglect of household sanitation	Failure to meet basic standards of housekeeping care and cleanliness	Allowing garbage and trash to accumulate in the home Failing to control vermin and insects Allowing surfaces in the home to become covered with dirt and filth Failing to provide clean bedding
Inadequate shelter	Failure to provide adequate physical shelter and/or a stable home	Refusing responsibilities of custody of child Not allowing runaway child to return home Failing to provide child with a stable and permanent home (i.e., homelessness) Providing child with an overcrowded home (e.g., 25 people living in a four-bedroom home) Throwing child out of the home

Subtype	Description	Examples
Abandonment	Physical desertion of the child	Placing child in a dumpster; leaving child in a park Failing to return after placing child in the care of others (e.g., babysitters, hospital personnel, relatives)
Supervisory neglect	Failure to provide a level of supervision necessary to avoid child injury	Leaving child in the home without adult parental supervision for prolonged periods Allowing child to roam the streets at night
Educational neglect	Failure to provide care and supervision necessary to promote education	Failing to enroll child of mandatory school age in school Permitting child's frequent and chronic truancy Failing to attend to child's special education needs
Emotional neglect	Failure to provide child with security, emotional support, and encouragement	Being unavailable to child emotionally Being indifferent to or rejecting child
Fostering delinquency	Encouragement of the development of illegal behaviors in the child	Rewarding child for stealing
Environmental neglect	Lack of environmental safety, opportunities, and resources	High-crime neighborhoods Few resources for children and families Accessible guns Unrestrained children in cars
Parental substance use and abuse	Adult behaviors contribute to a child's exposure to or use of illicit or controlled substances	Parents manufacture a controlled substance in the presence of a child Prenatal exposure of a child to harm due to the mother's use of an illegal drug or other substance Allowing a child to be present where the chemicals or equipment for the manufacture of controlled substances are used or stored Selling, distributing, or giving drugs or alcohol to a child Use of a controlled substance by a caregiver that impairs the caregiver's ability to adequately care for the child

Sources: A representative but not exhaustive list of sources for the information displayed in this table includes the following: Child Welfare Information Gateway, 2014; Dubowitz, Pitts, & Black, 2004, 2012; Hegar & Yungman, 1989; A. M. Jackson, Kissoon, & Greene, 2015; Mennen, Kim, Sang, & Trickett, 2010; Mitchell & Guichon, 2019; Munkel, 1994; Sedlak & Broadhurst, 1996; Wolock & Horowitz, 1984; Zuravin, 1991.

a cancerous growth on his tongue (Linebaugh, 2013). **Educational neglect** and **developmental neglect** (also sometimes referred to as **cognitive neglect**) are generally defined as failure to provide a child with the experiences necessary for growth and development, such as intellectual and educational opportunities (Sedlak et al., 2010). An example of educational neglect is a child who is chronically truant or not enrolled in school.

The category of **emotional neglect** has stimulated the greatest disagreement among scholars in terms of defining what it encompasses. Although most agree on broad conceptual parameters of emotional neglect that include failure to provide a child with emotional support, security, and encouragement, they disagree on the specific operationalization of such behaviors. The NIS-4, for example, categorized intimate partner violence (IPV) as emotional neglect (i.e., Sedlak et al., 2010), whereas others have classified it as a form of psychological maltreatment (i.e., R. Herrenkohl, 2005). There is also considerable overlap between definitions of emotional neglect and child psychological maltreatment, but we have chosen to include most of our discussion of emotional neglect (including exposure to IPV) in our discussion of psychological maltreatment in Chapter 6, because we agree with others that emotional neglect is conceptually similar to other forms of psychological maltreatment (e.g., A. Baker & Festinger, 2011).

Some have proposed an additional category of **prenatal neglect**, or neglect that occurs even before a child is born (see Box 5.1). Another type of child neglect that has perhaps received the least amount of attention is **environmental neglect**. In 2003, the National Research Council characterized environmental neglect as "a lack of environmental safety, opportunities, and resources associated with living in a neighborhood burdened by crime, lack of civility, and few resources for children and families" (quoted in Dubowitz et al., 2012, p. 165).

Several researchers have attempted to empirically validate various typologies of neglect. Dubowitz and colleagues (2011), for example, administered a self-report survey that assessed neglectful behavior by parents as recalled by adults or as experienced by adolescents. The original measure assessed four common domains including physical (providing adequate food, hygiene, clothing, etc.), emotional (providing comfort, help, praise, etc.), supervisory (monitoring activities, friendships, misbehavior, etc.), and cognitive neglect (monitoring homework, school attendance, etc.). A group of 593 adolescents participating in the **Longitudinal Studies of Child Abuse and Neglect (LONGSCAN)** consortium were surveyed at 12 years of age and then again at age 14 (272 adolescents completed the process). Results suggested a three-factor model of neglect that included physical needs, emotional support, and parental monitoring. In another study, Dubowitz and colleagues (2004) examined the relationship between environmental neglect, physical neglect, and psychological neglect among 73 children and their families. In this study, environmental neglect was measured using a self-report survey completed by mothers, which assessed negative neighborhood characteristics such as open drug abuse; fear of

BOX 5.1
NEGLECTING THE UNBORN CHILD

The term *prenatal neglect* refers generally to any actions of a pregnant woman that can potentially harm her unborn child. Most conceptualizations of prenatal neglect focus on women who abuse illicit drugs (e.g., opiates such as heroin and morphine, marijuana, amphetamines, cocaine) as well as legal substances such as alcohol and nicotine during pregnancy, exposing infants to the effects of these substances in utero. Although some have referred to prenatal substance exposure as a form of *abuse* (fetal abuse; McCoy & Keen, 2013), it is most commonly seen as a form of child neglect. Many legislators, for example, view this problem as an act of omission or as a failure to provide adequate prenatal care (Child Welfare Information Gateway, 2016b). Estimates of the numbers of substance-exposed infants (SEIs) in the United States vary widely, in part because no state requires the uniform testing of infants for substance exposure. According to the National Survey on Drug Use and Health (NSDUH), approximately 5.4 percent of pregnant women aged 15–44 years reported using illicit drugs in the past month while 9 percent of pregnant women reported current alcohol use and 3 percent reported heavy or binge drinking (Substance Abuse and Mental Health Services Administration, 2014).

In 2016, the Comprehensive Addiction and Recovery Act (CARA) included an amendment to the Child Abuse Prevention and Treatment Act (CAPTA) to collect and report the number of infants with prenatal substance exposure, thereby improving our understanding of rates of prenatal infant drug exposure. The National Child Abuse and Neglect Data System first began collecting these data in 2018, and based on reports for that year from 45 states, approximately 30,000 children were identified as SEIs, which represents 4 percent of all victims for that year (U.S. DHHS, 2020).

What are the consequences of prenatal exposure to substances on the subsequent health of the child? This, of course, is a very difficult question to answer. The quantity of the substance that pregnant women consume and the timing of consumption (i.e., during first, second, or third trimester), for example, may determine whether any negative effects manifest in their infants. Maternal substance use also often occurs in association with polydrug use and poor maternal nutrition, so it is difficult to determine which variable is responsible for negative developmental outcomes. Results of such studies are also difficult to interpret when researchers do not consider the influence of environment on infants' development subsequent to birth. Recent research findings suggest that the postnatal environment influences the developmental outcomes of SEIs. Characteristics of an SEI's environment that contribute to negative developmental outcomes include high levels of parental stress, continued parental substance abuse, and postnatal drug exposure (Keegan, Parva, Finnegan, Gerson, & Belden, 2010). For example, a child may be exposed to cigarette or marijuana smoke in utero as well as in the environment after birth when the mother continues to smoke.

An increasing number of studies have demonstrated a relationship between prenatal substance exposure and pregnancy complications, infant drug withdrawal, and negative child developmental outcomes (Brickner, 2019; CRC Health Group, 2016; Holbrook & Nguyen, 2015). The most compelling evidence comes from studies that have examined the effects of fetal exposure to alcohol. Research has consistently demonstrated that children born of mothers who consumed large quantities of alcohol during pregnancy face definitive and irreversible effects, including growth deficiency, anomalies of brain structure and function, mental retardation, and abnormalities of the head and face (Popova et al., 2016). One emerging concern of opiate abuse is **neonatal abstinence syndrome (NAS)**.

(Continued)

(Continued)

NAS refers to a constellation of drug withdrawal symptoms, such as irritability, restlessness, tremors, weight loss, and poor feeding and sleep patterns, shortly after birth due to drug exposure in utero (D. Wilson & Shiffman, 2015). Although NAS is treatable, there is some evidence of longer-term effects of opioid abuse including risk for cognitive and motor delays through the preschool years (Holbrook & Nguyen, 2015; R. Hunt, Tzioumi, Collins, & Jeffery, 2008). Studies of maternal use of cocaine demonstrate similar outcomes suggestive of withdrawal in addition to direct impacts on birth weight and head size (Keegan et al., 2010; Shankaran et al., 2007). There is also evidence that prenatal cocaine exposure is associated with arousal, attention, and response inhibition as well as behavioral problems, at least through age 7 (e.g., Bada et al., 2007; Behnke & Smith, 2013). The possible long-term impact of prenatal exposure to these substances is less clear.

In response to the problem of prenatal substance exposure, many have called for substance testing of newborns, asserting that such testing could identify infants at risk for developmental problems. Several problems are associated with infant substance screening, however. Drawbacks to both universal testing (testing of all newborn infants) and targeted testing (testing of specific groups of infants identified as high risk) include financial costs, potential avoidance of medical care by pregnant substance users, limited ability of some tests to detect certain substances, and the potential for discriminatory screening practices (Anthony, Austin, & Cormier, 2010; Burke, 2007; National Institute on Drug Abuse, 2018). The overwhelming majority of newborn infants exposed to drugs and alcohol prenatally are not tested (Anthony et al., 2010; S. Christian, 2004).

Some observers argue that substance-abusing pregnant women should be held criminally liable for any ill effects their substance abuse causes their children. Punishment could include legal sanctions, court-ordered treatment, and removal of the infant from the home. The **Keeping Children and Families Safe Act** of 2003, an amendment to CAPTA, actually required

states to report infants who were born exposed to illegal substance abuse or who exhibited withdrawal symptoms. The act also included eligibility requirements for child welfare funding to encourage states to create policies requiring Child Protective Services (CPS) notification of infants prenatally exposed to illegal drugs (P.L. 108–36). The problem with the act, as Burke (2007) notes, is that although "states are to have protocols requiring reporting of positive tests, there is no mandate on testing . . . so if hospitals do not test any newborns or their mothers, none would be identified as substance-exposed, and there would be no one to report" (p. 1504). Another problem with the original act is that it does not address the role of alcohol exposure (Anthony et al., 2010), although a 2010 amendment provided for inclusion of infants affected by fetal alcohol spectrum disorder. Some states explicitly define infants born with positive drug toxicology as abused or neglected. In the United States, 14 states and the District of Columbia include substance exposure in their definitions of child abuse or neglect, and approximately 19 states and the District of Columbia have specific reporting procedures for infants who show evidence at birth of having been exposed to drugs, alcohol, or other controlled substances (Child Welfare Information Gateway, 2016b, 2019b).

One reason for the lack of uniformity in states' responses to prenatal neglect is the ongoing debate surrounding the relative significance of the rights of the unborn child versus the rights of the pregnant woman. Another source of confusion is the ambiguity of some states' statutes concerning the circumstances under which a pregnant woman can be legally sanctioned for causing possible harm to her fetus. A number of scholars have questioned the use of punitive responses toward substance-abusing pregnant women on practical, constitutional, therapeutic, and empirical grounds (e.g., Schroedel & Fiber, 2001).

Perhaps in response to such criticisms, more recent policy focuses on meeting the *treatment needs* of *both* infant and caregiver. The Keeping Children and Families Safe Act of 2003 included a requirement for the development of a **Plan of Safe Care** for infants identified as being born impacted by illegal substance abuse or withdrawal symptoms. Safe Care plans call for the provision of services and supports to ensure the safety and well-being of an infant affected by substance abuse, withdrawal, or fetal alcohol spectrum disorder (National Center on Substance Abuse and Child Welfare, 2018, p. 12). In 2016, a CAPTA amendment added a requirement that a Plan of Safe Care address not only the safety and treatment needs of infants impacted by substance use disorder, but also the treatment needs of the affected family or caregiver. Indeed, these recent changes in CAPTA are intended to strengthen an "approach that is grounded in early identification and intervention to keep infants safe and strengthen families by ensuring parents/caregivers have support and access to services to address their substance use disorder and other challenges" (Casey Family Programs, 2019, p. 9).

being raped, robbed, mugged, or murdered; and property damage. These researchers found only moderate to modest correlations among the three subtypes of neglect. In addition, findings indicated that the three subtypes of neglect were differentially related to child outcomes. Other studies have confirmed the independent nature of various subtypes of neglect (Dubowitz et al., 2012). These findings suggest that subtypes may represent unique dimensions of child neglect and that recognizing various subtypes of neglect might be helpful to furthering our understanding of child neglect and intervening in the problem.

Estimates of Child Neglect

Child neglect is the most frequently reported and substantiated form of child maltreatment. Approximately 61 percent of all child maltreatment cases reported to CPS in 2018 were for child neglect, compared to approximately 11 percent for physical abuse and 7 percent for sexual abuse (U.S. DHHS, 2020). In the NIS-4, child neglect comprised 61 percent of identified maltreatment according to the NIS harm standard and 77 percent of maltreatment according to the NIS endangerment standard (Sedlak et al., 2010). Between NIS-1 and NIS-3, rates of child neglect increased from 1.6 to 19.9 per 1,000 children (Sedlak & Broadhurst, 1996). Although child neglect has shown a small overall decline since NIS-3, declines in child neglect have trailed behind the declines for child physical and sexual abuse and shown mixed patterns (i.e., child neglect has declined in some states but increased in others; L. Jones, Finkelhor, & Halter, 2012). These trends are discussed further in Chapter 11.

The second National Survey of Children's Exposure to Violence (NatSCEV II) measured self-reported child neglect in a nationally representative sample of nearly 4,500 U.S. children ages 1 month to 17 years in 2011 (Finkelhor, Turner, Shattuck, & Hamby, 2015). In this study, child neglect was defined as parents' inability to look after a child (due to drug or alcohol abuse or psychological problems), child abandonment, presence in the home of persons who made the child fearful, unsafe or unsanitary conditions in the home, and failure to attend to the child's cleanliness or grooming. Rates of child neglect were among the highest when comparing all forms of child maltreatment, with rates of approximately 7 percent for all children and youth in the past year, and 22.3 percent for 14- to 17-year-olds in their lifetimes. The NatSCEV III, conducted three years later in 2014, showed slightly lower rates for neglect of approximately 5 percent for all children and youth in the past year, and 18.4 percent for 14- to 17-year-olds in their lifetimes, although this decrease was not statistically significant (Finkelhor, Turner, Shattuck, & Hamby, 2015).

Other studies have examined estimates of different forms of child neglect. Straus and colleagues used the Parent–Child Conflict Tactics Scales to estimate child neglect in a national random sample of parents (Straus, Hamby, Finkelhor, Moore, & Runyan, 1998). Child neglect was defined by several questions that focused on lack of parental supervision, nutritional neglect, alcohol abuse, medical neglect, and emotional neglect. Of parents responding to this survey, 27 percent reported engaging in some form of child neglect at least once during the past year. In this sample, 11 percent of the parents reported that they were unable to ensure that their children obtained the food they needed, and approximately 2 percent reported an inability to care for their children adequately because of problem drinking. The most common form of neglect, reported by approximately 20 percent of parents, was "supervisory neglect," which the authors defined as leaving a child alone even when the parent thought an adult should be present.

Consider, for example, Auwin Dargin, a young father who was charged with child abuse after passersby noticed an unattended baby girl crying in a parked car in a California city. The father left his 9-month-old daughter in the car for nearly an hour while he paid a visit to a strip club for lap dances two blocks away. Dargin pled no contest and was sentenced to 10 days in county jail, five years' probation, 52 weeks of parenting classes, and 45 days of community service (Judge, 2017; Los Angeles County District Attorney's Office, 2017). Other researchers have confirmed that supervisory neglect appears to be one of the most frequently reported subtypes of child neglect (Mennen et al., 2010; Vanderminden et al., 2019).

RISK FACTORS ASSOCIATED WITH CHILD NEGLECT

What are the specific characteristics and traits of neglecting adults and their children? Although the studies we describe are limited by various methodological weaknesses described in previous chapters on other forms of child maltreatment, their findings nonetheless shed some light on the general characteristics of children who are neglected and their parents (for reviews, see Giardino, Lyn, & Giardino, 2019; Mulder, Kuiper, van der Put, Stams, & Assink, 2019).

Characteristics of Neglected Children

For obvious reasons, the risk for child neglect declines with age. Older children are less dependent on parents and are therefore far less vulnerable. Data from the NIS-4 indicate that the incidence rate for 15- to 17-year-olds was 8.7 per 1,000 children, compared to 15.3 or more per 1,000 for 3- to 8-year-olds (Sedlak et al., 2010). Children under 3 years of age appear to be the most vulnerable and to suffer the most significant consequences (Scannapieco & Connell-Carrick, 2002; U.S. DHHS, 2020). Race may be a factor, with black children more frequently reported (18 per 1,000) than white children (12 per 1,000) or Hispanic children (10 per 1,000) (Sedlak et al., 2010). However, as we note in the next section, poverty is a significant risk factor for child neglect, and there is evidence that racial disproportionality in child neglect among black and white children is largely attributable to differences in poverty (H. Kim & Drake, 2018). Few differences appear between sexes in rates of child neglect (Sedlak et al., 2010).

Characteristics of Neglecting Parents

Birth parents account for 91 percent of reported cases, and the majority (87%) are identified as mothers (Sedlak et al., 2010). The higher proportion of females reported for neglect likely reflects the fact that mothers spend more time with children than fathers, as well as a general social attitude that mothers, rather than fathers, are responsible for meeting the needs of their children. Even in two-parent families it is not uncommon for only mothers (and not fathers) to be labeled as neglectful (Azar, Povilaitis, Lauretti, & Pouquette, 1998). In general, the research suggests that younger parents are, on average, more neglectful, with teen mothers being at especially high risk (J. Brown, Cohen, Johnson, & Salzinger, 1998; Fantuzzo, Perlman, & Dobbins, 2011).

A number of researchers have examined the psychological and behavioral characteristics of neglecting parents. Neglecting parents generally interact less with their children, and when they do interact, the interactions are less positive (e.g., Stith et al., 2009). For example, they engage in less verbal instruction and play behavior with their children, show their children less nonverbal affection, and exhibit less warmth in discussions with their children. They are also less empathetic, more angry, exhibit more stress about parenting, and are more likely to engage in verbal aggression and spanking of their children (e.g., Stith et al., 2009; Polansky, Gaudin, & Kilpatrick, 1992; Slack et al., 2011). Like other forms of child maltreatment, there is some evidence that neglecting parents are neglectful because they received inadequate parenting in their own childhoods (Mulder et al., 2018; Widom & Massey, 2015).

Not surprisingly, neglecting mothers also report more personal problems such as depressive symptoms, impulsivity, low self-esteem, low empathy, and chronic health problems than do nonneglecting mothers (Christensen et al., 1994; Éthier, Lacharite, & Couture, 1995; Polansky et al., 1992; Slack et al., 2011). Others have evaluated specific psychiatric symptoms and diagnoses such as depressive disorders and obsessive compulsive disorder and found that neglecting parents in their sample were more likely to receive such diagnoses than were nonneglecting parents (Chaffin, Kelleher, & Hollenberg, 1996; Mulder et al., 2018; Rahman, Lovel, Bunn, Iqbal, & Harrington, 2004). Other studies have found that a history of antisocial behavior/criminal offending and health problems is associated with neglectful parenting behaviors (Mulder et al., 2018).

There is also mounting evidence that substance abuse contributes to child neglect. Slack and colleagues (2011) identified parental drug use as a significant risk factor for child neglect. In addition, a study conducted by Chaffin and colleagues (1996) indicated that neglecting parents were more likely to receive a diagnosis of substance abuse than were nonneglecting parents. According to a report released by the National Center on Addiction and Substance Abuse at Columbia University (2005), parents who abused alcohol and drugs were 4 times more likely to neglect their children than were parents who did not abuse such substances.

Social Ecological Factors

Low socioeconomic status (SES) is the most powerful predictor of neglect; it is more powerfully predictive of neglect than of any other form of child maltreatment (Sedlak et al., 2010). Studies consistently indicate that rates of neglect are higher in families characterized by unemployment, social welfare, limited access to doctors, and trouble paying rent and utility bills (Fantuzzo et al., 2011; Slack et al., 2011; Slack, Holl, Altenbernd, McDaniel, & Stevens, 2003). It was clear that the family in the opening case history had financial troubles, for example, as neither parent was employed and the parents sent Will and Mark out into the neighborhood to beg for money. Various correlates of low SES, including single-parent families and large family size, are also predictive of child neglect (Sedlak et al., 2010). Children who have been neglected are also more likely to be homeless at some point in their lives (Fantuzzo et al., 2011). Some speculate that the empirical link between SES and neglect reflects, at least in part, a reporting bias. The behaviors of the poor and disadvantaged tend to be more visible, so perhaps their neglectful behavior is merely more likely to be noticed. Research suggests, however, that reporting bias cannot explain away the class link (Chaffin et al., 1996).

Other social factors such as family functioning and a family's level of community integration and social support may also play a role in child neglect. Adolescents who are neglected, for example, perceive their families as being less cohesive compared to adolescents who are not neglected, and both adolescents who are neglected and their mothers are more likely to report high levels of stress compared to their counterparts (Williamson, Borduin, & Howe, 1991). Others have found that strained parent–child interactions and domestic violence are associated with child neglect (Hartley, 2012b; Slack et al., 2011).

Neglecting mothers are less involved in social networks, participate less in social and community activities, describe themselves as more lonely, and also perceive themselves to be less supported and involved in the lives of others (Polansky, Ammons, & Gaudin, 1985; Williamson et al., 1991). In a fascinating study that controlled for SES, Polansky, Gaudin, Ammons, and Davis (1985) interviewed a sample of neglecting parents who were receiving welfare benefits as well as a sample of nonneglecting families who were also receiving welfare benefits. A third sample included the next-door neighbors of the neglecting families. They found that neglecting mothers viewed their neighborhoods as less supportive than did both their next-door neighbors and the comparison mothers.

Protective Factors and Resilience

As we have noted in previous chapters, there are various risk factors that can increase the likelihood of both the occurrence of various forms of child maltreatment and the likelihood of various negative psychological outcomes. Likewise, there are various resilience factors that, when present, might serve a protective function. Slack and colleagues (2011) identified two **protective factors** in their analysis of findings across three large-scale probabilistic longitudinal samples of low-income families. One of their most robust findings indicated that across studies, higher levels of self-efficacy were associated with lower rates of self-reported or CPS reports of child neglect. In addition, involvement of parents in their child's activities also served as a protective factor against the occurrence of child neglect.

Others have suggested that positive relationships might function as a protective factor. Reynolds and Ou (2003), for example, studied a large sample of high-risk children and found that high-quality day care served as a protective factor for the children. Others have identified positive relationships with both teachers and peers as a protective factor for high-risk children (Elder & Conger, 2000; Hamre & Pianta, 2001). Studies examining the potential protective role of relationships have not yet been carried out specifically with child neglect samples.

CONSEQUENCES ASSOCIATED WITH CHILD NEGLECT

Although considerable research has evaluated the negative consequences associated with other forms of child maltreatment, relatively little has examined the unique effects of child neglect. The limited research in this area is surprising given that child neglect is the most frequently reported form of child maltreatment and can have serious consequences for children. Indeed, some speculate that child neglect may have differential outcomes compared to other forms of maltreatment (Humphreys & Zeanah, 2015) and actually may be associated with more serious harm than either physical or sexual abuse (e.g., Erickson & Egeland, 2002; Sroufe, Egeland, Carlson, & Collins, 2005).

Similar to our discussions of outcomes in earlier chapters, it is helpful to distinguish between the immediate impact of neglect on children and the effects that endure into adulthood. Most studies that have examined the effects associated with child neglect have consistently uncovered several problems associated with child neglect, including social difficulties, cognitive deficits, emotional and behavioral problems, and physical consequences (Gardner, Thomas, & Erskine, 2019; Lippard & Nemeroff, 2020; Twardosz & Lutzker, 2010; S. Tyler, Allison, & Winsler, 2006). Many of these problems appear to be somewhat unique to child neglect when compared with problems associated with physical abuse (Hildyard & Wolfe, 2002). Table 5.2 provides a summary of the possible negative effects that have been found to be associated with child neglect.

The Immediate Impact of Child Neglect

The most immediate and tragic *physical consequence* of child neglect is, of course, death. In 2018, 1,770 children died as a result of child abuse and neglect in the United States,

TABLE 5.2 ■ Possible Negative Effects Associated With Child Neglect	
Effects	**Examples**
Social and attachment difficulties	Disturbed parent–child attachment (e.g., anxious and disorganized)
	Disturbed parent–child interactions (e.g., child is passive and withdrawn; parent exhibits low sensitivity to and involvement with child)
	Disturbed peer interactions (e.g., deficits in prosocial behavior, social withdrawal, isolation, few reciprocal friendships)
Cognitive and academic deficits	Receptive and expressive language deficits
	Low academic achievement
	Grade repetitions
	Low academic engagement
	Deficits in overall intelligence
	Low level of creativity and flexibility in problem solving
	Deficits in language comprehension and verbal abilities

Effects	Examples
Emotional and behavioral problems	Apathy and withdrawal
	Low self-esteem
	Ineffective coping
	Difficulty recognizing and discriminating emotion
	Negative affect (e.g., anger, frustration, depression)
	Physical and verbal aggression
	Violent delinquency and other antisocial behavior
	Attention problems
	Post-traumatic stress symptoms (PTSD)
	Conduct problems and noncompliance
	Personality disorder symptoms
	Psychiatric symptoms (e.g., anxiety, depression, PTSD)
	Internalizing and externalizing emotional and behavior problems
Physical consequences	Death
	Failure to thrive
	Obesity
Long-term consequences	Cognitive deficits (e.g., low IQ scores and reading ability)
	Illegal behavior (e.g., delinquency, prostitution, violent assault)
	Psychiatric disorders (e.g., dysthymia, PTSD, major depressive disorder, anxiety disorders, disruptive disorders, antisocial personality disorder)
	Trauma symptoms
	Suicidal ideation
	Substance use
	Violent behavior

Sources: A representative but not exhaustive list of sources for the information displayed in this table includes the following: Bland, Lambie, & Best, 2018; Di Sante, Sylvestre, Bouchard, & Leblond, 2019; Dubowitz et al., 2019; Erickson & Egeland, 2002; Degli Esposti, Pereira, Humphreys, Sale, & Bowes, 2020; Fantuzzo, Perlman, & Dobbins, 2011; Gardner, Thomas, & Erskine, 2019; R. Gilbert, Kemp, et al., 2009; R. Gilbert, Widom, et al., 2009; Hecker, Boettcher, Landolt, & Hermenau, 2019; Kotch et al., 2008; McGuigan, Luchette, & Atterholt, 2018; Mersky & Reynolds, 2007; Milot, Éthier, St-Laurant, & Provost, 2010; Nelson, Klumparendt, Doebler, & Ehring, 2017; Petrenko, Friend, Garrido, Taussig, & Culhane, 2012; Sroufe, Egeland, Carlson, & Collins, 2005; C. Thomas, Hyponnen, & Power, 2008; Tyler, Allison, & Winsler, 2006; Twardosz & Lutzker, 2010; Vanderminden et al., 2019; Villodas et al., 2015; R. Whitaker, Phillips, Orzol, & Burdette, 2007.

for a rate of 2.39 children per 100,000 children (U.S. DHHS, 2020). These children were disproportionately very young (71% were under 3) and victims of neglect rather than physical abuse (73%; U.S. DHHS, 2020).

Another tragic physical consequence often associated with neglect in infants is **failure to thrive (FTT)**, a syndrome characterized by marked retardation or cessation of growth during the first three years of life (Burge, Louis, & Giardino, 2019). This syndrome develops in a significant number of children as a result of child neglect involving inadequate nutrition and disturbed social interactions (Block & Krebs, 2005). Others have identified some forms of childhood obesity as a physical symptom of child neglect (e.g., Harper, 2014; A. M. Jackson et al., 2015).

In an attempt to identify the more subtle effects of neglect, the Minnesota Mother–Child Project followed a sample of children who were *physically neglected* (e.g., caregivers failed to provide adequate physical care or protection for their children) as well as those who were *emotionally neglected* (e.g., caregivers exhibited emotional detachment and unresponsiveness to their children's needs for care). The researchers then compared these children with a comparison group of children who were not maltreated for several years—extending into adolescence. The results of the Minnesota Mother–Child Project and similar developmentally sensitive studies suggest that the experience of child neglect results in significant developmental problems that are cumulative across development, and these problems manifest similarly across developmental stages (Hildyard & Wolfe, 2002; Sroufe et al., 2005).

One of the most frequently cited problems associated with child neglect is difficulty in *social adjustment*. A number of studies, for example, suggest a relationship between neglect and disturbed patterns of infant–caretaker attachment. Investigators have observed mother–infant pairs during several interactions including feeding and play situations, a stressful situation in which a stranger was introduced into the environment, and a problem-solving task. Results indicated that, compared with children in a control group, a significantly higher proportion of children who were neglected displayed an **anxious attachment style** (e.g., overly dependent, clingy, and prone to crying) at both 12 and 18 months, and the social difficulties these children experienced continued throughout elementary school (Erickson & Egeland, 2002; Sroufe et al., 2005). In addition to anxious attachment styles, child neglect is associated with a disorganized attachment style, as described in Chapter 3 (Baer & Martinez, 2006; Hildyard & Wolfe, 2002), which is a form of attachment characterized by a lack of a coherent style or pattern for coping. Children who are neglected also show deficits in interactions and social adjustment with peers, with many exhibiting more socially withdrawn behavior, decreased prosocial behavior, greater conflict with friends, and fewer reciprocated friendships than children who are not neglected (e.g., Bolger, Patterson, & Kupersmidt, 1998; Crittenden, 1992; Prino & Peyrot, 1994).

Child neglect also impacts *intellectual ability* and *academic achievement*. Findings from a large group of studies comparing infants, children, and adolescents who were neglected with matched comparisons have indicated that victims of neglect show deficits in language abilities, academic skills, intelligence, and problem-solving skills (e.g., Di Sante, Sylvestre, Bouchard, & Leblond, 2019; Erickson & Egeland, 2002; Slack et al., 2003; Wodarski, Kurtz, Gaudin, & Howing, 1990). Fantuzzo and colleagues (2011) examined academic achievement and engagement of 11,835 second graders enrolled in public schools. This study was unique in that the researchers examined the impact of physical abuse and neglect as well as the timing of the child maltreatment (pre-kindergarten vs. post-kindergarten). The researchers controlled for a number of other risk factors known to correlate with academic achievement. Children who experienced neglect prior to kindergarten were 31 percent more likely to have poor outcomes on a standardized reading assessment, 42 percent more likely to have poor language outcomes, and 35 percent more likely to have poor science outcomes compared to their peers who were not neglected. Findings related to academic engagement indicated that experiences of child neglect, both prior to kindergarten and after kindergarten, were significantly associated with each of the academic engagement outcomes, including poor classroom learning behaviors, poor social skills, and low attendance.

Victims of child neglect also frequently exhibit *emotional and behavioral difficulties.* Several studies have found that both psychological and physical neglect are associated with both internalizing and externalizing symptomatology (Petrenko, Friend, Garrido, Taussig, & Culhane, 2012; Villodas et al., 2015). Studies have also demonstrated that neglecting mothers are more likely than nonneglecting mothers to rate their children as having behavioral problems in general (Erickson & Egeland, 2002). Researchers have also documented differences in specific behavioral and emotional problems between adolescent, school-age, and preschool children who are neglected and not neglected (e.g., J. Johnson, Smailes, Cohen, Brown, & Bernstein, 2000; Manly, Kim, Rogosch, & Cicchetti, 2001; Toth, Cicchetti, Macfie, Maughan, & Vanmeenen, 2000).

Long-Term Outcomes

Much of what is known about the long-term effects associated with child neglect comes from the prospective longitudinal research of Cathy Spatz Widom and her colleagues. Recall from earlier discussions of Widom's work in Chapters 2 and 3 that she has been following a large number of child abuse and neglect victims ($N = 908$ in the original sample), along with a sample of matched comparisons ($N = 667$ in the original sample) for almost 50 years. Over much of the course of their study, the investigators have not distinguished between individuals with histories of physical abuse and those with histories of neglect, yet the findings are powerful in demonstrating a connection between child maltreatment (either physical abuse or neglect, or both) and deficits in cognitive abilities (e.g., lower intelligence test scores and reading ability), increased illegal behavior (e.g., delinquency, criminal behavior, and violent criminal behavior), and increased likelihood of running away from home (R. Gilbert, Kemp, et al., 2009; R. Gilbert, Widom, et al., 2009; J. Kaufman & Widom, 1999; Perez & Widom, 1994; Widom, 1989; Widom & Kuhns, 1996). Other more recent studies have corroborated these findings (e.g., Degli Esposti et al., 2020).

Other studies investigating the long-term effects of child neglect have examined the relationship between maltreatment in childhood and personality and psychiatric disorders in adulthood. Widom and colleagues once again provide much of the evidence, which links child neglect with **dysthymia**, **antisocial personality disorder**, and alcohol problems in adults, although once the researchers controlled for other stressful life events, they found that childhood maltreatment had little impact on mental health outcome (Horwitz, Widom, McLaughlin, & White, 2001). Widom (1999) also found evidence of lifetime incidence of post-traumatic stress disorder in her sample of adults who had experienced child neglect specifically. Additional prospective longitudinal studies have also confirmed the presence of various psychiatric diagnoses in adults with histories of child neglect. P. Cohen, Brown, and Smailes (2001), for example, assessed mental disorders from early childhood to adulthood in a community sample of individuals who were later identified as neglected by official reports. Findings indicated that adults with official records of child neglect exhibited elevated symptoms of disruptive disorders and major depressive disorder relative to adults in the normative sample. The cases of child neglect in this study, however, showed some partial remission in symptoms from adolescence to adulthood.

Recall from Chapter 3 that one topic that has increasingly become the focus of research attention is the adult health risks associated with child maltreatment. The Adverse Childhood Experiences (ACE) Study is a population-based effort to assess associations between adverse childhood experiences such as child maltreatment, including child neglect, and health and well-being in later life (Centers for Disease Control and Prevention, n.d.a). The ACE Study and the role of traumatic childhood experiences are described in Box 5.2.

BOX 5.2
ACES RESEARCH

The original Adverse Childhood Experiences (ACE) Study, supported by the Centers for Disease Control and Prevention (CDC) and Kaiser Permanente, is a population-based effort to assess associations between adverse, or stressful, childhood experiences and health and well-being in later life (CDC, n.d.a). The original study utilized survey questions that asked adult participants to respond to a series of questions and indicate whether or not they experienced various stressful childhood experiences during the first 18 years of their lives (Felitti et al., 1998):

Did a parent or other adult in the household often . . . Swear at you, insult you, put you down, or humiliate you? or Act in a way that made you afraid that you might be physically hurt?

Did a parent or other adult in the household often . . . Push, grab, slap, or throw something at you? or Ever hit you so hard that you had marks or were injured?

Did an adult or person at least 5 years older than you ever . . . Touch or fondle you or have you touch their body in a sexual way? or Try to or actually have oral, anal, or vaginal sex with you?

Did you often feel that . . . No one in your family loved you or thought you were important or special? or Your family didn't look out for each other, feel close to each other, or support each other?

Did you often feel that . . . You didn't have enough to eat, had to wear dirty clothes, and had no one to protect you? or Your parents were too drunk or high to take care of you or take you to the doctor if you needed it?

Were your parents ever separated or divorced?

Was your mother or stepmother: Often pushed, grabbed, slapped, or had something thrown at her? or Sometimes or often kicked, bitten, hit with a fist, or hit with something hard? or Ever repeatedly hit over at least a few minutes or threatened with a gun or knife?

Did you live with anyone who was a problem drinker or alcoholic or who used street drugs?

Was a household member depressed or mentally ill or did a household member attempt suicide?

Did a household member go to prison?

As you can see, these questions focused on various child maltreatment experiences including physical, sexual, and psychological abuse/maltreatment (including witnessing IPV) and neglect as well as serious mental health and legal troubles within the household such as substance use, mental illness and suicide, and incarceration. Results from the ACE Study indicated that experiencing multiple adverse childhood experiences (ACEs) was strongly correlated with a number of negative health behaviors and outcomes such as less physical activity, tobacco use, depression, and chronic health conditions (Felitti et al., 1998). In addition, those with multiple ACEs experienced a 4- to 12-fold increase in alcoholism, drug abuse, depression, and suicide attempts compared to those with no ACEs in their childhood history.

Numerous ACEs research studies over the past 20 years have found similar findings suggesting that ACEs are associated with both negative physical health outcomes (including most major causes of death) and especially mental health problems, and that the more ACEs to which children are exposed, the greater the negative outcomes in adulthood (see Kochanek, Murphy, Xu, & Arias, 2017; Petruccelli, Davis, & Berman, 2019; Wang et al., 2019). In addition, research suggests that experiencing ACEs in childhood is relatively common. One recent study using a 25-state telephone survey found that approximately 61 percent of adults experienced at least one type of ACE while approximately 16 percent experienced four or more ACEs (Merrick et al., 2019).

In an effort to prevent ACEs, some researchers have examined how positive childhood experiences (e.g., high parental education, two-parent family composition, residential stability, familial warmth), sometimes referred to as counter-ACEs, might serve as protective factors and diminish the risks associated with ACEs. Such positive experiences may help build resilience in children and, as a result, help them to withstand stressful experiences (J. Poole, Dobson, & Pusch, 2017; Sege et al., 2017). Crandall et al. (2019), for example, found that counter-ACEs protected against poor adult health and led to better adult wellness. Other researchers have suggested various resiliency interventions that use a psychoeducational approach and attempt to increase active coping, build strengths, enhance cognitive flexibility, and increase social supports (Chandler, Roberts, & Chiodo, 2015). Other interventions include parenting interventions to teach parents about ACEs and how to help children cope, mindfulness interventions to reduce mental health symptoms and improve health behaviors, and educating health care professionals about screening for ACEs and then linking families to appropriate community resources (Dubowitz, Feigelman, Lane, & Kim, 2009; Ortiz & Sibinga, 2017; Petruccelli et al., 2019).

INTERVENTION AND PREVENTION OF CHILD NEGLECT

Most intervention and prevention strategies address child maltreatment generally, and are not uniquely focused on child neglect (for a review, see National Research Council, 2014). Indeed, many of the approaches described in previous chapters (e.g., interventions with adults to enhance parenting skills, interventions with children to reduce effects associated with maltreatment) have been suggested for child neglect. As a result, in this chapter we focus on additional approaches not discussed previously and/or strategies that have specifically targeted child neglect. The discussion here focuses on formal programs and strategies; personal responses to address the problem are included in Chapter 11.

The Role of Child Protective Services

One element that we have not discussed in much detail up to this point is the various issues surrounding child welfare policy in the United States. Because child neglect is by far the most commonly reported form of child maltreatment, this chapter seems like the appropriate one to engage the reader in this conversation. As noted in Chapter 1, federal and state laws provide for the protection of children who are at risk for child abuse or neglect via a division within state departments of social services. These state-level services are typically referred to as Child Protective Services, or CPS. (Some states use other names, such as Children and Family Services, or simply Social Services.) As noted previously, CPS agencies investigate alleged child maltreatment and respond to substantiated findings. In some cases families receive services while the child remains in the home; in other cases the CPS response is to remove the child from the home and place the child in some form of out-of-home care.

Removing a child from the home is never a desirable option, so ideally the goal of CPS is to preserve families *and* protect children. The controversy surrounding the effectiveness of the **family preservation** goal of CPS is far from settled, and bears significantly on the ongoing debate concerning family reunification as a primary goal of child protection (see Box 5.3). In more recent years, in addition to child protection and family preservation, federal child welfare policy has added an emphasis on child well-being, providing an impetus for the provision of mental health services (Zeanah & Humphreys, 2018; see also U.S. DHHS, 2012).

CPS has long been criticized as a failing system due to a number of identified problems in the implementation of its goals. The average response time from report to investigation, for example, is 92 hours or 3.8 days, a lapse in time many find unacceptable (U.S. DHHS, 2020). In addition, findings from both the United States and Canada suggest that CPS investigates only approximately one-fourth to one-half of children reported for abuse, under even the most stringent definition of maltreatment (Fallon et al., 2010; Sedlak & Broadhurst, 1996).

There is also some evidence that the services provided to children and parents are often lacking or inappropriate to their particular needs. CPS offered no post-investigative services at all, for example, in almost half (42%) of substantiated cases in 2018 (U.S. DHHS, 2020). As noted previously, it is well established that children who are neglected are at greater risk for various emotional, behavioral, and developmental problems, which may require specific services (Casanueva et al., 2012). In one study, however, 50 percent of the children with demonstrated mental health needs did not receive services, and 84 percent with demonstrated educational needs did not receive needed services (Petrenko, Culhane, Garrido, & Taussig, 2011). Understanding why CPS sometimes fails children is, no doubt, a complicated matter. Many would argue that CPS is woefully underfunded, and that systemic inadequacies mostly stem from societal indifference. Data from the 2008–2011 National Survey of Child and Adolescent Well-Being II, for example, indicated a commitment by caseworkers to children's well-being as 80 percent of child welfare caseworkers reported feeling very responsible for the behavioral health management of children (Jolles, Givens, Lombardi, & Cuddeback, 2019). In other words, most caseworkers really care about the welfare of children.

In the most tragic and most highly publicized cases, caseworker error is the most immediate reason for the system's failure (Jones & Kaufman, 2003). Consider, for example, the death of Anthony Avalos reported in various news sources that claim that CPS failed this young boy (e.g., Bloom, 2019). In 2018, paramedics found 10-year-old Anthony in his family's apartment in full cardiac arrest, with traumatic brain injuries, and bruises and abrasions all over his body. The boy died in the hospital after enduring several days of torture while his siblings were forced to not only watch, but also participate. The boy's mother and her boyfriend have been charged with murder and torture, and prosecutors are seeking the death penalty (Bloom, 2019). According to news reports, Anthony was just 4 years old when Children and Family Services investigated the family for child abuse and neglect. Reports showed that Anthony had endured beatings with a cord and belt, starvation and force-feedings, having hot sauce poured in his mouth, being locked up, and being dangled upside down from a staircase. The agency was involved in Anthony's case since 2013—with at least 16 different reports—removing Anthony from his home temporarily but ultimately returning him to his family when his caseworkers believed reunification was appropriate. Anthony's family filed a $50 million lawsuit against Children and Family Services for wrongful death (Bloom, 2019).

Some of the information presented here may read as a criticism of the child welfare system as unable to provide adequate protection and services for children who have been reported as victims of child maltreatment. However, there are several factors that contribute to the difficulties the child welfare system faces in providing protection and services to victims. Mandatory reporting laws (see Chapter 1) and public education about child maltreatment have led to consistent increases in child abuse reports and resulting increases in CPS workloads. For example, during 2018, CPS agencies received an estimated 4.3 million referrals, which represented an approximate 16.4 percent increase since 2014 (U.S. DHHS, 2020). For many child welfare caseworkers, large caseloads and excessive workloads make it difficult to effectively serve children and families (Child Welfare Information Gateway, 2016a). Additionally, caseworkers face other challenges such as inadequate training and preparation, high caseworker turnover, and insufficient supervision (see Schelbe, Radey, & Panisch, 2017).

In contrast to those critical of CPS, others see the missteps by CPS as an inevitability. According to a medical director of a health center with years of experience working with children who are abused, quoted in the article about Anthony Avalos's death, many children are victims of failed oversight by child welfare agencies: "They fall through the cracks of an overworked protective service system . . . Protective Services is underfunded, understaffed, undertrained, undercompensated and expected to do society's work on a scale which is probably impossible" (Ramgopal, 2018). Indeed, CPS workers are charged with a diversity of tasks including investigating reports of child maltreatment, providing needed services to victims, protecting children, and providing support for families. CPS workers attempt to do all these things in a highly stressful environment. Indeed, many of the decisions that child welfare workers must make *on a daily basis* can have significant consequences for children and their families. In addition to working under emotionally stressful circumstances, child welfare workers are doing so for very little compensation (see also Chapter 11). According to the most recent U.S. Bureau of Labor Statistics (2018) numbers, the average annual salary of people who work in the Child, Family, and School Social Workers category, which would include child welfare services, was $49,760 for those working in individual and family services, which is more than $12,000 less than those working in elementary and secondary schools. These circumstances are likely to lead to low staff morale and high turnover rates.

Several researchers have argued for a radical change in approach to child welfare reform. Bartholet (2015), for example, has argued that not only does the United States need to strengthen the CPS system through increased resources (to monitor parents, provide more parents with more rehabilitative services, and enhance protection of children through removal where necessary), but current approaches are proposing false solutions by avoiding the real causes of child maltreatment. According to these policy reformers, certain policies and services are doomed to failure because they don't focus on the true problems producing child maltreatment, which are "rooted in poverty, unemployment, inadequate housing, substance abuse, and severe and persistent mental illness" (Littell, 1997, p. 36).

BOX 5.3
FAMILY PRESERVATION VERSUS OUT-OF-HOME CARE

One of the most controversial issues within child protection circles is the question of when families should be preserved and when children should be temporarily or permanently removed from their homes (see Vischer, Knorth, Grietens, & Post, 2019). CPS agencies are mandated to make child protection their top priority, and no one questions this mandate. But when a child is at risk, what course of action will serve the best interests of the child? Should CPS attempt to maintain the family unit, offering support and training in hopes that abuse will not occur again in the future? Or should CPS remove the child from the home and place the child in a temporary setting with the hope of eventually returning the child to the home? Or should the state seek a more permanent solution for the child, such as adoption or placement in an orphanage?

A brief review of federal policy on family preservation helps put this debate in context. Federal child welfare policy has, since the passage of the Adoption Assistance and Child Welfare Act of 1980 (P.L. 96–272), embraced the goal of family preservation as its guiding principle. The 1980 act, sometimes referred to as the Reunification Act, requires that states, as a condition of receiving federal child welfare funding, make every reasonable effort to rehabilitate abusive parents and keep families together. If one were going to select key concepts that describe the mandates of the 1980 act, they would be *reunification* and *family preservation services* (U.S. DHHS, 2002; Wattenberg, Kelley, & Kim, 2001).

The **Adoption and Safe Families Act (ASFA)** of 1997 (P.L. 105–89) changed and clarified a number of policies established in the 1980 act, subtly moving federal policy away from preservation as the only goal (Gelles, 2005). The 1997 law explicitly established child safety as a "paramount concern" and encouraged expedited permanency decisions for children who are abused. In the

1997 act, therefore, there is a slight change in focus that emphasizes concepts like safety, permanency, and adoption (U.S. DHHS, 2002; Wattenberg et al., 2001).

These policy commitments remind us that, in many respects, there is consensus regarding the core values of our child welfare system. All sides acknowledge, for example, that the nuclear family is the best place to raise a family, and federal law reflects this recognition. All sides also acknowledge that parents should be given considerable latitude in decisions regarding their own children, and again federal law also reflects this recognition. Indeed, the courts, citing the Fourteenth Amendment, recognize the blood relationship as a constitutionally protected human right (Gelles, 2005). In contrast, the concept of *parens patriae* (introduced in Chapter 1) dictates that the state has a responsibility to protect vulnerable children. Given the level of agreement, it should not surprise us to learn that even those who argue that child welfare policy overemphasizes preservation acknowledge that there should be a "'high bar' that restrains and restricts state intervention into the parent–child relationship. This has been the law of the land for more than 200 years, and it has worked reasonably well for the majority of families and children" (Gelles, 2005, p. 331).

Ultimately, of course, the debate centers on those middle-ground cases where risk is difficult to assess. Proponents of the family preservation model maintain that ASFA moved policy too far away from family preservation. Children can be safely left in their homes if their communities offer vulnerable families the social services and training they need. These advocates point out that the foster care system is not a panacea, noting the relatively high rates of abuse and/or neglect in foster families (Carr et al., 2019). There is also evidence that foster care does more harm than good. In an important article published in the

(*Continued*)

(Continued)

prestigious *American Economic Review*, Doyle (2007) found that children "on the margins of placement" (i.e., cases of neglect where the foster care versus family preservation decision is far from clear) who were placed in foster care fared worse in the long term (in terms of teen motherhood rates, juvenile delinquency, and employment earnings) than did children who were similarly neglected but were left in the home, although some have argued that his findings are overstated and might not hold up under contemporary circumstances (e.g., recent reductions in the number of children in foster care) (Font & Gershoff, 2020).

Another potential problem with the foster care system is that it targets the poor. Approximately 70 percent of children in foster care are placed there for neglect, which critics charge is too often synonymous with poverty and homelessness (Cytryn, 2010). Richard Wexler, executive director of the National Coalition for Child Protection Reform, argues that the greatest sin of many maltreating families may be that they are poor. These families don't need to have their children taken from them; they need social services and support (Wexler, 2005).

Critics of the "single-minded" goal of family preservation, on the other hand, argue that family preservation and unification goals too often put children at risk. Several highly publicized child deaths in recent years serve as a reminder of the potential dangers of reuniting children with parents who have been abusive in the past (see the case of Anthony Avalos noted earlier). An overcommitment to reunifying families also sometimes leaves children in long-term temporary settings—moving them in and out of foster care—which is rarely in the best interests of the child and results in a "revolving door" phenomenon that is harmful to children (see Davidson, Tomlinson, Beck, & Bowen, 2019; Gelles, 2005).

Much of the disagreement centers on when families can or should be offered family preservation services and whether these services can successfully rehabilitate abusive parents. Family preservation programs most typically focus on intervention before the child is removed, offering services in the home rather than in an office or agency that focus on the entire family and are crisis oriented, with help available to families 24 hours a day, every day of the week (Cash, 2008). Such programs also seek to provide family support and resource connections within their larger communities. One of the first family preservation programs, often referred to as **home visiting programs**, is **Homebuilders**, which began in the state of Washington in the early 1970s and has now been implemented in various locales across the country. The Homebuilders model calls for intensive home-based services for families in the midst of crisis, assuming that parents who are about to lose a child will be more open to receiving services and learning new behaviors. Caseworker loads are very low (typically two families per caseworker) and the interactions extensive (up to 20 hours per week) (for a review see Kinney, Haapala, Booth, & Leavitt, 2017).

A number of family preservation, or home visiting, programs now exist that have demonstrated success. Evaluations of these programs are described in our discussion of intervention and prevention of child neglect in the next section. Certainly, nobody is suggesting that the family preservation goal be abandoned. In less serious cases of abuse, where the parents are poor, young, stressed, and needy—and are likely to benefit from social services—family reunification should be the goal, and supportive intervention should be the means to achieving that end. In more serious cases, where rehabilitation is not likely to be successful, the goal of family reunification should be questioned. Determining which response is most appropriate is a matter of considerable research attention and debate (see a special issue of the *APSAC Advisor*, 2016, on **differential response**). Hopefully, future research will help us distinguish between the two.

Out-of-Home Care

As noted earlier, **out-of-home care** is one potential CPS response to child maltreatment and includes foster care placement, **kinship care**, and placement in residential treatment centers and institutions. In 2018, approximately 23 percent of identified victims of child maltreatment were removed from their homes and placed in one of these out-of-home placements (U.S. DHHS, 2020). According to the **Adoption and Foster Care Analysis and Reporting System (AFCARS)**, which collects data from the 50 U.S. states on the number of children placed in out-of-home care, there were over 400,000 children living in out-of-home placements as of September 30, 2019 (U.S. DHHS, 2019b). Thirty-two percent of these children were in kinship care (i.e., in the homes of relatives approved by child welfare agencies), 46 percent were in foster care (i.e., private homes of nonrelatives who are licensed and supervised by child welfare agencies), 10 percent were in residential/group care, and 8 percent were in other types of placement such as adoptive homes (U.S. DHHS, 2019b).

According to 2018 AFCARS data (U.S. DHHS, 2019b), the mean age of children in foster care was approximately 8 years, with the most frequently represented age group being children 7 years of age or younger (52%). There were slightly more males (52%) than females (48%). In terms of race and ethnicity, 44 percent were white, 23 percent black, and 21 percent Hispanic, with the remaining children being of other ethnicities/races.

Several factors likely influence the decision to place a child in foster care. Of most importance is the child's health and safety. Children who are prior victims of maltreatment are, therefore, more likely than first-time victims to be placed in foster care (Dolan, Casanueva, Smith, Lloyd, & Ringeisen, 2012). In addition, foster care placement is more common in younger children (44% of children entering foster care in 2018 were 4 years of age or younger), when parental drug use is present, and for child victims of neglect compared to other forms of child maltreatment (U.S. DHHS, 2019b).

According to the AFCARS report, the case disposition of children in foster care varies in terms of their length of stay in foster care and whether or not they reunite with their families (U.S. DHHS, 2019b). Consistent with CPS philosophy, the case goal in 56 percent of cases in 2018 was reunification with the parent(s) or principal caretaker(s). Of the children who left foster care in 2018, 49 percent were returned to parent(s) or primary caretaker(s), 7 percent were placed with other relatives, and 25 percent were adopted (other outcomes included emancipation and guardianship). The mean number of months in care during 2018 was 19.2, and the median was approximately 15 months. Nearly one-half (43%) of children were in foster care for less than a year, another 30 percent were in out-of-home care from one to two years, and 28 percent were in foster care for two years or more.

A number of different factors likely influence whether children are eventually reunited with their parents. Children placed in kinship care (with relatives), as opposed to other placements, are less likely to be reunited with parents. Additionally, children placed in out-of-home care due to neglect as opposed to other forms of child maltreatment are also less likely to reunite with their parents (e.g., M. Harris & Courtney, 2003). Children and youth identified as having more mental health and developmental problems are also less likely to reunite with their parents (e.g., Landsverk, Davis, Ganger, Newton, & Johnson, 1996). Given the overlap between the factors associated with reunification and those associated with victim placement in foster care, it is difficult to determine whether these specific factors are critical in such decisions or whether general risk determines both placement and reunification.

During the past 20 years, the number of children placed in out-of-home care, particularly in nonrelative foster care, has led to concern and considerable debate about out-of-home placement decisions (see Box 5.3). Many professionals are troubled about the potential negative adjustment of foster care youth because of the unstable circumstances that often surround foster care placement. For example, children in foster care on average move from one placement to another at least once, and for some children it is not uncommon to change foster placements three or more times (Doyle, 2007). Foster care placement instability has been shown to increase the risk of behavioral and developmental problems in children (Konijn et al., 2019) and is especially concerning because of the potentially negative impact on developing secure attachment relationships (Konijn et al., 2019). These concerns have led some to recommend that the United States bring back orphanages as an alternative to foster care. B. Allen and Vacca (2011), for example, argue that what is needed are long-term placements for these children—placements that last until adulthood: "What we are suggesting is that we as a society consider bringing back orphanages—well run facilities that provide a stable environment over time, good educational opportunities, and the chance for the children to develop emotionally in a secure, nurturing environment" (p. 1067). They suggest the development of more long-term residential programs, such as the Milton Hershey School, where students live in homes on campus with their house parents. Another exemplar, according to these researchers, is Boys Town located in Nebraska. This facility provides services ranging from a residential treatment facility (Village of Boys Town) to outpatient treatment clinics. Although no randomized controlled trial studies have been conducted on these programs, early outcome evaluations show promise (Casey Family Programs, 2009).

Intervention and Prevention Strategies Aimed at Families

Parent training interventions, as discussed in Chapter 3, hold promise as an effective strategy to address not only child physical abuse but child neglect as well. Recall that one such intervention is Incredible Years (IY), a multitiered program targeted at young children with behavior problems. The program includes child-focused, parent-focused, and teacher-focused modules (Webster-Stratton, Reid, & Beauchaine, 2011, 2013).

The IY parent intervention aims to reduce coercive parent–child interactions by providing parents with information about child development along with strategies to enhance parent–child interactions, such as the use of positive discipline, the reduction of negative affect during parenting interactions, and the reinterpretation of negative cognitive attributions about the parent–child relationship. Several randomized controlled trials of IY show that it is effective at reducing physical punishment and at enhancing parent–child interactions, which in turn leads to improvements in the behavior of young children, including neglected children (Letarte, Normandeau, & Allard, 2010).

Another common parent training/support approach, discussed briefly, is the many home visiting programs that bring community resources into the homes of at-risk families. Hundreds of thousands of at-risk children in the United States are reached annually by home visiting programs (National Home Visiting Resource Center, 2019). Such programs have flourished under the **Maternal, Infant, and Early Childhood Home Visiting Program (MIECHV)**, created by Obamacare or the Patient Protection and Affordable Care Act of 2010 (H.R. 3590), which expired in 2017 but was reauthorized for an additional five years in early 2018. In 2018, for example, over 300,000 children received home visiting services (National Home Visiting Resource Center, 2019). Although the specifics of such programs vary, the Child Welfare Information Gateway (2011, p. 7) identified several primary issues addressed during home visits, including (a) the parent's personal health and life choices; (b) child health and development; (c) environmental concerns such as income, housing, and community violence; (d) family functioning, including adult and child relationships; and (e) access to services. There is a substantial body of research evidence that suggests that home visiting programs result in a number of child- and family-related positive outcomes including promotion of maternal and child health, prevention of child abuse and neglect, enhanced positive parenting and child development, and improved school readiness (National Academies of Science, Engineering, and Medicine, 2019).

One of the most well-known home visiting programs was established by Olds and colleagues and is recognized as an important success story in child maltreatment prevention (MacMillan & Waddell, 2012). Originally called the Prenatal/Early Infancy Project, the program began in the 1970s and pairs young single mothers with public health nurses beginning prenatally and continuing until 2 years of age (Olds, Sadler, & Kitzman, 2007). The project is currently referred to as the **Nurse–Family Partnership (NFP)** and provides prenatal and early childhood services to young mothers to help them understand child health and development and to strengthen their confidence in themselves and in their capacity for change. More specifically, the program is designed to accomplish the following goals: (a) enhance the health of the infant, (b) improve parental caregiving, and (c) provide life course development support (e.g., educational, occupational, and pregnancy planning) (Olds, 1997). The NFP program has undergone a number of carefully controlled evaluations and demonstrated its effectiveness in preventing child maltreatment. In a 15-year follow-up, child abuse and neglect were identified less often in the families who received home visitation compared to those who had not (Olds, Eckenrode, et al., 1997; Olds, Henderson, et al., 1998). In another follow-up of a randomized controlled trial, women receiving home visiting were 58 percent less likely to have been arrested and 43 percent less likely to have been convicted compared to a comparison (Eckenrode et al., 2010). One recent study examined potential mediators of the effectiveness of the NFP program and found that having fewer children and staying off of public assistance decreased the risk of child maltreatment (Eckenrode et al., 2017).

Other home visitation programs include multicomponent approaches that serve both to intervene in child neglect and to prevent it, and are ideal for neglecting families because of the multiproblem nature of such families. Most such interventions have an ecological emphasis—that is, they offer diverse community services with the aim of improving the family's social environment. Such programs attempt to alter the social factors that increase stress and affect a family's ability to function effectively in order to prevent future abuse and neglect from reoccurring in substantiated cases of child maltreatment or to prevent the occurrence of child maltreatment in high-risk families. **SafeCare** (formerly Project 12-Ways) is a noteworthy example of a multicomponent intervention; it includes a variety of services for families, such as parent–child training, stress reduction, marital counseling, employment assistance, and training in money management (Chaffin, Hecht, Bard, Silovsky, & Beasley, 2012; Lutzker & Chaffin, 2012). Evaluation studies of SafeCare have demonstrated its effectiveness in reducing the number of hazards in the home, improving parent engagement and retention, reducing domestic violence in the home, and preventing child welfare recidivism (Chaffin et al., 2012; Jabaley, Lutzker, Whitaker, & Self-Brown, 2011; Silovsky et al., 2011; Tertinger, Greene, & Lutzker, 1984). Parents who participate in the program also believe that the program was helpful to their parenting skills, which might influence parents' motivation to complete the program (Gallitto, Romano, & Drolet, 2017).

Studies of a number of other home visiting programs have also found positive results, such as enhanced parenting knowledge and skills—including increased positive parenting, more appropriate developmental expectations, safer home environments, fewer child injuries and reduced likelihood of maltreatment, and less use of physical punishment among program participants compared to controls (Casillas, Fauchier, Derkash, & Garrido, 2016; Chaiyachati et al., 2018; A. Culp, Culp, Anderson, & Carter, 2007; A. Culp et al., 2004; Daro, 2011). A review of the home visiting literature conducted under the guidance of a U.S. DHHS interagency working group as part of the **Home Visiting Evidence of Effectiveness (HomVEE)** initiative summarized various home visiting models in terms of their evidence of effectiveness and found that out of 45 models, 19 programs (including NFP and SafeCare) met DHHS criteria for evidence of effectiveness (Sama-Miller et al., 2016).

Many other reviews of evaluation studies assessing the effectiveness of home visiting programs, however, have been mixed (e.g., Daro, 2011; National Research Council, 2014). Although several evaluations of such programs conducted in the 1990s demonstrated their success (e.g., Bath & Haapala, 1993; Fraser, Walton, Lewis, & Pecora, 1996), other research (much of which is experimental and includes random assignments) has not found them to be effective either in reducing out-of-home placements, in protecting children who are at risk for abuse, or in changing the behavior of parents (Gelles, 2000; Lindsey, Martin, & Doh, 2002; U.S. DHHS, 2005). Lindsey and colleagues (2002) assert that earlier reports of the success of home visiting programs were based not only on methodologically flawed studies but also on the exaggerated enthusiasm of program advocates. The U.S. Preventive Services Task Force (2018) recently reviewed a total of 22 randomized clinical trials of programs from 33 publications of "good or fair quality," including home visitation–based interventions, and concluded that there was insufficient evidence to assess either the benefits or the harms of such programs on preventing child maltreatment among youth without a known history of child maltreatment. This group of researchers acknowledged, however, that they did not assess the effectiveness of home visiting programs for other outcomes such as improving child and maternal health, encouraging positive parenting, or promoting child development. Daro (2011) has argued that regardless of whether such programs directly prevent child maltreatment, some home visitation programs have been shown to improve child and family functioning; they have been effective in producing positive effects on parenting and parent–child interactions as well as maternal behavior, attitudes, and educational attainment (Bull, McCormick, Swann, & Mulvihill, 2004; Geeraert, Van den Noortgate, Grietens, & Onghena, 2004; Sweet & Applebaum, 2004).

The controversy surrounding the effectiveness of home visiting programs is far from settled and bears significantly on the ongoing debate concerning family reunification and preservation as a primary goal of child protection (Gelles, 2005; see Box 5.3). It may be that programs need further refinement before their effectiveness can be adequately demonstrated through rigorous research designs (R. Hahn, Mercy, Bilukha, & Briss, 2005). In addition, because home visiting programs vary from one to the other, it is important to consider the effectiveness of individual programs rather than evaluating them collectively (MacMillan & Waddell, 2012). In addition, mixed findings may be the result of differences in the manner in which such programs are implemented, such as the way staff are trained, the type and amount of supervision offered, and **fidelity monitoring** (the faithfulness with which the program is implemented) (Casillas et al., 2016). Future research should attempt to determine the specific conditions associated with program success, such as the types of families that benefit and the specific components of intervention that are effective, as well as the effectiveness of various implementation practices.

Law and Policy

Another strategy in efforts to reduce or eliminate child neglect involves policy initiatives with the potential to impact the occurrence of child neglect. Many of these policies have been discussed earlier in this chapter or in previous chapters. Another example of an important policy initiative is **safe-haven laws**, which allow biological mothers to give up their newborn infants anonymously in specific safe locations (e.g., hospitals, fire stations) with full immunity from prosecution. Prior to the implementation of these laws, parents in need of assistance often had nowhere to turn.

Consider, for example, the case of Emmanuelle, an 18-year-old high school senior, who was desperate. The father of her child had abandoned her, she was unable to support herself and her child with her waitressing job, and her family was unwilling to help. With nowhere to turn, she left her 2-and-one-half-year-old child at a Brooklyn hospital with a note:

> *To Whom It May Concern:*
>
> *I am an 18-year-old student and I also work. I can't handle the pressure. I sometimes take it out on her. I love her and would not like to hurt her. Please find her a good home where she'll get the love she desires.*

The next day Emmanuelle realized she had made a mistake and called the hospital to ask for her baby back. When she arrived, she was arrested and charged with child abandonment (Fontana & Moohnan, 1994, pp. 227–228).

Notice that this story dates to the mid-1990s. In more recent years there has been a fairly dramatic shift in how we view situations like this, and safe-haven laws reflect this shift. All 50 U.S. states have passed such legislation (Child Welfare Information Gateway, 2013c). Although the focus of such laws is on protecting newborns, one wonders why these age restrictions should be so limited. What if the parents of a 5-year-old, for example, are in distress and recognize their inability to parent their child? Is it not in everyone's best interest to provide safe haven for that child? Although such laws have their detractors, they do provide a solution that protects children from abandonment that could lead to death, and such laws might be expanded in the future to protect an even greater number of children.

CHAPTER SUMMARY

Child neglect is one of the most elusive forms of child maltreatment and, as a result, has received less attention than other forms. The vague nature of child neglect is evident in the fact that a significant proportion of the research devoted to this topic has focused on definitional issues. At present, no single definition of child neglect is universally accepted. Although experts generally agree on conceptual definitions of child neglect (i.e., failure to provide for a child's basic needs), little consensus exists regarding operational definitions.

Given these definitional complexities, the true incidence of child neglect is largely undetermined, as are the characteristics of victims of child neglect. Child neglect is the most frequently reported form of child maltreatment, accounting for 61 percent to 77 percent of reported maltreatment cases. The majority of victims of child neglect are under the age of 5, and the risk for neglect appears to decline as children become older. Children whose families are experiencing a variety of financial stressors (e.g., low income or unemployment) are at higher risk than children in financially better-off families. For this form of child maltreatment, there appears to be little difference in risk between boys and girls. Studies that have examined the negative effects associated with child neglect have consistently shown it to be related to a variety of problems including social difficulties, intellectual deficits, and emotional and behavioral problems.

Neglecting parents can be distinguished from nonneglecting parents by several characteristics. One consistent finding in families of neglect is that parent–child interactions are disturbed, and parents have increased levels of stress, with few social supports and limited integration into the community. Neglecting parents are also characterized by low educational achievement and often have become parents at a young age. Further research is needed to determine additional factors contributing to child neglect, given that not all parents with the characteristics noted neglect their children.

Few intervention and prevention strategies have been devised to address the unique aspects of child neglect, and as a result, research evaluating the effectiveness of interventions for victims of this form of maltreatment, in particular, is limited. Efforts to address child neglect primarily focus on parental competency programs that include home visitation, parent education, and parent support. A great deal of research has been conducted on home visitation programs, which often incorporate a multicomponent approach designed to include a variety of services for families. Such programs operate on the assumption that by enhancing parental support and parents' knowledge about parenting and child development, they can improve family functioning, which will result in lower levels of child neglect. Although the effectiveness of home visitation programs has been debated, there is increasing evidence that such programs are generally effective in meeting many of their goals. Another strategy in efforts to reduce or eliminate child neglect involves policy initiatives, such as safe-haven laws, which have the potential to significantly improve the lives of children.

Recommended Resources

Daro, D. (2011). Prevention of child abuse and neglect. In J. E. B. Myers (Ed.), *The APSAC handbook on child maltreatment* (3rd ed., pp. 17–37). Thousand Oaks, CA: Sage.

DePanfilis, D. (2018). *Child protective services: A guide for caseworkers*. U.S. Department of Health and Human Services. Retrieved from https://www.childwelfare.gov/pubPDFs/cps2018.pdf

Font, S. A., & Gershoff, E. T. (2020). Foster care and the "Best Interests of the Child": Integrating research, policy and practice. *Advances in Child and Family Policy and Practice*.

Giardino, A. P., Lyn, M. A., & Giardino, E. R. (Eds.). (2019). *A practical guide to the evaluation of child physical abuse and neglect*. New York, NY: Springer.

Green, A. E., Trott, E., Willging, C. E., Finn, N. K., Ehrhart, M. G., & Aarons, G. A. (2016). The role of collaborations in sustaining an evidence-based intervention to reduce child neglect. *Child Abuse & Neglect, 53*, 4–16.

Mulder, T. M., Kuiper, K. C., van der Put, C. E., Stams, G. J. J., & Assink, M. (2018). Risk factors for child neglect: A meta-analytic review. *Child Abuse & Neglect, 77*, 198–210.

National Research Council. (2014). *New directions in child abuse and neglect research*. Washington, DC: National Academies Press. https://doi.org/10.17226/18331

6

CHILD PSYCHOLOGICAL MALTREATMENT

LEARNING OBJECTIVES

1. Describe the definition and scope of child psychological maltreatment, including problems inherent in measuring this form of abuse.

2. Identify the various risk factors associated with child psychological maltreatment.

3. Summarize the consequences of child psychological maltreatment, including both short- and long-term outcomes.

4. Discuss the various intervention and prevention efforts that have been developed to address child psychological maltreatment, including evidence of their effectiveness.

CASE HISTORY

TOUGH LOVE OR CHILD PSYCHOLOGICAL MALTREATMENT?

By most outward appearances, the Machnicks were a typical all-American family. Grady Machnick was a sergeant with the Los Angeles County Sheriff's Department, and Deborah Machnick was an elementary school principal. They were raising three children, one of whom was a 14-year-old boy, Grady Machnick's biological son and Deborah Machnick's stepson. The Machnicks lived in a two-story home in a well-kept Southern California neighborhood. By all accounts they were a "normal" upper-class family, hardly fitting the stereotype of an abusive family. And indeed, there was no indication that the Machnicks ever physically or sexually abused their son. But they were in fact arrested for child abuse, in a case that can be most accurately described as child psychological maltreatment (CPM). At the time the charges were filed, Grady Machnick denied any inappropriate mistreatment of his son, and his attorney stated that "any actions that were taken were appropriate to the circumstances of disciplining a teenager." The allegations included the following:

- The parents required the teenage boy to spend nights outside, sleeping on a dog mat, as punishment for not completing his homework.

- The parents did not allow the teen to use the bathroom located in the home, instead requiring him to use a public restroom at a nearby park.

- The parents poured water on the teen to wake him from sleep.

- The parents sent the teen to school with dog feces in his backpack as punishment for not cleaning up after the family dog.

- The parents forced the teen to strip and be photographed naked as a form of punishment.

- The parents forced the teen out of the house at 3:30 a.m. when the parents needed to go out because, they said, he could not be trusted in the home alone.

- The parents confiscated the teen's belongings (e.g., clean clothing) and required that he earn the items back through good behavior.

- The parents withheld the teen's lunch money.

At trial, Grady and Deborah Machnick testified that they employed the parenting practices they did because they were attempting to discipline their defiant son. The teen reportedly earned poor grades in school, refused to help with chores at home, and was often caught lying and stealing. Grady Machnick summed up his son's behavior by testifying that his son "reminded him of inmates." Throughout their trial, the Machnicks insisted that their efforts at discipline were designed to keep their son from continuing to engage in questionable behavior.

The Machnicks were ultimately acquitted on felony charges of conspiring to abuse their teenage son. The jurors agreed that the parents' discipline was inappropriate and inconsistent with their own parenting practices, but they were reluctant to condemn the Machnicks' behavior as criminal or to judge the couple based on their own value systems. Although the jurors agreed that the Machnicks' behavior did not rise to the level of a felony, they could not agree on whether to convict the Machnicks of the lesser charge of misdemeanor child abuse. One juror who voted to convict both parents stated in an interview, "Breaking someone down mentally, that's what they tried to do. There were no bruises, but the whole behavior of Grady and Deborah was to break him down mentally."

In his closing argument, one of the Machnicks' attorneys described the couple's parenting behavior as follows: "It's not a great parenting technique. If you're grading, A, B, C, D, or F, maybe it's an F. But it's not a crime" ("Judge OKs Retrial in Alleged Abuse Case," 2003; see also Leonard, 2001; Pfeifer, 2002; Pfeifer & Anton, 2002).

Despite the lack of overt physical aggression, sexual behavior, or physical signs of maltreatment in the case history just described, many observers would agree that the parents' behavior was abusive. Cases such as this have led researchers to address CPM, a form of child maltreatment that differs from the other forms already discussed in this book.

Relative to other forms of child maltreatment, CPM has received considerably less attention. One explanation for the relative neglect of the topic is that the other forms of child maltreatment are more likely to result in immediate and observable harm. The negative consequences of CPM, while more elusive, are no less insidious. Research has shown that the negative effects of CPM are just as serious, if not more so, as those related to physical and sexual abuse (Cecil, Viding, Fearon, Glaser, & McCrory, 2017; Fung, Chung, & Ross, 2020; Hodgdon et al., 2018; Spinazzola et al., 2014). Indeed, CPM may be the most destructive form of child abuse. In addition to possibly being the most harmful form of child maltreatment, CPM may be the most pervasive, based on a variety of different forms of reporting as we will discuss in this chapter. One of the unique characteristics of CPM is that it often co-occurs with other forms of child maltreatment (K. Kim, Mennen, & Trickett, 2017; Pynoos et al., 2014; Vachon, Krueger, Rogosch, & Cicchetti, 2015) and, as some have argued, exists as a component of all forms of child maltreatment (e.g., Garbarino, 2011; S. Hart & Brassard, 2019; S. Hart et al., 2011).

To illustrate these points, let's return to the case of Adrian Peterson discussed in Chapter 1. Recall that Peterson's abuse was discovered when medical personnel found cuts and bruises on his son's legs. Let's imagine, for the sake of argument, that other than physically hurting his child, Peterson was a model parent. He loved, nurtured, respected, protected, and cared for his child. Let's also assume that Peterson's son likewise understood his father to be a model parent, and that he accepted that his father was hitting him "for his own good." CPM experts would suggest that these circumstances could cause harm to the child because once the physical pain subsides, and the physical injuries heal, the potential psychological damage to the child might not heal as easily. In addition, it is hard to imagine that a parent could create welts and cuts without also demeaning and belittling the child.

Scholars have thus increasingly come to understand CPM as a discrete form of child maltreatment worthy of scientific study (see Brassard, Hart, Baker, & Chiel, 2019). The realization that CPM may be the most pervasive and damaging form of child maltreatment has spurred research interest in the topic. In the following sections, we address the current state of knowledge regarding CPM. Much of the literature to date aims at clarifying definitional issues, and our discussion reflects that emphasis. We also attempt to address what the research so far reveals about children who experience CPM, the characteristics of maltreating parents, and the consequences associated with CPM. We conclude the chapter with descriptions of various prevention and intervention strategies that scholars have proposed to address the problem.

SCOPE OF THE PROBLEM

CPM has received less attention than other forms of abuse, in part, because it is so difficult to define. Where should we draw the line between less-than-adequate parenting, or parental error, or parental frustrations, and psychological maltreatment? Many, if not most, parents ignore, criticize, or are unsupportive of their children from time to time. Under what circumstances do these behaviors constitute psychological maltreatment?

What Is Child Psychological Maltreatment?

Would you characterize the following behaviors as abusive? Why or why not?

- A mother locks her 3-year-old son in a dark attic as a method of punishment.

- A father shackles his 7-year-old son to his bed at night to prevent him from getting out of bed repeatedly.

- A mother says to her daughter, "You are the stupidest, laziest kid on Earth. I can't believe you're my child. They must have switched babies on me at the hospital."

- A father tells his daughter that he will kill her new puppy if she or the puppy misbehaves.

- A father repeatedly states to one of his children, "I don't love you."

- A mother refuses to look at or touch her child.

The difficulty in determining what behaviors constitute CPM may contribute to the idea that it is the most ambiguous form of child abuse. It is likely that nearly all parents, to some degree, treat their children in inappropriate ways at some time or another by saying or doing hurtful things they later regret. Such mistakes are a characteristic of most intimate relationships. Few assert, however, that most children are victims of CPM. Indeed, parenting occurs on a continuum that ranges from healthy parenting to poor or dysfunctional parenting to psychological maltreatment (Wolfe & McIsaac, 2011).

One of the most significant areas of confusion is related to the inconsistency of terms used to describe this form of child maltreatment. Various researchers use the word *psychological* while others use the term *emotional*. Although these two terms seem to be used interchangeably, the lack of consistency creates confusion. In addition, there is confusion about whether or not this form of child maltreatment refers only to *acts of commission* that a parent might engage in against a child or whether *acts of omission* should also be included (e.g., Baker & Festinger, 2011). A mother who tells her child that she is "the stupidest, laziest kid on Earth," as in the third scenario, is committing an act of commission (commonly identified as **verbal abuse**) while, as in the last scenario, a mom who "refuses to look at or touch her child" is engaging in an act of omission (failing to nurture her child, typically referred to, as discussed in Chapter 5, as emotional neglect). The terms used for these various forms of child maltreatment vary across studies and among researchers. These are important matters to resolve, as they can significantly impact methods of estimation and measurement and hamper understanding about the problem. In this chapter, we use the broader term *psychological maltreatment* to refer to acts of both omission and commission to include all forms of psychological and/or emotional abuse and neglect.

A second conceptual dilemma is whether to include *child outcomes* as well as *parental behaviors* in definitions of CPM. Notice that all of the scenarios listed earlier focus exclusively on parental behavior. Some researchers have argued, however, that child outcomes such as *mental injury or impaired psychological functioning and development* should be included in our definitions of CPM (Hamarman, Pope, & Czaja, 2002; S. Hart, Brassard, Binggeli, & Davidson, 2002). This approach is problematic for several reasons. One problem is that a definition requiring demonstration of harm precludes the possibility of preventing the harm before it occurs (Glaser, 2002). In addition, the harm associated with psychological maltreatment may not be evident immediately; it could take months or even years to develop. Measurable problems might, in fact, never appear. But if a father repeatedly says to his daughter, "I don't love you," is he not engaged in psychologically abusive behavior, even if his behavior does not demonstrably harm the daughter?

The **American Professional Society on the Abuse of Children (APSAC)** in 2017 defined CPM, primarily based on parent behaviors, as "a repeated pattern or extreme incident(s) of caretaker behavior that thwart the child's basic psychological development needs (e.g., safety, socialization, emotional and social support, cognitive stimulation, respect) and convey a child is worthless, defective, damaged, unloved, unwanted, endangered, primarily useful in meeting another's needs, and/or expendable" (p. 3). APSAC (2017) and others have also identified several major subtypes of CPM, which we review later in this chapter (Glaser, 2011; Kairys & Johnson, 2002; Wolfe & McIsaac, 2011). According to most researchers and practitioners, one of the primary factors that distinguishes CPM from nonabusive dysfunctional parenting is the fact that patterns of CPM are typically chronic, severe, and escalating (Wolfe & McIsaac, 2011).

Whether CPM refers to behavior on the part of parents or to the consequences that result for the child is related to the core conceptual problem concerning the meaning of the term *psychological* in CPM. The key area of confusion has to do with whether *psychological* refers to parental behavior and/or child outcomes that are nonphysical (or psychological/emotional) in nature. McGee and Wolfe (1991) have constructed a matrix to explain the multiple conceptual perspectives from which scholars view CPM. In this model, CPM can be defined based on *both* child outcomes and parental behaviors. Table 6.1 displays a modified version of this matrix, which shows various combinations and possibilities for understanding the concept of CPM. As this matrix shows, parent behaviors can be physical or nonphysical and can result in either physical or nonphysical (e.g., psychological or emotional) consequences to the child. Parent behaviors that are physical and result in physical consequences (e.g., touching a child with a cigarette that results in a burn) fit the commonly accepted view of child physical abuse. According to McGee and Wolfe, researchers have defined CPM using the remaining combinations of parenting behaviors and psychological outcomes. Some would classify a situation in which a parent engages in physical behavior (e.g., touching a child with a cigarette) that

TABLE 6.1 ■ Conceptual Perspectives on Psychological Maltreatment

Consequences to the Child	Parent Behaviors	
	Physical	**Nonphysical**
Physical	Physical abuse	Psychological maltreatment
	Example: Choking a child results in injury to the child's trachea.	Example: A parent's lack of supervision results in a child's being poisoned.
Nonphysical	Psychological maltreatment	Psychological maltreatment
	Example: Repeatedly beating a child leads to low self-esteem in the child.	Example: Repeatedly yelling and screaming at a child leads to low self-esteem in the child.

Source: Adapted from McGee & Wolfe, 1991.

results in physical as well as nonphysical outcomes (e.g., anxiety and fear) as CPM. On the basis of this model, additional physical behaviors carried out by parents (such as sexual abuse or physical neglect) that result in negative psychological outcomes would also be considered CPM.

In contrast, some parental behaviors can be nonphysical in nature and still result in either physical or nonphysical harm to the child. For example, insensitive parenting (e.g., not responding to a child's needs for nurturance and attention), which we described in Chapter 5 as a form of emotional neglect, has been linked to both physical (e.g., malnutrition) and nonphysical (e.g., deficits in cognitive or emotional development) negative outcomes in children. Finally, the combination of nonphysical parental behavior (e.g., swearing at a child) and nonphysical outcomes (e.g., decreased self-esteem) reflects the conceptualization of CPM as a distinct or pure form of child maltreatment (McGee & Wolfe, 1991).

The Centers for Disease Control and Prevention define CPM as

intentional caregiver behavior that conveys to a child that he or she is worthless, flawed, unloved, unwanted, endangered, or valued only in meeting another's needs. Psychologically maltreating behaviors may include blaming, belittling, degrading, intimidating, terrorizing, isolating, restraining, confining, corrupting, exploiting, spurning, or otherwise behaving in a manner that is harmful, potentially harmful, insensitive to the child's developmental needs, or can potentially damage the child psychologically or emotionally. (Leeb, Paulozzi, Melanson, Simon, & Arias, 2008, p. 11)

The advantage of this definition is that it recognizes both parent behavior and child outcomes and that in considering child outcomes, both harm and *potential* harm are identified rather than evidence of *actual* harm (Wolfe & McIsaac, 2011). In addition, this definition describes specific parental behaviors that constitute CPM. These specific dimensions of parent behavior are described in the following section.

Proposed Subtypes of Child Psychological Maltreatment

There is much debate about the most appropriate organizational framework to accurately capture the multidimensional nature of CPM. As noted in the previous section of this chapter, one definitional approach is to focus on specific parental behaviors that we might deem abusive. Table 6.2 summarizes the subtypes and provides examples of CPM commonly reported in the literature. It is important to note, however, that different subtypes of CPM can overlap conceptually and can also co-occur (S. Brown, Rienks, McCrae, & Watamura, 2019; Dubowitz, Pitts, & Black, 2012; Hodgdon et al., 2018). Consider, for example, the Machnicks' teen son from the opening case history. This teen was clearly exposed to a number of forms of CPM consisting of being rejected, degraded, and isolated, among others. Eight subtypes have been consistently reported: **rejecting**, **degrading** (i.e., verbal abuse), **terrorizing**, **isolating**, **missocializing** (i.e., corrupting), **exploiting**, **denying emotional responsiveness** (i.e., ignoring), and **close confinement**. Other models have additionally suggested a ninth subtype—**parental inconsistency** (Kairys & Johnson, 2002). Some frameworks simply list categories of parental behaviors while others consider the developmental needs of the child; others focus on a continuum of developmentally appropriate/inappropriate parent–child interactions.

One of the most widely recognized frameworks was offered by APSAC in 1995 and revised in its *Guidelines for the Investigation and Determination of Suspected Psychological Maltreatment in Children and Adolescents* (APSAC, 2017). These guidelines list six categories of parental behaviors that constitute CPM:

- Spurning (e.g., verbal and nonverbal hostile rejecting/degrading behaviors)

- Terrorizing (e.g., caregiver behaviors that harm or threaten harm to a child or child's loved ones or possessions)

- Exploiting/corrupting (e.g., encouraging inappropriate behaviors in a child)

- Emotional unresponsiveness (e.g., ignoring a child's needs or failing to express positive affect toward a child)

- Isolating (e.g., denying a child opportunities to interact/communicate with others)

- Mental health/medical/educational neglect (e.g., failing to provide for a child's needs in these areas)

TABLE 6.2 ■ Subtypes of Child Psychological Maltreatment		
Subtype	**Description**	**Examples**
Rejecting	Verbal or symbolic acts that express feelings of rejection toward the child	Singling out a specific child for criticism and/or punishment Refusing to help a child Routinely rejecting a child's ideas
Degrading (i.e., verbally abusing)	Actions that deprecate a child	Insulting a child or calling a child names Publicly humiliating a child Constantly criticizing a child
Terrorizing	Actions or threats that cause extreme fear and/or anxiety in a child	Continually yelling or swearing at a child Threatening to harm a child Threatening to harm a child's loved one Exposing a child to interpersonal violence Punishing a child by playing on normal childhood fears Threatening suicide or to leave a child Using cruel or harsh control methods
Isolating	Preventing a child from engaging in normal social activities	Locking a child in a closet or room Refusing to allow a child to interact with individuals outside the family Refusing to allow a child to interact with other relatives
Missocializing (i.e., corrupting)	Modeling, permitting, or encouraging antisocial behavior in a child	Encouraging delinquent behavior in a child Encouraging alcohol or substance abuse in a child Indoctrinating a child in racist values
Exploiting	Using a child for the needs, advantages, or profits of the caretaker	Treating a child as a surrogate parent Using a child for child pornography or prostitution Using a child to pursue the caretaker's unfulfilled dreams

(*Continued*)

TABLE 6.2 ■ (Continued)		
Subtype	**Description**	**Examples**
Denying emotional responsiveness (i.e., ignoring)	Acts of omission whereby the caretaker does not provide a child with necessary stimulation and responsiveness	Behaving toward a child in a detached and uninvolved manner Interacting with a child only if absolutely necessary Failing to express affection, caring, and love toward a child Refusing to look at a child or call a child by name
Close confinement	Restricting a child's movement by binding limbs	Tying a child's arms and legs together Tying a child to a chair, bed, or other object
Parental inconsistency	Parent responds unreliably and inconsistently to a child	Sporadic or capricious rule- or limit-setting Responds unpredictably, accompanied by emotional outburst
Other	Forms of psychological maltreatment not specified under other categories	Withholding food, shelter, sleep, or other necessities from a child as a form of punishment Chronically applying developmentally inappropriate expectations to a child (sometimes referred to as *overpressuring*)

Sources: A representative but not exhaustive list of sources for the information displayed in this table includes the following: APSAC, 2017; Baily & Baily, 1986; Brassard et al., 2019; Garbarino, Guttman, & Seeley, 1986; S. Hart & Brassard, 1991; S. Hart, Germain, & Brassard, 1987; R. Herrenkohl, 2005; Heyman & Smith Slep, 2009; Kairys & Johnson, 2002; Potter, Nasserie, & Tonmyr, 2015; M. Schneider, Ross, Graham, & Zielinksi, 2005; U.S. Department of Health and Human Services, 1988; Wolfe & McIsaac, 2011.

Wolfe and McIsaac (2011) suggest that we imagine parental behavior on a continuum ranging from healthy parenting behavior to poor/dysfunctional (but nonabusive) behavior to more extreme and potentially more harmful parental behaviors that would be considered CPM. Based on this continuum model, CPM includes parenting deficiencies in stimulation and emotional expression (e.g., expressing conditional love and ambivalent feelings toward a child), interactions (e.g., emotionally or physically rejecting a child's attention), consistency and predictability (e.g., responding unpredictably, with emotional discharge), rules and limits (e.g., rules and limits are sporadic or capricious), disciplinary practices (e.g., cruel and harsh control methods that frighten a child), and emotional delivery and tone (e.g., frightening, denigrating, threatening, or insulting a child). At the healthy end of parenting behavior are appropriate and healthy forms of child-rearing that are child-centered and promote child development, whereas the opposite end of the continuum includes CPM parenting behaviors that violate children's basic needs and dependency status and represent harsh, insensitive, and ineffective forms of child-rearing.

The typologies displayed in Table 6.2 illustrate the subjective nature of definitions of CPM. Definitions and typological systems represent compilations of the various behaviors and circumstances that researchers in the field have identified. As such, these conceptualizations reflect the values of those who created them, with various advocates and researchers determining the types of parent–child interactions that should be considered inappropriate. For example, one researcher may see "refusing to help a child" as abusive, whereas another may see such behavior on the part of a parent as important in helping a child gain independence.

There are several problems inherent in many classification systems. One is that the subtypes are not mutually exclusive: One behavior can be categorized under more than one subtype. Insulting a child by shouting, "You're nothing but a fat, lazy pig," for instance, could be considered not only an act of degrading but also an act of rejecting. Another problem is that many typologies do not consider parental behavior on a continuum such that they include *normative* parental behaviors. Harsh control methods that frighten a child, such as physical punishment or spanking, although not an ideal parenting behavior, are one that a large percentage of U.S. parents support and employ at some time during a child's development (Child Trends Databank, 2015; Zolotor, Robinson, Runyan, Barr, & Murphy, 2011). Another criticism is that some of the typologies used to describe CPM include some subtypes that are defined by their outcomes. *Missocializing*, for example, is defined as stimulating the child to engage in destructive and antisocial behavior. One final criticism is that although there is generally good conceptual agreement across the proposed classification systems about various types of CPM, there is some inconsistency. Not all classification systems, for example, conceptually include exposure to intimate partner violence as a form of CPM (see Box 6.1).

Despite the numerous difficulties in defining CPM, in recent years researchers and clinicians have made significant progress toward consistency, reliability, and validity of definitions of CPM both in the United States and abroad (see Baker & Brassard, 2019; Brassard et al., 2019; Lansford & Deater-Deckard, 2012; Potter, Nasserie, & Tonmyr, 2015). Research is also appearing that supports various distinctions among subtypes of psychological maltreatment (e.g., Baker & Festinger, 2011; S. Hart et al., 2002). In addition, scholars have demonstrated that both laypeople and professionals are consistent in how they conceptualize CPM. Burnett (1993), for example, surveyed 452 social workers and 381 members of the general public regarding their opinions about 20 vignettes depicting possible CPM. Both groups generally agreed that the adults' behaviors in 18 of

BOX 6.1

IS CHILDREN'S EXPOSURE TO INTIMATE PARTNER VIOLENCE A FORM OF CHILD PSYCHOLOGICAL MALTREATMENT?

Historically, the fields of child maltreatment and intimate partner violence (IPV) have developed as separate entities. As Graham-Bermann (2002) notes, "Researchers in the areas of child abuse and domestic violence have occupied different spheres of inquiry, used disparate sources of data, received funding from different agencies, reported results at different conferences, and published their work in different journals" (p. 119). Increasingly, however, researchers have begun to see the two issues as interconnected. For example, as we have noted in previous chapters, IPV frequently co-occurs with the various forms of child maltreatment. Domestic violence in the home has been identified by the National Child Abuse and Neglect Data System (NCANDS) as a risk factor that increases the likelihood of abuse, with more than one-quarter of victims (27.2%) demonstrating this risk factor (U.S. Department of Health and Human Services [U.S. DHHS], 2019b). In one review of several studies, child maltreatment was shown to co-occur with IPV in as many as 67 percent of some families (Jouriles, McDonald, Smith Slep, Heyman, & Garrido, 2008).

Data from nationally representative samples suggest that 6 to 11 percent of U.S. children have been exposed to IPV in the past year and about 25 percent of children have been exposed to IPV in their lifetime (Finkelhor, Turner, Shattuck, & Hamby, 2015; Hamby, Finkelhor, Ormrod, & Turner, 2010). Many of these children have been exposed to severe violence, including witnessing a parent being beaten up, threatened with a gun or knife, stabbed, or shot (McDonald, Jouriles, Ramisetty-Mikler, Caetano, & Green, 2006). Is exposure to IPV its own specific form of CPM? Although disagreement on this issue exists (Victor, Henry, Gilbert, Ryan, & Perron, 2019), many experts suggest the answer is yes, in part because of the negative outcomes for children that result from such exposure.

A number of controlled studies have found that children exposed to IPV experience a variety of negative psychosocial, cognitive, and neurodevelopmental problems across the life span (e.g., Bair-Merritt et al., 2015; Costa & Gomes, 2018; Howell, Barnes, Miller, & Graham-Bermann, 2015; Shepard, 2019). Some would argue that the harm that befalls such children is the result of an omission in care, and thus exposure to IPV should be classified as emotional neglect (e.g., failure to protect). Others would argue that the emotional harm that such children experience results from a parental act of commission, and thus exposure to IPV should be viewed as a form of abuse—a form of terrorizing, whereby parental actions or threats cause a child to experience extreme fear and anxiety. In a recent study of Child Protective Services (CPS) referrals, childhood exposure to IPV was primarily classified as emotional abuse (Henry, 2018) while the most common maltreatment types substantiated for childhood exposure to IPV in another similar study were neglect-based rather than abuse-based (Victor et al., 2019). Regardless of the classification system used, it is clear that children exposed to IPV experience multiple threats (A. Campbell & Thompson, 2015).

Children's exposure to IPV has received increasing recognition by legislators, with some states enacting specific laws that criminalize exposure to IPV. To date, approximately 25 U.S. states and territories mention children's exposure to IPV in their state statutes (Child Welfare Information Gateway, 2016b). Some state statutes increase the penalty for IPV if it happens in the presence of a child; fewer actually indicate that exposing a child to IPV is a crime. Several states, for example, consider a child's exposure to IPV in their sentencing guidelines for domestic violence as an "aggravating circumstance" (Child Welfare Information Gateway, 2016b, p. 2). Utah laws, on the other hand, are more explicit and state that it is a crime to commit an act of IPV in the presence of a child (UAC 76-5-109.1). Whether or not exposure to IPV should be legally criminalized, however, is a matter of some debate because of the special circumstances that sometimes characterize these families as well as the limitations in funding associated with carrying out such legislation (Edleson, Gassman-Pines, & Hill, 2006; G. Kantor & Little, 2003).

Recognizing exposure to IPV as child maltreatment presents many significant policy, practice, and legal implications. Because all U.S. states mandate reporting of suspected cases of child abuse, defining exposure to violence as child abuse makes IPV involving children grounds for mandatory reporting. This broadening definition of abuse has led to an increase in CPS referrals, which threatens to overwhelm already overburdened state child protection systems in this country (G. Kantor & Little, 2003). In Minnesota, for example, a law mandating reporting of all cases of IPV exposure overwhelmed CPS and had to be repealed. IPV exposure laws also put adult victims in a difficult position. Knowing that they may be seeking help from professionals mandated to report the IPV as child abuse, many victims may choose not to seek help (Jaffe, Crooks, & Wolfe, 2003).

Even more controversial is the question of who should be identified as the perpetrator in IPV exposure cases. Presumably, a physically abusive father or boyfriend would be culpable. But would the woman be culpable if, for example, she chose to reunite with her abuser, thus potentially exposing her child to further harm? These are difficult questions that sometimes pit family violence advocates against one another. Many child advocates maintain that a mother who remains with an abusive husband or boyfriend should be held accountable for her failure to protect. Women's advocates, on the other hand, argue that responsibility for the exposure should not fall on the woman, who is herself a victim. Any number of special circumstances might create obstacles to a woman leaving a violent relationship (LaViolette & Barnett, 2013).

For example, women may lack the financial resources necessary to leave their homes or fear that leaving the relationship will incite more severe violence from the abuser. There is also the possibility that, because of the patriarchal assumption about the primacy of the mother's role, women who allow their children to witness IPV will be judged more harshly. Linda Mills, who has trained child welfare workers on methods of assessment and intervention, concludes that "in no uncertain terms, the mother is still viewed as the primary caretaker and is therefore judged more harshly by the child protection agency than her husband or partner" (Mills, 2000, p. 200).

In a widely publicized case on the subject, a New York district court ruled in *Nicholson v. Scoppetta* that child protection authorities acted in error when they removed children from the home of three battered women (Nowling, 2003). In each case, the primary grounds for removal were that the mother, who had been routinely assaulted, had failed to protect the child from exposure to the violence. The case hinged in large part on expert testimony from social scientists who offered differing opinions about what would likely cause the child more harm, separation from the mother or exposure to the violence. Experts called by the state testified to the various negative effects of exposure to violence, arguing in essence that removal was less traumatic and disruptive to the children than witnessing the violence. Experts called by the plaintiffs disagreed, arguing that "taking a child whose greatest fear is separation from his or her mother and in the name of 'protecting' that child by forcing on them what is, in effect, their worst nightmare, is tantamount to pouring salt on an open wound" (psychologist David Pelcovitz, as quoted in Nowling, 2003, p. 518). In its decision, the court defended the mother–child relationship, ruling that child protection authorities "shall not remove a child from the mother's custody without a court order solely because the mother is the victim of domestic violence, except in cases where the child is in such imminent danger of life or health" (Nowling, 2003, p. 518).

(Continued)

(Continued)

Many saw the case as a victory for women's rights. Whereas child protection authorities had argued in court that "women were at fault for 'engaging' in domestic violence," defenders saw the decision as recognition by the courts that battered women do not engage in domestic violence; they are victims of it (Nowling, 2003, p. 526). The word *engage* requires the consent and effort of both parties to actively participate in an activity. The dynamics of domestic violence clearly show that the victim does not actively participate in the abuse and certainly does not consent to it. Defenders of children, on the other hand, criticized the decision, arguing that the courts had not adequately addressed the problems associated with children who witness this violence as "they are victims in this situation whose rights must be protected and whose safety must be a primary concern of the courts" (Nowling, 2003, p. 526). Several state-level child welfare agencies have found a balance between these competing interests and have adopted policies that both exclude childhood exposure to IPV as an actionable form of child maltreatment (i.e., IPV does not inherently constitute child maltreatment) *and* require exposure to IPV to result in demonstrable harm or a threat of harm to be classified as child maltreatment (see, for example, Vermont Department for Children and Families, 2017).

Defining exposure to IPV as child maltreatment involves complex issues that require greater knowledge than is currently available, particularly with regard to possible legal statutes that might be affected (L. Harris, 2010). Rather than defining all cases of exposure to IPV as child abuse, legislators and others may find it more useful to consider the specific circumstances under which exposure should be defined as criminal child abuse. Several scholars have advocated for a reasoned approach on reaching this balance given the practical realities of defining child maltreatment so broadly, the fact that many children exhibit resilience under such circumstances, and because of the potential infringement on parental rights, particularly survivors of IPV (Edleson, 2004; Henry, 2017; G. Kantor & Little, 2003).

Recent years have seen a number of gains in terms of furthering research linking IPV exposure and child maltreatment and increasing collaboration between IPV and child abuse programs, between battered-women advocates and CPS workers, between child maltreatment and IPV interventions within the child welfare system, and between researchers and practitioners (Edleson & Malik, 2008; Hartley, 2012a; Lawson, 2019; Lessard & Alvarez-Lizotte, 2015; Postmus & Ortega, 2005). Although progress in coordinating the efforts of both these fields is growing, greater collaborative efforts are needed. In addition, further research is needed to determine what conceptualization of the relationship between IPV and child maltreatment will best serve children exposed to such violence.

the 20 vignettes constituted psychological maltreatment. In another study, Schaefer (1997) asked parents and mental health professionals to rate the acceptability of 10 categories of verbal behavior of parents toward children and found 80 percent agreement between the groups about the definition of these categories as never acceptable. There is also recent evidence that training programs, specifically for future child protection professionals, can be effective in helping trainees identify psychological and emotional abuse (Parker, McMillan, Olson, Ruppel, & Veith, 2019). More work in this area is necessary, however, as CPM, relative to other forms of child maltreatment, continues to be the least recognized and reported form of child maltreatment (Schols, De Ruiter, & Öry, 2013; Vanderfaeillie, De Ruyck, Galle, Van Dooren, & Schotte, 2018).

Legal Issues

As the case history that opens this chapter illustrates, although we might agree that CPM is potentially harmful and represents less-than-ideal parenting, there is far less agreement on its illegality. A total of 44 U.S. states include some reference to CPM, but it is not addressed in the statutes of 6 states (Brassard et al., 2019). In addition, when CPM is referenced, it is done so ambiguously. The original 1974 federal Child Abuse Prevention and Treatment Act (CAPTA, introduced in Chapter 3) referred to CPM (as "mental injury") and delegated the responsibility for more specific definitions to the individual states. The current version of CAPTA does little to improve on clarity and references "emotional harm" (Baker & Brassard, 2019). According to a recent assessment of U.S. state statutes, the ambiguous term "mental injury" from the original CAPTA legislation was used, and a full two-thirds of states do not define the term at all (Baker & Brassard, 2019). In addition, few court decisions have addressed cases in which CPM has occurred in the absence of any other form of child maltreatment, such as physical or sexual abuse (S. Hart et al., 2011), further hampering the recognition of CPM.

Problems of defining CPM from a legal perspective mirror those that impact the conceptual and operational definitions described at the beginning of this chapter. Nearly every state mentions acts of commission in its child abuse statutes, for example, but acts of omission are less frequently included. Most state statutes also focus on the demonstration of harm to the child as opposed to parental behavior (Brassard et al., 2019). As discussed earlier, this is potentially problematic because the effects of psychological maltreatment may only rarely be identifiable, or they may be identifiable only after years of maltreatment. Pennsylvania, for example, provides a specific and narrow definition for its category of *serious mental injury*: "a psychological condition . . . which renders the child chronically sick and severely anxious, agitated, depressed, socially withdrawn, psychotic, or in fear that his/her life is threatened" (Cons. Stat. Tit. 23, § 6303). Other states require that a child's injuries be *substantial* and *observable*. The state of Oregon added a broad definition of *mental injury* to its child abuse reporting law in 1985. This law states that any mental injury to a child "shall include only observable and substantial impairment of the child's mental or psychological ability to function caused by cruelty to the child, with due regard to the culture of the child" (ORS 419B.005).

Other state definitions emphasize the parental behaviors that lead to child injury. Minnesota's statute, for instance, includes injury that results from either overt acts of commission that are consistently and deliberately inflicted or a parent's omissions in caring for a child (Minn. Stat. Ann. 260C.007). Florida's statute provides even greater definitional specificity with regard to which parental acts of commission and omission should be regarded as CPM. For example, it recognizes various forms of isolation, such as the use of unreasonable restraints or subjecting the child to extended periods of isolation in order to control the child (Fla. Stat. Ann. 39.01).

It goes without saying that the lack of clear and consistent legal definitions contributes to problems in identifying and intervening to protect vulnerable children (Baker & Brassard, 2019; Hamarman et al., 2002; S. Hart et al., 2002). In one study, for example, Hamarman and colleagues (2002) found that states in which the laws are more likely to recognize caretaker culpability report higher rates of CPM than do other states. In contrast, states that include a harm standard in definitions have lower rates of CPM (Baker & Brassard, 2019). Clear legal definitions and definitional consensus concerning CPM are needed across the United States so that lawmakers can develop appropriate statutes to identify children at risk and intervene effectively.

Estimates of Child Psychological Maltreatment

National reporting statistics have consistently demonstrated that CPM is the least common form of reported and substantiated child maltreatment. Only 2 percent of all reported cases of child maltreatment in 2018 were identified as CPM, as distinct from child physical abuse, child sexual abuse, or child neglect (U.S. DHHS, 2020). There are several reasons to believe that this percentage is a significant underestimate. NCANDS defines CPM narrowly as "acts or omissions—other than physical abuse or sexual abuse—that caused or could have caused—conduct, cognitive, affective, or other behavioral or mental disorders. Frequently occurs as verbal abuse or excessive demands on child's performance" (p. 118). In addition, when one evaluates the "other only" category of maltreatment, which states reporting to NCANDS can use to classify other types of abuse, these cases included an additional 3 percent of children—a category that included abuse that might be considered forms of CPM such as "threatened abuse or neglect" or parent's "drug/alcohol addiction" (p. 22). It is unclear, however, how many of the children in this "other" category suffered from CPM since this category has included experiences not considered CPM (e.g., "safe relinquishment of a newborn") (U.S. DHHS, 2016, p. 25). Finally, the data used in the 2018 NCANDS report analyzed maltreatment types differently than prior editions. The 2018 NCANDS report counted only unique victims of a certain form of maltreatment (e.g., child experienced psychological maltreatment only) rather than duplicate counts (e.g., child experienced multiple forms of child maltreatment). In 2018, nearly 16 percent of children were classified as experiencing multiple maltreatment types (U.S. DHHS, 2020). Given the overlap between CPM and other forms of child maltreatment noted previously, it is likely that many of the children classified as experiencing multiple forms of maltreatment also experienced CPM.

Other evidence that rates of CPM might be higher than the 2018 estimate of 2 percent comes from data that examined caregiver alcohol or drug abuse as a risk factor. As we have noted previously, some definitions of CPM include caretaker alcohol and drug abuse as CPM, and the percentage of children in the most recent NCANDS data whose caregivers were identified as abusing alcohol or drugs was approximately 12 percent and 31 percent, respectively (U.S. DHHS, 2020).

The National Incidence Study (NIS), which uses a broader definition of CPM, suggests considerably higher rates (Sedlak & Broadhurst, 1996; Sedlak et al., 2010; U.S. DHHS, 1981, 1988). In the NIS-2, CPM (defined as psychological abuse and emotional neglect) accounted for 28 percent of all cases of child maltreatment (Sedlak, 1990). NIS data indicated that between 1980 (NIS-1) and 1986 (NIS-2), the rate of psychological abuse increased by 43 percent, and the rate of emotional neglect more than doubled. Results of the NIS-3 indicated that the rate of both psychological abuse and emotional neglect nearly tripled between 1986 and 1993 (Sedlak & Broadhurst, 1996). Results of the most recent study, the NIS-4 (2005–2006), show a different pattern (Sedlak et al., 2010). In 2005–2006, rates of CPM showed a significant increase, primarily accounted for by an increase in cases of emotional neglect.

The first National Family Violence Survey, using the Conflict Tactics Scales (CTS), found that 45 percent of parents reported insulting or swearing at their children (Daro & Gelles, 1992). Analysis of data from the second National Family Violence Survey indicated that approximately 63 percent of parents surveyed reported using one form of CPM, defined to include both verbal (e.g., insulting or swearing) and nonverbal (e.g., sulking or refusing to talk) forms of interaction with a child. One study using the CTS to estimate global prevalence of psychological aggression across residents of several low- and middle-income countries found that approximately 65 percent of parents "shouted, yelled, screamed" at, or "called dumb, lazy, or another name" their 2- to 4-year-old children (Cuartas et al., 2019). A revised version of the CTS, the Parent-Child Conflict Tactics Scales (CTSPC), was created to improve upon items assessing various forms of CPM, referred to as psychological aggression in this instrument (Straus, Hamby, Finkelhor, Moore, & Runyan, 1998). Results of a telephone survey of 1,000 parents that used the CTSPC as its measurement instrument indicated that approximately 85 percent of parents reported shouting, yelling, or screaming at their child; 54 percent reported threatening to spank or hit their child; 24 percent reported swearing or cursing at their child; 16 percent called their child a name (e.g., "dumb or lazy"); and 6 percent threatened to send their child away or "kick" them out of the house during the previous year (Straus et al., 1998).

According to the first National Survey of Children's Exposure to Violence (NatSCEV I), administered in 2008 to a nationally representative sample of 4,549 American children (Finkelhor, Turner, et al., 2009), CPM was the most frequently reported form of child maltreatment (compared to physical abuse or neglect). In this study, approximately 6 percent of the youth and parents surveyed reported some experience of CPM in the previous year, and nearly 12 percent reported having experienced CPM at some point during their lifetime. In this study, psychological maltreatment was defined as feeling "scared or bad" when "grown-ups in your life called you names, said mean things to you, or said they didn't want you" (Finkelhor, Turner, et al., 2009, p. 1418). The rates of CPM by a caregiver in the NatSCEV II, conducted in 2011, were slightly higher, with rates of CPM at 8 percent for the full sample reporting CPM in the past year and 15 percent for the full sample reporting CPM at some point during their lifetime, although these increases were not significant (Finkelhor, Turner, Shattuck, & Hamby, 2013). Similar rates for past-year and lifetime emotional abuse, 9 and 15 percent, respectively, were found in the NatSCEV III, conducted in 2014 (Finkelhor, Turner, Shattuck, & Hamby, 2015). In this study, the highest past-year and lifetime rates were observed for emotional abuse compared to physical and sexual abuse as well as neglect.

Taken as a whole, these data lead to a remarkably consistent picture. Approximately 5 percent to 10 percent of children report feeling "scared or bad" when adults in their life call them "names," say "mean things" to them, or say "they didn't want" them. These rates inch closer to 15 percent if the child is asked about lifetime experiences. This leads us to conclude that CPM is not uncommon, and is likely the most underreported form of child maltreatment. In fact, it is likely the most common form of child maltreatment (Finkelhor et al., 2013; Sedlak et al., 2010).

RISK FACTORS ASSOCIATED WITH CHILD PSYCHOLOGICAL MALTREATMENT

In this section, we describe the various risk factors associated with CPM identified to date. Because of the lack of definitional consensus for CPM and the small percentage of CPM cases reported, however, the current knowledge about its risk factors is tentative at best.

Characteristics of Psychologically Maltreated Children

Data from the NIS-4 as well as the NatSCEV III indicate that older children are at a much greater risk of CPM (Finkelhor, Turner, Shattuck, & Hamby, 2015; Sedlak et al., 2010). Results from the NatSCEV III, for example, show that approximately 16 percent of 14- to 17-year-olds were victims of emotional abuse compared to approximately 7 percent of children ages both 6–9 years and 10–13 years (Finkelhor, Turner, Shattuck, & Hamby, 2015). It is difficult to interpret these data, however, given the difficulties in reporting associated with young age.

Official estimates from the NIS-4 found no significant differences in the incidence rate of emotional abuse or emotional neglect for females and males (Sedlak et al., 2010). In contrast, findings from community surveys as well as clinical studies have found slightly higher rates for females (Finkelhor, Turner, et al., 2009; Flory et al., 2009). Data from the NatSCEV I, for example, indicated that girls (8.8%) were slightly more at risk than boys (5.5%) for CPM in the previous year as well as over their lifetime (15.7% of girls and 10.9% of boys). The NatSCEV II and III found similar trends without statistical significance (Finkelhor, Turner, Shattuck, & Hamby, 2013, 2015). These findings suggest that boys and girls are equally likely to come to the attention of mandated professionals, whereas girls are generally at greater risk for CPM than boys in self-report surveys.

Findings from several of the National Incidence Studies suggest that race and ethnicity are associated with CPM. The NIS-4 found that for emotional abuse, Hispanic children were at least risk, with both white and black children showing greater incidence than Hispanic children (Sedlak et al., 2010). In this study, black children were also at greater risk of emotional neglect than white children. One study examined race and ethnicity in a large sample (N = 1,401) of young adults ranging in age from 18 to 25 years and also found that black children reported higher levels of maternal psychological maltreatment, as measured by the CTSPC, compared to white children (Malkin & McKinney, 2019).

Very little is known about special characteristics of children, such as physical disabilities, gender identity confusion, and sexual orientation, that may put children at increased risk for CPM. Research on this topic is very limited. There is every reason to believe, however, that children who, in one way or another, are deemed "abnormal" may be at particular risk for emotional abuse and neglect. Consider, for example, the case of Evenaud Julmeus, age 30, who was arrested in late 2019 after abandoning his son on the side of the road at night because he believed the boy to be gay (Jensen, 2019). Julmeus reportedly became angry with the boy after he found him watching gay pornography on his phone and told him "the police will find you a new home" (Ng, 2019). According to news reports, the boy had no food, water, phone, or money and only a duffel bag with a few items of clothing. Given that we know that higher rates of bullying by peers (including both traditional and cyber forms of bullying) are more likely to be directed at youth who identify as lesbian, gay, bisexual, transgender, or queer (LGBTQ) compared to non-LGBTQ youth (Abreu & Kenny, 2018; Kosciw, Greytak, Giga, Villenas, & Danischewski, 2016), it stands to reason that such children may also be at greater risk of CPM by their parents. Future research should examine other potential variables that may put children at risk for CPM such as heteronormative discrimination.

Characteristics of Psychologically Maltreating Parents

Some research has examined the characteristics of psychologically maltreating parents including demographic characteristics as well as various psychosocial qualities of parents who psychologically maltreat their children. The NIS-4, for example, found that biological parents are the primary perpetrators of CPM, accounting for 73 percent of reported emotional abuse cases and 90 percent of reported emotional neglect cases

(Sedlak et al., 2010). The sex distributions of reported cases indicate that females (80%) are about twice as likely to be reported as perpetrators of emotional neglect compared to males (41%), whereas males (60%) are more likely than females (50%) to be reported for emotional abuse.

Psychologically maltreating parents exhibit more difficulties with interpersonal and social interactions, problem solving, and psychiatric adjustment. Hickox and Furnell (1989), for example, studied a group of parents legally established as emotionally abusive and found that these parents were characterized by more problematic psychosocial and background factors when compared with a matched comparison group of parents identified as needing assistance with child care and management. Emotionally abusive parents had more difficulty building relationships, exhibited poor coping skills, and displayed deficits in child management techniques. In addition, emotionally abusive mothers demonstrated a lack of support networks (both personal and community) as well as greater levels of perceived stress. Lesnik-Oberstein, Koers, and Cohen (1995) evaluated psychologically abusive and nonabusive mothers on a variety of measures of adjustment and found that the psychologically abusive mothers exhibited a greater number of psychiatric symptoms (e.g., depression, aggression, hostility), personality disturbances (e.g., social anxiety, neuroticism, low self-esteem), and physical illnesses. In addition, relative to nonabusive mothers, psychologically abusive mothers scored lower on a measure of verbal reasoning ability and reported engaging in fewer social activities. Other researchers have identified additional caregiver risk factors including substance abuse and learning disabilities (Glaser, 2011; Hickox & Furnell, 1989; Simmel & Shpiegel, 2013).

A recent meta-analysis of several studies comparing emotionally maltreating parents to nonmaltreating parents confirmed many of these earlier findings. In particular, Lavi and colleagues (2019) found that parents who emotionally maltreated their children reported higher levels of negative affect, depression, verbal aggression, and anger compared to their nonmaltreating counterparts. In addition, emotionally maltreating parents reported lower levels of emotional control, emotion regulation, and coping strategies. These findings have particular relevance to understanding the factors that might contribute to causal processes underlying CPM, and emotional maltreatment in particular, and suggest that emotional processes, including emotion reactivity and regulation, may underlie the propensity to emotionally maltreat children (Lavi et al., 2019). Lavi and colleagues suggested that the presence of negative emotions (i.e., anger and depression), coupled with poor regulation of these emotions (i.e., experiencing overwhelming emotions, cognitive difficulties when experiencing strong emotions, negative behavior when experiencing negative emotions, poor inhibition of emotional experience, and aggressive expression of emotion), put parents at risk for emotionally maltreating their own children and disrupting attachment bonds. That similar high levels of negative emotion, emotion dysregulation, and disrupted attachment are outcomes associated with experiencing

CPM (see the section of this chapter on consequences associated with CPM) gives rise to the question of intergenerational transmission of CPM.

Several studies have examined the intergenerational transmission of child maltreatment, as noted in previous chapters. Assink and colleagues (2018), for example, conducted a meta-analysis of intergenerational transmission of all types of maltreatment and found that the odds of child maltreatment in families of parents who experienced maltreatment in their own childhood were nearly 3 times the odds of child maltreatment in families of parents without a history of experiencing child maltreatment. Other studies have found that child emotional abuse is associated with greater parental psychological control (Zalewski, Cyranowski, Cheng, & Swartz, 2013), punitiveness, and psychological abuse of one's own children (Haapasalo & Aaltonen, 1999). Although a history of CPM in one's childhood serves as a risk factor for psychologically maltreating one's own children, there is also evidence that the presence of safe, stable, nurturing relationships can serve as a significant protective factor against the intergenerational transmission of child maltreatment (Merrick & Guinn, 2018; Schofield, Lee, & Merrick, 2013).

Family and Community Risk Factors

In terms of family income, the National Incidence Studies have consistently found that lower-income families are significantly more likely than higher-income families to psychologically mistreat their children (Sedlak et al., 2010). In the NIS-4, rates of abuse and neglect were 4–5 times higher for children from families of low socioeconomic status (SES) than for high-SES children (Sedlak et al., 2010).

With regard to family composition, NIS-4 data indicate differences in terms of family structure and size (Sedlak et al., 2010). Children living with a single parent are more likely to be abused and neglected than children living with two married biological parents. In terms of family size, rates of emotional abuse and emotional neglect were highest for children in the largest families (e.g., those with four or more children).

There is also an association between CPM and family dysfunction including marital discord and IPV (Hickox & Furnell, 1989; Kohl, Edleson, English, & Barth, 2005; Simmel & Shpiegel, 2013). As noted previously, witnessing IPV is sometimes viewed as a form of CPM in and of itself; however, studies also indicate that IPV is associated with occurrences of psychological maltreatment that include forms of CPM other than witnessing IPV. Simmel and Shpiegel (2013), for example, examined exposure to IPV as a risk factor for CPM using NCANDS data that included CPM cases reported to CPS. Recall from our earlier discussion that the NCANDS defined CPM as acts or omissions that caused or could have caused negative child outcomes, but that frequently involved verbal abuse or excessive demands on a child's performance. Using these data, Simmel and Shpiegel identified significant overlap between the occurrence of witnessing IPV and

CPM. Others have noted that the combination of witnessing IPV and the presence of verbal abuse results in greater negative outcomes for children than the isolated experience of either form of violence (Teicher, Samson, Polcari, & McGreenery, 2006).

It is interesting to note that Simmel and Shpiegel (2013) also found in their analysis of contextual risk factors that for a significant number of reported cases, there was a complete absence of any risk factors associated with CPM reports. These findings suggest that additional research is needed to uncover as yet undiscovered risk factors associated with CPM.

CONSEQUENCES ASSOCIATED WITH CHILD PSYCHOLOGICAL MALTREATMENT

A growing body of research studies have examined both the short-term effects associated with CPM observed in infants and children and the long-term effects observed in adolescents and adults. The *APSAC Monograph on Psychological Maltreatment* recently reached the following conclusion after providing a review of the literature on consequences associated with CPM: "Because these outcomes are found internationally, in both community and clinical samples; in correlational, prospective, and retrospective longitudinal research; in natural experiments; as well as in clinician and biographical accounts, very strong evidence establishes that the damaging correlates or consequences of [CPM] are common among those who experience it" (Brassard et al., 2019, p. 17). Table 6.3 lists the effects that have received the most consistent empirical support, which we review in the following section (for reviews, see Brassard et al., 2019, and Maguire et al., 2015).

Short-Term Effects

The short-term effects associated with CPM include a variety of problems that have been observed in infants as well as children, such as interpersonal maladjustment, learning problems, and affective-cognitive-behavioral problems. In the *interpersonal realm*, researchers have documented maladjustment in psychologically maltreated infants and children in the areas of attachment, social adjustment, and peer relationships. Psychologically maltreated children, for example, are significantly more likely than their nonmaltreated peers to experience insecure attachment to a parent (e.g., Egeland, 1997; Finzi, Ram, Har-Even, Shnit, & Weizman, 2001). Several investigators have also found that psychologically maltreated children exhibit lower levels of social competence and adjustment (e.g., have trouble making friends) than do their nonmaltreated counterparts (e.g., J. Kim & Cicchetti, 2010).

Specific *intellectual and learning problems* also distinguish psychologically maltreated children from controls (e.g., Erickson & Egeland, 2002; Fishbein et al., 2009).

TABLE 6.3 ■ Possible Outcomes Associated With Child Psychological Maltreatment	
Outcomes Observed in Infants and Children	
Interpersonal maladjustment	Insecure attachment to caregiver
	Low social competence/skills and adjustment; difficulty initiating/developing friendships
	Difficulties with peers
Intellectual and learning problems	Academic problems (including reduced literacy and numeracy)
	Deficits in problem solving and intelligence
	Poor executive decision making
Affective-cognitive-behavioral problems	Externalizing behavior (aggressive, assaultive, destructive, antisocial/delinquent)
	Internalizing behavior (withdrawn, somatic complaints, anxiety/depression)
	Less prosocial behavior
	Hostility, anger
	Suicidality
	Noncompliant behavior
	Nonsuicidal self-injury (NSSI)
	Low self-esteem, shame, guilt
	Post-traumatic stress symptoms
	Emotion dysregulation and misattribution of emotion
	Conduct disorder
	Hyperactivity, inattention, impulsivity, distractibility
	External locus of control
	Overdependence on adults for help, support, and nurturance
Outcomes Observed in Adolescents and Adults	
Health and health-related behaviors	Health problems (e.g., obesity, diabetes, coronary heart disease)
	Health-risk behavior (e.g., smoking, risky HIV behavior)
	Impaired brain limbic system
Affective-behavioral-cognitive problems	Juvenile delinquency and conduct problems
	Aggression
	Emotion dysregulation
	Negative life views and self-perceptions
	Low dispositional optimism

(Continued)

TABLE 6.3 ■ (Continued)

Outcomes Observed in Adolescents and Adults

	Low self-esteem and self-efficacy
	Anxiety
	Depression
	Suicidal ideation and behavior
	NSSI
	Dissociation
	School and learning problems (e.g., school absences)
	Sexual problems
	Substance use (binge drinking, alcohol abuse, drug use)
	Maladaptive cognitive styles
	Decreased life satisfaction
Interpersonal and parenting difficulties	Interpersonal sensitivity
	Attachment problems
	IPV (including teen dating violence, both perpetration and victimization of IPV)
	Parenting problems (e.g., hostility toward children; parenting stress; decreased caregiver responsivity, availability, self-efficacy, and positive parent–child interactions)
	Relationship difficulties, poor adjustment, low satisfaction
	Marital dissatisfaction
Mental disorders	Post-traumatic stress disorder (PTSD)
	Anxiety disorders
	Major depressive disorder
	Psychotic disorders (e.g., schizophrenia spectrum disorders)
	Eating disorders
	Personality disorders (e.g., paranoid, borderline, schizotypal)

Sources: A representative but not exhaustive list of sources for the information displayed in this table includes the following: Afifi et al., 2011; Alink, Cicchetti, Kim, & Rogosch, 2012; Bai & Han, 2016; Banducci, Felton, Bonn-Miller, Lejuez, & MacPherson, 2017; Banducci, Lejuez, Dougherty, & MacPherson, 2017; Bigras, Godbout, Hébert, Runtz, & Daspe, 2015; Bounoua et al., 2015; J. Campbell, Walker, & Egede, 2016; Caslini et al., 2016; Chapman et al., 2004; Gardner, Thomas, & Erskine, 2019; Kuo, Khoury, Metcalfe, Fitzpatrick, & Goodwill, 2015; J. Liu et al., 2017; S. Liu, Zhou, Dong, Wang, & Hao, 2019; Maguire et al., 2015; Martins, Baes, de Carvalho Tofoli, & Juruena, 2014; Massing-Schaffer, Liu, Kraines, Choi, & Alloy, 2015; Nanda, Reichert, Jones, & Flannery-Schroeder, 2016; S. Riggs, Cusimano, & Benson, 2011; S. Riggs & Kaminski, 2010; Shin, Lee, Jeon, & Wills, 2015; Spinazzola et al., 2014; Taillieu, Brownridge, Sareen, & Afifi, 2016; Wekerle, Wolfe, Cohen, Bromberg, & Murray, 2009; Yuhui et al., 2015.

Recall the longitudinal Minnesota Mother–Child Project described in Chapter 5. Researchers in that study included two psychologically maltreating groups of mothers: *verbally abusive* mothers and *psychologically unavailable* mothers (Erickson & Egeland, 2002). The children of verbally abusive mothers exhibited difficulty learning and solving problems as well as low levels of creativity relative to comparison children. The children of psychologically unavailable mothers appeared to show even greater deficits, including declines in intellectual ability and low educational achievement. A more recent Australian study examining over 19,000 kindergarten-age children found lower reading readiness among children who experienced substantiated forms of CPM (M. Bell, Bayliss, Glauert, & Ohan, 2018).

Affective, cognitive, and behavioral problems include more internalizing and externalizing behavior problems and higher levels of specific problems such as conduct problems, attention difficulties, disruptive classroom behavior, nonsuicidal self-injury, hostility and anger, anxiety, and depression (e.g., Alink, Cicchetti, Kim, & Rogosch, 2012; Cullerton-Sen et al., 2008; Schneider et al., 2005; Thomassin, Shaffer, Madden, & Londino, 2016). Such children also exhibit higher levels of emotion dysregulation, misattribution of emotion, low self-esteem, and negative cognitive styles (APSAC, 2017; Fishbein et al., 2009; J. Kim & Cicchetti, 2006, 2010).

Long-Term Effects

There is now significant consensus that CPM is associated with a number of psychological difficulties that extend into adolescence and adulthood (see Table 6.3). The Adverse Childhood Experiences (ACE) Study, described in Chapters 3 and 5 (see also Box 5.2), established CPM as a significant adverse childhood experience on par with both physical and sexual abuse (Anda et al., 1999). Since the original study, many studies, conducted both nationally and internationally, and using a variety of methodologies similar to the original ACE format, have found significant independent effects of CPM on both physical and mental health outcomes among adults (e.g., Almuneef, Qayad, Aleissa, & Albuhairan, 2014; Anderson et al., 2018; J. Campbell et al., 2016; Chapman et al., 2004; J. Poole, Dobson, & Pusch, 2017; Ramiro, Madrid, & Brown, 2010). Researchers have also conducted a number of studies of adolescents assessing both current and lifetime childhood adversities and a number of mental health outcomes and also found independent effects for CPM (e.g., Cecil et al., 2017; Hagborg, Berglund, & Fahlke, 2018). Several studies indicate that emotional or verbal abuse has the most significant and broad impact (e.g., J. Campbell et al., 2016; S. Dube et al., 2001).

Various affective-behavioral-cognitive difficulties such as low self-esteem, alcohol problems, anxiety, depression, identity problems, and suicidal ideation and behavior are more common in adults with histories of CPM (e.g., J. Campbell et al., 2016; Chapman et al., 2004; J. Liu et al., 2017; Shin, Lee, Jeon, & Wills, 2015). Adults with such histories also experience interpersonal difficulties such as problematic attachment, parenting, and general relationship functioning (Bigras, Godbout, Hébert, Runtz, & Daspe, 2015; S. Riggs, Cusimano, & Benson, 2011; S. Riggs & Kaminski, 2010). In addition to these specific problems, other research has demonstrated the presence of a number of psychological disorders such as eating disorders, major depression, and PTSD, among others (Caslini et al., 2016; Taillieu, Brownridge, Sareen, & Afifi, 2016).

It is important to remember that CPM is a broad term that represents a number of qualitatively different experiences (Berzenski, Madden, & Yates, 2019). Waxman and colleagues (Waxman, Fenton, Skodol, Grant, & Hasin, 2014), for example, found that acts of commission—emotional abuse—were associated with certain personality disorders (e.g., **schizotypal**, borderline, **narcissistic**) while acts of omission—emotional neglect—were associated with other personality disorders (e.g., **paranoid**, **schizoid**, **avoidant**). In contrast, Taillieu et al. (2016) found in a large (N = 34,653) nationally representative U.S. sample that all categories of emotional maltreatment (including both emotional abuse and neglect) were associated with increased odds of nearly every mental disorder assessed (independent of sociodemographic characteristics, other forms of child maltreatment, and family history of dysfunction), although the effects were greater for emotionally abusive acts of commission than those of omission. Other studies have consistently found that acts of degradation (e.g., verbally aggressive and abusive parenting) in particular, as compared to other forms of emotional abuse and other forms of child maltreatment, result in particularly damaging impacts (Miller-Perrin, Perrin, & Kocur, 2009; Paul & Eckenrode, 2015; Teicher et al., 2006). These discrepant findings may be due to variability in CPM experiences such as the perceived frequency, intensity, and meaning of the abuse experiences. Research examining child emotional abuse, for example, has revealed that specific characteristics of such abuse experiences, such as frequency and intensity, are independent characteristics of abuse, and are associated with different outcomes (Berzenski et al., 2019). Berzenski and colleagues (2019), for example, found in a sample of female caregivers with a history of emotional abuse that higher frequency of abuse predicted increased adult psychopathology, while higher intensity of abuse predicted dysfunctional views of the parent–child relationship.

While there is considerable research examining the long-term effects associated with CPM, there is less understanding about the mechanisms that explain why CPM leads to certain outcomes. Several studies are emerging that suggest specific pathways that explain why CPM leads to the various outcomes listed in Table 6.3 (Arslan, 2016; Bigras et al., 2015; Paul & Eckenrode, 2015). Sachs-Ericsson and colleagues (2010), for example, found that self-criticism mediated the relationship between parental verbal abuse and depression/anxiety symptoms. Other studies have found that CPM is related to poor relationship adjustment through its impact on unhealthy attachment styles, impaired sense of self, and the experience of greater conflicts in relationships (Bigras et al., 2015; S. Riggs et al., 2011).

One recent longitudinal study with implications for the intergenerational transmission of CPM (discussed earlier) found that negative emotional expressiveness mediated the relationship between a mother's own emotional maltreatment experiences and her infant's emotional dysregulation and behavioral problems in children as young as 14 months of age (S. Liu, Zhou, Dong, Wang, & Hao, 2019). Research has also suggested that these specific pathways may vary depending on whether the victim is male or female as well as the developmental stage of the victim (Paul & Eckenrode, 2015). Clearly, additional research is needed to untangle the complicated relationships between CPM and its outcomes.

INTERVENTION AND PREVENTION OF CHILD PSYCHOLOGICAL MALTREATMENT

Few unique research efforts have been directed toward possible solutions and interventions for CPM. In addition, CPM has not been a significant focus in either child welfare or public health (Altafim & Linhares, 2016; Coore Desai, Reece, & Shakespeare-Pellington, 2017). As a result, studies concerned with intervention and prevention approaches unique to CPM have been nearly nonexistent, although many of the strategies discussed in previous chapters (e.g., parenting programs, home visitation, individual and group therapies) may also be applicable to CPM. As noted previously and discussed in the opening case history of the Machnick family, criminal prosecution is rarely a viable option in CPM. In addition, separating the child from the maltreating caregiver(s) is rarely a first response (Glaser, 2011); therefore, most efforts focus on intervention approaches directed at children and parents and on public education about the problem. In an attempt to move the field of CPM forward, experts in the field have also offered suggestions for the development of innovative intervention and prevention efforts specific to CPM (for reviews, see Brassard et al., 2019; Chiel & Fiorvanti, 2019). The discussion here focuses on formal programs and strategies; personal responses to address the problem are included in Chapter 11.

Brassard and colleagues (2019) offer a three-tiered framework for interventions that is directly relevant to CPM. The three tiers include the following (p. 47):

Tier 1 encompassing universal well-being promotion and violence prevention efforts,

Tier 2 concentration on pointed intervention for at-risk populations, and

Tier 3 focused on correction where [psychological maltreatment] has occurred and requires intensive targeted intervention due to the failure or insufficiency of the other tiers.

Efforts to address all three of these tiers as they relate to child maltreatment have been addressed in Chapters 3, 4, and 5. We discussed media campaigns, child-focused education programs, and universal parenting programs (Tier 1), as well as home visiting programs and community-based programs (both Tier 1 and Tier 2). Tier 3 approaches have also been discussed in previous chapters including interventions that focus on children who are maltreated, their parents, or both children and parents of maltreating families (e.g., trauma-focused cognitive behavioral therapy [TF-CBT], Alternatives for Families: A Cognitive Behavioral Therapy [AF-CBT], and Parent–Child Interaction Therapy [PCIT]). We therefore focus this section on available efforts that specifically address CPM and attempt to correct difficulties associated with CPM for both children and parents (Tier 3). We then briefly consider the role of schools and public education in combatting CPM, specifically (Tier 1).

Interventions for Psychologically Maltreated Children

Given the many forms that CPM can take, it is likely that no single treatment intervention will be effective for all victims. Binggeli, Hart, and Brassard (2001) recommend treatment interventions that focus on three domains that correspond to the negative outcomes associated with CPM. The first domain concerns intrapersonal issues, including identity, self-esteem, and dysfunctional attributions of self. The second domain focuses on social and interpersonal issues, including relationship problems and deficits in attachments to significant others. The third domain consists of behavior and emotional problems, such as depression, anxiety, aggression, and poor impulse control.

Glaser (2011) recommends that children who remain in families where the CPM continues need ongoing support to cope with the maltreatment, including addressing issues of intrapersonal concern (self-blame and low self-esteem). Additional issues that may need to be addressed include acknowledging the reality of the children's experiences and explaining the parents' difficulties, enhancing the children's problem-solving skills to cope with the maltreatment, ensuring the children are able to fulfill their educational potential to enhance self-esteem, and encouraging the development of a positive, enduring, and meaningful relationship with another adult(s). Other intervention strategies focus on the behavioral and emotional difficulties of the child as well as parental responses to the child. These strategies include enhancing the developmental and adaptive abilities of the child (e.g., social skills and assertiveness training), enhancing appropriate expectations for child compliance, increasing effective parenting skills, and promoting anger management techniques (Iwaniec, 2006; Wolfe, 1991).

Although there is no intervention outcome literature on these treatment strategies that are designed specifically for CPM, studies have documented the effectiveness of various treatment strategies with other child maltreatment groups, such as TF-CBT. (See Chapters 3–5 for discussions of treatment outcome research for other forms of child maltreatment.) These strategies may not prove effective in addressing all of the problems associated with CPM, but they do hold some promise.

Interventions to Enhance Sensitive Parenting

As noted by Binggelli and colleagues (2001), as well as other experts on CPM (Brassard et al., 2019; S. Hart, 2019), one domain that should be addressed in psychologically maltreating families is relationship problems, including deficits in attachment to significant others. Several relational interventions have been developed because they potentially promote *resilient* functioning by supporting the development of more positive parent–child interactions (Toth & Manly, 2019). Attention to resilience in addressing the issues facing child maltreatment victims, including those who have experienced CPM, has increased within the context of research on adverse childhood experiences. Resilience, for example, has been defined as a dynamic process that includes positive adaptation within the context of significant adversity (Luthar & Ciciola, 2015; Masten, 2014) such as CPM specifically and other forms of child maltreatment more generally. Furthermore, "resilience relies fundamentally on relationships, and this is true for children and adults" (National Academies of Science, Engineering, and Medicine, 2019). Relational interventions include a number of promising approaches for both preventing and addressing the sequelae of child maltreatment for children at various ages such as during infancy and toddlerhood (child–parent psychotherapy [Lieberman, Ghosh Ippen, & Van Horn, 2015], Attachment and Biobehavioral Catch-Up [Bernard et al., 2012; Dozier, 2003], and brief attachment-based intervention [Moss et al., 2011]), as well as for older children (PCIT [discussed in Chapter 4] and multisystemic therapy for child abuse and neglect [Swenson, Penman, Henggeler, & Rowland, 2010]).

Relational interventions for psychologically maltreating parents, particularly those who emotionally neglect their children, are based on **attachment theory** (Erickson & Egeland, 2011). The development of a secure attachment relationship between child and caregiver is critical to a child's early healthy development and has a significant impact on the development of current as well as future behavior and relationships. As noted previously, children who are maltreated are at increased risk for developing insecure attachments, and therefore, it is important to provide relationally based interventions to infants and children who are maltreated (Guild, Toth, Handley, Rogosch, & Cicchetti, 2017; Toth & Manly, 2019). Such interventions typically center on improving parental sensitivity, attunement, and responsiveness to children's needs in the first five years of life (Toth & Manly, 2019). In particular, treatment strategies focus on enhancing parental sensitivity and enjoyment of the child through child observation, child-centered activities, and play and stimulation techniques, among other targets (Barlow & McMillan, 2010; Iwaniec, 2006; Toth & Manly, 2019). One specific approach is child–parent psychotherapy (CPP), which uses active dyadic sessions with parents and children in an effort to restore or establish parents' ability to protect and care for their children through processing emotions, facilitating attention to children's emotional needs, and supporting the development of positive relationships and attachment security (Lieberman et al., 2015). Furthermore, this approach is designed to address trauma in both parent and child (Lieberman et al., 2015), which is particularly helpful given our earlier discussion about the frequency with which parents who engage in CPM have their own histories of emotional abuse.

In an initial randomized controlled trial of CPP with anxiously attached infants and their mothers (not those specifically exposed to CPM), results indicated a reduction in children's avoidance, resistance, and anger, and enhanced mother–child relationships, compared to a control group (Lieberman, Weston, & Pawl, 1991). Another evaluation study examined CPP, along with a psychoeducational parenting intervention, specifically with maltreating families, and found the combination to be effective in changing early parent–child attachment relationships from insecure to secure, and efficacy of CPP was sustained at a one-year follow-up (Cicchetti, Rogosch, & Toth, 2006; Stronach, Toth, Rogosch, & Cicchetti, 2013). As evidence of CPP's long-term effectiveness, a follow-up study of CPP found positive effects of the treatment approach on peer relationships of school-age children years after treatment (Guild et al., 2017). A meta-analysis examining the effectiveness of several different attachment-based interventions, ranging from home visiting programs to parent–infant psychotherapy, demonstrated that these programs show promise in improving both sensitive parenting and infant attachment security (Bakermans-Kranenburg, van IJzendoorn, & Juffer, 2003). In one study, 1-year-old infants (approximately 70% of whom had been emotionally maltreated) were randomly assigned to receive either infant–parent psychotherapy, a psychoeducational home visitation parenting intervention, or a community standard control intervention that did not include enhanced services (Cicchetti et al., 2006). Compared to infants in the control condition, infants in both intervention conditions showed significant increases in secure attachment at a 26-month post-intervention follow-up. Others have implemented cognitive behavioral therapy approaches with psychologically maltreating parents to help parents manage difficult child behavior, decrease parental anger, and correct misattributions of child behavior (Sanders et al., 2004). Relative to other forms of child maltreatment, very few published interventions and evaluations specifically target psychologically maltreating parents, and there is no direct evidence that these interventions *prevent* CPM (Hibbard et al., 2012; MacMillan et al., 2009). More research is needed in this area in order to effectively enhance parenting behaviors as well as to prevent psychological maltreatment from reoccurring.

The Role of Schools and Day Cares

Day cares, schools, and their respective personnel can play an important role in addressing CPM. First, we know that a significant number of official reports of CPM and other forms of child maltreatment come from school personnel. In one study conducted in Brussels, 38 percent of reports of suspected child maltreatment came from school personnel (Vanderfaeillie et al., 2018). In the United States in 2018, the highest percentage (20.5%) of child maltreatment reports were from education personnel (U.S. DHHS, 2020). Clearly, these educators are in a position to identify cases of CPM that might otherwise go undetected. Second, because children spend so much of their time in school, the school setting provides a natural environment for promoting healthy interpersonal interactions. Preschool and elementary school teachers, for example, can help both children and parents by developing secure attachments with the children they encounter and by serving as models of appropriate adult–child interaction for parents (S. Hart et al., 2002). Schools are also ideal environments for developing and nurturing specific social and academic skills. As S. Hart and colleagues (2002) note, "Schools that give at-risk students a sense of competence through successful experience in academics, art, music, athletics, or social interaction and that teach them to plan and make conscious choices about important events in their lives have significantly better student outcomes" (p. 97). Schools can also develop intervention programs that target various protective factors, such as resilience and self-esteem, and that include children and adolescents as participants as well as parents (Arslan, 2016).

Public Engagement and Education

A number of experts in the field recommend a public health model for addressing CPM that includes universal interventions aimed to broadly promote positive parent–child relationships and healthy child development (Brassard et al., 2019; Hibbard et al., 2012; Wolfe & McIsaac, 2011). Core elements of this approach involve increasing public awareness about what constitutes positive parenting and healthy child development, and providing community-based support for young parents. The Triple P and Incredible Years programs, discussed in Chapters 3 and 5, respectively, provide good examples of this approach that have demonstrated effectiveness. Another strategy would be educating the public about CPM through various media-based campaigns including leaflets, books, posters, social media, and videos (Brassard et al., 2019; Hibbard et al., 2012; Wolfe & McIsaac, 2011). A number of media campaigns also include informational websites (for examples, see https://preventchildabuse.org/resource/preventing-emotional-abuse/ and https://bapa.org/campaign-brings-awareness-to-child-abuse-prevention/). One media campaign, *Breaking the Cycle*, served to educate the general public regarding the benefits of not maltreating children and helping parents understand the cycle of maltreatment (i.e., children learn from their parents). This program was effective in changing parents' emotionally abusive behaviors as a post-campaign survey showed that up to 44 percent of parents had considered changing their behavior and up to 16 percent had tried to stop yelling at, screaming at, or putting down their child (Stannard, Hall, & Young,

1998). Other campaigns focusing on positive parenting have been similarly successful in de-stigmatizing the notion that parents need help in parenting (Henley, Donovan, & Morehead, 1998).

Another important step in preventing CPM should be to educate various professionals about the problem. Legal professionals, medical and mental health practitioners, legislators, educators, and government officials need to become aware of the existence of CPM as an independent form of child maltreatment that is associated with detrimental child outcomes. As we have noted, although improvements are happening in knowledge and understanding of CPM among professionals, CPM continues to be the least recognized and reported form of child maltreatment; greater awareness among professionals about CPM is clearly needed. One study found that such awareness is particularly needed for professionals who might encounter emotional abuse as school personnel identified emotional abuse less frequently and viewed it as less severe relative to other forms of child maltreatment (Vanderfaeillie et al., 2018). Indeed, enhancing awareness and understanding of the problem of child maltreatment, including CPM, among both professionals and the lay public is a primary goal of many professional organizations (see Box 6.2). Currently, many organizations and their professional members are working diligently to increase awareness about this social problem. APSAC, one of the premier professional groups focusing on child maltreatment, has recently revised its practice guidelines on CPM in an effort to help professionals understand what constitutes CPM and to improve practice in this area (APSAC, 2017) and also recently published its *APSAC Monograph on Psychological Maltreatment* to help provide information about what is known about CPM and its assessment, prevention, and intervention (Brassard et al., 2019). Once influential professionals and society at large become convinced of the importance of the problem, greater support for intervention and prevention efforts should emerge.

BOX 6.2

THE AMERICAN PSYCHOLOGICAL ASSOCIATION'S DIVISION 37 SECTION ON CHILD MALTREATMENT

The American Psychological Association (APA) is the largest scientific and professional organization of psychologists in the world, with more than 100,000 members and 54 divisions representing the many diverse areas within the field of psychology. Each APA division contains various sections made up of members who are interested in special topics within psychology. APA's Division 37 (Society for Child and Family Policy and Practice) is the home of members of the Section on Child Maltreatment.

The Section on Child Maltreatment is the only permanent organization within the APA specifically created to address issues related to child physical and sexual abuse, CPM, and child neglect. The section was established in 1994 to support and promote scientific inquiry, training, professional practice, and advocacy in the area of child maltreatment. In the short time of its existence, the section has accomplished a great deal. A team of section members, for example, has developed curriculum guidelines to improve education and training in the area of child maltreatment at the undergraduate, graduate, and postgraduate levels. Another team has developed a lesson plan on child maltreatment for use with high school students. Members of the section also organized a congressional briefing on Capitol Hill in an effort to increase federal funding for child abuse prevention activities. A section team also helped to develop an amicus brief for the U.S. Supreme Court on the long-term effects of child sexual abuse.

The Section on Child Maltreatment welcomes new members, including both students and professionals, who are interested in furthering research, practice, and policy issues related to the area of child maltreatment. Section members receive the section newsletter, which contains updates on section activities as well as columns on best practices and other information on research and policy. Members are also eligible to receive section awards for outstanding early career contributions to research and practice, promising dissertation proposals, and exemplary APA poster presentations by students. Interested readers can get more information on joining the Section on Child Maltreatment by contacting the APA's Division Services Office at (202) 216-7602 or by visiting the section's website at www .apadivisions.org/division-37/sections/index .aspx.

CHAPTER SUMMARY

Child psychological maltreatment is arguably the most elusive form of maltreatment and, as a result, has received the least amount of attention. The vague nature of this form of maltreatment is evident by the fact that a significant proportion of the research directed toward CPM focuses on definitional issues. At present, no single definition of CPM is universally accepted. Establishing the parameters of CPM has proved quite difficult and confusing. Researchers disagree about whether definitions should be broad or narrow and about the relative importance of parental behaviors versus child outcomes.

Given these definitional complexities, the true incidence of CPM is largely undetermined, as are victim characteristics associated with this form of child maltreatment. Researchers have obtained much of their information about rates and correlates of psychological maltreatment from official reports made to CPS agencies. Although the quality of information available on this problem is limited, it is clear that many children are reported as victims of CPM each year in the United States. CPM, however, is the least commonly reported form of child maltreatment, accounting for 6 percent to 28 percent of reported cases.

Research conducted to date indicates that reports of CPM increase as children become older. The research has shown no consistent gender differences among victims, nor is there a clear pattern of racial differences. Studies have shown a link, however, between CPM and low income. Most reported cases indicate that female parents are about twice as likely to be identified as the perpetrators of emotional neglect compared to males, while males are more often reported as perpetrators of emotional abuse compared to females. Consistent findings have also been observed with regard to psychosocial variables in psychologically maltreating parents, who are characterized as exhibiting interpersonal and social difficulties, poor problem-solving skills, substance abuse, and psychiatric maladjustment. Additional research is needed, however, to replicate current findings and expand understanding of risk factors associated with CPM.

Studies of the negative effects associated with CPM are limited in both number and quality, making interpretation of findings difficult. Research has, however, consistently uncovered a variety of associated problems in victims, including social, emotional, and behavioral difficulties and intellectual deficits. Many scholars believe that the negative effects of child CPM extend into adulthood, but more research is necessary to establish the relationship between childhood histories of CPM and adjustment problems in adulthood.

Few intervention and prevention approaches have been developed to address the unique aspects of CPM, and research evaluating the effectiveness of such approaches is limited. Professionals in the field of child maltreatment should focus their future efforts on increasing public awareness and understanding of CPM to garner support and resources for efforts aimed at reducing the incidence and harmful effects associated with this form of child maltreatment.

Recommended Resources

American Professional Society on the Abuse of Children. (2017). *APSAC practice guidelines for the investigation and determination of suspected psychological maltreatment in children and adolescents.* Chicago, IL: Author.

Barlow, J., & McMillan, A. S. (2010). *Safeguarding children from emotional maltreatment: What works.* London, England: Jessica Kingsley.

Brassard, M. R., Hart, S. N., Baker, A., & Chiel, Z. (2019). *The APSAC monograph on psychological maltreatment.* Columbus, OH: American Professional Society on the Abuse of Children. Retrieved from www.apsac.org/single-post/2019/12/16/Now-Available-The-APSAC-Monograph-on-Psychological-Maltreatment

Glaser, D. (2011). How to deal with emotional abuse and neglect: Further development of a conceptual framework (FRAMEA). *Child Abuse & Neglect, 35*(10), 866–875.

Maguire, S. A., Williams, B., Naughton, A. M., Cowley, L. E., Tempest, V., Mann, M. K., . . .

Kemp, A. M. (2015). A systematic review of the emotional, behavioural and cognitive features exhibited by school-aged children experiencing neglect or emotional abuse. *Child: Care, Health and Development, 41*(5), 641–653.

National Academies of Science, Engineering, and Medicine. (2019). *Vibrant and healthy kids: Aligning science, practice, and policy to advance health equity.* Washington, DC: National Academies Press. https://doi.org/10.17226/25466

Toth, S. L., & Manly, J. T. (2019). Developmental consequences of child abuse and neglect: Implications for intervention. *Child Development Perspectives, 13*(1), 59–64.

Wolfe, D. A., & McIsaac, C. (2011). Distinguishing between poor/dysfunctional parenting and child emotional maltreatment. *Child Abuse & Neglect, 35*(10), 802–813.

7

ABUSE IN ADOLESCENT AND EMERGING ADULT RELATIONSHIPS

Peer Sexual Harassment, Sexual Assault, Dating Violence, and Stalking

LEARNING OBJECTIVES

1. Describe the definition and scope of peer sexual and gender harassment, sexual assault, and teen dating violence and stalking, including problems inherent in measuring these forms of abuse.

2. Identify the various risk factors associated with peer sexual and gender harassment, sexual assault, and teen dating violence and stalking.

3. Summarize the consequences of peer sexual and gender harassment, sexual assault, and teen dating violence and stalking.

4. Discuss the various intervention and prevention efforts that focus on peer sexual and gender harassment, sexual assault, and teen dating violence and stalking, including evidence of their effectiveness.

CASE HISTORY
TROY "LIKES" TONYA

Shortly after he started sixth grade, 12-year-old Troy told all of his friends how much he liked the new girl at their school, Tonya, and he boasted that soon she would be his girlfriend. Troy spent a lot of time following Tonya around school, and he made sure he sat next to her in every class they had in common. Whenever she walked by him, he stared at her and made comments about her body, which became increasingly sexually suggestive, especially if he was in the company of his friends. For her part, Tonya tried ignoring Troy and, on several occasions, including in the presence of his friends, told him to "Stop it" and "Shut up," but he just laughed and taunted her more. When he started touching her, she complained to her teachers, and she also told her parents. School officials said they would talk to Troy, but he remained undeterred. One day, in front of his friends, he came up behind her and began rubbing his genitals against her buttocks while explicitly asking her for sex.

Tonya, who up to this point had always been a good student, started missing school, and her grades dropped dramatically. Her worried parents noticed that she wasn't eating and that she was spending most of her time in her room, isolating herself from family and friends. Tonya's parents' alarm grew when they found what appeared to be a suicide note written by Tonya. They acted quickly to get her counseling, but they also filed a criminal complaint against Troy as well as a federal civil rights lawsuit against the school district. The grounds for the civil suit rested on the argument that school officials were aware of Troy's behavior, but did little to stop it, thereby violating Tonya's civil rights. The court agreed with Tonya and her parents, emphasizing that the behavior of her male classmate was not "bullying," but rather sexual harassment, which is a violation of Title IX of the 1972 Education Amendments Act. By not responding appropriately, the court ruled, school officials had created a hostile and abusive learning environment, thus limiting Tonya's ability to fully participate in, and benefit from, school.

Some people might read about Troy's behavior and, while conceding it was boorish, nevertheless shrug it off as "normal" for an adolescent male. Adolescence, after all, is presumed by many to be a time when young men are coping with their "raging hormones," but don't know yet how to effectively communicate with those in whom they are romantically interested. Adolescent awkwardness may end up getting expressed through aggression, which could result in "misunderstandings." But as depicted in the case history and as we will continue to discuss throughout this chapter, behavior such as Troy's has serious negative consequences for those subjected to it. It is more than simply a manifestation of immaturity; it is a form of sexual harassment.

Adolescence and emerging adulthood is recognized as a distinct developmental stage of the life course. It is the transitional period that spans the onset of puberty through young adulthood (roughly ages 12–24). It is important to keep in mind that there is a good deal of diversity among young people during this developmental stage. For instance, as Table 7.1 shows, some adolescents end their formal education at age 16 or younger, and even more at 17 or 18; they move out of their parents' homes and seek employment or other ways to financially support themselves and, perhaps, significant others in their lives. Others, like many of you who are reading this book, continue their formal education during this developmental period, enrolling in college part-time or full-time, and delay living totally independently for at least several more years. Regardless of the trajectory toward adulthood, however, this is the period when young people are expected to assert greater autonomy, become more self-reliant, and engage in more self-directed decision making. It is also the time

TABLE 7.1 ■ Enrollment Status of the Population, Ages 10–24 Years, 2017	
Age (in Years)	% Enrolled in School
10–13	97.8
14–15	98.2
16–17	92.9
18–19	68.2
20–21	55.0
22–24	28.4

Source: U.S. Census Bureau, Table 1. Enrollment Status of the Population 3 Years Old and Over by Sex, Age, Race, Hispanic Origin, Foreign Born, & Foreign-Born Parentage: October 2017. Retrieved June 23, 2019, from http://www.census.gov/data/tables/2017/demo/school-enrollment/2017-cps.html.

when young people become involved in romantic relationships with opposite-sex or same-sex peers. Indeed, for most youth, adolescence and emerging adulthood is a period of active sexual exploration and, often, intense emotional interactions.

On national surveys, about one-quarter to more than one-half of 12- to 18-year-olds in the United States report being in some type of "special" romantic or dating relationship (Furman & Winkles, 2011; Lenhart, Smith, & Page, 2015). While most of these youth do not label their romantic relationships as "serious" (Lenhart et al., 2015), many of them are sexually active. The Centers for Disease Control and Prevention (CDC) reports that among high school students surveyed in 2017 as part of the Youth Risk Behavior Surveillance System (YRBSS), just over one-third (39.5%) said they had ever had sexual intercourse, and 9.7 percent of these young people had had sex with four or more different partners so far during their lives (Kann et al., 2018; see Table 7.2). Not surprisingly, older teens (in 12th grade) are more likely to report having ever had sex (58.9% of males and 55.8% of females); nevertheless, about one-fifth of teens in ninth grade (23.3% of males and 17.2% of females) also report having had sex (Kann et al., 2018).

Adolescents and young adults see their intimate partners as a major source of social and emotional support, and the importance of this support increases from adolescence to young adulthood. Research shows, for instance, that in a hierarchical ranking of the supportive people in one's life, romantic partners move from fourth place among seventh graders, to third place among tenth graders, to first place among college men and tied for first among college women (Furman & Winkles, 2011). But, as we will learn in the

TABLE 7.2 ■ U.S. High School Students Who Are Sexually Active, by Sex and Grade, 2017				
	Currently Sexually Active (%)*		Sexual Intercourse With > 4 Partners, Lifetime (%)	
Grade	Males	Females	Males	Females
9	14.1	11.7	6.0	1.8
10	25.3	24.6	9.7	5.1
11	34.7	35.8	12.2	9.1
12	43.5	45.1	19.5	16.5

*Currently sexually active: Had sexual intercourse with at least one person during the 3 months before the survey.

Source: Centers for Disease Control and Prevention (CDC), Youth Risk Behavior Surveillance—United States, 2017. Retrieved from https://www.cdc.gov/mmwr/volumes/67/ss/ss6708a1.htm.

following pages, intimate relationships may also be stressful and have serious negative consequences for adolescents and young adults.

In this chapter, we will examine various types of peer-to-peer abuse, including sexual harassment as described in the opening case history, as well as sexual assault and violence and stalking in dating relationships. Although many youth navigate this developmental stage with minimal crises and emerge with a strong and positive sense of self and with the skills needed for healthy adult relationships, adolescence and emerging adulthood is a period of high risk for these problematic behaviors and experiences. Risk, however, is not distributed equally among all teens and young adults. One of our goals in this chapter, then, is not only to discuss the incidence and prevalence of various types of abuse in adolescence and young adulthood, but also to identify the most salient risk factors, which, in turn, suggest effective prevention and intervention strategies.

PEER SEXUAL HARASSMENT

In the case history that opened this chapter, we read that the court, in deciding in favor of Tonya and her parents in their civil suit against the school district, noted that Troy's behavior was sexual harassment, not bullying. How are the two different? **Bullying** is aggressive or mean-spirited behavior that occurs repeatedly over time and has the underlying intent to harm or disturb the person or group at whom it is targeted. Bullying is perpetrated by a person or group who is perceived as having more power (physical or psychological) than the weaker, less powerful individual or peer group that is targeted (Nansel et al., 2001). **Sexual harassment**, in contrast, is defined as unwelcome sexual advances, requests for sexual favors, or other verbal, nonverbal, or physical conduct of a sexual nature (U.S. Department of Education, 2010). As shown in Table 7.3, sexual harassment includes a wide range of unwanted and unwelcome behaviors such as sexual comments, jokes, gestures, or rumors; showing sexual pictures or writing sexual messages in private (e.g., notes, text messages), on public spaces (e.g., bathroom walls, locker rooms), or through social media posts; and being touched or grabbed, or being forced to touch someone else, in a sexual way. Being called gay or lesbian in a malicious way is also a form of sexual harassment although it is usually referred to as **gender harassment** rather than sexual harassment (J. Gruber & Fineran, 2007; U.S. Department of Education, 2010). As we learned in Chapter 4, adults may do these things to children, but in this chapter we will focus on young men and women who do these things to each other. Moreover, while bullying is inappropriate and harmful and may be perpetrated using behaviors (e.g., physical assaults) that are illegal, bullying in and of itself is not a legally prohibited activity. Sexual harassment is illegal discrimination that violates the victim's civil rights (L. Brown, Chesney-Lind, & Stein, 2007; J. Gruber & Fineran, 2016; U.S. Department of Education, 2010). However, researchers report that both bullying and

TABLE 7.3 ■ Examples of Sexually Harassing Behaviors
• Making unwanted and unwelcome sexual comments, jokes, or gestures, or telling stories or spreading rumors of this nature
• Repeatedly asking a person out on a date or to hook up, even though that person has already refused
• Showing or sending sexual pictures or images to someone the person in the pictures or images does not want to see them
• Sending unwanted sexual messages (e.g., emails, texts, notes) or writing such messages about someone in public spaces (e.g., graffiti in public restrooms) or on social media
• Touching or grabbing someone in a sexual way without the other person's consent, or forcing someone to touch or grab another person against that person's will
• Using sexual body language to embarrass or upset someone
• Calling people gay or lesbian or a pejorative term for homosexual in a malicious way or taunting people about their sexuality (also called gender harassment)

Sources: J. Gruber & Fineran, 2007; N. Henry & Flynn, 2019; U.S. Department of Education, 2010.

sexual harassment can have devastating effects on the victimized, especially for girls and for lesbian, gay, bisexual, transgender, and queer (LGBTQ) youth (J. Gruber & Fineran, 2016; Riese, 2016).

Prevalence of Peer Sexual Harassment

Estimates of peer sexual harassment among adolescents and emerging adults vary widely, ranging from 23 percent to more than 80 percent (Clear et al., 2014). This variation is largely due to the characteristics of the samples surveyed, the definitions used, the way questions were worded, and the time period examined. For instance, the percentages, not surprisingly, are higher if one asks about experiences that occurred during the respondents' "school years" versus during the past school year. But questions that ask if a respondent has ever been "sexually harassed" yield lower percentages than those that are behaviorally specific, asking, for example, if the respondent has experienced unwanted sexual comments from a classmate (see also Box 7.1).

One recent study of students attending 26 high schools throughout the state of Kentucky asked behaviorally specific questions about sexual harassment experiences that had occurred during the past 12 months (Clear et al., 2014). These experiences included a classmate who told the respondent sexual jokes or stories that made the respondent feel uneasy; made gestures, made rude remarks, or used sexual body language to embarrass or upset the respondent; and kept asking the respondent out on a date or to hook up, even though the respondent had already said no. Of the 20,806 students who completed surveys, 37.1 percent of girls and 21.4 percent of boys reported having experienced at least one form of sexual harassment from a classmate over the past 12 months. These findings support those of other studies that consistently show that girls experience more sexual harassment than boys, although it may be surprising to some readers that about one in five boys report sexual harassment by a classmate (J. Gruber & Fineran, 2016; C. Hill, Kearl, & American Association of University Women, 2011). Far fewer students admit to perpetrating sexual harassment, but the findings again show gender differences: About twice as many boys as girls have sexually harassed a classmate—for example, 12.4 percent of boys compared with 5.1 percent of girls in the Kentucky high school study (Clear et al., 2014).

Researchers also report other important differences in sexual harassment victimization and perpetration. For instance, students of color, especially female students of color, are more likely than white students to experience sexual harassment (Kann et al., 2018; J. Miller, 2008), and students with disabilities, especially girls with disabilities, experience more sexual harassment than students who do not have disabilities (K. Brown, Peña, & Rankin, 2017; J. Gruber & Fineran, 2007). Studies also show that LGBTQ students experience more sexual harassment than heterosexual students do (J. Gruber & Fineran, 2007; Kann et al., 2018). Clear et al. (2014), for example, found that students who identified as not exclusively attracted to partners of the opposite sex had significantly higher rates of sexual harassment victimization (40.1%) than students who identified as exclusively attracted to partners of the opposite sex (28.1%). Moreover, researchers report that sexual minority youth are significantly more likely to experience chronic (as opposed to infrequent) sexual harassment (McGinley, Wolff, Rospenda, Lu, & Richman, 2016) and to experience polyvictimization (i.e., multiple types of harassment and sexual violence) (Sterzing et al., 2019).

Risk Factors Associated With Peer Sexual Harassment

Several risk factors associated with peer sexual harassment have been identified (see Table 7.4). We mentioned previously, for example, that on surveys, both girls and boys

TABLE 7.4 ■ Risk Factors for Adolescent Peer Sexual Harassment Perpetration
• Bullying at a young age
• Witnessing and/or experiencing abuse at home
• Adherence to norms of hegemonic masculinity
• Peer support and reinforcement for harassing behaviors

Sources: Clear et al., 2014; Espelage et al., 2011; J. Gruber & Fineran, 2016; Wolfe, Jaffe, & Crooks, 2006.

admit to having perpetrated sexual harassment against their peers, but boys have significantly higher perpetration rates than do girls. In fact, in sexual harassment studies, while boys typically harass girls, they are rarely the victims of sexual harassment by girls (J. Gruber & Fineran, 2016). Rates of sexual harassment perpetration by nonwhite students are somewhat higher than for white students (11.9% and 7.8%, respectively). Although little research is available on same-sex peer sexual harassment, studies show that LGBTQ students admit to perpetrating sexual harassment more often than do heterosexual students (Clear et al., 2014; Eisenberg, Gower, McMorris, & Bucchianeri, 2015).

Studies of peer sexual harassment have identified several other risk markers for both perpetration and victimization. Interestingly, although bullying is distinct from sexual harassment in important ways, it is also a significant risk factor for sexual harassment. Espelage, Basile, De La Rue, and Hamburger (2015), for example, identified the **bullying/ sexual violence pathway**, in which bullying of peers at a young age eventually changed to aggressive homophobia and sexual harassment in adolescence. In their study, bullying behavior in fifth grade predicted perpetration of sexual harassment and other forms of sexual violence in seventh grade (see also Espelage, Basile, Leemis, Hipp, & Davis, 2018; Pepler, 2012). At the same time, individuals who report being bullied also report high rates of peer sexual harassment victimization (Clear et al., 2014; Pepler, 2012).

Another risk factor is witnessing parents' intimate partner violence (IPV) and abuse and/or experiencing child maltreatment. For instance, Clear et al. (2014) found that 42.2 percent of the students in their study who reported sexual harassment victimization and 13 percent of those who reported perpetrating sexual harassment also disclosed exposure to IPV at home. Similarly, in research reported by Wolfe, Jaffe, and Crooks (2006), witnessing or experiencing abuse at home impacts adolescent relationships, although the pattern is gendered: Adolescent boys are at greater risk of perpetrating sexual harassment, and adolescent girls are at greater risk of being victims of sexual harassment. As these researchers put it, youth who have witnessed or experienced such maltreatment "have formed a view of relationships that involves power differentials and control tactics, encased in emotions of fear, anger, and mistrust. Beyond these behavioral and cognitive distortions, the impact encompasses a disruption in the child's ability to regulate emotions heightened by traumatic experiences in the family that can persist into adolescence and adulthood," which might lead to peer sexual harassment (Wolfe et al., 2006, p. 11; see also Foshee et al., 2016).

Wolfe et al. (2006) emphasize the psychological impact of exposure to violence in the home, but their finding that this impact is gendered reminds us that there are structural and cultural risk factors for peer sexual harassment as well. One of the most important is adherence to specific norms of masculinity that some researchers have labeled **hegemonic masculinity** (Connell, 1995; DeKeseredy & Schwartz, 2013). Hegemonic masculinity includes the notion that males are superior to females and, therefore, males should have more power, status, and privileges than females. It also holds that masculinity and femininity are opposites. "Masculine men" are unemotional, tough, competitive, and willing to take risks; any male who displays traits associated with femininity—for example, fear, physical frailty, or passivity—is derided as weak, and called a sissy or any of the many demeaning slurs that are used to refer to women. Most of these slurs are sexualized; women and girls in the hegemonic masculine frame are sexually objectified. It is not difficult to make a connection between adherence to such norms and perpetration of peer sexual harassment. As J. Gruber and Fineran (2016) point out, "hegemonic masculinity accounts for the sharp [gender] imbalance in perpetration that we and others have documented" (p. 128). Moreover, adherence to hegemonic masculinity is also associated with perpetration of gender harassment, given the myriad ways "in which adolescent boys (and adult men) unmercifully police each other with rigid conventional notions of masculinity and the imposition of compulsive heterosexuality" (L. Brown et al., 2007, p. 1261). As Lyn Mikel Brown and her colleagues (2007) argue, a primary operating feature of "boy culture" is for boys and young men to work tirelessly to ensure that their peers define them as "not gay." The pressure that young men put on one another to demonstrate their acceptable masculinity further reinforces a school environment conducive to both sexual and gender harassment (L. Brush & Miller, 2019; DeKeseredy & Schwartz, 2013; E. Miller, 2018).

Consequences of Peer Sexual Harassment

As Tonya's case history shows, peer sexual harassment negatively affects victims in multiple ways. The psychological and physical impacts of sexual harassment on victims include depression, anxiety, lowered self-esteem, lowered self-confidence, loss of appetite, sleep disturbances, and substance use (C. Hill et al., 2011; McGinley et al., 2016; Sterzing et al., 2019). Like Tonya, sexual harassment victims often lose interest in their regular activities and isolate themselves from family and friends. Their schoolwork suffers as well; their academic performance declines along with their grades (Hand & Sanchez, 2000; Robers et al., 2012). Sexual harassment victims are also more likely to miss school, often because they feel threatened and afraid (Hand & Sanchez, 2000; Robers, Zhang, Truman, U.S. Department of Justice, & National Center for Education Statistics, 2012).

As noted earlier, these negative outcomes appear to be more frequent and more severe for female sexual harassment victims (J. Gruber & Fineran, 2016). This is not to say that heterosexual boys are unharmed by sexual harassment victimization. Studies indicate, however, that among heterosexual students, girls report being more upset by sexual harassment than boys, and they admit to taking it more personally (Chiodo, Wolfe, Crooks, Hughes, & Jaffe, 2009; Gadin & Hammarstrom, 2005; J. Gruber & Fineran, 2016). This may be not only because girls are more likely to experience sexual harassment, but also because girls experience *more frequent* and *more severe* harassment.

More specifically, girls more often than boys report experiencing repeated (i.e., 3 or more) incidents of sexual harassment, and are more likely to be touched or grabbed sexually or to have sexual rumors spread about them (Chiodo et al., 2009; Clear et al., 2014; J. Gruber & Fineran, 2016). But even when girls and boys are victims of the same type of harassment (e.g., sexual comments), girls report being more upset by the experience and find it more frightening (J. Gruber & Fineran, 2016). Given that sexual minority youth are more likely than cisgender, heterosexual boys to experience chronic sexual harassment (McGinley et al., 2016) and polyvictimization (Sterzing et al., 2019), it is likely that they suffer more severe negative consequences as well, although more research with sexual minority youth is needed to understand their sexual harassment victimization and its consequences.

Victims of gender harassment also suffer serious consequences. Like victims of sexual harassment, victims of gender harassment report depression, lower self-esteem, and lower self-confidence. They are also at high risk for missing school and for dropping out of school due to safety concerns (Kann et al., 2018; Riese, 2016). LGBTQ students, however, are more likely than heterosexual students to experience suicidal thoughts, to attempt suicide, and to actually kill themselves, and a significant percentage of these suicides are related to their experiences of gender harassment, especially among boys (Riese, 2016). For example, Nigel Shelby, an African American ninth grader from Alabama, killed himself in 2019 after experiencing severe gender harassment and homophobic bullying at school (K. Allen, 2019). Similarly, Jamel Myles, a fourth grader in Colorado, committed suicide in 2018, shortly after coming out as gay, which his mother said had prompted increased gender harassment at his school (Turkewitz, 2018). Researchers estimate, however, that about 75 percent of students who experience peer gender harassment do not identify as LGBTQ (Riese, 2016).

Prevention and Intervention Strategies

Given the prevalence of peer sexual harassment and its negative short- and long-term consequences for victims, effective responses when it occurs—and, perhaps more importantly, programs to *prevent* it from occurring—are essential. As we saw in the case of Tonya, sexual harassment is illegal discrimination, so students and their parents can turn to the courts for relief should they choose to do so. But the law places considerable responsibility on schools to address sexual harassment and to ensure that the education of all students occurs in a safe learning environment. Indeed, as we learned from Tonya's case, schools can be held liable by the courts if they are made aware that sexual harassment is occurring and they do not respond appropriately (L. Brown et al., 2007).

Apart from holding perpetrators accountable and providing victims with treatment and accommodations (e.g., assistance in making up missed classes and schoolwork), some schools, particularly in the lower grades, try to proactively address sexual and gender harassment by offering more general bullying prevention programs. Evaluations of these programs, however, show that they are *not* effective in preventing either sexual or gender harassment. Some speculate that they are ineffective because they typically do not address sexism and homophobia explicitly (L. Brown et al., 2007; Espelage, Basile, & Hamberger, 2011; Stein & Mennemeier, 2011). Most adolescents understand that physical and verbal abuse is "bad" and hurtful, but they often don't label behaviors such as making sexual gestures or comments to peers, "rating" their peers' bodies or physical attractiveness, and intentionally grabbing their peers' clothes or rubbing up against them as sexual harassment. Instead, they typically dismiss such behaviors as "teasing" or "just joking," and this interpretation is frequently reinforced by their friends as well as by adults in their environment, who excuse it as "boys will be boys" or with the claim that the harasser "didn't mean any harm." It therefore becomes normative, which makes it extremely difficult for anyone, especially another adolescent, to denounce such behavior or intervene to stop it (DeKeseredy & Schwartz, 2013; Wolfe et al., 2006).

Consequently, researchers and professionals have argued that programs are needed that (1) explicitly challenge hegemonic masculine norms and replace them with an alternative, more egalitarian set of core beliefs and behavioral norms; (2) provide opportunities to learn and practice healthy relationship skills; (3) address sexual health and other relevant issues, such as substance use; and (4) empower young people to recognize and intervene to stop sexual harassment (Crooks, Goodall, Hughes, Jaffe, & Baker, 2007; but for a different perspective, see L. Brush & Miller, 2019). A number of these programs— e.g., Green Dot (https://alteristic.org/services/green-dot/), Coaching Boys Into Men (www.coachescorner.org), Expect Respect (Ball et al., 2012), and Safe Dates (Foshee & Langwick, 2010)—are also designed to prevent sexual assault and dating violence, so we will discuss them later in the chapter (see also Chapter 11). Here we will highlight just one program, the *Fourth R* (https://youthrelationships.org), that may be particularly helpful in addressing peer sexual harassment as well as other types of abuse and violence during adolescence and emerging adulthood.

The Fourth R is a comprehensive, school-based curriculum that consists of 21 lessons designed to promote healthy relationships and reduce risky sexual behaviors and substance use by adolescents and young adults (Wolfe et al., 2009; Wolfe et al., 2006). A basic principle of the program is that relationship skills ("the fourth *R*") can be taught to youth just like "the first three *R*s" (i.e., reading, 'riting, and 'rithmetic). But while most programs already emphasize educating youth by providing them with accurate information on the harmfulness of certain behaviors, developers of the Fourth R curriculum recognize that simply conveying information is not sufficient to produce behavioral change (Wolfe et al., 2006). Information sharing is certainly an element of the program, but considerable attention is given to ensuring that the information is disseminated by individuals who will have the greatest credibility with this audience (e.g., older peers) and in a way that has high salience (e.g., using interactive, rather than lecture, methods). In addition to information sharing, however, youth are given opportunities to learn skills, such as assertiveness, effective communication, and problem solving, and, perhaps more importantly, to practice using these skills in a variety of situations so they grow more confident in their ability to affect a situation in which they may find themselves. One method for doing this is through role play; another is through what is called forum theater, in which young actors perform plays about harassment and violence (Jaffe, Wolfe, Crooks, Hughes, & Baker, 2004; K. S. Mitchell & Freitag, 2011). A play is performed from start to finish once, but then the audience is given a chance during a second performance to intervene either to stop the action when something objectionable happens or to replace the victim or the offender, which lets them try to change the outcome of the scene. The program is also "gender strategic" in that it challenges hegemonic masculinity and traditional gender norms, including homophobia, through activities such as "media deconstruction" exercises and discussions of gendered expectations and standards. And while the Fourth R curriculum recognizes the need to include parents, teachers, and the wider community in prevention efforts, the central focus is on youth ownership, empowerment, and leadership.

Research evaluating the effectiveness of the Fourth R curriculum has been encouraging. When compared to a control group, Fourth R participants engaged in greater negotiation and less violence as well as less sexual risk-taking behavior (Crooks, Jaffee, Dunlop, Kerry, & Exner-Cortens, 2019; Wolfe et al., 2012). They are also better able to resist the coercive pressures of their peers, and the program has a protective effect for high-risk adolescents, including those who have a history of multiple forms of maltreatment (Crooks et al., 2019; Wolfe, Crooks, Chiodo, Hughes, & Ellis, 2012). While the Fourth R and other prevention programs we will discuss later in this chapter appear promising, it is unclear if they can be effective in reducing technology-facilitated harassment (B. Henson, Fisher, & Reyns, 2019), which we consider in the next section.

Technology-Facilitated Peer Harassment

It will likely come as no surprise to our readers that research suggests that almost all teens (95%) have an "online presence" (Lenhart et al., 2011; Lenhart et al., 2015). Although most teens do not meet their romantic partners online, social media is the primary means they use to flirt with and show interest in a potential romantic partner. Lenhart and colleagues (2015), for example, found that 63 percent of dating teens, aged 13–17, reported that they have sent flirtatious messages to someone they were interested in romantically, and 23 percent said they had sent sexy or "flirty" pictures or videos (sometimes referred to as "sexting"). Most teens (63% total; 71% of girls and 57% of boys) also use social media to express support of their friends' romantic relationships, although many (69%) feel that social media posts give others too much information about their private romantic lives (Lenhart et al., 2015).

The majority of teens using social media (69%) say that their peers are mostly kind to one another on these sites, but 88 percent nevertheless reported having witnessed peers being mean or cruel, and 15 percent said they themselves had been the target of negative, harassing, or cruel messages and posts (Lenhart et al., 2011; see also B. Henson et al., 2019; C. Hill & Johnson, 2019). Such behavior is referred to as **technology-facilitated peer harassment**. Not surprisingly, these experiences are gendered. Just as young women are more likely than young men to be victims of in-person peer sexual harassment, they are also more likely to experience unwanted and uncomfortable flirting and sexual harassment online (N. Henry & Flynn, 2019; Lenhart et al., 2015). Data on these experiences are just beginning to become available, since much of the research to date has focused on adult sexual exploitation of children online. However, the studies that are available show a range of harassing behaviors that include repeatedly emailing or text messaging someone to pressure that person into hooking up or other sexual activity; electronically distributing sexually explicit, intimate, or embarrassing images or videos of a person without consent; bombarding a targeted person with "flirtatious" or sexually explicit messages or images via text or instant messaging; changing or deleting a partner or ex-partner's social media profile; and name-calling or spreading sexual rumors about someone on social media sites (Drouin, Ross, & Tobin, 2015; N. Henry & Flynn, 2019; Reed, Wong, & Raj, 2019).

Young people who experience technology-facilitated peer harassment are often advised to just turn off their devices, change their security settings, or block the harasser on their smartphones or social media sites. In fact, over one-third of girls (35%) and 16 percent of boys report having blocked or "unfriended" someone who has made them uncomfortable when "flirting" online (Lenhart et al., 2015). But as N. Henry and Flynn (2019) point out, such responses do not address the serious harm that can result from technology-facilitated harassment. For example, harassment via electronic technology offers perpetrators some anonymity and has a "force multiplying effect" because images, rumors, and sexist and heterosexist hate speech may be distributed instantaneously to millions of internet users, who not only see and hear the damaging content, but may then join in the harassment (N. Henry & Flynn, 2019; C. Hill & Johnson, 2019). Victims use a variety of strategies to cope with the harassment (Scarduzio, Sheff, & Smith, 2018), but the consequential psychological impact of such harassment can be severe: depression, anxiety, and fear, including fear that threats made online (e.g., "You deserve to be raped") will be carried out in physical space (C. Hill & Johnson, 2019). Technology-facilitated harassment may also lead victims to engage in self-harm and has prompted some to consider or commit suicide (N. Henry & Flynn, 2019; C. Hill & Johnson, 2019). For example, in

September 2010, Tyler Clementi, a first-year student at Rutgers University, killed himself after his roommate and another dormitory resident streamed live video of Clementi having sex with a man in his dorm room, and subsequently tweeted details of the incident, inviting others to tune in (I. Parker, 2012). Similarly, Jessica Logan, an 18-year-old Ohio student, hanged herself in 2008 after her former boyfriend circulated a nude photo she had texted to him when they were dating, which resulted in her being severely harassed by classmates (*Huffington Post*, 2017). This latter example is a case of revenge porn, which researchers maintain is a growing problem (Branch, Hilinski-Rosick, Johnson, & Solano, 2017; McGlynn, Rackley, & Houghton, 2017).

Currently, both the law and prevention programming appear to be lagging behind the development and proliferation of the technology and its applications, raising serious concerns about our ability to effectively address technology-facilitated perpetration and victimization. Victims of technology-facilitated harassment have been encouraged to preserve the offensive messages or posts, since these can be used as evidence in criminal prosecutions and civil litigation (N. Henry & Flynn, 2019). At the same time, programs to prevent in-person sexual and gender harassment need to be expanded to include prevention of technology-facilitated harassment. The technology itself may be used in these programming efforts, which include social media campaigns to teach bystanders how to intervene if they witness online harassment, how to challenge harassers, and how to support victims. B. Henson and colleagues (2019) found that students who score high in self-control, who have previously experienced online victimization, and/or who have seen their peers help others in physical space (e.g., helped an intoxicated friend or a sexual assault victim) are more likely to intervene when they witness someone being sexually harassed online.

Technology is also being used to mobilize against sexual harassment and other forms of violence online and in physical space. Social media platforms, such as Twitter, have become vehicles for sharing personal stories of victimization and influencing public opinion. "The use of hashtags as a way for marginalized individuals to come together to protest on social media through a united word, phrase, or sentence" is known as **hashtag activism** (Maas, McCauley, Bonomi, & Leija, 2018, p. 1741). Hashtags, such as #MeToo and #NotOkay, are being used by victims and antiviolence activists to call out perpetrators and to challenge power relations as well as sexist, racist, and homophobic social discourse around sexual harassment and assault. It is too early to determine whether hashtag activism will produce the policy and behavior changes advocated by victims and other activists, although initial research indicates that it appears to be successful in promoting public awareness of sexual harassment and other forms of violence, both independently and through mainstream media coverage of specific hashtags (Maas et al., 2018). Nevertheless, analysts are concerned about the potential for overexposure, desensitization, and retraumatization of victims to undermine the effectiveness of hashtag activism (Maas et al., 2018; McCauley, Bogen, & Bonomi, 2017).

RAPE AND SEXUAL ASSAULT

Sexual assault encompasses various forms of *nonconsensual* sexual contact, such as kissing or fondling a person without consent or when the person is unable to consent. The most severe form of sexual assault is **rape** nonconsensual attempted or completed penetration, "no matter how slight, of the vagina or anus with any body part or object, or oral penetration by a sex organ of another person" (Federal Bureau of Investigation, 2012). Sexual assault may be accomplished through the use of physical force or the threat of force, but perpetrators may also use intimidation or the imposition of authority to make the victim have sex with them. In addition, sexual assault can be perpetrated with the use of alcohol or drugs such that the victim is rendered unconscious or is too drunk or high to be able to consent to sex.

Prevalence of Rape and Sexual Assault

Estimates of the prevalence of rape and sexual assault vary widely. For example, official law enforcement statistics, such as those collected by the Federal Bureau of Investigation from reports by police departments throughout the United States, indicate that in 2017 there were about 41.7 rape victims per 100,000 people in the U.S. population (Federal Bureau of Investigation, 2017). In contrast, the National Crime Victimization Survey (NCVS), an ongoing survey that asks a random sample of U.S. households about their criminal victimization experiences (see Chapter 2), found that in 2017 there were 140 rape victims per 100,000 people 12 years old and older in the United States (Morgan & Truman, 2018). How can these estimates be so different? One answer to this question has to do with the fact that sexual assault is one of the violent crimes victims are least likely to report to the police (Fisher, Daigle, Cullen, & Turner, 2003; Ullman, Starzynski, Long, Mason, & Long, 2008). For instance, only 40.4 percent of sexual assaults are reported to the police compared with 49 percent of robberies and 79 percent of car thefts (Morgan & Truman, 2018). To some extent, this is because many people, including rape victims themselves, adhere to a set of beliefs, commonly referred to as **rape myths**, about what constitutes "real rape" and "worthy victims" (see Table 7.5). A "real rape" is perpetrated by a stranger who attacks a lone woman on an isolated street or in a dark alley and inflicts serious physical injuries. A "worthy rape victim" is one who did nothing to "invite" or precipitate the assault, who was not drinking or using drugs prior to the assault, who was dressed and behaving modestly, who tried desperately to fight off the assailant, and who reported the assault promptly after it happened.

In reality, however, most sexual assaults are perpetrated by someone the victim knows—a phenomenon referred to as **acquaintance rape** In fact, about 73 percent of rapes are acquaintance rapes (Truman & Langton, 2015). But because most victims accept the myth of stranger rape, they label what has happened to them a "bad date"

TABLE 7.5 ■ Common Rape Myths
• If a girl is raped while she is drunk, she is at least somewhat responsible for letting things get out of hand.
• If a guy is drunk, he might rape someone unintentionally.
• If both people are drunk, it can't be rape.
• When girls go to parties wearing slutty clothes, they are asking for trouble.
• If a girl goes to a room alone with a guy at a party, it is her own fault if she is raped.
• When girls get raped, it's often because the way they said "no" was unclear.
• If a girl initiates kissing or hooking up, she should not be surprised if a guy assumes she wants to have sex.
• Rape happens when a guy's sex drive goes out of control.
• If a girl doesn't physically resist or fight back, you can't really say it was rape.
• A rape probably didn't happen if a girl doesn't have any bruises or marks.
• A lot of times, girls who say they were raped agreed to have sex and then regretted it.
• Rape accusations are often used as a way of getting back at guys.
• A lot of times, girls who claim they were raped have emotional problems.
• Girls who are caught cheating on their boyfriends sometimes claim it was rape.

Sources: McMahon & Farmer, 2011; Payne, Lonsway, & Fitzgerald, 1999.

or "miscommunication" and frequently blame themselves, especially if they had been partying before the assault or they had willingly gone with the assailant to a private place or invited the assailant into their homes. Indeed, victims of acquaintance rape—the majority of rape victims—often excuse or justify the perpetrator's behavior (Amacker & Littleton, 2013; Littleton, Breitkopf, & Berenson, 2008; Weiss, 2009; see also Box 7.1).

Research shows that adolescents and young adults are particularly vulnerable to rape and other types of sexual assault. As Table 7.6 shows, for example, the 2017 YRBSS study found that 11.3 percent of girls and 3.5 percent of boys in grades 9–12 throughout the United States disclosed that they had been forced to have sexual intercourse when they did not want to at some time in their lives (Kann et al., 2018). We see here that gender as well as sexual identity matters with regard to sexual assault risk. Gay, lesbian, bisexual, and transgender youth, both girls and boys, are significantly more likely than heterosexual youth to have been victimized. Youth who are unsure of their sexual identity, both girls and boys, also have significantly higher rates of victimization than youth who identify as heterosexual, but much lower rates than their LGBTQ peers. Age is also an important factor. Twelfth-grade girls are more likely to have been victimized than girls

BOX 7.1

HOW WE ASK THE QUESTIONS MAKES A DIFFERENCE IN THE ANSWERS WE RECEIVE

In the 1980s, Mary Koss and her colleagues were commissioned by the *Ms. Magazine* Campus Project on Sexual Assault to conduct a survey of a nationally representative sample of college women about their experiences of rape and other forms of unwanted sex. To collect the data, Koss developed the Sexual Experiences Survey (SES), a 10-item instrument that measured rape and sexual coercion in a way that no other survey instrument had ever done before: The items on the SES asked *behaviorally specific* questions about the women's unwanted sexual experiences. Koss realized that many young women subscribe to myths about "real rape" and "worthy victims," so if they were asked, "Have you ever been raped?" they would likely respond, "No." Instead, she asked, "Have you ever had sexual intercourse when you didn't want to because a man threatened or used some degree of physical force (twisting your arm, holding you down, etc.) to make you?" Koss and her colleagues received a significantly higher number of positive answers to these behaviorally specific questions than those obtained by interviewers for the NCVS (which, at that time, was the NCS—the National Crime Survey): 15 percent of respondents reported attempted rape by a man who used threats or physical force; 12 percent reported attempted rape by a man who used drugs or alcohol; 9 percent reported completed rape (sexual intercourse) by a man who used threats or physical force; 8 percent reported completed rape (sexual intercourse) by a man who used drugs or alcohol; and 6 percent reported completed rape (oral or anal sex or penetration with an object other than a penis) by a man who used threats or physical force (Koss, Gidycz, & Wisniewski, 1987; see also Koss et al., 2007).

Koss's research ignited a debate among sexual assault researchers regarding the most accurate methods for measuring victimization and perpetration of rape and other forms of coerced sex. Numerous studies have been undertaken to test a variety of methodological issues, such as question wording and research design (Bachman, 2000; Hamby & Koss, 2003; Jaquier, Johnson, & Fisher, 2011). One recent study (Fisher, 2009), for example, compared two surveys—the National College Women Sexual Victimization (NCWSV) study and the National Violence Against College Women (NVACW) study—to determine how differences in question wording might affect estimates of completed, attempted, and threatened rape. The NCWSV asked 12 behaviorally specific questions, whereas the NVACW used questions identical to those in the NCVS; apart from differences in number of questions and question wording, the methodology of the two studies was identical. Fisher's (2009) analysis of the data from these surveys led her to conclude that "the use of behaviorally specific questions cannot be overemphasized, not necessarily because they produce larger estimates of rape but because they use words and phrases that describe to the respondent exactly what behavior is being measured" (p. 143). In other words, behaviorally specific questions help respondents better understand what the researcher is asking and help them remember their experiences.

Fisher (2009) pointed out that using behaviorally specific questions does not make a rape or sexual assault measure "perfect," but it does appear to be a significant methodological improvement toward greater measurement reliability and accuracy. Still, Michael D. Smith's (1987) characterization of measuring rape as one of the "biggest methodological challenge(s) in survey research" (p. 185) remains as well founded today as it was in the 1980s.

TABLE 7.6 ■ Percentage of U.S. High School Students Ever Physically Forced to Have Sexual Intercourse, by Sex, Race/Ethnicity, Grade, and Sexual Identity, 2017		
Race/Ethnicity	**% Female**	**% Male**
White	11.2	3.3
Black	11.7	3.4
Hispanic	11.2	3.6
Grade		
9	8.1	2.7
10	11.2	3.5
11	12.1	2.8
12	13.9	4.8
Sexual Identity		
Heterosexual (Straight)	8.6	2.3
Gay, Lesbian, or Bisexual	23.7	15.6
Not Sure	12.7	11.8
Total	11.3	3.5

Source: Centers for Disease Control and Prevention (CDC), Youth Risk Behavior Surveillance—United States, 2017. Retrieved from https://www.cdc.gov/mmwr/volumes/67/ss/ss6708a1.htm.

in grades 9–11 and boys in all grades, although 12th-grade boys are more likely to have been victimized than boys in grades 9–11.

Additional data reinforce the importance of gender when considering the prevalence of rape and sexual assault: 82 percent of rape victims under the age of 18 are females, and girls aged between 16 and 19 years are 4 times more likely than the general community to be victimized by rape, attempted rape, or another form of sexual assault (Rape, Abuse & Incest National Network, 2016). In a nationally representative survey of adults, among women who disclosed having been raped, 42.2 percent were first victimized before their 18th birthday, and 29.9 percent were first victimized between the ages of 11 and 17 years. Among adults first raped when they were 10 years old or younger, males had a higher victimization rate than females, 27.8 percent and 12.3 percent, respectively (Black et al., 2011). Importantly, female and male victims are significantly more likely to be assaulted by someone they know (e.g., an intimate partner such as a boyfriend or girlfriend, a relative, or an acquaintance); only 13.8 percent of female rape victims and 15.1 percent of male rape victims were assaulted by strangers (Black et al., 2011).

Given the high rate of rape and sexual assault among adolescents and emerging adults, it is important to identify specific risk factors that contribute to increased vulnerability during this stage of the life course.

Risk Factors Associated With Rape and Sexual Assault

As we have already noted, simply being female is a risk factor for sexual assault victimization, and being young and female significantly escalates the risk. That being said, not all young women have an equal likelihood of being sexually assaulted. Young women of color—particularly, African American and American Indian young women—face greater risk than other groups of women (J. Miller, 2008; Rennison, 2002). In Jody Miller's (2008) study of gendered violence among African American teens in a St. Louis, Missouri, neighborhood, more than half of the young women she interviewed, who, on average, were just 16 years old, reported having experienced some type of sexual coercion or assault, and nearly one-third of these young women (31%) disclosed multiple victimizations. As Miller emphasizes, however, race is not the risk factor; the risk derives from the fact that racial minorities are disproportionately represented among the poor and are more likely to live in economically disadvantaged neighborhoods. Figure 7.1 shows results from Callie Rennison's (2017) analysis of national sexual violence victimization data.

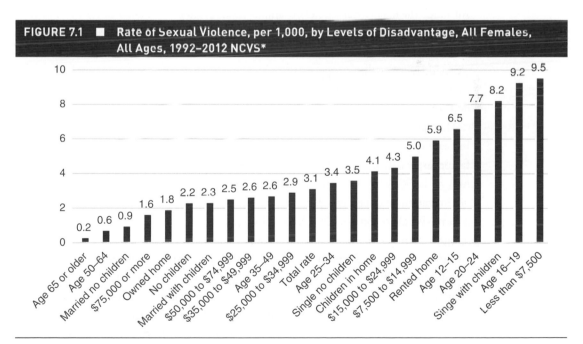

FIGURE 7.1 ■ Rate of Sexual Violence, per 1,000, by Levels of Disadvantage, All Females, All Ages, 1992–2012 NCVS*

*NCVS = National Crime Victimization Survey

Source: Rennison, 2018, p. 104.

Like Miller, Rennison found that poor women are nearly 4 times more likely to be sexually victimized than middle-class women and 6 times more likely to be sexually victimized than women in the highest income bracket. Education is also related to economic status, so not surprisingly, the education status of young women is related to their sexual victimization risk. Young women 18–24 years old who are not enrolled in college have a sexual victimization rate 1.4 times higher than their college-enrolled peers: 7.5 versus 5.6 per 1,000 women, respectively (Rennison, 2017). Single mothers in this age group who are not enrolled in college are sexually victimized at a rate more than 3 times greater than that for single mothers 18–24 years old who are enrolled in college: 10.6 versus 3.4 per 1,000 women, respectively (Rennison, 2017).

Despite these data, considerable attention has been given recently to sexual assault on college campuses. A frequently cited statistic regarding campus sexual assault is that one in five (20%) female college students have been sexually victimized (see Krebs, Lindquist, Warner, Fisher, & Martin, 2007). This statistic, however, is derived from a study of a small number of universities using voluntary samples of respondents and measured not only rape, but also unwanted kissing and fondling. Other studies of campus sexual assault have arrived at very different estimates. For instance, in a review of campus sexual assault studies that were completed between 2000 and 2015, Fedina, Holmes, and Backes (2018) found that prevalence rates for unwanted sexual contact since entering college ranged from 1.8 percent to 34 percent for women and 4.8 percent to 30 percent for men. Although the majority of studies of campus sexual assault have data primarily from white, heterosexual students, the relatively few studies that examine the experiences of sexual minority students show that gay male, bisexual, unsure, and transgender students are at elevated risk of multiple types of sexual victimization on college campuses (L. Johnson, Matthews, & Napper, 2016). Fedina et al. (2018), however, note the wide variation in definitions of sexual assault across studies along with other methodological challenges.

There are, however, several features of college and university environments that increase the risk of sexual victimization for students. Campus social life is one such risk factor, especially given that much of it includes alcohol use. Alcohol use, particularly heavy drinking and binge drinking, significantly increases both sexual assault victimization and perpetration (Dowdall, 2008; Hirsch & Khan, 2020; Messman-Moore, Ward, & Brown, 2009). Sorority membership is also related to sexual assault victimization risk, perhaps because sorority members are more likely to attend parties, consume alcohol, and engage in other high-risk behaviors (Franklin, 2016; Minow & Einolf, 2009; Ullman & Najdowski, 2011). At the same time, fraternity membership is related to sexual assault perpetration, not only because of the social life associated with fraternities, but also because of the rape-supportive hegemonic masculinity that typically characterizes fraternities (DeKeseredy & Schwartz, 2013). In fact, in studies of risk factors for rape perpetration, one of the most consistent findings is that rape-supportive attitudes, acceptance of violence against women, hostility toward women, and desire to be in control are strongly related to sexual aggression (Knight & Sims-Knight, 2011). Not unrelated to these attitudes and beliefs is pornography use, which has also been found to increase sexual assault perpetration and adherence to rape myths (DeKeseredy & Schwartz, 2013; Knight & Sims-Knight, 2011).

Hirsch and Khan (2020) emphasized that the "sexual geographies" of the campus environment—that is, the physical environment, including living and socializing spaces, furniture, and access to particular spaces—also contribute to risk of sexual assault. Consider, for example, that one of the few places where students, including couples, can be together privately is in a small dorm room with the bed as the most accommodating seating.

Consequences of Rape and Sexual Assault

Sexual assault has a very serious impact on victims, including negative physical and psychological health consequences (see Table 7.7). Among the physical health outcomes experienced by sexual assault victims are physical injuries, ranging from scratches and bruises to broken bones and head and spinal cord injuries; various gynecological problems (e.g., dysmenorrhea, sexually transmitted infections [STIs]); headaches; gastrointestinal disorders; and insomnia and disordered sleep (Martin, Macy, & Young, 2011). Research

TABLE 7.7 ■ Consequences of Sexual Assault for Adolescent and Young Adult Victims
• Physical injuries in addition to the sexual assault itself (e.g., bruises, scratches, broken bones, head trauma, spinal cord injuries)
• Gynecological problems (e.g., STIs, dysmenorrhea)
• Chronic headaches
• Gastrointestinal disorders
• Sleeping disorders (e.g., insomnia)
• PTSD symptoms
• Anxiety
• Hypervigilance
• Depression
• Substance use
• Suicidal ideation
• Sexual revictimization as an adult

Sources: Gidycz, Orchowski, King, & Rich, 2008; Martin et al., 2011; Ullman & Najdowski, 2011.

shows that certain psychological impacts are especially common among young women and sexual minority youth, including post-traumatic stress disorder (PTSD) symptoms and suicidal ideation (Martin et al., 2011; Ullman & Brecklin, 2002).

One of the most significant consequences of sexual assault victimization during childhood and adolescence is increased risk for revictimization as an adult. As noted in Chapter 4, researchers have also found that victims of sexual abuse during childhood who are revictimized when they are adolescents are at greater risk of further sexual victimization as adults (Ullman & Najdowski, 2011). The underlying mechanisms for these revictimization pathways are not well understood, but clearly more research is warranted, not only to improve responses to victims and help them heal from the trauma of the assault, but also to prevent later revictimization.

Some researchers have hypothesized that revictimization may be due in part to increased substance use by sexual assault victims. In other words, substance use, as we mentioned earlier, is a risk factor for sexual assault, but it is also one of the negative consequences for sexual assault victims, perhaps making them vulnerable to revictimization (Angelone, Marcantonio, & Melillo, 2017; Martin et al., 2011; Ullman & Najdowski, 2011). Sexual assault victims may use alcohol and drugs—both prescription and illegal drugs—to self-medicate as a way to cope with the distress and trauma of the assault (Bonomi, Nichols, Kammes, & Green, 2018; Ehlke & Kelley, 2019; J. Mitchell, Macleod, & Cassisi, 2017).

Prevention and Intervention Strategies

Historically, responses to sexual assault by the legal, health care, and education systems, as well as by victims' friends and family, have been woefully inadequate and, at times, even harmful. Police, for example, tended to "unfound" many rape complaints—that is, they chose not to investigate them because they did not think there was enough evidence that a "real" rape had occurred or they doubted victims' accounts of the crime. Any indication that the victim may have "precipitated" the assault—for instance, by her dress or behavior or because she had previously had consensual sex with the perpetrator—was grounds for unfounding the complaint (Angelone, Mitchell, & Pilafova, 2007; Caringella, 2009; Whatley, 2005). The suspicion of victim culpability has affected male victims, too; a commonly held rape myth is that men are "unrapeable," especially by women. As we noted previously, some state statutes still have gender restrictions in their rape laws, defining victims as females and perpetrators as males, thereby rendering cisgender male and noncisgender victims legally invisible (Levine, 2018). It is hardly surprising, then, that victims are reluctant to report sexual assaults to the police, but as Figure 7.2 shows, even when they do, fewer than 1 in 5 complaints result in an arrest; of those arrested, only about 20 percent are formally charged and prosecuted, and just 54 percent of these are convicted. It is estimated, in fact, that when one factors in unreported

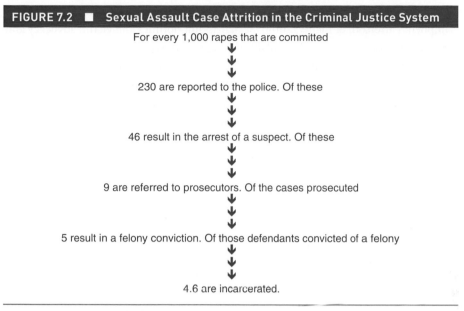

FIGURE 7.2 ■ Sexual Assault Case Attrition in the Criminal Justice System

For every 1,000 rapes that are committed

230 are reported to the police. Of these

46 result in the arrest of a suspect. Of these

9 are referred to prosecutors. Of the cases prosecuted

5 result in a felony conviction. Of those defendants convicted of a felony

4.6 are incarcerated.

Source: Rape, Abuse, and Incest National Network (RAINN), 2016.

and reported sexual assaults, only 1 in 16 results in a perpetrator being held accountable by the criminal justice system (Seidman & Pokorak, 2011).

In studies of rape cases on college and university campuses, findings show that victim complaints may not be treated seriously or are sometimes dismissed as simply a "he said–she said" argument, particularly if the accused assailant is a star athlete or the child of a prominent alumnus. Victims also report harsh treatment by health care providers in emergency rooms and clinics, while friends and family, who also buy into many rape myths, may question victims about their actions and decisions, implying that they are at least partially responsible for what happened to them (R. Campbell & Patterson, 2011; Maier, 2008; Orchowski & Gidycz, 2012). Importantly, studies show that victims who receive negative or unsupportive responses from formal and informal help providers to whom they disclose the assault experience poorer mental health outcomes, including greater depression (Deitz, Williams, Rife, & Cantrell, 2015; Kaukinen & DeMaris, 2009; Orchowski & Gidycz, 2015).

Reforms instituted since the 1990s have helped considerably to improve the treatment of sexual assault victims by the criminal justice system and other social service providers, such as medical personnel. Most police officers, for example, now receive special training to sensitize them to the trauma of victims, and many hospitals now use Sexual Assault Nurse Examiners (SANEs) to collect physical evidence from victims in emergency rooms. Research has shown that these developments have positive outcomes, not only for victims, but also for the successful prosecution of perpetrators (Caringella, 2009; R. Campbell, Patterson, & Lichty, 2005). Sexual assault hotlines and victim advocacy and support services are now widely available throughout the country, including on college and university campuses, although these specialized services are rare in high schools and middle schools (R. Campbell, 2006). The federal government has also taken steps to improve responses to sexual assault on college and university campuses, including developing a model reporting and confidentiality protocol; providing a checklist schools can use to develop a comprehensive sexual misconduct policy; developing trauma-informed training for school personnel, including campus police and health services staff; and increasing transparency with regard to the campus climate and safety (White House Task Force to Protect Students From Sexual Assault, 2014).

Despite the many reforms, however, victims continue to encounter difficulties report-ing to police and obtaining help, and as Figure 7.2 shows, the attrition rate of sexual assault cases in the criminal justice system remains high (Alderden & Ullman, 2012; Patterson, 2011; Spohn & Tellis, 2012). Accused offenders from prominent families, for example, continue to receive more lenient treatment by the police and the courts, and the harm done to victims by their assailants is minimized. Consider, for example, a 2018 case in which a New Jersey family court judge refused prosecutors' motion to try a teenager accused of rape as an adult, saying that such treatment was unwarranted for the young man, who was from a good family, attended an excellent school, had terrific grades, and was an Eagle Scout. The judge also chastised prosecutors for not informing the victim and her family that pressing charges would likely ruin the young man's life. The accused had videotaped himself raping an intoxicated 16-year-old girl at a party, sharing the video with friends on social media and tweeting, "When your first time having sex was rape." The judge questioned whether the incident was a "real" rape and whether the victim was actually so intoxicated that she did not know what was happening. In 2019, an appeals court overturned the judge, allowing the case to be referred to a grand jury where the offender would be treated as an adult. The appeals court also rebuked the family court judge, noting his bias in favor of "privileged youth" (Ferre-Sadurni, 2019). Although the judge subsequently resigned from the bench and the New Jersey Supreme Court ordered all judges to receive mandatory training on sexual assault, domestic violence, implicit bias, and diversity, observers note that this case is not exceptional (Bosman, 2019).

Perhaps the best-known case in which class privilege benefited an offender con-victed of sexual assault is that of Brock Turner, a former swimmer at Stanford University. Turner was discovered by two graduate students sexually assaulting an intoxicated and unconscious 22-year-old woman behind a dumpster. When the graduate students interrupted him, he fled, but one chased and apprehended him, and they held him until the police arrived and arrested him. Turner was originally charged with two counts of rape, two counts of felony sexual assault, and one count of attempted rape, but the two rape charges were eventually dropped. He was convicted of the remaining three sexual assault charges, which potentially carried a sentence of 14 years. But Turner was sentenced in 2016 to six months in jail and three years of probation, and was later released from jail after only three months (see www.documentcloud.org/documents/2852615-Stanford-Victim-Letter-Impact-Statement-From.html for the survivor's victim impact statement, read at Turner's sentencing). The judge in that case was recalled by California voters in 2018 (Bosman, 2019). There are also numerous cases from colleges and universities across the country (e.g., Michigan State University, Baylor University) in which the institutions' administrators and sexual misconduct adjudication systems quashed or minimized victims' reports and, in effect, allowed offenders to victimize others.

The incidence of sexual assault across all population groups in the United States is concerning, but the greater vulnerability of adolescents and young adults, especially by their peers and acquaintances, is particularly troubling. Some observers have argued that one way to protect young people, especially young women, is to teach them self-defense tactics (Hollander, 2009, 2014; Thompson, 2014; White & Rees, 2014). Research shows that resisting sexual assault—through verbal assertiveness, screaming, and physical actions, including fighting—reduces the likelihood of rape completion and does not affect the likelihood of additional physical injuries (Gidycz et al., 2015; Jordan & Mossman, 2018; Tark & Kleck, 2014).

Some experts, however, caution that focusing resources on self-defense training places the burden of safety on potential victims rather than holding perpetrators accountable, and fails to address the critical need to change rape-supportive attitudes in our culture, especially among young men. The primary goal from this perspective is preventing sexual assault from occurring in the first place. Self-defense and assertiveness training are, then, just one element of a multidimensional approach to sexual assault prevention (see also Chapter 11).

There are a number of prevention programs currently employed in various settings, including middle schools, high schools, and colleges and universities. Some are referred to as awareness-based programs, which employ speakers, such as sexual assault survivors, victim advocates, or even local celebrities, to give a presentation that raises awareness among the audience about the seriousness of the problem and its consequences. Awareness-based programs, though, have been critiqued because they don't teach audience members specific skills or offer them the opportunity to practice those skills, which, as we noted in our discussion of peer sexual harassment, are necessary to program effectiveness (Gidycz, Orchowski, & Edwards, 2011). Other important components of prevention programs are that they are peer-led; are delivered to intact peer groups, such as athletic teams, fraternities and sororities, clubs, and residence halls; use interactive and multiple methods of teaching ideas, skills, and behaviors; and offer a curriculum broken down into multiple segments or lessons (Brecklin & Forde, 2001; Gidycz et al., 2011; Wolfe et al., 2006).

One type of program that includes all of these components is **bystander intervention programs**. As Cook-Craig and colleagues (2014) explain, "As a prevention strategy, the bystander approach trains individuals to respond to situations in which norms or behaviors that promote violence are present. Because the majority of individuals do not perpetrate [sexual violence], the bystander approach increases the likelihood of not just individual change but also community and norms change, as the target population for change is everyone in the community, rather than just perpetrators or victims" (p. 1167). Bystander programs have been implemented in high schools and on college and university campuses in recent years, with evaluations indicating some success in terms of increasing bystanders' confidence and willingness to intervene when they witness a risky social interaction unfolding (Banyard, Moynihan, & Plante, 2007; see also Chapter 11). For example, an evaluation of one such program, the Green Dot active bystander intervention program, found that students who had received the training showed lower rape myth acceptance and an increase in active bystander intervention behavior (Coker et al., 2011). Perhaps most importantly, in comparison with students at two universities without the Green Dot program, students at a university where the program was offered reported less violent victimization (Coker et al., 2015). Of course, further evaluation of these and other sexual assault prevention programs is needed, but the results to date suggest that at least some peer sexual violence is preventable.

Most colleges and universities have incorporated a unit on "healthy relationships" into their campus orientation programs for first-year students, and in these sessions, students may receive some bystander training as well as learn about the institution's student code of conduct that includes the consent policy. Typically, the consent policy requires students to obtain the affirmative and unambiguous consent of their partners before engaging in any type of sexual behavior with them. This usually means that the consent must be a verbal "yes" and that it must be continuous throughout the sexual encounter (i.e., as the type of sexual behavior changes from, for example, kissing to undressing to oral sex, consent is obtained at each stage) (A. Gruber, 2020). Although these sessions and consent requirements are intended to reduce campus sexual assault and unwanted sexual contact, the research findings call their effectiveness into question. For instance, Hirsch and Khan (2020) found that while most of the students in their study were "acutely attuned to the importance of consent" (p. 115) and could recite their institution's legal consent standard verbatim, their actual behavior did not reflect this knowledge. The vast majority, particularly heterosexual students, relied on contextual and behavioral cues (e.g., moaning, pushing one's body in closer, beginning to undress) to determine their partner's consent and considered explicitly asking for consent awkward at best. Needless to say, many of the students with whom Hirsch and Khan spoke had engaged in nonconsensual sex. As a result of their research, therefore, Hirsch and Khan (2020) maintain that campus prevention programs are too narrow and, more importantly, start too late. They advocate for comprehensive sex education in grades K–12, as well as sexual socialization by parents, that teaches "sex as a critical life skill" (p. 266) and that promotes "sexual citizenship"—that is, "the recognition of one's own right to sexual self-determination and, importantly, acknowledges the equivalent right in others" (p. xvi). It is uncertain whether these and similar recommendations will be adopted in most schools and homes in the United States, but given the limited success of current programs and practices, additional research to evaluate these alternatives seems warranted.

TEEN DATING VIOLENCE AND STALKING

Teen dating violence is physical, psychological, or sexual violence, as well as stalking, perpetrated within a dating relationship. **Stalking** is a form of teen dating violence that involves a pattern of unwanted, harassing, or threatening tactics that generate fear in the victim. These definitions encompass a wide range of behaviors, including hitting and slapping, threats, forced sexual activity, and following a person, but some researchers maintain that the specific act must also be considered in the context in which it occurs, the motivation of the actor, the meaning it has to the parties involved, and the impact or consequences it has. For example, a person who hits his intimate partner to punish her for defying his wishes is being abusive, but if she pushes him to get him to stop hitting her, she is acting in self-defense. A person who leaves a gift for her boyfriend after they've just broken up may be trying to apologize or reestablish the relationship, but if she leaves gifts every day, even after he tells her to stop, and he becomes afraid of what she might do next, she is stalking him. Dating violence and stalking may be perpetrated in person or electronically, and may involve current or former dating partners.

Prevalence of Teen Dating Violence and Stalking

Estimates of the incidence of teen dating violence vary, depending on the sample of teens surveyed and the behaviors they are asked about. Victimization rates reported in various studies range from about 6 percent to nearly 16 percent; self-reported perpetration rates range from 6.4 percent to about 19 percent (Coker et al., 2014; Haynie et al., 2013). In a study of more than 14,000 high school students, Coker and her colleagues (2014) reported that 33.4 percent of the teens disclosed victimization and 20.2 percent disclosed perpetration of partner violence. Importantly, in many of these studies girls' reports of partner victimization *and* perpetration are similar to and, in some studies, slightly higher than those of boys. As Table 7.8 shows, however, in the 2017 YRBSS survey, female high school students were victimized at rates significantly higher than male high school

TABLE 7.8 ■ Percentage of U.S. High School Students Who Experienced Physical Dating Violence or Sexual Dating Violence by Sex, Race/Ethnicity, Grade, and Sexual Identity, 2017				
	Physical Dating Violence*		Sexual Dating Violence*	
	Females	Males	Females	Males
Race/Ethnicity				
White	8.0	5.9	11.1	2.6
Black	13.1	7.1	8.8	2.7
Hispanic	9.2	5.9	11.4	2.5
Grade				
9	8.1	5.6	11.0	2.2
10	10.1	6.5	10.6	2.9
11	8.4	4.8	11.5	1.8
12	9.5	8.9	9.4	4.0
Sexual identity				
Heterosexual (Straight)	7.1	5.8	9.3	2.1
Gay, Lesbian, or Bisexual	16.9	16.8	16.3	13.5
Not Sure	11.3	14.1	15.5	9.2
Total	13.0	7.4	14.4	6.2

*Among the 69.0% of students nationwide who dated or went out with someone during the 12 months before the survey.

Source: Centers for Disease Control and Prevention (CDC), Youth Risk Behavior Surveillance—United States, 2017. Retrieved from https://www.cdc.gov/mmwr/volumes/67/ss/ss6708a1.htm.

students, particularly with regard to sexual dating violence (10.7% and 2.8%, respectively) (Kann et al., 2018), which is a consistent finding across studies (Molidor, Tolman, & Kober, 2000; Swahn, Simon, Arias, & Bossarte, 2008). The YRBSS, however, measures only physical and sexual dating violence. Psychological and emotional abuse in teen dating relationships is even more common than physical and sexual abuse, with rates of victimization for both girls and boys in one study at 23 percent (Coker et al., 2014; Foshee, McNaughton Reyes, & Wyckoff, 2009).

As Table 7.8 shows, there is some variation across racial and ethnic groups with regard to dating violence, with black teens, especially girls, experiencing a higher rate of physical violence. The greatest differences, however, occur across sexual identity groups. Teens who are unsure of their sexual identity experience greater rates of both physical and sexual violence compared to heterosexual teens. Gay, lesbian, and bisexual teens, however, have the highest rates of physical and sexual dating violence across sexual identity groups (Kann et al., 2018).

A disturbing trend emerging in the research literature is the prevalence among teens of using cell phones or the internet to control and stalk their dating partners. For example, among teens who responded to a survey by the Pew Research Center, 22 percent reported that a current or former partner used the internet or a cell phone to call them names, put them down, or say "really mean" things about them; 21 percent reported that a current or former dating partner had read their text messages without permission; 16 percent were required by a dating partner to remove former dating partners from their friends list on social media; 15 percent reported that a current or former dating partner spread rumors about them using a cell phone or the internet; 13 percent said a current or former dating partner demanded to know their passwords to their email and internet accounts; 11 percent reported that a current or former dating partner used a cell phone or the internet to threaten to hurt them; and 8 percent said a current or former dating partner used information posted on the internet against them, to harass them, or to embarrass them (Lenhart et al., 2015; see also N. Henry & Powell, 2015; C. Hill & Johnson, 2019).

These are, without a doubt, troubling statistics, but as we have seen with regard to the other forms of abuse and violence discussed in this chapter, risk for dating violence and stalking is not equally distributed across all groups of teens.

Risk Factors Associated With Teen Dating Violence and Stalking

In many studies, victimization rates of teen dating violence and stalking do not show significant variation across racial and ethnic groups (compare, for example, Kann et al., 2018, with Coker et al., 2014). Social class, however, is consistently associated with teen dating violence: youth who are poor are more likely to report victimization as well as perpetration (Coker et al., 2014; J. Miller, 2008). As we have already noted, LGBTQ teens report particularly high rates of victimization; they also report higher rates of perpetration relative to their heterosexual peers (Coker et al., 2014; DiFulvio, 2015; Gillum & DiFulvio, 2012; Kann et al., 2018).

The factors found to be associated with peer sexual harassment and sexual assault also emerge in research as significant contributing factors to teen dating violence and stalking. Researchers have found, for instance, that teens who begin using alcohol at a young age and those who report binge drinking are at greater risk of both dating violence victimization and perpetration (Coker et al., 2014; Haynes, Strauss, Stuart, & Shorey, 2018; Vagi et al., 2013). Witnessing parental IPV or experiencing maltreatment as a child also increases the likelihood that a teen will be the victim or perpetrator of dating violence (Coker et al., 2014; Foshee et al., 2016; Vagi et al., 2013). Sexual proprietariness, jealousy, and the belief that dating violence is acceptable under specific circumstances also elevate risk of dating violence and stalking perpetration (Foshee et al., 2016; Ozaki & Otis, 2017; Vagi et al., 2013). Finally, peers play a role in risk of dating violence and stalking: Having a friend involved in dating violence increases a teen's risk of victimization and perpetration (Adelman & Kil, 2007; DeKeseredy & Schwartz, 2013; J. Miller, 2008; Vagi et al., 2013). Ball and her colleagues (2012) summarize these findings: "Multiple experiences of violence in relationships across social contexts, lack of positive role models, and violence-supportive peer group norms . . . appear to be interacting factors that increase the risk for experiencing or inflicting peer and dating violence" (p. 748).

Crooks and her colleagues (2019) point out that there is now considerable research that demonstrates the increased risk for teen dating violence among socially marginalized groups of teens, including LGBTQ youth and youth with disabilities. Many of the factors that increase risk for heterosexual youth and youth without disabilities apply to socially marginalized groups as well, although their marginalization in itself constitutes a risk factor. Crooks et al., however, argue it is time to place more research effort into working with marginalized teens and young adults to identify programs and services that will meet their needs and reduce their vulnerability. We will return to the topic of prevention and intervention shortly.

Consequences of Teen Dating Violence and Stalking

We have noted that many studies show similar rates of dating violence perpetration by girls and boys. Nevertheless, girls experience more long-term and severe physical and psychological health problems as a result of dating violence and stalking victimization, including depression; social withdrawal; anxiety; suicidal ideation and attempts; eating disorders; increased use of tobacco, alcohol, and drugs; and poor school performance (Chiodo et al., 2009; Exner-Cortens, Eckenrode, & Rothman, 2013; Haynie et al., 2013). Girls who are victims of teen dating violence and stalking are also at elevated risk of being revictimized by an intimate partner as adults (P. Smith, White, & Holland, 2003; Stroem, Aakvaag, & Wentzel-Larson, 2019).

Girls are also significantly more likely than boys to be injured or killed by a dating partner (J. Miller, 2008; Swahn et al., 2008). In 2018, for example, University of Utah senior Lauren McCluskey was shot to death by her ex-boyfriend after she had blocked his calls and refused to give him money to keep him from distributing suggestive pictures of her. McCluskey had filed complaints with the campus police, notifying them that her ex-boyfriend was stalking her, but the police did not act until she reported the extortion attempt. Even then, they told her an investigation would take time. Her friends reported the problem to university housing officials, but they decided not to "overstep" because McCluskey had not spoken to them herself. McCluskey's parents are now suing the University of Utah for the "deliberate indifference" shown toward their daughter's safety and well-being on the campus, in violation of the provisions of Title IX (Pettit, 2019). Commentators on this case point out that although campus sexual assault has received a great deal of attention in recent years, IPV has not been a focal concern at most institutions. Unfortunately, Lauren McCluskey is one of dozens of student victims killed by their intimate partners or ex-partners, signaling the need for more training for campus police, student life personnel, and other campus officials and for better coordination of campus services to provide timely and effective responses (Pettit, 2019). We look at other prevention and intervention efforts in the next section.

Intervention and Prevention Strategies

Research indicates that adolescents are unlikely to seek help to address dating violence (Hedge, Sianko, & McDonell, 2017). In one study, for instance, 60 percent of adolescent victims and 79 percent of adolescent perpetrators of dating violence did not seek any type of help (Ashley & Foshee, 2005). Among adolescents who do seek help, most disclose to their friends or family members, rather than professionals such as teachers, school nurses, doctors, or clergy (Fry et al., 2013). Many youth express the belief that individuals should handle personal problems on their own (Sawyer et al., 2000), but they also report with regard to disclosure that they do not trust or feel close to adult professionals, and they also worry about privacy, confidentiality, and being blamed or stigmatized (Clement et al., 2015; Ocampo, Shelley, & Jaycox, 2007). Importantly, however, adolescents who perceive that they have high levels of support from family and friends are more likely to seek professional help than those who perceive little or no social support (Hedge et al., 2017).

Given that many of the risk factors for teen dating violence and stalking are the same as those for the other forms of abuse and violence we have discussed in this chapter, it is not surprising that advocates and researchers have applied some of the same programs to *preventing* these problems. For example, Crooks and colleagues (2019) found that the Fourth R program, discussed earlier in this chapter, significantly reduced physical dating violence among a sample of 14- to 15-year-olds compared with their peers who did not participate in the program, and also increased condom use in sexually active boys. Students who participated in the program also increased their skills at resisting peer pressure, and as we noted earlier, there is additional evidence that the program may be especially beneficial to high-risk youth (i.e., those with a history of child maltreatment). Another prevention program, the Youth Relationships Project (YRP), has also been shown to produce positive outcomes for 14- to 16-year-olds who were at elevated risk of dating violence because they had histories of child maltreatment (Crooks et al., 2019). The YRP is an

18-lesson program that addresses gender norms and offers alternatives to aggression for solving interpersonal problems. Evaluation findings show that, compared with teens who were not exposed to the YRP, the teens who participated in the program had lower rates of both physical and emotional abuse as well as fewer symptoms of emotional distress over time (Crooks et al., 2019).

Expect Respect is another program designed primarily for at-risk teens. It is composed of 24 sessions that focus on five themes: developing group skills, choosing equality and respect for others, learning to recognize abusive relationships, developing healthy relationship skills, and becoming active proponents for safe and healthy relationships (Ball et al., 2012). Expect Respect uses many of the teaching methods of the YRP and the Fourth R. In an evaluation of the program, Ball and her colleagues (2012) found that participants showed an increase in healthy relationship skills by the time they completed the program. With regard to victimization and perpetration rates, however, the findings were mixed. Overall, levels of both victimization and perpetration did not change over the course of the program, but among the participants who, at the start of the program, disclosed the highest rates of victimization and perpetration, these rates significantly declined by completion of the program.

One theme addressed by the Expect Respect program—learning to recognize abusive relationships—has been found to be particularly important for young women. Chung (2007) found in her study of young women who had been in abusive dating relationships that there was strong reluctance on their part to label the relationships abusive or to describe their boyfriends as violent or controlling. In addition, Chung found that the young women tended to blame themselves for their "relationship problems" and their boyfriends' behavior—major reasons they do not seek help to address the abuse and its impact. She recommends, therefore, that dating violence prevention programs include not only peer education and support, but also components that address "the broader social context of dating relationships, such as heterosexual dominance, the social pressure to be in a relationship, the tactics of sexual coercion and abuse, and the myths and barriers that prevent women from seeking help" (p. 1294).

The programs discussed here are certainly not the only programs or efforts currently underway to address dating violence and stalking as well as peer sexual harassment and sexual assault. However, as we noted earlier, Crooks and her colleagues (2019), in a review of such programs, identify significant gaps, especially in culturally competent programming for teens and young adults of color; for LGBTQ teens and young adults; and for teens and young adults with physical, developmental, or psychological disabilities. Moreover, they emphasize the need to include members of each target group in the development and evaluation of programs, rather than imposing programming on them. We will return to the issue of prevention in Chapter 11, where we will discuss additional policies and programs for promoting a violence-free future.

CHAPTER SUMMARY

Adolescence and emerging adulthood is a transitional stage in the life course when young people assert greater autonomy, become more independent, make more decisions for themselves, develop intimate relationships with opposite-sex or same-sex peers, and become sexually active. The research we reviewed in this chapter shows, however, that this is also a developmental stage when peer sexual and gender harassment, sexual assault, dating violence, and stalking are not uncommon.

We defined sexual harassment as unwelcome sexual advances, requests for sexual favors, or other verbal, nonverbal, or physical conduct of a sexual nature; it includes gender harassment, which refers to being called gay or lesbian or derogatory names or slurs for gays or lesbians in a malicious way. Sexual assault encompasses various forms of sexual contact without a person's consent or when one is unable to consent. The most severe form of sexual assault is rape, or nonconsensual attempted or completed penetration. Finally, we defined dating violence as physical, psychological, or sexual violence, including stalking, which involves a pattern of unwanted, harassing, or threatening tactics that generate fear in a victim. Estimates of these forms of violence and abuse vary widely mostly due to the samples surveyed, the definitions used, the way questions were worded, and the time period examined. What is clear, however, is that a significant number of adolescents and young adults are affected by these forms of violence each year.

These forms of adolescent violence are important to study, not only because they represent a violation of human rights, but because such violence is associated with a number of negative physical, psychological, and social consequences. There are significant impacts on victims, particularly associated with rape and dating violence, ranging from scratches and bruises to broken bones, spinal cord injuries, and even death as a result of homicide. Rape victims also suffer from various gynecological problems (e.g., STIs) as well as headaches, gastrointestinal disorders, and insomnia and disordered sleep. Adolescent violence can also be associated with psychological problems including depression, lowered self-esteem, lowered self-confidence, social withdrawal, a decline in school achievement, loss of appetite, and increased use of tobacco, alcohol, and drugs. More severe outcomes include PTSD, suicidal ideation, and attempted and completed suicide.

Although girls and boys may be perpetrators and victims of these behaviors, girls are at greater risk of victimization, and boys are at greater risk of perpetration. We discussed various risk and protective factors to better understand adolescent victimization and perpetration experiences. Although specific risk factors vary depending on the type of adolescent violence, there are commonalities, such as adherence to norms of hegemonic masculinity, witnessing parental IPV, early use of alcohol or drugs, having a history of child maltreatment, and LGBTQ identity.

Identifying risk factors is important for guiding the development and implementation of prevention and intervention programs to improve responses to victims and perpetrators and to reduce the incidence of these problem behaviors. Importantly, research shows that effective prevention programs must do more than simply raise awareness. The programs that researchers have found to be most successful are peer-led, emphasize gender-egalitarian attitudes and values, teach nonviolent problem-solving skills as well as strategies for intervening (i.e., active bystanding) in potentially harmful incidents, and provide opportunities for practicing and, therefore, reinforcing these values, attitudes, skills, and strategies.

Recommended Resources

Crooks, C. V., Jaffe, P., Dunlop, C., Kerry, A., & Exner-Cortens, D. (2019). Preventing gender-based violence among adolescents and young adults: Lessons from 25 years of program development and evaluation. *Violence Against Women, 25*(1), 29–55.

Follingstad, D. R. (2017). The challenges of measuring violence against women. In C. M. Renzetti, J. L. Edleson, & R. K. Bergen (Eds.), *Sourcebook on violence against women* (3rd ed., pp. 57–77). Thousand Oaks, CA: Sage.

Hirsch, J. S., & Khan, S. (2020). *Sexual citizens: A landmark study of sex, power, and assault on campus.* New York, NY: W. W. Norton.

Miller, C. (2019). *Know my name: A memoir.* New York, NY: Viking.

Powell, A., & Henry, N. (2017). *Sexual violence in a digital age.* London, England: Palgrave Macmillan.

Renzetti, C. M., & Follingstad, D. R. (Eds.). (2020). *Adjudicating campus sexual misconduct and assault: Controversies and challenges.* San Diego, CA: Cognella.

8

INTIMATE PARTNER VIOLENCE IN ADULT RELATIONSHIPS

Focusing on Victims

LEARNING OBJECTIVES

1. Describe the definition and scope of intimate partner violence (IPV), from the perspective of victimization, including problems inherent in measuring this form of abuse.

2. Identify the various risk factors associated with IPV victimization.

3. Summarize the consequences of IPV for victims.

4. Discuss the various intervention and prevention efforts that focus on IPV victims, including evidence of their effectiveness.

CASE HISTORY

SHELBY AND MARCUS: A DEADLY OUTCOME

Shelby was 20 years old and Marcus was 24 years old when they met. Marcus worked as a lineman for the local utility company and nearly every morning came to the restaurant where Shelby worked as a waitress during the breakfast shift. In fact, Shelby became "his" waitress; she'd start bringing a pot of coffee to his table and filling his cup when she saw him sauntering toward the front door from the parking lot. They flirted with each other, and—finally—Marcus asked her out. A whirlwind romance ensued, and in less than a year, they were engaged.

Shelby moved into Marcus's small bungalow on the outskirts of town before the wedding. The first time Marcus had taken her to his home, she was shocked by his décor; hanging on the walls of his living room were a variety of knives. Marcus was very proud of his collection of rare and exotic knives, but Shelby found them a little frightening. This was now the home she was going to share full-time with Marcus.

Over time, Marcus became increasingly possessive of Shelby. He would accuse her of flirting with his friends or with other customers and, when she denied it, would get very angry and call her a liar and a slut, although later he would apologize and tell her he wouldn't get so upset if he didn't love her so much. He started to call her at work, and if she didn't answer the phone—usually because she was busy serving customers—he would come to the restaurant to check up on her. Shelby's boss warned her that Marcus was interfering with her ability to do her job well, and when Shelby told Marcus he needed to stop checking up on her at work, he argued that her boss was trying to break them up so he could have Shelby to himself. Marcus insisted Shelby quit her job, and although she didn't really want to, she complied, rationalizing that she would then have more time to plan their wedding.

Following the wedding reception, which lasted until midnight, Shelby and Marcus drove two hours to their honeymoon destination. Marcus wanted to have sex, but Shelby, tired from the day's events and the long drive, told him she just wanted to go to sleep. Marcus flew into a rage, held Shelby down by her arms, and told her, "You're mine now. When I say I want sex, we're having sex." Marcus then forced Shelby to have sex.

As their marriage continued, Marcus became increasingly controlling, imposing more "rules" on Shelby. If she disobeyed, or even complained, he would "punish" her with a slap, or by pulling her hair. He frequently called her names or made fun of her opinions or how she dressed. He told her to stop taking her birth control pills because he wanted a baby, but Shelby secretly continued to take them, thinking that she wanted their relationship to improve before she brought a child into it. During a routine check-up, Shelby's doctor told her she had a sexually transmitted infection (STI). She then realized that Marcus must be cheating on her, since she had not had sex outside their marriage. She dared not tell him about the STI, however, because she knew he would likely accuse *her* of infidelity. But Marcus grew more impatient as the months passed and Shelby did not get pregnant. He began to threaten her. For instance, he would make her sit with him while he cleaned his knives, mentioning how they could kill a person with just one quick swipe across the neck. He would add a comment about how husbands used to be able to kill their wives for not bearing them children. Just before her 23rd birthday, Marcus asked Shelby what her favorite color was; when she told him pink, he replied that for her birthday he was going to buy her a pink casket.

Marcus didn't buy Shelby a pink casket for her birthday that year, but one evening a few weeks after her birthday, as she sat next to him watching him clean his knives, he made a quick move toward her with a knife to frighten her. She instantly jumped back, but her leg accidentally hit the table, causing the polish to spill. Marcus began screaming at Shelby, calling her horrible names, and he backhanded her hard across her face. She ran to the bedroom and locked herself in, but he pounded on the door and said he would break it down if she didn't come out. When she emerged from the bedroom, Marcus grabbed Shelby by her hair and dragged her into the living room, yelling for her to clean up the mess she had made. As she got up from the floor to get something to wipe up the polish, he kicked her back down. He put his hand on her neck and pushed her face into the spilled polish while telling her he could kill her if that was what he wanted to do. Shelby then grabbed a knife and stabbed Marcus in the stomach. She had seriously injured him, but she had also made him even angrier. He reached for her, but she stabbed him again, and again—13 times in all. She continued to stab him after he fell to the floor, because, as she told the police later, she was convinced she couldn't kill him; she just wanted him to stop hurting her. When Marcus stopped moving, Shelby went out to the front porch of the house, sat on the steps, and called 9-1-1 to report the incident.

Shelby was arrested and tried for the murder of her husband. Her court-appointed attorney argued that she had acted in self-defense. A neighbor testified for the defense that she had noticed bruises on Shelby's arms on one of the rare occasions Shelby was not wearing a long-sleeved blouse and that, when asked about them, Shelby had said that Marcus had grabbed her hard during an argument but hadn't meant any harm. Shelby confided to a counselor appointed by the court that Marcus had made it clear that if she ran away from him, he would "hunt her down" and kill her; she believed him and felt "trapped." Nevertheless, the jury convicted Shelby of second-degree murder. They had heard evidence from the prosecution that Shelby had never called the police; she had never sought help from a battered women's shelter. If the marriage was so bad, why hadn't she tried to get help? And surely it wasn't necessary to stab Marcus 13 times to get him to stop, even if he had been hitting her. It appeared to the jury that Shelby was the violent partner in the marriage. Shelby is serving a sentence of 30 years in a women's state correctional facility; she will be eligible for a parole hearing in 10 years.

Certainly, in hindsight at least, it appears clear that Shelby and Marcus's relationship was plagued by intimate partner violence, but the jury's verdict against Shelby raises one of the most controversial questions that has surrounded the study of and responses to IPV: Who is a *legitimate* victim? In this chapter, we will explore answers to that question by considering the definition of IPV and victimization rates across various groups and in different contexts. We will also discuss the consequences of victimization for those who experience IPV, and both criminal justice and social service responses to IPV victims. Victimization, of course, is closely related to perpetration, but we will limit our focus primarily to victimization issues in this chapter and take up perpetration in Chapter 9.

SCOPE OF THE PROBLEM

What Is IPV?

Intimate partner violence (IPV) includes any threatened or completed acts of physical, sexual, or psychological abuse committed by a spouse, ex-spouse, or current or former boyfriend or girlfriend. We will elaborate on this general definition throughout the chapter. Even though most people think they know which behaviors obviously constitute IPV—for example, pushing, hitting, slapping, throwing things at one's partner to hurt her or him—there is actually a great deal of disagreement over what "counts" as IPV. We will learn in this chapter that many researchers and practitioners argue that in addition to the specific behavior in question, the context, meaning, motivation, and consequences of the behavior must be considered before any specific act is labeled IPV (see also Chapter 7).

Definitions of IPV are further complicated by domestic violence laws, which vary from state to state. Some states do not have laws specifically prohibiting IPV, or domestic violence, but instead subsume it under general assault, aggravated assault, and battery laws. In other states, individuals may be charged with misdemeanor or felony domestic violence, depending on the severity of the assault and the nature of the relationship between the individuals involved. (Individual state laws may be examined at statelaws.findlaw.com/family-laws/domestic-violence.html.) In 1994, Congress passed the federal Violence Against Women Act (VAWA), which must be reauthorized every five years. VAWA's provisions include components intended to reduce IPV, as well as other forms of violence that disproportionately affect women, largely through criminal justice remedies, such as increasing perpetrator accountability (D. Ford, Bachman, Friend, & Meloy, 2002). In 2018, VAWA expired, and although reauthorization passed with bipartisan support in the U.S. House of Representatives, as of April 2020 the Senate still had not reauthorized the law. Elements of the reauthorization bill that are opposed by some senators include added protections for transgender people and American Indian and Alaska Native women, and the provision that prohibits anyone convicted of abuse from owning a gun. Although federal funding for many programs is still available, the expiration of the law raises concerns among many service providers and legal professionals. Nevertheless, because the U.S. Constitution grants certain powers to the federal government and certain powers to state governments—a principle called federalism—passage of VAWA did not produce uniform state laws on IPV, although it did make certain behaviors, such as crossing state lines to commit IPV—commonly referred to as **interstate domestic violence**—a federal crime with serious penalties. We will discuss several significant impacts of VAWA later in this chapter.

Estimates of IPV

Given our ongoing discussions of how difficult it is to define and measure violence and maltreatment in intimate relationships (VMIR), it should come as no surprise that determining the rate of IPV victimization is not a straightforward task. One approach would be to ask a random sample of the U.S. population if their intimate partner has done various things to them and, if so, how many times. Then, the researcher could count up the incidents of IPV and get the rate for the sample as well as use this rate to extrapolate to the entire population. This is precisely what a number of national surveys—for instance, the National Family Violence Survey (Straus & Gelles, 1990), the National Violence Against Women Survey (NVAWS; Tjaden & Thoennes, 2000), and the National Intimate Partner and Sexual Violence Survey (NISVS; Black et al., 2011)—have done. Based on the findings of these surveys, it is estimated that approximately 8–12 percent of men and 12–25 percent of women are physically and/or sexually assaulted by an intimate partner each year (Black et al., 2011; Tjaden & Thoennes, 2000).

Notice, however, that this method results in rather large ranges in victimization rates. As we have discussed, *how* we define IPV and the questions that we ask will affect findings. Table 8.1 shows some of the methodological differences across several national surveys that have tried to measure IPV. In some studies, what "counts" as IPV is narrowly defined (e.g., only physical acts that can result in harm), whereas in other studies, a broader approach is adopted (e.g., in addition to physical acts, psychological or verbal aggression is measured). Studies that use broader, more inclusive definitions of IPV will generally produce higher estimates of victimization (DeKeseredy & Schwartz, 2011). Studies that restrict the definition of IPV to only

TABLE 8.1 ■ Methodological Differences Across National Surveys That Measure IPV				
Methodology	**Survey Title**			
	National Crime Victimization Survey (NCVS)	**National Women's Study (NWS)**	**National Family Violence Survey**	**National Violence Against Women Survey (NVAWS)**
Sample	National probability sample of individuals, age ≥ 12	National probability sample of women, age ≥ 18	National probability sample of married or cohabiting heterosexual couples, age ≥ 18	National probability sample of women, age ≥ 18
Asks specifically about violence perpetrated by current and former intimate partners	No. Asks about victimizations perpetrated by "friends" and/or "family members"	No. Asks about victimizations perpetrated by "friends" and/or "family members"	Asks only about victimizations perpetrated by "current partner"	Yes. Asks about victimizations perpetrated by current and former partners
Behaviors included in screening questions about violence	Attacked or threatened; attacked or threatened with any weapon; with anything like a baseball bat, frying pan, scissors, or a stick; by something thrown such as a rock or bottle; any grabbing, punching, or choking; any rape or sexual attack; any face-to-face threats; any attack or threat or use of force	Attacked with a gun, knife, or some other weapon, or attacked without a weapon but with no intent to seriously injure	Threw something at partner; pushed, grabbed, or shoved; slapped, kicked, bit, or hit with fist; hit or tried to hit with something; beat up; choked; threatened with a knife or gun; used a knife or fired a gun	Threw something that could hurt; pushed, grabbed, or shoved; pulled hair; slapped or hit; kicked or bit; choked or attempted to drown; hit with an object; beat up; threatened with a gun; threatened with a knife or other weapon; used a gun, knife, or other weapon
Asks about stalking	No	No	No	Yes
Context of the survey	Questions asked in context of a "crime survey"	Questions asked in context of "stressful events" experienced	Questions asked in context of "personal conflicts" between family members	Questions asked in context of issues related to "personal safety"

TABLE 8.1 ■ (Continued)				
	Survey Title			
Methodology	National Crime Victimization Survey (NCVS)	National Women's Study (NWS)	National Family Violence Survey	National Violence Against Women Survey (NVAWS)
Identifies injuries resulting from violence	Yes	No	No	Yes
Identifies context of violence	Yes. Asks questions to distinguish acts of self-defense	No. Does not distinguish acts of self-defense	No. Does not distinguish acts of self-defense	Yes. Asks questions that distinguish acts of self-defense

Source: Ford, Bachman, Friend, & Meloy, 2002.

physical acts, however, overlook important types of IPV that can have serious negative consequences for victims. For example, many studies do not include **economic (financial) abuse** in which perpetrators deliberately try to weaken or destroy their partner's financial solvency by, for example, purposely ruining the partner's credit rating or running up large debts for which the partner may be held responsible. This type of abuse may lead to the victim's impoverishment, or at least a lowered standard of living, and sometimes may lead to homelessness (Tutty, Ogden, Giurgiu, & Weaver-Dunlop, 2014).

Another type of IPV that typically is not measured in standard surveys designed to estimate IPV is **coercive control** Coercive control is an ongoing pattern of domination, in which the abusive partner uses intimidation, isolation, and similar tactics to erode the freedom of the victim (Stark, 2009). Evan Stark (2009), who has written extensively about coercive control, maintains that it is the most pervasive type of IPV and often the first type inflicted by an abusive partner, as we saw in the case of Marcus and Shelby. In 2015, England and Wales recognized the devastating impact of coercive control, particularly on victims' mental health, and became the first countries in the world to criminalize it as an illegal form of IPV (for more information on this law, see https://rightsofwomen.org.uk/get-information/violence-against-women-and-international-law/coercive-control-and-the-law/). We will learn more about coercive control later in this chapter, but for now suffice it to say that it is not illegal in the United States and often not even "counted" in IPV prevalence studies.

Who is asked about IPV victimization experiences also matters. For instance, studies that use random, nonclinical samples—that is, samples drawn from the general community—often show only very small differences in victimization rates between women and men. In contrast, studies that use clinical or criminal justice system–involved samples usually result in significantly higher victimization rates for women than for men (Hamby, 2017). Indeed, as we will see in Chapter 9, the gendered nature of IPV victimization is hotly debated among researchers and practitioners.

RISK FACTORS ASSOCIATED WITH IPV VICTIMIZATION

During the 1970s and 1980s, as victim advocacy groups sought to raise public awareness about the severity of IPV in the United States, a common claim was that IPV victims are found among all sociodemographic groups. Of course, there is some truth to this statement, but it also masks the greater vulnerability to victimization among members of some social groups. Here we consider some differences in victimization risk across various groups.

Sex

Are men as likely as women to be victimized by an intimate partner? As we discussed earlier, if we simply count acts of IPV, women's reports of IPV *perpetration* against their male partners are as high as—and, in some studies, higher than—men's reports of IPV perpetration against their female partners (Archer, 2000). These data, however, obscure some important differences in women's and men's IPV victimization experiences (Hamby, 2017).

First, women's victimization is usually more severe than men's victimization, which is likely why women express greater fear of bodily harm from IPV than men do (Hamby, 2017). About 1 in 4 women, compared with 1 in 7 men, are victims of severe physical IPV (Black et al., 2011). Women are also significantly more likely to be sexually assaulted by an intimate partner (Black et al., 2011). Polyvictimization is also more common among women; over 33 percent of female victims of IPV report experiencing two or more types of abuse (e.g., physical violence, sexual violence, psychological abuse, and stalking) compared with under 10 percent of male IPV victims (Black et al., 2011; Gover, Richards, & Patterson, 2018). In light of these findings, it is not surprising that women are more likely than men to be injured by an intimate partner, and that their injuries are more serious and more likely to require medical treatment or hospitalization (Hamby, 2018; Menard, Anderson, &

Godboldt, 2009; Sorenson, 2017). Furthermore, women are more likely than men to be killed by an intimate partner (Hamby, 2018; Sorenson, 2017). We will return to this issue later in this chapter and in Chapter 9.

Age

Young age is the most consistent demographic risk factor for IPV victimization. In a review of large-scale studies using adult samples, for example, the researchers reported that the most vulnerable group was younger women, aged 18–29 years (J. Campbell, Alhusen, Draughton, Kub, & Walton-Moss, 2011). Of course, this does not mean that older couples do not experience IPV, a topic we will explore in Chapter 10.

Race and Ethnicity

Most studies do not include multiple racial and ethnic groups, but instead compare one or two racial or ethnic minority groups with whites. Several studies, such as the NISVS (see Table 8.2), which is the most recent comprehensive study of IPV in the United States, have reported higher rates of IPV victimization for African Americans compared to whites (Black et al., 2011; see also Azziz-Baumgartner, McKeown, Melvin, Quynh, & Reed, 2011). However, because African Americans are disproportionately represented among the financially disadvantaged and people living in poverty, it may be that race is less important than social class with regard to IPV victimization risk. Studies that compare the IPV victimization rates of African Americans and whites with similar incomes have produced inconsistent findings, with a number of studies showing that differences in IPV rates between African Americans and whites disappear when socioeconomic factors, such as annual household income, are held constant (Capaldi, Knoble, Shortt, & Kim, 2012; Cho, 2012; H. Clark, Galano, Grogran-Kaylor, Montalvo-Liendo, & Graham-Berman, 2016).

Similar inconsistencies are reported in studies of Hispanics and Asian Americans (H. Clark et al., 2016; C. A. Field & Caetano, 2003; Grossman & Lundy, 2007; see also Table 8.2). Some of these differences are likely due to differences in samples and methods across studies, but they are also likely a result of diversity within Hispanic and Asian American groups as well as other factors such as immigration status and recency of immigration.

Two groups for whom consistently high rates of victimization have been found across studies are American Indians and Alaska Natives (see Table 8.2). In fact, studies of American Indian and Alaska Native women and men repeatedly show that these groups have the highest rates of IPV victimization of any racial or ethnic group (Black et al., 2011; M. Jones, Worthen, Sharp, & McLeod, 2020; Luna-Firebaugh, 2006). Again, however, it is important to consider the intersection of race with social class inequality, given

TABLE 8.2 ■ Lifetime Prevalence of Rape, Physical Violence, and/or Stalking by an Intimate Partner, for U.S. Women and Men, 2010						
Women (%)						
IPV Type	Hispanic	Black	White	Asian or Pacific Islander	American Indian or Alaska Native	Multiracial
Rape	8.4	12.2	9.2	*	*	20.1
Physical violence	35.2	40.9	31.7	*	45.9	50.4
Stalking	10.6	14.6	10.4	*	*	18.9
Rape, physical violence, and/or stalking	37.1	43.7	34.6	19.6	46.0	53.8
Men (%)						
IPV Type	Hispanic	Black	White	Asian or Pacific Islander	American Indian or Alaska Native	Multiracial
Rape	*	*	*	*	*	*
Physical violence	26.5	36.8	28.1	8.4	45.3	38.8
Stalking	*	*	1.7	*	*	*
Rape, physical violence, and/or stalking	26.6	38.6	28.2	*	45.3	39.3

*Estimate is not reported; relative standard error > 30% or cell size < 20.

Source: Black et al., 2011.

that American Indians and Alaska Natives have higher rates of poverty than other U.S. racial and ethnic groups (Macartney, Bishaw, & Fontenot, 2013). In addition, American Indians and Alaska Natives have higher rates of adverse childhood experiences and lifetime trauma, which are also significantly associated with IPV in adulthood (M. Jones et al., 2020).

It is also important to note that most research that has examined IPV victimization rates across racial and ethnic groups has assumed that both partners in a couple are the same race or ethnicity. Very little research has examined IPV among interracial couples. One exception is a study conducted by Hattery (2009), which examined IPV among interracial couples using data from the NVAWS. She found low rates of IPV among heterosexual couples in which the male partner was white and the female partner was black, but relatively high rates of IPV among couples in which the male partner was black and the female partner was white. Of course, there are many more combinations of interracial couples in the United States and a variety of potential mediating factors, such as social class, for which Hattery did not control. C. J. Field, Kimuna, and Lang (2015) examined IPV among a racially diverse sample of college students and found that interracial couples, in which one partner identified as black and the other as white, had higher rates of IPV than interracial couples of "other races." The subsample of "other interracial couples," however, was too small to tease out differences across various interracial combinations. Additional research that examines IPV among interracial couples and that attempts to account for other intervening factors is clearly warranted, as is research with multiracial women and men, considering their high victimization rates reported in the NISVS (see Table 8.2).

Socioeconomic Status

Most of the research on socioeconomic status or social class and IPV victimization has focused on financial strain and the effects of living in economically disadvantaged neighborhoods. Overall, the research points to the conclusion that there is a strong relationship between indicators of economic distress and IPV, but also that the associations are complex.

A large body of data shows high IPV victimization rates among individuals with low financial resources (Bonomi, Trabert, Anderson, Kernic, & Holt, 2014). For example, analyses of data from the National Crime Victimization Survey show that households in the lowest annual income category had an IPV rate 5 times greater than that of households in the highest income category (Greenfeld et al., 1998). Moreover, among those who are poor, data also indicate that it is the poorest of the poor who experience the highest rates of IPV victimization (see, for instance, Browne, Salomon, & Bassuk, 1999; Lloyd, 1997; Tolman & Rosen, 2001). But even among couples who are not living in poverty, financial strain has been found to be associated with IPV. Benson and Fox (2004) found, for example, that among couples who reported subjective feelings of strong financial strain the IPV rate was 9.5 percent, compared with 2.7 percent among couples who reported subjective feelings of low financial strain. Nevertheless, Leguizamon, Leguizamon, and Howden (2017) reported that the impact of economic stress on IPV may vary across racial and ethnic groups. They discovered that economic uncertainty (e.g., a mass layoff) increased the risk of IPV among whites, but decreased it among blacks.

It is important to keep in mind as well that research shows that the relationship between economic hardship and IPV may be *reciprocal* in that while economic stress may increase the risk of IPV, at least among some social groups, the experience of IPV may lead victims into and entrap them in poverty as well as the abusive intimate relationship. Women are especially vulnerable in this way, since they have lower incomes on average than men and are more likely than men to live in poverty (DeNavas-Walt & Proctor, 2014).

As we noted in our discussion of estimating rates of IPV, perpetrators may engage in economic abuse to deliberately weaken or destroy their partner's financial solvency, leading to impoverishment or a substantially lower standard of living. Perpetrators, for instance, may withhold money from their partner or force the partner to turn over earnings, purposely ruin the partner's credit rating, or, as we saw in the case history that opened this chapter, interfere with the partner's ability to work (A. Adams, Littwin, & Javorka, 2019; A. Adams, Tolman, Bybee, Sullivan, & Kennedy, 2012; Allstate Foundation, 2009). We'll return to a discussion of the impact of IPV on victims' employment later in this chapter.

Additional research has documented that living in an economically disadvantaged neighborhood is a major risk factor for IPV victimization (Bonomi et al., 2014). Studies show that neighborhoods with a high concentration of poverty and high male unemployment rates have higher rates of IPV as well as other types of violent crime (Benson, Fox, DeMaris, & Van Wyk, 2003; DeKeseredy, Alvi, Schwartz, & Tomaszewski, 2003; Raghavan, Mennerich, Sexton, & James, 2006). Some researchers have argued that financially distressed neighborhoods are characterized by social incivilities (e.g., public intoxication, drug dealing) and a variety of other types of crimes such as assaults because residents of these neighborhoods, unlike those in more financially affluent neighborhoods, have little political power, feel socially isolated, and mistrust one another (Sampson, Raudenbusch, & Earls, 1997). Social support networks in such neighborhoods are weak, and members of those networks may themselves be involved in harmful behaviors or relationships (James, Johnson, & Raghavan, 2004; D. Rosen, 2004). Raghavan and her colleagues (2006), for instance, found in their study of women living in financially disadvantaged neighborhoods that IPV victimization was widespread *among members of the women's social networks*, and this factor increased their study participants' own likelihood of being IPV victims. Raghavan et al. hypothesize that when IPV is common among one's friends and relatives, it becomes incorporated into one's "cognitive landscape" and becomes viewed as a "normal" part of intimate relationships or even, as Marcus tried to tell Shelby, an expression of love or caring. But at least one research team that looked at IPV incidents over time found that the use of a weapon during the baseline IPV incident was a stronger predictor of repeated incidents than was neighborhood income (Bonomi et al., 2014).

Sexual Orientation and Gender Identity

Until very recently, many gay men, lesbian women, and bisexual men and women were not open about their sexual orientation—and some still are not. Consequently, large, nationally representative samples of gay, lesbian, and bisexual individuals are simply unavailable (with the exception of the NISVS; see Walters, Chen, & Breiding, 2013), making it difficult, if not impossible, to get a relatively accurate estimate of the prevalence of IPV in same-sex and bisexual relationships. Some researchers argue that it occurs at the same rate as, or even at a higher rate than, IPV in heterosexual relationships (Badenes-Ribera, Frias-Navarro, Bonilla-Campos, Pons-Salvador, & Monterde-i-Bort, 2015; Walters et al., 2013). But these findings are often based on studies of convenience samples; people who self-select to participate in a study often do so because they have a strong vested interest in the topic. Consequently, the findings are not representative of the experiences of the general gay, lesbian, and bisexual populations. These studies have demonstrated, however, that gays, lesbians, and bisexuals do experience IPV at significant rates and, as with heterosexual women and men, their victimization is typically not a onetime, situational event. Once it occurs, it is likely to reoccur, and it may grow more severe over time (Badenes-Ribera et al., 2015; R. Lewis, Milletich, Kelley, & Woody, 2012; Walters et al., 2013).

Studies of IPV in same-sex and other sexual minority relationships indicate that the types of violence and abuse that victims experience are similar to those experienced by heterosexual victims. At the same time, however, there are types of abuse unique to gay and lesbian relationships. For example, **homophobic control**, which involves behaviors such as threatening to "out" a lesbian or gay man to family, friends, employers, coworkers, or others whom the individual does not want to know about her or his sexuality, is a type of abuse unique to same-sex relationships (B. Hart, 1986; Renzetti, 1992). Gay men may use HIV-positive status as a way to control an intimate partner. For instance, if the abused intimate partner is HIV-positive, the abuser may withhold critical drugs, refuse to take the sick partner to treatment, or psychologically abuse the sick partner by telling him no one else will take care of him or love him because of his HIV status. Conversely, if the abusive partner is HIV-positive, he may use guilt to psychologically control the victim—for example, "You can't leave me now that I'm sick," or "I wouldn't be sick if it weren't for you." These examples remind us that same-sex IPV occurs in the context not only of sexism, but also of **heterosexism** and **homophobia**. Research shows a significant relationship between sexual minority stressors, including heterosexism and consciousness of stigma, and IPV in same-sex relationships (Carvalho, Lewis, Derlega, Winstead, & Viggiano, 2011; Sutter et al., 2019). Moreover, as we will see shortly, heterosexism and homophobia have serious consequences for sexual minority victims of IPV.

Recent research also indicates that transgender people, especially trans women who are young and black or Latina, are at elevated risk of IPV victimization (James et al., 2016; Waters & Yacka-Bible, 2017). Even more so than data on other sexual minorities, reliable data on the IPV experiences of transgender individuals are difficult to come by, since they are typically excluded from most studies of IPV, which tend to rely on the gender binary when identifying IPV victims and perpetrators (Guadalupe-Diaz, 2019;

S. Jordan, Mehrotra, & Fujikawa, 2019). The U.S. Trans Survey (USTS) is perhaps the largest national study of trans and gender-nonconforming adults in the country. The most recent USTS, conducted in 2015, found that 54 percent of the 27,715 respondents reported having experienced IPV in their lifetime and 24 percent reported severe physical violence inflicted by an intimate partner (James et al., 2016). In addition to widespread trans stigma, S. Jordan and colleagues (2019) point out that social and structural inequities increase the vulnerability of trans people to violent victimization and, as we will discuss later in the chapter, reduce their ability to obtain victim services.

Immigration Status

Immigrants and refugees, especially women, are at elevated risk of IPV victimization; estimates of immigrant women's victimization rates range from 40 percent to 50 percent (Murshid & Bowen, 2018). Their increased vulnerability is due to several reasons. One reason is that men often immigrate first and then their female partners follow, which means the women have lower immigration standing than their male partners. The men are their wives' sponsors, which gives them control over their wives' ability to remain in the United States (Orloff & Garcia, 2013; Raj & Yore, 2018; Zadnik, Sabina, & Cuevas, 2016). This situation affords men a mechanism of tremendous control over their wives and may actually facilitate IPV. Lack of English language skills, social isolation, economic dependence, anti-immigrant bias, and lack of familiarity with or mistrust of the police and the legal system also increase the vulnerability of immigrant women to IPV victimization (Dutton, Ammar, Orloff, & Terrell, 2006; Hass, Dutton, & Orloff, 2000; Menjivar & Salcido, 2002). Undocumented immigrant women are particularly vulnerable, since their fear of deportation may be used by abusive partners to control them and fear also prevents them from reporting abuse or seeking help (Murshid & Bowen, 2018).

Some observers blame immigrants' cultural backgrounds for their greater risk of IPV victimization, drawing on stereotypes of gender relations among specific ethnic groups. For instance, some have argued that women with certain cultural backgrounds passively accept male dominance and control because they come from societies in which patriarchal gender relations are valued and enforced (Mahoney, Williams, & West, 2001). It is certainly the case that cultural ideology with regard to such issues as the meaning of marriage, the importance of intact families, and **fatalism** contributes to entrapping IPV victims in abusive relationships. But this does not mean that women from these cultures do not resist violence and abuse, or do not want help to address it. Furthermore, cultural ideologies do not operate in a vacuum; they are reinforced and facilitated by some of the same structural constraints we have previously identified. Together, these factors inhibit immigrant and refugee victims' ability *to get help* for the abuse (Fontes & McCloskey, 2011; Murshid & Bowen, 2018; Raj & Yore, 2018).

Military Status

Recently, there has been considerable media attention to sexual harassment and sexual assault of women in the U.S. military by male military members, but there has been less discussion of IPV victimization among intimate partners of military members. Most, though not all, studies that compare IPV rates among military and civilian samples have shown higher rates for intimate partners of military members (see, for example, A. Marshall, Panuzio, & Taft, 2005; L. Rosen, Kaminski, Parmely, Knudson, & Fancher, 2003). These studies focus on male military personnel as perpetrators and their civilian partners/spouses as victims (Sparrow et al., 2018).

There are a number of reasons why researchers have hypothesized elevated risk of IPV victimization for intimate partners of military personnel. For instance, younger couples are at greater risk of IPV than older couples (see Chapter 10), and as we have discussed, couples from lower socioeconomic groups also have higher rates of IPV. Given that the military has a high concentration of young people from lower socioeconomic groups whose intimate partners share similar demographic characteristics, it is not surprising that their rates of IPV are higher. Heavy alcohol use by intimate partners in the military also increases vulnerability to IPV victimization (N. Bell, Harford, McCarroll, & Senier, 2004; Dobie et al., 2004).

There are also experiences unique to involvement in the military that increase risk of IPV, including the hypermasculine environment of the military and the stresses associated with frequent relocations and deployment (Basile & Black, 2011; McCarroll, Newby, & Dooley-Bernard, 2008). In addition, exposure to and participation in combat and experiences of war-related trauma have been found to be strongly related to IPV perpetration by military men (Taft et al., 2005). Given the multiple deployments of many U.S. military personnel to war and conflict zones in the Middle East, it is critical to recognize and attempt to proactively address the increased risk of IPV victimization for intimate partners in military contexts. One systematic literature review, however, also emphasized the need for more research on military personnel as *victims* of IPV. Sparrow and colleagues (2018) conducted a meta-analysis of 28 studies with a total of 69,808 military participants and found the rate of self-reported IPV victimization to be 21 percent for men and 13.6 percent for women. Psychological abuse was the most prevalent type of IPV across these samples, which is comparable to findings for the general civilian population.

CONSEQUENCES OF IPV FOR VICTIMS

Not surprisingly, in addition to the risk of physical injuries and even death at the hands of an abusive partner, IPV has numerous direct and indirect consequences for victims.

Outcomes for victims of IPV are influenced, of course, by a number of factors, including the frequency, severity, and, as described in Box 8.1, type of IPV they experience.

Physical and Mental Health Consequences of IPV for Victims

There is now a large body of research that documents the relationship between IPV victimization and a variety of negative physical and mental health outcomes (see Table 8.3). IPV victimization, for example, is consistently associated with a number of physical outcomes including irritable bowel syndrome (IBS) and other gastrointestinal disorders (Becker-Dreps et al., 2010; Loxton, Schofield, Hussain, & Mishra, 2006), arthritis (Black & Breiding, 2008), and chronic fatigue syndrome (Lowe, Humphreys, & Williams, 2007; Loxton et al., 2006; Patel et al., 2005). Additional studies have found elevated risk for hypertension, diabetes, high cholesterol, and heart disease among IPV victims, especially women (Black & Breiding, 2008; Diaz-Olavarrieta, Ellertson, Paz, Ponce de Leon, & Alarcon-Segovia, 2002). IPV victimization is also associated with various gynecological and obstetric problems, including unwanted pregnancies, miscarriages, chronic pelvic or abdominal pain, menstrual irregularity, HIV, and, as we saw with Shelby in the case history, STIs (A. Coker, 2007; A. Coker, Willams, Follingstad, & Jordan, 2011). Researchers emphasize, however, that the relationship between IPV and poor physical health may not be a direct one for some victims. For example, women with a history of IPV are more likely than women who have not experienced IPV to engage in various health-compromising behaviors, such as smoking and binge drinking (Bosch, Weaver, Arnold, & Clark, 2017). Bosch et al. (2017), in fact, found no significant relationship between IPV and high blood pressure and high cholesterol, but pointed out that victims' greater likelihood of engaging in health-compromising behaviors puts them at

BOX 8.1

MARITAL RAPE

In Chapter 7, we defined rape as *nonconsensual* attempted or completed vaginal or anal penetration with any body part or object, or oral penetration by the sex organ of another person. Recall from Chapter 1 that historically, however, husbands were exempt from charges of raping their wives—a legal principle known as **spousal exemption**—even if they used considerable force, because upon marriage, women give their husbands **irrevocable consent** to have sex with them (Bergen, 2016).

Moreover, rape laws in the United States were originally enacted and enforced as property laws—that is, as laws to protect a father's property (his unmarried daughter) and a husband's property (his wife) from "theft" by other men (D. Russell, 1982). Consequently, a man could not be charged with raping his wife because he could not be charged with "stealing" something he already owned.

It was not until 1978 that a husband, John Rideout, was successfully prosecuted in the

United States (specifically, in Oregon) for raping his wife while they were still living together (Bergen, 2016). It took another 15 years for marital rape to become a crime in all 50 states. Still, as of 2019, a number of states continued to have some type of spousal exception in their rape laws: for example, if the husband did not use "excessive force" or a weapon, or if his wife was unable to consent (she was asleep or in some way impaired) (Garvey, Fuhrman, & Long, 2019; Hirsch & Khan, 2020). The latter exception is curious, given that in all other circumstances, the inability to consent is not a defense in the crime of rape but rather a part of its definition. Marital rape, then, continues to be treated differently—and, frequently, more leniently—than other types of sexual assault (Bergen & Barnhill, 2006). Yllö (2010) reported that this attitude is shared by a majority of Americans, who view marital rape as considerably less serious than stranger or even acquaintance rape. This view is also reflected in state statutes that reduce the penalty when a spouse is convicted of sexual assault; for instance, in Virginia, rape, forcible sodomy, and object sexual penetration are punishable with imprisonment from five years to life, but when the convicted defendant is married to the complainant, the judge may place the defendant on probation with a condition of completing counseling and therapy (Levine, 2018).

Despite public and legal perceptions, however, the findings from research on rape in marriage show that it is quite serious. Researchers report that marital rape often takes place in the context of an already physically and psychologically abusive relationship; the sexual violence is one more type of abuse inflicted on the victim (Finkelhor & Yllö, 1985; D. Russell, 1982). Such was the case with Shelby and Marcus in the opening case history. But rape may also occur *after* physical violence, when abusive partners force or coerce their partners into what the abusers claim is "makeup sex" (Bergen & Barnhill, 2006; DeKeseredy, Schwartz, Fagen, & Hall, 2006). Research has also shown that sexual abuse in marriage may occur without other types of physical violence, although it is often a tactic of coercive control and typically accompanies psychological and emotional abuse (Basile, 2002; Stark, 2009).

Studies of marital rape survivors document the severe and long-term trauma of this type of victimization. Victims of marital rape experience immediate traumatic effects similar to those of other rape victims—for example, shock, fear, anxiety, and depression (Bergen, 2016). Long-term outcomes include post-traumatic stress disorder (PTSD), depression, sleeping disorders, anxiety, distorted body image, and hypervigilance (Bergen & Barnhill, 2006; J. Campbell, 1989; Kilpatrick, Best, Saunders, & Vernonen, 1988; Stermac, del Bove, & Addison, 2001). Research that has compared women IPV victims who have been raped by their intimate partners with women IPV victims who have not been raped by their intimate partners has found the former group to have more severe diagnoses of anxiety, depression, and other psychological disorders (J. Campbell, 1989; Plichta & Falik, 2001). Clinicians and researchers attribute these severe long-term consequences to several factors: (1) the fact that marital rape victims typically experience multiple sexual assaults over the course of the relationship; (2) the deep sense of betrayal and violation of trust that victims experience as a result of having been raped by someone they have loved and who they thought loved them; and (3) the lack of support and assistance victims receive from both informal and formal help providers, including the legal system, who, as we have noted, often do not view this crime as serious (Bergen, 2016).

Despite increased attention to marital rape in recent years, it is also important to note that most research, along with many state statutes, continues to define marital rape in terms of the gender binary and nearly always frames perpetrators as male and victims as female. Many states address rape between same-sex partners in "counterpart" laws that describe identical offenses and carry similar penalties but name the offense differently (e.g., "criminal sexual act") (Levine, 2018). These classifications generate a hierarchy of perpetrators and victims based on sexist and heterosexist assumptions of severity and "worthiness" (Levine, 2018).

TABLE 8.3 ■ Physical and Mental Health Problems Associated With IPV Victimization

- Gastrointestinal disorders (e.g., IBS)
- Arthritis
- Chronic fatigue syndrome
- Hypertension
- Diabetes
- High cholesterol and heart disease
- Gynecological and obstetric problems (e.g., unwanted pregnancy, miscarriage, chronic pelvic or abdominal pain, menstrual problems)
- HIV/AIDS and other STIs
- Anxiety
- Depression
- PTSD
- Substance use
- Suicidal ideation and suicide attempts

Sources: References are representative rather than exhaustive: Becker-Dreps et al., 2010; Black & Breiding, 2008; Carbone-Lopez, Kruttschnitt, & MacMillan, 2006; Chang, Kahle, & Hirsch, 2015; A. Coker, 2007; A. Coker et al., 2011; Lipsky, Kernic, Qiu, & Hasin, 2016; Loxton et al., 2006.

greater risk of developing high blood pressure and high cholesterol, which, in turn, can contribute to other chronic health problems.

Researchers have also documented extensive mental health consequences of IPV victimization, although A. Coker et al. (2011) caution that having a serious preexisting mental illness significantly increases the risk of IPV victimization. This appears to be the case for both women and men. For example, in one four-state study, researchers compared rates of past-year physical and sexual assault in a sample of women and men diagnosed with a severe mental illness (SMI) with assault rates of women and men in the general population. Combining physical and sexual assaults over the past year, the researchers found that women with an SMI were 16 times more likely to be victimized than women in the general population, and men with an SMI were 10 times more likely to be victimized than men in the general population (Goodman et al., 2001). Nevertheless, studies show that IPV often leads to anxiety, high rates of depression, and diagnoses of PTSD in victims (Bosch et al., 2017; Lipsky, Kernic, Qiu, & Hasin, 2016; Stampfel, Chapman, & Alvarez, 2010; Wathen, MacGregor, & MacQuarrie, 2018). IPV victims also engage in higher rates of suicidal ideation and suicide attempts

(Chang, Kahle, & Hirsch, 2015; Reviere et al., 2007; Silva-Martinez, 2016; Wong, Tiwari, Fong, & Bullock, 2016).

As previously noted, IPV victimization has been linked to a number of unhealthy behaviors, such as smoking and substance use (Black & Breiding, 2008; Bosch et al., 2017). This is perhaps not surprising, given the strong associations of IPV victimization with anxiety, depression, and PTSD; IPV victims may use cigarettes, alcohol, and drugs to self-medicate as a means to cope with the trauma (Gezinski, Gonzalez-Pons, & Rogers, 2019; Watson-Singleton et al., 2019). Substance use, however, also increases the risk of victimization (A. Coker et al., 2011; see also DeVries et al., 2014). Although the specific mechanisms of this association are not well understood, it is hypothesized that substance use impairs a person's ability to recognize danger cues, employ communication skills that might de-escalate a conflict, or act to remove oneself from an unsafe interaction (Freeman, 2018). Couples in which both partners are heavy alcohol or drug users may be especially volatile, given that both partners may frequently be impaired and also because conflicts may arise over procuring and sharing alcohol or drugs (Andrews, Cao, Marsh, & Shin, 2011). Substance use may also make it difficult for a victim to leave an abusive partner (Andrews et al., 2011). However, many studies that have examined the relationship between substance use and IPV victimization have been cross-sectional, so more prospective longitudinal studies are needed to tease out the reciprocal effects of IPV and substance abuse and to understand variations in the relationship across different social groups, including sexual and gender minorities (A. Coker et al., 2011; Freeman, 2018; R. Lewis, Winstead, Braitman, & Hitson, 2018).

Economic Consequences of IPV Victimization

As we saw in the case of Marcus and Shelby, IPV victims are sometimes forced to quit their jobs or are fired because the IPV (or their abusive partner) interferes with their ability to fulfill their work responsibilities. Reduced income, material hardship, and, for some women, impoverishment are consequences of IPV victimization (L. Brush, 2011; Gilroy, Nava, & McFarlane, 2019; O'Connor & Nepomnyaschy, 2019). More than one-third of IPV victims, the vast majority of whom are women with children, become homeless when they leave an abusive partner, given that few affordable or subsidized housing options are available (B. Brush, Gultekin, Dowdell, Saint Arnault, & Satterfield, 2018; Jasinski, Wesley, Wright, & Mustaine, 2010). Many turn to friends and relatives for temporary housing, but others must use battered women's shelters or homeless shelters, a topic to which we will return shortly.

IPV has economic consequences not only for individual victims, but also for society more generally. One study, for instance, estimated the cost of IPV in the United States for adult female and male victims (individual economic burden) and for the total population (total economic burden) (C. Peterson et al., 2018). C. Peterson and colleagues

(2018) reported that the estimated lifetime cost of IPV is $103,767 per female victim and $23,414 per male victim; and the population economic burden is nearly $3.6 trillion (in 2014 U.S. dollars). Their estimates include $2.1 trillion in medical expenses (59%), $1.3 trillion in lost productivity among victims and perpetrators (37%), $73 billion in criminal justice expenses (2%), and $62 billion in other expenses including victims' property loss or damage. Despite the enormity of the total economic burden, these estimates are nevertheless considered conservative because they do not include all costs, such as social services associated with IPV (Basile & Black, 2011).

INTERVENTIONS AND PREVENTION OF IPV FOCUSING ON VICTIMS

In the case history that opened this chapter, we read that the jury at Shelby's trial reasoned that if she had been abused by Marcus, and the abuse was as severe as she claimed it was, then she should have left him and sought help. Historically, this has been a common reaction to IPV victims: "If it's so bad, just leave." As Box 8.2 explains, however, there are many reasons why IPV victims do not leave an abusive partner or, if they do leave, why

BOX 8.2

COMMON OBSTACLES TO LEAVING AN ABUSIVE PARTNER

Sarah Buel, an attorney, law professor, and survivor of IPV, points out that the question "Why doesn't she just leave?" is indicative of the widespread belief that IPV victims who stay with, or return to, an abusive partner must be stupid, masochistic, or "codependent." But, Buel (1999) argues, labeling victims culpable for the abuse because they remain in the relationship absolves batterers of responsibility for their crimes and ignores the many barriers victims face if they try to leave. Buel compiled a list of 50 obstacles to leaving an abusive relationship although, as she notes, the list is hardly exhaustive. Some of the reasons Buel enumerates include the following:

- The victim believes the *abuser's threats to kill her and the children* if she leaves. Research shows that such beliefs are not unfounded, given that lethal risk

increases when the victim leaves or tries to leave (Dobash & Dobash, 2015).

- The victim is *afraid of losing custody* of the children if she leaves. Abusive partners often threaten victims with custody litigation, and again, research indicates that these are not idle threats. Moreover, even in cases involving IPV, the majority of fathers who request some form of custody are granted it by the courts (Dragiewicz, 2011; Kernic, Monary-Einsdorff, Koepsell, & Holt, 2005; Morrill, Dai, Dunn, Sung, & Smith, 2005; D. Saunders, Faller, & Tolman, 2016).

- The victim realizes that she is *unable to provide for her children* without the abuser's income. Buel (1999) cites a study from Texas that found that 85 percent of IPV victims who called crisis hotlines or went to emergency rooms or shelters had left their abusive partners multiple times but gave financial despair as the primary reason for having returned.

- The victim *feels guilty and responsible for the abuse*, often because the abuser has convinced her that it is her fault. If only she would do something—or not do something—he wouldn't become so angry with her. She may also believe it is her responsibility to maintain family harmony and keep the family intact.

- The victim is *socially isolated*. Restricting the victim's interactions with family, friends, neighbors, and coworkers is a common tactic of coercive control used by abusive partners. The victim may feel like she has no one to whom she can turn for help, and such

feelings may be exacerbated if *family members pressure her to stay* with the abuser because they believe divorce is wrong or a "sin" or that it will harm the children.

- The victim *feels embarrassed and ashamed*. The victim may come from a cultural background that values "family privacy" and discourages family members from "airing their dirty laundry." If the victim is middle class or more affluent, she may believe that IPV only occurs in working-class or poor families, and fears the stigma she will incur if the abuse is discovered. She also may not want to tarnish the abusive partner's reputation or cause problems for him at work, in their church, or with relatives and friends.

Source: Adapted from Buel, 1999.

they return to that partner, sometimes repeatedly. One reason victims frequently give for not leaving an abusive partner is a lack of safe, viable alternatives, but that does not mean they do not seek help. Most IPV victims turn initially to family or friends—whom researchers refer to as **informal help providers**—for emotional support as well as material assistance. Many also seek help from **formal help providers,** such as battered women's shelters and **victim advocacy services** (e.g., residential services, assistance with filing a protection order), health care professionals, and the police and legal system. In this section, we will focus on these formal sources of help for IPV victims.

Shelters and Other Victim Services

Many readers, like the jurors in Shelby's case, probably assume that crisis services, such as battered women's shelters, are readily available and easily accessible. But, in fact, only within the past 40 years have battered women's shelters become an option for women wanting to leave an abusive partner (C. Sullivan, 2011). As we learned in Chapter 1, IPV was not recognized as a social problem in the United States until the 1970s. At that time, social activists, especially those involved in the women's liberation movement, organized the first emergency services for women fleeing abusive intimate partners (Ake & Arnold, 2018; Schechter, 1982). Although these services provided shelter to battered women, they were not shelters as we know them today; they were typically rooms offered by private citizens, primarily women opening their homes to other women who needed help (N. Allen, Larson, & Walden, 2011; C. Sullivan, 2011). As public and political awareness of the problem grew, more shelters and other services for IPV victims became available, supported by both private and public funding (Ake & Arnold, 2018; Schechter, 1982).

According to Theresa's Fund (2020), a nonprofit organization that provides a free searchable directory of domestic violence shelters and programs, there are more than 2,000 battered women's shelters in the United States (see DomesticShelters.org). Shelters offer a variety of programs and services, including 24-hour hotlines, counseling, support groups, transitional housing programs, financial education, employment training and assistance, legal advocacy, and programs specially designed for children (Renzetti & Follingstad, 2015; C. Sullivan, 2011). Some shelters also offer programs for underserved groups, such as lesbians, immigrant women, and women with substance use problems (Theresa's Fund, 2020; N. Allen et al., 2011). Shelters specifically for cisgender men and transgender men and women are scarce, although many programs provide other types of victim services for these populations (Guadalupe-Diaz, 2019; S. Jordan et al., 2019).

Transitional housing programs provide IPV victims and their children with a private, low-cost living space for a set period of time, typically a year or two, so they have time to secure permanent housing and attain greater financial stability. This is particularly important given the problem of economic abuse and the risk of homelessness among this population (Melbin, Sullivan, & Cain, 2003). Economic empowerment and advocacy programs teach financial literacy (i.e., the knowledge and skills necessary to make sound financial decisions and acquire resources) and foster both economic self-efficacy (i.e., confidence in one's ability to achieve financial security) and economic self-sufficiency (i.e., the ability to independently meet one's daily needs) (Postmus, 2010; Renzetti & Follingstad, 2015). This is especially important because research and the frontline experience of shelter staff indicate that financial instability, the threat or actual experience of poverty, and economic dependence on an intimate partner, in addition to the negative mental health impacts of IPV, are among the factors that motivate women to return to abusive partners, thus increasing their risk of revictimization (L. Brush, 2011; Farber & Miller-Cribbs, 2014; Goodman & Epstein, 2009; Thomas, Joshi, Wittenberg, & McCloskey, 2008).

Most shelters and nonresidential victim service programs offer individual and/or group counseling to IPV victims. C. Sullivan (2011) points out that most provide **empowerment counseling**, which is designed to help victims gain or restore their sense of personal power and control, which is severely diminished by repeated abuse. Other types of counseling and therapeutic practices, such as cognitive behavioral therapy, meditation and relaxation therapies, therapeutic horticulture, and art therapy, may also be used alone or in conjunction with empowerment counseling, depending on victims' individual needs (Renzetti & Follingstad, 2015; C. Sullivan, 2011).

Evaluations of these and other trauma-focused counseling programs indicate that they improve victims' sense of well-being, self-esteem, self-efficacy, and coping skills, and reduce anxiety, depression, and PTSD symptoms (J. Beck et al., 2016; C. Sullivan, Goodman, Virden, Strom, & Ramirez, 2018). Nevertheless, most shelters and nonresidential victim services do not screen for or treat more severe mental health problems. Although there is recognition of the need for such services for some IPV victims, as we noted earlier in the chapter, many shelters and services do not have the resources or trained staff to provide these more specialized services. Typically, they must refer victims to mental health providers who do not necessarily specialize in treating IPV victims. But some IPV service providers and victim advocates are also hesitant to screen victims for severe mental health problems out of concern for how being officially labeled "mentally ill" may be used against them in court proceedings, custody litigation, and other interactions with the abuser (Simmons, Craun, Farrar, & Ray, 2016).

Despite the growth of shelters, not all victims have equal access. As we have already stated, cisgender men and sexual and gender minorities have few service options. It is important to keep in mind as well that most shelters continue to be located in urban and suburban areas. Consequently, victims who live in rural areas not only have fewer shelters and services available to them, but also must deal with the challenges of geographic distance and transportation (Coy, Kelly, Foord, & Bowstead, 2011; Eastman, Bunch, Williams, & Carawan, 2007; C. Lanier & Maume, 2009). Space at specific shelters is also limited, and need continues to exceed capacity (Theresa's Fund, 2020; Lyon, Lane, & Menard, 2008; C. Sullivan, 2011). At the same time, available services may be structured according to a specific cultural model that is not compatible with the values and needs of diverse groups of victims. For example, we have noted that many programs are designed to prevent victims from returning to their partners. Some victims, however, want to preserve the relationship for a variety of reasons—for example, they love their partner and believe the positive aspects of the relationship outnumber the negatives; they believe their children would be harmed by divorce; or they come from cultures with collectivist, family-preservationist values. In such cases, services should focus on strategies for increasing victims' safety and preventing abusive partners from perpetrating IPV in the future (C. Sullivan, 2011; Yoshioka & Choi, 2005).

Immigrant victims, in particular, may have difficulty using services such as shelters, because they don't speak English and do not understand how such services work, because they are undocumented and fear deportation, or because they cannot practice their religious or cultural traditions at a specific shelter (Abu-Ras, 2007; Fowler, Faulkner, Learman, & Runnels, 2011). Cultural competence is especially important for shelters and other victim advocacy services, since victims may be reluctant to use such services or discontinue using them if the programs and staff seem alienating or hostile to their values, beliefs, and behaviors (Donnelly, Cook, Van Ausdale, & Foley, 2005; C. Sullivan, 2011). Additional populations who may find shelter and victim advocacy services inaccessible, irrelevant, or inhospitable are victims of color (Donnelly et al., 2005; Gillum, 2009);

lesbian, gay, and bisexual victims (Renzetti, 1989; Ristock, 2002); substance-using victims (Martin, Moracco, Chang, Council, & Dulli, 2008; J. Tucker, Wenzel, Straus, Ryan, & Golinelli, 2005); elderly victims and victims with disabilities (Ballan, Freyer, Powledge, & Marti, 2016; Vinton, 2001; Zweig, Schlichter, & Burt, 2002; see also Chapter 10); and, as we have noted, victims with severe mental health problems (Simmons et al., 2016).

Despite these limitations, shelters and nonresident services for IPV victims are, without a doubt, significantly better than they were 40 years ago. A recent review of research evaluating the effectiveness of shelter services and programs supports this observation (C. Sullivan, 2011). In addition to providing a violence-free space for victims and their children, shelters and other programs offer victims counseling and therapy, distribute helpful information and referrals for additional services (e.g., legal aid), provide emotional and sometimes financial support, and teach victims how to increase their safety once they leave the shelter or if they return home (see Box 8.3). Evaluation studies have documented a number of positive outcomes for IPV victim services users including increased knowledge about their rights, options, and community resources; increased understanding of various strategies they can use to remain safe; and greater hopefulness and optimism about their future (C. Sullivan et al., 2018; C. Sullivan, O'Halloran, & Lyon, 2008). Most important, perhaps, IPV victims themselves have high praise for the assistance they have received from shelters and other victim services (Goodman, Manyard, Woulfe, Ash, & Mattern, 2016; Lyon et al., 2008). Nevertheless, additional, more rigorous evaluation research is needed in order to improve shelters and IPV victim services, especially for marginalized and underserved populations.

Health Care Responses to IPV Victims

Recognizing IPV as a widespread and serious public health problem, several national medical organizations and agencies—including the U.S. Department of Health and Human Services, the National Academy of Medicine, the American College of Obstetricians and Gynecologists, and the American Medical Association—have recommended IPV screening, counseling, and treatment referrals by health care providers as routine practice (E. Miller, Decker, & Glass, 2018). In fact, IPV screening and brief counseling for patients who screen positive were among the free preventive services mandated by the Affordable Care Act (E. Miller et al., 2018). Nevertheless, research shows that some health care providers are hesitant to screen and counsel because they feel uncomfortable asking patients about IPV, they feel they lack the knowledge and confidence to provide effective counseling and intervention, or they don't think they have enough time to screen or intervene effectively (Semin, Skrundevskiy-Coburn, Smith, & Rajaram, 2019; Sprague et al., 2014). Indeed, studies indicate that health care providers need specific training on how to screen and respond appropriately to patients' disclosures of IPV

BOX 8.3
SAFETY PLANNING

Jill Davies and Eleanor Lyon (2014) report that the decisions women who have experienced IPV make for themselves, for their children, and in relation to their abusive partner depend to a large extent on four primary factors: (1) the victim's understanding of the abuse and its severity, (2) the victim's relationship with her children and her concern for their well-being, (3) the victim's relationship with the abusive partner, and (4) the victim's financial and social resources. J. Davies and Lyon also point out that these factors are not the same for all victims and they frequently change over time, which results in a shift in a victim's priorities. All IPV victims, however, make plans in response to these factors, and although they are not likely to refer to them as "safety plans," their goals are to reduce or end the abuse, improve stability, and increase well-being. Assisting IPV victims in safety planning, then, requires flexibility as well as recognition that the victim is the "expert" on her situation, since she has more firsthand knowledge of the circumstances than anyone else. That said, victims may need help sorting out their priorities relative to their available resources, developing effective responses to immediate crises versus short-term problems versus long-term goals, and identifying the costs and benefits of specific strategies.

J. Davies and Lyon (2014) point out that variations in safety plans are "endless" (p. 88). Indeed, Sherry Hamby (2014), in her examination of battered women's protective strategies, identifies a multitude of actions that IPV victims take in response to both immediate and long-term threats to their safety and the safety of their children. These include

- setting up a prearranged signal with a child, neighbor, or friend that will let the other person know that help is needed or the police should be called;

- getting an emergency phone;

- asking family members or friends for help getting guns or other weapons out of the house;

- teaching children to call the police;

- placing pets in a kennel or a "foster home";

- keeping copies of important financial and legal documents in a safe place (e.g., at the home of a friend or relative) where the batterer cannot take them or destroy them;

- keeping spare clothes for oneself and one's children at the home of a friend or relative;

- explaining the situation to one's employer and coworkers and asking for a security plan in the workplace; and

- identifying and accessing formal help providers (e.g., keeping the hotline number in one's phone).

None of these strategies, of course, guarantees safety, and should they fail, the victim is not to blame. But helping IPV victims identify which strategies may be most effective for their particular circumstances, as well as the risks and benefits that may accompany each strategy, can provide victims with a stronger sense of self-efficacy in responding to a specific situation and ultimately improve their safety.

victimization, yet training varies widely in frequency and duration with many health professionals reporting that they received less than three hours of training on domestic violence (Semin et al., 2019). Not surprisingly, screening rates remain low. One recent study found that only 1.5 percent to 15 percent of female patients in primary care clinics were screened for IPV (S. Hill & Ousley, 2017); another study showed that among a sample of women who had seen any health care provider in the past year, only 39 percent were screened (Swailes, Lehman, & McCall-Hosenfield, 2017).

Is health care screening effective at identifying IPV and reducing recidivism? This is a matter of debate, with some researchers arguing that there is no unequivocal evidence to support universal IPV screening in health care settings (MacMillan et al., 2009). However, there is evidence that screening and brief interventions in health care settings result in a number of benefits including providing victims with a connection to people who may provide help, allowing victims to unburden themselves, and assisting them in taking steps to increase safety behaviors, which can reduce revictimization (Macy, Ermentrout, & Johns, 2011; Spangaro, Koziol-McLain, Rutherford, & Zwi, 2019). E. Miller et al. (2018) point out that family planning clinics are health care settings in which it is particularly important to educate female patients about, and screen for, IPV. This is because patients at family planning clinics are women in the age group at highest risk for IPV victimization. Moreover, as we saw in the case of Shelby and Marcus, IPV may involve **reproductive coercion**: pressure to get pregnant or, alternatively, to abort a pregnancy. Evaluations of interventions in family planning clinics have shown reductions in reproductive coercion and increases in safety behaviors among patients (E. Miller et al., 2011).

Absent any evidence that screening is harmful, and given the potential role health care providers might play in alleviating the problem, many argue that all female patients should receive information about IPV and victim services. Doing so as a routine part of care educates patients about the problem and available assistance, sends the message that the physician's office or clinic is a safe place to discuss such issues, and informs appropriate care for patients (E. Miller et al., 2018; Spangaro et al., 2019). It is important to keep in mind, however, that other patient groups, including men, the elderly, and adults with disabilities, may also benefit from education, screening, and intervention, given that they face significant barriers to disclosure and IPV victimization may be even more likely to go undetected in these populations (Semin et al., 2019; see also Chapter 10).

Responses by the Police and the Legal System

Assault and battery of another person, including one's intimate partner, is a crime. Until the late 1970s, however, arrests and prosecutions for IPV were few and far between. Police typically viewed IPV as a "spat" that "got out of hand," and were afforded tremendous discretion in how to handle such calls. Today, police officers in most jurisdictions are *required* (known as **mandatory arrest policies**) or are at least encouraged (known as **preferred arrest policies**) to make an arrest when responding to a call if they have probable cause to believe that IPV has occurred. What changed in the intervening years?

According to Goodmark (2018), in the late 1970s, women in various U.S. cities filed lawsuits against their police departments for failing to enforce the law when they did not arrest the women's husbands for assaulting and battering them. Perhaps the most famous suit was *Thurman v. City of Torrington, CT* (1984), in which Tracey Thurman was awarded $2.3 million in damages following an incident in which her husband repeatedly stabbed her and kicked her in the head as the police stood by and did nothing to stop him. It was not the first time Thurman had called the police for help and they failed to appropriately respond. Another significant event in 1984 was the publication of the Minneapolis Domestic Violence Experiment, a randomized controlled study, which reported that IPV perpetrators who were arrested had lower recidivism rates. This study contributed to a national conversation that led the U.S. Attorney General's Task Force on Family Violence to recommend that police departments adopt the policy of arresting IPV perpetrators when responding to domestic violence calls. Ten years later, the federal VAWA recommended appropriation of millions of dollars to police, prosecutors, and courts to strengthen the legal system's response to IPV, especially by holding perpetrators accountable for their illegal behavior (Goodmark, 2018).

While mandatory and preferred arrest policies send the message not only to perpetrators but also to the general public that IPV *is* a crime and will be taken seriously by the criminal justice system, they also have some significant limitations. Some IPV victims, particularly those who have had negative experiences with the police—for example, those from disadvantaged communities and communities of color (Richie, 2012); undocumented immigrants; and lesbian, gay, bisexual, transgender, and queer victims (Guadalupe-Diaz, 2019; Renzetti, 1992)—may be reluctant to call the police and may worry about how their partners will be treated if arrested. Another serious criticism of mandatory and preferred arrest policies is that they have resulted in a sharp increase in **dual arrests**—that is, the arrest of both partners for IPV—even though victims may have been acting in self-defense, or abusers may have injured themselves to get their partners arrested (S. L. Miller, 2005). Arresting victims may result in them being less likely to call the police for help in the future. It may also jeopardize their housing and welfare benefits, immigration status, employment, and parental rights (Goodmark, 2018).

Goodmark (2018) notes that although arrests for IPV increased following the adoption of mandatory and preferred arrest policies, prosecutions remained low into the 1990s. Prosecutors blamed victims' unwillingness to participate in prosecution for these low rates. Victims refused to cooperate with the prosecution for various reasons: for example, fear of the abuser, a desire to preserve their relationship with the abuser, financial dependence on the abuser, or pressure from family members. As a result, **victimless** or **evidence-based prosecution** was instituted. Victimless prosecution allows prosecutors to build a case using police reports, photographs, and physical and other evidence, without relying on victims' testimony. Another remedy to low prosecution rates is **no-drop prosecution**, which requires prosecutors to proceed with a case regardless of whether a victim agrees to participate. In addition to ensuring that the law is enforced, supporters of no-drop prosecution argue that other benefits of the policy include protecting victims from coercion by abusers to drop charges.

Although victimless and no-drop prosecution policies have increased the number of IPV prosecutions, they are not without their critics. Some observers maintain, for instance, that instead of empowering victims, these policies have the opposite effect by ignoring the wishes of victims and not allowing them to make critical decisions about their lives and relationships. In addition, studies that have examined whether prosecution reduces recidivism have produced conflicting findings, with some studies showing no significant reduction in IPV recidivism associated with prosecution (Kingsnorth, 2006; O'Sullivan, Davis, Farole, & Rempel, 2007). Concerns have also been raised about whether pro-prosecution policies are racially biased in light of evidence that prosecutors are more likely to pursue cases against minority than white defendants (Henning & Feder, 2005; Kingsnorth & Macintosh, 2004).

In the aftermath of an IPV incident, particularly if victims seek help from a shelter or a victim service provider, they may file for a **protection order** (also known as a **restraining order** or a **domestic violence order**). Such orders are obtained in the civil courts, rather than the criminal courts. They allow judges to impose specific restrictions on the abusive partner, depending on the concerns of the victim and the circumstances of the case. These orders typically include restrictions on contact with the victim and/or with one's children, but because they were established to allow for individualized responses, they may cover a range of issues, such as financial support, access to property, and mandatory counseling for the abusive partner. Protection orders are in effect for a limited period of time—usually one to three years—but they may be extended if judged to be necessary (Goodman & Epstein, 2011). The primary purpose of a protection order is to keep victims safe. VAWA provisions also make crossing state lines to violate a protection order a federal crime, and require criminal justice authorities in one state to recognize and enforce protection orders issued in another state (D. Ford et al., 2002).

Although issued by the civil courts, protection orders are enforced by the criminal justice system. The effectiveness of protection orders, then, depends not only on their specific content, but also on how the police and the courts respond to violations (S. L. Miller, Iovanni, & Kelley, 2011). Research indicates that violations are not uncommon; between 23 percent and 70 percent of abusers violate protection orders, and most of these violations occur within the first three months the order is in effect (Goodman & Epstein, 2011; Spitzberg, 2002). Nevertheless, it appears that protection orders do help to improve victim safety; for example, women with permanent orders of protection tend to have lower rates of revictimization over time compared with women without protection orders, and they also report feeling safer (Holt, Kernic, Wolf, & Rivara, 2003; Logan & Walker, 2009; Messing, O'Sullivan, Cavanaugh, Webster, & Campbell, 2017). Still, as Goodman and Epstein (2011, p. 223) point out, "One of the most significant obstacles to greater effectiveness of the protection order system stems from the failure to enforce these orders" (see also Diviney, Parekh, & Olson, 2009; Logan & Walker, 2009).

In Chapter 9, we will discuss other criminal justice responses to IPV offenders, but for now, two additional points are worth noting. First, IPV victims appear to benefit most when help providers—police, as well as health care professionals, victim advocacy service providers, and shelter staff—provide them with information about the options available to them, which they can then use to inform their decision making. In other words, help providers should take a **victim-centered approach**, in which they *consult* with victims, rather than tell them what they should do. A number of victim-centered, community-based programs have been established that involve collaborations across service organizations and agencies, such as victim advocacy service providers and the police, or victim advocacy service providers and health care providers (N. Allen et al., 2011; Fleury-Steiner & Brady, 2011). Although these programs confront a number of challenges, such as meeting the needs of diverse clients with limited resources, evaluation research indicates that they also have several benefits. These benefits include increasing victims' access to services, which in turn increases victims' safety, and improving responses to victims by the police, the legal system, and health care providers (see, for example, Hovell, Seid, & Liles, 2006; Stover, Rainey, Berkman, & Marans, 2008; Ulbrich & Stockdale, 2002)

Second, it is important to keep in mind that although many help providers assume that the best outcome for victims is to end their relationship with their abusive partners, leaving does not necessarily mean the abuse will stop (Fleury, Sullivan, & Bybee, 2000; S. L. Miller & Smolter, 2011; Orenstein & Rickne, 2013). As we stated earlier, leaving and post-separation are actually the most dangerous times for IPV victims. Abusive partners will sometimes step up their coercive control tactics and violence in response to what they perceive as the victim's challenge to their authority. Stalking may begin or worsen following separation (Logan & Walker, 2009). And victims who have children with their abusive partners may find that parental visitations are used by abusers as opportunities to extract information from the children or as ways to force contact with their victims (T. Parker, Rogers, Collins, & Edleson, 2008). Consequently, the critical question to ask with regard to IPV is not why doesn't the victim just leave, but rather, why do some people abuse their partners, whom they claim to love, and how can the abuse be stopped? We will explore the answers to these questions in Chapter 9.

CHAPTER SUMMARY

In this chapter, we examined the problem of IPV in adult relationships from the perspective of victims. We defined IPV as any threatened or completed acts of physical, sexual, or psychological abuse committed by a spouse, ex-spouse, or current or former boyfriend or girlfriend. This definition encompasses a wide range of behaviors, including economic abuse and coercive control, but we also discussed the challenges of measuring IPV and how the measures chosen affect estimates of IPV prevalence. Estimates of IPV also vary depending on the population from which the sample surveyed is selected (e.g., clinical populations vs. the general population).

Both women and men may be victims of IPV, but the majority of studies show that women are at greater risk of victimization, and men are at greater risk of perpetration. We discussed other social and demographic factors that are associated with IPV victimization, including age, race and ethnicity, socioeconomic status, sexual orientation and gender identity, immigration status, and military status.

IPV may cause physical injuries and may even result in the death of the victim. IPV has many other direct and indirect consequences for victims that vary by the frequency, severity, and type of IPV experienced. These consequences include physical health problems, such as gastrointestinal illnesses, chronic fatigue syndrome, and gynecological and obstetric disorders, as well as mental health problems, such as anxiety, depression, PTSD, and substance use. IPV victims may also experience economic consequences, including unemployment, high debt, and homelessness.

In light of these consequences, it is not surprising that IPV victims actively seek help from multiple informal and formal sources. Shelter and other victims' services, which were virtually nonexistent only 40 years ago, are now widely available throughout the United States, although need still exceeds capacity. Shelters and other programs provide a variety of services to IPV victims, including hotlines, housing, and counseling, which we found have positive impacts on victims' health, safety, and well-being.

The health care system's response to IPV victims has also improved, although there is still reluctance among health care providers to screen patients for IPV and to intervene if IPV is disclosed. Even greater change has occurred in the legal system. Mandatory and preferred arrest policies, along with victimless and no-drop prosecution, have produced dramatic increases in arrests and prosecutions of IPV offenders. Supporters of these reforms argue that they send a powerful message that IPV is a crime that will be taken seriously by the criminal justice system and perpetrators will be held accountable. However, critics note that these policies have had negative impacts on some victims and have also largely failed to reduce recidivism.

Taken together, the research discussed in this chapter indicates that significant improvements have occurred in the identification of IPV and in responses to victims, but that there continues to be room for considerable improvement.

Recommended Resources

Goodmark, L. (2018). *Decriminalizing domestic violence: A balanced policy approach*. Berkeley: University of California Press.

Hamby, S. (2014). *Battered women's protective strategies: Stronger than you know*. New York, NY: Oxford University Press.

Messinger, A. M., & Guadalupe-Diaz, X. (2020). *Transgender intimate partner violence: A comprehensive introduction*. New York: New York University Press.

Renzetti, C. M., Edleson, J. L., & Bergen, R. K. (Eds.). (2018). *Sourcebook on violence against women* (3rd ed.). Thousand Oaks, CA: Sage.

Yllö, K., & Torres, M. G. (Eds.). (2016). *Marital rape: Consent, marriage, and social change in global context*. New York, NY: Oxford University Press.

INTIMATE PARTNER VIOLENCE IN ADULT RELATIONSHIPS

Focusing on Perpetrators

LEARNING OBJECTIVES

1. Describe the definition and scope of intimate partner violence (IPV) in adult relationships, from the perspective of perpetration, including problems inherent in measuring this form of abuse.

2. Identify the various risk factors associated with perpetration of IPV in adult relationships.

3. Discuss the various intervention and prevention efforts that focus on perpetration of IPV in adult relationships, including evidence of their effectiveness.

CASE HISTORY

MARIA AND VICTOR: "I AM *NOT* A BATTERER!"

Maria and Victor got married in their early 20s. According to Maria, shortly after their wedding Victor began to treat her as if she were his "servant." For example, he expected her to do all the household chores and to have dinner ready within 30 minutes of his arrival home from work, even though she also had a full-time job. Within two years of their marriage, Maria got pregnant, but Victor's demands did not decline. After their son was born, Maria felt that Victor was jealous of the attention she gave the baby. Although Maria was doing nearly all the child care, including getting up several times each night for feedings, Victor became increasingly critical of her housekeeping, her cooking, and her appearance. He began to go out with his friends after work, returning home late at night, often drunk. He told Maria he couldn't stand having to listen to a crying baby, in a "dirty" house with a wife who "didn't take care of herself anymore"; he deserved to have fun with his friends and to relax because he worked hard to support his family.

One weekend morning, when Victor returned home after having been out all night, Maria angrily confronted him about his behavior. Victor flew into a rage and pushed Maria into a kitchen cabinet, causing her to fall and hit her head. While she was on the floor, Victor kicked her repeatedly, while insulting her and calling her names. The noise awakened the baby, and Victor stormed off to their bedroom, yelling at Maria to "shut the baby up" so he could get some sleep. Maria went to get the baby, but while she was soothing him, she called the police and then her sister, Alicia. When the police arrived, they saw Maria's injuries and took her report of what had happened; they arrested Victor. Alicia took Maria to the emergency room, where she was treated for two broken ribs, a cut on her head that required five stitches to close, and multiple contusions on her back and legs.

When they left the hospital, Alicia took Maria and the baby to her house and called the local crisis hotline, which put Maria in contact with a victim advocate. With the help of the advocate, Maria filed for and was granted an emergency protection order. Victor was subsequently convicted of misdemeanor assault and was mandated to a 26-week batterer intervention program. Although Victor complied with the court's order, he stated in both individual and group sessions that it made him angry to attend the program. He insisted that his wife had "provoked" him into hitting her and that she had "put on an act" to convince the judge that she was a "battered woman." But, Victor repeatedly insisted, "I am *not* a batterer!"

In this chapter, we will discuss intimate partner violence (IPV) *perpetration* in adult relationships. As we see in the case history of Maria and Victor, many individuals who push, hit, kick, or do something to physically injure their intimate partners do not consider themselves batterers or even violent people. In fact, researchers and clinicians report that IPV perpetrators often refer to themselves as "victims"—for instance, victims of an unfair criminal justice system, victims of abusive parents, victims of their own "demons" such as alcohol use and abuse, or victims of vengeful partners (Nason-Clark & Fisher-Townsend, 2015). Obviously, as the case history illustrates, batterers' behaviors have serious consequences for the partners they victimize (see Chapter 8), for those who witness the abuse (such as children; see Chapter 6), and for the batterers themselves. For instance, research indicates that batterers are more likely than nonbatterers to miss work and to be less productive at work (Rothman & Corso, 2008). And as we will discuss later in this chapter, they may also be arrested, prosecuted on criminal charges, and sentenced to jail, supervision (e.g., probation), or a batterer intervention program. It is not surprising, therefore, that researchers have invested considerable effort and resources in trying to understand why some people physically, sexually, and psychologically abuse those they claim to love. These studies have produced an extensive list of risk factors, which we will review. We also describe in this chapter the various prevention and intervention strategies recommended to address IPV perpetration.

SCOPE OF THE PROBLEM

Defining IPV Perpetration

Given that many people who engage in abusive behavior do not see themselves as "batterers," how do we identify an IPV perpetrator? We adopt the definition of L. Bancroft, Silverman, and Ritchie (2012, p. 4): A **batterer** or **IPV perpetrator** is "a person who exercises a pattern of coercive control in a partner relationship, punctuated by one or more acts of intimidating physical violence, sexual assault, or credible threat of physical violence. This pattern of control and intimidation may be predominantly psychological, economic, or sexual in nature or may rely primarily on the use of physical violence." This definition recognizes that IPV perpetration is not homogeneous; that is, batterers do not all behave in exactly the same ways or use the same abusive tactics (Aldarondo & Castro-Fernandez, 2011). Furthermore, this definition allows for the fact that IPV may be perpetrated by both males and females and may occur in heterosexual and same-sex relationships. In addition, this definition does not require individuals to "beat" their partners in order to be batterers; IPV perpetrators may rely exclusively on psychological abuse to control and coerce their partners (L. Bancroft et al., 2012). Examples of the types of coercive and harmful behaviors perpetrated by batterers are discussed in Chapter 8.

Estimates of IPV Perpetration

Estimates of IPV victimization were discussed in Chapter 8, where we learned that national surveys of large, nationally representative samples estimate that approximately 8–12 percent of men and 12–25 percent of women are physically and/or sexually assaulted by an intimate partner each year (Black et al., 2011; Tjaden & Thoennes, 2000). As described in the opening case history, batterers often don't recognize their own behavior as abusive and also typically underestimate the severity of their abusive behavior and its negative impact on those they victimize. They also overestimate the prevalence of others' abusive behaviors—that is, they believe that IPV is normative and more common than it actually is (Neighbors et al., 2010). In one study of men from the general population who admitted to engaging in various types of physical and sexual abuse over the past 90 days, the participants' mean estimates of the percentage of men who perpetrate seven different types of IPV (e.g., beat up their partner, throw something at their partner to inflict injury, choke their partner) were more than double national survey findings. With regard to forced sex, the men's estimate was nearly 3 times higher than national survey findings (Neighbors et al., 2010). It is important to understand, therefore, what factors contribute to these distorted perceptions and harmful behaviors.

RISK FACTORS ASSOCIATED WITH IPV PERPETRATION

Although we will discuss a variety of risk factors that have been found to be strongly associated with IPV perpetration, we must emphasize that no *single* factor produces abusive and violent behavior. Rather, IPV perpetration is the result of the interaction of multiple factors, both individual and structural. Importantly, the factors that have been most extensively studied are individual ones; we know far less about social and community risk factors and how these may interact with individual factors to influence IPV perpetration. Moreover, the observation that IPV perpetration is not homogeneous applies to risk factors as well. In other words, not all IPV perpetrators are influenced by the same set of factors in the same way (Aldarondo & Castro-Fernandez, 2011). In the sections that follow, then, we examine factors that have been shown to elevate risk of IPV perpetration, but it is important to keep in mind that most people who are in these risk categories are *not* abusive or violent. In addition, as discussed in Box 9.1, predicting specific violent outcomes using risk assessment instruments remains an imperfect science.

Sex and Sexual Orientation

One of the most consistent findings in criminological and public health research is that men commit more violent crime than women do. Yet, for about 40 years, IPV researchers have argued about whether women are as violent as men (see also Chapter 1). This is referred to as the **gender symmetry** (or **gender parity**) **debate**. The data that prompted the debate were generated using one of the most commonly used measures of IPV, the Conflict Tactics Scales (CTS; Straus, 1979), which were revised in the 1990s to include measures of sexual assault and injury (CTS2; Straus, Hamby, Boney-McCoy, & Sugarman, 1996). Studies that use the CTS and CTS2 frequently find that women and men perpetrate IPV at nearly equivalent rates; in fact, some of these studies show that women perpetrate more IPV than men (Archer, 2000; Straus, 2007). Critics of the CTS and CTS2, however, point out that such measures ignore important contextual factors and outcomes (DeKeseredy & Schwartz, 1998). For instance, given the average size and strength differences between women and men, if a woman pushes a man, she is not likely to do him much harm, but if a man pushes a woman, he could seriously injure her. Yet, on the CTS and CTS2, both actions would be equivalent. Sherry Hamby (2018), one of the coauthors of the CTS2, further points out that nearly all other indicators of IPV perpetration—for example, arrests, police reports, homicides, witness reports—show

BOX 9.1
ASSESSING DANGEROUSNESS

Perhaps the most important reason for identifying risk factors for IPV perpetration is to *prevent* the violence from occurring in the first place. Certainly, if we could use risk factors to distinguish individuals who are likely to inflict severe violence from those who may be considered less dangerous, we could effectively improve safety and reduce victimization, while also directing perpetrators to the most appropriate interventions. With these goals in mind, researchers have developed a variety of **dangerousness assessment instruments**, some of which are administered to victims to assist with their safety

planning, and others of which are administered to perpetrators (or potential perpetrators) by clinicians in treatment settings or even by police responding to calls for help to identify risk of reoffending.

Among the most widely used dangerousness assessment instruments are the Danger Assessment Scale (DAS; J. Campbell, 1986) and the Spousal Assault Risk Assessment (SARA; Kropp, Hart, Webster, & Eaves, 1995). These and similar assessment tools consist of questions about a perpetrator's behavior; usually they cover areas such as history of violent behavior toward others (e.g., children, friends, strangers); history of abusive behavior (physical, sexual, psychological) toward intimate partners (both the current and previous intimate partners); access to lethal weapons; antisocial attitudes and behaviors; affiliations with antisocial peers; relationship instability, particularly whether the partner is currently separating from or divorcing the perpetrator; presence of various life stressors (e.g., financial problems); history of family of origin abuse; symptoms of mental health problems; resistance to changing the abusive behavior or obtaining treatment for it; and attitudes supportive of violence against women (Kropp, 2004).

The DAS is designed to be administered by a victim service provider, who asks the IPV victim 20 questions of this sort about the perpetrator, but also asks the victim to complete a calendar that charts the frequency and severity of the abuse over the past year (J. Campbell, 2005). The DAS seeks to identify the most dangerous IPV perpetrators, but primarily for the purpose of assisting victims with safety planning (Hamby & Cook, 2011). Research has shown the DAS to be fairly successful in distinguishing between high- and low-risk groups, and J. Campbell and her colleagues (2003) report that the DAS may be useful in identifying perpetrators at high risk of committing lethal violence. The SARA also consists of 20 items, but it is administered to perpetrators by clinicians who can make professional determinations of psychological health (Hamby & Cook, 2011). Kropp and Hart (2000) report that the SARA can distinguish IPV perpetrators from other types of offenders, as well as recidivists from nonrecidivists (see also Olver & Jung, 2017).

Despite this evidence, however, researchers and clinicians urge that extreme caution must be exercised in using dangerousness assessment instruments to predict who will perpetrate IPV, especially serious or lethal IPV (Dinwiddie et al., 2019; Messing, Campbell, Wilson, Brown, & Patchell, 2017; Monckton Smith, 2019). As Hamby and Cook (2011) emphasize, no dangerousness assessment instrument is 100 percent accurate, and mistakes are not infrequent. These researchers point to one test of the SARA, for example, in which 32 percent of nonrecidivists were

identified as high risk, and 40 percent of recidivists were identified as moderate or low risk. The first error, in which a relatively nondangerous offender is labeled dangerous (nonrecidivists identified as high risk), is known as a **false positive**; the second error, in which a relatively dangerous offender is labeled nondangerous (recidivists identified as moderate or low risk), is known as a **false negative**. False positives could result in mistreatment of perpetrators (e.g., unwarranted harsher punishments), while false negatives could leave serious batterers unaccountable for their abusive behavior and potentially put their intimate partners at severe risk of revictimization or even death. As Kropp (2004, p. 677) warns, "there is no such thing as no risk in the context of spousal violence. Risk assessments should not be used to marginalize the concerns of those victims believed to be at lower risk: All spousal assaulters are dangerous to some degree, and risk assessment does not allow us to rule out danger." Indeed, Dinwiddie and colleagues (2019) emphasize the need to include victims' own perceptions of risk, since research has shown these to be fairly accurate in predicting future abuse. Victims have "unique knowledge of their abuser's personal traits, relationship patterns, and cycles of violence," so their perceptions are valuable in predicting future risk (Dinwiddie et al., 2019, p. 3). Of course, victims sometimes minimize or overlook signs of risk for various reasons, including fear of retaliation by the abusive partner, their desire to preserve the relationship, or their desire to protect the abusive partner, so risk assessment tools should be used *in conjunction with* victims' personal assessments of risk (Dinwiddie et al., 2019).

Additional concerns with risk assessment tools are that they may miss culturally specific or relationship-specific risk markers. For example, these instruments were designed to compare an individual to a normed reference group, which is typically white and heterosexual (Dinwiddie et al., 2019; Kimmes et al., 2019). Moreover, as Monckton Smith (2019) points out, analyzing clusters of risk markers is more important in assessing risk, especially risk of lethal violence, than counting numbers of risk markers on a list (see also Monckton Smith, Szymanska, & Haile, 2017).

significantly greater male perpetration with more severe outcomes. Does this mean that women *never* perpetrate IPV, serious or otherwise? No experienced IPV researcher would answer that question affirmatively, but they would respond that, as with other types of violent crime, men make up the majority of the offender population. "Most indicators fall in the range of about two to four male perpetrators for one female perpetrator, although a few indicators have even lower rates of female-perpetrated violence" (Hamby, 2018, p. 3).

Men's and women's IPV perpetration varies not only quantitatively, but qualitatively as well. Consider threats, for example. Women commonly threaten to (or actually do) harm themselves (e.g., commit suicide) or destroy their partner's valued property (e.g., scratching or crashing the partner's car), whereas men more often threaten to (or actually do) kill not only their partner, but also the partner's children, the partner's relatives (e.g., the partner's parents), or other people close to the partner (e.g., friends, coworkers) (Hamby, 2014, 2018; Meyer & Post, 2013; S. Smith, Fowler, & Niolon, 2014). Studies also show that women's and men's motivations for using violence against an intimate partner differ. Men are more likely to use violence when they perceive themselves losing control of the relationship or when they interpret their partner's words or behavior as challenges to their authority. In contrast, women are more likely to use violence, especially severe physical violence, in self-defense, when they believe they are in imminent danger of being attacked, or in retaliation for being attacked (O. Barnett, Lee, & Thelan, 1997; R. P. Dobash, Dobash, Cavanaugh, & Lewis, 1998; S. Miller, 2001; Rajan & McCloskey, 2007). This is perhaps why female perpetrators who have used violence against a male partner in a heterosexual relationship are significantly less likely than male perpetrators in heterosexual relationships to reoffend (Gerstenberger, Stansfield, & Williams, 2019). Consequently, in this chapter, we will usually refer to IPV perpetrators as men, but we will also address women's use of violence in intimate relationships.

The focus on male batterers in heterosexual relationships is not intended to overlook or minimize IPV in same-sex or noncisgender relationships. IPV perpetrators in same-sex relationships have not been studied as extensively, so we have far less data available with regard to perpetration risk factors in same-sex relationships. For instance, in a systematic review of the literature on IPV among men who have sex with men, Finneran and Stephenson (2014) found that less than a third (9 of 28 studies reviewed) even asked participants about their IPV perpetration. Drawing on the limited data available, it appears that the factors that influence the abusive behavior of lesbian and gay male batterers correspond closely to those that influence heterosexual batterers (L. Bancroft et al., 2012; Leventhal & Lundy, 1999; Renzetti, 1992).

Despite the similarities between heterosexual and same-sex IPV perpetration, there also appears to be at least one significant difference: the potential for internalized homophobia to contribute to IPV in same-sex relationships. **Internalized homophobia** is the acceptance and internalization to one's identity of negative (homophobic) societal attitudes and beliefs about lesbians and gay men (Pharr, 1986). According to Renzetti (1992), there are at least two ways that internalized homophobia is hypothesized to contribute to IPV perpetration in same-sex relationships. First, internalized homophobia may be used by a perpetrator to control an intimate partner; for example, the abuser may threaten to out the partner to family, friends, teachers, or coworkers (see also Chapter 8). Second, internalized homophobia lowers self-esteem, induces feelings of powerlessness, and leads to an obsessive closeting of one's sexual orientation as well as a tendency to deny differences between oneself and heterosexuals. Internalized homophobia has been linked to self-destructive behaviors, such as substance use, but researchers posit that the self-destructive behavior may be displaced to an intimate partner in the form of abuse (Renzetti, 1992; see also Sutter et al., 2019). Kimmes and colleagues (2019), for instance, found that internalized homophobia was the strongest predictor of IPV perpetration among gay men in their sample. Although Renzetti (1992) found evidence of internalized homophobia in her study of IPV in lesbian relationships, Kimmes et al. (2019) reported that the strongest predictor of IPV perpetration among lesbians in their sample was *fusion*, which involves intense focus on one's partner and anxiety over any desire by the partner for autonomy or separation in the relationship (Gold, 2003). Importantly, Renzetti's (1992) data also indicated that extreme dependency of one partner on the other was associated with IPV perpetration in lesbian relationships. Of course, this anxious dependency could be a defense against external homophobia, but it should be kept in mind that the concept of fusion in lesbian relationships has been extensively criticized (Gold, 2003).

To date, there is very limited research that empirically tests the relationship between internalized homophobia and perpetration of IPV in same-sex relationships. This research would require the development of a reliable and valid measure of internalized homophobia, which is no simple task. Moreover, this research would need to tease out the factors that cause some gay men and lesbian women to internalize homophobia while others do not, given that all live in a heterosexist and homophobic society. It may be that low self-esteem and perceived powerlessness are antecedents, rather than consequences, of internalized homophobia. Both low self-esteem and perceived powerlessness have also been associated with IPV perpetration, but it may be that both are risk factors not only for IPV, but for other dysfunctional outcomes as well (Renzetti, 1992). Clearly, more research on same-sex IPV perpetration is needed.

Even less is known about IPV in relationships in which one or both partners are transgender. The empirical research that is available indicates that transgender people experience high rates of violence in intimate relationships, that this violence is often severe, and that while it includes many of the same types of violence that occur in cisgender heterosexual relationships and same-sex relationships, it also takes unique forms (Guadalupe-Diaz, 2019). These unique forms of abuse include **genderist attacks** intended to regulate victims' daily behavior by criticizing how they perform with regard to gendered behavior (e.g., critiquing a trans woman for not behaving in traditionally feminine ways, or claiming masculine superiority over a victim who is femininely identified) (Guadalupe-Diaz, 2019). **Transphobic abuse**, particularly by nontrans partners, is also common—for instance, ridiculing a trans person's body, destroying items used by victims to communicate their gender (e.g., breast binders or enhancers), and isolating and shaming the victim (N. Brown, 2011; Guadalupe-Diaz, 2019). Transphobic attacks by nontrans partners may be extremely violent, even lethal. In 2015, for instance, Mercedes Williamson, a trans teenage girl, was murdered by her former boyfriend, 29-year-old Joshua Vallum, after he learned that one of his friends, a fellow member of the Latin Kings gang, knew he had had a sexual relationship with a young trans woman and he was worried other gang members would find out. Vallum lured Williamson into his car, drove her from her home in Alabama to his father's home in Mississippi, and then killed her using a stun gun, a knife, and a hammer. Although Vallum initially used a "trans panic defense," claiming he didn't know Mercedes was transgender but "snapped" and killed her when he discovered she was, he ended up pleading guilty and admitted that he had planned the homicide (S. Allen, 2018). Vallum was the first defendant in the United States to be successfully prosecuted for the murder of a transgender person under the federal Matthew Shepard and James Byrd Jr. Hate Crimes Prevention Act. He was sentenced to 49 years in prison.

Age, Race and Ethnicity, and Socioeconomic Status

Given that young women are at greatest risk for IPV victimization (see Chapter 8), it is not surprising that most studies show that young men, 18 to 29 years old, are at high risk for IPV perpetration, particularly physical violence. In at least one international study, however, the researchers reported that older men, aged 40 to 59, were nearly twice as likely to report IPV perpetration than men aged 18 to 28 (Fleming et al., 2015). This finding, though, may be due to the fact that the researchers asked participants whether they had *ever* perpetrated IPV; simply by virtue of having lived longer, older men will have higher odds of having ever engaged in the behavior. Moreover, a multitude of factors intersect with age to elevate perpetration risk, although how various combinations of factors may influence risk for different age groups or during different life stages is currently unknown (Aldarondo & Castro-Fernandez, 2011; Cancio, 2020).

Numerous studies report variations in IPV perpetration across racial and ethnic groups, with racial and ethnic minorities usually having higher rates of perpetration than whites (Sutton et al., 2020). The exception is Asian Americans, who typically have significantly lower rates than all other racial and ethnic groups (Breiding, Black, & Ryan, 2008; Tjaden & Thoennes, 2000). One significant problem with these studies, however, is that they typically collapse multiple and highly diverse racial and ethnic subgroups into a small number of very broad categories. For instance, African Americans, Afro-Caribbeans, and Africans are usually assessed as a single group (i.e., blacks). Similarly, Mexican Americans, Puerto Ricans, Cubans, and individuals from any Latin American country are all considered Hispanics or Latinx, even though their history, culture, and present social and economic circumstances may be vastly different. Findings from the relatively few studies that have disaggregated the broad racial and ethnic categories show considerable variation in IPV perpetration rates across diverse racial and ethnic subgroups. For example, Aldarondo, Kaufman Kantor, and Jasinski (2002) examined perpetration rates and risk factor differences among a sample of Puerto Ricans, Mexicans, Mexican Americans, and Anglo-Americans. Some of their findings are shown in Table 9.1. Interestingly, they found that when men reported on their IPV perpetration, the rate was highest for Mexican Americans, but when reports of female partners were used, Puerto Rican men had the highest perpetration rate, followed by Mexican American and Mexican men. Moreover, although Anglo-American men had the lowest rates of perpetration regardless of whether the men or the women were reporting, the women's reports were higher than those of the men. These findings indicate that men in some groups may underreport or simply underestimate their abusive behavior, which we noted previously is not uncommon. Aldarondo et al. also found that Mexican men who had been abused themselves by their parents, and Anglo men who had witnessed abuse in their families of origin, were more likely to perpetrate IPV, whereas among Mexican American men, risk of IPV perpetration increased in relation to a decrease in economic resources.

Another criticism of research on race and ethnicity as a risk factor for IPV perpetration is that it often fails to take socioeconomic status into account. Racial and ethnic minorities are disproportionately represented among the poor and near-poor, and studies consistently show that poverty, low income, low occupational status, and low educational attainment all elevate IPV perpetration risk (Breiding et al., 2008; Cho, 2012). L. Bancroft et al. (2012), however, caution that the research with regard

TABLE 9.1 ■ Reports of Husband-to-Wife Violence by Gender and Ethnicity of Respondent (Percent)		
Ethnicity	Male Respondents	Female Respondents
Puerto Rican	21.9	25.7
Mexican	17.6	13.4
Mexican American	26.0	16.7
Anglo-American	10.6	11.3
Total sample	14.1	13.2

Source: Aldarondo, Kaufman Kantor, & Jasinski, 2002.

to educational attainment is equivocal, and, based on their clinical experience with batterers, they concluded that those who are better educated tend to "rely less on physical violence and draw more on sophisticated techniques of psychological abuse that they have at their disposal" (p. 31).

Sutton and colleagues (2020) have drawn attention to the relationship between racial discrimination and IPV perpetration by African American men, particularly those who live in high-crime and economically disadvantaged neighborhoods. In their prospective longitudinal study with 200 young African American men, they hypothesized that repeated experiences of racial discrimination generate strong negative emotional reactions, including anger at the perceived injustice. Moreover, individuals who have these experiences come to expect exploitation and harm in their interactions with others and are primed to respond to hostility with aggression, perhaps even toward intimate partners whom they perceive are acting maliciously toward them. Importantly, however, Sutton et al. found that the men in their study who, during adolescence, had caregivers who displayed love and support along with appropriate behavioral control experienced some protection from the stress induced by racial discrimination and, in turn, had a lower likelihood of perpetrating IPV. In contrast, the men most at risk for IPV perpetration were those who experienced high levels of racial discrimination in adolescence or high levels of anger in young adulthood, coupled with frequent corporal punishment from caregivers during adolescence. Sutton et al.'s (2020) research illustrates the complex interactions between demographic, family, and structural risk factors for IPV perpetration.

Similarly, concerns have been raised with regard to IPV risk among immigrant populations. As we noted in Chapter 8, immigrant women are at increased risk of IPV victimization for a number of reasons, including factors related to their immigration status (e.g., language proficiency, social isolation). We also noted that immigrant men may threaten their intimate partners with deportation as a tool of coercive control. The assumption is often made that immigrants from countries with rigid patriarchal gender norms are at elevated risk of IPV because they import their cultural beliefs to the host country. There is research, however, that indicates that IPV risk increases post-immigration because of various **immigration-related stressors**, such as the inability to find work or to attain financial stability (Dutton, Orloff, & Hass, 2000; Pan et al., 2006), which may be exacerbated by beliefs about appropriate gender roles (Gupta et al., 2010).

Nevertheless, there is a great deal of diversity across immigrant groups, and most studies of immigrants use samples that are too small to allow for analyses of specific subgroups. One exception is a study by Vaughn and colleagues (Vaughn, Salas-Wright, Cooper-Sadlo, Maynard, & Larson, 2015), who examined data from a large, nationally representative sample of U.S. residents aged 18–49 (*N* = 19,073), which included immigrants categorized by their *region* of origin (i.e., Asia, Africa, Europe, or Latin America).

The researchers found that immigrants as a group were significantly more likely to perpetrate IPV than native-born Americans, but when they disaggregated the immigrant group by region of origin, they discovered that most IPV perpetration was accounted for by immigrants from Latin America; immigrants from Asia, Africa, and Europe had lower IPV perpetration rates than native-born Americans. At the same time, however, Vaughn et al. found that immigrants who perpetrated IPV were significantly more likely than nonperpetrators to exhibit mood, anxiety, personality, and substance use disorders; they were twice as likely to receive a diagnosis of a psychiatric disorder. The longer the immigrants were in the United States, the greater their likelihood of IPV perpetration, indicating perhaps that post-immigration stressors are major contributing factors to lowered mental health and IPV perpetration risk.

In sum, the research discussed in this section highlights the challenge of teasing out the relative contribution of a host of factors to IPV perpetration risk. Moreover, this research points to the serious limitations in relying on individual demographic characteristics to predict IPV perpetration risk.

Psychological Functioning

It is commonly assumed that batterers are mentally ill. Research consistently shows, however, that except for a very small group of extremely physically violent individuals, batterers do not have significantly higher rates of psychopathology than nonbatterers, and most individuals diagnosed with a mental illness do not perpetrate IPV (L. Bancroft et al., 2012). Although some batterers exhibit various emotional or psychological problems, such as depression, low self-esteem, high levels of trait anger and trait jealousy, and rigid and maladaptive cognitive styles, there is no specific personality disorder or mental illness that characterizes batterers in comparison with nonbatterers (Birkley & Eckhardt, 2015; Brem, Shorey, Rothman, Temple, & Stuart, 2018; Doumas, Pearson, Elgin, & McKinley, 2008; Langhinrichsen-Rohling, Huss, & Ramsey, 2000). There are studies indicating that IPV perpetrators may have low self-control, but this finding is countered by research and clinical observations that show that most IPV perpetrators are not violent or abusive outside their homes and that they often exhibit strong self-control (L. Bancroft et al., 2012; L. Bennett & Bland, 2008; Holtzworth-Munroe & Meehan, 2004).

Jasinski (2001, p. 9) argues that assuming disordered psychological functioning or personality traits cause IPV "satisfies most people's need to view violence as a behavior exhibited by someone who is different from themselves." This explanation of IPV perpetration may also be used to absolve perpetrators from responsibility for their abusive behavior (e.g., "He can't help himself; he's sick"), and it overlooks important social and environmental factors that contribute to IPV perpetration. At least one recent study (Armenti, Snead, & Babcock, 2018), for example, has found that the association between certain psychological problems and IPV perpetration may be related to problematic substance use, an issue we discuss next.

Substance Use

One of the most commonly cited contributing factors to IPV, which was illustrated in the opening case history, is substance use, particularly problematic alcohol use (Eckhardt, Parrott, & Sprunger, 2015; Lipsky, Kernic, Qiu, Wright, & Hasin, 2014; but see Cafferky, Mendez, Anderson, & Stith, 2018, whose meta-analysis indicated that both alcohol and drug use [amphetamines, cocaine, and marijuana] are similarly related to IPV perpetration). Studies that examine the role of alcohol use in IPV typically show that men who are heavy or problem drinkers, especially men who binge drink, are at significantly greater risk of perpetrating IPV than men who are light or moderate drinkers or who abstain from alcohol (C. A. Field, Caetano, & Nelson, 2004; O'Leary & Schumacher, 2003; Peralta, Tuttle, & Steele, 2010; see also Testa & Derrick, 2014, who found that perpetration of verbal and physical aggression by heterosexual female partners also increased when they drank). Moreover, IPV perpetrated by men who abuse alcohol tends to be more frequent and more severe than IPV perpetrated by men who are not problem drinkers; severity of problematic alcohol use predicts severity of IPV perpetrated by problem drinkers (K. Graham, Bernards, Wilsnack, & Gmel, 2011; Stuart et al., 2006; Testa, Quigley, & Leonard, 2003). H. Johnson (2001), for example, reports that the men in her study who drank heavily or were intoxicated at the time of the IPV incident were more likely than nondrinkers to use very serious forms of violence against their intimate partners (e.g., choking, threatening with a weapon, sexual assault) and were more likely to inflict physical injuries, including injuries that required medical attention. Indeed, there is evidence that having a substance abuse problem is a risk marker for perpetration of lethal IPV (J. Campbell, 2007).

Nevertheless, researchers emphasize that a correlation between substance use and IPV perpetration does not mean that substance use such as heavy drinking *causes* IPV (L. Bennett & Bland, 2008; see also Chapter 8). Brem et al. (2018) note, for instance, that alcohol is *not* involved in a majority (55% or more) of IPV incidents. Other researchers point out that some perpetrators start drinking or getting high *after* an IPV incident or use their alcohol or drug use as an excuse or justification for their abusive behavior (Gelles, 1993; Lewis, Winstead, Braitman, & Hitson, 2018). Interestingly, clinicians have found that some batterers become more abusive when they stop drinking or using drugs, presumably because they are more irritable or perhaps because they are better able to monitor their partners' behavior (L. Bancroft et al., 2012). L. Bancroft and his colleagues (2012) also report that some batterers even incorporate concepts they learn in 12-step substance abuse recovery programs into their verbally abusive tactics (e.g., accusing their partners of "being in denial" about their own problems or of being "codependent").

And Lewis and colleagues (2018) point out that drinking per se may have less of an effect on IPV risk than *discrepant* drinking—that is, a pattern in which one partner drinks more than or away from (e.g., in a bar, like Victor in the opening case history) the other partner. Lewis et al. state that research with heterosexual couples indicates that light drinking and shared drinking (presumably not shared binge or problematic drinking) may be adaptive. Research indicates, however, that discrepant drinking increases the likelihood of various negative relationship interactions, including IPV (Fischer & Wiersma, 2012). Lewis et al. (2018) found this to be the case among lesbian couples as well, but for psychological abuse, not physical abuse.

Although common sense may tell us that substance use probably raises the risk of IPV perpetration for many couples, the mechanisms by which this occurs are not well understood (Eckhardt et al., 2015). Eckhardt and colleagues (2015) propose integrating two theoretical models as the most promising way to understand *how* substance use—and, specifically, alcohol use—increases risk of IPV perpetration. They begin with I^3 **(I-Cubed) theory**, which identifies three *interactive* factors that are needed to predict alcohol-induced IPV perpetration: instigation, impellance, and inhibition (i.e., the "three *Is*"). An *instigating* factor is a situational or contextual experience, such as an argument with an intimate partner, that serves as a provocation or trigger for aggression. An *impelling* factor is a dispositional or situational factor—for example, high trait and/or state anger, high trait jealousy, or a tendency toward hostile rumination—that psychologically primes an individual to respond to an instigating factor with aggression. As Eckhardt et al. (2015) explain, "instigating and impelling factors interact with each other and share a relationship akin to a match and gasoline; the gasoline alone will not ignite, but the introduction of a flame produces a reaction of exaggerated magnitude" (p. 943). But *inhibitory* factors, such as high self-awareness, enable an individual to resist the urge to respond to an instigation with aggression. Of course, *disinhibiting* factors can reduce the effectiveness of inhibitory factors. One potent disinhibitor is alcohol; alcohol intoxication affects cognitive functioning and reduces individuals' ability to regulate their emotions and behavior (Eckhardt et al., 2015).

Eckhardt and colleagues (2015) then turn their attention to the way alcohol lowers inhibitory factors and essentially fuels the fire of the interaction of instigating and impelling factors. To do so, they draw on **alcohol myopia theory (AMT)**. AMT posits that alcohol creates a myopic or narrowing effect on intoxicated individuals' attention and ability to process meaning from informational cues they perceive in their environment. This limited "allocation of attention" causes the intoxicated persons to focus narrowly on only the most salient cues in an interaction (e.g., an instigating factor, such as their partner calling them derogatory names), while simultaneously screening out less immediate cues (e.g., an inhibiting factor, such as the fact they could be arrested for responding with violence).

Eckhardt et al. (2015) conclude that "it follows from AMT that alcohol use should potentiate IPV by narrowing attention onto salient, provocative cues—particularly in already high-risk persons" (p. 944). This explanatory model, in fact, has received considerable empirical support. For instance, consistent with AMT, Brem et al. (2018) found that problematic alcohol use was positively related to both physical and sexual IPV perpetration among men with high, but not low, trait jealousy. Armenti et al. (2018) reported that problematic alcohol use (but not drug use) moderated the relationship between both borderline personality disorder and antisocial personality disorder and IPV. And Ngo et al. (2018) found that mindfulness, especially awareness of one's actions and being nonjudgmental toward others, reduced the risk of IPV perpetration.

One risk factor found to fairly consistently moderate the relationship between substance use and IPV perpetration is adherence to traditional patriarchal gender norms. For instance, researchers have explored how men's need for power, especially power over other people, may be related to both their alcohol use and IPV perpetration. Peralta and colleagues (2010) found that alcohol use in combination with the use of violence against an intimate partner was seen by the men in their study—men who had been officially identified as batterers—as a marker of masculine dominance and control. Other researchers have found that the correlation between substance use and IPV perpetration is strongest among men who endorse male dominance, who hold hostilely sexist attitudes toward women, and who believe that IPV is appropriate behavior in certain situations (C. A. Field et al., 2004; H. Johnson, 2001; Renzetti, Lynch, & DeWall, 2015). We will examine these attitudes as risk factors in more detail shortly.

Family of Origin Abuse

An old adage states that "children learn what they live." Recall from Chapter 2 that in the literature on violence and maltreatment in intimate relationships, this idea is known as intergenerational transmission. Intergenerational transmission suggests that children, especially boys, who witness their fathers abusing their mothers are likely to abuse their own intimate partners when they grow up. And, as noted in Chapter 8, girls who witness IPV by their fathers are at increased risk of becoming IPV victims when they grow up. Intergenerational transmission theory derives from classic **social learning theory** (Bandura, 1978), which posits that children learn by **modeling** or imitating those around them. Their parents are their first and most important role models. In addition, behaviors that receive **reinforcement** or are rewarded, rather than punished, are more likely to be learned and internalized. Although the research findings are inconsistent with regard to whether children are more inclined to model the behavior of their same-sex parent, there is evidence that the perceived power of the model influences the degree to which children will imitate the model's behavior (Jacklin, 1989).

A substantial number of studies provide support for the intergenerational transmission of IPV (see Delsol & Margolin, 2004; Murrell, Chistoff, & Henning, 2007). Boys exposed to IPV or who are abused themselves tend to be more aggressive toward their peers and engage in more bullying than boys who do not witness IPV or experience abuse (see Chapter 7). There is also evidence that both boys and girls who live in homes with IPV are more likely to try to get what they want by using manipulation, pressure, and coercion (Graham-Bermann, 1998). Additional research shows that the more frequent and more severe a man's abuse is toward the mother of the children in the household, the more likely the children are to believe that men are superior to women and are entitled to privileges in the family, and that violence against family members is not only acceptable, but also often necessary (Graham-Bermann & Brescoll, 2000).

It is the batterer's transmission of attitudes about women and intimate relationships to children that most concerns many clinicians. These attitudes include victim-blaming, violence as an acceptable way to get one's way or to resolve conflicts, and sexism. Boys who closely identify with abusive men who model or explicitly teach these attitudes are at greater risk of growing up to be IPV perpetrators themselves (L. Bancroft et al., 2012). In fact, in a study that examined the effect of experiencing (not just witnessing) abuse on likelihood to later abuse one's intimate partner, O'Hearn and Margolin (2000) found that only boys who had adopted their abusive father's attitude supportive of IPV were at increased risk of growing up to be IPV perpetrators themselves. Abused boys who did not internalize this attitude were at no greater risk of perpetrating IPV as an adult than boys who had not been abused.

Given the role that traditional patriarchal attitudes play in fostering IPV perpetration, we will examine them more closely. First, though, it is important to note that children are not passive recipients of socialization messages and do not unquestioningly imitate adult role models. Many children actively resist and bravely stand up to abusers, and intervene on behalf of their abused mothers (L. Bancroft et al., 2012; Mbilinyi, Edleson, Hagemeister, & Beeman, 2007). Moreover, a number of factors may counter the negative influence of the batterer, including the child's development of a specific talent from which the child derives personal satisfaction as well as approval of others, and the development of close relationships with other positive adult role models (L. Bancroft et al., 2012; Kerig, 2003). In short, the pathway from childhood exposure to parental IPV to adult IPV perpetration (or victimization) is by no means inevitable.

Attitudes and Beliefs Supportive of IPV

Certain attitudes and beliefs have been found to be strongly associated with men's IPV perpetration against women (see Table 9.2). Among these are the beliefs that men are superior to women and that women are weak, incompetent, manipulative of men, untrustworthy, and stupid (L. Bancroft et al., 2012). We saw this superiority in the opening case history in which Victor treated Maria like his "servant." These traditional patriarchal attitudes are indicative of a general hostility toward women (L. Bancroft et al., 2012;

TABLE 9.2 ■ IPV Perpetration Risk Factors Related to Patriarchal Gender Norms
• The belief that men are superior to women
• Generally hostile attitudes toward women (e.g., beliefs that women are weak, incompetent, manipulative of men, untrustworthy, and stupid)
• The belief that a man's wife or girlfriend is his possession
• Extreme jealousy and sexual proprietariness
• The belief that a man must control his wife or girlfriend because women are not trustworthy
• A strong sense of male entitlement
• Peer support for hostile attitudes toward women and approval of abusive behavior to punish or control intimate partners

Sources: References are representative rather than exhaustive: Aldarondo, Kaufman Kantor, & Jasinski, 2002; L. Bancroft, Silverman, & Ritchie, 2012; L. Bennett & Bland, 2008; Breiding, Black, & Ryan, 2008; DeKeseredy & Schwartz, 2013; Hamby, 2018; Murrell, Christoff, & Henning, 2007; Pan et al., 2006; Renzetti, 1992; L. Rosen, Kaminski, Parmely, Knudson, & Fancher, 2003.

Ozaki & Otis, 2017). Researchers note that hostility toward women is significantly correlated with IPV perpetration by men (Holtzworth-Munroe, Meehan, Herron, Rehman, & Stuart, 2000). C. Anderson and Anderson (2008) report, in fact, that men who are highly hostile toward women specifically target women for aggression.

Based on their clinical experience, L. Bancroft and colleagues (2012) have identified other attitudes and beliefs that are common among male IPV perpetrators, all of which reflect an adherence to traditional patriarchal gender norms. For example, L. Bancroft et al. have found that batterers typically think of their intimate partners as possessions or "owned objects." They report that their clients sometimes struggle to use an intimate partner's name and instead call her "my wife" or "my girl." This possessiveness often manifests as extreme jealousy, sexual proprietariness, and the use of control tactics, which the batterer may justify as necessary due to his partner's untrustworthiness. Should the woman resist his control, the batterer will characterize her behavior as further evidence of her infidelity, mental instability, or her abusiveness toward him. Bancroft et al. also note that IPV perpetrators are, not surprisingly, selfish and self-centered, but they see these characteristics as stemming from the perpetrators' strong sense of **entitlement**. "Entitlement is the belief that one has special rights and privileges without accompanying reciprocal responsibilities" (L. Bancroft et al., 2012, p. 8). The IPV perpetrator's entitlement derives in large part from his sense of male superiority and his belief that his partner is his possession, whose primary purpose is to meet his needs.

Importantly, these attitudes and beliefs, which support and justify IPV, are often shared by a perpetrator's friends (DeKeseredy & Schwartz, 2013). As we learned in

Chapter 7, male peer support for abusive behavior is predictive of dating violence. Young men who frequently talk with their peers about women in demeaning, hostile, and sexist ways have been found to be more likely to perpetrate IPV later in their adult relationships (Capaldi, Dishion, Stoolmiller, & Yoerger, 2001; DeKeseredy & Schwartz, 2013). Adult peer groups are no less important in this regard, suggesting that membership in certain types of communities may contribute to risk of IPV perpetration.

High-Risk Communities

As we noted at the outset of our discussion of IPV perpetration risk, most research has focused on identifying individual characteristics, rather than on social, community, or structural factors. The research on attitudes and beliefs supportive of IPV is an exception in that it focuses on attitudes and beliefs grounded in patriarchal gender norms, which reflect gender inequalities embedded in social institutions. Although in most social contexts today blatantly hostile sexism is frowned upon (Swim, Aiken, Hall, & Hunter, 1995), gender inequality remains a feature of most major social institutions, such as the workplace. We saw an example of this in Chapter 8 when we noted the fact that women continue to earn on average less than men and are disproportionately represented among the poor (DeNavas-Walt & Proctor, 2014).

In recent years, there has been an increase in studies that include community or structural risk markers for IPV perpetration, as a result of growing recognition of the importance of examining how community characteristics and organization may reinforce and perpetuate gender inequality, including gendered violence and aggression (DeKeseredy & Schwartz, 2013). For example, several recent studies, using both quantitative and qualitative data collection methods, have identified neighborhood characteristics associated with elevated IPV rates. Specifically, IPV perpetration risk is higher in neighborhoods characterized by concentrated poverty; high unemployment, especially among male residents; low levels of trust among neighbors; and a reluctance by neighbors to intervene if they see or hear problematic or potentially criminal behavior taking place (Benson & Fox, 2004; Bourgois, 1999; Browning, 2002). It has been hypothesized that the economic disadvantage of such environments is emasculating for male residents who, in turn, abuse women to reassert dominance and control (DeKeseredy & Schwartz, 2013). At the same time, the male subcultures of these neighborhoods provide men "with a vocabulary that defines women as legitimate targets of abuse," and the unwillingness of neighbors to intervene imbues confidence in perpetrators that their behavior will probably go unsanctioned (DeKeseredy & Schwartz, 2013, p. 116; see also J. Miller, 2008; Sutton et al., 2020). In one study, researchers found that some residents in public housing developments even helped batterers get away before the police arrived on the scene (Renzetti & Maier, 2002).

Another risky community for IPV perpetration is the military. As we discussed in Chapter 8, studies comparing IPV rates between military and civilian samples report higher rates by military members (see, for example, Cancio, 2020; Novaco & Chemtob, 2015). Among the individual risk factors associated with elevated rates of IPV perpetration in the military are age and socioeconomic status (the armed forces have a high concentration of young men from lower socioeconomic groups) and high rates of heavy alcohol use (N. Bell, Harford, McCarroll, & Senier, 2004; Dobie et al., 2004). We also previously noted that the stress produced by frequent relocations and deployments has been associated with IPV perpetration (Basile & Black, 2011; McCarroll, Newby, & Dooley-Bernard, 2008), and this stress appears to be particularly high among post-9/11 veterans (Morin, 2011). Exposure to and participation in combat along with war-related trauma and subsequent post-traumatic stress disorder (PTSD) have been shown to be significant risk factors for IPV perpetration by military men (Heinz, Makin-Byrd, Blonigen, Reilly, & Timko, 2015; Taft, Stafford, Watkins, & Street, 2011). Researchers also point out that military recruits are socialized into a culture of hypermasculinity that encourages emotional distancing from others and provides peer support for denigrating attitudes toward women (L. Rosen, Kaminski, Parmely, Knudson, & Fancher, 2003). Military training also imbues hypervigilance to perceived threats. Research indicates that active duty military personnel as well as veterans are more likely to interpret events and interactions in an overly hostile way and subsequently respond to perceived threats or challenges with aggression (O. Gonzalez, Novaco, Reger, & Gahm, 2016; Novaco & Chemtob, 2015). At the same time, however, Cancio (2020) reported that not all veterans are at elevated risk of IPV perpetration. In his study of post-9/11 veterans, military status appeared to serve as a protective factor for Asian American and Pacific Islander as well as American Indian men in that they were less likely than their civilian peers to perpetrate either physical or sexual IPV. In contrast, military status was a risk factor for white men, who were more likely than their civilian peers to perpetrate both physical and sexual IPV. Military status was a protective factor for physical IPV perpetration among Latinos, but a risk factor for sexual IPV perpetration by this group, and there were no differences between black post-9/11 veterans and civilians for risk of perpetrating either type of IPV. As Cancio argues, considerably more research is needed to understand how military service may contribute to (or protect against) IPV perpetration across various groups of male active duty and veteran military service members.

Although the U.S. Department of Defense has taken steps to address IPV in the military, these efforts have been criticized for their failure to distinguish IPV from "normal marital disputes" and to properly hold perpetrators accountable for the abuse (Rosenthal & McDonald, 2003). At the same time, we know very little about IPV perpetration by active duty and veteran military women. Women make up an increasing percentage of all branches of the U.S. armed forces and are one of the fastest-growing groups of veterans in the country (Creech et al., 2020; Manning, 2019). Research shows that women service members experience high rates of all forms of intimate violence, including sexual harassment, acquaintance sexual assault, and IPV (Bonnes, 2019; Dichter, Wagner, & True, 2018; U.S. Department of Defense, 2019) and that their victimization experiences have serious negative consequences, including PTSD and problematic substance use (Creech et al., 2020; Dichter et al., 2018). It may be that gendered differences in coping with and managing military-related stressors protect women from responding with aggression when confronted with a perceived threat or challenge by their intimate partners. Before this hypothesis and others may be empirically tested, however, research must first be conducted that compares perpetration rates across diverse groups of service members and veterans.

Clearly, contextual risk factors are important in understanding how and why IPV occurs. Despite the recent increase in studies of community-level and structural risk factors for IPV perpetration, there is a need for more research that analyzes the interrelated, cumulative impacts of individual, social, community, and structural variables on IPV perpetration risk (M. Whitaker, 2014).

INTERVENTION AND PREVENTION OF IPV PERPETRATION

The importance of holding perpetrators accountable has been a prominent theme in the anti–violence against women movement since the 1970s. As we have noted in other chapters in this book, historically IPV was viewed as a private family matter in which the police, courts, and other public institutions did not want to intervene. Activists in the 1970s, who lobbied the public and legislatures to view IPV as a social problem, argued that men abused their wives and girlfriends because they could get away with it—that is, abusers shared the view that what they did in their intimate relationships was their "own business" and they knew they would rarely, if ever, suffer negative consequences as a result. As we learned in Chapter 8, this situation changed in the late 1970s, not only because of consciousness-raising efforts by social activists, but also because of successful lawsuits brought by IPV victims against municipalities for failure of their police departments to enforce the law when responding to a domestic violence call. Today, use of the legal system is the standard formal response to IPV (Goodmark, 2018), although other responses include treatment interventions for batterers and prevention strategies.

The Police and Legal System Response

In addition to successful lawsuits against municipalities, we also learned in Chapter 8 that research on police responses to IPV showed that arresting perpetrators was more effective at reducing recidivism than simply separating the partners briefly or mediating the conflict (Sherman & Berk, 1984). The Minneapolis Domestic Violence Experiment, as it was called, had a tremendous impact on public policy in that following publication of the initial findings, most jurisdictions enacted mandatory arrest or preferred arrest policies. These policies either *require* or *encourage* officers to arrest the individual they believe is the perpetrator if there is probable cause, regardless of whether the officers witnessed the offense and even if the victim does not want the perpetrator arrested. However, subsequent studies in six cities to replicate the Minneapolis experiment—collectively known as the Spouse Assault Replication Program (SARP)—produced more equivocal findings (Maxwell, Garner, & Fagan, 2002). These studies showed that arrest was only an effective deterrent for some subgroups of perpetrators. Specifically, those perpetrators who had a "high stake in conformity"—that is, had a good deal to lose by being arrested for IPV (e.g., their jobs)—were more likely to be deterred from re-assaulting their partners, while perpetrators who had a "low stake in conformity" (e.g., were unemployed, unmarried, or had a previous criminal record) were unlikely to be deterred from re-assaulting their partners by being arrested (S. Miller, Iovanni, & Kelley, 2011; Sherman et al., 1992). These findings led to the conclusion that while arrest generally has a stronger deterrent effect than separating the partners or mediating the conflict, other factors, such as the perpetrator's criminal history, play a bigger role in determining likelihood of re-assault (Maxwell et al., 2002). Nevertheless, arrest remains the typical outcome when police respond to an IPV call.

We noted in Chapter 8 that victims sometimes do not want their partners arrested because it may have negative consequences for them and their children (e.g., they fear the perpetrator will retaliate against them, or they don't want to lose the perpetrator's wages). Victims often call the police not because they want the perpetrator arrested and jailed, but because they want help making the abuse occurring in that moment to stop (Goodmark, 2012). Mandatory and preferred arrest policies have also resulted in a dramatic increase in the number of women arrested for IPV perpetration (see Box 9.2), which may eventually deter them from calling the police during an IPV episode.

Once charges are brought against an offender—and the specific charges will depend on a number of factors, including previous IPV arrests, whether a weapon was used, and injuries to the victim—the case moves to prosecution. Until the 1980s, most prosecutors would automatically drop the charges against an IPV offender at the victim's request without investigating whether the victim was being coerced into making this request by the offender or the offender's family. But not long after the adoption of mandatory or preferred arrest policies, many jurisdictions adopted victimless or no-drop prosecution policies. Victimless prosecution allows prosecutors to build a case using police reports, photographs, and physical and other evidence, without relying on victims' testimony. No-drop prosecution mandates prosecutors to proceed with a case regardless of whether a victim agrees to participate. Supporters of these policies maintain that they ensure that

BOX 9.2

THE PROBLEM OF DUAL ARRESTS

One of the unanticipated consequences of mandatory and preferred arrest laws was a dramatic increase in the number of women, especially black women, arrested for IPV perpetration (Larance, Goodmark, Miller, & Dasgupta, 2019). Sometimes women are arrested as the sole perpetrator, but more often, it appears, police arrest both intimate partners, a practice known as dual arrest (DeLeon-Granados, Wells, & Binsbacher, 2006; Hirschel, Buzawa, Pattavina, Faggiani, & Reuland, 2007; S. Miller, 2005). As we noted earlier, men and women usually have different motivations for using force against their intimate partners: Men are more often motivated by a desire to maintain control over their partner, whereas women more often act in defense of themselves or their children, or in retaliation for abuse (O. Barnett et al., 1997; R. P. Dobash et al., 1998; S. Miller, 2001; Rajan & McCloskey, 2007). Some researchers have also found that abusive men, aware of the mandatory or preferred arrest law, call the police themselves to make sure they are perceived as the victim; they may even self-injure to ensure that their partner is arrested (S. Miller, 2005), although a man who has actually been victimized might also be deterred from calling the police for fear of being arrested under the assumption that men are typically the abusive partners.

When injuries are serious and obvious, the police must arrest whoever appears to have inflicted those injuries. To reduce the risk of an IPV victim being arrested along with a perpetrator, however, many jurisdictions have enacted **primary aggressor laws**, which require responding officers to distinguish the party who initiated the aggression from the party who likely acted as a defensive response to that aggression, and offensive injuries from defensive injuries (Hirschel & Deveau, 2016). Today, at least 34 states have adopted primary aggressor laws (Hirschel & Buzawa, 2013). A study by Finn and

her colleagues found that police officers said they would be less likely to engage in dual arrest if their department encouraged arrest of the primary aggressor only (Finn, Blackwell, Stalans, Studdard, & Dugan, 2004). Research evaluating the impact of primary aggressor laws on dual arrests supports this finding; dual arrests decline significantly following the enactment of primary aggressor laws or once police receive special training on identifying primary aggressors when responding to a domestic violence call (Dichter, Marcus, Morabito, & Rhodes, 2011; Meloy & Miller, 2011). In a study of factors that influence officers' likelihood of making an arrest in an IPV case, Hirschel and Deveau (2016) found that the existence of a state primary aggressor law had a greater impact on officers' decision making than the presence of injuries or the perpetrator's use of a weapon. However, these researchers also found that the existence of the state primary aggressor law lowered the chances that either party would be arrested. They concluded that "an unintended consequence of a state enacting a primary aggressor law is that officers may be deciding to arrest neither of the involved parties instead of determining who the primary aggressor is" (p. 16). If this conclusion bears out after further testing, the police response to IPV may be becoming more similar to what it was prior to the enactment of mandatory and preferred arrest laws.

Identifying the primary aggressor and avoiding dual arrests that include the victim is a significant justice issue. Research shows that female IPV victims who are arrested and processed as offenders fare rather poorly in the court system. Many of the women, for example, are unfamiliar with the court process, have limited knowledge of their options, and cannot afford to hire an attorney, so they have to rely on the assistance of a public defender, who may have little experience with IPV cases. They are frightened and want to

(Continued)

(Continued)

get the case over with so they can just go home. Consequently, instead of opting for a criminal trial where they can present evidence of self-defense, they accept a guilty plea without fully understanding that they will now have a criminal record that could, among other things, prevent them from working in certain jobs, cause them to lose federal benefits, and have the conviction held against them in a custody hearing (S. Miller, 2005).

Stand your ground laws have been used successfully in many states where women arrested for IPV are found to have been defending themselves from an abusive partner. Twenty-one states have stand your ground laws, which permit individuals to use force, including deadly force, without the obligation to retreat, if they reasonably believe that it is necessary to prevent someone who is attacking them in their home from killing them or inflicting serious bodily injury (FindLaw.com, n.d.). Prosecutors in Florida, however, have argued that the state's stand your ground law should not be applied in IPV cases, and the courts have generally agreed (Larance et al., 2019). In 2011, for instance, the stand your ground defense of Marissa Alexander, a black woman, who was arrested after firing a single gunshot into the ceiling of her home to warn off her husband who was attacking her, was rejected by the court. Following a subsequent jury trial, she was convicted and sentenced to 20 years in prison, even though no one was injured by the warning shot and Alexander had no previous criminal record or arrests. She spent three years in prison before her conviction was overturned on the grounds that the judge in the case had erred in instructing the jury prior to their deliberations, but she then faced the possibility of a second trial, in which the prosecutor threatened to seek three consecutive 20-year prison sentences if Alexander was convicted a second time. Instead, Alexander agreed to plead guilty to three counts of aggravated assault in exchange for a sentence that capped her prison time to the three years she had already served, but which required her to serve two years under house arrest during which time her movements were monitored electronically. She completed this sentence in January 2017 (Hauser, 2017).

IPV victims arrested and convicted as perpetrators are more likely to be mandated to a batterer intervention program (BIP) than sentenced to jail or prison. Given that the majority of victims are women, that women and men typically use force differently in intimate relationships, and that most BIPs are designed to treat abusive men, the content and treatment approach of the programs are usually inappropriate for women (Larance, 2018; Larance et al., 2019; Meloy & Miller, 2011). This does not mean that these women cannot benefit from treatment; rather, it means that the content and treatment approach must be specifically designed to meet their unique needs. Otherwise, the program is likely to be revictimizing and traumatizing and, therefore, ineffective and perhaps even harmful (Larance, 2018). In short, a gender-responsive intervention to women's and men's differential use of force in their intimate relationships is the solution advocated by most practitioners. (See Larance, 2018, and Larance et al., 2019, for a discussion of programming resources for women who use force.)

IPV perpetrators are held accountable while also protecting victims from threats and coercion by perpetrators (Goodman & Epstein, 2011).

One outcome of these arrest and prosecution policies is that they have increased the number of IPV offenders who are processed through the criminal justice system, which some observers argue is beneficial because it sends a strong message that IPV is a crime that has serious consequences (Goodmark, 2018). Nevertheless, some researchers have questioned whether formal criminal justice processing of these cases is successful in reducing IPV (Goodmark, 2018). Research examining the impact of formal case processing and disposition on recidivism rates has produced inconsistent results, with some studies showing no appreciable effect of prosecution on lowering IPV recidivism (Kingsnorth, 2006; O'Sullivan, Davis, Farole, & Rempel, 2007) and other studies showing that a formal disposition of some kind (e.g., a trial even if it resulted in acquittal, a mandatory batterer intervention or other counseling program, probation, or jail time) is better than doing nothing (i.e., not filing charges) and can even result in significant reductions in IPV recidivism (Sechrist & Weil, 2018; Wooldredge & Thistlewaite, 2002). But the fact that many victims, especially victims of color, do not wish to engage with the criminal justice system (see Chapter 8) has led some researchers and practitioners to seek out alternative responses to IPV perpetrators.

Restorative Justice as an Alternative to the Criminal Justice System

Members of immigrant communities and communities of color have been subjected to disproportionately harsh and, in some cases, brutal treatment by the police and the legal system. Studies of pro-prosecution policies, for example, have raised concerns about racial bias, given findings that prosecutors are more likely to pursue cases against racial and ethnic minority defendants than white defendants (Henning & Feder, 2005; Kingsnorth & Macintosh, 2004; Larance et al., 2019). Negative stereotypes about the criminality of men of color may also lead to prejudicial outcomes when these men appear in court on IPV charges (L. Bancroft et al., 2012). Consequently, some analysts have proposed the use of alternative justice models to respond to IPV perpetration, particularly in communities where members fear or are alienated from the criminal justice system. One such alternative is restorative justice.

Restorative justice, broadly defined, involves the practice of informal conflict mediation (Ptacek, 2005). This rather simple definition masks a diverse array of programs and practices that de-emphasize punishment in favor of making amends to victims and reintegrating offenders into their communities (Hayden, 2016). These goals are pursued through meetings or "conferences" that typically include the victim; the offender; support people (often family members and friends) who serve as supporters for the victim and the offender, respectively; community members; and a facilitator. The meetings are essentially structured dialogues in which the victim, the victim's supporters, and community members can express the impact that the crime has had on them and on others, and to figure out a way for the offender to repair the harm done, including by apologizing and by making reparations of some kind (Goodman & Epstein, 2011). Restorative justice has been used primarily with juvenile offenders and has not been recommended—indeed, it is not permitted in some jurisdictions—for use in cases of violent crime, including IPV. Yet, an increasing number of feminist researchers, legal scholars, and practitioners have called for a closer examination of the use of restorative justice for at least some IPV cases (Curtis-Fawley & Daly, 2005; Pennell & Francis, 2005).

There has been very limited research on the use of restorative justice methods in IPV cases (Curtis-Fawley & Daly, 2005; S. Miller, 2011; Pennell & Francis, 2005). The most commonly voiced criticism of restorative justice with regard to IPV perpetration is that it downplays or completely ignores the power imbalances in abusive intimate relationships as well as the broader social and structural inequalities (e.g., gender inequality) that facilitate and perpetuate IPV (Goodman & Epstein, 2011). In fact, by bringing in the offender's supporters, the process may reinforce abusive behavior that may be integral to the support group's norms (D. Coker, 2002).

Other critics of restorative justice maintain that it largely serves as a way to divert offenders from the courts, jails, and prisons, but is still overseen by the criminal justice system (M. Kim, 2020; S. Miller, 2011). These critics press the need for more radical changes to IPV intervention and prevention (M. Kim, 2020). One alternative model is **transformative justice**, which challenges elements of the conventional approach to IPV intervention that emphasize individualized service delivery to victims and arrest, prosecution, and punishment (e.g., incarceration) of perpetrators. Transformative justice, in contrast, is a collective model that emphasizes **community accountability** in which community organizations replace professionalized services and state-based (especially criminal justice) interventions, and community members, including victims' and perpetrators' social networks, serve as both a support and an accountability system (M. Kim, 2020). Although there are few alternative, community-based, transformative justice interventions currently available in the United States, M. Kim (2020) conducted an implementation study of one, the Strengthening Social Network Approaches to Domestic Violence initiative. This initiative was developed and led by experienced domestic violence service providers, which increased its appeal to peer service providers. M. Kim (2020) reports that many participating providers were committed to increasing community engagement and accountability and reducing criminal justice involvement, but she also identified several obstacles to implementation, including lack of funding, overworked staff, and, perhaps most important, a strong, unanimous reluctance to engage with perpetrators.

It is unlikely that the controversy over the use of alternative justice models to respond to IPV perpetration will be resolved soon, particularly since there are no empirically rigorous evaluations to gauge the effectiveness of such programs. Goodman and Epstein (2011, p. 230) have called for the development of "a variety of carefully structured demonstration projects . . . as a potential complement to justice system remedies" (see also M. Kim, 2020; S. Miller, 2011). These demonstration projects would perhaps be most useful in socially and economically marginalized communities where negative attitudes toward the criminal justice system are widespread.

Batterer Intervention Programs

Like Victor in the opening case history, most individuals arrested for IPV, especially for the first time and on a misdemeanor charge, are not sentenced to jail or prison, but rather are mandated to attend a treatment program, usually called a **batterer intervention program (BIP)**. Although all states have BIPs, state standards are quite varied; some states require that the provider and the program content be certified by a state body, and other states simply offer guidelines on best practices (Bennett & Vincent, 2002; Tolman & Edleson, 2011). There is also tremendous variation across programs in terms of length of treatment. Programs vary from a weekend "retreat" to 52 weeks of 90- to 120-minute sessions, with the average program length being 26 weeks (Bent-Goodley, Rice, Williams, & Pope, 2011; Tolman & Edleson, 2011).

The content and therapeutic models also differ, although the majority of programs concentrate on challenging sexism and rigid gender norms, developing relational skills that are nonviolent and nonabusive, accepting responsibility for the abusive behavior, and identifying the social and emotional antecedents of the perpetrator's coercion and violence. Most of the work in BIPs is done in groups, although group sessions may be supplemented in some programs with individual counseling and therapy. The most popular therapeutic models combine didactic teaching with cognitive behavioral therapy or **motivational interviewing** (Roffman, Edleson, Neighbors, Mbilinyi, & Walker, 2008; Tolman & Edleson, 2011). Psychotherapy is less frequently used because it has been found to be relatively ineffective (L. Bancroft et al., 2012).

Arguably, the most pressing question with regard to BIPs is whether they "work." In other words, are they successful in changing abusers' attitudes about their intimate partners and relationships, and are they effective in reducing IPV recidivism? The answer is an unsatisfying one: sometimes. To date, there have been numerous evaluations of BIPs—more than 70 by one count (Tolman & Edleson, 2011)—and the findings, taken together, indicate that in general BIPs reduce or eliminate violence and abuse by men who complete them (L. Bancroft et al., 2012; Tolman & Edleson, 2011). The extent of this change, however, depends on the type of data collected and the length of follow-up after program completion. According to Tolman and Edleson (2011), the greatest positive change is detected when researchers compare program completers to noncompleters using police reports of re-arrest for a period of time (e.g., 6 months, 12 months). When victim reports are used instead, the success of the BIPs declines, but nonetheless remains positive (Babcock, Green, & Robie, 2004; Tolman & Edleson, 2011).

One of the most optimistic assessments of BIP success was reported by Gondolf (2002), who followed 840 male participants in BIPs in four cities, along with their partners, for four years. Gondolf found that four years after the baseline measure (i.e., start of the BIP), about 90 percent of the men had not re-assaulted their intimate partner.

Unfortunately, other studies provide less sanguine assessments. Klein and Tobin (2008), for example, followed 342 men over a 10-year period (1995–2005), examining arrests for IPV as well as any other crime. They found that within one year of their initial court arraignment (baseline for this study), only 32 percent had re-abused and 42 percent had been arrested for any crime. But as the follow-up period increased, so did the arrest rates, such that over the decade examined, 60 percent re-abused, and nearly 75 percent were re-arrested for a domestic abuse or non–domestic abuse offense. The researchers concluded, therefore, that "success" in the short term, regardless of the intervention (arrest, prosecution, probation, supervision, incarceration, or batterer treatment), does not predict long-term behavior change. It is important to remember that program content and approach vary, so it is difficult to compare "success" across programs. Tolman and Edleson (2011) point out that the available data do not allow us to determine which specific characteristics and components of BIPs produce the greatest positive change.

Considerable attention has been given to the need for programs to address additional components such as culture, gender and sexual orientation diversity, and comorbid problems such as substance abuse. Some have stressed the need for programs to be culturally competent and to address the unique concerns and experiences of men of color (Bent-Goodley et al., 2011). But research that has compared "color blind" programs with "culturally specific" and "culturally centered" programs has not demonstrated that one approach is any more effective than the other (Gondolf, 2007). Most BIPs are designed to respond to abuse by cisgender men against cisgender women; there are few programs specifically for gay men or lesbian women and none for transgender people. With regard to substance abuse, L. Bancroft and colleagues (2012) caution that because there is little evidence that substance use *causes* IPV perpetration, treatment for a substance use problem should not preclude simultaneous treatment for IPV. Recall the clinical observations noted previously that recovery from substance abuse sometimes increases abusive behavior due to the discomfort and stress caused by addiction treatment. Moreover, addiction recovery is not sufficient to ensure long-term reductions in abusive and violent behaviors; such an assumption could give the abused partner a dangerously false sense of safety. Perpetrators with a substance use problem need *both* substance abuse treatment *and* a BIP.

One strategy that does appear to increase positive outcomes from BIPs is to coordinate them with criminal justice responses. The way this works is to ensure that an offender begins BIP participation soon after arrest (e.g., in less than three weeks), is actively monitored by the court for treatment compliance (e.g., through periodic court appearances or check-ins), and experiences a swift and consequential response for any violations or noncompliance. Evaluations of such coordinated interventions suggest that they result in more consistent BIP attendance, reduced dropout rates, and lower IPV recidivism (Gondolf, 2004; Klein & Crowe, 2008; Sechrist & Weil, 2018).

Prevention Approaches Focused on IPV Perpetration

One limitation of BIPs is that they are purely reactive; a comprehensive response to ending IPV includes strategies to prevent it from occurring in the first place. In Chapter 7, we discussed several programs that have been developed for youth in middle school, high school, and college. These programs target youth because, as we noted previously, attitudes and behavior that support IPV are acquired through socialization, both at home and at school, and young people are at especially high risk of perpetration. The most popular school-based prevention programs include the Fourth R, Green Dot, Coaching Boys Into Men, Expect Respect, and the Youth Relationships Project (see Chapters 7 and 11).

Unfortunately, there is little research on the effectiveness of non-school-based programs in preventing IPV, although there are a number of such programs being implemented throughout the United States (Tolman & Edleson, 2011). Some of these programs target men who are at particularly high risk for IPV perpetration—for example, young, unemployed men who may have criminal histories and who are noncustodial fathers, new fathers, or fathers-to-be. Examples include the Responsible Fatherhood Program and Con Los Padres, both of which use weekly meetings to teach high-risk men about effective parenting and techniques for developing and maintaining healthy relationships (Tolman & Edleson, 2011).

Broader prevention programs that target the general population include media campaigns to raise awareness of IPV and the harm it causes, and pledge campaigns, which enlist men as allies in preventing IPV by asking them to publicly denounce violence against women and children, promote a more respectful culture, and share these messages with coworkers and others by distributing brochures and other resources in their workplaces, clubs, and other venues (Tolman & Edleson, 2011). The White Ribbon Campaign, which was founded in Canada in 1991 and has since spread to more than 60 countries throughout the world, is an example of a pledge campaign.

The White Ribbon Campaign was cited by the United Nations as a successful strategy for involving men in IPV prevention (Tolman & Edleson, 2011). At the same time, however, this and other programs target primarily cisgender men and overlook sexual minority populations. Moreover, while it is certainly the case that the White Ribbon Campaign, among others, has enlisted male allies worldwide in the fight against IPV specifically and violence against women more generally, there is no evaluative research that measures the success of these types of campaigns in actually reducing violence. Studies designed to gauge the effectiveness of general and targeted prevention strategies are badly needed.

CHAPTER SUMMARY

This chapter focused on IPV perpetration in adult relationships. We defined an IPV perpetrator or a batterer as a person who uses or threatens to use physical, sexual, or psychological abuse against a partner, which constitutes a pattern of coercive control. Yet we also noted that batterers often depict themselves as victims, rather than perpetrators, and they typically underestimate the frequency, severity, and harmful effects of their abuse.

Both men and women may perpetrate IPV, but claims of gender symmetry or parity in IPV perpetration are not supported by the majority of empirical studies. The evidence shows that men are significantly more likely to perpetrate IPV than women. Research also demonstrates gender differences in the types of IPV perpetrated and in the motivations for using force against an intimate partner.

We reviewed research on a variety of perpetration risk factors, which, in addition to sex, sexual orientation, and gender identity, include age, race and ethnicity, socioeconomic status, immigration status, psychological functioning, substance use, family of origin abuse, and attitudes and beliefs supportive of IPV. While most studies of risk factors have focused on individuals, more attention is now being given to community and structural risk factors, including patriarchal gender norms in the larger society and neighborhood characteristics that increase risk for residents.

Although historically the response to IPV perpetrators was weak at best, legal reforms during the 1980s and 1990s—for example, mandatory and preferred arrest policies, victimless prosecution, and no-drop prosecution—resulted in a significant increase in IPV arrests, prosecutions, and convictions. Today, the legal system is the standard formal response to IPV, although critics have raised concerns about problems such as dual arrests and disproportionately harsher treatment of minority men, leading some to call for the use of alternative interventions, such as restorative justice and transformative justice programs.

Most IPV perpetrators, we learned, are mandated to treatment in batterer intervention programs (BIPs), which vary in length, treatment approach, and curriculum. Evaluations of BIPs in terms of their effectiveness in reducing recidivism have shown short-term success, but the extent to which they produce genuine, long-term behavioral change is less clear. Research is also needed on targeted and more general IPV prevention programs, which to date remain largely unevaluated.

Recommended Resources

DeKeseredy, W. S., & Schwartz, M. D. (2013). *Male peer support and violence against women: The history and verification of a theory.* Boston, MA: Northeastern University Press.

Dobash, R. E., & Dobash, R. P. (2015). *When men murder women.* New York, NY: Oxford University Press.

Fleury-Steiner, R. E., Hefner, M. K., & Miller, S. L. (Eds.). (2020). *Civil court responses to intimate partner violence and abuse.* San Diego, CA: Cognella.

Nason-Clark, N., & Fisher-Townsend, B. (2015). *Men who batter.* New York, NY: Oxford University Press.

National Clearinghouse for the Defense of Battered Women. http://www.ncdbw.org

Ptacek, J. (Ed.). (2010). *Restorative justice and violence against women.* New York, NY: Oxford University Press.

INTIMATE ABUSE OF PEOPLE WITH DISABILITIES AND THE ELDERLY

INTIMATE ABUSE OF PEOPLE WITH DISABILITIES

Little attention has been given to intimate abuse of people with disabilities. Intimate violence researchers typically have neglected to purposely recruit people with disabilities, or have failed to ask study participants if they have specific disabilities, and then compare their experiences with those of people without disabilities. Disabilities researchers and service providers often do not ask about intimate violence, although they may ask about other types of abuse, such as mistreatment by physical therapists and health care providers. Until recently, studies of abuse of people with disabilities have focused almost exclusively on sexual abuse of people with developmental disabilities, especially children (Curry, Hassouneh-Phillips, & Johnston-Silverberg, 2001; see also Chapter 4). There is now empirical evidence, however, that people with disabilities are particularly vulnerable to intimate abuse. In this chapter, we will discuss what is currently known about intimate abuse of people with disabilities, but as we will see, there are still significant gaps in the knowledge base about this problem.

This chapter also examines intimate abuse of the elderly, which similarly remains understudied. Until recently, this problem was largely met with apathy, not only by the general public, but also by researchers and service providers (S. Jackson & Hafemeister, 2013). Although more attention is now being given to intimate abuse of the elderly, far less is known about this problem than violence and maltreatment in other intimate relationships. With the elderly population in the United States projected to nearly double over the next 30 years, it behooves us to understand elder intimate abuse and to develop effective prevention and intervention strategies (Ortman, Velkoff, & Hogan, 2014).

CASE HISTORY

JULIE'S DILEMMA

Julie was diagnosed with Becker muscular dystrophy (MD) when she was 15 years old. Becker MD progresses slowly, causing a gradual weakening of the muscles, especially in the thighs, hips, pelvis, and shoulders. For several years after her diagnosis, Julie's symptoms were fairly mild, although she would sometimes get severe muscle cramps during physical activities and her friends would often remark that she walked "funny," because she tended to walk on her toes.

Julie married her college sweetheart, Rick, shortly after their graduation and they both quickly found jobs in the same city, but they had to relocate away from family and longtime friends. Rick worked as an engineer for a construction company, and Julie taught social studies at a middle school. As the MD progressed and she found it harder to stand for long periods, Julie moved from the classroom to the school library, where she could spend most of her time seated, assisting students with computer searches and other online research.

By the age of 27, Julie was using a cane to help her maintain her balance and get around, but she began using a walker not long after her 32nd birthday. She relied on a fellow teacher to take her to and from work, but she also increasingly needed Rick's assistance at home with routine tasks, such as personal hygiene and getting dressed. Because Julie had always prided herself on being independent, her growing reliance on Rick was a blow to her self-esteem. She would struggle to take care of herself, but this sometimes resulted in Rick having to clean up after her or "come to her rescue" if she started a task and couldn't complete it. Rick grew more impatient with Julie, which, in turn, caused her to try even harder to do things on her own. They argued frequently, and Julie began to notice that when Rick was helping her, he was increasingly aloof or, worse, angry. He would sometimes be rough when he bathed her, helped her in and out of her clothes, or brushed her hair. During one particularly heated argument, Julie threatened to leave him, but Rick actually laughed at her, asking, "And how do you think you're going to do that? You can't walk. You certainly can't run. You can't even put your coat on without my help. And where are you going to go? Who else would ever do what I do for you? Look at yourself. You're a mess!" Rick's words hurt Julie deeply, but they also reinforced her sense of self-loathing and entrapment. She believed what Rick said: that no one else would want her and she was essentially dependent on him now for her survival. For better or for worse, Julie decided she would have to remain in what was becoming an increasingly abusive marriage.

Defining Intimate Abuse of People With Disabilities

In order to define intimate abuse of people with disabilities, we must first specify what we mean by **disability**. There is, however, a general lack of uniformity in how disability is defined across studies (J. Hahn, McCormick, Silverman, Robinson, & Koenen, 2014). For instance, some studies only include conditions that cause activity limitations, sensory limitations (e.g., sight, hearing), and physical limitations and exclude other physical conditions, such as arthritis, as well as mental health problems. Other studies use a much broader definition of disability and include any condition that causes difficulty in mobility, sensory perception, or cognition, along with mental health problems and conditions that prevent performance of everyday activities, such as work and personal care (J. Hahn et al., 2014).

Most researchers now adopt the standard specified by the Americans With Disabilities Act (ADA), which defines a disability as a physical or mental impairment that substantially limits a major activity of daily living. This definition further specifies types of disability: physical, psychiatric or mental, developmental, and sensory. **Physical disabilities** include any mobility limitations or illnesses that affect physical functioning. Julie's Becker MD is an example of this type of disability. **Psychiatric or mental disabilities** encompass all mental illnesses (e.g., schizophrenia, bipolar disorder). **Developmental disabilities** are physical and/ or mental conditions that manifest before age 22 (e.g., mental retardation, autism, cerebral palsy). Finally, **sensory disabilities** are those that affect sensory functions of hearing and sight (Ballan et al., 2014). It is important to keep in mind that these categories are not mutually exclusive; an individual may have multiple disabilities. Clearly, people with disabilities are not a homogeneous group.

People with disabilities, then, may experience all of the types of intimate abuse that we have discussed in other chapters: physical, sexual, or psychological abuse or threats of such abuse, perpetrated by an individual with whom they have an intimate relationship. They may also experience economic abuse and coercive control (see Chapter 8). But it is also important to point out that in addition to the types of intimate abuse typically examined by researchers, people with disabilities often experience **disability-related abuse**—that is, abuse specific to their particular limitation. For instance, a batterer may deliberately withhold medications, such as insulin injections that a person with diabetes needs to regulate blood sugar. Other examples of disability-related abuse include removing batteries from the wheelchair that a person with paralysis depends on for mobility, or rearranging furniture to deliberately cause a blind person to fall. Batterers may also treat partners with disabilities roughly or coldly when they assist with daily hygiene tasks, like Rick did with Julie in the case history. Or they may simply refuse to assist at all, or fail to take their partners with disabilities to doctor's appointments or medical treatments (Plummer & Findley, 2012; Shah, Tsitsou, & Woodin, 2016). In one study, participants with disabilities reported that their abusive partners exploited their disability in order to "punish" or control them. One person with diabetes, for instance, said that her partner would force-feed her sugar; another, who needed a wheelchair to get around, said that her partner would drive her to an isolated wooded area and leave her there without the wheelchair (Renzetti, 1992). These examples suggest that those who are abusive may actually tailor their abuse to the specific vulnerabilities of their partners.

Estimates of Intimate Abuse of People With Disabilities

Estimates of rates of intimate abuse of people with disabilities vary tremendously, depending on the source of the statistics and the definitions employed. Using the ADA definition, about 12.6 percent of the U.S. population has a disability, 12.7 percent of females and 12.5 percent of males (U.S. Census Bureau, 2018). Studies using the ADA definition of disability or some part of it (e.g., physical limitations) have found that both women and men with disabilities are at higher risk for intimate partner violence (IPV), particularly severe forms of physical abuse (e.g., being kicked, punched, or bitten), than women and men without disabilities (Ballan et al., 2014; Curry et al., 2001; Plummer & Findley, 2012). Although some researchers maintain that people with disabilities may be as much as 2–5 times more likely to be victimized, others have been critical of these estimates because most studies use small, convenience samples, usually of people with one type of disability, which are not representative of the population of people with disabilities (Bowen & Swift, 2019; J. Hahn et al., 2014).

There have been only a few studies that use large, population-based samples to examine the problem of intimate abuse against people with disabilities, although those that are available show smaller differences in risk between people with and without disabilities. For example, J. Hahn et al. (2014) analyzed two waves of data from the National Epidemiologic Survey on Alcohol and Related Conditions (NESARC; N = 34,563 adults). Some of their findings are shown in Table 10.1. They found that 4.4 percent of women with physical and mental health impairments reported past-year IPV victimization compared to 3 percent of women without impairments. More men than women in this study reported past-year IPV victimization, although similar to the findings of other IPV studies, women experienced more IPV that caused injuries serious enough to require medical attention. The differences in IPV rates between men with and without disabilities were not large: 4.9 percent of men with physical and mental health impairments and 3.6 percent of men without impairments reported IPV victimization in the past year.

Rates also vary by type of abuse and by characteristics of victims. In J. Hahn et al.'s (2014) study, for instance, women with physical and mental disabilities had higher rates of IPV than women without these disabilities, whereas men with only mental disabilities had higher rates of IPV than men without such disabilities (see also Ballan, Freyer, & Powledge, 2017; Mitra & Mouradian, 2014). Using data from the Massachusetts Behavioral Risk Factor Surveillance System (N = 25,756), Mitra, Mouradian, and McKenna (2011) found that women and men with disabilities were significantly more likely than women and men without disabilities to report past-year and lifetime sexual violence

TABLE 10.1 ■ Past-Year Rates of IPV Among Women and Men With Physical and Mental Health Disabilities		
IPV Victimization	Women (%)	Men (%)
Partner pushed, grabbed, or shoved you	3.9	4.3
Partner slapped, kicked, bit, or punched you	1.8	2.3
Partner threatened you with a weapon	0.4	0.6
Partner cut or bruised you	1.0	0.7
Partner forced sex from you	0.8	0.5
Partner injured you to the level that required medical care	6.3	0.2
Total IPV victimization	4.4	4.9

Source: Compiled from J. Hahn, McCormick, Silverman, Robinson, & Koenen, 2014.

victimization, although women with disabilities had the highest rates of past-year and lifetime sexual violence victimization compared with women without disabilities and men with and without disabilities. Similarly, Platt et al. (2015) report that in their study of 350 adults with developmental disabilities, both men and women reported high rates of abuse as adults: 63.7 percent and 68.2 percent, respectively. More women than men reported sexual abuse and IPV, but the gender differences in victimization rates were not large overall, leading Platt and her colleagues to conclude that abuse is a serious and widespread problem for both women and men with disabilities.

Risk Factors Associated With Intimate Abuse of People With Disabilities

The factors that put people with disabilities at risk of victimization are similar to the factors that put people without disabilities at risk (see Chapter 8), although these risk factors may be exacerbated by disability status. We noted, for example, that low income and poverty are risk factors for IPV victimization. Since the likelihood of being unemployed and living in persistent poverty is significantly greater for 21- to 64-year-olds with disabilities than it is for their peers without disabilities, their risk for IPV victimization is also greater (U.S. Census Bureau, 2018). Unfortunately, however, we have no data on whether risk for intimate abuse among people with disabilities varies across diverse racial and ethnic groups or among sexual minority groups.

The probability of developing a disability increases with age. For instance, 12.5 percent of people 35–64 years of age have a disability, 24.4 percent of people 65–74 years of age have a disability, and 47.5 percent of people 75 years of age and older have a disability. In contrast, only 6.4 percent of people 18–34 years old have a disability (U.S. Census Bureau, 2018). The likelihood of being victimized by intimate violence, however, is higher for younger women and men, with or without disabilities (J. Hahn et al., 2014). Nevertheless, as we will see later in this chapter, the elderly are not immune from intimate violence and abuse.

There are several risk factors that research shows to be more specific to people with disabilities (see Table 10.2). One risk factor that affects people with disabilities more than most other social groups is their increased exposure to multiple potential perpetrators. As for people without disabilities, the most common perpetrator of intimate abuse against someone with a disability is an intimate partner or a relative. But many people with disabilities must have frequent—sometimes, daily—contact with others responsible for their care, including **personal assistance services (PAS) providers**. Many people, when they think of PAS providers, think of formal paid professionals, but Saxton and her colleagues (2001) report that the majority of people with disabilities who live in their own homes in the community, rather than in group or nursing homes, rely mostly on informal PAS providers, including relatives, friends, and neighbors, or a combination of formal and informal providers.

TABLE 10.2 ■ Risk Factors Associated With Intimate Abuse of People With Disabilities	
Risk Factors Associated With the Victim	**Risk Factors Associated With the Perpetrator**
Greater likelihood of being unemployed and living in poverty	Desire for a partner who is easily dominated, controlled, and manipulated
Young age	Behaves in a patriarchal, dominating manner
Exposure to multiple potential perpetrators due to assistance needs	Engages in sexually proprietary behaviors
Social isolation	Stress from responsibilities associated with caring for a disabled person (but this factor has not received strong empirical support)
Dependency (physical, financial, emotional)	

Sources: References are representative rather than exhaustive: Brownridge, 2006; Martin et al., 2006; Nosek, Hughes, Taylor, & Taylor, 2006; Plummer & Findley, 2012; Powers, Curry, Oschwald, & Maley, 2002; Saxton et al., 2001.

The nature of the relationship between individuals with disabilities and their PAS providers is usually quite intimate, given that the PAS provider typically spends at least several hours a day with the individual with disabilities or may live in the individual's home, and is responsible for such tasks as feeding, toileting, and bathing. Although the majority of PAS providers may provide compassionate care, people, especially women, with disabilities report a high lifetime incidence of physical and sexual abuse by PAS providers (Powers, Curry, Oschwald, & Maley, 2002; Saxton et al., 2001). For instance, in one study of women with physical disabilities or with cognitive and physical disabilities, Saxton and her colleagues (2001) found that the abusive behavior these women experienced often involved personal boundary violations, such as unwanted or ambiguous sexual contact. These interactions were often subtle, making it difficult for the women to identify them as abusive, even though they typically made the women feel uncomfortable and vulnerable. Most common, however, was emotional abuse, including yelling and screaming, threats of abandonment or physical harm, and being ignored or neglected.

Researchers also report that perpetrators of intimate abuse against people with disabilities may deliberately seek out a partner with disabilities for an intimate relationship because they believe people with disabilities are easy to dominate, control, and manipulate (Martin et al., 2006; Shah et al., 2016). Brownridge (2006), in his study of risk factors for IPV among a large, nationally representative sample of women in Canada, found that one of the strongest predictors of increased risk of IPV victimization for women with disabilities was male partners who behaved, as Brownridge described, in a "patriarchal dominating manner" and engaged in sexually proprietary behaviors (p. 818). Many IPV victims with disabilities report that their partners exploited their physical or mental limitations to dominate and control them (Shah et al., 2016; K. Thomas, Joshi, Wittenberg, & McCloskey, 2008).

Another factor that increases victimization risk for people with disabilities is their greater likelihood of social isolation (Gilson, DePoy, & Cramer, 2001; Nosek, Hughes, Taylor, & Taylor, 2006). Individuals with a disability often have less mobility than their peers without disabilities, so they may have fewer opportunities to go out to meet and socialize with others. In addition, depending on their specific limitation, their ability to communicate with others may be hampered; they may not be able to use a phone or the internet to reduce isolation (Plummer & Findley, 2012). Isolation also inhibits their ability to get help for abuse, as we will see shortly.

Related to isolation is dependency. As we noted, people with disabilities need assistance; they depend on others—usually intimate partners, other relatives, and friends—to help them meet their daily needs, such as personal hygiene, administration of medications or treatments, transportation, meal preparation, and household chores. In addition to this physical dependency, individuals with disabilities may be financially dependent on their intimate partner or other relatives, and the social isolation they experience may increase their emotional dependency as well (Martin et al., 2006).

It has been hypothesized that the burden of caring for a partner or relative with disabilities causes stress in the primary caregiver, which in turn may cause abusive behavior on the caregiver's part (Petersilia, 2001). There is not a lot of empirical support for this hypothesis, however. Stress may occasionally cause anger or impatience in caregivers, as we saw with Rick in the opening case history, but it is unlikely to be at the root of persistent neglect and abuse of a person with disabilities (Brownridge, 2006). Dependency, though, does make it more difficult for people with disabilities who are abused to seek help (Plummer & Findley, 2012).

Consequences of Intimate Abuse of People With Disabilities

There has been little research on the consequences of intimate violence for victims with disabilities (Plummer & Findley, 2012). Available evidence indicates that victims with disabilities experience the same negative outcomes as victims without disabilities, but some researchers point out that abuse may worsen existing conditions for victims with disabilities—for example, through physical injuries or psychological distress, or by withholding or interfering with medications or treatment (Bonomi, Nichols, Kammes, & Green, 2018; C. Thomas et al., 2008). Victims with disabilities show elevated rates of depression, anxiety, and suicidal ideation (Hassouneh-Phillips, 2005; Mitra & Mouradian, 2014). However, researchers caution that without longitudinal studies, it is difficult to determine the extent to which the stress of living with a disability, especially in a society marked by **ableism** (prejudice and discrimination against people with disabilities in favor of the able-bodied), contributes to these negative health conditions and how much is the product of the abuse (Plummer & Findley, 2012). Longitudinal research would also help us distinguish situations in which people with disabilities are victimized by intimate violence and abuse from situations in which intimate violence and abuse cause disabilities (J. Hahn et al., 2014).

Interventions for Intimate Abuse of People With Disabilities

In Chapter 8, we noted that observers who have little or no understanding of the dynamics and constraints of abusive intimate relationships frequently assume that victims can quickly and easily leave their abusers and get effective help to address the abuse. We discussed the inaccuracy of this belief and its consequences for IPV victims. The isolation and dependency experienced by intimate violence victims who have disabilities make it even more difficult for them to terminate the relationship and to get help. Leaving the abuser, for example, presumes that the victim has other housing and care options available. However, a recent research review found that some domestic violence shelters and agencies still are not fully ADA compliant, and some lack access to various disability resources such as sign language interpreters (Plummer & Findley, 2012). Friends and relatives of the victim may lack the space, time, and knowledge to take on caregiving responsibilities, or the victim may resist "burdening" them in this way. Victims with disabilities may also be afraid that reporting the abuse or leaving the abuser will only increase their social isolation, given that their social networks may already be limited, and abusers may reinforce this vulnerability (Gilson et al., 2001; Hassouneh-Phillips, 2005). Recall from the opening case history what Rick said to Julie when she threatened to leave him. Moreover, people who were disabled at birth or during childhood are often taught from an early age to be compliant and agreeable, which may inhibit them from challenging the abuser, although the disability itself may make such a challenge practically impossible (Nosek et al., 2006).

Even when victims with disabilities report the abuse, they may receive unhelpful responses. We live in a society that devalues and marginalizes people with disabilities. As we noted earlier, this prejudice and discrimination against people with disabilities is called ableism. Ableism often intersects with sexism, producing negative responses to intimate violence victims with disabilities. There may be reluctance on the part of service providers and others to see men as victims (J. Hahn et al., 2014). Men with disabilities who are abused may not self-identify as victims because they share stereotypes about masculinity and are ashamed of their "weakness" (Mitra & Mouradian, 2014). Ballan and colleagues (2017) report that nearly 50 percent of the men with disabilities in their sample had contact with health care providers due to the abuse they had experienced, but only 15.8 percent of these men received a referral from the health care provider for IPV services.

Women with disabilities are frequently stereotyped as asexual or undesirable, which may contribute to the tendency of service providers to overlook the possibility that they may be victims of intimate violence, especially sexual abuse (Ballan et al., 2014; Mays, 2006). Perpetrators may also manipulate others into believing that victims' accusations of abuse are symptomatic of their disability: The victim is mentally ill or "imagines" things (Saxton et al., 2001). Relatives, friends, and service providers may even feel sorry for the perpetrator, perceiving the perpetrator as a trustworthy person who selflessly bears the burden of caring for an intimate partner or relative with disabilities (Plummer & Findley, 2012).

Researchers who study intimate violence against people with disabilities emphasize the acute need to improve service responses to this victim population. Box 10.1 discusses programs designed to increase safety-promotion behaviors among people with disabilities, but the responsibility for effectively preventing and responding to intimate violence against people with disabilities does not lie with victims. Consequently, researchers urge professionals who provide services to people with disabilities to universally screen their clients, including their male clients, for intimate abuse (Curry et al., 2009; Mitra & Mouradian, 2014). In addition, such professionals should receive training specifically on the dynamics of abusive intimate relationships, how to detect abuse, and how to communicate with women and men who are disabled about their experiences of abuse

BOX 10.1
PROMOTING SAFETY AMONG PEOPLE WITH DISABILITIES

There are currently a wide variety of programs available to raise awareness of the problems of sexual assault and IPV (see Chapters 7 and 8). Most of these programs, however, are designed for women and men without special needs and limitations. Researchers and practitioners concerned with intimate abuse of people with disabilities have argued for programs that address the unique concerns and safety issues faced by this population. For instance, because, as we have noted, people with disabilities may be socialized to be compliant, programs that increase assertiveness and safety self-efficacy would be particularly helpful. A recent review (Lund, 2011), however, found that there are few such programs available, and those that are available have not been properly evaluated to determine their effectiveness (see also Mikton, Maguire, & Shakespeare, 2014). An exception is **A Safety Awareness Program (ASAP)**, although this program has only been evaluated with regard to its effectiveness for women with disabilities (R. Hughes et al., 2010).

According to the program evaluators (Robinson-Whelen et al., 2014), the goals of ASAP for Women are to raise awareness and knowledge of intimate abuse, build safety skills, improve safety self-efficacy, and increase social support, which together should increase women's safety behavior and ultimately reduce victimization (although the latter has not yet been evaluated). Participants in the program attend eight 2½-hour classes that meet once per week. Classes incorporate both didactic and interactive methods to teach problem solving and action planning with regard to each of the goals. Each class also concludes with affirming messages and relaxation training. One of the most important elements of the program is that it is peer-led; women with disabilities who are staff members at **centers for independent living (CILs)** receive intensive training on the ASAP curriculum among other topics and subsequently lead the ASAP classes (Robinson-Whelen

et al., 2014). As we noted in Chapter 7, peer-led prevention and intervention programs appear to be more effective than programs led by authority figures or outside "experts" (Jaffe, Wolfe, Crooks, Hughes, & Baker, 2004).

Robinson-Whelen and her colleagues (2014) evaluated ASAP for Women using a randomized controlled trial, which, as noted in Chapter 2, is considered the "gold standard" in evaluation research design. Women with diverse disabilities were recruited to participate and were randomly assigned to either ASAP or usual care at a CIL. All participants completed measures to gauge abuse and safety knowledge, safety skills, safety self-efficacy, social networks, and safety-promoting behaviors at baseline, eight weeks (post-ASAP completion), and six months later (follow-up). The ASAP and control groups did not differ on baseline measures, but there were significant differences at eight weeks and follow-up. The women who completed ASAP scored higher on all protective measures at either eight weeks or follow-up or both, indicating that the program appears to be effective in achieving its goals. The researchers did note that the program appeared less effective for women with cognitive disabilities, but that their outcomes could perhaps be improved with supplemental classes that offer opportunities to practice and reinforce lessons learned.

ASAP shows promise as a prevention and intervention program to potentially reduce intimate violence victimization of women with disabilities. As Robinson-Whelen et al. (2014) point out, however, the program still needs to be evaluated with men with disabilities, whose needs and concerns may require revisions to the ASAP curriculum. In addition, while it is important to improve safety promotion among people with disabilities, we must also address the attitudes and behavior of perpetrators, who ultimately are responsible for the violence and abuse (see Chapter 9).

(Ballan et al., 2017; Ruiz-Perez, Pastor-Moreno, Escriba-Aguir, & Maroto-Navarro, 2018). Similarly, IPV and sexual assault victim service providers should receive training about the diverse needs and experiences of people with disabilities. In fact, researchers suggest that IPV and disabilities service providers be trained together—an approach referred to as cross-training—not only to improve their knowledge about each other's fields, but also to foster collaboration among agencies (Mitra & Mouradian, 2014; Ruiz-Perez et al., 2018). Given the unique needs of victims with disabilities, service providers face special challenges in these cases, such as locating accessible housing, obtaining appropriate adaptive equipment and assistive devices, and enlisting a PAS provider with specific training in working with trauma survivors (Ballan et al., 2014).

INTIMATE ABUSE OF THE ELDERLY

CASE HISTORY
MARJORIE BECOMES A PARENT AGAIN AT AGE 68

Marjorie has lived alone since her husband, Sam, passed away eight years ago from lung cancer. Marjorie and Sam had one child together: their daughter, Alice. As Marjorie describes her, Alice has always been "a handful." She dropped out of high school just before graduating and had her first child when she was 19 years old. By the time she was 30 years old, she had three more children and had been involved in a series of abusive relationships with the children's fathers. Alice also had a "drug problem" and had been arrested for possession of a controlled substance. She had been sentenced to probation and a drug treatment program, instead of being incarcerated, but not long after she completed probation and the treatment program, she was again "running with the wrong crowd." Last year, the police raided Alice's trailer after they received a tip from a neighbor who suspected Alice was "cooking meth." The police did find a meth lab in Alice's home; they arrested her and she was eventually convicted and sentenced to seven years in the state correctional facility. At that time, three of Alice's four

children were adults, but her youngest child, her son Luke, was just 15 years old. Luke went to live with his grandmother, Marjorie.

Marjorie realized that parenting a teenager at the age of 68 would be challenging, especially in light of her chronic health problems, including diabetes and osteoarthritis, but she hoped that by providing a home to Luke, her daughter could focus on finally getting her life together. Luke, however, quickly proved to be more of a "handful" than his mother had been at his age. He refused to obey Marjorie's rules, and he frequently yelled at her and called her names. One day Marjorie noticed that a ring and a bracelet were missing from the jewelry box in her bedroom. She suspected Luke had taken the jewelry, but when she asked him about it, he claimed he didn't know what she was talking about and suggested that she had probably just forgotten where she had put the items. She didn't think she had misplaced the jewelry, but she also knew she could be forgetful, so she decided to let the incident pass. A few weeks later, though, Marjorie caught Luke stealing money from a small purse she kept hidden in her closet. She told Luke to give her the money and to leave the room, but he taunted her, saying, "What are you going to do about it, old lady?" He then pushed her out of his way, causing Marjorie to fall, and because the osteoarthritis made her bones quite fragile, she broke her wrist and fractured several vertebrae.

Luke left the apartment, but Marjorie was able to call a neighbor for help. She was taken to the local emergency room, but when asked about the circumstances of the fall, she said simply that she had lost her balance. The doctor tending to her injuries didn't ask her any further questions, nor did Marjorie volunteer additional information. She reasoned that Luke hadn't meant to harm her. He was going through a tough time with his mother in prison, and his disrespectful behavior wasn't really his fault; her daughter had just never taught him to respect his elders. Marjorie couldn't imagine reporting Luke's behavior to the doctor or anyone else. After all, he was still her grandson.

Defining Intimate Abuse of the Elderly

Elder abuse is any maltreatment or neglect of a person aged 60 or older by a caregiver or another person in a trust relationship with the elder (Centers for Disease Control and Prevention [CDC], 2016a). This definition includes people in many roles who may be potential perpetrators: for example, nurses, physicians, home health aides, bankers, and lawyers. However, research shows that perpetrators are most often a family member—an intimate partner, an adult son or daughter, or, as we saw in the case history, a grandchild (Hildreth, Burke, & Glass, 2009; National Center on Elder Abuse, 1998). Consequently, most elder abuse incidents involve *intimate abuse* of an elderly person.

One definitional challenge in the field is disagreement over how to define "elder." Many people define an elder as someone aged 65 and older, but the CDC (2016a), whose definition we cited in the previous paragraph, maintains that the elderly population includes individuals as young as 60. Obviously, the age demarcation affects prevalence estimates; a broader age range means that more individuals will be included as potential victims. What "counts" as abuse also affects prevalence estimates (see Chapters 2 and 8).

Most researchers and practitioners agree that intimate abuse of the elderly includes physical abuse, sexual abuse or abusive sexual contact, psychological or emotional abuse, neglect, abandonment, and financial abuse or exploitation (CDC, 2016a), but the specific behaviors that should be included in each of these categories continue to be debated. Some behaviors—for example, demanding a kiss before fulfilling a request by an elderly person—may be playful and loving or manipulative and threatening depending on the context and meaning of the interaction to both parties and the motives of the actor. Certainly, even if such behavior elicited discomfort in recipients, they probably would not report it as "abuse," and if they did report it, authorities probably would not treat it seriously. Even reports of interactions that more closely conform to popular ideas of "abuse" may not be taken seriously or be investigated thoroughly, particularly if the accused appears more credible than the accuser or successfully exploits stereotypes of the elderly, such as the belief that most elderly people suffer from dementia (Nerenberg, 2006).

Despite the fact that individuals aged 65 and older constitute the fastest-growing segment of the U.S. population, as noted at the beginning of this chapter, intimate abuse of the elderly is arguably the most understudied form of intimate violence. Some researchers maintain that it is the most underreported and underprosecuted form of intimate violence as well (Caccamise & Mason, 2004; Meloy & Cunningham, 2018). There has been little academic, governmental, media, or public attention to the problem of intimate abuse of the elderly. The federal government began funding Adult Protective Services (APS) in the 1960s, but it was not until 1985 that all states had APS. By the close of the 1980s, most states had also enacted mandatory elder abuse reporting laws, and in 2010, Congress passed the Elder Justice Act, analogous to the Child Abuse Prevention and Treatment Act and Violence Against Women Act, but without any monetary appropriations to accompany the law (S. Jackson & Hafemeister, 2013; see Chapter 1). Rigorous empirical research on intimate abuse of the elderly has also lagged well behind research on child abuse, adolescent dating violence, and sexual assault and IPV among younger adults (Bows, 2018; S. Jackson & Hafemeister, 2013).

This apparent apathy toward the problem of intimate abuse of the elderly may be attributed at least in part to **ageism**—that is, negative prejudicial attitudes toward and discrimination against the elderly. In addition, there is no powerful interest group, professional organization, or social movement championing the cause and coalescing widespread support for calls to address it, as has occurred with many other forms of intimate violence (S. Jackson & Hafemeister, 2013; Leroux & Petrunik, 1990). As "baby boomers" age and the elderly population grows significantly, this situation could change dramatically. People aged 65 and older as a percentage of the total U.S. population grew from 12.4 percent in 2000 to 13.7 percent in 2012, and as Table 10.3 shows, this group is expected to exceed 20 percent by 2030 (Ortman et al., 2014). The current state of affairs, however, means that knowledge of intimate abuse of the elderly is limited, which in turn hinders prevention and intervention efforts.

Estimates of Intimate Abuse of the Elderly

The underreporting of intimate abuse of the elderly makes it difficult to estimate prevalence. These incidents are not likely to be reported for a variety of reasons, including, as we saw in the case history that opened this section of the chapter, lack of understanding of the abuse as a crime, especially if it is perpetrated by an intimate partner or a family

TABLE 10.3 ■ Percentage Distribution and Projections of the U.S. Population by Age, 2012–2050					
Age	**2012**	**2020**	**2030**	**2040**	**2050**
Under 18 years	23.5	22.8	22.4	21.7	21.5
18–64 years	62.8	60.4	57.3	57.3	57.6
65 years and over	13.7	16.8	20.3	21.0	20.9

Source: Ortman, Velkoff, & Hogan, 2014.

member, as well as emotional commitment to the perpetrator, shame, fear of retaliation, and physical or financial dependency on the perpetrator (Paranjape, Corbie-Smith, Thompson, & Kaslow, 2009; Zink, Regan, Jacobson, & Pabst, 2003).

Despite the difficulty of accurately measuring intimate violence against the elderly, several nationally representative studies have produced what may be considered "best estimates." The most comprehensive study of elder abuse to date is the National Elder Mistreatment Study, which was conducted in 2009 and included a nationally representative sample of 5,777 elderly respondents, aged 60–97 (Acierno et al., 2010). This study found that about 1 in 10 (11.4%) respondents had experienced physical, emotional, or sexual abuse or neglect in the year preceding the survey. Despite this disturbingly high rate, however, relatively few of these incidents were reported to police or other authorities: Approximately 31 percent of physical abuse incidents, 16 percent of sexual abuse incidents, and 7.9 percent of emotional abuse incidents were reported to authorities by respondents to this survey. Other studies show even lower reporting rates (see Bows & Westmarland, 2017; Pillemer & Finkelhor, 1988).

Risk Factors Associated With Intimate Abuse of the Elderly

Women are at greater risk of intimate elder abuse simply by virtue of having a longer average life expectancy than men; in 2018, there were 80 men aged 65 and older for every 100 women in this age group (U.S. Census Bureau, 2018). Although this ratio is expected to narrow over the next few decades as men's life expectancy improves, the current sex ratio means that there are more potential elderly female victims of intimate violence than male elderly victims.

Women are at greater risk of all types of elder abuse, but they are especially vulnerable to sexual abuse (Bows, 2018; Meloy & Cunningham, 2018). Unfortunately, however, our understanding of sexual abuse of the elderly is limited by the fact that few studies specifically examine this problem (Bows, 2018; A. Burgess, 2006), and stereotypes of elders' sexuality (e.g., elderly women are asexual; elderly men are hypersexual "dirty old men") also appear to impede successful prosecution of such cases (Hodell et al., 2009).

Apart from gender, one of the strongest risk factors for intimate abuse of the elderly is low social support concomitant with high social isolation. The National Elder Mistreatment Study, for example, showed that low social support more than tripled the likelihood respondents indicated any type of abuse had been perpetrated against them in the year prior to the survey (Acierno et al., 2010). Interestingly, even among elderly individuals living in group settings (e.g., assisted-living facilities, nursing homes), low social support and high social isolation increase abuse risk; residents who have few or no regular visitors are more likely to experience abuse (Bachman & Meloy, 2008). This may be due to the fact that isolated elders with low social support have fewer concerned others monitoring their safety and in whom they can confide should abuse occur. As Acierno et al. point out, however, it is likely that low social support accompanied by high social isolation not only puts the elderly at risk of victimization, but also is probably an *outcome* of victimization. Bows (2018), in fact, notes that elderly victims of sexual violence often withdraw from social networks following victimization.

Importantly, physical and financial dependence on others are risk factors for *all* forms of intimate abuse against the elderly, not simply financial abuse and exploitation (Meloy & Cunningham, 2018). It is also the case, however, that the financial dependence of other adults (e.g., adult sons and daughters) on the elderly individual is a risk factor for all types of abuse (Paranjape et al., 2009). Other perpetrator risk characteristics include substance use and mental health problems (Nadien, 2006). Some researchers have also hypothesized that elder abuse may be the result of the perpetrator's experience of abuse as a child. Paranjape and her colleagues (2009) report that this hypothesis has not received empirical support.

There is also limited empirical support for the popular idea that **cognitive functional impairment**—that is, partial or complete loss of significant cognitive abilities, such as decision making, facial recognition, and memory—increases risk of elder abuse, at least among the elderly who do not live in institutions. For instance, in the National Elder Mistreatment Study, cognitive functional impairment was associated with verbal and financial abuse, but not with other forms of abuse (Acierno et al., 2010). Among the institutionalized elderly, however, cognitive functional impairment appears to increase risk of abuse, particularly if there is a small number of skilled staff relative to the number of residents needing substantial care and attention (Bachman & Meloy, 2008).

Consequences of Intimate Abuse of Elderly Victims

As we have noted, the majority of perpetrators of elder abuse are family members, most of whom—76 percent in cases of physical abuse—are intimate partners (National Center on Elder Abuse, 1998). Moreover, as is the case with sexual abuse generally, elders are more likely to be sexually assaulted by someone they know than by a stranger; in one study, 40 percent of sexual abuse perpetrators were intimate partners and 40 percent were acquaintances of the victim (National Center on Elder Abuse, 1998; see also Bows, 2018; Paranjape et al., 2009). Consequently, as previously mentioned, elderly victims frequently do not report their abuse. As a result, perpetrators of intimate abuse against the elderly are unlikely to be held accountable for their behavior or experience any negative consequences because of it.

In contrast, elderly victims of intimate abuse and violence may experience numerous negative consequences. For instance, given that many elderly people already experience significant health problems and may be physically frail, it is not surprising that they are at greater risk of severe injury and death as a result of abuse (Dong et al., 2009; Hackenberg, Sallinen, Koljonen, & Handolin, 2017; Mouton, 2003). In addition, elderly victims of abuse experience high rates of depression and other mental health problems (Dyer, Pavlik, Murphy, & Hyman, 2000). Elderly sexual abuse victims, in particular, experience severe psychological trauma with symptoms that include flashbacks and nightmares, anxiety, and fear, but they may also suffer more serious physical injuries than younger sexual assault victims, as research indicates that perpetrators may be especially brutal toward elderly victims and use far greater physical force than is necessary to subdue and restrain them (Bows, 2018; Jeary, 2005). Bows (2018) reported that the physical and emotional effects of sexual victimization on elderly adults lead them to curtail their lifestyles, disengage from social networks, and use negative coping strategies.

Intervention and Prevention of Intimate Abuse of the Elderly

Despite the serious negative outcomes of victimization experienced by the elderly, there are few specialized services for this victim population, and official responses remain woefully inadequate. As we noted previously, the federal government began funding Adult Protective Services in the 1960s, but it was not until 1985 that all states had APS. By the close of the 1980s, most states had also enacted mandatory elder abuse reporting laws, although there is tremendous variation in reporting systems throughout the United States (Nerenberg, 2006).

APS is typically the agency to which suspected elder abuse cases are initially reported. Although reports to APS have increased significantly since the late 1990s, it is unclear whether this is the result of more incidents of elder abuse or simply an artifact of greater awareness of the problem and mandatory reporting laws (Teaster, Lawrence, & Cecil, 2007). What is more certain, however, is that the increase in reports has led to a sharp rise in APS caseloads that has not been matched with additional funding. Some cases—for example, sexual assault, poisoning, and complex forms of financial abuse and fraud—require extensive investigations by individuals with specialized skills and knowledge, which most APS workers simply do not have

(Nerenberg, 2006). Further complicating the work of APS is the fact that reporting requirements, abuse definitions, service eligibility requirements for victims, and how cases are assessed, prioritized, and responded to vary across the United States and even within individual states, which makes it difficult for each APS agency to determine service demands and staffing needs (Nerenberg, 2006).

When intimate elder abuse cases are brought to the attention of the criminal justice system, an aggressive investigation is unlikely, and relatively few cases are actually prosecuted (Hodell et al., 2009; Nerenberg, 2006). To some extent, this is due to the fact that elderly victims, as illustrated in the case history, often do not want to identify, let alone prosecute, their abusers. In addition, the stress of a criminal trial, including facing their abuser in court and revisiting the trauma of the abuse in order to testify for the prosecution, could pose a health risk to a frail or already sick elder. Nerenberg (2006) notes that some jurisdictions have established programs to improve elderly victims' access to court and to improve police officers' and prosecutors' understanding of the unique needs and challenges of this population. These programs, however, are still not widely available throughout the United States.

Health care providers are one professional group that is most likely to come into contact with elders who are abused, since older women and men are more likely to have health conditions that require them to see health care providers more often than younger people, and also because when they are abused, they may suffer injuries that require medical attention. For instance, in a recent study of victims of severe IPV presenting for treatment at one hospital, 17 percent (n = 5) were aged 65 or older; two of these elderly patients had the highest injury severity score in the entire study sample (n = 29; Hackenberg et al., 2017). Yet, in a systematic review of screening tools for IPV, elder abuse, and abuse of vulnerable adults, Feltner and colleagues (2018) found only one screening tool for elder abuse, but the study assessing it rated it as poor in terms of its accuracy in detecting physical or verbal abuse.

We noted earlier in the chapter that public recognition of the problem of intimate elder abuse is generally lacking (S. Jackson & Hafemeister, 2013; Nerenberg, 2006). Media campaigns are being used to increase public awareness of the problem, and the National Center on Elder Abuse (NCEA) has been leading this effort. Table 10.4 provides an example of an NCEA public education tool: a list of elder abuse warning signs for which the public can watch.

Home visitation programs for the elderly, in which caseworkers regularly check in on elders who are still living in their own homes, have shown some promising results in terms of identifying and intervening in potential intimate elder abuse cases (Davis, Medina, & Avitabile, 2001). Programs to increase elders' social networks are also needed, in light of empirical evidence showing that low social support and high social isolation combine as a significant risk factor for all types of elder abuse

TABLE 10.4 ■ Warning Signs of Elder Abuse or Neglect

- Presence of a "new best friend" who is willing to care for the elder for little or no cost
- Recent changes in banking or spending patterns
- The older person is isolated from friends and family
- The elder's caregiver has problems with drugs, alcohol, anger, and/or emotional instability
- The caregiver is financially dependent on the elder
- The family pet seems neglected or abused
- There is an abundance of mail and/or phone solicitations for money
- The elder seems afraid of the caregiver
- The elder has unexplained bruises, cuts, or other injuries
- The elder has "bed sores" (i.e., pressure sores from lying in one position for too long)
- The elder appears dirty, undernourished, dehydrated, or over- or undermedicated, or is not receiving care for problems with eyesight, hearing, dental issues, or incontinence

If you suspect an elder is at risk of abuse or neglect, call your local Adult Protective Services center or Office on Aging. You can find the numbers for your state at https://ncea.acl.gov/Resources/State.aspx.

Source: National Center on Elder Abuse (n.d.). Retrieved from https://ncea.acl.gov/resources/docs/Home-for-Holidays.pdf.

(Aday, Kehoe, & Farney, 2006; Teaster, Roberto, & Dugar, 2006). Programs for elders, like programs addressing other types of intimate abuse, should be culturally competent, since the status of the elderly varies across cultures as do prescriptions regarding family members' privileges and obligations and the meanings of abuse (Nerenberg, 2006). And all programs should be rigorously evaluated. Partnerships between researchers and service providers will facilitate program evaluation (S. Jackson & Hafemeister, 2013), but service providers also need training and practice experience specifically focusing on responding to and supporting older survivors of sexual and intimate partner violence, since research shows that such training and experience are currently limited (Bows, 2018; Brossoie & Roberto, 2016).

Although more attention is finally being given to intimate abuse of the elderly, it remains an understudied and poorly understood social problem. More research is needed to improve knowledge of the frequency and severity of intimate abuse of the elderly, risk factors for victimization and perpetration, consequences for victims and perpetrators, and improved responses and prevention strategies. Understanding how experiences differ across diverse social groups of elders is also critically important, given that research with younger people shows that prevalence, risk, consequences, help-seeking, and effective prevention strategies are not identical for all groups (see Chapters 7 and 8). This research is especially urgent given the projected growth in the elderly population over the next 30 years. The National Institute of Justice currently funds the **Elder Mistreatment Research Program**, which is supporting research on such topics as the collection and evaluation of forensic evidence of elder physical and sexual abuse (S. Jackson & Hafemeister, 2013). The Bureau of Justice Statistics is also developing a data collection instrument designed to improve the analysis of the frequency, severity, and risk factors for elder abuse (Office of Justice Programs, 2011). Such initiatives give us reason to be optimistic that our knowledge and responses to intimate abuse of the elderly will significantly improve in the near future.

CHAPTER SUMMARY

In this chapter, we discussed intimate violence and abuse against two understudied and underserved groups, people with disabilities and the elderly. We noted that one challenge in studying intimate abuse of people with disabilities is inconsistent definitions of the term *disability*. A disability is a physical or mental impairment that substantially limits a major activity of daily living. In addition to physical and mental impairments, disabilities may be developmental or sensory.

People with disabilities may experience all of the types of abuse we have discussed throughout this book, but they also often experience disability-related abuse, which is abuse specific to their particular limitation. Accurate estimates of intimate abuse of people with disabilities are difficult to calculate because most studies use small, nonrandom, nonrepresentative samples. Nevertheless, the best data available indicate that both men and women with disabilities are at elevated risk of intimate violence victimization.

Risk factors for intimate abuse of people with disabilities are similar to the risk factors for people without disabilities—for example, low income, unemployment, and poverty. Additional victimization risk factors that we examined include increased exposure to multiple potential perpetrators, greater social isolation, low social support, and dependency. Perpetrator risk factors include a desire to dominate one's partner and sexual proprietariness.

Although there has been relatively little research on the consequences of intimate abuse for victims with disabilities, available data show the potential for worsening existing conditions and elevated rates of depression, anxiety, and suicidal ideation. We learned that despite these serious outcomes, however, interventions for victims with disabilities are limited, and to some extent this is because of widespread ableism in our society. More programs are needed to meet the unique service needs of this population and to increase their safety-promotion behaviors.

In this chapter, we also examined the problem of intimate abuse of the elderly, which we learned is arguably the most understudied form of intimate abuse. Elder abuse is any maltreatment or neglect of a person aged 60 or older by a caregiver or another person in a trust relationship with the elder, but most perpetrators are family members. One of the reasons intimate abuse of the elderly has not been extensively studied is societal ageism (i.e., negative prejudicial attitudes toward and discrimination against the elderly).

Intimate abuse of the elderly is difficult to estimate at least in part because victims often do not report it for a variety of reasons. Risk factors for elder intimate abuse victimization include being female, low social support, high social isolation, and physical and financial dependence on others. Perpetrator risk factors include financial dependence on the elderly victim, substance use, and mental health problems.

Elderly victims of intimate abuse experience numerous negative consequences, including high rates of depression and other mental health problems, severe injury, and even death. Their abusers, however, may not experience any consequences because the abuse goes largely unreported.

The most common intervention in elder intimate abuse is an investigation by APS. However, we noted that underfunding and inconsistencies across states and jurisdictions hamper these efforts. Law enforcement and prosecutors do not consider elder intimate abuse cases a high priority, so arrest and prosecution rates are low, but many elderly victims also do not wish to prosecute their abusers. More public awareness campaigns, home visitation programs, and programs to increase elders' social networks are needed, but these programs must be rigorously evaluated to determine their success in reducing intimate abuse of the elderly.

Recommended Resources

Anetzberger, G. (2004). *The clinical management of elder abuse*. New York, NY: Hawthorne.

Centers for Disease Control and Prevention. (2016). *Elder abuse surveillance: Uniform definitions and recommended core data elements*. Atlanta, GA: Author.

Centers for Disease Control and Prevention. (n.d.). *Victimization of persons with traumatic brain injury or other disabilities: A fact sheet for professionals*. Available at http://www.cdc.gov/traumaticbraininjury/pdf/VictimizationTBI_Fact%20Sheet4Pros-a.pdf

Chenoweth, L., & Cook, S. (Guest Eds.). (2001). Special issue: Violence against women with disabilities. *Violence Against Women, 7*(4).

Hughes, C. (2003). *Stop the violence, break the silence: A training guide—Building bridges between domestic violence and sexual assault agencies, disability services agencies, people with disabilities, families and caregivers*. Austin, TX: Disability Services ASAP of SafePlace.

National Clearinghouse on Abuse in Later Life. www.ncall.us

11

SOCIETAL RESPONSES TO VIOLENCE AND MALTREATMENT IN INTIMATE RELATIONSHIPS

Some Concluding Thoughts

I f we imagine ourselves sitting in a coffee shop a century ago discussing "social problems," it is not likely we would have been discussing many of the topics addressed in this book. The hitting of children? Unwanted touches? Marital rape? Husbands hitting wives? Men having sex with underage girls? These social problems did not even exist a century ago. The behaviors obviously occurred back then, though. In fact, we have every reason to assume they occurred then more commonly than now. But they were yet to be "discovered." They were not viewed as *social problems*.

Today, however, our coffee shop discussion would be very different. Violence and maltreatment in intimate relationships (VMIR), as a social problem, has clearly arrived.

Given the current status of VMIR as a well-recognized social problem, it seems fitting for this concluding chapter to include our reflections on the current state of VMIR as a social problem, our views about how we see the field moving forward, and our suggestions about how you, the reader, can help to alleviate the problem.

Throughout this book we have tried to approach our subject matter as empirical social scientists, and have avoided openly engaging in claims making. Although undoubtedly we have not always succeeded (passions are often hard to hide), our intent has been to remain relatively dispassionate in our discussion of the social *science* relating to VMIR. The tone of this final chapter, however, is decidedly different. We plan to sprinkle some passion into the discussion, and we also plan to actually offer our insights about how to alleviate the problem. Indeed, in this chapter we intend to engage in a little claims making ourselves.

VMIR RATES ARE DECLINING!

When we discuss social problems, it is easy to assume that social problems are *always* getting worse. It makes sense that this might be our perception because claims makers, in an attempt to draw attention and concern, often employ alarmist language, make dire predictions, and call for immediate action (Best, 2001). But it is important to remember that social problems are not always "getting worse." For almost all of the forms of VMIR discussed in this text, in fact, it seems reasonable to conclude that things are getting better! Think of it this way. Awareness about VMIR is closely connected to the rising status of children and women. Child abuse could not be recognized as a social problem until childhood was discovered. Intimate partner violence (IPV), sexual assault, and marital rape could not be discovered until gender equality became an expectation.

The #MeToo movement provides a perfect illustration. The movement began in the fall of 2017, in the days following a *New York Times* article alleging that famed movie producer Harvey Weinstein had sexually exploited women (Kantor & Twohey, 2017). Almost overnight, many women, some of whom were themselves quite accomplished and powerful (for example, actresses Ashley Judd, Gwyneth Paltrow, and Uma Thurman, to name but a few), suddenly felt empowered to tell stories they had mostly kept to themselves for years. What had been "normal" (men exploiting positions of power for sex) suddenly became a national conversation.

As the #MeToo movement rapidly evolved, we found ourselves rethinking history, even very modern history. President Bill Clinton, for example, was impeached by the U.S. House of Representatives in 1998 for perjury and obstruction of justice. He had lied about his sexual relationship with Monica Lewinsky. What was ignored, unmentioned, and clearly unimportant (at least at the time) was the fact that the sexual encounter he lied about had occurred with a workplace subordinate—a violation, we might reasonably assume, that would have most certainly led to his removal from office in the #MeToo era.

In the aftermath of the tragic helicopter crash that claimed the life of Kobe Bryant and eight others in January 2020, some writers felt it important to mention, if only in passing, that Bryant had been charged with sexual assault in 2003. One week before the trial was scheduled to begin, Bryant and his accuser agreed to a financial settlement, with the added condition that he make a public apology: "After months of reviewing discovery, listening to her attorney, and even her testimony in person, I now understand how she feels that she did not consent to this encounter" (J. Henson, 2020). Would Bryant have survived an admission of a nonconsensual sexual encounter in today's #MeToo era?

One final example of rapid change is Jeffrey Epstein, the convicted sex offender who is alleged to have committed suicide in his jail cell in 2019. We now know that Epstein had been engaging in sexual activities with underage girls for many years. Seemingly, his close associates knew, but nobody cared. In 2018, during the quickly evolving #MeToo movement, Epstein's history of sexual abuse began to attract national attention. His 2008 conviction for teenage prostitution, in particular, was scrutinized (J. Brown, 2018). Prosecutors had agreed to reduce the underage sex charges to felony prostitution charges, which effectively minimized the victimization status of the teenage girls who had been abused. Why? Epstein's conviction would typically have resulted in a trip to state prison. Instead, he spent most of his 18-month sentence in some form of work release or house arrest. Why? The short answer, of course, is that he had the power and resources to avoid the most serious consequences. But just a few years later, in the shadow of the #MeToo movement, Epstein's status and power were suddenly irrelevant. He died, alone, in a New York City jail cell.

The point is that the #MeToo movement radically altered the social landscape. And, importantly, the responses to other topics discussed in this text, while perhaps not as dramatic and sudden as the #MeToo movement, have also changed radically. Today, children have greater legal status, and are offered more legal protection, than at any time in human history. Consider the United Nations Convention on the Rights of the Child (UNCRC). It is a stunning document. Suddenly, the world community formally recognized the human rights of children, including their right to be loved, protected, cared for, and *not* hit. Women, likewise, have more status and are offered more legal protections than at any time in human history. Consider the Declaration of Rights and Sentiments (1848). It, too, is a stunning document: "We hold these truths to be self-evident: that all men *and women* are created equal!"

Our point is that change has been dramatic. Things *are* better. But can we observe these changes in VMIR rates? Do we have empirical data that VMIR is declining?

Consider child maltreatment. Are child maltreatment rates declining? The number of child abuse incidents *reported* to Child Protective Services (CPS), called "referrals," have steadily increased over the last 25 years. In 2018, there were 4.2 million child maltreatment referrals to CPS, a 5 percent increase from the year before. This increase is consistent with trends over the past few decades (U.S. Department of Health and Human Services, 2020). But, of course, rising reports tell us very little. Public awareness has risen, definitions have become more inclusive, and mandatory reporting laws have been strengthened. Of course reports have risen.

As we piece together the very complicated puzzle of victimization rates, we do indeed find some evidence of decline in maltreatment. For example, from 1990 to 2013, the rate of substantiated child neglect declined by 13 percent, the rate of substantiated physical abuse declined by 55 percent, and the rate of child sexual abuse (CSA) declined by 64 percent (Finkelhor, Saito, & Jones, 2016). Self-report surveys, while limited, also suggest declines. Keep in mind that the ideal way to study trends would be with self-report surveys that define and measure VMIR over time using *the exact same questions*. The 1975 National Family Violence Survey and the 1985 National Family Violence Resurvey did exactly this; both measured VMIR with the Conflict Tactics Scales. Gelles and Straus (1988) have written that they did not anticipate any changes in rates of VMIR over the 10 years that separated the two studies. What they found, however, was that rates of self-reported child physical abuse (CPA) and marital violence *declined* significantly during the 10-year period.

The National Survey of Children's Exposure to Violence (NatSCEV), another self-report survey, is a victim survey that has been conducted 3 times (2003, 2008, and 2011). The survey instrument used in the NatSCEV, the Juvenile Victimization Questionnaire, estimates *polyvictimization*, and many of the variables relate specifically to our focus on VMIR. Results from this survey suggest that child maltreatment within the family, sexual victimization of children, dating violence, and bullying have all decreased (Finkelhor, Shattuck, Turner, & Hamby, 2014a).

The National Crime Victimization Survey (NCVS) also provides trend data (specifically for IPV). The NCVS defines *intimate* as a current or former spouse, boyfriend, or girlfriend, and defines *violence* as rape or sexual assault, robbery, aggravated assault, or simple assault. From 1996 to 2011, IPV declined by over 60 percent for both males and females (Catalano, 2012). NCVS data suggest that crimes against the elderly have also declined (Morgan & Mason, 2014).

Finally, according to the National Incidence Study (NIS), which is a survey of mandated reporters and sits between official and self-report statistics, the overall rate of CPA declined for the 12-year period between the NIS-3 and the NIS-4 by 29 percent. NIS data also show declines in CSA (Sedlak et al., 2010). The only exception to this downward trend is child psychological maltreatment, which the NIS data suggest has increased in recent years. Of course, this is the most recently recognized form of child maltreatment, so it would stand to reason that mandated professionals have submitted more reports in recent years (Sedlak et al., 2010).

Several factors lead us to conclude that the declines are real (Finkelhor et al., 2014a; L. Jones, Finkelhor, & Halter, 2012; Sedlak et al., 2010). First, the declines appear in both self-report studies and official statistics. Second, declines have occurred broadly across a variety of violence and maltreatment subtypes. Third, a variety of other child welfare indicators, including suicide, juvenile delinquency, running away, and teen pregnancy, have also declined (Finkelhor, Turner, Ormrod, & Hamby, 2010).

The reader might recall that we began this book with a claim: Women, children, and the elderly are more likely to be victimized in their own homes than they are on the streets of America's most dangerous cities. In the wake of the COVID-19 pandemic, this statement took on even greater relevance. Stay-at-home orders are difficult enough for relatively harmonious families. But for families where maltreatment and violence are common, it was feared that COVID-19 would, almost certainly, lead to an increase in VMIR.

Several factors are driving concern about VMIR and the COVID-19 pandemic. First, as we learned in earlier chapters, family strain and stress, including financial strain, are correlated with VMIR. The uncertainty and stress of the pandemic itself, coupled with the unemployment and financial worries many have experienced, is a troubling reality. Second, in families where VMIR is not uncommon, being trapped at home reduces access to resources and social support systems that could potentially mitigate increased tension in the home. Perhaps even more importantly, being stuck at home increases contact time. A violent father and husband, who spends much of his week at work, and spends a lot of time drinking with his buddies in the local bar, is now stuck at home 24/7. His wife and children are also home 24/7. We can only assume that in troubled families already prone to maltreatment, COVID-19 puts the vulnerable at increased risk (Campbell, 2020).

Research from past traumatic events and natural disasters, including Mt. Saint Helens in Washington State (P. Adams & Adams, 1984) and Hurricane Katrina in New Orleans (Serrata & Hurtado, 2019), found an increase in IPV in the months following these disasters. In the early stages of the COVID-19 pandemic, furthermore, several countries were indeed observing increases in reports of IPV (Campbell, 2020). And while reports of child abuse actually declined in the United States during the early stages of the pandemic, experts speculated that with schools and other community organizations closed, child abuse had merely become more invisible (Campbell, 2020). While conclusive research on the impact of COVID-19 on violence and maltreatment inside the home will have to wait, there is every reason to believe that the pandemic will be a difficult time for vulnerable family members.

WHAT DO WE VALUE?

Do we commit enough resources to prevention and intervention? This is a very complicated question, and we are in no position to fully address it in this concluding chapter. We do, however, have some observations.

Keep in mind that prevention and intervention occur at the local level. The federal government can pass laws and can provide funding to states, but it does not provide direct services. In the end, prevention and intervention most typically occur at the county level. If you need to report a case of suspected child or elder abuse, you do so by contacting the local Department of Social Services. Because social services are so decentralized, it is difficult to generalize about "the system." Some counties are very good, and some counties are not. Some counties commit tremendous resources to prevention and intervention, and some do not.

But sometimes it does feel like "the system" is undervalued, underfunded, and broken. Too often, it seems, victims fall through the cracks. Tight budgets and high caseloads are not the only reason why victims sometimes fall through the cracks. In the most tragic and most highly publicized cases, in fact, caseworker error is the most immediate reason for the system's failure (R. Jones & Kaufman, 2003). At the same time, however, there are instances when the financial neglect of the social services system is difficult to ignore. In 2003, in the aftermath of several highly publicized child abuse deaths, the *New York Times* reported that the caseworker assigned to 2-year-old victim Alfredo Montez had a caseload of 50 children and made an annual salary of only $28,000. In New Jersey, the caseworker assigned to 7-year-old Faheem Williams, who starved to death after being locked in a basement by his parents, had juggled as many as 100 cases at one time during her career. Current and former caseworkers in the New Jersey office where she worked complained that they were under tremendous pressure to close investigations and reduce caseloads (L. Kaufman & Kocieniewski, 2003). The Williams case was so dramatic, and so traumatic, that it was still being discussed in New Jersey years later (Mabrey, 2014). Despite highly publicized cases like this, as noted in Chapter 5, the challenges to the child welfare system continue today (e.g., Bloom, 2019).

The problem, of course, is that there are not enough big hearts to go around, and even those with big hearts who set out to help can grow disillusioned with the social service and legal systems, overwhelmed by the human tragedy they see, and burn out (Child Welfare Information Gateway, 2016a). We see this dilemma in our students all the time. Their hearts tell them that they want to make a difference in the world, but given the reality of workload, stress, and dealing with tragedy, combined with low salaries and low prestige, it is difficult for them to commit to working in social services. Who can blame them? After all, they have student loans to repay, families to raise, and homes to purchase.

A search of PayScale.com, an online compensation information company, helps illustrate the problem of insufficient resources. An entry-level "social services case manager" (a career category option on the website) with a bachelor's degree in social work from the University of Southern California (USC) earned approximately $43,000 per year in Los Angeles in 2020. With 20 years of experience and a master's degree in social work from USC, the estimated salary would be $48,000. (Keep in mind, of course, that the cost of living is quite high in Los Angeles, and salaries tend to be higher than they would be in other parts of the country.) For comparative purposes, we searched PayScale.com for firefighters. A Los Angeles firefighter with the same education (bachelor's degree in social work from USC) and no other specialized training earned approximately $57,000 in 2020. Twenty years of experience bumped the salary to $90,000.

Firefighters are very important, of course, and it is not our intent to devalue what they do. But social services workers are also very important, and the fact that salaries in the social services system generally fall below salaries for nurses, public school teachers, police, and firefighters surely says something about what we do, and do not, value in society.

Lower social worker salaries, high caseloads, and high career turnover rates have received considerable media attention in recent years. In interviews, child welfare workers describe a job that is highly stressful and rarely rewarding (e.g., Galofaro, 2015):

> "How do you ever stop thinking about those kids? I wasn't able to sleep. It was so consuming." (Sara Barth, explaining why she quit)

> "It's not a glamorous job. It's a job where you don't deal in a lot of positives. It takes a special person to do child welfare." (Bruce Lender, describing his difficult work)

> "I was taking chances with children's lives, and I was not comfortable doing that. There is not enough money in the world to send me back there, under those conditions." (Anonymous worker, describing what it was like to have 48 cases when she resigned)

> "There's not many of us left. And when we're gone I don't know what's going to happen to these kids. There are kids and families out there that really need help, and that's going to fall on somebody else's shoulders." (Patricia Pregliasco, lamenting the departure of experienced workers)

We end this section with the question we began with: What do we value? During halftime of football games it is not uncommon to honor people who serve our common interests. Most typically this means the military, or firefighters, or police. We honor them because we value their contribution. Perhaps it is time we started honoring *other heroes in our society—those who run battered women's shelters, child and adult welfare workers, and advocates for victims of VMIR.*

WHAT CAN WE DO?

Those of us who want to help can do so in a number of ways. We can be a resource for our friends and family. We can know the signs of abuse. We can write letters to our local, state, and federal representatives. We can visit their offices. We can talk to colleagues, friends, and family members. We can write opinion pieces for our local newspapers.

We can join or give money to organizations we believe in. We can advocate for children and the elderly in court. We can volunteer at battered women's shelters. We can take in foster children. We can adopt unwanted children. We can vote for people who will take our concerns seriously. There are some larger and less obvious ways we can help as well.

Take a Stand Against Culturally Accepted Violence

One thing we can all do is to take a stand against culturally accepted violence. Several years ago, the musician Eminem recorded the song "Kim," which appeared on his 2000 album *The Marshall Mathers LP*. In the song, Eminem expresses his anger about his wife's infidelity by detailing his plans to beat her and kill her. He writes of beating the s_ _ _ out of her and how she needs to shut the f_ _ _ up and get the punishment she deserves. In perhaps the most disturbing line in the song, he tells of his plans to take her for a car ride. His prediction that they will be back soon but that she will be in the trunk of the car seems to refer to his intention to kill her. The song concludes with the words "Now bleed, bitch, bleed" repeated numerous times. *The Marshall Mathers LP* sold 1.76 million copies in its first week of release.

How should we respond to a song like "Kim"? In this section, we would like to briefly address this question. At issue, at least in part, are the various ways we condone, either explicitly or implicitly, VMIR. Perhaps change begins with us and our response to violent themes and actions that are so common in our society they are perceived as normal.

Normative Violence

There is considerable agreement, at least on a theoretical level, that violence begets violence (Tolan & Guerra, 1998). That is, societal acceptance and glorification of violence might increase the level of violence in intimate relationships and in society more generally. Establishing an empirical link is complicated, and there is certainly disagreement on the subject, but at the very least one could reasonably argue that aggression and violence in the home mirror society's tolerance for violence.

In what ways is violence accepted in the home? The most obvious way is **spanking**. Some might object to the use of the word *violence* in this context. For caring parents who spank *because* they love their children and want to be good parents, the word feels harsh. But recall from Chapter 1 that we defined violence as "an act carried out with the intention of, or an act perceived as having the intention of, physically hurting another person" (Steinmetz, 1987, p. 729). Is it not true that a father who spanks a child has intentions of physically hurting that child? He does not want to injure that child, but doesn't he want to inflict pain? Isn't that the point? So, yes, spanking is a form of violence. However, since it is an *acceptable* form of violence, we do not see it as violence (see Box 11.1).

Is spanking harmful? Yes, it *can* be. Not for everyone who has been spanked, of course. But, yes, research consistently suggests that spanking causes more harm than

BOX 11.1

TEN MYTHS THAT PERPETUATE CORPORAL PUNISHMENT

It is difficult to overestimate the impact of University of New Hampshire sociologist Murray Straus, who is widely regarded as the founder of the field of family violence. Straus died in 2016 at the age of 86. He devoted much of his later career to the study of corporal punishment. His 1994 book, *Beating the Devil Out of Them: Corporal Punishment in American Families*, was, at the time of its publication, the most comprehensive statement on the problem of spanking as a discipline technique. His "Ten Myths That Perpetuate Corporal Punishment" have only become more pertinent with the passage of time.

Myth 1: Spanking works better. There is no evidence that spanking works better than other forms of discipline. What little evidence has been collected suggests that spanking may be less effective than nonviolent forms of discipline (e.g., time-outs or loss of privileges).

Myth 2: Spanking is needed as a last resort. If one accepts the argument that spanking is no better than other forms of discipline, then it stands to reason that there are no situations in which spanking is necessary. Straus argues that much of the time when parents resort to hitting, they are doing so out of their own frustration. Essentially, the parent who hits is sending a message to the child that if one is angry, hitting is justified.

Myth 3: Spanking is harmless. According to Straus, hitting is so firmly entrenched in American culture that it is difficult for us to admit that it is wrong. To do so would be to admit that our parents were wrong or we have been wrong. The evidence suggests, however, that on average, spanking does more harm than good. Certainly, most people who were spanked "turn out fine," but this does not disprove the general pattern. That most smokers do not die of lung cancer does not disprove the evidence on the harmful effects of smoking.

Myth 4: Spanking one or two times won't cause any damage. It is true that the evidence suggests that spanking is most harmful when it is frequent and severe. If spanking is harmful in large quantities, however, how can it be good in small quantities?

Myth 5: Parents can't stop without training. Eliminating spanking would be easy, Straus maintains, if society would embrace the belief that a child should never be hit. Parent educators and social scientists are reluctant to take this stand, however, because of the belief that parents cannot be expected to stop spanking unless they are presented with alternative parenting techniques. Straus counters that parents do not need training in alternative parenting techniques—they simply need to embrace the belief that spanking is wrong. Everyone agrees, for example, that directing demeaning and insulting language toward children (i.e., psychological abuse) is wrong, and no one argues that parents cannot be expected to avoid this behavior without training. "Rather than arguing that parents need to learn certain skills before they can stop using corporal punishment," Straus (1994) argues, "I believe that parents are more likely to use and cultivate those skills if they decide or are required to stop spanking" (p. 156).

Myth 6: If you don't spank, your children will be spoiled or will run wild. It is true that some children who are not spanked run wild, but it is equally true that some children who are spanked run wild. The key to having well-behaved children is being a consistent disciplinarian, not being a physical disciplinarian.

Myth 7: Parents spank rarely or only for serious problems. It is true that many parents perceive that they reserve spanking for serious problems, but Straus maintains that parents simply do not realize how often they hit their children. This is especially true for parents who use spanking as their primary discipline technique.

Myth 8: By the time a child is a teenager, parents have stopped spanking. The national child maltreatment surveys indicate that more than half of parents of 13- and 14-year-olds had hit their children in the preceding 12 months. With teenagers, corporal punishment is more likely to be a slap to the face than a slap to the bottom.

Myth 9: If parents don't spank, they will verbally abuse their children. Parents who spank frequently are actually more likely than nonspanking parents to be verbally abusive.

Myth 10: It is unrealistic to expect parents never to spank. Straus (1994) is clearly frustrated by the level of acceptance of corporal punishment

in the United States. He asks, "Is it unrealistic to expect husbands not to hit their wives? Why is violence unacceptable between strangers but acceptable between a parent and child?" Straus concedes that it is probably not feasible to criminalize spanking in this culture, but he asserts that scholars who oppose spanking can make some progress "by showing parents that spanking is dangerous, that their children will be easier to bring up if they do not spank, and by clearly saying that a child should never, under any circumstances, be spanked" (p. 162).

good (Gershoff et al., 2018; Straus, Douglas, & Medeiros, 2014). There are those who disagree with this conclusion, arguing that "appropriate" spanking (e.g., open hand, leaving no marks, accompanied by explanation and love) does indeed do more good than harm (Larzelere & Baumrind, 2010). But theirs is rapidly becoming a minority voice in the academic world. It has also become the minority voice around the world. Article 19 of the UNCRC, which was adopted in 1989, encourages member states to take "all appropriate legislative, administrative, social and educational measures to protect the child from all forms of physical or mental violence" (United Nations General Assembly, 1989). According to the Global Initiative to End All Corporal Punishment of Children (2020), 58 countries, beginning with Sweden in 1979, prohibit corporal punishment in the home.

The United States is the only member nation yet to ratify the UNCRC. Critics fear that ratification of the treaty would undermine the rights of the parents to, for example, spank or homeschool their children. While it is not clear that the UNCRC would necessarily produce these results, it is clear that the rhetoric of "parental rights" has stalled ratification efforts in the United States. However, as Gary Melton (2008) points out, parents have no specially protected rights. The core of his argument comes from the Universal Declaration of Human Rights (1948), which states that "recognition of the inherent dignity and of the equal and inalienable rights of all members of the human family is the foundation of freedom, justice, and peace in the world" (Melton, 2008, p. 907). Noticeably absent from the declaration, Melton points out, are age-related qualifiers. Everyone—adults and children—is guaranteed these inalienable rights. Parents have rights *and* children have rights. We call them human rights. "Those who would pit parents against children fail to see that respect for children implies no diminution of respect for the adults who care for them" (Melton, 2008, p. 912).

Another form of VMIR that is common and too often tolerated is between siblings. This form of violence and maltreatment is often rationalized as a "normal" and "inevitable" part of sibling interaction. As with spanking, observers often avoid the perceived harshness of terms like *violence* or *abuse*, preferring instead to talk about sibling *conflict* or *aggression* (Kettrey & Emery, 2006).

Tucker, Finkelhor, Turner, and Shattuck (2013) found that approximately 50 percent of children between the ages of 2 and 9 report sibling violence. These rates decline with age. Children are more likely to be the recipients of maltreatment when they are young, and then, as they get older, they become the aggressor.

The issues are much the same with adult violence and maltreatment. Gavey (2013), for example, described a "cultural scaffolding of rape" that produces "forms of heterosex that set up the preconditions for rape—women's passive, acquiescing sexuality, and men's forthright, urgent pursuit of sexual 'release'" (p. 3). These a priori assumptions contribute to a "rape myth" that women "ask for it" and ultimately "like it." We see these gendered assumptions about sexuality illustrated in a fraternity party culture that sometimes exists on college campuses, where upperclassmen, in search of sexual conquests, provide alcohol, transportation, and a place to party for underage women. The women, who are themselves seeking social status and attention, are vulnerable in these male-dominated settings (Armstrong, Hamilton, & Sweeney, 2006). Some readers might recall that Old Dominion University was in the news in the fall of 2015 after members of the Sigma Nu fraternity hung banners outside their fraternity hall saying things like "Hope your baby girl is ready for a good time" and "Freshman daughter dropoff." As the *Huffington Post* reported with a series of pictures a few days after the Old Dominion story broke, Old Dominion was not the only university where this had occurred (Kingkade, 2015).

It is very important to remember that this form of objectification of women is not the norm with college men. Nor, obviously, is this behavior limited to college men. In October 2016, the reader will no doubt remember, a 2005 audio recording surfaced of Donald Trump bragging about behavior that constitutes sexual assault. In the recording, Trump tells entertainment reporter Billy Bush: "You know, I'm automatically attracted to beautiful women. I just start kissing them. It's like a magnet. Just kiss. I don't even wait. And when you're a star, they let you do it. Grab 'em by the p_ _ _ y. You can do anything" ("Transcript: Donald Trump's Taped Comments About Women," 2016). Trump dismissed the quote as nothing more than "locker-room talk," saying he never actually did any of the behaviors he describes on the tape. But for our purposes, that defense is irrelevant. "Locker-room talk" that objectifies women inevitably contributes to a cultural acceptance of sexual assault.

What could sibling violence and President Trump possibly have in common? Our point is that violence and maltreatment, both in attitude and in behavior, are too often tolerated. Obviously, this conclusion applies to some forms of violence and maltreatment more than others. Spanking and sibling violence, for example, are very *common:* They are normative. Acceptance of the rape myth, hitting one's spouse, or bragging about sexual assault may not be the norm, but these things are *not uncommon*. And since none of these behaviors produce positive outcomes, perhaps it is time to take a stand; *in this relationship, in this family, we do not sexually objectify, we do not verbally abuse, and we do not hit!*

The Media and Violence

The potential negative effect of media violence is hotly debated and widely discussed. While a thorough review of the research literature on this topic is well beyond the scope of this book, it seems reasonable to consider briefly the possible implications of media violence on VMIR. On the one hand, explanations of VMIR that reduce the source of the problem to the presence of violence in the media clearly oversimplify a very complex issue. However, research points to the negative effects of violence in the media, and the possible causal significance is difficult to ignore (Huesmann, Moise-Titus, Podolski, & Eron, 2003). There is a growing body of research suggesting that exposure to media violence contributes to real-world violence, including violence within intimate relationships (Anderson, Bushman, Donnerstein, Hummer, & Warburton, 2015). Also compelling is research suggesting that exposure to nonabusive sexual media contributes to sexual victimization (Ybarra, Strasburger, & Mitchell, 2014). There are also anecdotal examples of harmful effects, including crimes committed by youth who acted out scenes from violent video games (Hollander, 2013).

Grand Theft Auto serves as a fascinating, and frankly very disturbing, example. In this video game, players earn points by picking up a prostitute, having sex with her, and killing her. Skeptical that the content of the game had been exaggerated, the second author of this book googled "grand theft auto 5 kill prostitutes," which led to several "how to" YouTube videos. The video "Effectively Killing Prostitutes in Grand Theft Auto 5" (as of April 2020, this video was still available at www.youtube.com/watch?v=FqVPootBNPU) takes the viewer through a "prostitute hunt," which ends when the prostitute is taken to a back alley, shot with a stun gun, stabbed to death, drenched in gasoline, and burned. The narration of the video is grotesque, and the misogynistic comments left by YouTube viewers are arguably worse.

The topic of violent video games, and specifically youth access to these games, received widespread attention in June 2011, when the U.S. Supreme Court, in a 7–2 ruling, invalidated a California law banning the sale of violent video games to minors. Citing the First Amendment, Justice Antonin Scalia wrote, "like the protected books, plays and movies that preceded them, video games communicate ideas—and even social messages—through many familiar literary devices (such as characters, dialogue, plot and music) and through features distinctive to the medium (such as the player's interaction with the virtual world)" (*Brown v. Entertainment Merchants Association*, 2011, p. 4). The Court ultimately concluded that "speech about violence is not obscene," and is therefore protected by the First Amendment (*Brown v. Entertainment Merchants Association*, 2011, p. 10).

Defenders of age restrictions, citing empirical evidence of the harmful effects, had argued that the state has an obligation to protect children from such harm. Age-related restrictions are not unprecedented, they argued, noting laws that protect children from sexually explicit material. In response, the Court acknowledged that the United States has a long history of restricting access to sexual content, but no such history exists for violent content. Citing the violent subplots of the stories of Snow White, Hansel and Gretel, and Cinderella, Justice Scalia noted that childhood exposure to violence is common and accepted. "Grimm's Fairy Tales, for example, are grim indeed," Justice Scalia reasoned (*Brown v. Entertainment Merchants Association*, 2011, p. 10). The Court seems to have concluded that *sex is obscene, but violence is not.*

One of the few positive outcomes in the *Brown v. Entertainment Merchants Association* decision was that it drew attention to the violent content in some video games. Justice Samuel Alito, who voted with the 7–2 majority, cited several alarming specifics. In one game, he noted, the objective is to rape a mother and her daughters. In other games, players attempt to assassinate President John F. Kennedy, reenact the Columbine High School killings, or engage in ethnic cleansing by killing African Americans, Latinos, or Jews (*Brown v. Entertainment Merchants Association*, 2011, pp. 34–35).

Grand Theft Auto is one of the most popular video games in the world. When it was released in September 2013, it sold over 11 million copies in the first 24 hours, breaking previous records for an entertainment product (www.guinnessworldrecords.com). How should we respond? It seems reasonable to wonder aloud whether we—as advocates of violence-free families—should support artists or games or movies that condone what we oppose. Consequently, we urge the reader to take another stand: *to choose not to buy, play, or watch materials that condone VMIR, and to speak out against materials that do so.*

Minimize Opportunity

Sociologists often remind us that the best way to prevent crime and other deviant behaviors is to limit the *opportunities* that are available to would-be criminals and deviants. "Opportunity theory," as it is sometimes called, shifts the theoretical focus away from deviant motivations, which are the focus of most deviance theory, and instead assumes that everyone is sufficiently motivated to commit (or capable of committing) a deviant act (Felson, 2006). Shifting the focus in this way redirects our attention to creating structures that limit opportunities.

A simple example will help illustrate the point. Let's assume that on your way home from school you decide to stop and eat dinner. You have valuables with you, including your computer, which you obviously do not want to have stolen. If you need to leave the computer in the car, what *shouldn't* you do? Notice that the answer to this question is *not* dependent on the presumed motivations of those who happen to walk by. It only focuses on what you should, and should not, do. And you know that if you leave your window open with the computer sitting on the driver's seat the computer is more likely to get stolen.

What would it look like to extend this perspective to the prevention of VMIR? First, we would assume everyone is capable of VMIR. This assumption need not be cynical; we can and should expect the best of people. But while we might be 100 percent sure that the male youth minister at our church would never have sex with a teen in his youth group, we should work under the assumption that he, and all youth ministers, *could* do it. We would then work to create a structure and rules that limit opportunities. This is exactly what happened with the sex scandals within the Catholic Church. The assumption that "men of God" would never betray the trust of a young believer created opportunities that ultimately led to abuse. Many Catholic dioceses have responded by creating guidelines that forbid priests and lay leaders from being alone with children (Hamilton, 2016).

The research discussed previously about fraternity culture is also relevant here (Armstrong et al., 2006). If men provide alcohol, transportation, and a place to party for underage women, abuses will inevitably occur. These "organizational arrangements" ensure it. We could approach the physical abuse of children or elders in much the same way. A wife who is caring for a husband with dementia will face difficult times, and it is not unreasonable to assume that she is capable of abuse. Again, if we assume that everyone is capable, our efforts to eliminate the problem focus on providing support and limiting opportunities.

Pay Attention and Step Up

A final suggestion for what we can all do to impact VMIR is to be good citizens and active bystanders. What would you do if you observed a man slap his wife at the mall? What about an inebriated college female heading upstairs with a man at a party? Or what if you were in a supermarket and you saw a father pushing a shopping cart pulling his daughter alongside him with her hair wrapped around the handle of the cart? What would you do? What *should* you do?

The scenario we just described about the young girl being pulled along by her hair is not a hypothetical. Erika Burch observed the father dragging his daughter by the hair in a Texas Walmart. She made national news when she took a picture, confronted the father, and called the police. She also posted pictures on Facebook (Mele, 2016). The photos attracted national attention. But what should one do in a situation like that?

Intervening in the affairs of others is no easy matter, of course. It may not be taken well, and we must surely pick our battles carefully. But victims have a right not to be abused. And, of course, we must also remember this: If this is how a parent treats a child in public, what goes on behind closed doors?

Looking to share advice on how best to intervene, *New York Times* writer Christopher Mele (2016) interviewed several child welfare workers and advocates. When possible, the experts argued, collect yourself, be warm and friendly, and withhold judgment. As for what to say, they suggest comments like "Hello, I don't mean to get into your business or tell you how to parent, but I noticed that . . ." or "I remember when my children were that age. They can be a handful. Do you need any help?"

In recent years, programs designed to promote bystander intervention have become more and more common across the country, and have received considerable attention in the academic literature. For example, in a meta-analysis of 12 bullying prevention programs, Polanian, Espelage, and Pigott (2012) found evidence of increased bystander intervention in bullying situations for students of all ages. Also common are intervention programs that target IPV, especially among teens and young adults (Cook-Craig et al., 2014; Storer, Casey, & Herrenkohl, 2016). In general, research suggests that students who have gone through bystander programs express more willingness to intervene and have more confidence in their ability to effectively intervene. Whether these attitudinal changes produce actual behavioral changes, and whether interventions effectively reduce maltreatment and violence, is not yet clear (Storer et al., 2016).

The most widely discussed bystander intervention programs focus on sexual assault on college campuses. The federal government has essentially mandated these programs in a report produced by the 2014 White House Task Force to Protect Students From Sexual Assault (see Box 11.2). For the most part, research findings evaluating the effectiveness of rape intervention programs are similar to those discussed earlier that focus on dating violence. Rape bystander intervention programs impact participants' attitudes toward *willingness to intervene*, but there is little indication that participants are more likely to *actually intervene* (Alegría-Flores, Raker, Pleasants, Weaver, & Weinberger, 2017; Cermele & McCaughey, 2015; Kleinsasser, Jouriles, McDonald, & Rosenfield, 2015).

Get Involved

According to the Research Corporation for National and Community Service, a federal agency that promotes service, approximately one-fourth of all Americans volunteered through an organization in 2015 ("New Report," 2015). Although this rate is high, at least in comparison with the rates in many other countries, volunteerism (measured in terms of both time and money) has declined significantly in the United States since 1960. Harvard political scientist Robert Putnam, in his widely read book *Bowling Alone* (2000), suggests that the decline can be attributed to the fact that Americans have become less

BOX 11.2

THE 2014 WHITE HOUSE TASK FORCE TO PROTECT STUDENTS FROM SEXUAL ASSAULT

No area of VMIR has evolved as quickly, and as dramatically, as has sexual assault and rape. The 2014 White House Task Force to Protect Students From Sexual Assault effectively illustrates this evolution. Then president Barack Obama, in announcing the creation of the task force, directed the Office of the Vice President and the White House Council on Women and Girls to "lead an interagency effort to address campus rape and sexual assault, including coordinating Federal enforcement efforts by executive departments and agencies and helping institutions meet their obligations under Federal law" ("Memorandum—Establishing a White House Task Force to Protect Students From Sexual Assault," 2014). The new federal policy, articulated in the report *Not Alone* (White House Task Force to Protect Students From Sexual Assault, 2014), requires colleges and universities, as a condition to receiving federal funds, to "step up their game" in rape education and prevention (Cermele & McCaughey, 2015).

The task force is not without its critics. Given the contentious history of rape definitions and measurement, it is not surprising that some have challenged that the statistical claim, unquestioningly accepted as an "article of faith" in the opening sentence of the *Not Alone* report, that "one in five women is sexually assaulted in college" (S. Harris, 2014). Some critics have charged that this statistic, which comes from a U.S. Department of Justice report (Krebs, Lindquist, Warner, Fisher, & Martin, 2007), exaggerates the issue on college

campuses. The *Not Alone* report also requires college campuses to use a "preponderance of evidence" (i.e., more likely than not) in adjudicating sexual assault cases. This relaxed standard of proof, combined with the complaints of some that the threat of rape is exaggerated on college campuses, has led to concerns about the due process rights of accused students (S. Harris, 2014).

The mandates of the task force have also attracted attention from the academic community. According to Cermele and McCaughey (2015), the *Not Alone* report requires colleges to implement evidence-based programming to help prevent sexual assault. However, the only primary prevention programs that are acknowledged and suggested are sexual assault education programs and bystander intervention programs. Missing, according to Cermele and McCaughey, are self-defense programs that teach women to intervene for themselves. Their concern is that bystander intervention programs require the presence of a third party, while self-defense models do not. Self-defense training "disrupts the script of sexual violence by offering women a range of verbal and physical strategies to thwart rape" and "does not require the presence of a bystander in order to prevent assault" (Cermele & McCaughey, 2015). Furthermore, they argue, there is evidence that self-defense training is effective at preventing sexual assaults, while there is little evidence that bystander intervention programs are effective.

---

invested and involved in group associations. As group membership rates have declined, volunteerism has become more individualized and, ultimately, more sporadic.

Giving of our money and our time often begins when we join an organization. Our voluntary associations provide us with networks of like-minded peers who encourage our giving, present us with opportunities to serve others, and provide us with the training we need to serve others. One of the ways we can bring about change is by becoming involved in organizations that are committed to serving the abused and neglected. Numerous national, state, and local organizations, including many faith communities, are committed to alleviating the problem of victimization.

CHAPTER SUMMARY

In this final chapter, we began with a discussion of the long-term empirical trends in VMIR. In general, these data lead to the conclusion that rates of VMIR are declining. This conclusion applies not only to the long-term historical patterns, but to the most recent past as well. It makes sense that this would be the case, as awareness and concern have grown. We simply pay more attention than we used to, and the declines are in many ways a sign that we care.

These trends, however, should not make us complacent. As we have maintained throughout this book, women, children, and the elderly are *still* more likely to be victimized *in their own home* than they are on the streets of America's most dangerous cities. We argue that this is a sign that, while we care, we do not care enough. There are many signs that we, as a society, simply do not value the protection of vulnerable populations as much as we should.

What can we do to help? Perhaps the best place to start is by taking a stand against mass media content that glorifies violence. Concerned citizens can choose not to support or condone violence, despite the wider culture's apparent acceptance of violent materials. We can choose not to watch or to buy these products, and we can encourage others to do likewise. We can also choose not to condone violence in our own families. Spouses and siblings can choose not to hit one another, and parents can choose not to hit their children.

The opportunities for involvement are limitless. We can give of our time and money. We can work to limit opportunities. We can intervene when intervention is required. We only need to keep our eyes open, look for opportunities to advocate, and look for opportunities to serve.

GLOSSARY

A Safety Awareness Program (ASAP) is an abuse prevention program for people with disabilities that is designed to raise awareness and knowledge of intimate abuse, build safety skills, improve safety self-efficacy, and increase social support, which together should increase safety behavior and ultimately reduce victimization of people with disabilities.

Ableism is prejudice and discrimination against people with disabilities in favor of the able-bodied.

Abusive head trauma (AHT) is injury to the head that can sometimes result from vigorously shaking a child, which is referred to as shaken baby syndrome.

Acquaintance rape is sexual assault perpetrated by someone the victim knows.

ACT (Adults and Children Together) Media Campaign is a violence prevention media campaign whose goal is to raise awareness about adult behaviors that can impact young children for better or worse.

Administration for Children and Families is a division of the Department of Health and Human Services and aims to promote the economic and social well-being of children, families, and communities through partnerships, funding, guidance, training, and technical assistance.

Adoption and Foster Care Analysis and Reporting System (AFCARS) is a reporting system that collects data from the 50 states of the United States on the number of children placed in out-of-home care.

Adoption and Safe Families Act (ASFA) is legislation that attempts to correct the problems inherent in the foster care system that attempted to preserve families and deter the adoption of children. This legislation shifted emphasis away from reuniting children with their abusive parents toward children's health and safety.

Adult Protective Services (APS) is the major state-level system of intervention for cases of adult abuse and neglect. APS agencies carry out their responsibility of protecting adults (typically the elderly or disabled) in four ways: (1) by investigating reports of maltreatment, (2) by providing treatment services, (3) by coordinating the services offered by other agencies in the community, and (4) by implementing preventive services.

Adverse Childhood Experiences (ACE) Study is a population-based study supported by the Centers for Disease Control and Prevention (CDC) and Kaiser Permanente to assess associations between adverse childhood experiences (e.g., child maltreatment, parental divorce, parental drug and alcohol abuse) and health and well-being in later life.

Advocacy statistics are statistics that are misused or exaggerated to further a particular cause.

Ageism is negative prejudicial attitudes toward and discrimination against the elderly.

Alcohol myopia theory (AMT) posits that alcohol creates a myopic or narrowing effect on intoxicated individuals' attention and ability to process meaning from informational cues they perceive in their environment

Alternatives for Families: A Cognitive Behavioral Therapy (AF-CBT) is an evidence-based intervention that targets (1) diverse individual child and caregiver characteristics related to conflict and intimidation in the home, and (2) the family context in which aggression or abuse may occur.

American Professional Society on the Abuse of Children (APSAC) is the leading national organization supporting professionals who work with children and families impacted by child maltreatment.

Antisocial personality disorder is a personality disorder involving a pattern of behavior that includes a disregard for, and violation of, the rights of others (sometimes commonly referred to as a sociopath or psychopath).

Anxious attachment style (also known as insecure-ambivalent) refers to a parent–child attachment style in which the child is characterized as overly dependent, clingy, fussy, and prone to crying (see also insecure-ambivalent under **attachment styles**).

Attachment styles describe the type of bond that develops between parent and child and include four major styles: (1) secure (e.g., seeks closeness to care-giver and feels safer and more secure in their presence), (2) insecure-ambivalent (e.g., fears strangers and displays distress when separated from caregiver but is not reassured or comforted in the caregiver's presence), (3) insecure-avoidant (e.g., avoids caregiver and does not seek comfort or contact from them), and (4) insecure-disorganized (e.g., shows no clear pattern of attachment behavior and often demonstrates a mix of behaviors including avoidance and resistance).

Attachment theory is a developmental theory that explains the tendency of infants and children to seek closeness to particular individuals and to feel safer and more secure in their presence. This theory suggests that child maltreatment interferes with the development of secure attachments between the parent and the child that extends into adult relationships.

Attention-deficit/hyperactivity disorder (ADHD) is a psychological disorder characterized by a consistent pattern of age-inappropriate behaviors, including inattention, impulsivity, and hyperactivity.

Avoidant personality disorder is a personality disorder involving a pattern of behavior that includes social inhibition, feelings of inadequacy, and hypersensitivity to negative evaluation.

Battered child syndrome is a term first used by Dr. Henry Kempe to describe young children who have been the victims of serious physical abuse.

Batterer is a person who exercises a pattern of coercive control in a partner relationship, punctuated by one or more acts of intimidating physical violence, sexual assault, or credible threat of physical violence.

Batterer intervention program (BIP) is a treatment program for perpetrators of intimate partner violence. BIPs vary in length, curriculum, and therapeutic methods.

Biological embedding is the idea that early childhood experiences such as child maltreatment can alter underlying biological systems to produce stable and long-lasting impacts.

Borderline personality disorder is a personality disorder involving a pattern of behavior that includes instability in interpersonal relationships, self-image, and emotion; the pattern also includes notable impulsivity.

Bullying is aggressive or mean-spirited behavior that occurs repeatedly over time and has the underlying intent to harm or disturb the person or group at whom it is targeted. It is perpetrated by a person or group

that is perceived as having more power (physical or psychological) than the weaker, less powerful individual or peer group that is targeted.

Bullying/sexual violence pathway describes the process whereby bullying of peers at a young age eventually changes to aggressive homophobia and sexual harassment of peers in adolescence.

Bystander intervention program is a violence prevention strategy that trains individuals to respond to situations in which norms or behaviors that promote violence are present. Because the majority of individuals do not perpetrate violence, the bystander approach increases the likelihood of individual change and community and norms change. The target population for change is everyone in the community, rather than just perpetrators or victims.

Centers for independent living (CILs) are community-based organizations that are operated and controlled by people with disabilities. They offer various services and peer support to help people with disabilities gain greater control over their lives.

Chemical castration is a treatment technique for child sexual abuse perpetrators involving the administration of various drugs to reduce sex drive.

Chicago Child–Parent Centers program is a school-based intervention for preschoolers and school-age children, which provides preschool education and a variety of family support services for low-income children and their families.

Child Abuse Prevention and Treatment Act (CAPTA) is legislation that provides federal funding to states to support prevention, assessment, investigation, prosecution, and treatment of child maltreatment. The legislation also sets forth a minimal definition of child maltreatment and identifies the role of the federal government in supporting research, evaluation, technical assistance, and data collection.

Child fatality review teams are typically composed of community professionals representing multiple agencies who retrospectively review the circumstances under which a child died, identify the prevalence of deaths from abuse and neglect, improve the policies and procedures of Child Protective Services to prevent future child deaths and serious injuries, protect siblings of children whose causes of death are unexplained, and increase professional and public awareness of child death due to maltreatment.

Child neglect refers to a form of child maltreatment described as deficits in meeting a child's basic needs, including basic needs in the broad categories of physical, emotional, medical, and educational needs.

Child physical abuse (CPA) is the intentional use of physical force against a child that results in or has the potential to result in physical injury.

Child pornography is a form of commercial sexual exploitation of children and refers to any visual depiction of a child, including computer-generated images, engaging in sexually explicit behavior such as in photographs, film, video, or pictures that are made or produced by electronic, mechanical, or other means.

Child Protective Services (CPS) is the major state-level system of intervention for cases of child abuse and neglect. CPS agencies carry out their responsibility of protecting children in four ways: (1) by investigating reports of maltreatment, (2) by providing treatment services, (3) by coordinating the services offered by other agencies in the community to child victims and their families, and (4) by implementing preventive services.

Child psychological maltreatment (CPM) is a form of child maltreatment that involves caregiver behavior that communicates to a child that the child is worthless, flawed, unloved, unwanted, endangered, or valued only in meeting another's needs including behaving in a manner that is harmful, potentially harmful, or insensitive to the child's developmental needs, or that can potentially be damaging to the child's development.

Child sex trafficking is a form of commercial sexual exploitation of children that involves activities such as recruitment, harboring, transportation, provision, or obtainment of a child for the purpose of a commercial sex act.

Child sexual abuse (CSA) as defined by the Centers for Disease Control and Prevention refers to "any completed or attempted (non-completed) sexual act, sexual contact with, or exploitation of (i.e., noncontact sexual interaction) a child" (Leeb, Paulozzi, Melanson, Simon, & Arias, 2008, p. 11).

Child Sexual Abuse and Pornography Act is legislation created in 1986 that provides for federal prosecution of individuals engaged in child pornography, including parents who permit their children to engage in such activities.

Child sexual abuse images is a recent term used to replace *child pornography* because the latter term trivializes inherently abusive content, implies consensual activity, and fails to recognize that such materials are not the same as adult pornography or erotica.

Child sexual assault refers to anal or vaginal penetration by the penis or another object, oral-genital and oral-anal contact, touching of the genitals or other intimate body parts whether clothed or unclothed, and genital masturbation of the perpetrator in the presence of a child.

Child sexual exploitation refers to noncontact activities involving pornography (preparing, accessing, or distributing obscene matter depicting a child) and activities that include the sexual exploitation of children for financial gain, such as selling child pornography or encouraging and/or coercing child prostitution.

Claims makers are interest groups and individuals who actively engage in the process of raising awareness and concern about a particular social condition.

Close confinement is a form of child psychological maltreatment that involves restricting a child's movement by binding limbs.

Coercive control is an ongoing pattern of domination, in which the abusive partner uses intimidation, isolation, and similar tactics to erode the freedom of the victim.

Cognitive behavioral therapy (CBT) is an intervention that combines principles from both behavioral and cognitive psychology. This approach targets distorted thoughts, maladaptive behaviors, and dysregulated emotion.

Cognitive distortions are distorted beliefs such as the belief that children are misbehaving to annoy the parent rather than as part of a normal developmental response.

Cognitive functional impairments cause the partial or complete loss of significant cognitive abilities, such as decision making, facial recognition, and memory.

Cognitive neglect (see also **developmental** and **educational neglect**) is generally defined as failure to provide a child with the experiences necessary for growth and development, such as intellectual and educational opportunities.

Commercial sexual exploitation of children (CSEC) includes sexual abuse by an adult for some form of compensation, financial or otherwise, to the child or a third person or persons and includes pornography, prostitution, and sex trafficking.

Community accountability is an element of the transformative justice model in which community organizations replace professionalized services and state-based (especially criminal justice) interventions, and community members, including victims' and perpetrators' social networks, serve as both a support and an accountability system.

Community awareness campaigns are public education advertisements and public service announcements designed to make people aware of violence and maltreatment in intimate relationships and the role they can play in protecting victims.

Conduct disorder is a type of disruptive behavior disorder in children whereby a child exhibits a consistent pattern of antisocial behaviors, including aggression toward people or property, stealing, lying, truancy, and running away.

Conflict Tactics Scales (CTS) are one of the most widely used scales in self-reported family violence research, originally designed to measure intimate partner violence.

Corporal punishment (CP) is a form of punishment in which physical force is used and intended to cause some degree of pain or discomfort in order to affect a child's behavior.

Correlational studies analyze the statistical association between two or more variables. It is very difficult to establish causality with correlational studies.

Cross-sectional studies are research designs that assess participants of various ages at one point in time.

Cultural relativism is the idea that beliefs and practices are culture specific, and should be accepted and not judged negatively.

Cyberexploitation refers to various sexually exploitive internet interactions, including propositioning children and adolescents for sexual activity, exposing them to various forms of sexually explicit material, or engaging them in online sexual harassment.

Dangerousness assessment instruments are screening tools designed to identify intimate partner violence perpetrators' risk of reoffending.

Dark figure is the numerical gap between the violence and maltreatment in intimate relationships (VMIR) that is actually committed in a society and the VMIR that is officially recognized and recorded.

Declaration of Sentiments is a statement on women's rights written by Elizabeth Stanton in 1848.

Degrading (see also **verbal abuse**) is a form of child psychological maltreatment that involves actions that deprecate a child, often referred to as verbal abuse.

Denying emotional responsiveness (i.e., ignoring) is a form of child psychological maltreatment that involves acts of omission whereby the caretaker does not provide the child with necessary stimulation and responsiveness.

Deterrence doctrine is the assumption that people will not engage in deviant behavior if they fear the consequences, especially the legal consequences.

Deterrence theory assumes humans are rational beings who attempt to avoid sanctions. The greater the perceived likelihood of getting caught and the perceived severity of the sanctions, the less likely the individual is to engage in a deviant behavior.

Developmental disabilities are physical and/or mental conditions that manifest before age 22 (e.g., mental retardation, autism, cerebral palsy).

Developmental neglect (see also **educational neglect**) is generally defined as failure to provide a child with the experiences necessary for growth and development, such as intellectual and educational opportunities.

Differential response is a system reform that enables Child Protective Services to differentiate its response to reports of child maltreatment based on a family's risk level and the safety of the referred child.

Disability is a physical or mental impairment that substantially limits a major activity of daily living.

Disability-related abuse is abuse specific to a particular physical, mental, or sensory limitation.

Disinhibitors include any agent that causes a reduction in one's inhibitions, such as drugs, alcohol, or distorted thought patterns.

Disorganized attachment style refers to a parent–child attachment characterized by child behavior that demonstrates a lack of a coherent style or pattern for coping (sometimes referred to as Type D attachment).

Dissociation is the separation of normally related mental processes.

Domestic violence orders (see **protection orders**)

Dual arrest is the arrest of both partners for intimate partner violence without regard for which partner was the primary aggressor.

Durham Family Initiative (DFI) is a community prevention program that attempts to expand universal assessments designed to identify families at risk for child maltreatment and then connect them to appropriate community-based services.

Dysthymia is a form of depression characterized by a low-grade, chronic pattern of symptoms.

Economic (financial) abuse occurs when perpetrators deliberately try to weaken or destroy their partner's financial solvency.

Educational neglect (see also **developmental neglect**) is generally defined as failure to provide a child with the experiences necessary for growth and development, such as intellectual and educational opportunities.

Elder abuse is any maltreatment or neglect of a person aged 60 or older by a caregiver or another person in a trust relationship with the elder.

Elder Justice Act (EJA) is a federal law enacted in 2010 as part of the Patient Protection and Affordable Care Act ("Obamacare") that promotes the prevention, detection, treatment, and intervention in cases of elder abuse.

Elder Mistreatment Research Program is a federally funded program in the National Institute of Justice that supports research on such topics as the collection and evaluation of forensic evidence of elder physical and sexual abuse.

Emotional neglect (see also **child psychological maltreatment**) is a form of child maltreatment that includes failure to provide a child with emotional support, security, and encouragement.

Empowerment counseling is designed to help victims gain or restore their senses of personal power and control, which are severely diminished by repeated abuse.

Endangerment standard is a reporting standard used in the National Incidence Studies that allows for the reporting of cases in which children demonstrate no actual harm (i.e., present evidence of injury) but in which it is reasonable to suspect potential harm (i.e., future risk of injury).

Enough Abuse Campaign is a statewide education and community mobilization effort in Massachusetts that provides information about conditions and social norms associated with the occurrence of child sexual abuse and offers training for parents and child care professionals in an attempt to prevent people from sexually abusing children now and to prevent children from developing sexually abusive behaviors in the future.

Entitlement is the belief that one has special rights and privileges without accompanying reciprocal responsibilities.

Environmental neglect is a form of child maltreatment that refers to a lack of environmental safety, opportunities, and resources associated with living in neighborhoods burdened by crime, lack of civility, and few resources for children and families.

Evidence-based prosecution (also called **victimless prosecution**) allows prosecutors to build a case using police reports, photographs, and physical and other evidence, without relying on victims' testimony.

Experimental design (see also **randomized controlled trial**) is a methodological procedure in which a researcher randomly assigns participants to two or more groups and then introduces an independent variable into one or more of the groups. Because the groups are randomly assigned, any observed outcome differences can then be attributed to the independent variable, thus eliminating the time-order and spuriousness problems that plague nonexperimental designs. The randomized controlled trial is the most powerful methodological design for establishing causal relationships.

Exploiting is a form of child psychological maltreatment that involves using a child for the needs, advantages, or profits of the caretaker.

Externalizing behavior problems are childhood behavior problems, considered to be acting-out behaviors, that include observable symptoms such as aggression, antisocial behavior, and impulsivity, among others.

Failure to thrive (FTT) is a syndrome characterized by marked retardation or cessation of growth during the first three years of life that develops in a significant number of children as a result of child neglect involving inadequate nutrition and disturbed social interactions.

False negative occurs when a relatively dangerous offender is labeled nondangerous (recidivists identified as moderate or low risk).

False positive occurs when a nondangerous offender is labeled dangerous (nonrecidivists identified as high risk).

Family preservation refers to federal law requiring that all states, as a condition of receiving federal child welfare funding, make every reasonable effort to rehabilitate abusive parents and keep families together by offering intensive rehabilitative services to preserve family unity.

Fatalism is an attitude of resignation with regard to future events that are thought to be inevitable and uncontrollable.

Feticide is the killing of a fetus.

Fidelity monitoring is the faithfulness with which a program is implemented.

Formal help providers are institutions and agencies whose official role is to provide assistance to victims of intimate partner violence.

Gender harassment is calling someone gay or lesbian in a malicious way.

Gender symmetry debate (also known as **gender parity debate**) is the argument among intimate partner violence researchers about whether women are as violent as men.

Genderist attacks are a type of abuse intended to regulate transgender victims' daily behavior by criticizing how they perform with regard to gendered behavior.

Grooming is a strategy employed by offenders whereby a child's trust and compliance are gained through the development of a relationship with the child that gradually crosses sexual boundaries by progressing from nonsexual to sexual conversation and/or touch.

Harm standard is a reporting standard used in the National Incidence Studies that allows for the reporting of cases in which children demonstrate harm as a result of maltreatment.

Hashtag activism is "the use of hashtags as a way for marginalized individuals to come together to protest on social media through a united word, phrase, or sentence" (Maas, McCauley, Bonomi, & Leija, 2018, p. 1741).

Hebephilia refers to child sexual abuse that involves adult-to-adolescent contact.

Hegemonic masculinity is the dominant set of gender norms that position males as superior to females, construct masculinity and femininity as opposites, and denigrate males perceived to display feminine traits.

Heterosexism is a set of attitudes, beliefs, and behaviors that privilege heterosexuality and heterosexual relationships over homosexuality and other sexual orientations and relationships.

Home Visiting Evidence of Effectiveness (HomVEE) is a review of the home visiting research literature, conducted by the U.S. Department of Health and Human Services, to provide an assessment of the evidence of effectiveness for home visiting program models that target families with pregnant women and children from birth through age 5.

Home visiting programs are programs that attempt to provide both intervention and prevention programming to preserve families and prevent abuse by bringing community resources to at-risk families. Such programs address the parent's personal health and life choices; child health and development; environmental concerns such as income, housing, and community violence; family functioning, including adult and child relationships; and access to services.

Homebuilders is one of the first and most widely discussed family preservation, or home visiting, programs, which calls for intensive home-based services for families in the midst of crisis.

Homophobia is an unreasonable fear of and hostility toward homosexuals.

Homophobic control is the use of people's fear of their homosexuality being known by others to control their behavior.

House of Refuge movement is a social movement during the early 1800s that recognized the need for the state to provide support and services to troubled and lawbreaking children (rather than put them in adult prisons). The House of Refuge movement eventually evolved into the juvenile justice system.

Hypothalamic-pituitary-adrenal (HPA) axis is a neurobiological system (including the hypothalamus, pituitary gland, and adrenal cortex) involved in the stress response system of the body.

I³ (I-Cubed) theory identifies three interaction factors that are needed to predict alcohol-induced intimate partner violence: instigation, impellance, and inhibition.

Immigration-related stressors are sources of strain or tension caused by experiences related to being an immigrant.

Incredible Years (IY) is a parent training program that targets children with behavior problems and aims to reduce coercive parent–child interactions by providing parents with information about child development along with strategies to enhance parent–child interactions, such as the use of positive discipline, the reduction of negative affect during parenting interactions, and the reinterpretation of negative cognitive attributions about the parent–child relationship.

Infanticide is the killing of an infant under the age of 1.

Informal help providers are friends and family of a victim of intimate partner violence who provide material and emotional assistance.

Insecure attachment style refers to two different types of parent–child attachment styles in which the child is characterized as either fearing strangers and displaying distress when separated from the caregiver, but not being reassured or comforted in the caregiver's presence (insecure-ambivalent), or avoiding and not seeking comfort or contact from the caregiver (insecure-avoidant) (see also **attachment styles**).

Integrative Treatment of Complex Trauma for Children (ITCT-C) is a comprehensive treatment approach that includes multiple components, is assessment driven, is responsive to contextual issues, and integrates theoretical and clinical approaches for the treatment of complex trauma in children.

Intergenerational transmission of abuse refers to a pattern of abuse that continues from one generation to the next (e.g., abusive parents were themselves abused as children).

Internalized homophobia is the acceptance and internalization to one's identity of negative (homophobic) societal attitudes and beliefs about lesbians and gay men.

Internalizing behavior problems are a dimension of childhood behavior problems that include typically nonobservable symptoms such as anxiety, depression, and low self-esteem, among others.

Interstate domestic violence is crossing state lines to commit intimate partner violence.

Intervention strategies refer to societal responses to help alleviate the problems that result from violence and maltreatment in intimate relationships, including but not limited to therapeutic interventions, education, support services, arrest and prosecution, and medical attention.

Intimate is a spouse, ex-spouse, current or former boyfriend or girlfriend, parent/child, or sibling relationship.

Intimate partner violence (IPV) is any threatened or completed act of physical, sexual, or psychological abuse committed by a spouse, ex-spouse, or current or former boyfriend or girlfriend.

IPV perpetrator (see **batterer**)

Irrevocable consent is the legal principle that when she marries, a woman consents to have sex with her husband and that consent cannot be withdrawn.

Isolating is a form of child psychological maltreatment that involves preventing a child from engaging in normal social activities, such as locking a child in a closet.

Juvenile Victimization Questionnaire (JVQ) is a poly-victimization measure of a wide variety of childhood

victimizations, including conventional crime, child maltreatment, peer and sibling victimization, sexual assault, and witnessing an indirect victimization.

Keeping Children and Families Safe Act is legislation that requires states to report infants who were born exposed to illegal substance abuse or who exhibit withdrawal symptoms and includes eligibility requirements for child welfare funding to encourage states to create policies requiring Child Protective Services notification of infants prenatally exposed to illegal drugs.

Kinship care is a form of out-of-home placement in which children are placed with relatives other than the maltreating parent.

Longitudinal designs are research designs that follow participants over time, collecting data across multiple assessment periods for the same cohort of people.

Longitudinal Studies of Child Abuse and Neglect (LONGSCAN) is a consortium of research studies initiated in 1990 and funded by grants from the National Center on Child Abuse and Neglect through the University of North Carolina Injury Prevention Research Center and five satellite sites. Through LONGSCAN all studies operate under common by-laws and procedures with each site conducting a separate and unique research project on the etiology and impact of child maltreatment. While each project can stand alone on its own merits, through the use of common assessment measures, similar data collection methods and schedules, and pooled analyses, LONGSCAN is a collaborative effort.

Maltreatment refers to all forms of inappropriate behavior and abuse, whether violent or not.

Mandated reporters are anyone required by state law to report cases of child or elder maltreatment.

Mandatory arrest policies require police officers to make an arrest when responding to a call if they have probable cause to believe that intimate partner violence has occurred.

Mandatory reporting laws refer to state legislation that requires certain classes of professionals to report cases of suspected child or adult abuse.

Marital exemption law held that by mutual matrimonial consent and contract, a wife had given her consent to sexual intercourse with her husband.

Masturbatory satiation is a treatment technique used with child sexual abuse perpetrators who are instructed to reach orgasm through masturbation as quickly as possible using *appropriate* sexual fantasies and then following ejaculation are told to switch their fantasies to images involving children, continuing to masturbate until the total masturbation time is one hour, thereby reinforcing the appropriate fantasies through the pleasurable feelings of orgasm and diminishing the inappropriate fantasies by associating them with nonpleasurable masturbation that occurs after ejaculation.

Matched control group is a comparison group in which each subject is matched as closely as possible for variables that might reasonably be predictive of the dependent variable (socioeconomic status, family stability, sex, age, etc.). For example, if we wanted to study the long-term effects of child abuse on child development, we could select a sample of children who have been abused and compare their development over time to that of a matched comparison group of children who have not been abused. This matched comparison group would make causal assertions about the effects of child abuse more reasonable.

Maternal, Infant, and Early Childhood Home Visiting (MIECHV) Program is a federal grant program that is a provision within the Patient Protection and Affordable Care Act ("Obamacare"). Beginning in 2010, this initiative has provided states with substantial resources for home visiting, including $1.5 billion over five years (FYs 2010–2014) with an option for reauthorization.

Medical neglect is the failure or delay in seeking needed health care, refusal to allow or provide needed care for diagnosed conditions, and noncompliance with medical recommendations.

Missocializing (i.e., corrupting) is a form of child psychological maltreatment that involves modeling, permitting, or encouraging antisocial behavior in a child.

Modeling is a process of learning by imitating others' behavior.

Modus operandi refers to the method of operation of offenders.

Moral entrepreneurs are claims makers who are engaged in what they see as purely moral crusades.

Motivational interviewing is a therapeutic approach that facilitates and engages individuals' intrinsic motivation to change their behavior.

Narcissistic personality disorder is a personality disorder involving a pattern of behavior that includes grandiosity, need for admiration, and lack of empathy.

National Child Abuse and Neglect Data System (NCANDS) is a data set originating with state Child Protective Services agencies that reports state-level data on the number of child abuse and neglect reports, the source of child abuse reports, investigation outcomes, types of maltreatment, description of the victims of maltreatment, and the relationship of perpetrators to victims.

National Coalition Against Domestic Violence, founded in 1978, is a women's rights organization committed to advocating for battered women on a national level.

National Crime Victimization Survey (NCVS) is a semiannual victim survey conducted by the U.S. Census Bureau on behalf of the U.S. Department of Justice. The NCVS has been conducted since 1973 and is the primary source of information in the United States on the characteristics of criminal victimization.

National Incidence Studies (NIS) are a series of congressionally appropriated surveys of mandated professionals conducted by the National Center on Child Abuse and Neglect. There have been four NIS studies, which occurred in 1981, 1988, 1996, and 2008.

National Intimate Partner and Sexual Violence Survey (NISVS) is a victimization survey that measures adult respondents' recollections about physical violence and sexual assault experienced by the respondent.

National Organization for Women (NOW), founded in 1976, is a women's rights organization that remains active today.

National Survey of Children's Exposure to Violence (NatSCEV) is an ongoing national survey conducted by David Finkelhor that measures youth violence using the Juvenile Victimization Questionnaire. It has been conducted 3 times, in 2008, 2011, and 2014.

Neonatal abstinence syndrome (NAS) refers to a constellation of drug withdrawal symptoms, such as irritability, restlessness, tremors, weight loss, and poor feeding and sleep patterns, shortly after birth due to drug exposure in utero.

No-drop prosecution policies require prosecutors to proceed with a case regardless of whether a victim agrees to participate.

Nonspuriousness is a condition of cause in correlated variables. A spurious relationship is one in which a third unknown and uncontrolled variable accounts for the correlation between the two variables in question.

Nurse–Family Partnership (NFP) is a home visitation program (originally called the Prenatal/Early Infancy Project) that focuses on enhancing the health of the infant, improving parental caregiving, and providing life course development support (e.g., educational, occupational, and pregnancy planning).

Official statistics refer to estimates of violence and maltreatment in intimate relationships (VMIR) derived from statistics that come from the Federal Bureau of Investigation, social service agencies, or professionals; these estimates represent the amount of VMIR that comes to the attention of authorities.

One-child policy is a family planning policy in China that places limits and restrictions on how many children Chinese families can have.

Online grooming is a grooming process (see **grooming**) that occurs online over the internet.

Oppositional defiant disorder is one of the disruptive behavior disorders of childhood and is characterized by a recurring pattern of negative, defiant, disobedient, and hostile behaviors directed toward authority figures.

Out-of-home care is one type of post-investigative services provided by Child Protective Services agencies and includes foster care placement, kinship care, and placement in residential treatment centers and institutions.

Paranoid personality disorder is a personality disorder involving a pattern of behavior that includes a level of distrust and suspiciousness to the degree that others' motives are interpreted as malevolent.

Parens patriae is a doctrine that dictates that the state has a responsibility to protect vulnerable children.

Parent–Child Conflict Tactics Scale (CTSPC) is a scale developed to measure various tactics or behaviors that parents might use when having a conflict with a child; these scales are a variation of the original CTS.

Parent–Child Interaction Therapy (PCIT) is form of therapy involving behavioral parent training whereby the parent is coached in parenting skills during live parent–child interactions.

Parental inconsistency is a form of child psychological maltreatment that involves a parent responding unreliably and inconsistently to a child.

Patriarchal is the power of men over women.

Pedophilia is a diagnostic term that refers to sexual fantasies, urges, or behaviors that involve adult-to-child sexual contact with a child younger than age 14 years.

Perpetration surveys are phone or face-to-face surveys of the general public concerning violence and maltreatment in intimate relationships (VMIR) and focus on obtaining information from VMIR perpetrators.

Personal assistance services (PAS) providers are individuals who help people with disabilities complete tasks of daily living.

Physical disabilities include any mobility limitations or illnesses that affect physical functioning.

Physical neglect is defined as failure to provide a child with basic necessities of life, such as food, clothing, and shelter.

Plan of Safe Care is a requirement of the Keeping Children and Families Safe Act of 2003 for the development of a plan for provision of services and supports to ensure the safety and well-being of infants identified as being born affected by substance abuse, withdrawal, or fetal alcohol spectrum disorder.

Polyvictimization is experiencing two or more types of abuse (e.g., physical violence, sexual violence, psychological abuse, and stalking).

Postpartum depression (PPD) is a form of clinical depression and can affect both men and women, following childbirth. Symptoms are similar to those of clinical depression, but it is often one of the leading causes of murder in children less than 1 year of age.

Post-traumatic stress disorder (PTSD) is an anxiety disorder produced by an extremely stressful event(s) (e.g., assault, rape, military combat, death camp); the disorder is characterized by a number of adverse reactions including re-experiencing the trauma in painful recollections or recurrent dreams; diminished responsiveness, or numbing, with disinterest in significant activities and with feelings of detachment and estrangement from others; and additional symptoms such as exaggerated startle response, disturbed sleep, difficulty in concentrating or remembering, guilt about surviving when others did not, and avoidance of activities that recall the traumatic event.

Preferred arrest policies encourage police officers to make an arrest when responding to a call if they have probable cause to believe that intimate partner violence has occurred.

Prenatal neglect is a form of child maltreatment that refers generally to any actions of a pregnant woman that can potentially harm her unborn child, such as substance abuse.

Prevention strategies are strategies that attempt to stop abuse before it occurs.

Primary aggressor laws require police officers responding to an intimate partner violence call to distinguish the party who initiated the aggression from the party who likely acted with a defensive response to that aggression, and offensive injuries from defensive injuries.

Primary caregiver is an adult in charge of a child's care including, but not limited to, a parent, adult, or babysitter.

Prospective cohort is a longitudinal cohort study in which researchers recruit subjects and collect baseline exposure data *before* any of the subjects have developed the outcome of interest. This is in contrast to a retrospective study, which examines factors that explain an event that has occurred in the past.

Prostitution of children is a form of commercial sexual exploitation of children that is defined by the United Nations Optional Protocol to the Convention on the Rights of the Child (2000, article 2[b]) as "the use of a child in sexual activities for remuneration or any other form of consideration."

Protect Our Kids Act is legislation to commission the development of a national strategy and recommendations for reducing fatalities resulting from child abuse and neglect.

Protection orders are obtained in civil court, rather than criminal court, and allow judges to impose specific restrictions on the abusive partner, depending on the concerns of the victim and the circumstances of the case, to allow for individualized responses. They are in effect for a limited period of time—usually one to three years—but they may be extended if judged to be necessary.

Protective factors are variables that precede a negative outcome and decrease the chances that the outcome will occur.

Psychiatric or mental disabilities encompass all mental illnesses (e.g., schizophrenia, bipolar disorder).

Randomized controlled trial (RCT) (see also **experimental design**) is a methodological procedure in which a researcher randomly assigns participants to two or more groups and then introduces an independent variable into one or more of the groups. Because the groups are randomly assigned, any observed outcome differences can then be attributed to the independent variable, thus eliminating the time-order and spuriousness problems that plague nonexperimental designs. The RCT is the most powerful methodological design for establishing causal relationships.

Rape is nonconsensual attempted or completed penetration of the vagina or anus with any body part or object, or oral penetration by a sex organ of another person.

Rape myths are a set of beliefs about what constitutes "real rape" and "worthy" rape victims.

Recidivism rates represent the likelihood that offenders will commit repeat offenses.

Recovered memories are traumatic events that are sometimes blocked from conscious memory.

Reinforcement occurs when a behavior is rewarded, rather than punished; reinforced behaviors are more likely to be learned and internalized.

Rejecting is a form of child psychological maltreatment that involves verbal or symbolic acts that express feelings of rejection toward the child.

Repressed memories are traumatic events that are sometimes blocked from conscious memory.

Reproductive coercion involves pressuring a partner to get pregnant or, alternatively, to abort a pregnancy.

Restorative justice involves the practice of informal conflict mediation used in a variety of programs and practices that de-emphasize punishment in favor of making amends to victims and reintegrating offenders into their communities.

Restraining orders (see **protection orders**)

Retrospective studies search for factors that explain an event that occurred in the past. This is in contrast to a prospective study, which follows subjects before any of them have developed the outcome of interest.

Risk factors are variables that precede a negative outcome and increase the chances that the outcome will occur.

SafeCare (formerly Project 12-Ways) is a noteworthy multicomponent child maltreatment intervention that includes a variety of services for families, such as parent–child training, stress reduction, marital counseling, employment assistance, and training in money management.

Safe-haven laws allow biological mothers to give up their newborn infants anonymously in specific safe locations, such as hospitals or fire stations, with full immunity from prosecution.

Schizoid personality disorder is a personality disorder involving a pattern of behavior that includes detachment from social relationships and a restricted range of emotional responses.

Schizotypal personality disorder is a personality disorder involving an acute pattern of behavior that includes discomfort in close relationships, cognitive or perceptual disturbances, and eccentric behavior.

Self-report surveys are mail, phone, or face-to-face surveys of the general public designed to measure rates of violence and maltreatment in intimate relationships.

Sensory disabilities are disabilities that affect sensory functions of hearing and sight.

Sexting refers to sending sexually explicit messages and/or photographs electronically either via text messaging or by posting photographs on the internet.

Sexual assault encompasses various forms of *nonconsensual* sexual contact, such as kissing or fondling a person without the person's consent or when the person is unable to consent.

Sexual harassment refers to unwanted sexual advances, requests for sexual favors, and other verbal or physical harassment of a sexual nature.

Sexualized behavior refers to overt sexual acting out toward adults or other children, compulsive masturbation, excessive sexual curiosity, sexual promiscuity, and precocious sexual play and knowledge.

Shaken baby syndrome (SBS) results from vigorously shaking a child and can cause the brain to move within the skull, resulting in injury or abusive head trauma.

Social construction is a perspective that holds that societal reactions to a social condition are central to the process of that condition's redefinition as a social problem.

Social control is the collective efforts of a society to ensure conformity and prevent deviance.

Social learning theory is an explanatory model of socialization, which posits that children learn by modeling or imitating those around them and that behaviors that are reinforced or rewarded, rather than punished, are more likely to be learned and internalized.

Spanking is the most minor and culturally acceptable form of physical punishment of children, which typically refers to hitting a child with an open hand.

Spousal exemption is the legal principle that a husband cannot be prosecuted for raping his wife.

Stalking is a form of intimate violence that involves a pattern of unwanted, harassing, or threatening tactics that generate fear in the victim.

Stand your ground laws are laws that permit individuals to use force, including deadly force, without the obligation to retreat, if they reasonably believe that it is necessary to prevent someone who is attacking them in their home from killing them or inflicting serious bodily injury.

Stop It Now! is a prevention program developed to encourage offenders and those at risk for offending to self-identify, report themselves to authorities, and enter treatment.

Substantiated is the determination, made by Adult Protective Services or Child Protective Services, that a preponderance of evidence suggests that a reported incident of abuse did in fact occur.

Technology-facilitated peer harassment is the use of the internet or social media to send negative, harassing, or cruel messages and posts to peers.

Teen dating violence is physical, psychological, or sexual violence, as well as stalking, perpetrated within a dating relationship.

Terrorizing is a form of child psychological maltreatment that involves actions or threats that cause extreme fear and/or anxiety in a child.

Time order is a condition of cause in correlated variables. In order to conclude that X causes Y, we must establish that X occurred before Y.

Transformative justice is an alternative justice model that challenges the conventional approach to intimate partner violence intervention and instead emphasizes community accountability.

Transphobic abuse is a type of intimate partner violence perpetrated against transgender people, particularly by nontrans partners, that focuses on the trans identity of the victim.

Trauma-focused cognitive behavioral therapy (TF-CBT) is an evidence-based intervention that aims to address the therapeutic needs of children and adolescents who are experiencing difficulties associated with experiencing traumatic events. The primary goal of TF-CBT is to provide psychoeducation to children and their parents in order to help identify and cope with emotions, thoughts, and behaviors. The approach combines trauma-sensitive interventions with cognitive behavioral strategies (see **cognitive behavioral therapy**).

Triple P—Positive Parenting Program is a multilevel parenting and family support program whose primary aim is to promote healthy family functioning and reduce parent–child conflict by helping parents develop nurturing environments by promoting positive, caring relationships and the development of effective, nonviolent child management strategies.

Uniform Crime Report (UCR) is a nationwide effort by the Federal Bureau of Investigation to collect and report crimes, number of arrests, and persons arrested. It is the most common and widely used form of official statistics.

United Nations Convention on the Rights of the Child (UNCRC), which was adopted in 1989, affirms the inherent dignity and inalienable rights of all members of the human family, including children.

United Nations Declaration on the Elimination of Violence Against Women, which was adopted in 1994, calls for a "universal application to women of the rights and principles with regard to equality, security, liberty, integrity and dignity of all human beings."

Verbal abuse (see also **degrading**) is a form of child psychological maltreatment that involves deprecating a child, such as insulting a child or calling a child names, publicly humiliating a child, or constantly criticizing a child.

Victim advocacy services is a type of formal help provider specifically designed to provide support and assistance to victims of intimate partner violence.

Victim-centered approach is a strategy whereby help providers consult with victims, rather than tell them what they should do.

Victimization surveys are phone or face-to-face surveys of the general public concerning violence and maltreatment in intimate relationships (VMIR) and focus on obtaining information from victims of VMIR.

Victimless prosecution (also called **evidence-based prosecution**) allows prosecutors to build a case using police reports, photographs, and physical and other evidence without relying on victims' testimony.

Violence can be defined as an act carried out with the intention of, or an act perceived as having the intention of, physically hurting another person.

Violence Against Women Act (VAWA) is a federal law with provisions intended to reduce intimate partner violence, as well as other forms of violence that disproportionately affect women, largely through criminal justice remedies, such as increasing perpetrator accountability. It was first passed in 1994 and was most recently reauthorized in 2013.

Youth Internet Safety Survey (YISS) is a survey conducted by the Crimes Against Children Research Center that attempts to determine the magnitude of online exploitation of children.

REFERENCES

Abreu, R. L., & Kenny, M. C. (2018). Cyberbullying and LGBTQ youth: A systematic literature review and recommendations for prevention and intervention. *Journal of Child & Adolescent Trauma, 11*(1), 81–97.

Abu-Ras, W. (2007). Cultural beliefs and service utilization by battered Arab immigrant women. *Violence Against Women, 13*, 1002–1028.

Acierno, R., Hernandez, M. A., Arnstadter, A., Resnick, H. S., Steve, K., Muzzy, W., & Kilpatrick, D. G. (2010). Prevalence and correlates of emotional, physical, sexual and financial abuse and potential neglect in the United States: The National Elder Mistreatment Study. *American Journal of Public Health, 100*, 292–297.

Adams, A. E., Littwin, A. K., & Javorka, M. (2019). The frequency, nature, and effects of coerced debt among a national sample of women seeking help for intimate partner violence. *Violence Against Women*. Advance online publication. http://doi.org/10.1177/1077801219841446

Adams, A. E., Tolman, R. M., Bybee, D., Sullivan, C. M., & Kennedy, A. M. (2012). The impact of intimate partner violence on low-income women's economic wellbeing: The mediating role of job stability. *Violence Against Women, 18*(12), 1345–1367.

Adams, P. R., & Adams, G. R. (1984). Mount Saint Helens's ashfall: Evidence for a disaster stress reaction. *American Psychologist, 39*(3), 252.

Aday, R. H., Kehoe, G. C., & Farney, L. A. (2006). Impact of senior center friendships on aging women who live alone. *Journal of Women and Aging, 18*, 57–73.

Adelman, M., & Kil, S. H. (2007). Dating conflicts: Rethinking dating violence and youth conflict. *Violence Against Women, 13*(12), 1296–1318.

Adler, N., & Schutz, J. (1995). Sibling incest offenders. *Child Abuse & Neglect, 19*, 811–819.

Afifi, T. O., Mather, A., Boman, J., Fleisher, W., Enns, M. W., MacMillan, H., & Sareen, J. (2011). Childhood adversity and personality disorders: Results from a nationally representative population-based study. *Journal of Psychiatric Research, 45*(6), 814–822.

Ainsworth, F. (2002). Mandatory reporting of child abuse and neglect: Does it really make a difference? *Child & Family Social Work, 7*(1), 57–63.

Ake, J., & Arnold, A. (2018). A brief history of anti-violence against women movements in the U.S. In C. M. Renzetti, J. L. Edleson, & R. K. Bergen (Eds.), *Sourcebook on violence against women* (3rd ed., pp. 3–25). Thousand Oaks, CA: Sage.

Alaggia, R., Collin-Vézina, D., & Lateef, R. (2019). Facilitators and barriers to child sexual abuse (CSA) disclosures: A research update (2000–2016). *Trauma, Violence, & Abuse, 20*(2), 260–283.

Aldarondo, E., & Castro-Fernandez, M. (2011). Risk and protective factors for domestic violence perpetration. In J. W. White, M. P. Koss, & A. E. Kazdin (Eds.), *Violence against women and children: Mapping the terrain* (pp. 221–242). Washington, DC: American Psychological Association.

Aldarondo, E., Kaufman Kantor, G. K., & Jasinski, J. L. (2002). Risk marker analysis for wife assault in Latino families. *Violence Against Women, 8*, 429–454.

Alderden, M. A., & Ullman, S. E. (2012). Creating a more complete and current picture: Examining police and prosecutor decision making when processing sexual assault cases. *Violence Against Women, 18*(5), 525–551.

Alegría-Flores, K., Raker, K., Pleasants, R. K., Weaver, M. A., & Weinberger, M. (2017). Preventing interpersonal violence on college campuses: The effect of One Act Training on bystander intervention. *Journal of Interpersonal Violence, 32*(7), 1103–1126.

Alessandri, S. M. (1991). Play and social behavior in maltreated preschoolers. *Development and Psychopathology, 3*(2), 191–206.

Algood, C. L., Hong, J. S., Gourdine, R. M., & Williams, A. B. (2011). Maltreatment of children with developmental disabilities: An ecological systems analysis. *Children and Youth Services Review, 33*, 1142–1148.

Alink, L. R., Cicchetti, D., Kim, J., & Rogosch, F. A. (2012). Longitudinal associations among child maltreatment, social functioning, and cortisol regulation. *Developmental Psychology, 48*, 224–236.

Allen, B., Timmer, S. G., & Urquiza, A. J. (2016). Parent–child interaction therapy for sexual concerns of maltreated children: A preliminary investigation. *Child Abuse & Neglect, 56*, 80–88.

Allen, B. S., & Vacca, J. S. (2011). Bring back orphanages—An alternative to foster care? *Children and Youth Services Review, 33*, 1067–1071.

Allen, K. (2019, April 30). "He loved everybody": Alabama community picks up pieces after bullied gay teen takes his own life, family says. *ABC News*. Retrieved from https://abcnews.go.com/US/loved-alabama-community-picks-pieces-bullied-gay-teen/story?id=62694866

Allen, N. E., Larson, S. E., & Walden, A. L. (2011). An overview of community-based services for battered women. In C. M. Renzetti, J. L. Edleson, & R. K. Bergen (Eds.), *Sourcebook on violence against women* (2nd ed., pp. 245–264). Thousand Oaks, CA: Sage.

Allen, S. (2018). Why did Joshua Vallum kill Mercedes Williamson, his transgender girlfriend? *Daily Beast*. Retrieved from https://www.the dailybeast.com/why-did-joshua-vallum-kill-mercedes-williamson-his-transgender-girlfriend

Allstate Foundation. (2009). *Crisis: Economic and domestic violence*. Retrieved July 1, 2009, from http://www.ClickToEmpower.org

Allwood, M. A., & Widom, C. S. (2013). Child abuse and neglect, developmental role attainment and adult arrests. *Journal of Research in Crime and Delinquency, 50*, 551–578.

Almond, D., Li, H., & Zhang, S. (2019). Land reform and sex selection in China. *Journal of Political Economy, 127*(2), 560–585.

Almuneef, M., Qayad, M., Aleissa, M., & Albuhairan, F. (2014). Adverse childhood experiences, chronic diseases, and risky health behaviors in Saudi Arabian adults: A pilot study. *Child Abuse & Neglect, 38*, 1787–1793.

Altafim, E. R. P., & Linhares, M. B. M. (2016). Universal violence and child maltreatment prevention programs for parents: A systematic review. *Psychosocial Intervention, 25*(1), 27–38.

Altman, R. L., Canter, J., Patrick, P. A., Daley, N., Butt, N. K., & Brand, D. A. (2011). Parent education by maternity nurses and prevention of abusive head trauma. *Pediatrics, 128*(5), e1164–e1172.

Alvarez-Alonso, M. J., Jurado-Barba, R., Martinez-Martin, N., Espin-Jaime, J. C., Bolaños-Porrero, C., Ordoñez-Franco, A., . . . Manzanares, J. (2016). Association between maltreatment and polydrug use among adolescents. *Child Abuse & Neglect, 51*, 379–389.

Amacker, A. M., & Littleton, H. L. (2013). Perceptions of similarity and responsibility attributions to an acquaintance sexual assault victim. *Violence Against Women, 19*(11), 1384–1407.

Amado, B. G., Arce, R., & Herraiz, A. (2015). Psychological injury in victims of child sexual abuse: A meta-analytic review. *Psychosocial Intervention, 24*(1), 49–62.

Amaro, Y. (2018, December 17). Is spanking child abuse? Fresno Assemblyman Arambula's arrest opens debate. *Fresno Bee*.

Amelung, T., Kuhle, L. F., Konrad, A., Pauls, A., & Beier, K. M. (2012). Androgen deprivation therapy of self-identifying, help-seeking pedophiles in the Dunkelfeld. *International Journal of Law and Psychiatry, 35*(3), 176–184.

American Professional Society on the Abuse of Children. (1995). *Guidelines for the psychosocial evaluation of suspected psychological maltreatment in children and adolescents*. Chicago, IL: Author.

American Professional Society on the Abuse of Children. (2013). *The commercial sexual exploitation of children: The medical provider's role in identification, assessment and treatment*. Retrieved from www.apsac.org

American Professional Society on the Abuse of Children. (2016). Special issue: Differential response. *APSAC Advisor, 28*(2).

American Professional Society on the Abuse of Children. (2017). *APSAC practice guidelines for the investigation and determination of suspected psychological maltreatment in children and adolescents*. Chicago, IL: Author.

American Psychiatric Association. (2013). *Diagnostic and statistical manual of mental disorders* (5th ed.). Washington, DC: Author.

American Psychological Association. (2007). *Report of the APA task force on the sexualization of girls*. Washington, DC: Author.

American Psychological Association. (2020). *ACT Raising Safe Kids Program*. Retrieved from https://www.apa.org/act

Anda, R. F., Croft, J. B., Felitti, V. J., Nordenberg, D., Giles, W. H., Williamson, D. F., & Giovino, G. A. (1999). Adverse childhood experiences and smoking during adolescence and adulthood. *JAMA, 282*(17), 1652–1658.

Anda, R. F., Felitti, V. J., Chapman, D. P., Croft, J. B., Williamson, D. F., Santelli, J., Dietz, P. M., & Marks, J. S. (2001). Abused boys, battered mothers, and male involvement in teen pregnancy: New insights for pediatricians. *Pediatrics, 107*, e19.

Anderson, C. A., & Anderson, K. B. (2008). Men who target women: Specificity of target, generality of aggressive behavior. *Aggressive Behavior, 34*(6), 605–622.

Anderson, C. A., Bushman, B. J., Donnerstein, E., Hummer, T. A., & Warburton, W. (2015). SPSSI research summary on media violence. *Analyses of Social Issues and Public Policy, 15*(1), 4–19.

Anderson, E. L., Fraser, A., Caleyachetty, R., Hardy, R., Lawlor, D. A., & Howe, L. D. (2018). Associations of adversity in childhood and risk factors for cardiovascular disease in mid-adulthood. *Child Abuse & Neglect, 76*, 138–148.

Andrews, C. M., Cao, D., Marsh, J. C., & Shin, H. (2011). The impact of comprehensive services in substance abuse treatment for women with a history of intimate partner violence. *Violence Against Women, 17*, 550–567.

Angelone, D. J., Marcantonio, T., & Melillo, J. (2018). An evaluation of adolescent and young adult (re)victimization experiences: Problematic substance use and negative consequences. *Violence Against Women, 24*(5), 586–602.

Angelone, D. J., Mitchell, D., & Pilafova, A. (2007). Club drug use and intentionality in perceptions of rape victims. *Sex Roles, 57*, 283–292.

Anthony, E. K., Austin, M. J., & Cormier, D. R. (2010). Early detection of prenatal substance exposure and the role of child welfare. *Children and Youth Services Review, 32*, 6–12.

Antonietti, J., Resseguier, N., Dubus, J. C., Scavarda, D., Girard, N., Chabrol, B., & Bosdure, E. (2018). The medical and social outcome in 2016 of infants who were victims of shaken baby syndrome between 2005 and 2013. *Archives de Pediatrie, 26*, 21–29.

Appleton, R. (2019, May 16). Assemblyman Arambula found not guilty in child abuse case. He returns to Capitol on Monday. *Fresno Bee.*

Apstein, S. (2019, October 22). Astros staffer's outburst at female reporters illustrates MLB's forgive-and-forget attitude toward domestic violence. *Sports Illustrated.* Retrieved from https://www.si.com/mlb/2019/10/22/houston-astros-roberto-osuna-suspension

Archer, J. (2000). Sex differences in aggression between heterosexual partners: A meta-analytic review. *Psychological Bulletin, 126*(5), 651–680.

Ard, K. L., & Makadon, H. J. (2011). Addressing intimate partner violence in lesbian, gay, bisexual, and transgender patients. *Journal of General Internal Medicine, 26*(8), 930–933.

Armenti, N. A., Snead, A. L., & Babcock, J. C. (2018). Exploring the moderating role of problematic substance use in the relations between borderline and antisocial personality features and intimate partner violence. *Violence Against Women, 24*(2), 223–240.

Armstrong, E. A., Hamilton, L., & Sweeney, B. (2006). Sexual assault on campus: A multilevel, integrative approach to party rape. *Social Problems, 53*(4), 483–499.

Arslan, G. (2016). Psychological maltreatment, emotional and behavioral problems in adolescents: The mediating role of resilience and self-esteem. *Child Abuse & Neglect, 52*, 200–209.

Ashley, O. S., & Foshee, V. A. (2005). Adolescent help-seeking for dating violence: Prevalence, sociodemographic correlates, and sources of help. *Journal of Adolescent Health, 36*, 25–31.

Assink, M., Spruit, A., Schuts, M., Lindauer, R., van der Put, C. E., & Stams, G. J. J. (2018). The intergenerational transmission of child maltreatment: A three-level meta-analysis. *Child Abuse & Neglect, 84*, 131–145.

Assink, M., van der Put, C. E., Meeuwsen, M. W., de Jong, N. M., Oort, F. J., Stams, G. J. J., & Hoeve, M. (2019). Risk factors for child sexual abuse victimization: A meta-analytic review. *Psychological Bulletin, 145*(5), 459–489.

Averdijk, M., Mueller-Johnson, K., & Eisner, M. (2011). *Sexual victimization of children and adolescents in Switzerland.* Rapport final pour la Fondation UBS Optimus.

Azar, S. T. (1997). A cognitive behavioral approach to understanding and treating parents who physically abuse their children. In D. A. Wolfe, R. J. McMahon, & R. D. Peters (Eds.), *Child abuse: New directions in prevention and treatment across the lifespan* (pp. 79–101). Thousand Oaks, CA: Sage.

Azar, S. T., Povilaitis, T. Y., Lauretti, A. F., & Pouquette, C. L. (1998). The current status of etiological theories in intrafamilial child maltreatment. In J. R. Lutzker (Ed.), *Handbook of child abuse research and treatment* (pp. 3–30). New York, NY: Plenum Press.

Azziz-Baumgartner, E., McKeown, L., Melvin, P., Quynh, D., & Reed, J. (2011). Rates of femicide in women of different races, ethnicities, and places of birth: Massachusetts, 1993–2007. *Journal of Interpersonal Violence, 26*(5), 1077–1090.

Babchishin, K. M., Hanson, R. K., & Hermann, C. A. (2011). The characteristics of online sex offenders: A meta-analysis. *Sexual Abuse: A Journal of Research and Treatment, 23*(1), 92–123.

Babcock, J. C., Green, C. E., & Robie, C. (2004). Does batterers' treatment work? A meta-analytic review of domestic violence treatment outcome research. *Clinical Psychology Review, 23*, 1023–1053.

Bachman, R. (2000). A comparison of annual incidence rates and contextual characteristics of intimate partner violence against women from the National Crime Victimization Survey (NCVS) and the National Violence Against Women Survey (NVAWS). *Violence Against Women, 6*, 839–867.

Bachman, R. (2015). We are making progress in measuring sexual violence against women? In H. Johnson, B. S. Fisher, & V. Jaquier (Eds.), *Critical issues on violence against women: International perspectives and promising strategies* (pp. 19–30). New York, NY: Routledge.

Bachman, R., & Meloy, M. (2008). The epidemiology of violence against the elderly: Implications for primary and secondary prevention. *Journal of Contemporary Criminal Justice, 2*, 189–197.

Bada, H. S., Das, A., Bauer, C. R., Shankaran, S., Lester, B., LaGasse, L., . . . Higgins, R. (2007). Impact of prenatal cocaine exposure on child behavior problems through school age. *Pediatrics, 119*(2), e348–e359. doi:10.1542/peds.2006.1404. Retrieved from http://pediatrics.aappublications.org/content/119/2/e348.short

Badenes-Ribera, L., Frias-Navarro, D., Bonilla-Campos, A., Pons-Salvador, G., & Monterde-i-Bort, H. (2015). Intimate partner violence in self-identified lesbians: A meta-analysis of its prevalence. *Sexuality Research and Social Policy, 12*, 47–59.

Baer, J. C., & Martinez, C. D. (2006). Child maltreatment and insecure attachment: A meta-analysis. *Journal of Reproductive and Infant Psychology, 24*(3), 187–197.

Bai, L., & Han, Z. R. (2016). Emotion dysregulation mediates relations between Chinese parents' histories of childhood emotional abuse and parenting stress: A dyadic data analysis. *Parenting, 16*, 187–205.

Baily, T. F., & Baily, W. H. (1986). *Operational definitions of child emotional maltreatment: Final report* (DHHS Publication No. 90-CA-0956). Washington, DC: Government Printing Office.

Bair-Merritt, M. H., Voegtline, K., Ghazarian, S. R., Granger, D. A., Blair, C., Johnson, S. B., & Family Life Project Investigators. (2015). Maternal intimate partner violence exposure, child cortisol reactivity and child asthma. *Child Abuse & Neglect, 48*, 50–57.

Baker, A. J. L., & Brassard, M. (2019). Predictors of variation in state reported rates of psychological maltreatment: A survey of statutes and a call for change. *Child Abuse & Neglect, 96*. doi:10.1016/j.chiabu.2019.104102

Baker, A. J. L., & Festinger, T. (2011). Emotional abuse and emotional neglect subscales of the CTQ: Associations with each other, other measures of psychological maltreatment, and demographic variables. *Children and Youth Services Review, 33*(11), 2297–2302. doi:10.1016/j.childyouth.2011.07.018

Bakermans-Kranenburg, M. J., van IJzendoorn, M. H., & Juffer, F. (2003). Less is more: Meta-analyses of sensitivity and attachment interventions in early childhood. *Psychological Bulletin, 129*, 195–215.

Ball, B., Tharp, A. T., Noonan, R. K., Valle, L. A., Hamburger, M. E., & Rosenbluth, B. (2012). Expect Respect support groups: Preliminary evaluation of a dating violence prevention program for at-risk youth. *Violence Against Women, 18*(7), 746–762.

Ballan, M. S., Freyer, M. B., Marti, C. N., Perkel, J., Webb, K. A., & Romanelli, M. (2014). Looking beyond prevalence: A demographic profile of survivors of intimate partner violence with disabilities. *Journal of Interpersonal Violence, 29*(17), 3167–3179.

Ballan, M. S., Freyer, M. B., & Powledge, L. (2017). Intimate partner violence among men with disabilities: The role of health care providers. *American Journal of Men's Health, 11*(5), 1436–1443.

Ballan, M. S., Freyer, M. B., Powledge, L., & Marti, C. N. (2016). Intimate partner violence among help-seeking deaf women: An empirical study. *Violence Against Women*. Advance online publication. doi:10.1177/1077801216664428

Bancroft, J. (2003). *Sexual development in childhood* (Vol. 7). Bloomington: Indiana University Press.

Bancroft, L., Silverman, J. G., & Ritchie, D. (2012). *The batterer as parent* (2nd ed.). Thousand Oaks, CA: Sage.

Banducci, A. N., Felton, J. W., Bonn-Miller, M. O., Lejuez, C. W., & MacPherson, L. (2017). A longitudinal examination of the impact of childhood emotional abuse on cannabis use trajectories among community youth. *Drug and Alcohol Dependence, 100*(171), e14–e15.

Banducci, A. N., Lejuez, C. W., Dougherty, L. R., & MacPherson, L. (2017). A prospective examination of the relations between emotional abuse and anxiety: Moderation by distress tolerance. *Prevention Science, 18*(1), 20–30.

Bandura, A. (1978). *Social learning theory of aggression*. Englewood Cliffs, NJ: Prentice Hall.

Banyard, V. L., Moynihan, M. M., & Plante, E. G. (2007). Sexual violence prevention through bystander education: An experimental evaluation. *Journal of Community Psychology, 35*, 463–481.

Barlow, K. M., Thomson, E., Johnson, D., & Minns, R. A. (2005). Late neurologic and cognitive sequelae of inflicted traumatic brain injury in infancy. *Pediatrics, 116*(2), e174–e185. http://dx.doi.org/10.1542/peds.2004–2739

Barner, J. R., & Carney, M. M. (2011). Interventions for intimate partner violence: A historical review. *Journal of Family Violence, 26*(3), 235–244.

Barnett, D., Ganiban, J., & Cicchetti, D. (1999). Maltreatment, negative expressivity, and the development of Type D attachments from 12 to 24 months of age. *Monographs of the Society for Research in Child Development, 64*(3), 97–118.

Barnett, O. W., Lee, C. Y., & Thelan, R. (1997). Gender differences in attributions of self-defense and control interpartner aggression. *Violence Against Women, 3*(5), 462–481.

Barr, R. G., Barr, M., Fujiwara, T., Conway, J., Catherine, N., & Brant, R. (2009). Do educational materials change knowledge and behavior about crying and shaken baby syndrome? A randomized controlled trial. *Canadian Medical Association Journal, 180*(7), 727–733.

Barr, R. G., Barr, M., Rajabali, F., Humphreys, C., Pike, I., Brant, R., . . . Singhal, A. (2018). Eight-year outcome of implementation of abusive head trauma prevention. *Child Abuse & Neglect, 84*, 106–114.

Barth, J., Bermetz, L., Heim, E., Trelle, S., & Tonia, T. (2013). The current prevalence of child sexual abuse worldwide: A systematic review and meta-analysis. *International Journal of Public Health, 58*(3), 469–483.

Bartholet, E. (2015). Differential response: A dangerous experiment in child welfare. *Florida State University Law Review, 42*(3). Retrieved from https://papers.ssrn.com/sol3/papers.cfm?abstract_id=2477089

Basile, K. C. (2002). Prevalence of wife rape and other intimate partner sexual coercion in a nationally representative sample. *Violence and Victims, 17*(5), 511–524.

Basile, K. C., & Black, M. C. (2011). Intimate partner violence against women. In C. M. Renzetti, J. L. Edleson, & R. K. Bergen (Eds.), *Sourcebook on violence against women* (2nd ed., pp. 111–131). Thousand Oaks, CA: Sage.

Bath, H. I., & Haapala, D. A. (1993). Intensive family preservation services with abused and neglected children: An examination of group differences. *Child Abuse & Neglect, 17*, 213–225.

Bebbington, P., Jonas, S., Kuipers, E., King, M., Cooper, C., Brugha, T., . . . Jenkins, R. (2011). Childhood sexual abuse and psychosis: Data from a cross-sectional national psychiatric survey in England. *The British Journal of Psychiatry, 199*(1), 29–37.

Beck, A. J., Harrison, P. M., & Guerino, P. (2010). *Sexual victimization in juvenile facilities reported by youth, 2008–2009*. Bureau of Justice Statistics Special Report, NCJ228416. Retrieved from http://bjs.ojp.usdoj.gov/index.cfm?ty-pbdetail&iid=2113

Beck, J. G., Tran, H. N., Dodson, T. S., Herschel, A. V., Woodward, M. J., & Eddinger, J. (2016). Cognitive Trauma Therapy for battered women: Replication and extension. *Psychology of Violence, 6*(3), 368–377.

Becker, H. W. (1963). *Outsiders*. New York, NY: Free Press.

Becker-Dreps, S., Morgan, D., Pena, R., Cortes, L., Marten, C. F., & Valladares, E. (2010). Association between intimate partner violence and irritable bowel syndrome: A population-based study in Nicaragua. *Violence Against Women, 16*, 832–845.

Behnke, M., & Smith, V. C. (2013). Prenatal substance abuse: Short- and long-term effects on the exposed fetus. *Pediatrics, 131*(3), e1009–e1024. doi:101.1542/peds.2012-3931. Retrieved from http://pediatrics.aappublications.org/content/131/3/e1009.short

Beier, K. M., Oezdemir, U. C., Schlinzig, E., Groll, A., Hupp, E., & Hellenschmidt, T. (2016). "Just dreaming of them": The Berlin Project for Primary Prevention of Child Sexual Abuse by Juveniles (PPJ). *Child Abuse & Neglect, 52*, 1–10.

Bell, E., Shouldice, M., & Levin, A. V. (2011). Abusive head trauma: A perpetrator confesses. *Child Abuse & Neglect, 35*, 74–77.

Bell, M. F., Bayliss, D. M., Glauert, R., & Ohan, J. L. (2018). School readiness of maltreated children: Associations of timing, type, and chronicity of maltreatment. *Child Abuse & Neglect, 76*, 426–439.

Bell, N. S., Harford, T., McCarroll, J. E., & Senier, L. (2004). Drinking and spouse abuse among U.S. army soldiers. *Alcoholism: Clinical and Experimental Research, 28*(12), 1890–1897.

Belson, K. (2014, November 18). Goodell bars Peterson for rest of season and says he could miss games in 2015. *New York Times*. Retrieved from https://www.nytimes.com/2014/11/19/sports/football/adrian-peterson-suspended-by-nfl-for-remainder-of-season.html

Bennett, L., & Bland, P. (2008). *Substance abuse and intimate partner violence*. Harrisburg, PA: VAWnet. Retrieved from http://www.vawnet.org

Bennett, L. W., & Vincent, N. (2002). Standards for batterer programs: A formative evaluation of the Illinois protocol. In R. A. Geffner & A. Rosenbaum (Eds.), *Domestic violence offenders: Current interventions, research, and implications for policies and standards* (pp. 181–197). New York, NY: Haworth.

Bensley, L. S., Eenwyk, J. V., & Simmons, K. W. (2000). Self-reported childhood sexual and physical abuse and adult HIV-risk behaviors and heavy drinking. *American Journal of Preventive Medicine, 18*, 151–158.

Benson, M. L., & Fox, G. L. (2004). *When violence hits home: How economics and neighborhood play a role*. Washington, DC: U.S. Department of Justice, National Institute of Justice.

Benson, M. L., Fox, G. L., DeMaris, A., & Van Wyk, J. (2003). Neighborhood disadvantage, individual economic distress and violence against women in intimate relationships. *Journal of Quantitative Criminology, 19*, 207–235.

Bent-Goodley, T. B., Rice, J., Williams, O. J., & Pope, M. (2011). Treatment for perpetrators of domestic violence. In M. P. Koss, J. W. White, & A. E. Kazdin (Eds.), *Violence against women and children: Navigating solutions* (pp. 199–213). Washington, DC: American Psychological Association.

Benuto, L. T., & O'Donohue, W. (2015). Treatment of the sexually abused child: Review and synthesis of recent meta-analyses. *Children and Youth Services Review, 56*, 52–60.

Bergen, R. K. (2016). An overview of marital rape research in the United States: Limitations and implications for cross-cultural research. In K. Yllo & M. G. Torres (Eds.), *Marital rape: Consent, marriage, and social change in global context* (pp. 19–28). New York, NY: Oxford University Press.

Bergen, R. K., & Barnhill, E. (2006). *Marital rape: New research and directions*. Harrisburg, PA: VAWnet. Retrieved from http://www.vawnet.org

Berger, L. M., Slack, K. S., Waldfogel, J., & Bruch, S. K. (2010). Caseworker-perceived caregiver substance abuse and child protective services outcomes. *Child Maltreatment, 15*(3), 199–210.

Berger, P. (1963). *Invitation to sociology*. Garden City, NY: Doubleday.

Berger, R. P., & Bell, M. J. (2014). Abusive head trauma. In *Pediatric Critical Care Medicine* (pp. 617–626). London, England: Springer.

Berkout, O. V., & Kolko, D. J. (2016). Understanding child directed caregiver aggression: An examination of characteristics and predictors associated with perpetration. *Child Abuse & Neglect, 56*, 44–53.

Berliner, L. (2011). Child sexual abuse: Definitions, prevalence, and consequences. In J. E. B. Myers (Ed.), *The APSAC handbook on child maltreatment* (3rd ed., pp. 215–232). Thousand Oaks, CA: Sage.

Berliner, L., & Conte, J. R. (1990). The process of victimization: The victim's perspective. *Child Abuse & Neglect, 14*, 29–40.

Berliner, L., & Elliott, D. M. (2002). Sexual abuse of children. In J. E. B. Myers, L. Berliner, J. Briere, C. T. Hendrix, C. Jenny, & T. A. Reid (Eds.), *The APSAC handbook on child maltreatment* (2nd ed., pp. 55–78). Thousand Oaks, CA: Sage.

Bernard, K., Dozier, M., Bick, J., Lewis-Morrarty, E., Lindhiem, O., & Carlson, E. (2012). Enhancing attachment organization among maltreated children: Results of a randomized clinical trial. *Child Development, 83*, 623–636. doi:10.1111/j.1467-8624.2011.01712.x

Bernard-Bonnin, A. C., Herbert, M., Daignault, I. V., & Allard-Dansereau, C. (2008). Disclosure of sexual abuse and personal and familial factors as predictors of post-traumatic stress disorder symptoms in school-aged girls. *Pediatrics and Child Health, 13*, 479–486.

Bert, S. C., Guner, B. M., Lanzi, R. G., & Centers for Prevention of Child Neglect. (2019). The influence of history of abuse on parenting knowledge and behavior. *Family Relations, 58*, 176–187.

Berzenski, S. R., Madden, A. R., & Yates, T. M. (2019). Childhood emotional abuse characteristics moderate associations with adult psychopathology and caregiving. *Child Abuse & Neglect, 87*, 77–87.

Best, J. (1989). Introduction: Typification and social problems construction. In J. Best (Ed.), *Images of issues: Typifying contemporary social problems* (pp. xv–xxii). New York, NY: Aldine de Gruyter.

Best, J. (2001). *Damned lies and statistics: Untangling numbers from the media, politicians, and activists.* Berkeley: University of California Press.

Best, J. (2012). *Damned lies and statistics: Untangling numbers from the media, politicians, and activists* (Updated ed.). Berkeley: University of California Press.

Bigras, N., Godbout, N., Hébert, M., Runtz, M., & Daspe, M. È. (2015). Identity and relatedness as mediators between child emotional abuse and adult couple adjustment in women. *Child Abuse & Neglect, 50,* 85–93.

Binggeli, N. J., Hart, S. N., & Brassard, M. R. (2001). *Psychological maltreatment of children.* Thousand Oaks, CA: Sage.

Birkley, E., & Eckhardt, C. I. (2015). Anger, hostility, internalizing negative emotions, and intimate partner violence perpetration: A meta-analytic review. *Clinical Psychology Review, 37,* 40–56.

Black, M. C., Basile, K. C., Breiding, M. J., Smith, S. G., Walters, M. L., Merrick, M. T., . . . Stevens, M. R. (2011). *The National Intimate Partner and Sexual Violence Survey (NISVS): 2010 summary report.* Atlanta, GA: National Center for Injury Prevention and Control, Centers for Disease Control and Prevention.

Black, M. C., & Breiding, M. J. (2008). Adverse health conditions and health risk behaviors associated with intimate partner violence, United States 2005 *Morbidity and Mortality Weekly Report, 57,* 113–117.

Blakey, J. M., Glaude, M., & Jennings, S. W. (2019). School and program related factors influencing disclosure among children participating in a school-based childhood physical and sexual abuse prevention program. *Child Abuse & Neglect, 96.* Advance online publication. doi:10.1016/j.chiabu.2019.104092

Blanchard, R., Kuban, M. E., Klassen, P., Dickey, R., Christensen, B. K., Cantor, J. M., & Blak, T. (2003). Self-reported head injuries before and after age 13 in pedophilic and nonpedophilic men referred for clinical assessment. *Archives of Sexual Behavior, 32*(6), 573–581.

Bland, V. J., Lambie, I., & Best, C. (2018). Does childhood neglect contribute to violent behavior in adulthood? A review of possible links. *Clinical Psychology Review, 60,* 126–135.

Block, R. W. (2002). Child fatalities. In J. E. B. Meyers, L. Berliner, J. Briere, C. T. Hendrix, C. Jenny, & T. A. Reid (Eds.), *The APSAC handbook on child maltreatment* (2nd ed., pp. 293–301). Thousand Oaks, CA: Sage.

Block, R. W., & Krebs, N. F. (2005). Failure to thrive as a manifestation of child neglect. *Pediatrics, 116*(5), 1234–1237.

Bloom, T. (2019, August 28). Death penalty sought against mother, her boyfriend in torture killing of Anthony Avalos: DA's office. *KTLA.* Retrieved from https://ktla.com/news/local-news/death-penalty-sought-against-mother-her-boyfriend-in-torture-killing-of-anthony-avalos-das-office/

Blow, C. M. (2014, September 17). On spanking and abuse. *New York Times.* Retrieved from https://www.nytimes.com/2014/09/18/opinion/charles-blow-on-spanking-and-abuse.html

Bolen, R. M., & Gergely, K. B. (2015). A meta-analytic review of the relationship between nonoffending caregiver support and postdisclosure functioning in sexually abused children. *Trauma, Violence & Abuse, 16*(3), 258–279. Retrieved from https://doi.org/10.1177/1524838014526307

Bolger, K. E., Patterson, C. J., & Kupersmidt, J. B. (1998). Peer relationships and self-esteem among children who have been maltreated. *Child Development, 69,* 1171–1197.

Bonnes, S. (2019). Service-women's responses to sexual harassment: The importance of identity work and masculinity in a gendered organization. *Violence Against Women.* Advance online publication. Retrieved from https://doi.org/10.1177/1077801219873433

Bonomi, A., Nichols, E., Kammes, R., & Green, T. (2018). Sexual violence and intimate partner violence in college women with a mental health and/or behavior disability. *Journal of Women's Health, 27*(3). Retrieved from https://doi.org/10.1089/jwh.2016.6279

Bonomi, A. E., Trabert, B., Anderson, L., Kernic, M., & Holt, V. L. (2014). Intimate partner violence and neighborhood income: A longitudinal analysis. *Violence Against Women, 20*(1), 42–58.

Boroughs, D. S. (2004). Female sexual abusers of children. *Children and Youth Services Review, 26,* 481–487.

Borrego, J., Timmer, S. G., Urquiza, A. J., & Follette, W. C. (2004). Physically abusive mothers' responses following episodes of child noncompliance and compliance. *Journal of Consulting & Clinical Psychology, 72,* 897–903.

Bosch, J., Weaver, T. L., Arnold, L. D., & Clark, E. M. (2017). The impact of intimate partner violence on women's physical health: Findings from the Missouri Behavioral Risk Factor Surveillance System. *Journal of Interpersonal Violence, 32*(22), 3402–3419.

Bosman, J. (2019, July 5). Elite kid justice: Are privileged teenagers more likely to get a slap on the wrist? *New York Times*. Retrieved from http://www.nytimes.com/2019/07/05/us/rich-privilege-courts.html.

Boston Globe. (2014, November 18). Full text of NFL's announcement of Adrian Peterson suspension. Retrieved from https://www.bostonglobe.com/sports/2014/11/18/full-text-nfl-announcement-adrian-peterson-suspension/CC3ZOiHHfYGW890cee14QN/story.html

Bounoua, N., Felton, J. F., Long, K., Stadnik, R. D., Loya, J. M., MacPherson, L., & Lejuez, C. W. (2015). Childhood emotional abuse and borderline personality features: The role of anxiety sensitivity among adolescents. *Personality and Mental Health, 9*(2), 87–95.

Bourgois, P. (1999). *In search of respect: Selling crack in El Barrio*. New York, NY: Cambridge University Press.

Bousha, D. M., & Twentyman, C. T. (1984). Mother–child interactional style in abuse, neglect, and control groups: Naturalistic observations in the home. *Journal of Abnormal Psychology, 93*, 106–114.

Bowen, E., & Swift, C. (2019). Prevalence and correlates of partner abuse used and experienced by adults with intellectual disabilities: A systematic review and call to action. *Trauma, Violence, & Abuse, 20*(5), 693–705.

Bowes, L., Wolke, D., Joinson, C., Lereya, S. T., & Lewis, G. (2014). Sibling bullying and risk of depression, anxiety, and self-harm: A prospective cohort study. *Pediatrics, 134*, 1–8.

Bows, H. (2018). Sexual violence against older people: A review of the empirical literature. *Trauma, Violence & Abuse, 19*(5), 567–583.

Bows, H., & Westmarland, N. (2017). Rape of older people in the United Kingdom: Challenging the "real rape" stereotype. *British Journal of Criminology, 57*(1), 1–17.

Branch, K., Hilinski-Rosick, C. M., Johnson, E., & Solano, G. (2017). Revenge porn victimization of college students in the United States: An exploratory analysis. *International Journal of Cyber Criminology, 11*(1), 128–142.

Brassard, M. R., Hart, S. N., Baker, A. A. L., & Chiel, Z. (2019). *The APSAC monograph on psychological maltreatment*. Columbus, OH: American Professional Society on the Abuse of Children. Retrieved from https://www.apsac.org/single-post/2019/12/16/Now-Available-The-APSAC-Monograph-on-Psychological-Maltreatment

Bratton, S. C., Ceballos, P. L., Landreth, G. L., & Costas, M. B. (2012). Child–parent relationship therapy with nonoffending parents of sexually abused children. In P. Goodyear-Brown (Ed.), *Handbook of child sexual abuse: Identification, assessment, and treatment* (pp. 321–339). Hoboken, NJ: John Wiley & Sons.

Bratton, S. C., Landreth, G. L., Kellam, T., & Blackard, S. (2006). *Child–Parent Relationship Therapy (CPRT) treatment manual: A 10-session filial therapy model for training parents*. New York, NY: Routledge.

Bratton, S., Landreth, G., & Lin, Y. (2010). What the research shows about filial therapy. In J. Baggerly (Ed.), *Evidence-based filial and child-centered research studies and guidelines*. New York, NY: John Wiley & Sons.

Brecklin, L. R., & Forde, D. R. (2001). A meta-analysis of rape education programs. *Violence and Victims, 16*, 303–321.

Breiding, M. J., Black, M. C., & Ryan, G. W. (2008). Prevalence and risk factors of intimate partner violence in eighteen U.S. states/territories, 2005. *American Journal of Preventive Medicine, 34*(2), 112–118.

Brem, M. J., Shorey, R. C., Rothman, E. F., Temple, J. R., & Stuart, G. L. (2018). Trait jealousy moderates the relationship between alcohol problems and intimate partner violence among men in batterer intervention programs. *Violence Against Women, 24*(10), 1132–1148.

Brickner, A. (2019). Prenatal substance exposure and implications for CPS. *Virginia Child Protection Newsletter, 115*, 3–6.

Briere, J. (2002). Treating adult survivors of severe childhood abuse and neglect: Further development of an integrative model. In J. E. B. Meyers, L. Berliner, J. Briere, C. T. Hendrix, C. Jenny, & T. A. Reid (Eds.), *The APSAC handbook on child maltreatment* (2nd ed., pp. 175–205). Thousand Oaks, CA: Sage.

Briere, J., & Lanktree, C. (2011). *Treating complex trauma in adolescents and young adults*. Thousand Oaks, CA: Sage.

Briere, J., Lanktree, C. B., & Semple, R. J. (2019). *Using ITCT-A to treat self-injury in traumatized youth*. Los Angeles: University of Southern California.

Brinkerhoff, M. B., & Lupri, E. (1988). Interpersonal violence. *Canadian Journal of Sociology, 13*, 407–434.

Brossoie, N., & Roberto, K. A. (2016). Community professionals' response to intimate partner violence against rural older women. *Journal of Elder Abuse & Neglect, 27,* 470–488.

Brown, E. J., & Kolko, D. J. (1999). Child victims' attributions about being physically abused: An examination of factors associated with symptom severity. *Journal of Abnormal Child Psychology, 27,* 311–322.

Brown, J. (2018, November 28). Even from jail, sex abuser manipulated the system. His victims were kept in the dark. *Miami Herald.*

Brown, J., Cohen, P., Johnson, J. G., & Salzinger, S. (1998). A longitudinal analysis of risk factors for child maltreatment: Findings of a 17-year prospective study of officially recorded and self-reported child abuse and neglect. *Child Abuse & Neglect, 22*(11), 1065–1078.

Brown, K. R., Peña, E. V., & Rankin, S. (2017). Unwanted sexual contact: Students with autism and other disabilities at greater risk. *Journal of College Student Development, 58*(5), 771–776.

Brown, L. M., Chesney-Lind, M., & Stein, N. (2007). Patriarchy matters: Toward a gendered theory of teen violence and victimization. *Violence Against Women, 13*(12), 1249–1273.

Brown, M. L., & Essay, S. (2016). When pros become cons: Ending the NFL's history of domestic violence leniency. *Family Law Quarterly, 50,* 193–212.

Brown, N. (2011). Holding tensions of victimization and perpetration. In J. L. Ristock (Ed.), *Intimate partner violence in LGBTQ lives* (pp. 153–168). New York, NY: Routledge.

Brown, S. M., Rienks, S., McCrae, J. S., & Watamura, S. E. (2019). The co-occurrence of adverse childhood experiences among children investigated for child maltreatment: A latent class analysis. *Child Abuse & Neglect, 87,* 18–27.

Brown v. Entertainment Merchants Association, 564 U.S. 786 (2011).

Browne, A., Salomon, A., & Bassuk, S. S. (1999). The impact of recent partner violence on poor women's capacity to maintain work. *Violence Against Women, 5,* 393–426.

Browning, C. R. (2002). The span of collective efficacy: Extending social disorganization theory to partner violence. *Journal of Marriage and Family, 64,* 833–850.

Brownlie, E. B., Graham, E., Bao, L., Koyama, E., & Beitchman, J. H. (2017). Language disorder and retrospectively reported sexual abuse of girls: Severity and disclosure. *Journal of Child Psychology and Psychiatry, 58*(10), 1114–1121.

Brownridge, D. A. (2006). Partner violence against disabilities: Prevalence, risk, and explanations. *Violence Against Women, 12*(9), 805–822.

Brush, B. L., Gultekin, L. E., Dowdell, E. B., Saint Arnault, D. M., & Satterfield, K. (2018). Understanding trauma normativeness, normalization, and help seeking in homeless mothers. *Violence Against Women, 24*(13), 1523–1539.

Brush, L. D. (2011). *Poverty, battered women, and work in U.S. public policy.* New York, NY: Oxford University Press.

Brush, L. D., & Miller, E. (2019). Trouble in paradigm: "Gender transformative" programming in violence prevention. *Violence Against Women, 25*(14), 1635–1656.

Buckley, C. (2015, October 29). China ends one-child policy, allowing families two children. *New York Times.* Retrieved from http://www.nytimes.com/2015/10/30/world/asia/china-end-one-child-policy.html

Budin, L. E., & Johnson, C. F. (1989). Sex abuse prevention programs: Offenders' attitudes about their efficacy. *Child Abuse & Neglect, 13,* 77–87.

Buel, S. M. (1999). Fifty obstacles to leaving, a.k.a., why abuse victims stay. *Colorado Lawyer, 28*(10), 19–28.

Bull, J., McCormick, G., Swann, C., & Mulvihill, C. (2004). Ante- and post-natal home visiting programs: A review of reviews. *Evidence Briefing.* Retrieved from www.hda.nhs.uk/evidence

Bureau of Justice Statistics. (2019). *Data collection: National Crime Victimization Survey (NCVS).* Retrieved from http://www.bjs.gov/index.cfm?ty=dcdetail&iid=245#Methodology

Burge, L. R., Louis, P. T., & Giardino, A. P. (2019). Neglect and failure to thrive. In *A practical guide to the evaluation of child physical abuse and neglect* (pp. 251–285). Cham, Switzerland: Springer.

Burgess, A. W. (2006). *Elderly victims of sexual abuse and their offenders.* Washington, DC: U.S. Department of Justice.

Burgess, A. W., & Hartman, C. R. (1987). Child abuse aspects of child pornography. *Psychiatric Annals, 17,* 248–253.

Burgess, E. S., & Wurtele, S. K. (1998). Enhancing parent-child communication about sexual abuse: A pilot study. *Child Abuse & Neglect, 22*(11), 1167–1175.

Burke, K. D. (2007). Substance-exposed newborns: Hospital and child protection responses. *Children and Youth Services Review*, *29*, 1503–1519.

Burnett, B. (1993). The psychological abuse of latency age children: A survey. *Child Abuse & Neglect*, *17*, 441–454.

Butler, A. C. (2013). Child sexual assault: Risk factors for girls. *Child Abuse & Neglect*, *37*, 643–652. doi:10.1016/j.chiabu.2013.06.009

Button, D. M., & Gealt, R. (2010). High risk behaviors among victims of sibling violence. *Journal of Family Violence*, *25*, 131–140.

Caccamise, P. L., & Mason, A. (2004). Policy paper: New York state summit targets elder abuse: The time to act is now. *Journal of Elder Abuse & Neglect*, *16*, 41–62.

Cafferky, B. M., Mendez, M., Anderson, J. R., & Stith, S. M. (2018). Substance use and intimate partner violence: A meta-analytic review. *Psychology of Violence*, *8*(1), 110–131.

Cahill, C., Llewelyn, S. P., & Pearson, C. (1991). Treatment of sexual abuse which occurred in childhood: A review. *British Journal of Clinical Psychology*, *30*, 1–12.

Camasso, M. J., & Jagannathan, R. (2019). Conceptualizing and testing the vicious cycle in child protective services: The critical role played by child maltreatment fatalities. *Children and Youth Services Review*, *103*, 178–189.

Campbell, A. M. (2020). *An increasing risk of family violence during the Covid-19 pandemic: Strengthening community collaborations to save lives*. Forensic Science International: Reports, 100089.

Campbell, A. M., & Thompson, S. L. (2015). The emotional maltreatment of children in domestically violent homes: Identifying gaps in education and addressing common misconceptions: The risk of harm to children in domestically violent homes mandates a well-coordinated response. *Child Abuse & Neglect*, *48*, 39.

Campbell, J. A., Walker, R. J., & Egede, L. E. (2016). Associations between adverse childhood experiences, high-risk behaviors, and morbidity in adulthood. *American Journal of Preventive Medicine*, *50*(3), 344–352.

Campbell, J. C. (1986). Nursing assessment for risk of homicide with battered women. *Advances in Nursing Science*, *8*, 36–51.

Campbell, J. C. (1989). Women's responses to sexual abuse in intimate relationships. *Health Care for Women International*, *10*(4), 335–346.

Campbell, J. C. (2005). *Danger assessment*. Retrieved from http://www.dangerassessment.org/WebApplication1/pages/da/

Campbell, J. C. (2007). Prediction of homicide of and by battered women. In J. C. Campbell (Ed.), *Assessing dangerousness* (pp. 85–104). New York. NY: Springer.

Campbell, J. C., Alhusen, J., Draughton, J., Kub, J., & Walton-Moss, B. (2011). Vulnerability and protective factors for intimate partner violence. In J. W. White, M. P. Koss, & A. E. Kazdin (Eds.), *Violence against women and children: Mapping the terrain* (pp. 243–263). Washington, DC: American Psychological Association.

Campbell, J. C., Webster, D., Koziol-McLain, J., Block, C. R., Campbell, D., Curry, M. A., et al. (2003). Assessing risk factors for intimate partner homicide. *NIJ Journal*, *250*, 14–19.

Campbell, R. (2006). Rape survivors' experiences with the legal and medical systems: Do rape victim advocates make a difference? *Violence Against Women*, *12*, 30–45.

Campbell, R., & Patterson, D. (2011). Services for victims of sexual violence. In M. P. Koss, J. W. White, & A. E. Kazdin (Eds.), *Violence against women and children* (Vol. 2, pp. 95–114). Washington, DC: American Psychological Association.

Campbell, R., Patterson, D., & Lichty, L. F. (2005). The effectiveness of sexual assault nurse examiner (SANE) programs: A review of psychological, medical, legal, and community outcomes. *Trauma, Violence & Abuse*, *6*, 313–329.

Cancian, M., Clack, K. S., & Yang, M. Y. (2010). The effect of family income on risk of children maltreatment. *Institute for Research on Poverty*, 1385–1410.

Cancio, R. (2020). Military cohorts, substance use, and male-perpetrated intimate partner violence. *Violence Against Women*. Advance online publication. https://doi.org/10.1177/1077801219893475

Cant, R. L., O'Donnell, M., Sims, S., & Harries, M. (2019). Overcrowded housing: One of a constellation of vulnerabilities for child sexual abuse. *Child Abuse & Neglect*, *93*, 239–248.

Cantor, J. M., Blanchard, R., Robichaud, L. K., & Christensen, B. K. (2005). Quantitative reanalysis of aggregate data on IQ in sexual offenders. *Psychological Bulletin*, *131*(4), 555.

Cantos, A. L., Neale, J. M., O'Leary, K. D., & Gaines, R. W. (1997). Assessment of coping strategies of child abusing mothers. *Child Abuse & Neglect*, *21*(7), 631–636.

Capaldi, D., Dishion, T., Stoolmiller, M., & Yoerger, K. (2001). Aggression toward female partners by at-risk young men: The contribution of male adolescent friendships. *Developmental Psychology, 37*(1), 61–73.

Carbone-Lopez, K., Kruttschnitt, C., & MacMillan, R. (2006). Patterns of intimate partner violence and their associations with physical health, psychological distress, and substance use. *Public Health Reports, 121*, 382–392.

Caringella, S. (2009). *Addressing rape reform in law and practice.* New York, NY: Columbia University Press.

Carr, A., Nearchou, F., Duff, H., Mhaoileoin, D. N., Cullen, K., O'Dowd, A., & Battigelli, L. (2019). Survivors of institutional abuse in long-term child care in Scotland. *Child Abuse & Neglect, 93*, 38–54.

Carter, C. (2016, July). Woman with postpartum depression pleads guilty. *ABC News.* Retrieved from http://abcnews.go.com/US/Depression/story?id=92935

Carvalho, A. F., Lewis, R. J., Derlaga, V. J., Winstead, B. A., & Viggiano, C. (2011). Internalized sexual minority stressors and same-sex intimate partner violence. *Journal of Family Violence, 26*, 501–509.

Casanueva, C., Wilson, E., Smith, K., Dolan, M., Ringeisen, H., & Horne, B. (2012). *NSCAW II wave 2 report: Child well-being (Report No. 2012-38).* Washington, DC: Office of Planning, Research and Evaluation, Administration for Children and Families, U.S. Department of Health and Human Services. Retrieved from https://www.acf.hhs.gov/sites/default/files/pre/nscaw_report_w2_ch_wb_final_june_2014_final_report.pdf

Casey Family Programs. (2009). *Fact sheet: Latino children in child welfare.* Retrieved from http://www.casey.org/Resources/Publications/pdf/LatinoChildren.pdf

Casey Family Programs. (2019). *The Child Abuse Prevention and Treatment Act: Keeping children safe and strengthening families in communities.* Retrieved from https://www.casey.org/child-abuse-prevention-treatment-act/

Cash, S. (2008). Family preservation services. In N. Coady & P. Lehmann (Eds.), *Theoretical perspectives for direct social work practice: A generalist-eclectic approach* (2nd ed., pp. 471–492). New York, NY: Springer.

Casillas, K. L., Fauchier, A., Derkash, B. T., & Garrido, E. F. (2016). Implementation of evidence-based home visiting programs aimed at reducing child maltreatment: A metaanalytic review. *Child Abuse & Neglect, 53*, 64–80.

Caslini, M., Bartoli, F., Crocamo, C., Dakanalis, A., Clerici, M., & Carrà, G. (2016). Disentangling the association between child abuse and eating disorders: A systematic review and meta-analysis. *Psychosomatic Medicine, 78*(1), 79–90.

Catalano, S. M. (2012). *Intimate partner violence, 1993–2010.* Washington, DC: U.S. Department of Justice, Office of Justice Programs, Bureau of Justice Statistics.

Cecil, C. A., Viding, E., Fearon, P., Glaser, D., & McCrory, E. J. (2017). Disentangling the mental health impact of childhood abuse and neglect. *Child Abuse & Neglect, 63*, 106–119.

Centers for Disease Control and Prevention. (2009). *Parent training programs: Insight for practitioners.* Atlanta, GA: Author. Available at http://www.cdc.gov/ViolencePrevention/pdf/Parent_Training_Brief-a.pdf

Centers for Disease Control and Prevention. (2016a). *Elder abuse surveillance: Uniform definitions and recommended core data elements.* Atlanta, GA: Author.

Centers for Disease Control and Prevention. (2016b). *Preventing multiple forms of violence: A strategic vision for connecting the dots.* Atlanta, GA: Division of Violence Prevention, National Center for Injury Prevention and Control, Centers for Disease Control and Prevention.

Centers for Disease Control and Prevention. (n.d.). *ACE study.* Retrieved from http://www.cdc.gov/violenceprevention/acestudy/index.html

Cermele, J., & McCaughey, M. (2015). What's wrong with the CDC's public health model for rape prevention. *Journal of Community Medicine & Health Education, 5*, 387.

Chaffin, M. (2008). Our minds are made up—Don't confuse us with the facts: Commentary on policies concerning children with sexual behavior problems and juvenile sex offenders. *Child Maltreatment, 13*(2), 110–121.

Chaffin, M., Funderbunk, B., Bard, D., Valle, L. A., & Gurwitch, R. (2011). A combined motivation and parent–child interaction therapy package reduces child welfare recidivism in a randomized dismantling field trial. *Journal of Consulting and Clinical Psychology, 79*, 84–85.

Chaffin, M., Hecht, D., Bard, D., Silovsky, J. F., & Beasley, W. H. (2012). A statewide trial of the SafeCare home-based services model with parents in Child Protective Services. *Pediatrics, 129*(3), 509–515.

Chaffin, M., Kelleher, K., & Hollenberg, J. (1996). Onset of physical abuse and neglect: Psychiatric, substance abuse, and social risk factors from prospective community data. *Child Abuse & Neglect, 20*, 191–203.

Chaffin, M., Silovsky, J., Funderburk, B., Valle, L. A., Brestan, E. V., Balachova, T., . . . Bonner, B. L. (2004). Parent–child interaction therapy with physically abusive parents: Efficacy for reducing future abuse reports. *Journal of Consulting and Clinical Psychology, 72*, 491–499.

Chaiyachati, B. H., Gaither, J. R., Hughes, M., Foley-Schain, K., & Leventhal, J. M. (2018). Preventing child maltreatment: Examination of an established state-wide home-visiting program. *Child Abuse & Neglect, 79*, 476–484.

Chan, Y. C. (1994). Parenting stress and social support of mothers who physically abuse their children in Hong Kong. *Child Abuse & Neglect, 18*, 261–269.

Chandler, G. E., Roberts, S. J., & Chiodo, L. (2015). Resilience intervention for young adults with adverse childhood experiences. *Journal of the American Psychiatric Nurses Association, 21*(6), 406–416.

Chaney, A., Carballedo, A., Amico, F., Fagan, A., Skokauskas, N., Meaney, J., & Frodl, T. (2014). Effect of childhood maltreatment on brain structure in adult patients with major depressive disorder and healthy participants. *Journal of Psychiatry & Neuroscience, 39*(1), 50.

Chang, E. C., Kahle, E. R., & Hirsch, J. K. (2015). Understanding how domestic abuse is associated with greater depressive symptoms in a community sample of female primary care patients: Does loss of belongingness matter? *Violence Against Women, 21*, 700–711.

Chao, F., Gerland, P., Cook, A. R., & Alkema, L. (2019). Systematic assessment of the sex ratio at birth for all countries and estimation of national imbalances and regional reference levels. *Proceedings of the National Academy of Sciences, 116*(19), 9303–9311.

Chapman, D. P., Whitfield, C. L., Felitti, V. J., Dube, S. R., Edwards, V. J., & Anda, R. F. (2004). Adverse childhood experiences and the risk of depressive disorders in adulthood. *Journal of Affective Disorders, 82*, 217–225.

Chartier, M., Walker, J., & Naimark, B. (2007). Childhood abuse, adult health, and health care utilization: Results from a representative community sample. *American Journal of Epidemiology, 165*(9), 1031–1038.

Chartier, M. J., Walker, J. R., & Naimark, B. (2010). Separate and cumulative effects of adverse childhood experiences in predicting adult health and health care utilization. *Child Abuse & Neglect, 34*(6), 454–464.

Cheung, K., Taillieu, T., Turner, S., Fortier, J., Sareen, J., MacMillan, H. L., . . . & Afifi, T. O. (2018). Individual-level factors related to better mental health outcomes following child maltreatment among adolescents. *Child Abuse & Neglect, 79*, 192–202.

Chevignard, M., & Lind, K. (2014). Long-term outcome of abusive head trauma. *Pediatric Radiology, 44*(Suppl. 4), S548–S558. Retrieved from http://dx.doi.org/10.1007/s00247-014-3169-8

Chiel, Z., & Fiorvanti, C. (2019). Widening the reach of clinical interventions to reduce psychological maltreatment. *APSAC Advisor, 31*(3), 46–55.

Child Trends Databank. (2015, November). *Attitudes toward spanking*. Bethesda, MD: Author.

Child Welfare Information Gateway. (2011). *Child maltreatment prevention: Past, present, and future*. Washington, DC: U.S. Department of Health and Human Services, Children's Bureau.

Child Welfare Information Gateway. (2012). *The risk and prevention of maltreatment of children with disabilities*. Washington, DC: U.S. Department of Health and Human Services, Children's Bureau.

Child Welfare Information Gateway. (2013a). *Infant safe haven laws*. Washington, DC: U.S. Department of Health and Human Services, Children's Bureau. Retrieved from https://www.childwelfare.gov/pubPDFs/whatiscan.pdf

Child Welfare Information Gateway. (2013b). *Preventing child abuse and neglect*. Washington, DC: U.S. Department of Health and Human Services, Children's Bureau. Retrieved from https://www.childwelfare.gov/pubPDFs/safehaven.pdf

Child Welfare Information Gateway. (2014). *Definitions of child abuse and neglect*. Washington, DC: U.S. Department of Health and Human Services, Children's Bureau. Retrieved from https://www.childwelfare.gov/pubpdfs/define.pdf

Child Welfare Information Gateway. (2015). Links to state and tribal child welfare law and policy. Washington, DC: U.S. Department of Health and Human Services, Children's Bureau. Retrieved from https://www.childwelfare.gov/pubPDFs/resources.pdf

Child Welfare Information Gateway. (2016a). *Caseload and workload management*. Retrieved from https://www.childwelfare.gov/pubPDFs/case_work_management.pdf

Child Welfare Information Gateway. (2016b). *Child witnesses to domestic violence*. Washington, DC: U.S. Department of Health and Human Services, Children's Bureau.

Child Welfare Information Gateway. (2019a). *About CAPTA: A legislative history*. Washington, DC: U.S. Department of Health and Human Services, Children's Bureau.

Child Welfare Information Gateway. (2019b). *Definitions of child abuse and neglect*. Washington, DC: U.S. Department of Health and Human Services, Children's Bureau.

Child Welfare Information Gateway. (2019c). *Mandatory reporters of child abuse and neglect*. Washington, DC: U.S. Department of Health and Human Services, Children's Bureau.

Chiodo, D., Wolfe, D. A., Crooks, C., Hughes, R., & Jaffe, P. (2009). Impact of sexual harassment victimization by peers on subsequent adolescent victimization and adjustment: A longitudinal study. *Journal of Adolescent Health, 45*, 246–252.

Cho, H. (2012). Racial differences in the prevalence of intimate partner violence against women and associated factors. *Journal of Interpersonal Violence, 27*(2), 344–363.

Choudhary, A. K., Servaes, S., Slovis, T. L., Palusci, V. J., Hedlund, G. L., Narang, S. K., . . . Silvera, V. M. (2018). Consensus statement on abusive head trauma in infants and young children. *Pediatric Radiology, 48*(8), 1048–1065.

Christensen, M. J., Brayden, R. M., Dietrich, M. S., McLaughlin, F. J., Sherrod, K. B., & Altemeier, W. A. (1994). The prospective assessment of self-concept in neglectful and physically abusive low-income mothers. *Child Abuse & Neglect, 18*, 225–232.

Christian, S. (2004). *Substance-exposed newborns: New federal law raises some old issues*. Washington, DC: National Conference of State Legislatures. Available from National Conference of State Legislatures, 444 North Capitol Street, N.W., Suite 515, Washington, DC.

Chung, D. (2007). Making meaning of relationships: Young women's experiences and understandings of dating violence. *Violence Against Women, 13*(12), 1274–1295.

Cicchetti, D. (2016). Socioemotional, personality, and biological development: Illustrations from a multilevel developmental psychopathology perspective on child maltreatment. *Annual Review of Psychology, 67*, 187–211.

Cicchetti, D., Rogosch, F. A., & Toth, S. L. (2006). Fostering secure attachment in infants in maltreating families through preventive interventions. *Development and Psychopathology, 18*(3), 623–649.

Cicchetti, D., Rogosch, F. A., Toth, S. L., & Sturge-Apple, M. L. (2011). Normalizing the development of cortisol regulation in maltreated infants through preventive interventions. *Development and Psychopathology, 23*(3), 789–800.

Cicchetti, D., & Toth, S. L. (1995). A developmental psychopathology perspective on child abuse and neglect. *Journal of the American Academy of Child and Adolescent Psychiatry, 34*, 541–565.

Cicchetti, D., & Toth, S. L. (2016). Child maltreatment and developmental psychopathology: A multilevel perspective. *Developmental Psychopathology*, 1–56.

Clark, H. M., Galano, M. M., Grogan-Kaylor, A. C., Montalvo-Liendo, N., & Graham-Berman, S. A. (2016). Ethnoracial variation in women's exposure to intimate partner violence. *Journal of Interpersonal Violence, 31*, 531–552.

Clark, K. A., Biddle, A. K., & Martin, S. L. (2002). A cost-benefit analysis of the Violence Against Women Act of 1994. *Violence Against Women, 8*, 417–428.

Clawson, H. J., Dutch, N., Solomon, A., & Grace, L. G. (2009). *Human trafficking into and within the United States: A review of the literature*. U.S. Department of Health and Human Services, Office of the Assistant Secretary for Planning and Evaluation.

Clear, E. R., Coker, A. L., Cook-Craig, P. G., Bush, H. M., Garcia, L. S., Williams, C. M., Lewis, A. M., & Fisher, B. S. (2014). Sexual harassment victimization and perpetration among high school students. *Violence Against Women, 20*(10), 1203–1219.

Clement, S., Schauman, O., Graham, T., Maggioni, F., Evans-Lacko, S., Bezborodovos, N., et al. (2015). What is the impact of mental health–related stigma on help-seeking? A systematic review of quantitative and qualitative studies. *Psychological Medicine, 45*, 11–27.

Clemente, J. (2013). Additional background on child sexual victimization. In W. Sollers, M. Jensen, A. Dial, & D. Crawford, *Critique of the Freeh Report: The rush to injustice regarding Joe Paterno* (Appendix B, pp. 1–8). Retrieved from https://assets.documentcloud.org/documents/602483/sollers-final report.pdf

CNN Staff. (2014, September 16). Key events in the Ray Rice story. *CNN*. Retrieved from https://www.cnn.com/2014/09/09/us/ray-rice-timeline/index.html

Cobbina, J. E., & Oselin, S. S. (2011). It's not only for the money: An analysis of adolescent versus adult entry into street prostitution. *Sociological Inquiry, 81*, 310–332. doi:10.1111/j.1475-682X.2011.00375.x

Cohen, J. A., Mannarino, A. P., & Murray, L. K. (2011). Trauma-focused CBT for youth who experience ongoing traumas. *Child Abuse & Neglect, 35*(8), 637–646.

Cohen, L. J., & Galynker, I. (2009). Psychopathology and personality traits of pedophiles: Issues for diagnosis and treatment. *Psychiatric Times, 26*(6), 25–30. Retrieved from http://www.psychiatrictimes.com/display/article/10168/1420331

Cohen, P., Brown, J., & Smailes, E. M. (2001). Child abuse and neglect and the development of mental disorders in the general population. *Development and Psychopathology, 13*, 981–999.

Coker, A. L. (2007). Does physical intimate partner violence affect sexual health? A systematic review. *Trauma, Violence & Abuse, 8*, 149–177.

Coker, A. L., Clear, E. R., Garcia, L. S., Aasaolu, I. O., Cook-Craig, P. G., Brancato, C. J., et al. (2014). Dating violence victimization and perpetration rates among high school students. *Violence Against Women, 20*(10), 1220–1238.

Coker, A. L., Cook-Craig, P. G., Williams, C. M., Fisher, B. S., Clear, E. R., Hegge, L. M., & Garcia, L. S. (2011). Does teaching bystanding behaviors increase bystanding and change social norms supporting violence? The University of Kentucky experience. *Violence Against Women, 16*, 777–796.

Coker, A. L., Fisher, B. S., Bush, H. M., Swan, S. C., Williams, C. M., Clear, E. R., & DeGue, S. (2015). Evaluation of the Green Dot bystander intervention to reduce interpersonal violence among college students across three campuses. *Violence Against Women, 21*(12), 1507–1527.

Coker, A. L., Williams, C. M., Follingstad, D. R., & Jordan, C. E. (2011). Psychological, reproductive and maternal health, behavioral, and economic impact of intimate partner violence. In J. W. White, M. P. Koss, & A. E. Kazdin (Eds.), *Violence against women and children: Mapping the terrain* (pp. 265–284). Washington, DC: American Psychological Association.

Coker, D. (2002). Transformative justice: Anti-subordination processes in case of domestic violence. In H. Strang & J. Braithwaite (Eds.), *Restorative justice and family violence* (pp. 128–152). Cambridge, UK: Cambridge University Press.

Colello, K. J. (2014). *The Elder Justice Act: Background and issues for Congress*. Washington, DC: Congressional Research Service.

Commission to Eliminate Child Abuse and Neglect Fatalities (CECANF). (2016). *Within our reach: A national strategy to eliminate child abuse and neglect fatalities*. Washington, DC: Government Printing Office.

Connell, R. W. (1995). *Masculinities*. Berkeley: University of California Press.

Connor, T. (2016, December 21). FBI says gymnastics doctor Larry Nassar recorded abuse on Go Pro. *NBC News*. Retrieved from https://www.nbcnews.com/news/us-news/gymnastics-doctor-larry-nassar-hit-new-sex-abuse-claim-n698741

Conte, J. R., Wolf, S., & Smith, T. (1989). What sexual offenders tell us about prevention strategies. *Child Abuse & Neglect, 13*, 293–301.

Coohey, C. (2000). The role of friends, in-laws, and other kin in father-perpetrated child physical abuse. *Child Welfare, 79*, 373–402.

Coohey, C., & O'Leary, P. (2008). Mothers' protection of their children after discovering they have been sexually abused: An information-processing perspective. *Child Abuse & Neglect, 32*(2), 245–259.

Cook-Craig, P. G., Millspaugh, P. H., Recktenwald, E. A., Kelly, N. C., Hegge, L. M., Coker, A. L., & Pletcher, T. S. (2014). From Empower to Green Dot: Successful strategies and lessons learned from developing comprehensive sexual violence primary prevention programming. *Violence Against Women, 20*(10), 1162–1178.

Coore Desai, C., Reece, J. A., & Shakespeare-Pellington, S. (2017). The prevention of violence in childhood through parenting programmes: A global review. *Psychology, Health & Medicine, 22*(S1), 166–186.

Costa, E. C., & Gomes, S. C. (2018). Social support and self-esteem moderate the relation between intimate partner violence and depression and anxiety symptoms among Portuguese women. *Journal of Family Violence, 33*(5), 355–368.

Courtois, C. A. (2010). *Healing the incest wound: Adult survivors in therapy* (2nd ed.). New York, NY: W. W. Norton & Co.

Covell, C. N., & Scalora, M. J. (2002). Empathic deficits in sexual offenders: An integration of affective, social, and cognitive constructs. *Aggression and Violent Behavior, 7*, 251–270.

Coy, M., Kelly, L., Foord, J., & Bowstead, J. (2011). Roads to nowhere? Mapping violence against women services. *Violence Against Women, 17*, 404–425.

Crandall, A., Miller, J. R., Cheung, A., Novilla, L. K., Glade, R., Novilla, M. L. B., . . . Hanson, C. L. (2019).

ACEs and counter-ACEs: How positive and negative childhood experiences influence adult health. *Child Abuse & Neglect, 96.* Advance online publication. doi:10.1016/j.chiabu.2019.104089

CRC Health Group. (2016). *FAQ: Opiates and pregnancy.* Retrieved from http://www.crchealth.com/addiction/heroin-addiction-treatment/heroin-detox/opiates_pregnancy/

Creech, S. K., Pulverman, C. S., Shin, M. E., Roe, K. T., Wernette, G. T., Orchowski, L. M., . . . Zlotnick, C. (2020). An open trial to test participant satisfaction with and feasibility of a computerized intervention for women veterans with sexual trauma histories seeking primary care treatment. *Violence Against Women.* Advance online publication. https://doi.org/10.1177/1077801219895102

Crittenden, P. M. (1992). Children's strategies for coping with adverse home environments: An interpretation using attachment theory. *Child Abuse & Neglect, 16,* 329–343.

Crooks, C. V., Goodall, G. R., Hughes, R., Jaffe, P. G., & Baker, L. L. (2007). Engaging men and boys in preventing violence against women: Applying a cognitive-behavioral model. *Violence Against Women, 13*(3), 217–239.

Crooks, C. V., Jaffe, P., Dunlop, C., Kerry, A., & Exner-Cortens, D. (2019). Preventing gender based violence among adolescents and young adults: Lessons from 25 years of program development and evaluation. *Violence Against Women, 25*(1), 29–55.

Crouch, J. L., Hiraoka, R., McCanne, T. R., Reo, G., Wagner, M. F., Krauss, A., . . . Skowronski, J. J. (2018). Heart rate and heart rate variability in parents at risk for child physical abuse. *Journal of Interpersonal Violence, 33*(10), 1629–1652.

Crowe, H. P., & Zeskind, P. S. (1992). Psychophysiological and perceptual responses to infant cries varying in pitch: Comparison of adults with low and high scores on the Child Abuse Potential Inventory. *Child Abuse & Neglect, 16,* 19–29.

Cuartas, J., McCoy, D. C., Rey-Guerra, C., Britto, P. R., Beatriz, E., & Salhi, C. (2019). Early childhood exposure to non-violent discipline and physical and psychological aggression in low- and middle income countries: National, regional, and global prevalence estimates. *Child Abuse & Neglect, 92,* 93–105.

Cullerton-Sen, C., Cassidy, A. R., Murray-Close, D., Cicchetti, D., Crick, N. R., & Rogosch, F. A. (2008). Childhood maltreatment and the development of relational and physical aggression: The importance of a gender-informed approach. *Child Development, 79,* 1736–1751.

Culp, A. M., Culp, R. E., Hechtner-Galvin, T., Howell, C. S., Saathoff-Wells, T., & Marr, P. (2004). First-time mothers in home visitation services utilizing child development specialists. *Infant Mental Health Journal, 25*(1), 1–15.

Culp, R. E., Little, V., Letts, D., & Lawrence, H. (1991). Maltreated children's self-concept: Effects of a comprehensive treatment program. *American Journal of Orthopsychiatry, 61*(1), 114–121.

Currie, J., & Tekin, E. (2012). Understanding the cycle: Childhood maltreatment and future crime. *Journal of Human Resources, 47*(2), 509–549.

Curry, M. A., Hassouneh-Phillips, D., & Johnston-Silverberg, A. (2001). Abuse of women with disabilities. *Violence Against Women, 7,* 60–79.

Curry, M. A., Renker, P., Hughes, R. B., Robinson-Whelen, S., Oschwald, M., Swank, P. R., & Powers, L. E. (2009). Development of measures of abuse among women with disabilities and the characteristics of their perpetrators. *Violence Against Women, 15*(9), 1001–1025.

Curtis-Fawley, S., & Daly, K. (2005). Gendered violence and restorative justice: The views of victim advocates. *Violence Against Women, 11*(5), 603–638.

Cytryn, S. M. (2010). What went wrong? Why family preservation programs failed to achieve their potential. *Cardozo Journal of Law & Gender, 17.*

Dank, M., Lachman, P., Zweig, J. M., & Yahner, J. (2014). Dating violence experiences of lesbian, gay, bisexual, and transgender youth. *Journal of Youth and Adolescence, 43*(5), 846–857.

Daro, D. (2011). Prevention of child abuse and neglect. In J. E. B. Myers (Ed.), *The APSAC handbook on child maltreatment* (3rd ed., pp. 17–37). Thousand Oaks, CA: Sage.

Daro, D. (2012). The promise of prevention: Expanding with quality. *APSAC Advisor, 24*(1/2), 44–47.

Daro, D., & Dodge, K. A. (2009). Creating community responsibility for child protection: Possibilities and challenges. *The Future of Children, 19*(2), 67–93.

Daro, D., & Gelles, R. J. (1992). Public attitudes and behaviors with respect to child abuse prevention. *Journal of Interpersonal Violence, 7,* 517–531.

Davidson, R. D., Tomlinson, C. S., Beck, C. J., & Bowen, A. M. (2019). The revolving door of families in the child welfare system: Risk and protective factors associated with families returning. *Children and Youth Services Review*, *100*, 468–479.

Davies, E. A., & Jones, A. C. (2013). Risk factors in child sexual abuse. *Journal of Forensic Legal Medicine*, *20*(3), 146–150. doi:10.1016/j.jflm.2012.06.005

Davies, J., & Lyon, E. J. (2014). *Domestic violence advocacy: Complex lives/difficult choices*. Thousand Oaks, CA: Sage.

Davies, M. (2002). Male sexual assault victims: A selective review of the literature and implications for support services. *Aggression and Violent Behavior*, *7*(3), 203–214.

Davis, R. C., Medina, J., & Avitabile, N. (2001). *Reducing repeat incidents of elder abuse: Results of a randomized experiment*. Washington, DC: U.S. Department of Justice, National Institute of Justice.

Dawson, S. J., Bannerman, B. A., & Lalumière, M. L. (2016). Paraphilic interests: An examination of sex differences in a nonclinical sample. *Sexual Abuse: A Journal of Research and Treatment*, *28*(1), 20–45.

De Bellis, M. D., Morey, R. A., Nooner, K. B., Woolley, D. P., Haswell, C. C., & Hooper, S. R. (2019). A pilot study of neurocognitive function and brain structures in adolescents with alcohol use disorders: Does maltreatment history matter? *Child Maltreatment*, *24*(4), 1–15.

De Bellis, M. D., & Zisk, A. (2014). The biological effects of childhood trauma. *Child and Adolescent Psychiatric Clinics*, *23*(2), 185–222.

Deblinger, E., Mannarino, A. P., Cohen, J. A., Runyon, M. K., & Heflin, A. H. (2015). *Child sexual abuse: A primer for treating children, adolescents, and their nonoffending parents* (2nd ed.). New York, NY: Oxford University Press. doi:10.1093/med:psych/9780199358748.001.0001

Deblinger, E., Mannarino, A. P., Cohen, J. A., & Steer, R. A. (2006). A follow-up study of a multisite, randomized, controlled trial for children with sexual abuse–related PTSD symptoms. *Journal of the American Academy of Child and Adolescent Psychiatry*, *45*, 1474–1484.

DeCou, C. R., & Lynch, S. M. (2019). Emotional reactivity, trauma-related distress, and suicidal ideation among adolescent inpatient survivors of sexual abuse. *Child Abuse & Neglect*, *89*, 155–164.

Degli Esposti, M., Pereira, S. M. P., Humphreys, D. K., Sale, R. D., & Bowes, L. (2020). Child maltreatment and the risk of antisocial behaviour: A population-based cohort study spanning 50 years. *Child Abuse & Neglect*,

99. Advance online publication. https://doi.org/10.1016/j.chiabu.2019.104281

Deitz, M. F., Williams, S. L., Rife, S. C., & Cantrell, P. (2015). Examining cultural, social, and self-related aspects of stigma in relation to sexual assault and trauma symptoms. *Violence Against Women*, *21*(5), 598–615.

DeKeseredy, W. S., Alvi, S., Schwartz, M. D., & Tomaszewski, E. A. (2003). *Under siege: Poverty and crime in a public housing community*. Lanham, MD: Lexington Books.

DeKeseredy, W. S., & Schwartz, M. D. (1998). *Measuring the extent of woman abuse in intimate heterosexual relationships: A critique of the Conflict Tactics Scales*. U.S. Department of Justice Violence Against Women Grants Office Electronic Resources.

DeKeseredy, W. S., & Schwartz, M. D. (2011). Theoretical and definitional issues in violence against women. In C. M. Renzetti, J. L. Edleson, & R. K. Bergen (Eds.), *Sourcebook on violence against women* (2nd ed., pp. 3–21). Thousand Oaks, CA: Sage.

DeKeseredy, W. S., & Schwartz, M. D. (2013). *Male peer support and violence against women: The history and verification of a theory*. Boston, MA: Northeastern University Press.

DeKeseredy, W. S., Schwartz, M. D., Fagen, D., & Hall, M. (2006). Separation/divorce sexual assault: The contribution of male peer support. *Feminist Criminology*, *1*, 228–250.

DeLeon-Granados, W., Wells, W., & Binsbacher, R. (2006). Arresting developments: Trends in female arrests for domestic violence and proposed explanations. *Violence Against Women*, *12*(4), 355–371.

Dell'Antonia, K. (2016). Who is to blame when a child wanders at the zoo? *New York Times*. Retrieved from https://well.blogs.nytimes.com/2016/05/31/who-is-to-blame-when-a-child-wanders-at-the-zoo/

Delsol, C., & Margolin, G. (2004). The role of family-of-origin violence in men's marital violence perpetration. *Clinical Psychology Review*, *24*, 99–122.

deMause, L. (1974). The evolution of childhood. In L. deMause (Ed.), *The history of childhood* (pp. 1–74). New York, NY: Psychotherapy Press.

DeNavas-Walt, C., & Proctor, B. D. (2014). *Income and poverty in the United States, 2013*. Washington, DC: U.S. Department of Commerce, Bureau of the Census.

Denniston, G. C., & Milos, M. F. (Eds.). (2013). *Sexual mutilations: A human tragedy*. New York, NY: Springer Science & Business Media.

DeVries, K. M., Child, J. C., Bacchus, L. J., Mak, J., Falder, G., Graham, K., . . . Heise, L. (2014). Intimate partner violence victimization and alcohol consumption in women: A systematic review and meta-analysis. *Addiction, 109,* 379–391.

Dias, M. S., Smith, K., DeGuehery, K., Mazur, P., Li, V., & Shaffer, M. L. (2005). Preventing abusive head trauma among infants and young children: A hospital-based, parent education program. *Pediatrics, 115*(4), 470–477. Retrieved from www.pediatrics.org/cgi/content/full/115/4/e470

Diaz-Olavarrieta, C., Ellertson, C., Paz, F., Ponce de Leon, S., & Alarcon-Segovia, D. (2002). Prevalence of battering among 1780 outpatients at an internal medicine institution in Mexico. *Social Science and Medicine, 55,* 1589–1602.

Dichter, M. E., Marcus, S. C., Morabito, M. S., & Rhodes, K. V. (2011). Explaining the intimate partner violence arrest decision: Incident, agency, and community factors. *Criminal Justice Review, 36,* 22–39.

Dichter, M. E., Wagner, C., & True, G. (2018). Women veterans' experiences of intimate partner violence and non-partner sexual assault in the context of military service: Implications for supporting women's health and well-being. *Journal of Interpersonal Violence, 33*(6), 843–864.

DiFulvio, G. T. (2015). Experiencing violence and enacting resilience: The case story of a transgender youth. *Violence Against Women, 21*(11), 1385–1405.

Dillon, G., Hussain, R., Loxton, D., & Rahman, S. (2013). Mental and physical health and intimate partner violence against women: A review of the literature. *International Journal of Family Medicine.* Article ID 313909. Retrieved from http://dx.doi.org/10.1155/2013/313909

Dinwiddie, K., Zawadzski, S., Ristau, K., Luneburg, A. F., Earley, T. A., Ruiz, M., . . . Coker, K. L. (2019). A sample of predominantly African American domestic violence victims' responses to objective risk assessments. *Violence Against Women.* Advance online publication. Retrieved from https://doi.org/10.1177/1077801219848485

Di Sante, M., Sylvestre, A., Bouchard, C., & Leblond, J. (2019). The pragmatic language skills of severely neglected 42-month-old children: Results of the ELLAN study. *Child Maltreatment, 24*(3), 244–253.

DiScala, C., Sege, R., Li, G., & Reece, R. M. (2000). Child abuse and unintentional injuries: A 10-year retrospective. *Archives of Pediatric Adolescent Medicine, 154,* 16–22.

Diviney, C., Parekh, A., & Olson, L. (2009). Outcomes of civil protective orders: Results from one state. *Journal of Interpersonal Violence, 24*(7), 1209–1221.

Dobash, R. E., & Dobash, R. P. (1979). *Violence against wives: A case against patriarchy.* New York, NY: Free Press.

Dobash, R. E., & Dobash, R. P. (2015). *When men murder women.* New York, NY: Oxford University Press.

Dobash, R. P., Dobash, R. E., Cavanagh, K., & Lewis, R. (1998). Separate and intersection realities: A comparison of men's and women's accounts of violence against women. *Violence Against Women, 4*(4), 382–414.

Dobie, D. J., Kivlahan, C., Maynard, C., Bush, R., Davis, T. M., & Bradley, K.A. (2004). Post-traumatic stress disorder in female veterans: Association with self-reported health problems and functional impairment. *Archives of Internal Medicine, 164,* 394–400.

Dodge, K. A., Berlin, L. J., Epstein, M., Spitz-Roth, A., O'Donnell, K., Kaufman, M., . . . Christopoulos, C. (2004). The Durham Family Initiative: A preventive system of care. *Child Welfare, 83*(2), 109.

Doidge, J. C., Higgins, D. J., Delfabbro, P., & Segal, L. (2017). Risk factors for child maltreatment in an Australian population-based birth cohort. *Child Abuse & Neglect, 64,* 47–60.

Dolan, M., Casanueva, C., Smith, K., Lloyd, S., & Ringeisen, H. (2012). *NSCAW II wave 2 report caregiver health and services* (No. OPRE Report #2012-58). Washington, DC: Office of Planning, Research and Evaluation, Administration for Children and Families, U.S. Department of Health and Human Services.

Dombrowski, S. C., LeMasney, J. W., Ahia, C. E., & Dickson, S. A. (2004). Protecting children from online sexual predators: Technological, psychoeducational, and legal considerations. *Professional Psychology: Research and Practice, 35*(1), 65.

Domhardt, M., Münzer, A., Fegert, J. M., & Goldbeck, L. (2015). Resilience in survivors of child sexual abuse: A systematic review of the literature. *Trauma, Violence, & Abuse, 16*(4), 476–493.

Dong, X., Simon, M., de Leon, C. M., Fulmer, T., Beck, T., Hebert, L., et al. (2009). Elder self-neglect and abuse and mortality risk in a community-dwelling population. *Journal of the American Medical Association, 302,* 517–526.

Donnelly, D. A., Cook, K. J., Van Ausdale, D., & Foley, L. (2005). White privilege, color blindness, and services to battered women. *Violence Against Women, 11*(1), 6–37.

Doumas, D. M., Pearson, C. L., Elgin, J. E., & McKinley, L. L. (2008). Adult attachment as a risk factor for intimate partner violence: The "mispairing" of partners' attachment styles. *Journal of Interpersonal Violence*, *23*, 616–634.

Dowd, M. (2014, September 13). Throw the bums out: Roger Goodell, Ray Rice and the N.F.L.'s culture. *New York Times*. Retrieved from http://www.nytimes.com/2014/09/14/opinion/sunday/maureen-dowd-throw-the-bums-out.html

Dowdall, G. W. (2008). *College drinking: Reframing a social problem*. Santa Barbara, CA: ABC-CLIO.

Doyle, J. J. (2007). Child protection and child outcomes: Measuring the effects of foster care. *The American Economic Review*, *97*, 1583–1610.

Dozier, M. (2003). Attachment-based treatment for vulnerable children. *Attachment & Human Development*, *5*(3), 253–257.

Dragiewicz, M. (2011). *Equality with a vengeance: Men's rights groups, battered women, and antifeminist backlash*. Boston, MA: Northeastern University Press.

Drouin, M., Ross, J., & Tobin, E. (2015). Sexting: A new digital vehicle for intimate partner aggression. *Computers in Human Behavior*, *50*, 197–204.

Duan, G., Chen, J., Zhang, W., Yu, B., Jin, Y., Wang, Y., & Yao, M. (2015). Physical maltreatment of children with autism in Henan province in China: A cross-sectional study. *Child Abuse & Neglect*, *48*, 140–147.

Dube, N. (2012). Mandatory reporting of elder abuse. *OLR Research Report*. Retrieved from https://www.cga.ct.gov/2012/rpt/2012-R-0437.htm

Dube, S. R., Anda, R. F., Felitti, V. J., Chapman, D. P., Williamson, D. F., & Giles, W. H. (2001). Childhood abuse, household dysfunction and the risk of attempted suicide throughout the life span: Findings from the Adverse Childhood Experiences Study. *Journal of the American Medical Association*, *286*, 3089–3096.

Dubowitz, H., Feigelman, S., Lane, W., & Kim, J. (2009). Pediatric primary care to help prevent child maltreatment: The Safe Environment for Every Kid (SEEK) Model. *Pediatrics*, *123*(3), 858–864.

Dubowitz, H., Pitts, S. C., & Black, M. M. (2004). Measurement of three major subtypes of child neglect. *Child Maltreatment*, *9*(4), 344–356.

Dubowitz, H., Pitts, S. C., & Black, M. M. (2012). Measurement of three major subtypes of child neglect. In J. E. B. Myers (Ed.), *Child maltreatment: A collection of readings* (pp. 164–181). Thousand Oaks, CA: Sage.

Dubowitz, H., Roesch, S., Arria, A. M., Metzger, R., Thompson, R., Kotch, J. B., & Lewis, T. (2019). Timing and chronicity of child neglect and substance use in early adulthood. *Child Abuse & Neglect, 94*. Advance online publication. doi:10.1016/j.chiabu.2019.104027

Dubowitz, H., Villodas, M. T., Litrownik, A. J., Pitts, S. C., Hussey, J. M., Thompson, R., Black, M. M., & Runyan, D. (2011). Psychometric properties of a youth self-report measure of neglectful behavior by parents. *Child Abuse & Neglect*, *35*(6), 414–424.

Durborow, N., Lizdas, K., Flaherty, A., & Marjavi, A. (2010). *Compendium of state statutes and policies on domestic violence and health care*. Retrieved from http://www.acf.hhs.gov/sites/default/files/fysb/state_compendium.pdf

Durfee, M., Durfee, D. T., & West, M. P. (2002). Child fatality review: An international movement. *Child Abuse & Neglect*, *26*, 619–636.

Dutton, M. A., Ammar, N., Orloff, L., & Terrell, D. (2006). *Use and outcomes of protection orders by battered immigrant women*. Washington, DC: U.S. Department of Justice, National Institute of Justice.

Dutton, M. A., Orloff, L., & Hass, G. A. (2000). Characteristics of help-seeking behaviors, resources and service needs of battered immigrant Latinas: Legal and policy implications. *Georgetown Journal of Poverty, Law, and Policy*, *7*(2), 30–49.

Duva, J., & Metzger, S. (2010). Addressing poverty as a major risk factor in child neglect: Promising policy and practice. *Protecting Children*, *25*(1), 63–74.

Dyer, C. B., Pavlik, V. N., Murphy, K. P., & Hyman, D. J. (2000). The high prevalence of depression and dementia in elder abuse and neglect. *Journal of the American Geriatrics Society*, *48*, 205–208.

Eastman, B. J., Bunch, S. G., Williams, A. H., & Carawan, L. W. (2007). Exploring the perceptions of domestic violence service providers in rural localities. *Violence Against Women*, *13*, 700–716.

Easton, S. D. (2013). Disclosure of child sexual abuse among adult male survivors. *Clinical Social Work Journal*, *41*(4), 344–355.

Eckenrode, J., Campa, M., Luckey, D. W., Henderson, C. R., Jr., Cole, R., Kitzman, H., . . . Olds, D. (2010). Long-term effects of prenatal and infancy nurse home visitation on the life course of youths: 19-year follow-up of a randomized trial. *Archives of Pediatric & Adolescent Medicine*, *164*(1), 9–15.

Eckenrode, J., Campa, M. I., Morris, P. A., Henderson, C. R., Jr., Bolger, K. E., Kitzman, H., & Olds, D. L. (2017). The prevention of child maltreatment through the nurse family partnership program: Mediating effects in a long-term follow-up study. *Child Maltreatment*, *22*(2), 92–99.

Eckenrode, J., Smith, E. G., McCarthy, M. E., & Dineen, M. (2014). Income inequality and child maltreatment in the United States. *Pediatrics*, *133*, 454–461. Retrieved from http://dx.doi.org/10.1542/peds.2013-1707

Eckhardt, C. I., Parrott, D. J., & Sprunger, J. G. (2015). Mechanisms of alcohol-facilitated intimate partner violence. *Violence Against Women*, *21*(8), 939–957.

Edleson, J. L. (2004). Should childhood exposure to adult domestic violence be defined as child maltreatment under the law? In P. G. Jaffe, L. L. Baker, & A. J. Cunningham (Eds.), *Protecting children from domestic violence*. New York, NY: Guilford.

Edleson, J. L., Gassman-Pines, J., & Hill, M. B. (2006). Defining child exposure to domestic violence as neglect: Minnesota's difficult experience. *Social Work*, *51*(2), 167–174.

Edleson, J. L., & Malik, N. M. (2008). Collaborating for family safety: Results from the Greenbook Multisite Evaluation. *Journal of Interpersonal Violence*, *23*(7), 871–875.

Edmiston, E. E., Wang, F., Mazure, C. M., Guiney, J., Sinha, R., Mayes, L. C., & Blumberg, H. P. (2011). Corticostriatal-limbic gray matter morphology in adolescents with self-reported exposure to childhood maltreatment. *Archives of Pediatric & Adolescent Medicine*, *165*(12), 1069–1077.

Egan, R. D., & Hawkes, G. L. (2008). Endangered girls and incendiary objects: Unpacking the discourse on sexualization. *Sexuality & Culture*, *12*(4), 291–311.

Egeland, B. (1997). Mediators of the effects of child maltreatment on developmental adaptation in adolescence. In D. Cicchetti & S. L. Toth (Eds.), *Rochester symposium on developmental psychopathology* (Vol. 8, pp. 403–434). Rochester, NY: University of Rochester Press.

Ehlke, S. J., & Kelley, M. L. (2019). Drinking to cope motivations as a mediator of the relationship between sexual coercion victimization and alcohol use among college women: The role of depressive symptoms. *Violence Against Women*, *25*(6), 721–742.

Eisenberg, M. E., Gower, A. L., McMorris, B. J., & Bucchianeri, M. M. (2015, August 7). Vulnerable bullies: Perpetration of peer harassment among youths across sexual orientation, weight, and disability status. *American Journal of Public Health*. Retrieved from ajph.aphapublications.org/doi/abs/10.2105/AJPH .2015.302704

Eismann, E. A., Pearl, E. S., Theuerling, J., Folger, A. T., Hutton, J. S., & Makoroff, K. (2019). Feasibility study of the calm baby gently program: An educational baby book intervention on safe practices related to infant crying. *Child Abuse & Neglect*, *89*, 135–142.

Elder, G. H., & Conger, R. D. (2000). *Children of the land: Adversity and success in rural America*. Chicago, IL: University of Chicago Press.

Elder Justice Act. (2009). Retrieved from http://www .ncea.aoa.gov/Resources/Publication/docs/ELDER_ JUSTICE_ACT_2010.pdf

Elliott, M., Browne, K., & Kilcoyne, J. (1995). Child sexual abuse prevention: What offenders tell us. *Child Abuse & Neglect*, *19*, 579–594.

Ellison, C. G., Musick, M. A., & Holden, G. W. (2011). Does conservative Protestantism moderate the association between corporal punishment and child outcomes? *Journal of Marriage and Family*, *73*, 946–961. doi:10.1111/j.1741-3737.2011.00854.x

Emery, R. E., & Laumann-Billings, L. (1998, February). An overview of the nature, causes, and consequences of abusive family relationships: Toward differentiating maltreatment and violence. *American Psychologist*, *53*(2), 121–135.

Empey, L. I., Stafford, M. C., & Hay, H. II. (1999). *American delinquency: Its meaning and construction*. Belmont, CA: Wadsworth.

Erickson, M. F., & Egeland, B. (2002). Child neglect. In J. E. B. Myers, L. Berliner, J. Briere, C. T. Hendrix, C. Jenny, & T. A. Reid (Eds.), *The APSAC handbook on child maltreatment* (2nd ed., pp. 3–20). Thousand Oaks, CA: Sage.

Erickson, M. F., & Egeland, B. (2011). Child neglect. In J. E. B. Myers (Ed.), *The APSAC handbook on child maltreatment* (3rd ed., pp. 103–124). Thousand Oaks, CA: Sage.

Espelage, D. L., Basile, K. C., De La Rue, L., & Hamburger, M. E. (2015). Longitudinal associations among bullying, homophobic teasing, and sexual violence perpetration among middle school students. *Journal of Interpersonal Violence*, *30*, 2541–2561.

Espelage, D., Basile, K., & Hamburger, M. (2011). Bullying perpetration and subsequent sexual violence perpetration among middle school students. *Journal of Adolescent Health*, *50*, 60–65.

Espelage, D. L., Basile, K. C., Leemis, R. W., Hipp, T. N., & Davis, J. P. (2018). Longitudinal examination of the bullying-sexual violence pathway across early to late adolescence: Implicating homophobic name-calling. *Journal of Youth and Adolescence, 47,* 1880–1893.

Éthier, L. S., Couture, G., & Lacharite, C. (2004). Risk factors associated with the chronicity of high potential for child abuse and neglect. *Journal of Family Violence, 19*(1), 13–24.

Éthier, L. S., Lacharite, C., & Couture, G. (1995). Childhood adversity, parental stress and depression of negligent mothers. *Child Abuse & Neglect, 19,* 619–632.

Euser, S., Alink, L. R., Tharner, A., van IJzendoorn, M. H., & Bakermans-Kranenburg, M. J. (2016). The prevalence of child sexual abuse in out-of-home care: Increased risk for children with a mild intellectual disability. *Journal of Applied Research in Intellectual Disabilities, 29*(1), 83–92.

Exner-Cortens, D., Eckenrode, J., & Rothman, E. (2013). Longitudinal associations between teen dating violence victimization and adverse health outcomes. *Pediatrics, 131,* 71–78.

Fallon, B., Trocme, N., Fluke, J., MacLaurin, B., Tonmyr, L., & Ying-Ying, Y. (2010). Methodological challenges in measuring child maltreatment. *Child Abuse & Neglect, 34,* 70–79.

Famularo, R., Fenton, T., Kinscherff, R. T., Ayoub, C. C., & Barnum, R. (1994). Maternal and child posttraumatic stress disorder in cases of child maltreatment. *Child Abuse & Neglect, 18,* 27–36.

Famularo, R., Kinscherff, R. T., & Fenton, T. (1991). Posttraumatic stress disorder among children clinically diagnosed as borderline personality disorder. *Journal of Nervous and Mental Disease, 179,* 428–431.

Fantuzzo, J. W. (1990). Behavioral treatment of the victims of child abuse and neglect. *Behavior Modification, 14,* 316–339.

Fantuzzo, J. W., delGaudio, W. A., Atkins, M., Meyers, R., & Noone, M. (1998). A contextually relevant assessment of the impact of child maltreatment on the social competencies of low-income urban children. *Journal of the American Academy of Child and Adolescent Psychiatry, 37,* 1201–1208.

Fantuzzo, J. W., Perlman, S. M., & Dobbins, E. K. (2011). Types and timing of child maltreatment and early school success: A population-based investigation. *Children and Youth Services Review, 33,* 1404–1411.

Fantuzzo, J. W., Sutton-Smith, B., Atkins, M., Meyers, R., Stevenson, H., Coolahan, K., . . . Manz, P. (1996). Community-based resilient peer treatment of withdrawn maltreated preschool children. *Journal of Consulting and Clinical Psychology, 64,* 1377–1386.

Farber, N., & Miller-Cribbs, J. E. (2014). Violence in the lives of rural, southern, and poor white women. *Violence Against Women, 20,* 517–538.

Farrow, R. (2017, October 10). From aggressive overtures to sexual assault: Harvey Weinstein's accusers tell their stories. *The New Yorker.*

Federal Bureau of Investigation. (2012, March 19). *UCR program changes definition of rape.* Retrieved from https://www.fbi.gov/services/cjis/cjis-link/ucr-program-changes-definition-of-rape

Federal Bureau of Investigation. (2017). *Crime in the United States.* Retrieved from https://ucr.fbi.gov/crime-in-the-u.s./2014/tables/table-16

Fedina, L., Holmes, J. L., & Backes, B. L. (2018). Campus sexual assault: A systematic review of prevalence from 2000 to 2015. *Trauma, Violence & Abuse, 19*(1), 76–93.

Feld, K., Banaschak, S., Remschmidt, H., & Rothschild, M. A. (2018). Shaken baby syndrome—what convicted perpetrators report. *Rechtsmedizin, 28*(6), 514–517.

Felitti, V. J., Anda, R. F., Nordenberg, D., Williamson, D. F., Spitz, A. M., Edwards, V., . . . Marks, J. S. (2019). Relationship of childhood abuse and household dysfunction to many of the leading causes of death in adults: The Adverse Childhood Experiences (ACE) Study. *American Journal of Preventive Medicine, 56*(6), 774–786.

Felson, M. (2006). *Crime and nature.* Thousand Oaks, CA: Sage.

Feltner, C., Wallace, I., Berkman, N., Kistler, C. E., Middleton, J. C., Barclay, C., Hiiginbotham, L., Green, J. T., & Jones, D. E. (2018). Screening for intimate partner violence, elder abuse, and abuse of vulnerable adults: Evidence report and systematic review for the U.S. Preventive Services Task Force. *Journal of the American Medical Association, 320*(16), 1688–1701.

Fergusson, D. M., McLeod, G. F., & Horwood, L. J. (2013). Childhood sexual abuse and adult developmental outcomes: Findings from a 30-year longitudinal study in New Zealand. *Child Abuse & Neglect, 37*(9), 664–674.

Ferre-Sandurni, L. (2019, July 2). Teenager accused of rape deserves leniency because he's from a "good family," judge says. *New York Times.* Retrieved from http://www.nytimes.com/2019/07/02/nyregion/judge-james-troiano-rape.html

Field, C. A., & Caetano, R. (2003). Longitudinal model predicting partner violence among white, black, and Hispanic couples in the United States. *Alcoholism: Clinical and Experimental Research, 27*, 1451–1458.

Field, C. A., Caetano, R., & Nelson, S. (2004). Alcohol and violence-related cognitive factors associated with the perpetration of intimate partner violence. *Journal of Family Violence, 19*(4), 249–253.

Field, C. J., Kimuna, M. M., & Lang, M. N. (2015). The relation of interracial relationships to intimate partner violence by college students. *Journal of Black Studies, 46*, 384–403.

FindLaw.com. (n.d.). *Stand your ground laws.* Retrieved from https://criminal.findlaw.com/criminal-law-basics/stand-your-ground-laws.html

Finkelhor, D. (1994). Current information on the scope and nature of child sexual abuse. *Future of Children, 4*(2), 31–53.

Finkelhor, D. (1996). Introduction. In J. Briere, L. Berliner, J. A. Bulkley, C. Jenny, & T. A. Reid (Eds.), *The APSAC handbook on child maltreatment* (pp. ix–xiii). Thousand Oaks, CA: Sage.

Finkelhor, D. (2008). *Childhood victimization: Violence, crime, and abuse in the lives of young people.* New York, NY: Oxford University Press.

Finkelhor, D. (2009). The prevention of childhood sexual abuse. *The Future of Children, 19*(2), 53–78.

Finkelhor, D., Asdigian, N., & Dziuba Leatherman, J. (1995). The effectiveness of victimization prevention programs for children: A follow-up. *American Journal of Public Health, 85*(12), 1684–1689.

Finkelhor, D., Mitchell, K., & Wolak, J. (2000). Online victimization: A report on the nation's youth. Retrieved June 20, 2003, from www.unh.edu/ccrc/Youth_Internet_info_page.html

Finkelhor, D., Mitchell, K., & Wolak, J. (2005). Online victimization: What youth tell us. In S. Cooper, R. J. Estes, A. P. Giardino, N. D. Kellog, & V. I. Vieth (Eds.), *Medical, legal, & social science aspects of child sexual exploitation: A comprehensive review of pornography, prostitution, and Internet crimes* (pp. 437–467). St. Louis, MO: G. W. Medical.

Finkelhor, D., Moore, D., Hamby, S. L., & Straus, M. A. (1997). Sexually abused children in a national survey of parents: Methodological issues. *Child Abuse & Neglect, 21*, 1–9.

Finkelhor, D., & Ormrod, R. K. (2001). Factors in the underreporting of crimes against juveniles. *Child Maltreatment, 6*(3), 219–229.

Finkelhor, D., Ormrod, R. K., & Turner, H. A. (2007). Poly-victimization: A neglected component in child victimization. *Child Abuse & Neglect, 31*(1), 7–26.

Finkelhor, D., Ormrod, R. K., & Turner, H. A. (2009). Lifetime assessment of poly-victimization in a national sample of children and youth. *Child Abuse & Neglect, 33*, 403–411.

Finkelhor, D., Saito, K., & Jones, L. (2016). *Updated trends in child maltreatment.* Durham, NH: Crimes Against Children Research Center.

Finkelhor, D., Shattuck, A., Turner, H. A., & Hamby, S. L. (2014a). Trends in children's exposure to violence, 2003 to 2011. *JAMA Pediatrics, 168*(6), 540–546.

Finkelhor, D., Shattuck, A., Turner, H. A., & Hamby, S. L. (2014b). The lifetime prevalence of child sexual abuse and sexual assault assessed in late adolescence. *Journal of Adolescent Health, 55*(3), 329–333.

Finkelhor, D., Turner, H., & Ormrod, R. (2006). Kid's stuff: The nature and impact of peer and sibling violence on younger and older children. *Child Abuse & Neglect, 30*, 1401–1421.

Finkelhor, D., Turner, H., Ormrod, R., & Hamby, S. L. (2009). Violence, abuse, and crime exposure in a national sample of children and youth. *Pediatrics, 124*(5), 1411–1423.

Finkelhor, D., Turner, H., Ormrod, R., & Hamby, S. L. (2010). Trends in childhood violence and abuse exposure: Evidence from 2 national surveys. *Archives of Pediatrics & Adolescent Medicine, 164*(3), 238–242.

Finkelhor, D., Turner, H. A., Shattuck, A., & Hamby, S. L. (2013). Violence, crime, and abuse exposure in a national sample of children and youth: An update. *JAMA Pediatrics, 167*(7), 614–621.

Finkelhor, D., Turner, H. A., Shattuck, A., & Hamby, S. L. (2015). Prevalence of childhood exposure to violence, crime, and abuse. *JAMA Pediatrics, 169*(8), 746–754.

Finkelhor, D., Turner, H., Shattuck, A., Hamby, S., & Kracke, K. (2015). Children's exposure to violence, crime, and abuse: An update. *Juvenile Justice Bulletin, 2015*(September), 1–13.

Finkelhor, D., & Yllö, K. (1985). *License to rape: Sexual abuse of wives.* New York, NY: Free Press.

Finn, M. A., Blackwell, B. S., Stalans, L. J., Studdard, S., & Dugan, L. (2004). Dual arrest decisions in domestic violence cases: The influence of department policies. *Crime and Delinquency, 50*, 565–589.

Finneran, C., & Stephenson, R. (2014). Intimate partner violence among men who have sex with men: A systematic review. *Trauma, Violence & Abuse*, *14*(2), 168–185.

Finzi, R., Ram, A., Har-Even, D., Shnit, D., & Weizman, A. (2001). Attachment styles and aggression in physically abused and neglected children. *Journal of Youth and Adolescence*, *30*(4), 769–786.

Fischer, J. L., & Wiersma, J. D. (2012). Romantic relationships and alcohol use. *Current Drug Abuse Reviews*, *5*(2), 98–116.

Fishbein, D., Warner, T., Krebs, C., Trevarthen, N., Flannery, B., & Hammond, J. (2009). Differential relationships between personal and community stressors and children's neurocognitive functioning. *Child Maltreatment*, *14*, 299–315.

Fisher, B. S. (2009). The effects of survey question wording on rape estimates: Evidence from a quasi-experimental design. *Violence Against Women*, *15*(2), 133–147.

Fisher, B. S., Daigle, L. E., Cullen, F. T., & Turner, M. G. (2003). Reporting sexual victimization to the police and others: Results from a national-level study of college women. *Criminal Justice and Behavior*, *30*, 6–38.

Fitzgerald, M. M., & Berliner, L. (2012). Evidence-based mental health treatment: A 25-year glance at past, present, and future. *APSAC Advisor*, *24*(1/2), 36–43.

Fitzgerald, M. M., Schneider, R. A., Salstrom, S., Zinzow, H. M., Jackson, J., & Fossel, R. V. (2008). Child sexual abuse, early family risk, and childhood parentification: Pathways to current psychosocial adjustment. *Journal of Family Psychology*, *22*(2), 320.

Fleming, P. J., McCleary-Sills, J., Morton, M., Levtov, R., Heilman, B., & Barker, G. (2015). Risk factors for men's lifetime perpetration of physical violence against intimate partners: Results from the International Men and Gender Equality Survey (IMAGES) in eight countries. *PLoS One*, *10*(3), e0118639. doi:10.1371/journal.pone.0118639

Fleury, R. E., Sullivan, C. M., & Bybee, D. I. (2000). When ending the relationship does not end the violence: Women's experiences of violence by former partners. *Violence Against Women*, *6*(12), 1363–1383.

Fleury-Steiner, R. E., & Brady, L. T. (2011). The importance of resources and information in the lives of battered mothers. *Violence Against Women*, *17*, 882–903.

Flory, J. D., Yehuda, R., Grossman, R., New, A. S., Mitropoulou, V., & Siever, L. J. (2009). Childhood trauma and basal cortisol in people with personality disorders. *Comprehensive Psychiatry*, *50*(1), 34–37.

Font, S. A., & Gershoff, E. T. (2020). Foster care and the "Best Interests of the Child": Integrating research, policy and practice. *Advances in Child and Family Policy and Practice*.

Font, S. A., & Maguire-Jack, K. (2016). Pathways from childhood abuse and other adversities to adult health risks: The role of adult socioeconomic conditions. *Child Abuse & Neglect*, *51*, 390–399.

Fontana, V. J., & Moohnan, V. (1994). Establish more crisis intervention centers. In D. Bender & B. Leone (Eds.), *Child abuse: Opposing viewpoints* (pp. 227–234). San Diego, CA: Greenhaven.

Fontes, L. A. (2008). *Child abuse and culture: Working with diverse families*. New York, NY: Guilford.

Fontes, L. A., & McCloskey, K. A. (2011). Cultural issues in violence against women. In C. M. Renzetti, J. L. Edleson, & R. K. Bergen (Eds.), *Sourcebook on violence against women* (2nd ed., pp. 151–168). Thousand Oaks, CA: Sage.

Ford, D. A., Bachman, R., Friend, M., & Meloy, M. (2002). *Controlling violence against women: A research perspective on the 1994 VAWA's criminal justice impacts. I. The convergence of advocacy, research and law.* Washington, DC: U.S. Department of Justice, National Institute of Justice.

Ford, J. D., Elhai, J. D., Connor, D. F., & Frueh, B. C. (2010). Poly-victimization and risk of posttraumatic, depressive, and substance use disorders and involvement in delinquency in a national sample of adolescents. *Journal of Adolescent Health*, *46*(6), 545–552.

Fortson, B. L., Klevens, J., Merrick, M. T., Gilbert, L. K., & Alexander, S. P. (2016). *Preventing child abuse and neglect: A technical package for policy, norm, and programmatic activities*. Atlanta, GA: National Center for Injury Prevention and Control, Centers for Disease Control and Prevention. Retrieved from https://www.cdc.gov/violenceprevention/pdf/can-prevention-technical-package.pdf

Foshee, V., & Langwick, S. (2010). *Safe dates: An adolescent dating abuse prevention curriculum*. Center City, MN: Hazelden.

Foshee, V. A., McNaughton Reyes, H. L., Chen, M. S., Ennett, S. T., Basile, K. C., DeGue, S., . . . Bowling, J. M. (2016). Shared risk factors for the perpetration of physical dating violence, bullying, and sexual harassment among adolescents exposed to domestic violence. *Journal of Youth and Adolescence*, *45*(4), 672–686.

Foshee, V. A., McNaughton Reyes, H. L., & Wyckoff, S. C. (2009). Approaches to preventing psychological,

[QU: Updated per list of crx. you have full info.?]

physical, and sexual partner abuse. In K. D. O'Leary & E. M. Woodin (Eds.), *Psychological and physical aggression in couples: Causes and interventions* (pp. 165–189). Washington, DC: American Psychological Association.

Fowler, D. N., Faulkner, M., Learman, J., & Runnels, R. (2011). The influence of spirituality on service utilization and satisfaction for women residing in a domestic violence shelter. *Violence Against Women, 17,* 1244–1259.

Franklin, C. A. (2016). Sorority affiliation and sexual assault victimization: Assessing vulnerability using path analysis. *Violence Against Women, 22*(8), 895–922.

Fraser, M. W., Walton, E., Lewis, R. E., & Pecora, P. J. (1996). An experiment in family reunification: Correlates of outcomes at one-year follow-up. *Children and Youth Services Review, 18,* 335–361.

Frazier, E. R., Liu, G. C., & Dauk, K. L. (2014). Creating a safe place for pediatric care: A no hit zone. *Hospital Pediatrics, 4*(4), 247–250.

Freeman, R. (2018). Guest editor's introduction. *Violence Against Women, 24*(10), 1115–1131.

Friedenberg, F. K., Makipour, K., Palit, A., Shah, S., Vanar, V., & Richter, J. E. (2013). Population-based assessment of heartburn in urban black Americans. *Dis Esophagus, 26,* 561–569.

Friedman, M. S., Marshal, M. P., Guadamuz, T. F., Wei, C., Wong, C. F., Saewyc, E. M., & Stall, R. (2011). A meta-analysis of disparities in childhood sexual abuse, parental physical abuse, and peer victimization among sexual minority and sexual nonminority individuals. *American Journal of Public Health, 101*(8), 1490. 10.2105/AJPH.2009.190009

Friedrich, W. N. (2007). *Children with sexual behavior problems: Family-based, attachment-focused therapy.* New York, NY: W. W. Norton & Company.

Friedrich, W. N., Fisher, J., Broughton, D., Houston, M., & Shafran, C. R. (1998). Normative sexual behavior in children: A contemporary sample. *Pediatrics, 101,* e9.

Friedrich, W. N., Jaworski, T. M., Huxsahl, J. E., & Bengtson, B. S. (1997). Dissociative and sexual behaviors in children and adolescents with sexual abuse and psychiatric histories. *Journal of Interpersonal Violence, 12,* 155–171.

Frodi, A., & Lamb, M. (1980). Child abusers' responses to infant smiles and cries. *Child Development, 51,* 238–241.

Fry, D. A., Messinger, A. M., Rickert, V. I., O'Connor, M. K., Palmetto, N., Lessel, H., & Davidson, L. I. (2013). Adolescent relationship violence: Help-seeking and help-giving behaviors among peers. *Journal of Urban Health, 91,* 320–334.

Fuchs, A., Mohler, E., Resch, F., & Kaess, M. (2015). Impact of a maternal history of childhood abuse on the development of mother-infant interaction during the first year of life. *Child Abuse & Neglect, 48,* 179-189.

Fuller-Thomson, E., & Lewis, D. A. (2015). The relationship between early adversities and attention-deficit/hyperactivity disorder. *Child Abuse & Neglect, 47,* 94–101.

Fuller-Thomson, E., Mehta, R., & Valeo, A. (2014). Establishing a link between attention deficit disorder/ attention deficit hyperactivity disorder and childhood physical abuse. *Journal of Aggression, Maltreatment & Trauma, 23*(2), 188–198.

Fung, H. W., Chung, H. M., & Ross, C. A. (2020). Demographic and mental health correlates of childhood emotional abuse and neglect in a Hong Kong sample. *Child Abuse & Neglect, 99,* 104288.

Furman, W., & Winkles, J. K. (2011). Transformations in heterosexual romantic relationships across the transition in to adulthood. In B. Laursen & W. A. Collins (Eds.), *Relationship pathways: From adolescence to young adulthood* (pp. 191–213). Thousand Oaks, CA: Sage

Futures Without Violence. (n.d.). Mandatory reporting of domestic violence to law enforcement by health care providers: A guide for advocates working to respond to or amend reporting laws related to domestic violence. Retrieved from https://www.futureswithoutviolence .org/userfiles/Mandatory_Reporting_of_DV_to_Law %20Enforcement_by_HCP.pdf

Gadin, K. G., & Hammarstrom, A. (2005). A possible contributor to the higher degree of girls reporting psychological symptoms compared with boys in grade nine? *European Journal of Public Health, 15,* 380–385.

Gallitto, E., Romano, E., & Drolet, M. (2018). Caregivers' perspectives on the SafeCare® programme: Implementing an evidence-based intervention for child neglect. *Child & Family Social Work, 23*(2), 307–315.

Gallmeier, T. M., & Bonner, B. L. (1992). University-based interdisciplinary training in child abuse and neglect. *Child Abuse & Neglect, 16*(4), 513–521.

Galofaro, C. (2015, February 10). Social worker turnover leads to high caseloads. *The Courier-Journal.* Retrieved from http://www.courier-journal.com/story/

news/local/2015/02/06/social-worker-turnover-le ads-high-caseloads/22983561/

Garbarino, J. (2011). Not all bad treatment is psychological maltreatment. *Child Abuse & Neglect*, 35(10), 797–801.

Garbarino, J., Guttman, E., & Seely, J. (1986). *The psychologically battered child*. San Francisco, CA: Jossey-Bass.

Gardner, M. J., Thomas, H. J., & Erskine, H. E. (2019). The association between five forms of child maltreatment and depressive and anxiety disorders: A systematic review and meta-analysis. *Child Abuse & Neglect*, 96. Advance online publication. doi:10.1016/j .chiabu.2019.104082

Garvey, T. M., Fuhrman, H. M., & Long, J. (2019, September). Charging considerations in the prosecution of marital rape. *Strategies in Brief*, 34. AEquitas. Retrieved from https://aequitasresource.org

Gavey, N. (2013). *Just sex? The cultural scaffolding of rape*. New York, NY: Routledge.

Gecewicz, C. (2019, June). Key takeaways about how Americans view the sexual abuse scandal in the Catholic Church. *FactTank*.

Geeraert, L., Van den Noortgate, W., Grietens, H., & Onghena, P. (2004). The effects of early prevention programs for families with young children at risk for physical child abuse and neglect. A meta-analysis. *Child Maltreatment*, 9(3), 277–291.

Gelles, R. J. (1993). Alcohol and drugs are associated with violence—They are not its cause. In R. J. Gelles & D. R. Loseke (Eds.), *Current controversies on domestic violence* (pp. 182–196). Newbury Park, CA: Sage.

Gelles, R. J. (2000). Controversies in family preservation programs. *Journal of Aggression, Maltreatment, & Trauma*, 3, 239–252.

Gelles, R. J. (2005). Protecting children is more important than preserving families. In D. R. Loseke, R. J. Gelles, & M. M. Cavanaugh (Eds.), *Current controversies on family violence* (2nd ed., pp. 329–340). Thousand Oaks, CA: Sage.

Gelles, R. J., & Cornell, C. P. (1990). *Intimate violence in families* (2nd ed.). Newbury Park, CA: Sage.

Gelles, R. J., & Straus, M. A. (1987). Is violence toward children increasing? A comparison of 1975 and 1985 national survey rates. *Journal of Interpersonal Violence*, 2, 212–222.

Gelles, R. J., & Straus, M. A. (1988). *Intimate violence*. New York, NY: Simon & Schuster.

Gershoff, E. T., Goodman, G. S., Miller-Perrin, C. L., Holden, G. W., Jackson, Y., & Kazdin, A. E. (2018). The strength of the causal evidence against physical punishment of children and its implications for parents, psychologists, and policymakers. *American Psychologist*, 73(5), 626.

Gershoff, E. T., & Grogan-Kaylor, A. (2016). Corporal punishment by parents and its consequences for children: Old controversies and new meta-analyses. *Journal of Family Psychology*, 30, 453–469. doi:10.1037/ fam0000191

Gershoff, E. T., Lansford, J. E., Sexton, H. R., Davis-Kean, P., & Sameroff, A. J. (2012). Longitudinal links between spanking and children's externalizing behaviors in a national sample of white, black, Hispanic, and Asian American families. *Child Development*, 83, 838–843. doi:10.1111/j.1467-8624.2011.01732.x

Gerstenberger, C., Stansfield, R., & Williams, K. R. (2019). Intimate partner violence in same-sex relationships: An analysis of risk and rearrest. *Criminal Justice and Behavior*, 46(11), 1515–1527.

Gewirtz-Meydan, A., & Finkelhor, D. (2019). Sexual abuse and assault in a large national sample of children and adolescents. *Child Maltreatment*. Advance online publication. Retrieved from https://doi.org/10 .1177/1077559519873975

Gewirtz-Meydan, A., Lahav, Y., Walsh, W., & Finkelhor, D. (2019). Psychopathology among adult survivors of child pornography. *Child Abuse & Neglect*, 98. Advance online publication. doi:10.1016/j.chiabu.2019.104189

Gezinski, L. B., Gonzalex-Pons, K. M., & Rogers, M. M. (2019). Substance use as a coping mechanism for survivors of intimate partner violence: Implications for safety and service accessibility. *Violence Against Women*. Advance online publication. Retrieved from https://doi.org/10.1177/1077801219882496

Giardino, A. P., Lyn, M. A., & Giardino, E. R. (Eds.). (2019). *A practical guide to the evaluation of child physical abuse and neglect*. New York, NY: Springer.

Gibson, L. E., & Leitenberg, H. (2000). Child sexual abuse prevention programs: Do they decrease the occurrence of child sexual abuse? *Child Abuse & Neglect*, 24(9), 1115–1125.

Gidycz, C. A., Orchowski, L. M., & Edwards, K. M. (2011). Primary prevention of sexual violence. In M. P. Koss, J. W. White, & A. E. Kazdin (Eds.), *Violence against women and children*: Vol. 2. Navigating solutions (pp. 159–180). Washington, DC: American Psychological Association.

Gidycz, C. A., Orchowski, L. M., King, C. R., & Rich, C. L. (2008). Sexual victimization and health-risk behaviors. *Journal of Interpersonal Violence, 23,* 744–763.

Gidycz, C. A., Orchowski, L. M., Probst, D. R., Edwards, K. M., Murphy, M., & Tansill, E. (2015). Concurrent administration of sexual assault prevention and risk reduction programming: Outcomes for women. *Violence Against Women, 21*(6), 780–800.

Gilbert, N. (1997). Advocacy research and social policy. In M. Tonry (Ed.), *Crime and justice: An annual review of research* (pp. 101–148). Chicago, IL: University of Chicago Press.

Gilbert, N. (1998). Realities and mythologies of rape [Electronic version]. *Society, 35,* 356–362.

Gilbert, R., Kemp, A., Thoburn, J., Sidebotham, P., Radford, L., Glaser, D., & MacMillan, H. L. (2009). Recognising and responding to child maltreatment. *Lancet, 373,* 167–180.

Gilbert, R., Widom, C. S., Browne, K., Fergusson, D., Webb, E., & Janson, S. (2009). Burden and consequences of child maltreatment in high-income countries. *Lancet, 373,* 68–81.

Gil-González, D., Vives-Cases, C., Ruiz, M. T., Carrasco-Portiño, M., & Álvarez-Dardet, C. (2008). Childhood experiences of violence in perpetrators as a risk factor of intimate partner violence: A systematic review. *Journal of Public Health, 30*(1), 14–22.

Gillum, T. L. (2009). Improving services to African American survivors of IPV: From the voices of recipients of culturally specific services. *Violence Against Women, 15,* 57–80.

Gillum, T. L., & DiFulvio, G. (2012). "There's so much at stake": Sexual minority youth discuss dating violence. *Violence Against Women, 18*(7), 725–745.

Gilroy, H., Nava, A., & McFarlane, J. (2019). Developing a theory of economic solvency for women who have experienced intimate partner violence. *Violence Against Women.* Advance online publication. doi:10.1177/1077801219853366

Gilson, S. F., DePoy, E., & Cramer, E. P. (2001). Linking the assessment of self-reported functional capacity with abuse experiences of women with disabilities. *Violence Against Women, 7,* 418–431.

Glamour. (2019, May 18). Post-Weinstein, these are the powerful men facing sexual harassment allegations. Retrieved from https://www.glamour.com/gallery/post-weinstein-these-are-the-powerful-men-facing-sexual-harassment-allegations

Glaser, D. (2002). Emotional abuse and neglect (psychological maltreatment): A conceptual framework. *Child Abuse & Neglect, 26,* 697–714.

Glaser, D. (2011). How to deal with emotional abuse and neglect—Further development of a conceptual framework (FRAMEA). *Child Abuse & Neglect, 35*(10), 866–875.

Global Initiative to End All Corporal Punishment of Children. (2017). *Countdown to universal prohibition.* Retrieved from http://www.endcorporalpunishment.org/progress/countdown.html

Godbout, N., Briere, J., Sabourin, S., & Lussier, Y. (2014). Child sexual abuse and subsequent relational and personal functioning: The role of parental support. *Child Abuse & Neglect, 38*(2), 317–325.

Godfrey, D. (2019, January). *Signs of abuse, neglect, and exploitation: The checklist.* National Center on Law and Elder Rights. Retrieved from https://ncler.acl.gov/ElderJustice-Toolkit/Screening-Intake.aspx

Gold, L. (2003). A critical analysis of fusion in lesbian relationships. *Canadian Social Work Review, 20*(2), 259–271.

Gomez, R., & Fliss, J. (2019). A community-based prevention approach: Examples from the field. *Child and Adolescent Social Work Journal, 36*(1), 65–74.

Gondolf, E. W. (2002). *Batterer intervention systems.* Thousand Oaks, CA: Sage.

Gondolf, E. W. (2004). Evaluating batterer counseling programs. *Aggression and Violent Behavior, 9,* 605–631.

Gondolf, E. W. (2007). Culturally focused batterer counseling for African American men. *Criminology & Public Policy, 6,* 341–366.

Gonzalez, A., & Oshri, A. (2019). Introduction to the special issue on understanding neurobiological implications of maltreatment: From preschool to emerging adulthood. *Child Maltreatment, 24*(4), 335–339.

Gonzalez, O., Novaco, R., Reger, M. A., & Gahm, G. (2016). Anger intensification with combat-related PTSD and depression comorbidity. *Psychological Trauma: Theory, Research, Practice, and Policy, 8,* 9–16.

Goodey, J. (2008). Human trafficking: Sketchy data and policy responses. *Criminology and Criminal Justice, 8,* 421–442.

Goodin, S. M., Van Denburg, A., Murnen, S. K., & Smolak, L. (2011). "Putting on" sexiness: A content analysis of the presence of sexualizing characteristics in girls' clothing. *Sex Roles, 65*(1–2), 1–12.

Goodman, L. A., & Epstein, D. (2009). *Listening to battered women: A survivor-centered approach to advocacy, mental health and justice.* Washington, DC: American Psychological Association.

Goodman, L. A., & Epstein, D. (2011). The justice system response to domestic violence. In M. P. Koss, J. W. White, & A. E. Kazdin (Eds.), *Violence against women and children: Navigating solutions* (pp. 215–235). Washington, DC: American Psychological Association.

Goodman, L. A., Manyard, V., Woulfe, J., Ash, S., & Mattern, G. (2016). Bringing a network-oriented approach to domestic violence services: A focus group exploration of promising practices. *Violence Against Women, 22,* 64–89.

Goodman, L. A., Salyers, M. P., Mueser, K. T., Rosenberg, S. D., Swartz, M., Essock, S. M., et al. (2001). Recent victimization in women and men with severe mental illness: Prevalence and correlates. *Journal of Traumatic Stress, 14,* 615–632.

Goodmark, L. (2012). *A troubled marriage: Domestic violence and the legal system.* New York: New York University Press.

Goodmark, L. (2018). Innovative criminal justice responses to intimate partner violence. In C. M. Renzetti, J. L. Edleson, & R. K. Bergen (Eds.), *Sourcebook on violence against women* (3rd ed., pp. 253–270). Thousand Oaks, CA: Sage.

Goodyear-Brown, P., Fath, A., & Myers, L. (2012). Child sexual abuse: The scope of the problem. In P. Goodyear-Brown (Ed.), *Handbook of child sexual abuse: Identification, assessment, and treatment* (pp. 3–28). Hoboken, NJ: John Wiley & Sons.

Gorka, A. X., Hanson, J. L., Radtke, S. R., & Hariri, A. R. (2014). Reduced hippocampal and medial prefrontal gray matter mediate the association between reported childhood maltreatment and trait anxiety in adulthood and predict sensitivity to future life stress. *Biology of Mood & Anxiety Disorders, 4*(1), 12.

Gover, A. R., Richards, T. N., & Patterson, M. J. (2018). Explaining violence against women within the context of intimate partner violence (IPV). In C. M. Renzetti, J. L. Edleson, & R. K. Bergen (Eds.), *Sourcebook on violence against women* (3rd ed., pp. 31–50). Thousand Oaks, CA: Sage.

Grady, M. D., Yoder, J., & Brown, A. (2018). Childhood maltreatment experiences, attachment, sexual offending: Testing a theory. *Journal of Interpersonal Violence.* Advance online publication. doi:10.1177/0886260518814262

Graham, K., Bernards, S., Wilsnack, S. C., & Gmel, G. (2011). Alcohol may not cause partner violence but it seems to make it worse: A cross national comparison of the relationship between alcohol and severity of partner violence. *Journal of Interpersonal Violence, 26*(8), 1503–1523.

Graham-Bermann, S. (1998). The impact of woman abuse on children's social development: Research and theoretical perspectives. In G. Holden, R. Geffner, & E. Jouriles (Eds.), *Children exposed to marital violence: Theory, research, and applied issues* (pp. 21–54). Washington, DC: American Psychological Association.

Graham-Bermann, S. A. (2002). Child abuse in the context of domestic violence. In J. E. B. Myers, L. Berliner, J. Briere, C. T. Hendrix, C. Jenny, & T. A. Reid (Eds.), *The APSAC handbook on child maltreatment* (2nd ed., pp. 119–129). Thousand Oaks, CA: Sage.

Graham-Bermann, S. A., & Brescoll, V. (2000). Gender, power, and violence: Assessing the family stereotypes of the children of batterers. *Journal of Family Psychology, 14*(4), 600–612.

Grant, B. J., Shakeshaft, C., & Mueller, J. (2019). Prevention of preK–12 school employee sexual misconduct and abuse. *Journal of Child Sexual Abuse, 28*(2), 125–128.

Grant, B. J., Shields, R. T., Tabachnick, J., & Coleman, J. (2019). "I didn't know where to go": An examination of Stop It Now!'s sexual abuse prevention helpline. *Journal of Interpersonal Violence, 34*(20), 4225–4253.

Gratz, K. L., Paulson, A., Jakupcak, M., & Tull, M. T. (2009). Exploring the relationship between childhood maltreatment and intimate partner abuse: Gender differences in the mediating role of emotion dysregulation. *Violence & Victims, 24,* 68–82.

Gray, A., Busconi, A., Houchens, P., & Pithers, W. D. (1997). Children with sexual behavior problems and their caregivers: Demographics, functioning, and clinical patterns. *Sexual Abuse, 9*(4), 267–290.

Greenfeld, L. A., Rand, M. R., Craven, D., Klaus, P. A., Perkins, C., & Warchol, G., et al. (1998). *Violence by intimates: Analysis of data on crimes by current or former spouses, boyfriends, and girlfriends.* Washington, DC: U.S. Department of Justice.

Greeson, J. K., Treglia, D., Wolfe, D. S., Wasch, S., & Gelles, R. J. (2019). Child welfare characteristics in a sample of youth involved in commercial sex: An exploratory study. *Child Abuse & Neglect, 94.* Advance online publication. Retrieved from https://doi.org/10.1016/j.chiabu.2019.104038

Greger, H. K., Myhre, A. K., Lydersen, S., & Jozefiak, T. (2015). Previous maltreatment and present mental health in a high-risk adolescent population. *Child Abuse & Neglect, 45,* 122–134.

Grossi, L. M., Lee, A. F., Schuler, A., Ryan, J. L., & Prentky, R. A. (2016). Sexualized behaviors in cohorts of children in the child welfare system. *Child Abuse & Neglect, 52,* 49–61.

Grossman, S. F., & Lundy, M. (2007). Domestic violence across race and ethnicity: Implications for social work practice and policy. *Violence Against Women, 13,* 1029–1053.

Groth, A. N., & Burgess, A. W. (1980). Male rape: Offenders and victims. *The American Journal of Psychiatry, 139,* 806–810.

Gruber, A. (2020). The complexity of college consent. In C. M. Renzetti & D. R. Follingstad (Eds.), *Adjudicating campus sexual misconduct and assault: Controversies and challenges* (pp. 25–49). San Diego, CA: Cognella.

Gruber, J., & Fineran, S. (2007). The impact of bullying and sexual harassment victimization on the mental and physical health of adolescents. *Violence Against Women, 13,* 627–643.

Gruber, J., & Fineran, S. (2016). Sexual harassment, bullying, and school outcomes for high school girls and boys. *Violence Against Women, 22*(1), 112–133.

Guadalupe-Diaz, X. (2019). *Transgressed. Intimate partner violence in transgender lives.* New York: New York University Press.

Guild, D. J., Toth, S. L., Handley, E. D., Rogosch, F. A., & Cicchetti, D. (2017). Attachment security mediates the longitudinal association between child–parent psychotherapy and peer relations for toddlers of depressed mothers. *Development and Psychopathology, 29*(2), 587–600.

Gupta, J., Acevedo-Garcia, D., Hemenway, D., Decker, M. R., Raj, A., & Silverman, J. G. (2010). Intimate violence perpetration, immigration status, and disparities in a community health center–based sample of men. *Public Health Reports, 125*(1), 79–87.

Gushwa, M., Bernier, J., & Robinson, D. (2019). Advancing child sexual abuse prevention in schools: An exploration of the effectiveness of the Enough! online training program for K–12 teachers. *Journal of Child Sexual Abuse, 28*(2), 144–159.

Haapasalo, J., & Aaltonen, T. (1999). Mothers' abusive childhood predicts child abuse. *Child Abuse Review, 8,* 231–250.

Hackenberg, E. A. M., Sallinen, V., Koljonen, V., & Handolin, L. (2017). Severe intimate partner violence affecting both young and elderly patients of both sexes. *European Journal of Trauma and Emergency Surgery, 43*(3), 319–327.

Haelle, T. (2019, May 21). Guidelines addressing physician sexual abuse long past due, experts say. *Medscape Medical News.*

Hagborg, J. M., Berglund, K., & Fahlke, C. (2018). Evidence for a relationship between child maltreatment and absenteeism among high-school students in Sweden. *Child Abuse & Neglect, 75,* 41–49.

Hahn, J. W., McCormick, M. C., Silverman, J. G., Robinson, E. B., & Koenen, K. C. (2014). Examining the impact of disability status on intimate partner violence victimization in a population sample. *Journal of Interpersonal Violence, 29*(17), 3063–3085.

Hahn, R. A., Mercy, J., Bilukha, O., & Briss, P. (2005). Letter to the editor. *Child Abuse & Neglect, 29*(3), 215–218.

Hallowell, E. S., Oshri, A., Liebel, S. W., Liu, S., Duda, B., Clark, U. S., & Sweet, L. H. (2019). The mediating role of neural activity on the relationship between childhood maltreatment and impulsivity. *Child Maltreatment, 24*(4), 389–399.

Halpern, S. C., Schuch, F. B., Scherer, J. N., Sordi, A. O., Pachado, M., Dalbosco, C., . . . Von Diemen, L. (2018). Child maltreatment and illicit substance abuse: A systematic review and meta-analysis of longitudinal studies. *Child Abuse Review, 27*(5), 344–360.

Hamarman, S., Pope, K. H., & Czaja, S. J. (2002). Emotional abuse in children: Variations in legal definitions and rates across the United States. *Child Maltreatment, 7,* 303–311.

Hamby, S. L. (2014). *Battered women's protective strategies: Stronger than you know.* New York, NY: Oxford University Press.

Hamby, S. L. (2017). A scientific answer to a scientific question: The gender debate on intimate partner violence. *Trauma, Violence & Abuse, 18,* 145–154.

Hamby, S. L. (2018). Are women really as violent as men? The "gender symmetry" controversy. In C. M. Renzetti, J. L. Edleson, & R. K. Bergen (Eds.), *Sourcebook on violence against women* (3rd ed., pp. 78–81). Thousand Oaks, CA: Sage.

Hamby, S. L., & Cook, S. L. (2011). Assessing violence against women in practice settings: Processes and tools practitioners can use. In C. M. Renzetti, J. L.

Edleson, & R. K. Bergen (Eds.), *Sourcebook on violence against women* (2nd ed., pp. 49–71). Thousand Oaks, CA: Sage.

Hamby, S., Finkelhor, D., Ormrod, R., & Turner, H. (2010). The overlap of witnessing partner violence with child maltreatment and other victimizations in a nationally representative survey of youth. *Child Abuse & Neglect, 34*, 734–741. doi:10.1016/j.chiabu.2010.03.001

Hamby, S. L., & Koss, M. P. (2003). Shades of gray: A qualitative study of terms used in the measurement of sexual victimization. *Psychology of Women Quarterly, 27*, 243–255.

Hamilton, G. (2016, June 23). New guidelines forbid Montreal Catholic priests, lay workers to be alone with children. *National Post*. Retrieved from http://news.nationalpost.com/news/religion/newguidelines-forbid-montreal-catholic-priests-lay-workers-to-be-alone-with-children

Hamre, B. K., & Pianta, R. C. (2001). Early teacher–child relationships and the trajectory of children's school outcomes through eighth grade. *Child Development, 72*(2), 625–638.

Hand, J., & Sanchez, L. (2000). Badgering or bantering? Gender differences in experiences of, and reactions to, sexual harassment among U.S. high school students. *Gender & Society, 14*, 718–746.

Hanson, J. L., Nacewicz, B. M., Sutterer, M. J., Cayo, A. A., Schaefer, S. M., Rudolph, K. D., . . . Davidson, R. J. (2015). Behavioral problems after early life stress: Contributions of the hippocampus and amygdala. *Biological Psychiatry, 77*(4), 314–323.

Harper, N. S. (2014). Neglect: Failure to thrive and obesity. *Pediatric Clinics of North America, 61*(5), 937–957.

Harris, L. J. (2010). Failure to protect from domestic violence in private custody contests. *Family Law Quarterly, 44*, 169–196.

Harris, M. S., & Courtney, M. E. (2003). The interaction of race, ethnicity, and family structure with respect to the timing of family reunification. *Child and Youth Services Review, 25*, 409–429.

Harris, S. (2014, May 7). One in five? The White House's questionable sexual assault data. *Forbes*. Retrieved from http://www.forbes.com/sites/realspin/2014/05/07/one-in-five-the-white-houses-questionable-sexual-assault-data/#7d5a165d2907

Hart, B. (1986). Lesbian battering: An examination. In K. Lobel (Ed.), *Naming the violence* (pp. 173–189). Seattle, WA: Seal Press.

Hart, H., & Rubia, K. (2012). Neuroimaging of child abuse: A critical review. *Frontiers in Human Neuroscience, 6*, 52.

Hart, S. (2019). Implications of psychological maltreatment for universal intervention. *APSAC Advisor, 31*(3), 33–45.

Hart, S. N., & Brassard, M. R. (1991). Psychological maltreatment: Progress achieved. *Development and Psychopathology, 3*, 61–70.

Hart, S. N., & Brassard, M. R. (2019). Psychological maltreatment: A major child health, development, and protection issue. *APSAC Advisor, 31*(3), 4–12.

Hart, S. N., Brassard, M. R., Binggeli, N. J., & Davidson, H. A. (2002). Psychological maltreatment. In J. E. B. Myers, L. Berliner, J. Briere, C. T. Hendrix, C. Jenny, & T. A. Reid (Eds.), *The APSAC handbook on child maltreatment* (2nd ed., pp. 79–103). Thousand Oaks, CA: Sage.

Hart, S. N., Brassard, M. R., Davidson, H. A., Rivelis, E., Diaz, V., & Binggeli, N. J. (2011). Psychological maltreatment. In J. E. B. Myers (Ed.), *The APSAC handbook on child maltreatment* (3rd ed., pp. 125–144). Thousand Oaks, CA: Sage.

Hart, S. N., Germain, R., & Brassard, M. R. (1987). The challenge: To better understand and combat psychological maltreatment of children and youth. In M. R. Brassard, R. Germain, & S. N. Hart (Eds.), *Psychological maltreatment of children and youth* (pp. 3–24). New York, NY: Pergamon Press.

Hartley, C. C. (2012a). The co-occurrence of child maltreatment and domestic violence: Examining both neglect and child physical abuse. *Child Maltreatment, 7*, 340–358.

Hartley, C. C. (2012b). The co-occurrence of child maltreatment and domestic violence: Examining both neglect and child physical abuse. In J. E. B. Myers (Ed.), *Child maltreatment: A collection of readings* (pp. 296–310). Thousand Oaks, CA: Sage.

Hasday, J. E. (2000). Contest and consent: A legal history of marital rape [Electronic version]. *California Law Review, 88*, 1373–1505.

Hasinoff, A. A. (2016, April 4). Teenage sexting is not child porn. *New York Times*, A19.

Hass, G. A., Dutton, M. A., & Orloff, L. E. (2000). Lifetime prevalence of violence against Latina immigrants: Legal and policy implications. *International Review of Victimology, 7*(1–3), 93–113.

Hassouneh-Phillips, D. (2005). Understanding abuse of women with physical disabilities: An overview of the abuse pathways model. *Advances in Nursing Science*, *28*(1), 70–80.

Hattery, A. J. (2009). *Intimate partner violence*. Lanham, MD: Rowman & Littlefield

Haugaard, J. J., & Reppucci, N. D. (1988). *The sexual abuse of children*. San Francisco, CA: Jossey-Bass.

Hauser, C. (2017). Florida woman whose "stand your ground" defense was rejected is released. *New York Times*. Retrieved from https://www.nytimes.com/2017/02/07/marissa-alexander-released-stand-your-ground.html

Hauser, C. (2018, February 5). Larry Nassar is sentenced to another 40 to 125 years in prison. *New York Times*. Retrieved from https://www.nytimes.com/2018/02/05/sports/larry-nassar-sentencing-hearing.html

Havlicek, J., Huston, S., Boughton, S., & Zhang, S. (2016). Human trafficking of children in Illinois: Prevalence and characteristics. *Children and Youth Services Review*, *69*, 127–135.

Hayden, A. (Ed.). (2016). *A restorative approach to family violence: Changing tack*. London: Routledge.

Haynes, E. E., Strauss, C. V., Stuart, G. L., & Shorey, R. C. (2018). Drinking motives as a moderator of the relationship between dating violence victimization and alcohol problems. *Violence Against Women*, *24*(4), 401–420.

Haynie, D. L., Farhat, T., Brooks-Russell, A., Wang, I., Barbieri, B., & Iannotti, R. J. (2013). Dating violence perpetration and victimization among U.S. adolescents: Prevalence, patterns, and association with health complaints and substance use. *Journal of Adolescent Health*, *53*, 194–201.

Hecker, T., Boettcher, V. S., Landolt, M. A., & Hermenau, K. (2019). Child neglect and its relation to emotional and behavioral problems: A cross-sectional study of primary school-aged children in Tanzania. *Development and Psychopathology*, *31*(1), 325–339.

Hedge, J. M., Sianko, N., & McDonell, J. R. (2017). Professional help-seeking for adolescent dating violence in the rural South: The role of social support and informal help-seeking. *Violence Against Women*, *23*(12), 1442–1461.

Hegar, R. L., & Yungman, J. J. (1989). Toward a causal typology of child neglect. *Children and Youth Services Review*, *11*, 203–220.

Heinz, A. J., Makin-Byrd, K., Blonigen, D. M., Reilly, P., & Timko, C. (2015). Aggressive behavior among military veterans in substance use disorder treatment: The roles of post-traumatic stress and impulsivity. *Journal of Substance Abuse Treatment*, *50*, 59–66.

Helton, J. J., & Cross, T. P. (2011). The relationship of child functioning to parental physical assault: Linear and curvilinear models. *Child Maltreatment*, *16*(2), 126–136.

Heneghan, A., Stein, R. E., Hurlburt, M. S., Zhang, J., Rolls-Reutz, J., Fisher, E., . . . Horwitz, S. M. (2013). Mental health problems in teens investigated by US child welfare agencies. *Journal of Adolescent Health*, *52*(5), 634–640.

Henley, N., Donovan, R. J., & Moorhead, H. (1998). Appealing to positive motivations and emotions in social marketing: Example of a positive parenting campaign. *Social Marketing Quarterly*, *4*(4), 48–53.

Henning, K., & Feder, L. (2005). A comparison of men and women arrested for domestic violence: Who presents the greater threat? *Journal of Family Violence*, *19*(2), 69–70.

Henry, C. (2017). Expanding the legal framework for child protection: Recognition of and response to child exposure to domestic violence in California law. *Social Services Review*, *91*, 203–232.

Henry, C. (2018). Exposure to domestic violence as abuse and neglect: Constructions of child maltreatment in daily practice. *Child Abuse & Neglect*, *86*, 79–88.

Henry, N., & Flynn, A. (2019). Online distribution channels and illicit communities of support. *Violence Against Women*, *25*(16), 1932–1955.

Henry, N., & Powell, A. (2015). Embodied harms: Gender, shame, and technology-facilitated sexual violence. *Violence Against Women*, *21*(6), 758–779.

Henschel, M. M., & Grant, B. (2019). Exposing school employee sexual abuse and misconduct: Shedding light on a sensitive issue. *Journal of Child Sexual Abuse*, *28*(14), 1–20.

Henson, B., Fisher, B. S., & Reyns, B. W. (2019). There is virtually no excuse: The frequency and predictors of college students' bystander intervention behaviors directed at online victimization. *Violence Against Women*. Advance online publication. Retrieved from https://doi.org/10.1177/1077801219835050

Henson, J. (2020, January 26). What happened with Kobe Bryant's sexual assault case. *Los Angeles Times*.

Herdt, G. (1987). *The Sambia: Ritual and gender in New Guinea*. New York, NY: Holt, Rinehart, & Winston.

Herrenkohl, E. C., Herrenkohl, R. C., Rupert, L. J., Egolf, B. P., & Lutz, J. G. (1995). Risk factors for behavioral dysfunction: The relative impact of maltreatment, SES, physical health problems, cognitive ability, and quality of parent–child interaction. *Child Abuse & Neglect, 19*, 191–203.

Herrenkohl, R. C. (2005). The definition of child maltreatment: From case study to construct. *Child Abuse & Neglect, 29*, 413–424.

Hesse, E., & Main, M. (2000). Disorganized infant, child, and adult attachment: Collapse in behavioral and attentional strategies. *Journal of the American Psychoanalytic Association, 48*, 1097–1127.

Heyman, R. E., & Smith Slep, A. M. (2009). Reliability of family maltreatment diagnostic criteria: 41 site dissemination field trial. *Journal of Family Psychology, 23*(6), 905.

Hibbard, R., Barlow, J., MacMillan, H., Christian, C. W., Crawford-Jakubiak, J. E., Flaherty, E. G., . . . Sege, R. D. (2012). Psychological maltreatment. *Pediatrics, 130*(2), 372–378.

Hickox, A., & Furnell, J. R. G. (1989). Psychosocial and background factors in emotional abuse of children. *Child: Care, Health and Development, 15*, 227–240.

Hildreth, C. J., Burke, A. E., & Glass, R. M. (2009). Elder abuse. *Journal of the American Medical Association, 302*, 588.

Hildyard, K. L., & Wolfe, D. A. (2002). Child neglect: Developmental issues and outcomes. *Child Abuse & Neglect, 26*, 679–695.

Hill, C., & Johnson, H. (2019). Online interpersonal victimization as a mechanism of social control of women: An empirical examination. *Violence Against Women*. Advance online publication. Retrieved from https://doi.org/10.1177/10778-1219870608

Hill, C., Kearl, H., & American Association of University Women. (2011). *Crossing the line: Sexual harassment at school*. Washington, DC: American Association of University Women.

Hill, S., & Ousley, L. (2017). Intimate partner violence screening behaviors of primary care providers. *Journal of Interprofessional Education and Practice, 8*, 20–22.

Hillson, J. M. C., & Kupier, N. A. (1994). A stress and coping model of child maltreatment. *Clinical Psychology Review, 14*, 261–285.

Hirsch, J. S., & Khan, S. (2020). *Sexual citizens: A landmark study of sex, power, and assault on campus*. New York, NY: W. W. Norton.

Hirschel, D., & Buzawa, E. (2013). The impact of offenders leaving the scene on the police decision to arrest in cases of intimate partner violence. *Violence Against Women, 19*, 1080–1104.

Hirschel, D., Buzawa, E., Pattavina, A., Faggiani, D., & Reuland, M. (2007). *Explaining the prevalence, context, and consequences of dual arrest in intimate partner cases*. Washington, DC: U.S. Department of Justice.

Hirschel, D., & Deveau, L. (2016). The impact of primary aggressor laws on single versus dual arrest in incidents of intimate partner violence. *Violence Against Women*. Advance online publication. doi:10.1177/1077801216657898

Ho, P. (1959). *Studies on the population of China, 1368–1953* (No. 4). Cambridge, MA: Harvard University Press.

Hodell, E. C., Golding, J. M., Yozwiak, J. A., Bradshaw, G. S., Kinstle, T. L., & Marsil, D. F. (2009). The perceptions of elder sexual abuse in the courtroom. *Violence Against Women, 15*, 678–698.

Hodgdon, H. B., Spinazzola, J., Briggs, E. C., Liang, L. J., Steinberg, A. M., & Layne, C. M. (2018). Maltreatment type, exposure characteristics, and mental health outcomes among clinic referred trauma-exposed youth. *Child Abuse & Neglect, 82*, 12–22.

Hodge, D. R., & Lietz, C. A. (2007). The international sexual trafficking of women and children: A review of the literature. *Affilia: Journal of Women and Social Work, 22*, 163–174.

Hoefnagels, C., & Baartman, H. (1997). On the threshold of disclosure: The effects of a mass media field experiment. *Child Abuse & Neglect, 21*, 557–573.

Hoefnagels, C., & Mudde, A. (2000). Mass media and disclosures of child abuse in the perspective of secondary prevention: Putting ideas into practice. *Child Abuse & Neglect, 24*, 1091–1101.

Hoffman, B. (2019, October 24). Brandon Taubman, Astros executive, is fired over outburst. *New York Times*. Retrieved from https://www.nytimes.com/2019/10/24/sports/baseball/brandon-taubman-fired-astros.html?searchResultPosition=1

Holbrook, A. M., & Nguyen, V. H. (2015). Medication-assisted treatment for pregnant women: A systematic review of the evidence and implications for social work practice. *Journal of the Society for Social Work & Research, 6*(1), 1–19.

Hollander, J. A. (2009). The roots of resistance to women's self-defense. *Violence Against Women, 15*(5), 574–594.

Hollander, J. (2013, September 17). Grand Theft Auto V: Does it train murderers, glorify torture, and hurt women? *Bustle.* Retrieved from https://www.bustle.com/articles/5252-grand-theft-auto-v-does-it-train-murderers-glorify-torture-and-hurt-women

Hollander, J. A. (2014). Does self-defense training prevent sexual violence against women? *Violence Against Women, 20*(3), 252–269.

Holt, V. L., Kernic, M., Wolf, M., & Rivara, F. (2003). Do protection orders affect the likelihood of future partner violence and injury? *American Journal of Preventive Medicine, 24*, 16–21.

Holtzworth-Munroe, A., & Meehan, J. C. (2004). Typologies of men who are martially violent: Scientific and clinical implications. *Journal of Interpersonal Violence, 19*, 1369–1389.

Holtzworth-Munroe, A., Meehan, J. C., Herron, K., Rehman, U., & Stuart, G. L. (2000). Testing the Holtzworth-Munroe and Stuart (1994) batterer typology. *Journal of Consulting and Clinical Psychology, 68*(6), 1000–1019.

Hopper, J. (2011, November 14). Jerry Sandusky to Bob Costas in exclusive "Rock Center" interview: "I shouldn't have showered with those kids." *NBC Rock Center.* Retrieved from http://rockcenter.nbcnews.com/_news/2011/11/14/8804779-jerry-sandusky-to-bob-costas-in-exclusive-rock-center-interview-i-shouldnt-have-showered-with-those-kids

Horwitz, A. V., Widom, C. S., McLaughlin, J., & White, H. R. (2001). The impact of childhood abuse and neglect on adult mental health: A prospective study. *Journal of Health and Social Behavior, 42*, 184–201.

Houtepen, J. A., Sijtsema, J. J., & Bogaerts, S. (2016). Being sexually attracted to minors: Sexual development, coping with forbidden feelings, and relieving sexual arousal in self-identified pedophiles. *Journal of Sex & Marital Therapy, 42*(1), 48–69.

Hovell, M. F., Seid, A. G., & Liles, S. (2006). Evaluation of a police and social services domestic violence program: Empirical evidence needed to inform public health policies. *Violence Against Women, 12*, 137–159.

Howe, T. R., Knox, M., Altafim, E. R. P., Linhares, M. B. M., Nishizawa, N., Fu, T. J., . . . Pereira, A. I. (2017). International child abuse prevention: Insights from ACT Raising Safe Kids. *Child and Adolescent Mental Health, 22*(4), 194–200. Retrieved from https://doi.org/10.1111/camh.12238

Howell, K. H., Barnes, S. E., Miller, L. E., & Graham-Bermann, S. A. (2015). Developmental variations in the impact of intimate partner violence exposure during childhood. *Journal of Injury and Violence Research, 8*(1), 43–57.

Huesmann, L. R., Moise-Titus, J., Podolski, C. L., & Eron, L. D. (2003). Longitudinal relations between children's exposure to TV violence and their aggressive and violent behavior in young adulthood: 1977–1992. *Developmental Psychology, 39*, 201–221.

Huffington Post. (2017, December 6). Jessica Logan suicide: Parents of dead teen sue school, friends over sexting harassment. Retrieved from http://www.huffpost.com/entry/jessica-logan-suicide-par_n_382825

Hughes, R. B., Robinson-Whelen, S., Pepper, A. C., Gabrielli, J., Lund, E. M., Legerski, J., & Schwartz, S. (2010). Development of a safety awareness group intervention for women with diverse disabilities: A pilot study. *Rehabilitation Psychology, 55*, 263–271.

Hughes, R. B., Robinson-Whelen, S., Raymaker, D., Lund, E. M., Oschwald, M., Katz, M., . . . Larson, D. (2019). The relation of abuse to physical and psychological health in adults with developmental disabilities. *Disability and Health Journal, 12*(2), 227–234.

Humphreys, K. L., & Zeanah, C. H. (2015). Deviations from the expectable environment in early childhood and emerging psychopathology. *Neuropsychopharmacology, 40*(1), 154–170.

Hunt, P., & Baird, M. (1990). Children of sex rings. *Child Welfare: Journal of Policy, Practice, and Program, 69*(3), 195–207.

Hunt, R. W., Tzioumi, D., Collins, E., & Jeffery, H. E. (2008). Adverse neurodevelopmental outcome of infants exposed to opiates in-utero. *Early Human Development, 84*(1), 29–35. doi:10.1016/j.earlhumdev.2007.01.013. Retrieved from http://www.sciencedirect.com/science/article/pii/S0378378207000278

Hyman, A., Schillinger, D., & Lo, B. (1995). Laws mandating reporting of domestic violence: Do they promote patient well-being? *Journal of the American Medical Association, 273*, 1781–1787.

Infurna, M. R., Reichl, C., Parzer, P., Schimmenti, A., Bifulco, A., & Kaess, M. (2016). Associations between depression and specific childhood experiences of abuse and neglect: A meta-analysis. *Journal of Affective Disorders, 190*, 47–55.

Institute of Medicine & National Research Council. (2013). *Confronting commercial sexual exploitation* and sex trafficking of minors in the United States. Washington, DC: National Academies Press.

International Labour Organization. (2017). *Global estimates of modern slavery: Forced labour and forced marriage*. Geneva, Switzerland: Author. Retrieved from https://www.ilo.org/global/publications/books/WCMS_575479/lang--en/index.htm

Ippen, C. G., Harris, W. W., Van Horn, P., & Lieberman, A. F. (2011). Traumatic and stressful events in early childhood: Can treatment help those at highest risk? *Child Abuse & Neglect, 35*(7), 504–513.

Isaacson, B. (2013). Child abuse hotline ad uses photographic trick that makes it visible only to children. *Huffington Post*. Retrieved from https://www.huffpost.com/entry/child-abuse-ad_n_3223311

Iwaniec, D. (2006). *The emotionally abused and neglected child: Identification, assessment and intervention: A practice handbook*. West Sussex, England: John Wiley & Sons.

Jabaley, J. J., Lutzker, J. R., Whitaker, D. J., & Self-Brown, S. (2011). Using iPhones™ to enhance and reduce face-to-face home safety sessions within SafeCare®: An evidence-based child maltreatment prevention program. *Journal of Family Violence, 26*(5), 377–385.

Jack, S., Munn, C., Cheng, C., & MacMillan, H. M. (2006). *Child maltreatment in Canada: Overview paper*. Ottawa, ON: National Clearinghouse on Family Violence, Public Health Agency of Canada.

Jacklin, C. N. (1989). Female and male: Issues of gender. *American Psychologist, 44*, 127–133.

Jackson, A. M., Kissoon, N., & Greene, C. (2015). Aspects of abuse: Recognizing and responding to child maltreatment. *Current Problems in Pediatric and Adolescent Health Care, 45*(3), 58–70.

Jackson, S. L., & Hafemeister, T. L. (2013). *Understanding elder abuse*. Washington, DC: U.S. Department of Justice, National Institute of Justice.

Jaffe, P. G., Crooks, C. V., & Wolfe, D. A. (2003). Legal and policy responses to children exposed to domestic violence: The need to evaluate intended and unintended consequences. *Clinical Child and Family Psychology Review, 6*, 205–213.

Jaffe, P. G., Wolfe, D. A., Crooks, C. V., Hughes, R., & Baker, L. (2004). The fourth R: Developing healthy relationships in families and communities through school-based interventions. In P. G. Jaffe, A. Cunningham, & L. Baker (Eds.), *Innovative strategies to end domestic violence for victims, perpetrators, and their children*. New York, NY: Guilford.

James, S. E., Herman, J. L., Rankin, S., Keisling, M., Mottet, L., & Amafi, M. (2016). *The report of the 2015 U.S. Transgender Survey*. National Center for Transgender Equality. Retrieved from https://www.transequality.org/sites/default/files/docs/USTS-Full-Report-Final-pdf

James, S., Johnson, J., & Raghavan, C. (2004). "I couldn't go anywhere": Contextualizing violence and drug abuse: A social network study. *Violence Against Women, 10*, 991–1014.

Jaquier, V., Johnson, H., & Fisher, B. S. (2011). Research methods, measures, and ethics. In C. M. Renzetti, J. L. Edleson, & R. K. Bergen (Eds.), *Sourcebook on violence against women* (2nd ed., pp. 23–45). Thousand Oaks, CA: Sage.

Jardim, G. B. G., Novelo, M., Spanemberg, L., von Gunten, A., Engroff, P., Nogueira, E. L., & Neto, A. C. (2018). Influence of childhood abuse and neglect subtypes on late-life suicide risk beyond depression. *Child Abuse & Neglect, 80*, 249–256.

Jasinski, J. L. (2001). Pregnancy and violence against women: An analysis of longitudinal data. *Journal of Interpersonal Violence, 16*(7), 712–733.

Jasinski, J. L., Wesely, J. K., Wright, J. D., & Mustaine, E. E. (2010). *Hard lives, mean streets: Violence in the lives of homeless women*. Boston, MA: Northeastern University Press.

Jeary, K. (2005). Sexual abuse and sexual offending against elderly people: A focus on perpetrators and victims. *Journal of Forensic Psychiatry and Psychology, 16*, 328–343.

Jehu, D., Klassen, C., & Gazan, M. (1986). Cognitive restructuring of distorted beliefs associated with childhood sexual abuse. *Journal of Social Work and Human Sexuality, 4*, 49–69.

Jenkins, P. (1998). *Moral panic: Changing concepts of the child molester in modern America*. New Haven, CT: Yale University Press.

Jensen, K. T. (2019, December 6). Florida man abandoned son on the side of the road because he thought the child was gay, police say. *Newsweek*. Retrieved from https://www.newsweek.com/florida-man-abandoned-child-side-road-gay-1475961

Jesperson, A. F., Lalumière, M. L., & Seto, M. C. (2009). Sexual abuse history among adult sex offenders and non-sex offenders: A meta-analysis. *Child Abuse & Neglect, 33*, 179–192. doi:10.1016/j.chiabu.2008.07.004

Jesse, D. (2019, September). MSU to pay record $4.5M fine in Larry Nassar sexual assault scandal. *Detroit Free Press*. Retrieved from https://www.freep.com/story/news/education/2019/09/05/msu-fine-larry-nassar-betsy-devos/2219/81001/

Jirik, S., & Sanders, S. (2014). Analysis of elder abuse statutes across the United States, 2011–2012. *Journal of Gerontological Social Work, 57*, 478–497.

Jogerst, G. J., Daly, J. M., Brinig, M. F., Dawson, J. D., Schmuch, G. A., & Ingram, J. G. (2003). Domestic elder abuse and the law. *American Journal of Public Health, 93*(12), 2131–2136.

John Jay College of Criminal Justice. (2004). *The nature and scope of sexual abuse of minors by Catholic priests and deacons in the United States 1950–2002*. U.S. Conference of Catholic Bishops. Retrieved from http://www.usccb.org/issues-and-action/child-and-youth-protection/upload/The-Nature-and-Scope-of-Sexual-Abuse-of-Minors-by-Catholic-Priests-and-Deacons-in-the-United-States-1950-2002.pdf

Johnson, C. F. (2004). Child sexual abuse. *Lancet, 364*, 462–470.

Johnson, H. (2001). Contrasting view of the role of alcohol in cases of wife assault. *Journal of Interpersonal Violence, 16*(1), 54–72.

Johnson, J. G., Smailes, E. M., Cohen, P., Brown, J., & Bernstein, D. P. (2000). Associations between four types of childhood neglect and personality disorder symptoms during adolescence and early adulthood: Findings of a community-based longitudinal study. *Journal of Personality Disorders, 14*, 171–187.

Johnson, L. M., Matthews, T. L., & Napper, S. L. (2016). Sexual orientation and sexual assault victimization among U.S. college students. *The Social Science Journal, 53*(2), 174–183.

Jolles, M. P., Givens, A., Lombardi, B., & Cuddeback, G. S. (2019). Welfare caseworkers' perceived responsibility for the behavioral needs of children: A national profile. *Children and Youth Services Review, 98*, 80–84.

Jones, E. (2018). *Working with adult survivors of child sexual abuse*. New York, NY: Routledge.

Jones, L., Bellis, M. A., Wood, S., Hughes, K., McCoy, E., Eckley, L., Bates, G., Mikton, C., Shakespeare, T., & Officer, A. (2012). Prevalence and risk of violence against children with disabilities: A systematic review

and meta-analysis of observational studies. *Lancet, 380*(9845), 899–907.

Jones, L., Engstrom, D. W., Hilliard, T., & Diaz, M. (2007). Globalization and human trafficking. *Journal of Sociology & Social Welfare, 24*(2), 107–122.

Jones, L. M., Finkelhor, D., & Halter, S. (2012). Child maltreatment trends in the 1990s: Why does neglect differ from sexual and physical abuse? In J. E. B. Myers (Ed.), *Child maltreatment: A collection of readings* (pp. 247–265). Thousand Oaks, CA: Sage.

Jones, M. S., Worthen, M. G. F., Sharp, S. F., & McLeod, D. A. (2020). Native American and non-Native American women prisoners, adverse childhood experiences, and the perpetration of physical violence in adult intimate relationships. *Journal of Interpersonal Violence*. Advance online publication. Retrieved from https:doi.org/10.1177/0886260519897328

Jones, R. L., & Kaufman, L. (2003, May 1). Foster care caseworkers' errors are detailed in New Jersey. *New York Times*.

Jonzon, E., & Lindblad, F. (2004). Disclosure, reactions, and social support: Findings from a sample of adult victims of child sexual abuse. *Child Maltreatment, 9*, 190–200. doi:10.1177/1077559504264263

Jordan, J., & Mossman, E. (2018). "Back off buddy, this is my body, not yours": Empowering girls through self-defense. *Violence Against Women, 24*(13), 1591–1613.

Jordan, S. P., Mehrotra, G. R., & Fujikawa, K. A. (2019). Mandating Inclusion: Critical trans perspectives on domestic and sexual violence advocacy. *Violence Against Women*. Advance online publication Retrieved from https://doi.org/10.1177/1077801219836728

Jouriles, E. N., McDonald, R., Smith Slep, A. M., Heyman, R. E., & Garrido, E. (2008). Child abuse in the context of domestic violence: Prevalence, explanations, and practice implications. *Violence and Victims, 23*(2), 221–235.

Joyce, K. (2013, November 9). Hana's story. *Slate*. Retrieved from http://www.slate.com/articles/double_x/doublex/2013/11/hana_williams_the_tragic_death_of_an_ethiopian_adoptee_and_how_it_could.html

Joyce, T., & Huecker, M. R. (2019). Pediatric abusive head trauma (shaken baby syndrome). *StatPearls*. Retrieved from https://www.ncbi.nlm.nih.gov/books/NBK499836/

Jud, A., Fegert, J. M., & Finkelhor, D. (2016). On the incidence and prevalence of child maltreatment: A research agenda. *Child and Adolescent Psychiatry and Mental Health, 10*(17), 1–5.

Judge, M. (2017, April 27). Calif. father gets 10 days in jail for leaving his baby in the car while he got lap dances at a strip club. *The Root.* Retrieved from https://www.theroot.com/calif-father-sentenced-to-10-days-in-jail-for-leaving-1794727358

Judge OKs retrial in alleged abuse case. (2003, February 1). *Los Angeles Times*, p. B3.

Jung, H., Herrenkohl, T. I., Klika, J. B., Lee, J. O., & Brown, E. C. (2015). Does child maltreatment predict adult crime? Re-examining the question in a prospective study of gender differences, education, and marital status. *Journal of Interpersonal Violence, 30*, 2238–2257.

Justice, B., & Calvert, A. (1990). Family environment factors associated with child abuse. *Psychological Reports, 66*, 458.

Justice for Victims of Trafficking Act of 2015, S. 178, 114th Cong. (2015).

Kaeser, F. (2011). *What your child needs to know about sex: A straight-talking guide for parents.* New York, NY: Celestial Arts.

Kairys, S. W., & Johnson, C. F. (2002). The psychological maltreatment of children—Technical report. *Pediatrics, 109*(4), e68. Retrieved from http://pediatrics.aappublications.org/content/109/4/e68.full

Kann, L., McManus, T., Harris, W. A., Shanklin, S. L., Flint, K. H., Queen, B., . . . Ethier, K. A. (2018). Youth Risk Behavior Surveillance—United States, 2017. *Surveillance Summaries, 67*(8), 1–114. Retrieved from https://www.cdc.gov/mmwr/volumes/67/ss/ss6708a1.htm

Kantor, G. K., & Little, L. (2003). Defining the boundaries of child neglect: When does domestic violence equate with parental failure to protect? *Journal of Interpersonal Violence, 18*, 338–355.

Kantor, J., & Twohey, M. (2017, October 5). Harvey Weinstein paid off sexual harassment accusers for decades. *New York Times.*

Kaplan, S. J., Pelcovitz, D., & Labruna, V. (1999). Child and adolescent abuse and neglect research: A review of the past 10 years: Part I. Physical and emotional abuse and neglect. *Journal of the American Academy of Child and Adolescent Psychiatry, 38*, 1214–1222.

Katz, C. (2013). Internet-related child sexual abuse: What children tell us in their testimonies. *Children and Youth Services Review, 35*, 1536–1542. http://dx.doi.org/10.1016/j.childyouth.2013.06.006

Kaufman, J. G., & Widom, C. S. (1999). Childhood victimization, running away, and delinquency. *Journal of Research in Crime and Delinquency, 36*, 347–370.

Kaufman, L., & Kocieniewski, D. (2003, January 10). Caseworkers say overload makes it risky for children. *New York Times*, p. B6.

Kaukinen, C., & DeMaris, A. (2009). Sexual assault and current mental health: The role of help-seeking and police response. *Violence Against Women, 15*(11), 1331–1357.

Kay-Phillips, J. (2016). Unnecessary roughness: The NFL's history of domestic violence and the need for immediate change. *Berkeley Journal of Entertainment & Sports Law, 5*, 65.

Kazdin, A. E. (2011). Conceptualizing the challenge of reducing interpersonal violence. *Psychology of Violence, 1*(3), 166.

Kearney, C. A., Wechsler, A., Kaur, H., & Lemos-Miller, A. (2010). Posttraumatic stress disorder in maltreated youth: A review of contemporary research and thought. *Clinical Child and Family Psychology Review, 13*(1), 46–76.

Keegan, J., Parva, M., Finnegan, M., Gerson, A., & Belden, M. (2010). Addiction in pregnancy. *Journal of Addictive Diseases, 29*(2), 175–191.

Keene, A. C., & Epps, J. (2016). Childhood physical abuse and aggression: Shame and narcissistic vulnerability. *Child Abuse & Neglect, 51*, 276–283.

Keiley, M. K., Howe, T. R., Dodge, K. A., Bates, J. E., & Pettit, G. S. (2001). The timing of child physical maltreatment: A cross-domain growth analysis of impact on adolescent externalizing and internalizing problems. *Development and Psychopathology, 13*, 891–912.

Keim, J. (2018, November 21). Despite child abuse suspension, Adrian Peterson uses belt on son. *ESPN Sports.* Retrieved from https://www.espn.com/nfl/story/_/id/25342741/adrian-peterson-uses-belt-discipline-son

Kelleher, K., Chaffin, M., Hollenberg, J., & Fischer, E. (1994). Alcohol and drug disorders among physically abusive and neglectful parents in a community-based sample. *American Journal of Public Health, 84*, 1586–1590.

Keller, M. H., & Dance, G. J. X. (2019). The internet is overrun with images of child sexual abuse. What went wrong? *New York Times*.

Kempe, C. H., Silverman, F. N., Steele, B. F., Droegemueller, W., & Silver, H. K. (1962). The battered child syndrome. *Journal of the American Medical Association, 17*, 17–24.

Kendall-Tackett, K. A. (2003). *Treating the lifetime health effects of childhood victimization.* Kingston, NJ: Civic Research Institute.

Kendall-Tackett, K. A., Williams, L. M., & Finkelhor, D. (1993). Impact of sexual abuse on children: A review and synthesis of recent empirical studies. *Psychological Bulletin, 113*, 164–180.

Kenny, M. C., & Abreu, R. L. (2015). Training mental health professionals in child sexual abuse: Curricular guidelines. *Journal of Child Sexual Abuse, 24*(5), 572–591.

Kenny, M. C., Helpingstine, C., Abreu, R. L., & Duberli, F. (2019). Understanding the needs of LGBTQ clients and their risk for commercial sexual exploitation: Training community mental health workers. *Journal of Gay & Lesbian Social Services, 31*(2), 166–181.

Kenny, M. C., Helpingstine, C., Long, H., Perez, L., & Harrington, M. C. (2019). Increasing child serving professionals' awareness and understanding of the commercial sexual exploitation of children. *Journal of Child Sexual Abuse, 28*(4), 417–434.

Kerig, P. (2003). In search of protective processes for children exposed to inter-parental violence. In R. Geffner, R. Spurling Ingelman, & J. Zellner (Eds.), *The effects of intimate partner violence on children* (pp. 149–181). New York, NY: Haworth Press.

Kernic, M. A., Monary-Ernsdorff, D. J., Koepsell, J. K., & Holt, V. L. (2005). Children in the crossfire: Child custody determinations among couples with a history of intimate partner violence. *Violence Against Women, 11*, 991–1021.

Kestin, S., & Williams, D. (2010, April 24). Teachers and sex: Scores in Florida have lost jobs due to improper conduct with students. *Sun Sentinel*. Retrieved from http://articles.sun-sentinel.com/2010-04-24/news/fl-teacher-student-sex-20100416_1_biology-teacher-teenage-student-female-middle-school-teacher

Kettrey, H. H., & Emery, B. C. (2006). The discourse of sibling violence. *Journal of Family Violence, 21*(6), 407–416.

Kilpatrick, D. G., Best, C. L., Saunders, B. E., & Vernonen, L. J. (1988). Rape in marriage and dating relationships: How bad is it for mental health? *Annals of the New York Academy of Sciences, 528*, 335–344.

Kim, H., & Drake, B. (2018). Child maltreatment risk as a function of poverty and race/ethnicity in the USA. *International Journal of Epidemiology, 47*(3), 780–787.

Kim, J. (2009). Type-specific intergenerational transmission of neglectful and physically abusive parenting behaviors among young parents. *Children and Youth Services Review, 31*, 761–767.

Kim, J., & Cicchetti, D. (2006). Longitudinal trajectories of self-system processes and depressive symptoms among maltreated and nonmaltreated children. *Child Development, 77*, 624–639.

Kim, J., & Cicchetti, D. (2010). Longitudinal pathways linking child maltreatment, emotion regulation, peer relations, and psychopathology. *Journal of Child Psychology and Psychiatry, and Allied Disciplines, 51*, 706–716.

Kim, K., Mennen, F. E., & Trickett, P. K. (2017). Patterns and correlates of co-occurrence among multiple types of child maltreatment. *Child & Family Social Work, 22*(1), 492–502.

Kim, M. (2020). Shifting the lens: An implementation study of a community-based and social network intervention to gender-based violence. *Violence Against Women*, Advance online publication. Retrieved from https://doi.org/10.1177/1077801219889176

Kimberg, L. S. (2008). Addressing intimate partner violence with male patients: A review and introduction of pilot guidelines. *Journal of General Internal Medicine, 23*, 2071–2078.

Kimmes, J. G., Mallory, A. B., Spencer, C., Beck, A. R., Cafferky, B., & Stith, S. M. (2019). A meta-analysis of risk markers for intimate partner violence in same-sex relationships. *Trauma, Violence & Abuse, 20*(3), 374–384.

King, A. R., Kuhn, S. K., Strege, C., Russell, T. D., & Kolander, T. (2019). Revisiting the link between childhood sexual abuse and adult sexual aggression. *Child Abuse & Neglect, 94*, 104022. https://doi.org/10.1016/j.chiabu.2019.104022

Kingkade, T. (2015, August 26). Male students in America are putting up horrible banners to welcome female freshers. *Huffington Post*. Retrieved from http://www.huffingtonpost.co.uk/2015/08/26/male-students-in-america-are-putting-up-horrible-banners-to-welcome-female-freshers_n_8041762.html

Kingsnorth, R. F. (2006). Intimate partner violence: Predictors of recidivism in a sample of arrestees. *Violence Against Women, 12*(10), 917–935.

Kingsnorth, R. F., & Macintosh, R. C. (2004). Domestic violence: Predictors of victim support for official action. *Violence and Victims, 21*(2), 301–328.

Kinney, J., Haapala, D., Booth, C., & Leavitt, S. (2017). The Homebuilders model. In *Reaching high-risk families* (pp. 31–64). New York, NY: Routledge.

Kirsch, L. G., Fanniff, A. M., & Becker, J. V. (2011). Treatment of adolescent and adult sex offenders. In J. E. B. Myers (Ed.), *The APSAC handbook on child maltreatment* (3rd ed., pp. 289–305). Thousand Oaks, CA: Sage.

Kitzrow, M. A. (2002). Survey of CACREP-accredited programs: Training counselors to provide treatment for sexual abuse. *Counselor Education and Supervision, 42*(2), 107–118.

Klein, A. R., & Crowe, A. (2008). Findings from an outcome examination of Rhode Island's specialized domestic violence probation supervision program: Do specialized supervision programs of batterers reduce reabuse? *Violence Against Women, 14*(2), 226–246.

Klein, A. R., & Tobin, T. (2008). A longitudinal study of arrested batterers, 1995–2005: Career criminals. *Violence Against Women, 14*(2), 136–157.

Klein, V., Schmidt, A. F., Turner, D., & Briken, P. (2015). Are sex drive and hypersexuality associated with pedophilic interest and child sexual abuse in a male community sample? *PLoS One, 10*(7): e0129730. doi:10.1371/journal.pone.012973

Kleinman, P. K. (2015). *Diagnostic imaging of child abuse*. Cambridge, England: Cambridge University Press.

Kleinsasser, A., Jouriles, E. N., McDonald, R., & Rosenfield, D. (2015). An online bystander intervention program for the prevention of sexual violence. *Psychology of Violence, 5*(3), 227.

Klevens, J., Luo, F., Xu, L., Peterson, C., & Latzman, N. E. (2016). Paid family leave's effect on hospital admissions for pediatric abusive head trauma. *Injury Prevention, 22*(6), 442–445. doi:10.1136/injuryprev-2015-041702

Klika, J. B., Haboush-Deloye, A., & Linkenbach, J. (2019). Hidden protections: Identifying social norms associated with child abuse, sexual abuse, and neglect. *Child and Adolescent Social Work Journal, 36*(1), 5–14.

Klika, J. B., Herrenkohl, T. I., & Lee, J. O. (2012). School factors as moderators of the relationship between physical child abuse and pathways of antisocial behavior. *Journal of Interpersonal Violence, 28*, 852–867.

Klonsky, E., & Moyer, A. (2008). Childhood sexual abuse and non-suicidal self-injury: Meta-analysis. *British Journal of Psychiatry, 192*(3), 166–170.

Knight, R. A., & Sims-Knight, J. (2011). Risk factors for sexual violence. In J. W. White, M. P. Koss, & A. E. Kazdin (Eds.), *Violence against women and children* (Vol. 1, pp. 125–150). Washington, DC: American Psychological Association.

Knox, M. S., Burkhart, K., & Hunter, K. E. (2011). ACT against violence parents raising safe kids program: Effects on maltreatment-related parenting behaviors and beliefs. *Journal of Family Issues, 32*(1), 55–74.

Kochanek, K. D., Murphy, S. L., Xu, J., & Arias, E. (2017). *Mortality in the United States, 2016* [NCHS data brief]. National Center for Health Statistics. Retrieved from https://www.cdc.gov/nchs/data/databriefs/db293.pdf

Kohl, P. L., Edleson, J. L., English, D. J., & Barth, R. P. (2005). Domestic violence and pathways into child welfare services: Findings from the National Survey of Child and Adolescent Well-Being. *Children and Youth Services Review, 27*(11), 1167–1182.

Kolko, D. J. (1996a). Clinical monitoring of treatment course in child physical abuse: Child and parent reports. *Child Abuse & Neglect, 20*, 23–43.

Kolko, D. J. (1996b). Individual cognitive behavioral treatment and family therapy for physically abused children and their offending parents: A comparison of clinical outcomes. *Child Maltreatment, 1*, 322–342.

Konijn, C., Admiraal, S., Baart, J., van Rooij, F., Stams, G. J., Colonnesi, C., . . . Assink, M. (2019). Foster care placement instability: A meta-analytic review. *Children and Youth Services Review, 96*, 483–499.

Kosciw, J. G., Greytak, E. A., Giga, N. M., Villenas, C., & Danischewski, D. J. (2016). *The 2015 national school climate survey: The experiences of lesbian, gay, bisexual, transgender, and queer youth in our nation's schools*. New York, NY: GLSEN.

Koss, M. P. (1992). The underdetection of rape: Methodological choices influence incidence estimates. *Journal of Social Issues, 48*(1), 61–76.

Koss, M. P. (1993). Detecting the scope of rape. *Journal of Interpersonal Violence, 8*, 198–222.

Koss, M. P., Abbey, A., Campbell, R., Cook, S., Norris, J., Testa, M., . . . White, J. (2007). Revising the SES: A collaborative process to improve assessment of sexual aggression and victimization. *Psychology of Women Quarterly, 31*, 357–370.

Koss, M. P., Gidycz, C. A., & Wisniewski, N. (1987). The scope of rape: Incidence and prevalence of sexual aggression and victimization in a national sample of higher education students. *Journal of Counseling and Clinical Psychology, 55*, 162–170.

Kotch, J. B., Lewis, T., Hussey, J., English, D., Thompson, R., Litrownik, A. J., . . . Dubowitz, H. (2008). Importance of early neglect for childhood aggression. *Pediatrics, 121*(4), 725–731.

Krebs, C. P., Lindquist, C. H., Warner, T. D., Fisher, B. S., & Martin, S. L. (2007). *The campus sexual assault (CSA) study: Final report.* Washington, DC: National Institute of Justice, U.S. Department of Justice.

Kreston, S. S. (2002). On-line crimes against children. *Section on Child Maltreatment Newsletter, 7*(2), 13.

Kropp, P. R. (2004). Some questions regarding spousal assault risk assessment. *Violence Against Women, 10*(6), 676–697.

Kropp, P. R., & Hart, S. D. (2000). The Spousal Assault Risk Assessment (SARA) guide: Reliability and validity in adult male offenders. *Law & Human Behavior, 24*, 101–118.

Kropp, P. R., Hart, S. D., Webster, C. D., & Eaves, D. (1995). *Manual for the Spouse Assault Risk Assessment guide* (2nd ed.). Vancouver: British Columbia Institute on Family Violence.

Krug, E. G., Dahlberg, L. L., Mercy, J. A., Zwi, A. B., & Lozno, R. (Eds.). (2002). *World report on violence and health.* Geneva, Switzerland: World Health Organization.

Krugman, S. D., & Lane, W. G. (2014). Fatal child abuse. In J. E. Korbin & R. D. Krugman (Eds.), *Handbook of child maltreatment* (pp. 99–114). New York, NY: Springer.

Kulish, N. (2012, June 26). German ruling against circumcising boys draws criticism. *New York Times.* Retrieved from http://www.nytimes.com/2012/06/27/world/europe/german-court-rules-against-circumcising-boys.html

Kuo, J. R., Khoury, J. E., Metcalfe, R., Fitzpatrick, S., & Goodwill, A. (2015). An examination of the relationship between childhood emotional abuse and borderline

personality disorder features: The role of difficulties with emotion regulation. *Child Abuse & Neglect, 39*, 147–155.

Kurtz, P. D., Gaudin, J. M., Howing, P. T., & Wodarski, J. S. (1993). The consequences of physical abuse and neglect on the school age child: Mediating factors. *Children and Youth Services Review, 15*, 85–104.

Kurtz, P. D., Gaudin, J. M., Wodarski, J. S., & Howing, P. T. (1993). Maltreatment and the school-aged child: School performance consequences. *Child Abuse & Neglect, 17*, 581–589.

Kurz, D. (1991). Corporal punishment and adult use of violence: A critique of "Discipline and Deviance." *Social Problems, 38*(2), 155–161.

Laaksonen, T., Sariola, N., Johansson, A., Jern, P., Varjonen, M., von der Pahlen, B., . . . Santtila, P. (2011). Changes in the prevalence of child sexual abuse, its risk factors, and their associations as a function of age cohort in a Finnish population sample. *Child Abuse & Neglect, 35*, 480–490. doi:10.1016/j.chiabu.2011.03.004

Lahey, B. B., Conger, R. D., Atkeson, B. M., & Treiber, F. A. (1984). Parenting behavior and emotional status of physically abusive mothers. *Journal of Consulting and Clinical Psychology, 52*, 1062–1071.

Lamela, D., & Figueiredo, B. (2018). A cumulative risk model of child physical maltreatment potential: Findings from a community-based study. *Journal of Interpersonal Violence, 33*(8), 1287–1305.

Landsverk, J., Davis, I., Ganger, W., Newton, R., & Johnson, I. (1996). Impact of child psychosocial functioning on reunification from out-of-home placement. *Children and Youth Services Review, 18*, 447–467.

Lang, A. J., Gartstein, M. A., Rodgers, C. S., & Lebeck, M. M. (2010). The impact of maternal childhood abuse on parenting and infant temperament. *Journal of Child and Adolescent Psychiatric Nursing, 23*, 100–110.

Langhinrichsen-Rohling, J., Huss, M., & Ramsey, S. (2000). The clinical utility of batterer typologies. *Journal of Family Violence, 15*(1), 37–53.

Langton, L., Krebs, C., Berzofsky, M., & Smiley-McDonald, H. (2013). *Female victims of sexual violence, 1994–2010.* U.S. Department of Justice, Office of Justice Programs, Bureau of Justice Statistics.

Lanier, C., & Maume, M. O. (2009). Intimate partner violence and social isolation across the rural/urban divide. *Violence Against Women, 15*, 1311–1330.

Lanier, P., Maguire-Jack, K., Mienko, J., & Panlilio, C. (2015). From causes to outcomes: Determining prevention can work. In D. Daro, A. C. Donnelly, L. A. Huang, & B. J. Powell (Eds.), *Advances in child abuse prevention knowledge: The perspective of new leadership*. Switzerland: Springer International.

Lanktree, C. B., & Briere, J. N. (2016). *Treating complex trauma in children and their families: An integrative approach*. Thousand Oaks, CA: Sage.

Lanning, K. V. (2010). *Child molesters: A behavioral analysis for professionals investigating the sexual exploitation of children* (5th ed.). Alexandria, VA: National Center for Missing & Exploited Children, U.S. Department of Justice.

Lansford, J. E., & Deater-Deckard, K. (2012). Childrearing discipline and violence in developing countries. *Child Development*, *83*(1), 62–75.

Larance, L. Y. (2018). Programs for women who have used force in intimate relationships. In C. M. Renzetti, J. L. Edleson, & R. K. Bergen (Eds.), *Sourcebook on violence against women* (3rd ed., pp. 314–316). Thousand Oaks, CA: Sage.

Larance, L. Y., Goodmark, L., Miller, S. L., & Dasgupta, S. (2019). Understanding and addressing women's use of force in intimate relationships. *Violence Against Women*, *25*(1), 58–80.

Larsson, I., & Svedin, C. G. (2002). Sexual experiences in childhood: Young adults' recollections. *Archives of Sexual Behavior*, *31*, 263–273.

Larzelere, R. E., & Baumrind, D. (2010). Corporal punishment of children: Are spanking injunctions scientifically supported? *Law & Contemporary Problems*, *73*, 57–87.

Lavi, I., Manor-Binyamini, I., Seibert, E., Katz, L. F., Ozer, E. J., & Gross, J. J. (2019). Broken bonds: A meta-analysis of emotion reactivity and regulation in emotionally maltreating parents. *Child Abuse & Neglect*, *88*, 376–388.

Laviola, M. (1992). Effects of older brother-young sister incest: A study of the dynamics of 17 cases. *Child Abuse & Neglect*, *16*, 409–421.

LaViolette, A. D., & Barnett, O. W. (2013). *It could happen to anyone: Why battered women stay*. Thousand Oaks, CA: Sage.

Lawson, J. (2019). Domestic violence as child maltreatment: Differential risks and outcomes among cases referred to child welfare agencies for domestic violence exposure. *Children and Youth Services Review*, *98*, 32–41.

Leclerc, B., Proulx, J., & McKibben, A. (2005). Modus operandi of sexual offenders working or doing voluntary work with children and adolescents. *Journal of Sexual Aggression*, *11*(2), 187–195.

Lee, J. O., Herrenkohl, T. I., Jung, H., Skinner, M. L., & Klika, J. B. (2015). Longitudinal examination of peer and partner influences on gender-specific pathways from child abuse to adult crime. *Child Abuse & Neglect*, *47*, 83–93.

Leeb, R. T., Paulozzi, L., Melanson, C., Simon, T., & Arias, I. (2008). *Child maltreatment surveillance: Uniform definitions for public health and recommended data elements*. Atlanta, GA: Centers for Disease Control and Prevention, National Center for Injury Prevention and Control.

Leguizamon, J. S., Leguizamon, S., & Howden, W. (2017). Revisiting the link between economic distress, race, and domestic violence. *Journal of Interpersonal Violence*. Advance online publication. Retrieved from https://doi.org/10.1177/0886260517711177

Lenhart, A., Madden, M., Smith, A., Purcell, K., Zickuhr, K., & Raine, L. (2011). *Teens, kindness and cruelty on social network sites: How American teens navigate the new world of "digital citizenship."* Washington, DC: Pew Research Center.

Lenhart, A., Smith, A., & Page, D. (2015). *Teens, technology, and romantic relationships*. Washington, DC: Pew Research Center.

Leonard, J. (2001, September 12). Sheriff's sergeant accused of child abuse. *Los Angeles Times*, p. B1.

Leroux, T. G., & Petrunik, M. (1990). The construction of elder abuse as a social problem: A Canadian perspective. *International Journal of Health Services*, *20*, 651–663.

Lesnik-Oberstein, M., Koers, A. J., & Cohen, L. (1995). Parental hostility and its sources in psychologically abusive mothers: A test of the three-factor theory. *Child Abuse & Neglect*, *19*(1), 33–49.

Lessard, G., & Alvarez-Lizotte, P. (2015). The exposure of children to intimate partner violence: Potential bridges between two fields in research and psychosocial intervention: Research and interventions often focus on a specific form of violence without considering other forms of victimization. *Child Abuse & Neglect*, *48*, 29–38.

Letarte, M. J., Normandeau, S., & Allard, J. (2010). Effectiveness of a parent training program "Incredible Years" in a child protection service. *Child Abuse & Neglect*, *34*, 253–261. doi:10.1016/j.chiabu.2009.06.003

Letourneau, E. J., Brown, D. S., Fang, X., Hassan, A., & Mercy, J. A. (2018). The economic burden of child sexual abuse in the United States. *Child Abuse & Neglect*, *79*, 413–422.

Letourneau, E. J., Eaton, W. W., Bass, J., Berlin, F. S., & Moore, S. G. (2014). The need for a comprehensive public health approach to preventing child sexual abuse. *Public Health Reports*, *129*, 222–228.

Letourneau, E. J., & Levenson, J. S. (2011). Preventing sexual abuse: Community protection policies and practice. In J. E. B. Myers (Ed.), *The APSAC handbook on child maltreatment* (3rd ed., pp. 307–321). Thousand Oaks, CA: Sage.

Letourneau, E. J., Nietert, P. J., & Rheingold, A. A. (2016). Initial assessment of stewards of children program effects on child sexual abuse reporting rates in selected South Carolina counties. *Child Maltreatment*, *21*(1), 74–79.

Leve, L. D., Khurana, A., & Reich, E. B. (2015). Intergenerational transmission of maltreatment: A multilevel examination. *Development and Psychopathology*, *27*(4, Pt. 2), 1429–1442.

Leventhal, B., & Lundy, S. (Eds.). (1999). *Same-sex domestic violence: Strategies for change*. Thousand Oaks, CA: Sage.

Levesque, R. J. R. (2001). *Culture and family violence*. Washington, DC: American Psychological Association

Levi, B. H., & Portwood, S. G. (2011). Reasonable suspicion of child abuse: Finding a common language. *The Journal of Law, Medicine & Ethics*, *39*(1), 62–69.

Levine, E. C. (2018). Sexual scripts and criminal statutes: Gender restrictions, spousal allowances, and victim accountability after rape law reform. *Violence Against Women*, *24*(3), 322–349.

Lewis, R. J., Milletich, R. J., Kelley, M. L., & Woody, A. (2012). Minority stress, substance use, and intimate partner violence in sexual minority women. *Aggression and Violence Behavior*, *17*, 247–256.

Lewis, R. J., Winstead, B. A., Braitman, A. L., & Hitson, P. (2018). Discrepant drinking and partner violence perpetration over time in lesbians' relationships. *Violence Against Women*, *24*(10), 1149–1165.

Lewis, T., McElroy, E., Harlaar, N., & Runyan, D. (2016). Does the impact of child sexual abuse differ from maltreated but non-sexually abused children? A prospective examination of the impact of child sexual abuse on internalizing and externalizing behavior problems. *Child Abuse & Neglect*, *51*, 31–40.

Lieberman, A. F., Ghosh Ippen, C., & Van Horn, P. (2015). *"Don't hit my mommy!": A manual for child parent psychotherapy with young children exposed to violence and other trauma* (2nd ed.). Washington, DC: Zero to Three.

Lieberman, A. F., Weston, D. R., & Pawl, J. H. (1991). Preventive intervention and outcome with anxiously attached dyads. *Child Development*, *62*(1), 199–209.

Lind, K., Toure, H., Brugel, D., Meyer, P., Laurent-Vannier, A., & Chevignard, M. (2016). Extended follow-up of neurological, cognitive, behavioural and academic outcomes after severe abusive head trauma. *Child Abuse & Neglect*, *51*, 358–367.

Lindsey, D., Martin, S., & Doh, J. (2002). The failure of intensive casework services to reduce foster care placements: An examination of family preservation studies. *Children and Youth Services Review*, *24*, 743–775.

Linebaugh, S. (2013). *Parker Jensen cancer free 10 years later*. Salt Lake City, UT: KSL Broadcasting. Retrieved from https://www.ksl.com/?sid-25601811

Lippard, E. T., & Nemeroff, C. B. (2020). The devastating clinical consequences of child abuse and neglect: Increased disease vulnerability and poor treatment response in mood disorders. *American Journal of Psychiatry*, *177*(1), 20–36.

Lipson, G., Grant, B., Mueller, J., & Sonnich S. (2019). Preventing school employee sexual misconduct: An outcome survey analysis of making right choices. *Journal of Child Sexual Abuse*, *28*(4), 1–15.

Lipsky, S., Kernic, M. A., Qiu, Q., & Hasin, D. S. (2016). Traumatic events associated with posttraumatic stress disorder: The role of race/ethnicity and depression. *Violence Against Women*, *22*, 1055–1074.

Lipsky, S., Kernic, M., Qui, Q., Wright, C., & Hasin, D.S. (2014). A two-way street for alcohol use and partner violence: Who's driving it? *Journal of Family Violence*, *29*, 815–828.

Littell, J. H. (1997). Effects of the duration, intensity, and breadth of family preservation services: A new analysis of data from the Illinois Family First Experiment. *Children & Youth Services Review*, *17*, 36.

Littleton, H. L., Breitkopf, C. R., & Berenson, A. (2008). Beyond the campus: Unacknowledged rape among low-income women. *Violence Against Women*, *14*(3), 269–286.

Liu, J., Fang, Y., Gong, J., Cui, X., Meng, T., Xiao, B., . . . Luo, X. (2017). Associations between suicidal behavior and childhood abuse and neglect: A meta-analysis. *Journal of Affective Disorders*, *220*, 147–155.

Liu, S., Zhou, N., Dong, S., Wang, Z., & Hao, Y. (2019). Maternal childhood emotional abuse predicts Chinese infant behavior problems: Examining mediating and moderating processes. *Child Abuse & Neglect*, *88*, 307–316.

Lloyd, S. (1997). The effects of domestic violence on women's employment. *Law & Policy*, *19*, 139–167.

Lobanov-Rostovsky, C. (2015). *Adult sex offender management*. Sex Offender Management Assessment and Planning Initiative. Retrieved from http://www.smart.gov/pdfs/AdultSexOffenderManagement.pdf

Loftus, E. F., & Davis, D. (2006). Recovered memories. *Annual Review of Clinical Psychology*, *2*, 469–498.

Logan, T. K., & Walker, R. (2009). Civil protective order outcomes: Violations and perceptions of effectiveness. *Journal of Interpersonal Violence*, *24*(4), 675–692.

London, K., Bruck, M., Wright, D. B., & Ceci, S. J. (2008). Review of the contemporary literature on how children report sexual abuse to others: Findings, methodological issues, and implications for forensic interviewers. *Memory*, *16*(1), 29–47.

Los Angeles County District Attorney's Office. (2017). *Van Nuys man pleads to leaving baby in car while attending strip club*. Retrieved from http://da.co.la.ca.us/media/news/van-nuys-man-pleads-leaving-baby-car-while-attending-strip-club

Lowe, P., Humphreys, C., & Williams, S. J. (2007). Night terrors: Women's experiences of (not) sleeping where there is domestic violence. *Violence Against Women*, *13*, 549–561.

Loxton, D., Schofield, M., Hussain, R., & Mishra, G. (2006). History of domestic violence and physical health in midlife. *Violence Against Women*, *12*, 715–731.

Lueger-Schuster, B., Kantor, V., Weindl, D., Knefel, M., Moy, Y., Butollo, A., . . . Glück, T. (2014). Institutional abuse of children in the Austrian Catholic Church: Types of abuse and impact on adult survivors' current mental health. *Child Abuse & Neglect*, *38*(1), 52–64.

Luna-Firebaugh, E. N. (2006). Violence against American Indian women and the Services-Training-Officers-Prosecutors Violence Against Women (STOP VAIW) Program. *Violence Against Women*, *12*, 125–136.

Lund, E. M. (2011). Community-based services and interventions for adults with disabilities who have interpersonal violence: A review of the literature. *Trauma, Violence & Abuse*, *12*, 171–182.

Lund, E. M., & Vaughn-Jensen, J. E. (2012). Victimisation of children with disabilities. *Lancet*, *380*(9845), 867–869.

Lundahl, B. W., Nimer, J., & Parsons, B. (2006). Preventing child abuse: A meta-analysis of parent training programs. *Research on Social Work Practice*, *16*, 251–262.

Luthar, S. S., & Ciciolla, L. (2015). Who mothers mommy? Factors that contribute to mothers' well-being. *Developmental Psychology*, *51*(12), 1812–1823.

Lutzker, J. R., & Chaffin, M. (2012). SafeCare: An evidence-based to constantly dynamic model prevent child maltreatment. In H. Dubowitz (Ed.), *World perspectives on child abuse* (10th ed., pp. 93–96). Aurora, CO: International Society on Child Abuse and Neglect.

Lyon, E., Lane, S., & Menard, A. (2008). *Meeting survivors' needs: A multi-state study of domestic violence shelter experiences*. Washington, DC: U.S. Department of Justice, National Institute of Justice.

Maas, M. K., McCauley, H. L., Bonomi, A. E., & Leija, S. G. (2018). "I was grabbed by my pussy and it's #NotOkay": A Twitter backlash against Donald Trump's degrading commentary. *Violence Against Women*, *24*(14), 1739–1750.

Mabrey, S. (2014, August 25). The New Jersey Child Welfare Reform—DCP&P and FAFS Working Together for a Brighter Future. Retrieved from http://history-of-foster-care-nj.org/tag/faheem-williams/

Macartney, S., Bishaw, A., & Fontenot, K. (2013). *Poverty rates for selected detailed race and Hispanic groups by state and place, 2007–2011*. Washington, DC: U.S. Department of Commerce.

Macdonald, A., Danielson, C. K., Resnick, H. S., Saunders, B. E., & Kilpatrick, D. G. (2010). PTSD and comorbid disorders in a representative sample of adolescents: The risk associated with multiple exposures to potentially traumatic events. *Child Abuse & Neglect*, *34*(10), 773–783.

MacMillan, H. L., Tanaka, M., Duku, E., Vaillancourt, T., & Boyle, M. H. (2013). Child physical and sexual abuse in a community sample of young adults: Results from the Ontario Child Health Study. *Child Abuse & Neglect*, *37*, 14–21.

MacMillan, H. L., & Waddell, C. (2012). Home visitation in the prevention of child maltreatment: An evidence-based overview. In H. Dubowitz (Ed.), *World perspectives on child abuse* (pp. 103–106). Aurora, CO: International Society for Prevention of Child Abuse and Neglect.

MacMillan, H. L., Wathen, C. N., Barlow, J., Fergusson, D. M., Leventhal, J. M., & Taussig, H. N. (2009).

Interventions to prevent child maltreatment and associated impairment. *Lancet, 373*, 250–266.

Macy, R. J., Ermentrout, D. M., & Johns, N. B. (2011). Health care for survivors of partner and sexual violence. In C. M. Renzetti, J. L. Edleson, & R. K. Bergen (Eds.), *Sourcebook on violence against women* (2nd ed., pp. 289–308). Thousand Oaks, CA: Sage.

Maguire, S. A., Williams, B., Naughton, A. M., Cowley, L. E., Tempest, V., Mann, M. K., . . . Kemp, A. M. (2015). A systematic review of the emotional, behavioural and cognitive features exhibited by school-aged children experiencing neglect or emotional abuse. *Child: Care, Health and Development, 41*(5), 641–653.

Mahoney, P., Williams, L. M., & West, C. M. (2001). Violence against women by intimate relationship partners. In C. M. Renzetti, J. L. Edleson, & R. K. Bergen (Eds.), *Sourcebook on violence against women* (1st ed., pp. 143–178). Thousand Oaks, CA: Sage.

Maier, S. L. (2008). "I have heard horrible stories . . ." Rape victim advocates' perceptions of the revictimization of rape victims by the police and medical system. *Violence Against Women, 14*, 786–808.

Malesky, L. A. (2005). The use of the Internet for child sexual exploitation. In S. Cooper, R. J. Estes, A. P. Giardino, N. D. Kellog, & V. I. Vieth (Eds.), *Medical, legal, & social science aspects of child sexual exploitation: A comprehensive review of pornography, prostitution, and Internet crimes* (pp. 469–487). St. Louis, MO: G. W. Medical.

Malkin, M. L., & McKinney, C. (2019). Racial differences in parental involvement and physical and psychological maltreatment: Processes related to regard for parents. *Journal of Family Issues, 40*(6), 739–763.

Malloy, L. C., Lyon, T. D., & Quas, J. A. (2007). Filial dependency and recantation of child sexual abuse allegations. *Journal of the American Academy of Child and Adolescent Psychiatry, 46*, 162–170.

Mammen, O., Kolko, D., & Pilkonis, P. (2003). Parental cognitions and satisfaction: Relationship to aggressive parental behavior in child physical abuse. *Child Maltreatment, 8*, 288–301.

Mancini, C., & Shields, R. T. (2014). Notes on a (sex crime) scandal: The impact of media coverage of sexual abuse in the Catholic Church on public opinion. *Journal of Criminal Justice, 42*(2), 221–232.

Manly, J. T., Kim, J. E., Rogosch, F. A., & Cicchetti, D. (2001). Dimensions of child maltreatment and children's adjustment: Contributions of development timing and subtype. *Development and Psychopathology, 13*, 759–782.

Manning, L. (2019). *Women in the military: Where they stand.* Washington, DC: Service Women's Action Network.

Manso, J. M. M., Garcia-Baamonde, M. E., & Alonso, M. B. (2011). Design of a language stimulation program for children suffering abuse. *Children and Youth Services Review, 33*(7), 1325–1331.

Marshall, A. D., Panuzio, J., & Taft, C. T. (2005). Intimate partner violence among military veterans and active duty servicemen. *Clinical Psychology Review, 25*(7), 862–876.

Marshall, L. L., & Rose, P. (1990). Premarital violence: The impact of family of origin violence, stress, and reciprocity. *Violence and Victims, 5*(1), 51–64.

Marshall, W. L. (1999). Current status of North American assessment and treatment programs for sexual offenders. *Journal of Interpersonal Violence, 14*, 221–239.

Marshall, W. L., & Laws, D. R. (2003). A brief history of behavioral and cognitive behavioral approaches to sexual offender treatment: Part 2. The modern era. *Sexual Abuse: A Journal of Research and Treatment, 15*, 93–120.

Marshall, W. L., & Marshall, L. E. (2000). The origins of sexual offending. *Trauma, Violence, & Abuse, 1*, 250–263.

Martin, S. L., Macy, R. J., & Young, S. K. (2011). Health and economic consequences of sexual violence. In J. W. White, M. P. Koss, & A. E. Kazdin (Eds.), *Violence against women and children: Vol. 1. Mapping the terrain* (pp. 173–195). Washington, DC: American Psychological Association.

Martin, S. L., Moracco, K. E., Chang, J. C., Council, C. L., & Dulli, L. S. (2008). Substance abuse issues among women in domestic violence programs: Findings from North Carolina. *Violence Against Women, 14*, 985–997.

Martin, S. L., Ray, N., Sotres-Alvarez, D., Kupper, L. L., Moracco, K. E., Dickens, P. A., Scandlin, D., & Gizlice, Z. (2006). Physical and sexual assault of women with disabilities. *Violence Against Women, 12*(9), 823–837.

Martin, T. (2017). Wake up call: How the Ray Rice incident opened the public's eyes to domestic violence in professional sports and the need for change. *Sports Law Journal, 24*, 183–213.

Martinez, G., & Abma, J. C. (2015). *Sexual activity, contraceptive use, and childbearing of teenagers aged 15–19 in the United States.* Washington, DC: U.S. Department of Health and Human Services, Centers for Disease Control and Prevention, National Center for Health Statistics.

Martins, C. M. S., Baes, C. V. W., de Carvalho Tofoli, S. M., & Juruena, M. F. (2014). Emotional abuse in childhood is a differential factor for the development of depression in adults. *The Journal of Nervous and Mental Disease*, *202*(11), 774–782.

Massachusetts Citizens for Children. (2010). *Enough Abuse Campaign*. Retrieved from http://www .enoughabuse.org

Massing-Schaffer, M., Liu, R. T., Kraines, M. A., Choi, J. Y., & Alloy, L. B. (2015). Elucidating the relation between childhood emotional abuse and depressive symptoms in adulthood: The mediating role of maladaptive interpersonal processes. *Personality and Individual Differences*, *74*, 106–111.

Masten, A. S. (2014). Global perspectives on resilience in children and youth. *Child Development*, *85*(1), 6–20.

Mathews, B., & Collin-Vézina, D. (2019). Child sexual abuse: Toward a conceptual model and definition. *Trauma, Violence, & Abuse*, *20*(2), 131–148.

Mathews, B., Lee, X. J., & Norman, R. E. (2016). Impact of a new mandatory reporting law on reporting and identification of child sexual abuse: A seven year time trend analysis. *Child Abuse & Neglect*, *56*, 62–79.

Maxwell, C. D., Garner, J. H., & Fagan, J. A. (2002). The preventive effects of arrest on intimate partner violence: Research, policy and theory. *Criminology & Public Policy*, *2*(1), 51–79.

Mays, J. M. (2006). Feminist disability theory: Domestic violence against women with a disability. *Disability & Society*, *21*, 147–158.

Mbilinyi, L., Edleson, J., Hagemeister, A., & Beeman, S. (2007). What happens to children when their mothers are battered? Results from a four city anonymous telephone survey. *Journal of Family Violence*, *22*, 309–317.

McAlinden, A. M. (2006). "Setting 'em up": Personal, familial and institutional grooming in the sexual abuse of children. *Social & Legal Studies*, *15*(3), 339–362.

McCanne, T. R., & Hagstrom, A. H. (1996). Physiological hyperreactivity to stressors in physical child abusers and individuals at risk for being physically abusive. *Aggression and Violent Behavior*, *2*(4), 345–358.

McCarroll, J. E., Newby, J. H., & Dooley-Bernard, M. (2008). *Responding to domestic violence in the U.S. Army: The family advocacy program*. Kingston, NJ: Civic Research Institute.

McCauley, H. L., Bogen, K. W., & Bonomi, A. E. (2017, September). *#MaybeHeDoesntHitYou: Using Twitter as a platform to subvert historically taboo discourse on intimate partner violence*. Paper presented at the National Conference on Health and Domestic Violence, Futures Without Violence, San Francisco, CA.

McCloskey, K. A., & Raphael, D. N. (2005). Adult perpetrator gender asymmetries in child sexual assault victim selection: Results from the 2000 National Incident-Based Reporting System. *Journal of Child Sexual Abuse*, *14*, 1–24.

McClure, F. H., Chavez, D. V., Agars, M. D., Peacock, M. J., & Matosian, A. (2008). Resilience in sexually abused women: Risk and protective factors. *Journal of Family Violence*, *23*(2), 81–88.

McCoy, M. L., & Keen, S. M. (2013). *Child abuse and neglect*. New York, NY: Psychology Press.

McCrory, E., De Brito, S. A., & Viding, E. (2012). The link between child abuse and psychopathology: A review of neurobiological and genetic research. *Journal of the Royal Society of Medicine*, *105*(4), 151–156.

McDonagh, A., Friedman, M., McHugo, G., Ford, J., Sengupta, A., Mueser, K., . . . Descamps, M. (2005). Randomized trial of cognitive-behavioral therapy for chronic posttraumatic stress disorder in adult female survivors of childhood sexual abuse. *Journal of Consulting and Clinical Psychology*, *73*(3), 515.

McDonald, R., Jouriles, E. N., Ramisetty-Mikler, S., Caetano, R., & Green, C. (2006). Estimating the number of American children living in partner-violent families. *Journal of Family Psychology*, *20*(1), 137–142.

McDonnell, C. G., Boan, A. D., Bradley, C. C., Seay, K. D., Charles, J. M., & Carpenter, L. A. (2019). Child maltreatment in autism spectrum disorder and intellectual disability: Results from a population based sample. *Journal of Child Psychology and Psychiatry*, *60*(5), 576–584.

McGee, R. A., & Wolfe, D. A. (1991). Psychological maltreatment: Toward an operational definition. *Development and Psychopathology*, *1*, 3–18.

McGinley, M., Wolff, J. H., Rospenda, K. M., Liu, L., & Richman, J. A. (2016). Risk factors and outcomes of chronic sexual harassment during the transition to college: Examination of a two-part growth mixture model. *Social Science Research*, *60*, 297–310.

McGlynn, C., Rackely, E., & Houghton, R. (2017). Beyond "revenge porn": The continuum of image-based sexual abuse. *Feminist Legal Studies*, *25*, 25–46.

McGuigan, W. M., Luchette, J. A., & Atterholt, R. (2018). Physical neglect in childhood as a predictor of violent behavior in adolescent males. *Child Abuse & Neglect*, *79*, 395–400.

McLeigh, J. D., McDonell, J. R., & Lavenda, O. (2018). Neighborhood poverty and child abuse and neglect: The mediating role of social cohesion. *Children and Youth Services Review*, *93*, 154–160.

McLeod, D. A. (2015). Female offenders in child sexual abuse cases: A national picture. *Journal of Child Sexual Abuse*, *24*(1), 97–114. doi:10.1080/10538712.2015.978925

McMahon, S., & Farmer, L. (2011). An updated measure for assessing subtle rape myths. *Social Work Research*, *35*(2), 71–81.

McPhate, M. (2016). Zoo's killing of gorilla holding a boy prompts outrage. *New York Times*. Retrieved from https://www.nytimes.com/2016/05/31/us/zoos-killing-of-gorilla-holding-a-boy-prompts-outrage.html

McPherson, A. V., Lewis, K. M., Lynn, A. E., Haskett, M. E., & Behrend, T. S. (2009). Predictors of parenting stress for abusive and nonabusive mothers. *Journal of Child and Family Studies*, *18*(1), 61–69.

Meagher, M. W. (2004). Links between traumatic family violence and chronic pain: Biopsychosocial pathways and treatment implications. In K. A. Kendall-Tackett (Ed.), *Health consequences of abuse in the family* (pp. 155–177). Washington, DC: American Psychological Association.

Melbin, A., Sullivan, C. M., & Cain, D. (2003). Transitional supportive housing programs: Battered women's perspectives and recommendations. *Affilia*, *18*, 445–460.

Mele, C. (2016, September 28). Should you intervene when a parent harshly disciplines a child in public? *New York Times*. Retrieved from http://www.nytimes.com/2016/09/29/us/should-you-intervene-when-a-parent-harshly-disciplines-a-child-in-public.html

Melendez-Torres, G. J., Leijten, P., & Gardner, F. (2019). What are the optimal combinations of parenting intervention components to reduce physical child abuse recurrence? Reanalysis of a systematic review using qualitative comparative analysis. *Child Abuse Review*, *28*, 181–197.

Meloy, M. L., & Cunningham, N. (2018). Sexual victimization and domestic violence against elderly women. In C. M. Renzetti, J. L. Edleson, & R. K. Bergen (Eds.), *Sourcebook on violence against women* (3rd ed., pp. 185–199). Thousand Oaks, CA: Sage.

Meloy, M. L., & Miller, S. L. (2011). *The victimization of women: Law, policies, and politics*. New York, NY: Oxford University Press.

Melton, G. B. (2002). Chronic neglect of family violence: More than a decade of reports to guide US policy. *Child Abuse & Neglect*, *26*, 569–586.

Melton, G. B. (2008). Beyond balancing: Toward an integrated approach to children's rights. *Journal of Social Issues*, *64*, 903–920.

Memorandum—Establishing a White House Task Force to Protect Students From Sexual Assault. (2014, January 22). Retrieved from https://www.whitehouse.gov/the-press-office/2014/01/22/memorandum-establishing-white-house-task-force-protect-students-sexual-a

Menard, K. S., Anderson, A. L., & Godboldt, S. M. (2009). Gender differences in intimate partner recidivism: A 5-year follow-up. *Criminal Justice and Behavior*, *36*(1), 61–76.

Mendelson, T., & Letourneau, E. J. (2015). Parent-focused prevention of child sexual abuse. *Prevention Science*, *16*(6), 844–852.

Menjivar, C., & Salcido, O. (2002). Immigrant women and domestic violence: Common experiences in different countries. *Gender & Society*, *16*(6), 898–920.

Mennen, F. E., Kim, K., Sang, J., & Trickett, P. K. (2010). Child neglect: Definition and identification of youth's experiences in official reports of maltreatment. *Child Abuse & Neglect*, *34*(9), 647–658.

Merdian, H. L., Curtis, C., Thakker, J., Wilson, N., & Boer, D. P. (2013). The three dimensions of online child pornography offending. *Journal of Sexual Aggression*, *19*(1), 121–132.

Merrick, M. T., Ford, D. C., Ports, K. A., Guinn, A. S., Chen, J., Klevens, J., . . . Ottley, P. (2019). Vital signs: Estimated proportion of adult health problems attributable to adverse childhood experiences and implications for prevention—25 states, 2015–2017. *Morbidity and Mortality Weekly Report*, *68*(44), 999–1005.

Merrick, M. T., & Guinn, A. S. (2018). Child abuse and neglect: Breaking the intergenerational link. *AJPH Editorials*, *108*(9), 1117–1118.

Merrill, L. L., Hervig, L. K., & Milner, J. S. (1996). Childhood parenting experiences, intimate partner conflict resolution, and adult risk for child physical abuse. *Child Abuse & Neglect*, *20*, 1049–1065.

Mersky, J. P., & Reynolds, A. J. (2007). Child maltreatment and violent delinquency: Disentangling main effects and subgroup effects. *Child Maltreatment*, *12*(3), 246–258.

Mersky, J. P., Topitzes, J. D., & Reynolds, A. J. (2011). Maltreatment prevention through early childhood intervention: A confirmatory evaluation of the Chicago Child–Parent Center preschool program. *Children and Youth Services Review, 33*, 1454–1463.

Messing, J. T., Campbell, J., Wilson, J. S., Brown, S., & Patchell, B. (2017). The Lethality Screen: The predictive validity of an intimate partner risk assessment for use by first responders. *Journal of Interpersonal Violence, 32*(2), 205–226.

Messing, J. T., O'Sullivan, C. S., Cavanaugh, C. E., Webster, D. W., & Campbell, J. (2017). Are abused women's protective actions associated with reduced threats, stalking, and violence perpetrated by their male partners? *Violence Against Women, 23*(3), 263–286.

Messman-Moore, T. L., Ward, R. M., & Brown, A. L. (2009). Substance use and PTSD symptoms impact the likelihood of rape and revictimization in college women. *Journal of Interpersonal Violence, 24*, 499–521.

Meyer, E., & Post, L. (2013). Collateral intimate partner homicide. *SAGE Open, 3*(2). doi:10.1177/2158244013484235

Mikton, C., Maguire, H., & Shakespeare, T. (2014). A systematic review of the effectiveness of interventions to prevent and respond to violence against persons with disabilities. *Journal of Interpersonal Violence, 29*(17), 3207–3226.

Miller, E. (2018). Reclaiming gender and power in sexual violence prevention in adolescence. *Violence Against Women, 24*(15), 1785–1793.

Miller, E., Decker, M. R., & Glass, N. (2018). Innovative health care responses to violence against women. In C. M. Renzetti, J. L. Edleson, & R. K. Bergen (Eds.), *Sourcebook on violence against women* (3rd ed., pp. 299–313). Thousand Oaks, CA: Sage.

Miller, E., Decker, M. R., McCauley, H. L., Tancredi, D. J., Levenson, R. R., Waldman, J., . . . Silverman, J. G. (2011). A family planning clinic partner violence intervention to reduce risk associated with reproductive coercion. *Contraception, 83*(3), 274–280.

Miller, J. (2008). *Getting played: African American girls, urban inequality and gendered violence*. New York: New York University Press.

Miller, P. (2018). The prevention of child maltreatment through the Nurse Family Partnership Program: Mediating effects in a long-term follow-up study (pp. 25–26). *The 2018 Research to Practice Brief Compendium*. The American Professional Society on the Abuse of Children.

Miller, S. L. (2001). The paradox of women arrested for domestic violence: Criminal justice professionals and service providers respond. *Violence Against Women, 7*(12), 1339–1376.

Miller, S. L. (2005). *Victims as offenders: The paradox of women's violence in relationships*. New Brunswick, NJ: Rutgers University Press.

Miller, S. L., Iovanni, L., & Kelley, K. D. (2011). Violence against women and the criminal justice response. In C. M. Renzetti, J. L. Edeson, & R. K. Bergen (Eds.), *Sourcebook on violence against women* (2nd ed., pp. 267–286). Thousand Oaks, CA: Sage.

Miller, S. L., & Smolter, N. L. (2011). "Paper abuse": When all else fails, batterers use procedural stalking. *Violence Against Women, 17*(5), 637–650.

Miller-Perrin, C. L., Perrin, R. D., & Kocur, J. L. (2009). Parental physical and psychological aggression: Psychological symptoms in young adults. *Child Abuse & Neglect, 33*, 1–11.

Miller-Perrin, C., & Wurtele, S. K. (2017a). Sex trafficking and the commercial sexual exploitation of children. *Women and Therapy, 40*, 123–151.

Miller-Perrin, C., & Wurtele, S. K. (2017b). Primary prevention of childhood sexual abuse. In R. Alexander & N. Guterman (Eds.), *Prevention of child maltreatment*. St. Louis, MO: STM Learning, Inc.

Mills, L. G. (2000). Woman abuse and child protection: A tumultuous marriage (Part I). *Children and Youth Services Review, 22*, 199–205.

Milner, J. S. (2003). Social information processing in high-risk and physically abusive parents. *Child Abuse & Neglect, 27*, 7–20.

Milot, T., St-Laurent, D., Ethier, L. S., & Provost, M. A. (2010). Trauma-related symptoms in neglected preschoolers and affective quality of mother-child communication. *Child Maltreatment, 15*(4), 293–304.

Miner, M., Marques, J., Day, D. M., & Nelson, C. (1990). Impact of relapse prevention in treating sex offenders: Preliminary findings. *Annals of Sex Research, 3*, 165–185.

Minow, J. C., & Einolf, C. J. (2009). Sorority participation and sexual assault risk. *Violence Against Women, 15*(7), 835–851.

Mitchell, I., & Guichon, J. R. (2019). I think someone has or is deliberating harming this child. I think there is neglect of the child. Help! In *Ethics in pediatrics* (pp. 197–217). Cham, Switzerland: Springer.

Mitchell, J. C., MacLeod, B. P., & Cassisi, J. E. (2017). Modeling sexual assault risk perception among heterosexual college females: The impact of previous victimization, alcohol use, and coping style. *Violence Against Women*, *23*(2), 143–162.

Mitchell, K. J., Finkelhor, D., & Wolak, J. (2003). Victimization of youths on the Internet. *Journal of Aggression, Maltreatment & Trauma*, *8*, 1–39.

Mitchell, K. S., & Freitag, J. L. (2011). Forum theater for bystanders: A new model for gender violence prevention. *Violence Against Women*, *17*(8), 990–1013.

Mitchell, P. D., Brown, R., Wang, T., Shah, R. D., Samworth, R. J., Deakin, S., . . . Latimer, M. (2019). Multicentre study of physical abuse and limb fractures in young children in the East Anglia Region, UK. *Archives of Disease in Childhood*, 1–6. doi:10.1136/archdischild-2018-315035

Mitra, M., & Mouradian, V. E. (2014). Intimate partner violence in the relationships of men with disabilities in the United States: Relative prevalence and health correlates. *Journal of Interpersonal Violence*, *29*(17), 3150–3166.

Mitra, M., Mouradian, V. E., & McKenna, M. (2011). Sexual violence victimization against men with disabilities. *American Journal of Preventive Medicine*, *41*, 494–497.

Mulldor, C., Tolman, R. M., & Kober, J. (2000). Gender and contextual factors in adolescent dating violence. *Prevention Researcher*, *7*(1), 1–4.

Mollerstrom, W. W., Patchner, M. A., & Milner, J. S. (1992). Family functioning and child abuse potential. *Journal of Clinical Psychology*, *48*, 445–454.

Monckton Smith, J. (2019). Intimate partner femicide: Using Foucaldian analysis to track an eight stage progression to homicide. *Violence Against Women*. Advance online publication. Retrieved from https://doi.org/10.1177/1077801219863876

Monckton Smith, J., Szymanska, K., & Haile, S. (2017). *Exploring the relationship between stalking and homicide*. Suzy Lamplugh Trust. Retrieved from http://eprints.glos.ac.uk/4553/

Morgan, R. E., & Mason, B. J. (2014). *Crimes against the elderly, 2003–2013*. Washington, DC: U.S. Department of Justice, Bureau of Justice Statistics.

Morgan, R. E., & Oudekerk, B. A. (2019). *Criminal Victimization, 2018*. Retrieved from https://www.bjs.gov/content/pub/pdf/cv18.pdf

Morgan, R. E., & Truman, J. L. (2018). *Criminal victimization, 2017*. Washington, DC: U.S. Department of Justice, Bureau of Justice Statistics.

Morin, R. (2011). *The difficult transition from military to civilian life*. Washington, DC: Pew Research Center.

Morina, N., Koerssen, R., & Pollet, T. V. (2016). Interventions for children and adolescents with posttraumatic stress disorder: A meta-analysis of comparative outcome studies. *Clinical Psychology Review*, *47*, 41–54.

Morrill, A. C., Dai, J., Dunn, S., Sung, I., & Smith, K. (2005). Child custody and visitation decisions when the father has perpetrated violence against the mother. *Violence Against Women*, *11*, 1076–1107.

Mouton, C. P. (2003). Intimate partner violence and health status among older women. *Violence Against Women*, *9*, 1465–1477.

Mulder, T. M., Kuiper, K. C., van der Put, C. E., Stams, G. J. J., & Assink, M. (2018). Risk factors for child neglect: A meta-analytic review. *Child Abuse & Neglect*, *77*, 198–210.

Munkel, W. I. (1994). Neglect and abandonment. In A. E. Brodeur & J. A. Monteleone (Eds.), *Child maltreatment: A clinical guide and reference* (pp. 241–257). St. Louis, MO: Medical Publishing.

Murrell, A. R., Christoff, K. A., & Henning, K. R. (2007). Characteristics of domestic violence offenders: Associations with childhood exposure to violence. *Journal of Family Violence*, *22*, 523–532.

Murshid, N. S., & Bowen, F. A. (2010). A trauma-informed analysis of the Violence Against Women Act's provisions for undocumented immigrant women. *Violence Against Women*, *24*(13), 1540–1556.

Myers, J. E. B. (Ed.). (2011). *The APSAC handbook on child maltreatment* (3rd ed.). Thousand Oaks, CA: Sage.

Nadien, M. B. (2006). Factors that influence abusive interactions between aging women and caregivers. *Annals of the Academy of the New York Academy of Sciences*, *1087*, 158–169.

Nanda, M. M., Reichert, E., Jones, U. J., & Flannery-Schroeder, E. (2016). Childhood maltreatment and symptoms of social anxiety: Exploring the role of emotional abuse, neglect, and cumulative trauma. *Journal of Child & Adolescent Trauma*, *9*(3), 201–207.

Nansel, T. R., Overpeck, M., Pilla, R. S., Ruan, W. J., Simons-Morton, B., & Scheidt, P. (2001). Bullying behaviors among U.S. youth: Prevalence and association with psychosocial adjustment. *Journal of the American Medical Association*, *285*, 2094–2100.

Narang, J., Schwannauer, M., Quayle, E., & Chouliara, Z. (2019). Therapeutic interventions with child and adolescent survivors of sexual abuse: A critical narrative review. *Children and Youth Services Review, 107*. Retrieved from https://doi.org/10.1016/j.childyouth.2019.104559

Nason-Clark, N., & Fisher-Townsend, B. (2015). *Men who batter.* New York, NY: Oxford University Press.

National Academies of Science, Engineering, and Medicine. (2019). *Vibrant and healthy kids: Aligning science, practice, and policy to advance health equity.* Washington, DC: National Academies Press. Retrieved from https://doi.org/10.17226/25466

National Center for Injury Prevention and Control, Division of Violence Prevention. (2014). *National Intimate Partner and Sexual Violence Survey (NISVS): 2011 Victimization Questions.* Atlanta, GA: Centers for Disease Control and Prevention. Retrieved from https://stacks.cdc.gov/view/cdc/24726

National Center for Prosecution of Child Abuse. (2014). *Child endangerment/failure to protect laws.* National District Attorneys Association. Retrieved from http://www.ndaa.org/pdf/Child%20Endangerment%202014_%208_25_2014_FINAL.PDF

National Center on Addiction and Substance Abuse at Columbia University. (2005). *Family matters: Substance abuse and the American family.* Retrieved from www.casacolumbia.org/absolutenm/templates/PressReleases.asp?articleid=383&zoneid=64

National Center on Elder Abuse. (1998). *The National Elder Abuse Incidence Study: Final report.* Retrieved from http://www.aoa.gov/eldfam/Elder_Rights/Elder_Abuse/AbuseReport_Final.pdf

National Center on Substance Abuse and Child Welfare. (2018). *A planning guide: Steps to support a comprehensive approach to plans of safe care.* Retrieved from https://www.cffutures.org/files/fdc/A-Planning-Guide-Steps-to-Support-a-Comprehensive-Approach-to-Plans-of-Safe-Care-3.21.18-final.pdf

National Home Visiting Resource Center. (2019). *2019 home visiting yearbook.* Arlington, VA: James Bell Associates and the Urban Institute. Retrieved from https://nhvrc.org/yearbook/2019-yearbook/

National Institute on Drug Abuse. (2018). *Substance use while pregnant and breastfeeding.* Retrieved from https://www.drugabuse.gove/publications/research-reports/substance-use-in-women/substance-use-while-pregnant-breastfeeding

National Research Council. (2014). *New directions in child abuse and neglect research.* Washington, DC: National Academies Press. Retrieved from https://doi.org/10.17226/18331

Nayak, M. B., & Milner, J. S. (1998). Neuropsychological functioning: Comparison of mothers at high- and low-risk for child abuse. *Child Abuse & Neglect, 22*, 687–703.

Neighbors, C., Walker, D. D., Mbilinyi, L. F., O'Rourke, A., Edleson, J. L., Zegree, J., & Roffman, R. A. (2010). Normative misperceptions of abuse among perpetrators of intimate partner violence. *Violence Against Women, 16*(4), 370–386.

Nelson, J., Klumparendt, A., Doebler, P., & Ehring, T. (2017). Childhood maltreatment and characteristics of adult depression: Meta-analysis. *The British Journal of Psychiatry, 210*(2), 96–104.

Nerenberg, L. (2006). Communities respond to elder abuse. *Journal of Gerontological Social Work, 46*, 5–33.

New report: 1 in 4 Americans volunteer; 3 in 5 help neighbors. (2015, December 8). Corporation for National and Community Service. Retrieved from http://www.nationalservice.gov/newsroom/press-releases/2015/new-report-1-4-americans-volunteer-3-5-help-neighbors

New York congressman: "The picture was of me, I sent it." (2011, June 6). *NBC News.* Retrieved from http://www.nbcnews.com/id/43299964/ns/politics-capitol_hill/t/new-york-congressman-picture-was-me-i-sent-it/#.Xo4G8NNKjOR

Ng, K. (2019, December 4). Man abandoned boy on side of road because he "thought he was gay." *Independent.* Retrieved from https://www.independent.co.uk/news/world/americas/man-abandoned-boy-gay-road-florida-lgbt-evenaud-julmeus-a9232566.html

Ngo, Q. M., Ramirez, J. I., Stein, S. F., Cunningham, R. M., Chermack, S. T., Singh, V., & Walton, M. A. (2018). Understanding the role of alcohol, anxiety, and trait mindfulness in the perpetration of physical and sexual dating violence in emerging adults. *Violence Against Women, 24*(10), 1166–1186.

Noll, J. G., Shenk, C. E., & Putnam, K. T. (2009). Childhood sexual abuse and adolescent pregnancy: A meta-analytic update. *Journal of Pediatric Psychology, 34*, 366–378.

Nosek, M. A., Hughes, R. B., Taylor, H. B., & Taylor, P. (2006). Disability, psychosocial, and demographic characteristics of abused women with physical disabilities. *Violence Against Women, 12*(9), 838–850.

Novaco, R., & Chemtob, C. (2015). Violence associated with combat-related post-traumatic stress disorder: The importance of anger. *Psychological Trauma: Theory, Research, Practice and Policy, 7*, 485–492.

Nowling, M. M. (2003). Protecting children who witness domestic violence: Is *Nicholson v. Williams* an adequate response? *Family Court Review, 41*, 507–526.

Nunes, K. L., Hermann, C. A., Malcolm, J. R., & Lavoie, K. (2013). Childhood sexual victimization, pedophilic interest, and sexual recidivism. *Child Abuse & Neglect, 37*, 703–711. doi:10.1016/j.chiabu.2013.01.008

Oates, K. (2015). Some reflections from the past and some ideas for the future: The 2014 Kempe Oration. *Child Abuse & Neglect, 43*, 1–7.

Oates, R. K., & Bross, D. C. (1995). What have we learned about treating child physical abuse? A literature review of the last decade. *Child Abuse & Neglect, 19*, 463–474.

Ocampo, B. W., Shelley, G. A., & Jaycox, L. H. (2007). Latino teens talk about help seeking and help giving in relation to dating violence. *Violence Against Women, 13*, 172–189.

O'Connor, J., & Nepomnyaschy, L. (2019). Intimate partner violence and material hardship among urban mothers. *Violence Against Women.* Advance online publication. Retrieved from https://doi.org/10.1177/1077801219854539

Office of Justice Programs. (2011). *Elder abuse and mistreatment: OJP fact sheet.* Retrieved from http://ojp.gov/newsroom/factsheets/ojpfs_elderabuse.html

O'Hearn, H. G., & Margolin, G. (2000). Men's attitudes condoning marital aggression: A moderator between family of origin abuse and aggression against female partners. *Cognitive Therapy and Research, 24*, 159–174.

Olafson, E. (2011). Child sexual abuse: Demography, impact, and interventions. *Journal of Child & Adolescent Trauma, 4*, 8–21. doi:10.1080/19361521.2011.545811

Olafson, E., Corwin, D. L., & Summit, R. C. (1993). Modern history of child sexual abuse awareness: Cycles of discovery and suppression. *Child Abuse & Neglect, 17*(1), 7–24.

Olds, D. L. (1997). The Prenatal/Early Infancy Project: Preventing child abuse and neglect in the context of promoting maternal and child health. In D. A. Wolfe, R. J. McMahon, & R. D. Peters (Eds.), *Child abuse: New directions in prevention and treatment across the life-span* (pp. 130–154). Thousand Oaks, CA: Sage.

Olds, D. L., Eckenrode, J., Henderson, C. R., Jr., Kitzman, H., Powers, J., Cole, R., . . . Luckey, D. (1997). Long-term effects of home visitation on maternal life course and child abuse and neglect: Fifteen-year follow-up of a randomized trial. *Journal of the American Medical Association, 278*, 637–643.

Olds, D. L., Henderson, C. R., Cole, R., Eckenrode, J., Kitzman, H., Luckey, D., . . . Powers, J. (1998). Long-term effects of nurse home visitation on children's criminal and antisocial behavior: 15-year follow-up of a randomized controlled trial. *Journal of the American Medical Association, 280*, 1238–1244.

Olds, D. L., Sadler, L., & Kitzman, H. (2007). Programs for parents of infants and toddlers: Recent evidence from randomized trials. *Journal of Child Psychology and Child Psychiatry and Allied Disciplines, 483*(3/4), 355–391.

O'Leary, K. D., & Schumacher, J. A. (2003). The association between alcohol use and intimate partner violence: Linear effect, threshold effect, or both? *Addictive Behaviors, 28*(9), 1575–1585.

Olson, L. N., Daggs, J. L., Ellevold, B. L., & Rogers, T. K. (2007). Entrapping the innocent: Toward a theory of child sexual predators' luring communication. *Communication Theory, 17*(3), 231–251.

Olver, M. E., & Jung, S. (2017). Incremental prediction of intimate partner violence: An examination of three risk measures. *Law & Human Behavior, 41*(5), 440–453.

Oram, S., Khondoker, M., Abas, M., Broadbent, M., & Howard, L. M. (2015). Characteristics of trafficked adults and children with severe mental illness: A historical cohort study. *The Lancet Psychiatry, 2*(12), 1084–1091.

Orchowski, L. M., & Gidycz, C. A. (2012). To whom do college women confide following sexual assault? A prospective study of predictors of sexual assault disclosure and social reactions. *Violence Against Women, 18*(3), 264–288.

Orchowski, L. M., & Gidycz, C. A. (2015). Psychological consequences associated with positive and negative responses to disclosure of sexual assault among college women: A prospective study. *Violence Against Women, 21*(7), 803–823.

Orenstein, P., & Rickne, J. (2013). When does intimate partner violence continue after separation? *Violence Against Women, 19*, 617–633.

Orloff, L., & Garcia, O. (2013). *Dynamics of domestic violence experienced by immigrant victims.* Retrieved from http://library.niwap.org/wp-content/uploads/2015/CULT-Man-Ch1.1-DynamicsDomesticViolence2016.pdf

Ornstein, A. E., & Ward, M. G. K. (2012). An overview of abusive head trauma prevention and parent education programs. In H. Dubowitz (Ed.), *World perspectives on child abuse* (10th ed., pp. 107–112). Aurora, CO:

International Society for Prevention of Child Abuse and Neglect.

Orth, M. (2019, March 1). 10 undeniable facts about the Michael Jackson sexual-abuse allegations. *Vanity Fair.* Retrieved from https://www.vanityfair.com/hollywood/2019/03/10-undeniable-facts-about-the-michael-jackson-sexual-abuse-allegations

Ortiz, R., & Sibinga, E. M. (2017). The role of mindfulness in reducing the adverse effects of childhood stress and trauma. *Children, 4*(3), 16.

Ortman, J. M., Velkoff, V. A., & Hogan, H. (2014). *An aging nation: The older population in the United States.* Washington, DC: U.S. Department of Commerce.

Oshri, A., Gray, J. C., Owens, M. M., Liu, S., Duprey, E. B., Sweet, L. H., & Mackillop, J. (2019). Adverse childhood experiences and amygdalar reduction: High-resolution segmentation reveals associations with subnuclei and psychiatric outcomes. *Child Maltreatment, 24*(4). Retrieved from https://doi.org/10.1177/1077559519839491

O'Sullivan, C. S., Davis, R. C., Farole, D. J., & Rempel, M. (2007). *A comparison of two prosecution policies in cases of intimate partner violence mandatory case filing vs. following the victim's lead.* Washington, DC: U.S. Department of Justice, National Institute of Justice.

Otto, R. K., & Melton, G. B. (1990). Trends in legislation and case law on child abuse and neglect. In R. T. Ammerman & M. Hersen (Eds.), *Children at risk: An evaluation of factors contributing to child abuse and neglect* (pp. 55–83). New York, NY: Plenum.

Ouyang, L., Fang, X., Mercy, J., Perou, R., & Grosse, S. D. (2008). Attention-deficit/hyperactivity disorder symptoms and child maltreatment: A population-based study. *The Journal of Pediatrics, 153*(6), 851–856.

Ozaki, R., & Otis, M. D. (2017). Gender equality, patriarchal cultural norms, and perpetration of intimate partner violence: Comparison of male university students in Asian and European cultural contexts. *Violence Against Women, 23*(9), 1076–1099.

Pagelow, M. D. (1984). *Family violence.* New York, NY: Praeger.

Palusci, V. J., & Covington, T. M. (2014). Child maltreatment deaths in the U.S. National Child Death Review Case Reporting System. *Child Abuse & Neglect, 38*(1), 25–36.

Palusci, V. J., Yager, S., & Covington, T. M. (2010). Effects of a citizens review panel in preventing child maltreatment fatalities. *Child Abuse & Neglect, 34*(5), 324–331.

Pan, A., Daley, S., Rivera, L. M., Williams, K., Lingle, D., & Reznik, V. (2006). Understanding the role of culture in domestic violence: The Ahimsa project for safe families. *Journal of Immigrant and Minority Health, 8*(1), 35–43.

Papalia, N. L., Luebbers, S., Ogloff, J. R., Cutajar, M., & Mullen, P. E. (2017). The long-term co-occurrence of psychiatric illness and behavioral problems following child sexual abuse. *Australian & New Zealand Journal of Psychiatry, 51*(6), 604–613.

Paranjape, A., Corbie-Smith, G., Thompson, N., & Kaslow, N. J. (2009). When older African American women are affected by violence in the home: A qualitative investigation of risk and protective factors. *Violence Against Women, 15*, 977–990.

Parker, I. (2012, February 6). The story of a suicide: Two college roommates, a webcam, and a tragedy. *The New Yorker.* Retrieved from http://www.newyorker.com/magazine/2012/02/06/the-story-of-a-suicide

Parker, J., McMillan, L., Olson, S., Ruppel, S., & Vieth, V. (2008). Responding to basic and complex cases of child abuse: A comparison study of recent and current Child Advocacy Studies (CAST) students with DSS workers in the field. *Journal of Child & Adolescent Trauma*, 1–8.

Parker, T., Rogers, K., Collins, M., & Edleson, J. L. (2008). Danger zone: Battered mothers and their families in supervised visitation. *Violence Against Women, 14*(11), 1313–1325.

Parrish, R. N. (2012). Prosecuting child physical abuse and homicide cases: How things have changed since the creation of APSAC. *APSAC Advisor, 24*(1/2), 33–35.

Patel, V., Kirkwood, B. R., Weiss, H., Pednekar, S., Fernandes, J., Pereira, B., et al. (2005). Chronic fatigue in developing countries: Population based survey of women in India. *British Medical Journal, 330*, 1190–1193.

Patterson, D. (2011). The impact of detectives' manner of questioning on rape victims' disclosure. *Violence Against Women, 17*(11), 1349–1373.

Paul, E., & Eckenrode, J. (2015). Childhood psychological maltreatment subtypes and adolescent depressive symptoms. *Child Abuse & Neglect, 47*, 38–47.

Payne, D. L., Lonsway, K. A., & Fitzgerald, L. F. (1999). Rape myth acceptance: Exploration of its structure and its measurement using the Illinois Rape Myth Acceptance Scale. *Journal of Research in Personality, 33*(1), 27–68.

Pelton, L. H. (1994). The role of material factors in child abuse and neglect. In G. B. Melton & F. D. Barry (Eds.),

Protecting children from abuse and neglect (pp. 166–181). New York, NY: Guilford.

Pennell, J., & Francis, S. (2005). Safety conferencing: Toward a coordinated and inclusive response to safeguard women and children. *Violence Against Women*, *11*(5), 666–692.

Pepler, D. (2012). The development of dating violence: What doesn't develop, how does it develop, and what can we do about it? *Prevention Science*, *12*, 402–409.

Peralta, R. L., Tuttle, L. A., & Steele, J. L. (2010). At the intersection of interpersonal violence, masculinity, and alcohol use: The experiences of heterosexual male perpetrators of intimate partner violence. *Violence Against Women*, *16*(4), 387–409.

Pereda, N., Guilera, G., Forns, M., & Gómez-Benito, J. (2009). The international epidemiology of child sexual abuse: A continuation of Finkelhor (1994). *Child Abuse & Neglect*, *33*(6), 331–342.

Perez, C. M., & Widom, C. S. (1994). Childhood victimization and long-term intellectual and academic outcomes. *Child Abuse & Neglect*, *18*, 617–633.

Pérez, Z. J., & Hussey, H. (2014). *A hidden crisis: Including the LGBT community when addressing sexual violence on college campuses*. Washington, DC: Center for American Progress.

Pérez-Fuentes, G., Olfson, M., Villegas, L., Morcillo, C., Wang, S., & Blanco, C. (2013). Prevalence and correlates of child sexual abuse: A national study. *Comprehensive Psychiatry*, *54*(1), 16–27.

Perrin, R. D., & Miller-Perrin, C. (2011). Interpersonal violence as social construction: The potentially undermining role of claims-making and advocacy statistics. *Journal of Interpersonal Violence*, *26*, 3033–3049.

Petersilia, J. R. (2001). Crime victims with developmental disabilities: A review essay. *Criminal Justice and Behavior*, *28*, 655–694.

Peterson, C., Kearns, M. C., McIntosh, W. L., Estefan, L. F., Nicolaidis, C., McCallister, K. E., et al. (2018). Lifetime economic burden of intimate partner violence among U.S. adults. *American Journal of Preventive Medicine*, *55*(4), 433–444.

Petrenko, C. L. M., Culhane, S. E., Garrido, E. F., & Taussig, H. N. (2011). Do youth in out-of-home care receive recommended mental health and educational services following screening evaluations? *Children and Youth Services Review*, *33*, 1911–1918.

Petrenko, C. L., Friend, A., Garrido, E. F., Taussig, H. N., & Culhane, S. E. (2012). Does subtype matter? Assessing the effects of maltreatment on functioning in preadolescent youth in out-of-home care. *Child Abuse & Neglect*, *36*(9), 633–644.

Petruccelli, K., Davis, J., & Berman, T. (2019). Adverse childhood experiences and associated health outcomes: A systematic review and meta-analysis. *Child Abuse & Neglect*, *97*. Advance online publication. doi:10.1016/j.chiabu.2019.104127

Pettit, E. (2019, June 12). In plain sight: The killing of a student, one in a growing list of victims, opened her university's eyes to the unseen danger of intimate-partner violence. *Chronicle of Higher Education*.

Pfeifer, S. (2002, November 21). Tough love or abuse? *Los Angeles Times*, p. A1.

Pfeifer, S., & Anton, M. (2002, December 17). Parents' action not conspiracy, jury says. *Los Angeles Times*, p. B1.

Pharr, S. (1986). Two workshops on homophobia. In K. Lobel (Ed.), *Naming the violence: Speaking out about lesbian battering* (pp. 207–222). Seattle, WA: Seal.

Piers, M. W. (1978). *Infanticide: Past and present*. New York, NY: W. W. Norton.

Pillemer, K., & Finkelhor, D. (1988). The prevalence of elder abuse: A random sample survey. *The Gerontologist*, *28*, 51–57.

Pithers, W. D., Gray, A., Busconi, A., & Houchens, P. (1998). Children with sexual behavior problems: Identification of five distinct child types and related treatment considerations. *Child Maltreatment*, *3*(4), 384–406.

Pithers, W., & Kafka, M. (1990). Relapse prevention with sex aggressors: A method for maintaining therapeutic gain and enhancing external supervision. In W. L. Marshall, D. R. Laws, & H. E. Barbaree (Eds.), *Handbook of sexual assault: Issues, theories, and treatment of the offender* (pp. 343–361). New York, NY: Plenum.

Platt, L., Powers, L., Leotti, S., Hughes, R. B., Robinson-Whelen, S., Osburn, S., . . . Partnering With People With Disabilities to Address Violence Consortium. (2015). The role of gender in violence experienced by adults with disabilities. *Journal of Interpersonal Violence*. Advance online publication. doi:10.1177/0886260515585534

Pleck, E. (1987). *Domestic tyranny: The making of American social policy against family violence from colonial times to present*. New York, NY: Oxford University Press.

Plichta, S. B., & Falik, M. (2001). Prevalence of violence and its implications for women's health. *Women's Health Issues, 11*(3), 244–258.

Plummer, S., & Findley, P. A. (2012). Women with disabilities' experience with physical and sexual abuse: A review of the literature and implications for the field. *Trauma, Violence & Abuse, 13*(1), 15–29.

Polanin, J. R., Espelage, D. L., & Pigott, T. D. (2012). A meta-analysis of school-based bullying prevention programs' effects on bystander intervention behavior. *School Psychology Review, 41*(1), 47–65.

Polansky, N. A., Ammons, P. W., & Gaudin, J. M. (1985). Loneliness and isolation in child neglect. *Social Casework, 66*, 38–47.

Polansky, N. A., Ammons, P. W., & Weathersby, B. L. (1983). Is there an American standard of child care? *Social Work, 28*, 341–346.

Polansky, N. A., Chalmers, M. A., & Williams, D. P. (1987). Assessing adequacy of rearing: An urban scale. *Child Welfare, 57*, 439–448.

Polansky, N. A., Gaudin, J. M., Ammons, P. W., & Davis, K. B. (1985). The psychological ecology of the neglectful mother. *Child Abuse & Neglect, 9*, 265–275.

Polansky, N. A., Gaudin, J. M., & Kilpatrick, A. C. (1992). The maternal characteristics scale: A cross-validation. *Child Welfare League of America, 71*, 271–280.

Polansky, N. A., & Williams, D. P. (1978). Class orientation to child neglect. *Social Work, 23*, 397–401.

Pollio, E., Deblinger, E., & Runyon, M. K. (2011). Mental health treatment for the effects of child sexual abuse. In J. E. B. Myers (Ed.), *The APSAC handbook on child maltreatment* (3rd ed., pp. 267–288). Thousand Oaks, CA: Sage.

Pontes, L. B., Siqueira, A. C., & de Albuquerque Williams, L. C. (2019). A Systematic Literature Review of the ACT Raising Safe Kids Parenting Program. *Journal of Child and Family Studies*, 1–14.

Poole, D. A., & Wolfe, M. A. (2009). Child development: Normative sexual and nonsexual behaviors that may be confused with symptoms of sexual abuse. In K. Kuehnle & M. Connell (Eds.), *The evaluation of child sexual abuse allegations* (pp. 101–128). Hoboken, NJ: John Wiley & Sons.

Poole, J. C., Dobson, K. S., & Pusch, D. (2017). Anxiety among adults with a history of childhood adversity: Psychological resilience moderates the indirect effect of emotion dysregulation. *Journal of Affective Disorders, 217*, 144–152.

Poole, K. L., MacMillan, H. L., & Schmidt, L. A. (2019). Trajectories of resting heart period and shyness in adolescent females exposed to child maltreatment. *Child Maltreatment, 24*(4), 364–373.

Popova, S., Lange, S., Shield, K., Mihic, A., Chudley, A. E., Mukherjee, R. A. S., . . . Rehm, J. (2016). *Comorbidity of fetal alcohol spectrum disorder: A systematic review and meta-analysis*. Retrieved from http://www.sciencedirect.com/science/article/pii/S0140673615013458

Postmus, J. L. (2010). *Economic empowerment of domestic violence survivors*. Harrisburg, PA: National Resource Center on Domestic Violence. Retrieved from http://www.vawnet.org

Postmus, J. L., & Ortega, D. (2005). Serving two masters: When domestic violence and child abuse overlap. *Families in Society: The Journal of Contemporary Social Services, 86*(4), 483–490.

Potter, D., Nasserie, T., & Tonmyr, L. (2015). A review of recent analyses of the Canadian Incidence Study of Reported Child Abuse and Neglect (CIS). *Health Promotion and Chronic Disability Prevention in Canada, 35*(8/9), 119–129.

Powell, M. (2014, July 24). Suspended for abuse, then patted on the back. *New York Times*. Retrieved from https://www.nytimes.com/2014/07/25/sports/football/a-penalty-for-abuse-is-less-than-for-steroids-.html

Powers, L. E., Curry, M. A., Oschwald, M., & Maley, S. (2002). Barriers and strategies in addressing abuse: A survey of disabled women's experiences. *Journal of Rehabilitation, 68*, 4–13.

Preventing Sex Trafficking and Strengthening Families Act, H.R. 4980, 113th Cong. (2013).

Priebe, G., Mitchell, K. J., & Finkelhor, D. (2013). To tell or not to tell? Youth's responses to unwanted Internet experiences. *Cyberpsychology: Journal of Psychosocial Research on Cyberspace, 7*(1), article 6.

Prino, C. T., & Peyrot, M. (1994). The effect of child physical abuse and neglect on aggressive, withdrawn, and prosocial behavior. *Child Abuse & Neglect, 18*, 871–884.

Prinz, R. J. (2016). Parenting and family support within a broad child abuse prevention strategy: Child maltreatment prevention can benefit from public health strategies. *Child Abuse & Neglect, 51*, 400–406.

Prinz, R. J., Sanders, M. R., Shapiro, C. J., Whitaker, D. J., & Lutzer, J. R. (2009). Population-based prevention of child maltreatment: The U.S. Triple P System Population Trial. *Prevention Science, 10*, 1–12.

Ptacek, J. (2005). Guest editor's introduction. *Violence Against Women*, *11*(5), 564–570.

Putnam, K. T., Harris, W. W., & Putnam, F. W. (2013). Synergistic childhood adversities and complex adult psychopathology. *Journal of Traumatic Stress*, *26*(4), 435–442.

Putnam, R. D. (2000). *Bowling alone: The collapse and revival of American community*. New York, NY: Simon & Schuster.

Putnam-Hornstein, E. (2011). Report of maltreatment as a risk factor for injury death: A prospective birth cohort study. *Child Maltreatment*, *16*(3), 163–174.

Putnam-Hornstein, E., Cleves, M. A., Licht, R., & Needell, B. (2013). Risk of fatal injury in young children following abuse allegations: Evidence from a prospective, population-based study. *American Journal of Public Health*, *103*(10), e39–e44. doi:10.2105/ AJPH.2013.301516

Pynoos, R. S., Steinberg, A. M., Layne, C. M., Liang, L. J., Vivrette, R. L., Briggs, E. C., . . . Fairbank, J. A. (2014). Modeling constellations of trauma exposure in the National Child Traumatic Stress Network Core Data Set. *Psychological Trauma: Theory, Research, Practice, and Policy*, *6*(S1), S9.

Raby, K. I., Roisman, G. I., Labella, M. H., Martin, J., Fraley, R. C., & Simpson, J. A. (2019). The legacy of early abuse and neglect for social and academic competence from childhood to adulthood. *Child Development*, *90*(5), 1684–1701.

Rafferty, Y. (2013). Child trafficking and commercial sexual exploitation: A review of promising prevention policies and programs. *American Journal of Orthopsychiatry*, *83*(4), 559–575.

Raghavan, C., Mennerich, A., Sexton, E., & James, S. E. (2006). Community violence and its direct, indirect, and mediating effects on intimate partner violence. *Violence Against Women*, *12*, 1132–1149.

Rahman, A., Lovel, H., Bunn, J., Iqbal, Z., & Harrington, R. (2004). Mothers' mental health and infant growth: A case–control study from Rawalpindi, Pakistan. *Child: Care, Health and Development*, *30*(1), 21–27.

Raj, A., & Yore, J. B. (2018). Gender-based violence against immigrant and refugee women: Heightened vulnerabilities and barriers to help seeking. In C. M. Renzetti, J. L. Edleson, & R. K. Bergen (Eds.), *Sourcebook on violence against women* (3rd ed., pp. 135–139). Thousand Oaks, CA: Sage.

Rajan, M., & McCloskey, K. A. (2007). Victims of intimate partner violence: Arrest rates across recent

studies. *Journal of Aggression, Maltreatment, & Trauma*, *15*(3–4), 27–52.

Ramgopal, K. (2018, July 8). Death of Anthony Avalos has parallels to another child abuse case in L.A. *NBC News*. Retrieved from https://www.nbcnews.com/ news/us-news/death-anthony-avalos-has-parallels-another-child-abuse-case-l-n888991

Ramiro, L. S., Madrid, B. J., & Brown, D. W. (2010). Adverse childhood experiences (ACE) and health-risk behaviors among adults in a developing country setting. *Child Abuse & Neglect*, *34*(11), 842–855.

Rape, Abuse & Incest National Network. (2016). *Children and teens: Statistics*. Retrieved from https:// www.rainn.org/statistics/children-and-teens

Rebbe, R. (2018). What is neglect? State legal definitions in the United States. *The 2018 Research to Practice Brief Compendium* (pp. 27–28). Columbus, OH: American Professional Society on the Abuse of Children.

Reed, E., Wong, A., & Raj, A. (2019). Cyber sexual harassment: A summary of current measures and implications. *Violence Against Women*. Advance online publication. Retrieved from https://doi.org/10.1177/ 1077801219880959

Rehan, W., Antfolk, J., Johansson, A., & Santtila, P. (2019). Do single experiences of childhood abuse increase psychopathology symptoms in adulthood? *Journal of Interpersonal Violence*, *34*(5), 1021–1038.

Reid, J. A., & Jones, S. (2011). Exploited vulnerability: Legal and psychological perspectives on child sex trafficking victims. *Victims and Offenders*, *6*(207), 207–231.

Reilly, M. (2017, November 6). Anthony Weiner begins prison sentence for sexting a minor. *Huffington Post*.

Reiter, S., Bryen, D. N., & Shachar, I. (2007). Adolescents with intellectual disabilities as victims of abuse. *Journal of Intellectual Disabilities*, *11*(4), 371–387.

Renner, L. M., & Slack, K. S. (2006). Intimate partner violence and child maltreatment: Understanding intra- and intergenerational connections. *Child Abuse & Neglect*, *30*, 599–617.

Rennison, C. M. (2002). *Rape and sexual assault: Reporting to police and medical attention*. Washington, DC: U.S. Department of Justice, Bureau of Justice Statistics.

Rennison, C. M. (2018). Disadvantage as a catalyst for sexual victimization. In C. M. Renzetti, J. L. Edleson, & R. K. Bergen (Eds.), *Sourcebook on violence against women* (3rd ed., pp. 102–107). Thousand Oaks, CA: Sage.

Renzetti, C. M. (1989). Building a second closet: Third party responses to victims of lesbian partner abuse. *Family Relations*, *38*, 157–163.

Renzetti, C. M. (1992). *Violent betrayal: Partner abuse in lesbian relationships*. Newbury Park, CA: Sage.

Renzetti, C. M., & Follingstad, D. R. (2015). From blue to green: The development and implementation of a therapeutic horticulture program for residents of a battered women's shelter. *Violence and Victims*, *30*, 676–690.

Renzetti, C. M., Lynch, K. R., & DeWall, C. N. (2015). Ambivalent sexism, alcohol use, and intimate partner violence perpetration. *Journal of Interpersonal Violence*. Advance online publication. doi:0886260515604412

Renzetti, C. M., & Maier, S. L. (2002). "Private" crime in public housing: Violent victimization, fear of crime, and social isolation among women public housing residents. *Women's Health and Urban Life*, *1*, 46–65.

Renzetti, C. M., & Miley, C. H. (Eds.). (2014). *Violence in gay and lesbian domestic partnerships*. New York, NY: Routledge.

Reppucci, N. D., Land, D., & Haugaard, J. J. (1998). Child sexual abuse prevention programs that target young children. In P. K. Trickett & C. J. Schellenbach (Eds.), *Violence against children in the family and the community* (pp. 317–337). Washington, DC: American Psychological Association.

Reviere, S. L., Faber, E. W., Twomey, H., Okun, A., Jackson, E., Zanville, H., & Kaslow, N. J. (2007). Intimate partner violence and suicidality in low-income African American women: A multimethod assessment of coping factors. *Violence Against Women*, *13*, 1113–1129.

Reynolds, A. J., & Ou, S. (2003). Promoting resilience through early childhood intervention. In S. S. Luthar (Ed.), *Resilience and vulnerability: Adaptation in the context of childhood adversities* (pp. 436–459). New York, NY: Cambridge University Press.

Reynolds, A. J., & Robertson, D. L. (2003). School-based early intervention and later child maltreatment in the Chicago longitudinal study. *Child Development*, *74*(1), 3–26.

Rheingold, A. A., Zajac, K., Chapman, J. E., Patton, M., de Arellano, M., Saunders, B., & Kilpatrick, D. (2015). Child sexual abuse prevention training for childcare professionals: An independent multi-site randomized controlled trial of stewards of children. *Prevention Science*, *16*(3), 374–385.

Richards, K. (2011). Misperceptions about child sex offenders. *Trends and Issues in Crime and Criminal Justice*, *429*, 1–8.

Riese, J. (2016). *Youth who are bullied based upon perceptions about their sexual orientation*. Hazelden Foundation. Retrieved from http://www.violencepreventionworks.org/public/bullying_sexual_orientation.page

Riggs, D. S., O'Leary, K. D., & Breslin, F. C. (1990). Multiple correlates of physical aggression in dating couples. *Journal of Interpersonal Violence*, *5*, 61–73.

Riggs, S. A., Cusimano, A. M., & Benson, K. M. (2011). Childhood emotional abuse and attachment processes in the dyadic adjustment of dating couples. *Journal of Counseling Psychology*, *58*(1), 126–138. Retrieved from http://dx.doi.org/10.1037/a0021319

Riggs, S. A., & Kaminski, P. (2010). Childhood emotional abuse, adult attachment, and depression as predictors of relational adjustment and psychological aggression. *Journal of Aggression, Maltreatment & Trauma*, *19*(1), 75–104. Retrieved from http://dx.doi.org/10.1080/10926770903475976

Ristock, J. (2002). *No more secrets: Violence in lesbian relationships*. London, England: Taylor & Francis.

Robers, S., Zhang, J., Truman, J., U.S. Department of Justice, & National Center for Education Statistics. (2012). *Indicators of school crime and safety: 2011*. Washington, DC: National Center for Education Statistics.

Robert, C. E., & Thompson, D. P. (2019). Educator sexual misconduct and Texas educator discipline database construction. *Journal of Child Sexual Abuse*, *28*(1).

Roberts, A. L., Koenen, K. C., Lyall, K., Robinson, E. B., & Weisskopf, M. G. (2015). Association of autistic traits in adulthood with childhood abuse, interpersonal victimization, and posttraumatic stress. *Child Abuse & Neglect*, *45*, 135–142.

Robinson-Whelen, S., Hughes, R. B., Gabrielli, J., Lund, E. M., Abramson, W., & Swank, P. R. (2014). A safety awareness program for women with diverse disabilities: A randomized controlled trial. *Violence Against Women*, *20*(7), 846–868.

Rodríguez, M. A., Wallace, S. P., Woolf, N. H., & Mangione, C. M. (2006). Mandatory reporting of elder abuse: Between a rock and a hard place. *The Annals of Family Medicine*, *4*(5), 403–409.

Roffman, R. A., Edleson, J. L., Neighbors, C., Mbilinyi, L., & Walker, D. (2008). The men's domestic abuse check-up: A protocol for reaching nonadjudicated and untreated man who batters and who abuses substances. *Violence Against Women, 14*, 589–605.

Rogosch, F., Cicchetti, D., & Abre, J. L. (1995). The role of child maltreatment in early deviations in cognitive and affective processing abilities and later peer relationships problems. *Development and Psychopathology, 7*, 591–609.

Romano, E., Moorman, J., Ressel, M., & Lyons, J. (2019). Men with childhood sexual abuse histories: Disclosure experiences and links with mental health. *Child Abuse & Neglect, 89*, 212–224.

Rosen, D. (2004). "I just let him have his way": Partner violence in the lives of low-income, teenage mothers. *Violence Against Women, 10*, 6–28.

Rosen, L. N., Kaminski, R. J., Parmely, A. M., Knudson, K. H., & Fancher, P. (2003). The effects of peer group climate on intimate partner violence among married male U.S. army soldiers. *Violence Against Women, 9*(9), 1045–1071.

Rosenbaum, A. (1988). Methodological issues in marital violence research. *Journal of Family Violence, 3*, 91–104.

Rosenthal, L., & McDonald, S. (2003). Seeking justice: A review of the second report of the Defense Task Force on Domestic Violence. *Violence Against Women, 9*(9), 1153–1161.

Rothman, F., & Corso, P. S. (2008). Propensity for intimate partner abuse and workplace productivity: Why employers should care. *Violence Against Women, 14*, 1054–1064.

Rouse, H., & Fantuzzo, J. W. (2009). Multiple risks and educational well being: A population-based investigation of threats to early school success. *Early Childhood Research Quarterly, 24*, 1–14.

Rudolph, J., & Zimmer-Gembeck, M. J. (2018). Reviewing the focus: A summary and critique of child-focused sexual abuse prevention. *Trauma, Violence, & Abuse, 19*(5), 543–554.

Ruggiero, K. J., McLeer, S. V., & Dixon, J. F. (2000). Sexual abuse characteristics associated with survivor psychopathology. *Child Abuse & Neglect, 24*, 951–964.

Ruiz-Perez, I., Pastor-Moreno, G., Escriba-Aguir, V., & Maroto-Navarro, G. (2018). Intimate partner violence in women with disabilities: Perceptions of healthcare and attitudes of health professionals. *Disability and Rehabilitation, 40*(9), 1059–1065.

Runyon, M. K., Deblinger, E., & Steer, R. A. (2010). Group cognitive behavioural treatment for parents and children at-risk for physical abuse: An initial study. *Child and Family Behavior Therapy, 32*(3), 196–218.

Runyon, M. K., Deblinger, E., & Steer, R. A. (2014). PTSD symptom cluster profiles of youth who have experienced sexual or physical abuse. *Child Abuse & Neglect, 38*(1), 84–90.

Runyon, M. K., & Urquiza, A. J. (2011). Interventions for parents who engage in coercive parenting practices and their children. In J. E. B. Myers (Ed.), *The APSAC handbook on child maltreatment* (3rd ed., pp. 195–212). Thousand Oaks, CA: Sage.

Russell, D. E. H. (1982). *Rape in marriage*. Bloomington, IN: Macmillan.

Russell, D. E. H. (1984). *Sexual exploitation: Rape, child sexual abuse, and workplace harassment*. Beverly Hills, CA: Sage.

Russell, D. E. H., & Bolen, R. M. (2000). *The epidemic of rape and child sexual abuse in the United States*. Thousand Oaks, CA: Sage.

Rutenberg, J., Abrams, R., & Ryzik, M. (2017, October 16). Harvey Weinstein's fall opens the floodgates in Hollywood. *New York Times*. Retrieved from https://www.nytimes.com/2017/10/16/business/media/harvey-weinsteins-fall-opens-the-floodgates-in-hollywood.html

Sabina, C., & Straus, M. A. (2008). Polyvictimization by dating partners and mental health among US college students. *Violence and Victims, 23*(6), 667–682.

Sachs-Ericsson, N., Gayman, M. D., Kendall-Tackett, K., Lloyd, D. A., Medley, A., Collins, N., . . . Sawyer, K. (2010). The long-term impact of childhood abuse on internalizing disorders among older adults: The moderating role of self-esteem. *Aging & Mental Health, 14*(4), 489–501.

Sama-Miller, E., Akers, L., Mraz-Esposito, A., Avellar, S., Paulsell, D., and Del Grosso, P. (2016). *Home visiting evidence of effectiveness review: Executive summary*. Office of Planning, Research and Evaluation, Administration for Children and Families, U.S. Department of Health and Human Services. Washington, DC.

Sampson, R. J., Raudenbush, S. W., & Earls, F. (1997). Neighborhoods and violent crime: A multilevel study of collective efficacy. *Science, 277*, 918–924.

Sanders, M. R., Pidgeon, A. M., Gravestock, F., Connors, M. D., Brown S., & Young, R. W. (2004). Does parental attributional retraining and anger management enhance the effects of the Triple P—Positive Parenting

Program with parents at risk of child maltreatment? *Behavior Therapy*, *35*, 513–535.

Sanders, M. R., & Prinz, R. J. (2012). Child maltreatment prevention through positive parenting. In H. Dubowitz (Ed.), *World perspectives on child abuse* (10th ed., pp. 113–119). Aurora, CO: International Society for Prevention of Child Abuse and Neglect.

Saunders, B. E. (2012). Determining best practice for treating sexually victimized children. In P. Goodyear-Brown (Ed.), *Handbook of child sexual abuse: Identification, assessment, and treatment* (pp. 173–197). Hoboken, NJ: John Wiley & Sons.

Saunders, B. E., Kilpatrick, D. G., Hanson, R. F., Resnick, H. S., & Walker, M. E. (1999). Prevalence, case characteristics, and long-term psychological correlates of child rape among women: A national survey. *Child Maltreatment*, *4*, 187–200. doi:10.1177/107755959 9004003001

Saunders, D. G., Faller, K. C., & Tolman, R. M. (2016). Beliefs and recommendations regarding child custody and visitation in cases involving domestic violence. *Violence Against Women*, *22*, 722–744.

Sawle, G. A., & Kear-Colwell, J. (2001). Adult attachment style and pedophilia: A developmental perspective. *International Journal of Offender Therapy and Comparative Criminology*, *45*(1), 32–50.

Sawyer, M. G., Arney, F. M., Baghurst, P. A., Clark, J. J., Graetz, B. W., Kosky, R. J., . . . Zubrick, S. R. (2000). The *mental health of young people in Australia*. Canberra, Australia: Mental Health and Special Programs Branch, Commonwealth Department of Health and Aged Care.

Saxton, M., Curry, M. A., Powers, L. E., Maley, S., Eckels, K., & Gross, J. (2001). "Bring my scooter so I can leave you": A study of disabled women handling abuse by personal assistance providers. *Violence Against Women*, *7*, 393–417.

Scannapieco, M., & Connell-Carrick, K. (2002). Focus on the first years: An eco-developmental assessment of child neglect for children 0 to 3 years of age. *Children and Youth Services Review*, *24*, 601–621.

Scarduzio, J. A., Sheff, S. E., & Smith, M. (2018). Coping and sexual harassment: How victims cope across multiple settings. *Archives of Sexual Behavior*, *47*(2), 327–340.

Schaefer, C. (1997). Defining verbal abuse of children: A survey. *Psychological Reports*, *80*, 626.

Schechter, S. (1982). *Women and male violence*. Boston, MA: South End Press.

Schelbe, L., Radey, M., & Panisch, L. S. (2017). Satisfactions and stressors experienced by recently-hired frontline child welfare workers. *Children and Youth Services Review*, *78*, 56–63.

Schiffer, B., Peschel, T., Paul, T., Gizewski, E., Forsting, M., Leygraf, N., . . . & Krueger, T. H. (2007). Structural brain abnormalities in the frontostriatal system and cerebellum in pedophilia. *Journal of Psychiatric Research*, *41*(9), 753–762.

Schneider, M. W., Ross, A., Graham, J. C., & Zielinski, A. (2005). Do allegations of emotional maltreatment predict developmental outcomes beyond that of other forms of maltreatment? *Child Abuse & Neglect*, *29*, 513–532.

Schneiderman, J. U., Negriff, S., & Trickett, P. K. (2016). Self-report of health problems and health care use among maltreated and comparison adolescents. *Children and Youth Services Review*, *61*, 1–5.

Schober, D. J., Fawcett, S. B., & Bernier, J. (2012). The Enough Abuse Campaign: Building the movement to prevent child sexual abuse in Massachusetts. *Journal of Child Sexual Abuse*, *21*(4), 456–469. doi:10.1080/105 38712.2012.675423

Schober, D. J., Fawcett, S. B., Thigpen, S., Curtis, A., & Wright, R. (2012). An empirical case study of a child sexual abuse prevention initiative in Georgia. *Health Education Journal*, *71*(3), 291–298. doi:10.1177/0017896911430546

Schofield, T. J., Lee, R. D., & Merrick, M. T. (2013). Safe, stable, nurturing relationships as a moderator of intergenerational continuity of child maltreatment: A meta-analysis. *Journal of Adolescent Health*, *53*(4), S32–S38.

Schols, M. W., De Ruiter, C., & Öry, F. G. (2013). How do public child healthcare professionals and primary school teachers identify and handle child abuse cases? A qualitative study. *BMC Public Health*, *13*(1), 807.

Schroedel, J. R., & Fiber, P. (2001). Punitive versus public health oriented responses to drug use by pregnant women. *Yale Journal of Health Policy, Law, and Ethics*, *1*, 217–235.

Scott, J. C., & Pinderhughes, E. E. (2019). Distinguishing between demographic and contextual factors linked to early childhood physical discipline and physical maltreatment among Black families. *Child Abuse & Neglect*, *94*. Advance online publication. doi:10.1016/j .chiabu.2019.05.013

Sechrist, S. M., & Weil, J. D. (2018). Assessing the impact of a focused deterrence strategy to combat intimate partner domestic violence. *Violence Against Women*, *24*(3), 243–265.

Sedlak, A. J. (1990). *Technical amendment to the study findings: National incidence and prevalence of child abuse and neglect: 1988*. Rockville, MD: Westat.

Sedlak, A. J., & Broadhurst, D. D. (1996). *Third National Incidence Study on Child Abuse and Neglect*. Washington, DC: U.S. Department of Health and Human Services.

Sedlak, A. J., Finkelhor, D., Hammer, H., & Schultz, D. J. (2002). *National estimates of missing children: An overview*. OJJDP NISMART Bulletin Series. Washington, DC: U.S. Department of Justice, Office of Justice Programs, Office of Juvenile Justice and Delinquency Prevention, NCJ 196465.

Sedlak, A. J., Mettenburg, J., Basena, M., Petta, I., McPherson, K., Greene, A., & Li, S. (2010). *Fourth National Incidence Study of Child Abuse and Neglect (NIS-4): Report to Congress*. Washington, DC: U.S. Department of Health and Human Services, Administration for Children and Families.

Sege, R., Bethell, C., Linkenbach, J., Jones, J., Klika, B., & Pecora, P. J. (2018). *Balancing adverse childhood experiences with HOPE: New insights into the role of positive experience on child and family development*. Boston, MA: The Medical Foundation.

Seidman, I., & Pokorak, J. J. (2011). Justice responses to sexual violence. In M. P. Koss, J. W. White, & A. E. Kazdin (Eds.), *Violence against women and children* (Vol. 2, pp. 137–158). Washington, DC: American Psychological Association.

Semin, J. N., Skrundevskiy-Coburn, A., Smith, L. M., & Rajaram, S. S. (2019). Understanding the needs and preferences of domestic and sexual violence education for professional health students. *Violence Against Women*. Advance online publication. Retrieved from https://doi.org/10.1177/1077801219890420

Seneca Falls Convention. (1848). *Seneca Falls Convention Declaration of Sentiments*. Retrieved from http://www.milestonedocuments.com/documents/view/seneca-falls-convention-declaration-of-sentiments/text

Serrata, J., & Hurtado, M. G. (2019). *Understanding the impact of Hurricane Harvey on family violence survivors in Texas and those who serve them*. Texas Council on Family Violence. Retrieved from https://tcfv.org/wp-content/uploads/2019/08/Hurricane-Harvey-Report-FINAL-and-APPROVED-as-of-060619.pdf

Seto, M. (2008). *Pedophilia and sexual offending against children: Theory, assessment, and intervention*. Washington, DC: American Psychological Association.

Seto, M. C., Hanson, R. K., & Babchishin, K. M. (2011). Contact sexual offending by men arrested for child pornography offenses. *Sexual Abuse: A Journal of Research and Treatment*, *23*(1), 124–145.

Seto, M. C., & Lalumière, M. L. (2010). What is so special about male adolescent sexual offending? A review and test of explanations through meta-analysis. *Psychological Bulletin*, *136*(4), 526–575. doi:10.1037/a0019700

Shah, S., Tsitsou, L., & Woodin, S. (2016). Hidden voices: Disabled women's experiences of violence and support over the life course. *Violence Against Women*, *22*(10), 1189–1210.

Shankaran, S., Lester, B. M., Das, A., Bauer, C. R., Bada, H. S., Lagasse, L., & Higgins, R. (2007). Impact of maternal substance use during pregnancy on childhood outcome. *Seminars in Fetal & Neonatal Medicine*, *12*(2), 143–150. doi:10.1016/j.siny.2007.01.002. Retrieved from www.sciencedirect.com/science/article/pii/S1744165X07000029#

Shared Hope International. (2009). *The national report on domestic minor sex trafficking: America's prostituted children*. Vancouver, WA: Shared Hope International.

Shepard, C. F. (2019). The neurological impact of witnessing intimate partner violence during early childhood. *Virginia Child Protection Newsletter*, *115*, 9–10.

Sherman, L. W., & Berk, R. A. (1984). The specific deterrent effects of arrest for domestic violence. *American Sociological Review*, *49*(2), 261–272.

Sherman, L. W., Schmidt, J. D., Rogan, D. P., Smith, D. A., Gartin, P. R., Cohn, E. G., et al. (1992). The variable effects of arrest in criminal careers: The Milwaukee Domestic Violence Experiment. *Journal of Criminal Law and Criminology*, *83*(1), 137–169.

Shimada, K., Kasaba, R., Yao, A., & Tomoda, A. (2019). Less efficient detection of positive facial expressions in parents at risk of engaging in child physical abuse. *BMC Psychology*, *7*(1), 56.

Shin, S. H., Lee, S., Jeon, S. M., & Wills, T. A. (2015). Childhood emotional abuse, negative emotion-driven impulsivity, and alcohol use in young adulthood. *Child Abuse & Neglect*, *50*, 94–103.

Shor, R. (2000). Child maltreatment: Differences in perceptions between parents in low income and middle income neighbourhoods. *British Journal of Social Work*, *30*, 165–178.

Shpiegel, S., Simmel, C., & Huang, C. C. (2013). Emotional maltreatment reports in children: The influence of state statutes and co-occurring maltreatment. *Journal of Aggression, Maltreatment & Trauma, 22*(6), 626–643.

Silovsky, J. F., Bard, D., Chaffin, M., Hecht, D., Burris, L., Owora, A., . . . Lutzker, J. (2011). Prevention of child maltreatment in high-risk rural families: A randomized clinical trial with child welfare outcomes. *Children and Youth Services Review, 33*(8), 1435–1444.

Silovsky, J. F., & Niec, L. (2002). Characteristics of young children with sexual behavior problems: A pilot study. *Child Maltreatment, 7*(3), 187–197.

Silva, C. S., & Calheiros, M. M. (2020). Maltreatment experiences and psychopathology in children and adolescents: The intervening role of domain-specific self-representations moderated by age. *Child Abuse & Neglect, 99*. Advance online publication. doi:10.1016/j.chiabu.2019.104255

Silva, J. (2009). *Parents Raising Safe Kids: ACT 8-Week Program for Parents.* Washington, DC: American Psychological Association.

Silva-Martinez, E. (2016). "El silencio": Conceptualizations of Latina immigrant survivors of intimate partner violence in the Midwest of the United States. *Violence Against Women, 22*, 523–544.

Silverman, W. K., Ortiz, C. D., Viswesvaran, C., Burns, B. J., Kolko, D. J., Putnam, F. W., et al. (2008). Evidenced-based psychosocial treatments for children and adolescents exposed to traumatic events. *Journal of Clinical Child and Adolescent Psychology, 37*(1), 156–183.

Simmel, C., & Shpiegel, S. (2013). Describing the context and nature of emotional maltreatment reports in children. *Children and Youth Services Review, 35*(4), 626–633.

Simmons, C. A., Craun, S. W., Farrar, M., & Ray, R. (2016). Differences and similarities in mother and child reports about IPV risks: Concordance is likely but cannot be assumed. *Violence Against Women.* Advance online publication. doi:10.1177/1077801216663656

Simon, T. R., Anderson, M., Thompson, M. P., Crosby, A. E., Shelley, G., & Sacks, J. J. (2001). Attitudinal acceptance of intimate partner violence among US adults. *Violence and Victims, 16*(2), 115–126.

Simon, T. R., Shattuck, A., Kacha-Ochana, A., David-Ferdon, C. F., Hamby, S., Henly, M., . . . Finkelor, D. (2018). Injuries from physical abuse: National Survey of Children's Exposure to Violence I–III. *American Journal of Preventive Medicine, 54*(1), 129–132.

Simons, D. A., Wurtele, S. K., & Durham, R. L. (2008). Developmental experiences of child sexual abusers and rapists. *Child Abuse & Neglect, 32*, 549–560. doi:10.1016/j.chiabu.2007.03.027

Slack, K. S., Berger, L. M., DuMont, K., Yang, M.-Y., Kim, B., Ehrhard-Dietzel, S., & Holl, J. L. (2011). Risk and protective factors for child neglect during early childhood: A cross-study comparison. *Children and Youth Services Review, 33*, 1354–1363.

Slack, K. S., Holl, J., Altenbernd, L., McDaniel, M., & Stevens, A. B. (2003). Improving the measurement of child neglect for survey research: Issues and recommendations. *Child Maltreatment, 8*, 98–111.

Slack, K. S., Holl, J. L., McDaniel, M., Yoo, J., & Bolger, K. (2004). Understanding the risks of child neglect: An exploration of poverty and parenting characteristics. *Child Maltreatment, 9*(4), 395–408.

Slopen, N., Chen, Y., Guida, J. L., Albert, M. A., & Williams, D. R. (2017). Positive childhood experiences and ideal cardiovascular health in midlife: Associations and mediators. *Preventive Medicine, 97*, 72–79.

Smallbone, S. W., Marshall, W. L., & Wortley, R. (2008). Explaining child sexual abuse: A new integrated theory. *Preventing Child Sexual Abuse: Evidence, Policy and Practice*, 21–45.

Smith, B. E. (1995). *Prosecuting child physical abuse cases: A case study in San Diego.* Washington, DC: U.S. Department of Justice, Office of Justice Programs, National Institute of Justice.

Smith, M. D. (1987). The incidence and prevalence of woman abuse in Toronto. *Violence and Victims, 2*, 173–187.

Smith, M., & Fong, R. (2004). *Children of neglect: When no one cares.* New York, NY: Brunner-Routledge.

Smith, N., & Harrell, S. (2013). *Sexual abuse of children with disabilities: A national snapshot.* Center on Victimization and Safety, Vera Institute of Justice. Retrieved from http://tinyurl.com/15jw928

Smith, P. H., White, J. W., & Holland, L. J. (2003). A longitudinal perspective on dating violence among adolescent and college-age women. *American Journal of Public Health, 93*(7), 1104–1109.

Smith, S. G., Fowler, K. A., & Niolon, P. H. (2014). Intimate partner homicide and corollary victims in 16 states: National Violent Death Reporting System, 2003–2009. *American Journal of Public Health, 104*(3), 461–466.

Smith, S. G., Zhang, X., Basile, K. C., Merrick, M. T., Wang, J., Kresnow, M., & Chen, J. (2018). *The National*

Intimate Partner and Sexual Violence Survey (NISVS): 2015 Data Brief—Updated Release. Atlanta, GA: National Center for Injury Prevention and Control, Centers for Disease Control and Prevention.

Smith, T., Davern, M., Freese, J., & Morgan, S. L. (2019). *General Social Survey, 1972–2018*. NORC at the University of Chicago. Retrieved from http://gss.norc.org/

Smokowski, P. R., & Evans, C. B. R. (2019). Playground politics at home: Child maltreatment and sibling violence. In *Bullying and victimization across the lifespan* (pp. 123–150). Retrieved from https://doi.org/10.1007/978-3-030-20293-4_6

Smolak, L., & Murnen, S. K. (2002). A meta-analytic examination of the relationship between child sexual abuse and eating disorders. *International Journal of Eating Disorders, 31*, 136–150.

Sorenson, S. B. (2017). Guns in intimate partner violence: Comparing incidents by type of weapon. *Journal of Women's Health, 26*(3). Retrieved from https://doi.org/10.1089/jwh.2016.5832

Sousa, C., Mason, W. A., Herrenkohl, T. I., Prince, D., Herrenkohl, R. C., & Russo, M. J. (2018). Direct and indirect effects of child abuse and environmental stress: A lifecourse perspective on adversity and depressive symptoms. *American Journal of Orthopsychiatry, 88*(2), 180.

Spangaro, J., Koziol-McLain, J., Rutherford, A., & Zwi, A. B. (2019). "Made me feel connected". A qualitative comparative analysis of intimate partner violence routine screening pathways to impact. *Violence Against Women*. Advance online publication. Retrieved from https://doi.org/10.1177/1077801219830250

Sparrow, K., Dickson, H., Kwan, J., Howard, L., Fear, N., & MacManus, D. (2018). Prevalence of self-reported intimate partner violence victimization among military personnel: A systematic review and meta-analysis. *Trauma, Violence & Abuse*. Retrieved from https://doi.org/10.1177/1524838018782206

Spataro, J., Mullen, P. E., Burgess, P. M., Wells, D. L., & Moss, S. A. (2004). Impact of child sexual abuse on mental health: Prospective study in males and females. *British Journal of Psychiatry, 184*(5), 416–421.

Speckhardt, R. (2011). The religious sex abuse epidemic. *Huffington Post*. Retrieved from http://www.huffingtonpost.com/roy-speckhardt/religious-sex-abuse-epidemic_b_1008805.html

Spector, M., & Kitsuse, J. I. (1977). *Constructing social problems*. Menlo Park, CA: Benjamin Cummings.

Spinazzola, J., Hodgdon, H., Liang, L. J., Ford, J. D., Layne, C. M., Pynoos, R., . . . Kisiel, C. (2014). Unseen wounds: The contribution of psychological maltreatment to child and adolescent mental health and risk outcomes. *Psychological Trauma: Theory, Research, Practice, and Policy, 6*(S1), S18.

Spitzberg, B. H. (2002). The tactical topography of stalking victimization and management. *Trauma, 3*, 261–288.

Spohn, C., & Tellis, K. (2012). The criminal justice system's response to sexual violence. *Violence Against Women, 18*(2), 169–192.

Sprague, S., Goslings, J. C., Hogentonen, C., de Milliano, S., Simunovic, N., Madden, K., & Bhandari, M. (2014). Prevalence of intimate partner violence across medical and surgical health care settings: A systematic review. *Violence Against Women, 20*, 118–136.

Sroufe, L. A., Egeland, B., Carlson, E. A., & Collins, A. (2005). *The development of the person: The Minnesota study of risk and adaptation from birth to adulthood*. New York, NY: Guilford.

Stampfel, C. C., Chapman, D. A., & Alvarez, A. E. (2010). Intimate partner violence and posttraumatic stress disorder among high-risk women: Does pregnancy matter? *Violence Against Women, 16*, 426–443.

Stannard, S., Hall, S., & Young, J. (1998). Social marketing as a tool to stop child abuse. *Social Marketing Quarterly, 4*(4), 64–68.

Stark, E. (2009). *Coercive control: How men entrap women in personal life*. New York, NY: Oxford University Press.

Stein, N., & Mennemeier, K. (2011). *Addressing the gendered dimensions of harassment and bullying: What domestic and sexual violence advocates need to know*. Washington, DC: National Resource Center on Domestic Violence & National Sexual Violence Resource Center.

Steine, I. M., Skogen, J. C., Krystal, J. H., Winje, D., Milde, A. M., Grønli, J., . . . Pallesen, S. (2019). Insomnia symptom trajectories among adult survivors of childhood sexual abuse: A longitudinal study. *Child Abuse & Neglect, 93*, 263–276.

Steinmetz, S. K. (1987). Family violence: Past, present, and future. In M. B. Sussman & S. K. Steinmetz (Eds.), *Handbook of marriage and the family* (pp. 725–765). New York, NY: Plenum.

Stermac, L., del Bove, G., & Addison, M. (2001). Violence, injury, and presentation patterns in spousal sexual assaults. *Violence Against Women, 7*(11), 1218–1233.

Sterzing, P. R., Gartner, R. E., Goldbach, J. T., McGeough, B. L., Ratliff, G. A., & Johnson, K. C. (2019). Polyvictimization rates for sexual and gender minority adolescents: Breaking down the silos of victimization research. *Psychology of Violence*, 9(4), 419–430.

Stevens, N. R., Gerhart, J., Goldsmith, R. E., Heath, N. M., Chesney, S. A., & Hobfoll, S. E. (2013). Emotion regulation difficulties, low social support, and interpersonal violence mediate the link between childhood abuse and posttraumatic stress symptoms. *Behavior Therapy*, 44, 152–161.

Stewart, J. B. (2019, August 12). The day Jeffrey Epstein told me he had dirt on powerful people. *New York Times*. Retrieved from https://www.nytimes.com/2019/08/12/business/jeffrey-epstein-interview.html

Stith, S. M., Liu, T., Davies, L. C., Boykin, E. L., Alder, M. C., Harris, J. M., . . . Dees, J. E. M. E. G. (2009). Risk factors in child maltreatment: A meta-analytic review of the literature. *Aggression and Violent Behavior*, 14(1), 13–29.

Stone, S. (2007). Child maltreatment, out-of-home placement and academic vulnerability: A fifteen-year review of evidence and future directions. *Children and Youth Services Review*, 29, 139–161.

Stop Exploitation Through Trafficking Act of 2013, S. 1733, 113th Congress (2013).

Stop It Now! (2010). *What do U.S. adults think about child sexual abuse? Measures of knowledge and attitudes among six states*. Retrieved from http://www.StopItNow.org/rdd_survey_reportfrt

Storer, H. L., Casey, E., & Herrenkohl, T. (2016). Efficacy of bystander programs to prevent dating abuse among youth and young adults: A review of the literature. *Trauma, Violence, & Abuse*, 17(3), 256–269.

Stover, C. S., Rainey, A. M., Berkman, M., & Marans, S. (2008). Factors associated with engagement in a police-advocacy home-visit intervention to prevent domestic violence. *Violence Against Women*, 14, 1430–1450.

Straus, M. A. (1979). Measuring intrafamily conflict and violence: The Conflict Tactics (CT) Scales. *Journal of Marriage and the Family*, 41(1), 75–88.

Straus, M. A. (1994). *Beating the devil out of them: Corporal punishment in American families*. Lexington, MA: Lexington Books.

Straus, M. A. (2007). Processes explaining the concealment and distortion of evidence on gender symmetry in partner violence. *European Journal on Criminal Policy*, 13, 227–232.

Straus, M. A., Douglas, E. M., & Medeiros, R. A. (2014). *The primordial violence: Spanking children, psychological development, violence, and crime*. New York, NY: Routledge.

Straus, M. A., & Gelles, R. J. (1986). Societal change and change in family violence from 1975 to 1985 as revealed by two national surveys. *Journal of Marriage and the Family*, 465–479.

Straus, M. A., & Gelles, R. J. (Eds.). (1990). *Physical violence in American families: Risk factors and adaptations to violence in 8,145 families*. New Brunswick, NJ: Transaction.

Straus, M. A., Gelles, R. J., & Steinmetz, S. K. (1980). *Behind closed doors: Violence in the American family*. Garden City, NY: Doubleday.

Straus, M. A., Hamby, S. L., Boney-McCoy, S., & Sugarman, D. B. (1996). The Revised Conflict Tactics Scales (CTS2): Development and preliminary psychometric data. *Journal of Family Issues*, 17(3), 283–316.

Straus, M. A., Hamby, S. L., Finkelhor, D., Moore, D. W., & Runyan, D. (1998). Identification of child maltreatment with the Parent–Child Conflict Tactics Scales: Development and psychometric data for a national sample of American parents. *Child Abuse & Neglect*, 22, 249–270.

Strickland, S. M. (2008). Female sex offenders: Exploring issues of personality, trauma, and cognitive distortions. *Journal of Interpersonal Violence*, 23(4), 474–489. doi:10.1177/0886260507312944

Stroem, I. F., Aakvaag, H. F., & Wentzel-Larsen, T. (2019). Characteristics of different types of childhood violence and the risk of revictimization. *Violence Against Women*, 25(14), 1696–1716.

Stronach, E. P., Toth, S. L., Rogosch, F., & Cicchetti, D. (2013). Preventive interventions and sustained attachment security in maltreated children. *Development and Psychopathology*, 25(4, Pt. 1), 919–930.

Strouse, P. J. (2018). Shaken baby syndrome is real. *Pediatric Radiology*, 48, 1043–1047.

Stuart, G. L., Meehan, J. C., Moore, T. M., Morean, M., Hellmuth, J., & Follansbee, K. (2006). Examining a conceptual framework of intimate partner violence in men and women arrested for domestic violence. *Journal of Studies on Alcohol*, 67, 102–112.

Studer, M. (1984). Wife-beating as a social problem: The process of definition. *International Journal of Women's Studies*, 7, 412–422.

Sturtz, R. (2014, December). *Unprotected*. Retrieved from https://www.outsideonline.com/o/outdoor-adventure/

water-activities/swimming/The-Sex-Abuse-Scandal-Plaguing-USA-Swimming.html

Substance Abuse and Mental Health Services Administration. (2014). *Results from the 2013 National Survey on Drug Use and Health: Summary of National Findings*, NSDUH Series H-48, HHS Publication No. (SMA) 14-4863. Rockville, MD: Substance Abuse and Mental Health Services Administration.

Sugaya, L., Hasin, D. S., Olfson, M., Lin, K. H., Grant, B. F., & Blanco, C. (2012). Child physical abuse and adult mental health: A national study. *Journal of Traumatic Stress, 25*(4), 384–392.

Sullivan, C. M. (2011). Victim services for domestic violence. In M. P. Koss, J. W. White, & A. E. Kazdin (Eds.), *Violence against women and children: Navigating solutions* (pp. 183–197). Washington, DC: American Psychological Association.

Sullivan, C. M., O'Halloran, S., & Lyon, E. (2008, September). *What women wanted and what they received from shelter: Findings from the United States and Ireland.* Paper presented at the First World Congress of Women's Shelters, Edmonton, Alberta, Canada.

Sutter, M. E., Rabinovitch, A. E., Trujillo, M. A., Perrin, P. B., Goldberg, L. D., Coster, B. M., & Calton, J. M. (2019). Patterns of intimate partner violence victimization and perpetration among sexual minority women: A latent class analysis. *Violence Against Women, 25*(5), 572–592.

Sutton, T. E., Simons, L. G., Martin, B. T., Klopack, E. T., Gibbons, F. X., Beach, S. R. H., & Simons, R. L. (2020). Racial discrimination as a risk factor for African American men's physical partner violence: A longitudinal test of mediators and moderators. *Violence Against Women, 26*(2), 164–190.

Svoboda, S. J., Adler, P. W., & Van Howe, R. S. (2019). Is circumcision unethical and unlawful? A response to Morris et al. *Journal of Medical Law and Ethics, 7*(1), 72–92.

Swahn, M. H., Simon, T. R., Arias, I., & Bossarte, R. M. (2008). Measuring sex differences in violence victimization and perpetration within date and same-sex relationships. *Journal of Interpersonal Violence, 23*, 1120–1138.

Swailes, A. L., Lehman, E. B., & McCall-Hosenfield, J. S. (2017). Intimate partner violence discussion in the healthcare setting: A cross-sectional study. *Preventive Medicine Reports, 8*, 215–220.

Swartz, M. K. (2014). Commercial sexual exploitation of minors: Overlooked and underreported. *Journal of Pediatric Health Care, 28*(3), 195–196.

Sweet, M., & Appelbaum, M. (2004). Is home visiting an effective strategy? A meta-analytic review of home visiting programs for families with young children. *Child Development, 75*, 1435–1456.

Swenson, C. C., & Chaffin, M. (2006). Beyond psychotherapy: Treating abused children by changing their social ecology. *Aggression and Violent Behavior, 11*, 120–137.

Swenson, C. C., & Kolko, D. J. (2000). Long-term management of the developmental consequences of child physical abuse. In R. M. Reece (Ed.), *Treatment of child abuse: Common ground for mental health, medical, and legal practitioners* (pp. 135–154). Baltimore, MD: Johns Hopkins University Press.

Swenson, C. C., Penman, J., Henggeler, S. W., & Rowland, M. D. (2010). *Multisystemic therapy for child abuse and neglect.* Charleston, SC: Family Services Research Center, MUSC.

Swim, J. K., Aikin, K. J., Hall, S., & Hunter, B. A. (1995). Sexism and racism: Old-fashioned and modern prejudices. *Journal of Personality and Social Psychology, 68*, 199–214.

Tabachnick, J. (2003). STOP IT NOW! An innovative social marketing campaign targeting sexual abusers and the people who know abusers. *Social Marketing Quarterly, 9*(1), 42–47.

Taft, C. T., Pless, A. P., Stalans, L. J., Koenen, K. C., King, L. A., & King, D. W. (2005). Risk factors for partner violence among a national sample of combat veterans. *Journal of Consulting and Clinical Psychology, 73*(1), 151–159.

Taft, C. T., Stafford, J., Watkins, L. E., & Street, A. E. (2011). Posttraumatic stress disorder and intimate relationship programs: A meta-analysis. *Journal of Consulting and Clinical Psychology, 79*, 22–33.

Taillieu, T. L., Brownridge, D. A., Sareen, J., & Afifi, T. O. (2016). Childhood emotional maltreatment and mental disorders: Results from a nationally representative adult sample from the United States. *Child Abuse & Neglect, 59*, 1–12.

Tark, J., & Kleck, G. (2014). Resisting rape: The effects of victim self-protection on rape completion and injury. *Violence Against Women, 20*(3), 270–292.

Taylor, J. E., & Harvey, S. T. (2010). A meta-analysis of the effects of psychotherapy with adults sexually abused in childhood. *Clinical Psychology Review, 30*, 749–767.

Teaster, P. B., Lawrence, S. A., & Cecil, K. A. (2007). Elder abuse and neglect. *Aging Health, 3*, 115–128.

Teaster, P. B., Roberto, K. A., & Dugar, T. A. (2006). Intimate partner violence of rural aging women. *Family Relations*, *55*, 636–648.

Teicher, M. H., Samson, J. A., Polcari, A., & McGreenery, C. E. (2006). Sticks, stones, and hurtful words: Relative effects of various forms of childhood maltreatment. *American Journal of Psychiatry*, *163*(6), 993–1000.

Teisl, M., & Cicchetti, D. (2008). Physical abuse, cognitive and emotional processes, and aggressive/disruptive behavior problems. *Social Development*, *17*, 1–23.

Tener, D., & Murphy, S. B. (2015). Adult disclosure of child sexual abuse: A literature review. *Trauma, Violence, & Abuse*, *16*(4), 391–400.

Tertinger, D. A., Greene, B. F., & Lutzker, J. R. (1984). Home safety: Development and validation of one component of an ecobehavioral treatment program for abused and neglected children. *Journal of Applied Behavior Analysis*, *17*(2), 159–174.

Testa, M., & Derrick, J. L. (2014). A daily process examination of the temporal association between alcohol use and verbal and physical aggression in community couples. *Psychology of Addictive Behaviors*, *28*(1), 127–138.

Testa, M., Quigley, B. M., & Leonard, K. E. (2003). Does alcohol make a difference? Within participants comparison of incidents of partner violence. *Journal of Interpersonal Violence*, *18*(7), 735–743.

Theresa's Fund. (2020). *Data center: State and province summaries.* Retrieved from https://www.domesticshelters.org/data-center/state-province-summaries

Thomas, C., Hyponnen, E., & Power, C. (2008). Obesity and type 2 diabetes risk in mid-adult life: The role of childhood adversity. *Pediatrics*, *121*, 1240–1249.

Thomas, K. A., Joshi, M., Wittenberg, E., & McCloskey, L. A. (2008). Intersections of harm and health: A qualitative study of intimate partner violence in women's lives. *Violence Against Women*, *14*(11), 1252–1273.

Thomassin, K., Shaffer, A., Madden, A., & Londino, D. L. (2016). Specificity of childhood maltreatment and emotion deficit in nonsuicidal self-injury in an inpatient sample of youth. *Psychiatry Research*, *244*, 103–108.

Thompson, M. E. (2014). Empowering self-defense training. *Violence Against Women*, *20*(3), 351–359.

Thornberry, T. P., & Henry, K. L. (2013). Intergenerational continuity in maltreatment. *Journal of Abnormal Child Psychology*, *41*(4), 555–569.

Timmer, S. G., Urquiza, A. J., & Zebell, N. (2006). Challenging foster caregiver–maltreated child relationships: The effectiveness of Parent Child Interaction Therapy. *Child & Youth Services Review*, *28*, 1–19.

Tjaden, P., & Thoennes, N. (2000). Prevalence and consequences of male-to-female and female-to-male intimate partner violence as measured by the National Violence Against Women Survey. *Violence Against Women*, *6*(2), 142–161.

Tolan, P. H., & Guerra, N. (1998). Societal causes of violence against children. In P. K. Trickett & C. J. Schellenbach (Eds.), *Violence against children in the family and the community* (pp. 195–209). Washington, DC: American Psychological Association.

Tolman, R. M., & Edleson, J. L. (2011). Intervening with men for violence prevention. In C. M. Renzetti, J. L. Edleson, & R. K. Bergen (Eds.), *Sourcebook on violence against women* (2nd ed., pp. 351–368). Thousand Oaks, CA: Sage.

Tolman, R. M., & Rosen, D. (2001). Domestic violence in the lives of women receiving welfare: Mental health, substance dependence, and economic well-being. *Violence Against Women*, *7*, 141–158

Torquati, J. C. (2002). Personal and social resources as predictors of parenting in homeless families. *Journal of Family Issues*, *23*, 463–485. doi:10.1177/0192513X02023004001

Toth, S. L., Cicchetti, D., Macfie, J., Maughan, A., & Vanmeenen, K. (2000). Narrative representations of caregivers and self in maltreated preschoolers. *Attachment and Human Development*, *2*, 271–305.

Toth, S. L., & Manly, J. T. (2019). Developmental consequences of child abuse and neglect: Implications for intervention. *Child Development Perspectives*, *13*(1), 59–64.

Transcript: Donald Trump's taped comments about women. (2016, October 8). *New York Times*. Retrieved from http://www.nytimes.com/2016/10/08/us/donald-trump-tape-transcript.html

Trickett, P. K., Negriff, S., Ji, J., & Peckins, M. (2011). Child maltreatment and adolescent development. *Journal of Research on Adolescence*, *21*(1), 3–20.

Trickett, P. K., Noll, J. G., & Putnam, F. W. (2011). The impact of sexual abuse on female development: Lessons from a multigenerational, longitudinal research study. *Development and Psychopathology*, *23*(2), 453–476.

Truman, J. L., & Langton, L. (2015). *Criminal victimization, 2014.* Washington, DC: U.S. Department of Justice, Bureau of Justice Statistics.

Truman, J. L., & Morgan, R. E. (2014). *Nonfatal domestic violence, 2003–2012*. Washington, DC: U.S. Department of Justice.

Tsioulcas, A. (2019, March 5). Michael Jackson: A quarter-century of sexual abuse allegations. *National Public Radio*. Retrieved from https://www.npr.org/2019/03/05/699995484/michael-jackson-a-quarter-century-of-sexual-abuse-allegations

Tsopelas, C., Spyridoula, T., & Athanasios, D. (2011). Review on female sexual offenders: Findings about profile and personality. *International Journal of Law and Psychiatry, 34*, 122–126.

Tsopelas, C., Tsetsou, S., Ntounas, P., & Douzenis, A. (2012). Female perpetrators of sexual abuse of minors: What are the consequences for the victims? *International Journal of Law and Psychiatry, 35*(4), 305–310.

Tucker, C. J., Finkelhor, D., Turner, H., & Shattuck, A. (2013). Association of sibling aggression with child and adolescent health. *Pediatrics, 132*(1), 79–84.

Tucker, J. S., Wenzel, S. L., Straus, J. B., Ryan, G. W., & Golinelli, D. (2005). Experiencing interpersonal violence: Perspectives of sexually active, substance-using women living in shelters and low-income housing. *Violence Against Women, 11*, 1319–1340.

Turkewitz, J. (2018, August 28). 9-year-old boy killed himself after being bullied, his mom says. *New York Times*. Retrieved from http://www.nytimes.com/2018/08/28/us/jamel-myles-suicide-denver.html

Turner, K. M. T., & Sanders, M. R. (2006). Dissemination of evidence-based parenting and family support strategies: Learning from the Triple P – Positive Parenting Program system approach. *Aggression and Violent Behavior, 11*, 176–192.

Turner, S., Taillieu, T., Cheung, K., & Afifi, T. O. (2017). The relationship between childhood sexual abuse and mental health outcomes among males: Results from a nationally representative United States sample. *Child Abuse & Neglect, 66*, 64–72.

Turniansky, H., Ben-Dor, D., Krivoy, A., Weizman, A., & Shoval, G. (2019). A history of prolonged childhood sexual abuse is associated with more severe clinical presentation of borderline personality disorder in adolescent female inpatients: A naturalistic study. *Child Abuse & Neglect, 98*. doi:10.1016/j.chiabu.2019.104222

Turton, J. (2010). Female sexual abusers: Assessing the risk. *International Journal of Law, Crime and Justice, 38*, 279–293.

Tuteur, J. M., Ewigman, B. E., Peterson, L., & Hosokawa, M. C. (1995). The maternal observation matrix and Mother–Child Interaction Scale: Brief observational screening instruments for physically abusive mothers. *Journal of Clinical Child Psychology, 24*, 55–62.

Tutty, L. M., Ogden, C., Giurgiu, B., & Weaver-Dunlop, G. (2014). I built my house of hope: Abused women and pathways into homelessness. *Violence Against Women, 19*, 1498–1517.

Twardosz, S., & Lutzker, J. R. (2010). Child maltreatment and the developing brain: A review of neuroscience perspectives. *Aggression and Violent Behavior, 15*(1), 59–68.

Tyler, R. P., & Stone, L. E. (1985). Child pornography: Perpetuating the sexual victimization of children. *Child Abuse & Neglect, 9*, 313–318.

Tyler, S., Allison, K., & Winsler, A. (2006, February). Child neglect: Developmental consequences, intervention, and policy implications. *Child and Youth Care Forum, 35*(1), 1–20.

Ulbrich, P., & Stockdale, J. (2002). Making family planning clinics an empowerment zone. *Women & Health, 35*, 83–100.

Ullman, S. E., & Brecklin, L. R. (2002). Sexual assault history and suicidal behavior in a national sample of women. *Suicide and Life-Threatening Behavior, 32*, 117–130.

Ullman, S. E., & Najdowski, C. J. (2011). Vulnerability and protective factors for sexual assault. In J. W. White, M. P. Koss, & A. E. Kazdin (Eds.), *Violence against women and children. Vol. 1. Mapping the terrain* (pp. 151–172). Washington, DC: American Psychological Association.

Ullman, S. E., Starzynski, L. L., Long, S. M., Mason, G. E., & Long, L. M. (2008). Exploring the relationships of women's sexual assault disclosure, social reactions, and problem drinking. *Journal of Interpersonal Violence, 23*(9), 1235–1257.

UNICEF. (2014). *Hidden in plain sight: A statistical analysis of violence against children*. Retrieved from http://www.unicef.org/publications/files/Hidden_in_plain_sight_statistical_analysis_EN_3_Sept_2014.pdf

United Nations. (2000). *Protocol to prevent, suppress and punish trafficking in persons, especially women and children, supplementing the United Nations Convention against transnational organized crime*. Retrieved from http://www.uncjin.org/Documents/Conventions/dcatoc/final_documents_2/convention_%2traff_eng.pdf

United Nations General Assembly, Convention on the Rights of the Child. (1989). Retrieved from http://www .ohchr.org/EN/ProfessionalInterest/Pages/CRC.aspx

United Nations Office on Drugs and Crime. (2009). *Annual report 2009*. Available from www.unodc.org/ documents/about-unodc/AR09_LORES.pdf

U.S. Bureau of Labor Statistics. (2018). *Monthly labor review*. Retrieved from https://www.bls.gov/opub/mlr/ 2018/

U.S. Census Bureau. (2018). *Percent of U.S. population with disabilities*. Retrieved from https://data .census.gov/cedsci/table?q=percent of us population with disabilities&g=&t=Disability&table=S1810&tid= ACSST1Y2018.S1810&hidePreview=fasle&lastDis playedRow=25&vintage=2018

U.S. Department of Defense. (2019). *Annual report on sexual assault in the military*. Retrieved from https:// www.sapr.mil/reports

U.S. Department of Education, Office for Civil Rights. (2010, October 26). *Dear colleague letter: Bullying and sexual harassment*. Retrieved from http://www2.ed .gov/about/offices/list/ocr/letters/colleague-201010 .pdf

U.S. Department of Health and Human Services, Administration on Children, Youth and Families. (1981). *Study findings: National study of the incidence and severity of child abuse and neglect* (DHHS Publication No. OHDS 81-30325). Washington, DC: Government Printing Office.

U.S. Department of Health and Human Services, Administration on Children, Youth and Families. (1988). *Study findings: Study of national incidence and prevalence of child abuse and neglect* (DHHS Publication No. ADM 20-01099). Washington, DC: Government Printing Office.

U.S. Department of Health and Human Services, Administration on Children, Youth and Families. (1996). *Child maltreatment 1994: Reports from the states to the National Child Abuse and Neglect Data System*. Washington, DC: Government Printing Office.

U.S. Department of Health and Human Services. (2002). *Evaluation of family preservation and reunification programs: Final report*. Retrieved from http://aspe .hhs.gov/hsp/evalfampres94/final/

U.S. Department of Health and Human Services, Administration on Children, Youth and Families. (2005). *Child maltreatment 2003*. Washington, DC: Government Printing Office.

U.S. Department of Health and Human Services. (2012, April 17). ACYF-CB-IM-12-04. Retrieved from https:// www.acf.hhs.gov/cb/resource/im1204

U.S. Department of Health and Human Services, Administration for Children and Families, Administration on Children, Youth and Families, Children's Bureau. (2016). *Child maltreatment 2014*. Retrieved from http:// www.acf.hhs.gov/programs/cb/research-data- technology/statistics-research/child-maltreatment

U.S. Department of Health and Human Services. (2019a). *The AFCARS Report*. Available from https:// www.acf.hhs.gov/cb

U.S. Department of Health & Human Services, Administration for Children and Families, Administration on Children, Youth and Families, Children's Bureau. (2019b). *Child maltreatment 2017*. Retrieved from https://www.acf.hhs.gov/cb/research-data-technology/ statistics-research/child-maltreatment

U.S. Department of Health & Human Services, Administration for Children and Families, Administration on Children, Youth and Families, Children's Bureau. (2019c). *Information memorandum*. Retrieved from https://www.acf.hhs.gov/sites/default/files/cb/ im1204.pdf

U.S. Department of Health and Human Services. (2019d). *Strong and thriving families: 2019 prevention resource guide*. Retrieved from https://www .childwelfare.gov/pubPDFs/guide_2019.pdf

U.S. Department of Health and Human Services, Administration for Children and Families, Administration on Children, Youth and Families, Children's Bureau. (2020). *Child Maltreatment 2018*. Retrieved from https://www .acf.hhs.gov/cb/research-data-technology/statistics- research/child-maltreatment

U.S. Department of Justice. (2012). *Attorney General Eric Holder announces revisions to the Uniform Crime Report's definition of rape*. Retrieved from http://www.justice .gov/opa/pr/attorney-general-eric-holder-announces- revisions-uniform-crime-report-s-definition-rape

U.S. Department of Justice, Federal Bureau of Investigation. (2019). *Crime in the United States, 2018*. Retrieved from https://ucr.fbi.gov/crime-in-the-u.s/ 2018/crime-in-the-u.s.-2018

U.S. Department of State. (2005). *The facts about human trafficking for forced labor*. Retrieved from http://www.state.gov/g/tip/rls/fs/2005/50861.htm

U.S. Department of State. (2019). *Trafficking in persons report*. Retrieved from https://www.state.gov/

wp-content/uploads/2019/06/2019-Trafficking-in-Persons-Report.pdf

U.S. Preventive Services Task Force. (2018). Interventions to prevent child maltreatment US preventive services task force recommendation statement. *JAMA, 320*(20), 2122–2128. Retrieved from https://jamanetwork.com/journals/jama/fullarticle/2716570

U.S. Sentencing Commission. (2012). *Report to Congress: Federal child pornography offenses.* Washington, DC: U.S. Sentencing Commission. Retrieved from http://ww.ussc.gov/legislative_and_public_affairs/congressional_testimony_and_reports/sex_offense_topics/201212_federal_child_pornography_offenses/

Vachon, D. D., Krueger, R. F., Rogosch, F. A., & Cicchetti, D. (2015). Assessment of the harmful psychiatric and behavioral effects of different forms of child maltreatment. *JAMA Psychiatry, 72*(11), 1135–1142.

Vagi, K. J., Rothman, E., Latzman, N. E., Tetan Tharp, A., Hall, D. M., & Breiding, M. (2013). Beyond correlates: A review of risk and protective factors for adolescent dating violence perpetration. *Journal of Youth and Adolescence, 42*, 633–649.

Vaillancourt-Morel, M. P., Godbout, N., Sabourin, S., Briere, J., Lussier, Y., & Runtz, M. (2016). Adult sexual outcomes of child sexual abuse vary according to relationship status. *Journal of Marital and Family Therapy, 42*(2), 341–356.

Van Berkel, S. R., Tucker, C. J., & Finkelhor, D. (2018). The combination of sibling victimization and parental child maltreatment on mental health problems and delinquency. *Child Maltreatment, 20*(3), 244–253.

Vanderfaeillie, J., De Ruyck, K., Galle, J., Van Dooren, E., & Schotte, C. (2018). The recognition of child abuse and the perceived need for intervention by school personnel of primary schools: Results of a vignette study on the influence of case, school personnel, and school characteristics. *Child Abuse & Neglect, 79*, 358–370.

Vanderminden, J., Hamby, S., David-Ferdon, C., Kacha-Ochana, A., Merrick, M., Simon, T. R., . . . Turner, H. (2019). Rates of neglect in a national sample: Child and family characteristics and impact. *Child Abuse & Neglect, 88*, 256–265.

Vaughn, M. G., Salas-Wright, C. P., Cooper-Sadlo, S., Maynard, B. R., & Larson, M. (2014). Are immigrants more likely than native-born Americans to perpetrate intimate partner violence? *Journal of Interpersonal Violence, 30*(11), 1888–1904.

Veneziano, C., & Veneziano, L. (2002). Adolescent sex offenders: A review of the literature. *Trauma, Violence, & Abuse, 3*(4), 247–260.

Vermont Department for Children and Families. (2017). Policy 51: Child safety interventions. In *Family services policy manual.* Retrieved from http://dcf.vermont.gov/sites/dcf/files/FSD/Policies/51.pdf

Victor, B. G., Henry, C., Gilbert, T. T., Ryan, J. P., & Perron, B. E. (2019). Child protective service referrals involving exposure to domestic violence: Prevalence, associated maltreatment types, and likelihood of formal case openings. *Child Maltreatment, 24*(3), 299–309.

Vieth, V. I. (2018). *On this rock.* Eugene, OR: Wipf & Stock.

Villodas, M. T., Litrownik, A. J., Thompson, R., Jones, D., Roesch, S. C., Hussey, J. M., . . . Dubowitz, H. (2015). Developmental transitions in presentations of externalizing problems among boys and girls at risk for child maltreatment. *Development and Psychopathology, 27*(1), 205–219.

Vinton, L. (2001). Violence against older women. In C. M. Renzetti, J. L. Edleson, & R. K. Bergen (Eds.), *Sourcebook on violence against women* (1st ed., pp. 179–192). Thousand Oaks, CA: Sage.

Vischer, A. F. W., Knorth, E. J., Grietens, H., & Post, W. J. (2019). To preserve or not to preserve: That is the question. Decision-making about family preservation among families in multi-problem situations. *Children and Youth Services Review, 99*, 441–450.

Walker, E., Downey, G., & Bergman, A. (1989). The effects of parental psychopathology and maltreatment on child behavior: A test of the diathesis-stress model. *Child Development, 60*, 15–24.

Walsh, K., Zwi, K., Woolfenden, S., & Shlonsky, A. (2018). School-based education programs for the prevention of child sexual abuse: A Cochrane systematic review and meta-analysis. *Research on Social Work Practice, 28*(1), 33–55.

Walters, M. L., Chen, J., & Breiding, M. J. (2013). *The National Intimate Partner and Sexual Violence Survey (NISVS): 2010 findings on victimization by sexual orientation.* Atlanta, GA: National Center for Injury Prevention and Control, Centers for Disease Control and Prevention.

Wamser-Nanney, R., & Campbell, C. L. (2019). Children's sexual behavior problems: An ecological model using the LONGSCAN data. *Child Abuse & Neglect, 96*, 104085.

Wang, Y. R., Sun, J. W., Lin, P. Z., Zhang, H. H., Mu, G. X., & Cao, F. L. (2019). Suicidality among young adults: Unique and cumulative roles of 14 different adverse childhood experiences. *Child Abuse & Neglect, 98*. Advance online publication. doi:10.1016/j.chiabu.2019.104183

Ward, T., & Beech, A. (2006). An integrated theory of sexual offending. *Aggression and Violent Behavior, 11*, 44–63.

Waters, E., Hamilton, C. E., & Weinfield, N. S. (2000). The stability of attachment security from infancy to adolescence and early adulthood: General introduction. *Child Development, 71*(3), 678–683.

Waters, E., & Yacka-Bible, S. (2017). *A crisis of hate: A mid-year report on lesbian, gay, bisexual, transgender, and queer hate violence.* National Coalition of Anti-Violence Programs. Retrieved from https://www.avp.org/wp-content/uploads/2017/08/NCAVP-A-Crisis-of-Hate-Final.pdf

Wathen, C. N., MacGregor, J. C. D., & MacQuarrie, B. J. (2018). Relationships among intimate partner violence, work, and health. *Journal of Interpersonal Violence, 33*(14), 2268–2290.

Watson-Singleton, N. N., Florez, I. A., McClunie, A. M., Silverman, A. L., Dunn, S. E., & Kaslow, N. J. (2019). Psychosocial mediators between intimate partner violence and alcohol abuse in low-income African American women. *Violence Against Women.* Advance online publication. Retrieved from https://doi.org/10.1177/1077801219850331

Wattenberg, E., Kelley, M., & Kim, H. (2001). When the rehabilitation ideal fails: A study of parental rights termination. *Child Welfare, 80*, 405–431.

Waxman, R., Fenton, M. C., Skodol, A. E., Grant, B. F., & Hasin, D. (2014). Childhood maltreatment and personality disorders in the USA: Specificity of effects and the impact of gender. *Personality and Mental Health, 8*(1), 30–41.

Weber, M. (1949). *The methodology of the social sciences.* New York, NY: Free Press.

Webster-Stratton, C. H., & Reid, M. J. (2010). The Incredible Years parents, teachers, and children training series: A multifaceted treatment approach for young children with conduct problems. In J. Weisz & A. Kazdin (Eds.), *Evidence-based psychotherapies for children and adolescents* (2nd ed., pp. 194–210). New York, NY: Guilford.

Webster-Stratton, C. H., Reid, M. J., & Beauchaine, T. (2011). Combining parent and child training for young children with ADHD. *Journal of Clinical Child & Adolescent Psychology, 40*(2), 191–203.

Webster-Stratton, C., Reid, M. J., & Beauchaine, T. P. (2013). One-year follow-up of combined parent and child intervention for young children with ADHD. *Journal of Clinical Child & Adolescent Psychology, 42*(2), 251–261.

Weiss, K. G. (2009). "Boys will be boys" and other gendered accounts: An exploration of victims' excuses for unwanted sexual contact and coercion. *Violence Against Women, 15*(7), 810–834.

Wekerle, C., Leung, E., MacMillan, H. L., Boyle, M., Trocme, N., & Waechter, R. (2009). The contribution of childhood emotional abuse to teen dating violence among child protective services-involved youth. *Child Abuse & Neglect, 33*(1), 45–58.

Wekerle, C., Wolfe, D. A., Cohen, J. A., Bromberg, D. S., & Murray, L. (2019). *Childhood maltreatment* (2nd ed.). Göttingen, Germany: Hogrefe.

Wexler, R. (2005). Family preservation is the safest way to protect children. In D. R. Loseke, R. J. Gelles, & M. M. Cavanaugh (Eds.), *Current controversies on family violence* (2nd ed., pp. 311–328). Thousand Oaks, CA: Sage.

Whatley, M. A. (2005). The effect of participant sex, victim dress, and traditional attitudes on causal judgments for marital rape victims. *Journal of Family Violence, 20*, 191–200.

Whitaker, D. J., Le, B., Hanson, R. K., Baker, C. K., McMahon, P. M., Ryan, G., . . . Rice, D. D. (2008). Risk factors for the perpetration of child sexual abuse: A review and meta-analysis. *Child Abuse & Neglect, 32*(5), 529–548.

Whitaker, M. P. (2014). Linking community protective factors to intimate partner violence perpetration. *Violence Against Women, 20*(11), 1338–1359.

Whitaker, R. C., Phillips, S. M., Orzol, S. M., & Burdette, H. L. (2007). The association between maltreatment and obesity among preschool children. *Child Abuse & Neglect, 3*, 1187–1199.

White, D., & Rees, G. (2014). Self-defense or undermining the self? Exploring the possibilities and limitations of a novel anti-rape technology. *Violence Against Women, 20*(3), 360–368.

White House Task Force to Protect Students From Sexual Assault. (2014). *Not alone.* Retrieved from https://www.notalone.gov/assets/report.pdf

Whitney, C. A. (2019). Federal policy status update from the APA Advocacy Team. *Section on Child Maltreatment Insider, 24*(3), 10–11.

Whittle, H., Hamilton-Giachritsis, C., Beech, A., & Collings, G. (2013). A review of online grooming: Characteristics and concerns. *Aggression and Violent Behavior, 18*(1), 62–70.

Wickham, R. E., & West, J. (2002). *Therapeutic work with sexually abused children.* London, England: Sage.

Widom, C. S. (1989). Child abuse, neglect, and violent criminal behavior. *Criminology, 27,* 251–271.

Widom, C. S. (1999). Posttraumatic stress disorder in abused and neglected children grown up. *American Journal of Psychiatry, 156,* 1223–1229.

Widom, C. S., Czaja, S. J., & DuMont, K. A. (2015). Intergenerational transmission of child abuse and neglect: Real or detection bias? *Science, 347*(6229), 1480–1485.

Widom, C. S., & Kuhns, J. B. (1996). Childhood victimization and subsequent risk for promiscuity, prostitution, and teenage pregnancy: A prospective study. *American Journal of Public Health, 86,* 1607–1612.

Widom, C. S., & Massey, C. (2015). A prospective examination of whether childhood sexual abuse predicts subsequent sexual offending. *JAMA Pediatrics, 169*(1), e143357. Retrieved from http://jamanetwork.com/journals/jamapediatrics/fullarticle/2086458

Widom, C. S., & Maxfield, M. G. (2001) *An update on the "Cycle of Violence"* (NCJ Publication No. 184894). Washington, DC: U.S. Department of Justice.

Widom, C. S., & Wilson, H. W. (2015). Intergenerational transmission of violence. In J. Lindert & I. Levav (Eds.), *Violence and mental health* (pp. 27–45). Netherlands: Springer.

Wiehe, V. R. (1990). *Sibling abuse: Hidden physical, emotional, and sexual trauma.* Lexington, MA: Lexington Books.

Wiehe, V. R. (1997). *Sibling abuse: Hidden physical, emotional, and sexual trauma* (2nd ed.). Thousand Oaks, CA: Sage.

Wijkman, M., Bijleveld, C., & Hendriks, J. (2010). Women don't do such things! Characteristics of female sex offenders and offender types. *Sexual Abuse: A Journal of Research and Treatment, 22*(2), 135–156.

Wilber, K. H., & McNeilly, D. P. (2001). Elder abuse and victimization. In J. E. Birren & K. W. Schai (Eds.), *Handbook of the psychology of aging* (5th ed., pp. 569–591). San Diego, CA: Academic Press.

Williamson, J. M., Borduin, C. M., & Howe, B. A. (1991). The ecology of adolescent maltreatment: A multilevel examination of adolescent physical abuse, sexual abuse, and neglect. *Journal of Consulting and Clinical Psychology, 59,* 449–457.

Wilson, D., & Shiffman, J. (2015). Newborns die after being sent home with mothers struggling to kick drug addictions. *Reuters.* Retrieved from http://www.reuters.com/investigates/special-report/baby-opioids/

Wilson, H. W., & Widom, C. S. (2010). The role of youth problem behaviors in the path from child abuse and neglect to prostitution: A prospective examination. *Journal of Research on Adolescence, 20*(1), 210–236.

Wodarski, J. S., Kurtz, P. D., Gaudin, J. M., & Howing, P. T. (1990). Maltreatment and the school age child: Major academic, socioemotional, and adaptive outcomes. *Social Work, 35,* 506–513.

Wolak, J., Finkelhor, D., & Mitchell, K. (2011). Child pornography possessors: Trends in offender and case characteristics. *Sexual Abuse: A Journal of Research and Treatment, 23*(1), 22–42.

Wolak, J., Mitchell, K. J., & Finkelhor, D. (2003). Escaping or connecting? Characteristics of youth who form close online relationships. *Journal of Adolescence, 26,* 105–119.

Wolf, R. S. (2000). The nature and scope of elder abuse. *Generations, 24*(2), 6–12.

Wolfe, D. A. (1991). *Preventing physical and emotional abuse of children.* New York, NY: Guilford.

Wolfe, D. A., Crooks, C. V., Chiodo, D., Hughes, R., & Ellis, W. (2012). Observations of adolescent peer resistance skills following a classroom-based healthy relationship program: A post-intervention comparison. *Prevention Science, 13*(2), 196–205.

Wolfe, D. A., Crooks, C. V., Jaffe, P. G., Chiodo, D., Hughes, R., Ellis, W., . . . Donner, A. (2009). A universal, school-based program to prevent adolescent dating violence: A cluster randomized trial. *Journal of Pediatric and Adolescent Medicine, 163,* 692–699.

Wolfe, D. A., Jaffe, P. G., & Crooks, C. V. (2006). *Adolescent risk behaviors: Why teens experiment and strategies to keep them safe.* New Haven, CT: Yale University Press.

Wolfe, D. A., & McIsaac, C. (2011). Distinguishing between poor/dysfunctional parenting and child emotional maltreatment. *Child Abuse & Neglect, 35*(10), 802–813.

Wolfe, D. A., & Wekerle, C. (1993). Treatment strategies for child physical abuse and neglect: A critical progress report. *Clinical Psychology Review, 13*, 473–500.

Wolock, T., & Horowitz, B. (1984). Child maltreatment as a social problem: The neglect of neglect. *American Journal of Orthopsychiatry, 54*, 530–542.

Wong, J. Y. H., Tiwari, A., Fong, D. Y., & Bullock, L. (2016). A cross-cultural understanding of depression among abused women. *Violence Against Women, 22*, 1371–1396.

Wooldredge, J., & Thistlewaite, A. (2002). Reconsidering domestic violence recidivism: Conditioned effects of legal controls by individual and aggregate levels of stake in conformity. *Journal of Quantitative Criminology, 18*(1), 45–70.

World Health Organization. (2014). *Global status report on violence prevention 2014*. Violence and Injury Prevention. Retrieved from http://www.who.int/violence_injury_prevention/violence/status_report/2014/report/report/en/

World Health Organization. (2018). *INSPIRE handbook: Action for implementing the seven strategies for ending violence against children*. Geneva, Switzerland: WHO.

Wortley, R., & Smallbone, S. (2012). *Internet child pornography: Causes, investigation, and prevention*. Santa Barbara, CA: ABC-CLIO.

Wurtele, S. K. (2012). Preventing the sexual exploitation of minors in youth-serving organizations. *Children and Youth Services Review, 34*(12), 2442–2453.

Wurtele, S. K., Kast, L. C., & Melzer, A. M. (1992). Sexual abuse prevention education for young children: A comparison of teachers and parents as instructors. *Child Abuse and Neglect, 16*, 865–876.

Wurtele, S. K., & Kenny, M. C. (2016). Technology-related sexual solicitation of adolescents: A review of prevention efforts. *Child Abuse Review, 25*(5), 332–344.

Wurtele, S. K., & Miller-Perrin, C. L. (2012). Global efforts to prevent sexual exploitation of minors. In H. Dubowitz (Ed.), *ISPCAN's world perspectives* (pp. 82–88). Colorado: International Society for Prevention of Child Abuse and Neglect.

Wurtele, S. K., & Miller-Perrin, C. (2014). Preventing technology-initiated sexual victimization of youth: Developmental perspective. In M. C. Kenny (Ed.), *Sex education: Attitude of adolescents, cultural differences and schools' challenges* (pp. 147–175). New York, NY: Nova.

Wurtele, S. K., Moreno, T., & Kenny, M. C. (2008). Evaluation of a sexual abuse prevention workshop for parents of young children. *Journal of Child & Adolescent Trauma, 1*(4), 331–340.

Yamaoka, Y., Wilsie, C., Bard, E., & Bonner, B. L. (2019). Interdisciplinary Training Program (ITP) in child abuse and neglect: Long term effects. *Child Abuse & Neglect, 94*. Advance online publication. doi:10.1016/j.chiabu.2019.104032

Yancey, C. T., Hansen, D. J., & Naufel, K. Z. (2011). Heterogeneity of individuals with a history of child sexual abuse: An examination of children presenting to treatment. *Journal of Child Sexual Abuse, 20*(2), 111–127.

Yang, B., Zhang, H., Ge, W., Weder, N., Douglas-Palumberi, H., Perepletchikova, F., & Kaufman, J. (2013). Child abuse and epigenetic mechanisms of disease risk. *American Journal of Preventive Medicine, 44*, 101–107.

Yardley, J. (2005, January 31). Fearing future, China starts to give girls their due. *New York Times*, p. A3.

Yardley, W. (2010, April 23). $18.5 million in liability for Scouts in abuse case. Retrieved July 25, 2010, from http://www.nytimes.com/2010/04/24/us/24scouts.html?_r=1

Yates, T. M., Carlson, E. A., & Egeland, B. (2008). A prospective study of child maltreatment and self-injurious behavior in a community sample. *Developmental Psychopathology, 20*, 651–671.

Ybarra, M. L., Strasburger, V. C., & Mitchell, K. J. (2014). Sexual media exposure, sexual behavior, and sexual violence victimization in adolescence. *Clinical Pediatrics, 53*(13), 1239–1247.

Yllö, K. (2010). Rape, marital. In B. Fisher & S. Lab (Eds.), *Encyclopedia of victimology and crime prevention* (pp. 719–723). Thousand Oaks, CA: Sage.

Yoshioka, M. R., & Choi, D. Y. (2005). Culture and interpersonal violence research: Paradigm shift to create a full continuum of domestic violence services. *Journal of Interpersonal Violence, 20*, 513–519.

Young, A., Pierce, M. C., Kaczor, K., Lorenz, D. J., Hickey, S., Berger, S. P., . . . Thompson, R. (2018). Are negative/unrealistic parent descriptors of infant attributes associated with physical abuse? *Child Abuse & Neglect, 80*, 41–51.

Yuhui, W., Jing, C., Ying, S., & Fangbiao, T. (2015). Impact of childhood abuse on the risk of non-suicidal self-injury in mainland Chinese adolescents. *PLOS One, 10*(6).

Zadnik, E., Sabina, C., & Cuevas, C. A. (2016). Violence against Latinas: The effects of undocumented status on rates of victimization and help-seeking. *Journal of Interpersonal Violence, 31*, 1141–1153.

Zalewski, M., Cyranowski, J. M., Cheng, Y., & Swartz, H. A. (2013). Role of maternal childhood trauma on parenting among depressed mothers of psychiatrically ill children. *Depression and Anxiety, 30*, 792–799.

Zeanah, C. H., & Humphreys, K. L. (2018). Child abuse and neglect. *Journal of the American Academy of Child & Adolescent Psychiatry, 57*(9), 637–644.

Zellman, G. L., & Fair, C. C. (2002). Preventing and reporting abuse. In J. E. B. Myers, L. Berliner, J. Briere, C. T. Hendrix, C. Jenny, & T. A. Reid (Eds.), *The APSAC handbook on child maltreatment* (2nd ed., pp. 449–475). Thousand Oaks, CA: Sage.

Zhu, W. X., Lu, L., & Hesketh, T. (2009). China's excess males, sex selective abortion, and one child policy: Analysis of data from 2005 national intercensus survey. *British Medical Journal, 338*, b1211. doi:10.1136/bmj.b1211

Zielinski, D. S. (2009). Child maltreatment and adult socioeconomic well-being. *Child Abuse & Neglect, 33*, 666–678.

Zink, T., Regan, S., Jacobson, C. J., & Pabst, S. (2003). Cohort, period, and aging effects: A qualitative study of older women's reasons for remaining in an abusive relationship. *Violence Against Women, 9*, 1429–1441.

Zolotor, A. J., Robinson, T. W., Runyan, D. K., Barr, R. G., & Murphy, R. A. (2011). The emergency of spanking among a representative sample of children under 2 years of age in North Carolina. *Frontiers in Psychiatry, 2*, 1–8. doi:10.2289/fpsyt.2011.00036

Zuravin, S. J. (1991). Research definitions of child physical abuse and neglect: Current problems. In R. H. Starr, Jr., & D. A. Wolfe (Eds.), *The effects of child abuse and neglect: Research issues* (pp. 100–128). New York, NY: Guilford.

Zweig, J. M., Schlichter, K. A., & Burt, M. R. (2002). Assisting women victims of violence who experience multiple barriers to services. *Violence Against Women, 8*, 162–180.

Zwi, K. J., Woolfenden, S., Wheeler, D. M., O'Brien, T., Tait, P., & Williams, K. J. (2007). School-based education programs for the prevention of child sexual abuse. *Cochrane Database for Systematic Reviews, 2*, 1–44. Retrieved from http://www.cfah.org/hbns/archives/viewSupportDoc.cfm?supportingDocID=429

INDEX